# HUGH THOMAS

The author was born in 1931 and educated at Sherborne, Dorset, and Queens' College, Cambridge. *The Spanish Civil War*, which gained the Somerset Maugham Prize, was published in 1961. His other main study of a hispanic revolutionary experience, *Cuba or the Pursuit of Freedom*, was published in 1971. His other books include *Europe: the Radical Challenge*; *Goya's 'Third of May, 1808'*; and a biography of John Strachey. His *Unfinished History of the World* was published in 1979. Hugh Thomas was Professor of History at the University of Reading from 1966 to 1976, and has been Chairman of the Centre for Policy Studies since 1979. He has been a member of the House of Lords since 1981 sitting as Lord Thomas of Swynnerton and has spoken on a variety of subjects including education, crime, defence policy and international policy. Hugh Thomas's novels include *The World's Game* (1961) and *Havannah* (1984).

'Remarkably successful in pinning down, in finest detail, a crucial turning-point in contemporary history'
*Financial Times*

'Few will fail to discover new insights and information. Furthermore, so comprehensive is the detail that readers will often be tempted to suggest their own reasons for the break-up of the Grand Alliance and to speculate on ways in which it might have been prolonged'
*The Times Higher Education Supplement*

'A splendid overview of the origins and surfacing of the Cold War'
*Zbigniew Brzezinski*

'Cool, lucid, meticulous'
*Bernard Levin*

Hugh Thomas

# ARMED TRUCE

## The Beginnings of the Cold War
1945–46

First published in Great Britain in 1986 by Hamish Hamilton Ltd.

*Sceptre edition, 1988*

Maps drawn by Isambard Thomas

Sceptre is an imprint of Hodder and Stoughton Paperbacks, a division of Hodder and Stoughton Ltd.

**British Library C.I.P.**

Thomas, Hugh, *1931–*
   Armed truce: the beginnings of the Cold War, 1945–46.
   1. Western bloc countries. Foreign relations with communist countries, 1945–46   2. Communist bloc countries. Foreign relations with Western bloc countries, 1945–1946
   I. Title
   327′.09171′3

ISBN 0-340-42146-0

Printed and bound in Great Britain for Hodder and Stoughton Paperbacks, a division of Hodder and Stoughton Ltd., Mill Road, Dunton Green, Sevenoaks, Kent TN13 2YA (Editorial Office: 47 Bedford Square, London WC1B 3DP) by Richard Clay Ltd., Bungay, Suffolk. Photoset by Rowland Phototypesetting Ltd., Bury St Edmunds, Suffolk.

For Inigo, Isambard and Isabella
in the hope that they will see an end
to the conflict whose beginning is here discussed

# ACKNOWLEDGEMENTS

The author would like to thank the following publishers and individuals for permission to quote from:

*THE PRICE OF VISION* by John M. Blum copyright © 1973 by the estate of Henry A. Wallace and John Morton Blum; reprinted by permission of Houghton Mifflin Company.

*SPECIAL ENVOY TO CHURCHILL AND STALIN 1941–1946* by W. Averell Harriman and Elie Abel copyright © 1975 by W. Averell Harriman and Elie Abel reprinted by permission of Random House Inc, John Hawkins Inc and John Farquharson Ltd.

*MEMOIRS: 1925–1950* by George F. Kennan copyright © 1967 by George F. Kennan; reprinted by permission of Little, Brown and Company.

*ROOSEVELT AND HOPKINS: AN INTIMATE HISTORY* by Robert Sherwood; reprinted by permission of Harper & Row Publishers Inc and Eyre and Spottiswoode Ltd.

*WITNESS TO HISTORY* by Charles Hohlen; copyright © 1973 by W. W. Norton and Company Inc reprinted by permission of Weidenfeld and Nicolson Ltd and W. W. Norton and Company Inc.

*CONVERSATIONS WITH STALIN* by Milovan Djilas copyright © 1962 by Harcourt Brace Jovanovich Inc; reprinted by permission of Harcourt Brace Jovanovich Inc and Grafton Books, a division of Collins Publishing.

*STALINISM* by George Urban: reprinted by permission of the original publishers, Maurice Temple Smith Ltd.

Acknowledgements for unpublished material in libraries

I wish to give thanks to the Library of Congress in Washington for enabling me to quote from the diaries of Joseph Davies and William Leahy, as well as a great deal of other assistance on numerous occasions; to the Harry Truman Library in Independence, Missouri for enabling me to do the same from the diaries of Eben Ayers and Harold Smith; the Library of Yale University for the use of some pages of the diaries of Henry K. Stimson; the Seeley Mudd Library Princeton for the use of the Frederick Ebenhardt papers and of the original Forrestal diaries; and the Library of the London School of Economics, for kindly allowing me to quote from the unpublished diaries of Hugh Dalton.

If, despite our efforts, we have failed to acknowledge anyone who feels that they should have been acknowledged, we hope they will accept our apologies.


Note
In respect of proper nouns I have kept the spelling used in each country save for certain well-known place names which have an English spelling: e.g. Prague, not Praha. I have kept generally to the old usage Persia instead of Iran, except where the latter usage is quoted in a document (see page 553).

If co-operation is impossible, 'there will be no organised peace but only an armed truce.'

DEAN ACHESON TO PRESIDENT TRUMAN<br>
SEPTEMBER 25, 1945.

'I now feel that the best that can be hoped for is a prolonged armed truce.'

LITVINOV, MAY 23, 1946 IN MOSCOW, TO<br>
GENERAL BEDELL SMITH.

# CONTENTS

# PREFACE

This volume, the first of several about the Cold War, is a picture of the world in early 1946 insofar as it was a battleground in an undeclared war between two new great powers, the Soviet Union and the United States, and their allies. The conflict was one of metaphor so far as the great powers were concerned but was violent at the level of the political life of small states.

The book is a narrative for only a few chapters at the end. The rest of the volume sets the scene at the beginning of a quarrel which is in many respects still with us and whose end cannot be foreseen. A characteristic of the book emphasised by me is the role of individuals. Marx made a major contribution to thought when, in the 1840s and 1850s, he worked out a scheme of history based on the importance of technology rather than personality. But after his day the development of technology under the control of governments has placed vast power in the hands of those who lead their nations. Hence the men – there were no women of political consequence at that time – who led the world in 1945 and 1946 require attention.

Book I in this volume discusses the view of the world in 1946 of the Soviet Union under Stalin: a nation which aspired to world influence if not hegemony. For this section, I seek to interrelate the joint importance of Russian imperialism and Marxist-Leninist ideology and how each gave support to one another. Given what I explain above, I have naturally laid special attention on the personality of Stalin. In Book II, I discuss the character of the United States and her leaders: in particular the new President Truman and his recently dead predecessor, Franklin D. Roosevelt. I devote a long chapter to the British under Clement Attlee and the Foreign Office under Ernest Bevin. I have some pages on the most prominent Commonwealth leader, Mackenzie King, the prime minister of Canada. In Book III, I consider, briefly, the different nations about which the world was quarrelling or about whose future there was a question mark. In this section, I include not only Poland and East Europe, already forcibly gathered under the Soviet umbrella, but the great nations of Western Europe including France, Italy, Germany, Spain and Austria whose future in 1946, despite two thousand years of civilisation, was not altogether easy to predict. I also discuss the East as it began to slip out of the direction exercised by the West for a century or more. Then, in Book IV, I consider the political and military significance of the atom bomb, used in 1945 for the first time. Finally, in Book V, I discuss how the Soviet Union and the West clashed over Persia and how they each sought to outmanoeuvre one another in the last days of March 1946. The Conclusion is an interim report of where things then stood.

I shall hope to treat the unrolling of the tragedy thus embarked upon in other volumes.

There may be those who will say that the ground of this book has already been covered. In separate volumes that may have been so. But I do not think it has been done in combination. It is the combination which appears to me to be interesting.

I must give my thanks to those who have assisted me: above all to those whose monographs or special studies have guided me in research. I hope that I have given due recognition to these forerunners in the notes. The pillars on which the book is constructed are, however, first, the magnificent collection of documents in the series called the 'Foreign Relations of the United States'; second, papers beyond those so published, in the National Archives of the United States; third, the official papers now lodged in the Public Record Office in London; fourth, the press of the time; fifth, memories and memoirs. I have to thank Dr Jill Edwards, a research assistant without parallel, whose knowledge of the archives in both London and Washington enabled her to make a major contribution to this book; second, Alexandra Boscawen who not only helped with research but also typed and retyped the manuscript, which I also had retyped by the admirable services of St Stephen's Secretariat in London. In addition to the libraries mentioned in the acknowledgements, I am grateful to the libraries of the House of Lords, the Royal Institute of International Affairs, and the London Library, as well as to the British Library, whose Round Reading Room continues to afford such admirable service. I am grateful to my friends in the Centre for Policy Studies for their patience, and encouragement, while I was at work on this book. Several friends of mine helped me in reading the manuscript in part or in total: I thank particularly Lord Gladwyn who read the book at an early stage and saved me from several rash misjudgements although he continued to be sceptical about many of my opinions; others who helped me I have thanked in the notes where appropriate. Oliver Knox kindly read the proofs and made invaluable suggestions. So did my wife, Vanessa Thomas, who also checked innumerable references. Isabella Thomas did other good work in this respect. I am most grateful to Isambard Thomas for drawing the maps. I thank finally Alfred Knopf Junior and Christopher Sinclair-Stevenson of Atheneum, New York, and Hamish Hamilton, London, respectively, for their patience in waiting for a manuscript long past the date due for its delivery, whose dimension changed shape several times in its infancy.

HUGH THOMAS, AUGUST 31, 1986

# CHRONOLOGY OF EVENTS 1939–1946

**1939**

| | |
|---|---|
| September 1 | Invasion of Poland by the Germans |
| September 3 | Britain and France declare war on Germany |
| September 17 | Soviet invasion of Poland |
| September 19 | Soviet and German troops meet at Brest-Litovsk |
| September 29 | Partition of Poland between Germany and Russia |
| September 29 <br> October 5 <br> October 10 } | Soviet 'treaties' with Estonia, Latvia and Lithuania |
| November 26 | Finland rejects Soviet offer of treaty on model of the above |
| November 30 <br> March 12 } | Russo-Finnish war |

**1940**

| | |
|---|---|
| April | Fall of Norway and Denmark to Germany |
| May 9 | Britain occupies Iceland |
| May 10 | German invasion of the Netherlands, Belgium and Luxemburg |
| June 10 | Italy declares war on France and Britain |
| June 22 | Franco-German armistice and subsequent partition of France |
| June | Soviet occupation of Baltic states |
| August 30 | Romanian government gives up Bessarabia and North Bukovina to the Soviet Union, under pressure from Berlin |
| September 2 | 'Destroyers for bases' agreement between US and Britain |

| | |
|---|---|
| September 8 | Romania cedes Southern Dobrudja to Bulgaria |
| September 27 | Japan joins Germany and Italy in Ten-Year tripartite pact |
| October 8 | German troops enter Romania to 'protect' oil fields |
| October 28 | Greece rejects Italian demands for bases and Italy invades Greece |
| November 12 | Molotov-Hitler discussions in Berlin |
| November 20 ⎫ November 23 ⎭ | Hungary and Romania join Berlin-Rome-Tokyo pact |
| December 3 | Germans reinforce Italy in Greece |

## 1941

| | |
|---|---|
| March 1 | Bulgaria joins Berlin-Rome-Tokyo pact and German troops occupy Sofia |
| March 11 | Lend Lease Act signed by President Roosevelt |
| March 26–28 | Yugoslav *coup d'état* against idea of signing Berlin-Rome-Tokyo pact |
| April 6 | German invasion of Yugoslavia |
| April 10 | US agreement with Denmark over Greenland (bases for defence) |
| April 13 | Russo-Japanese non-aggression pact |
| April 17 | Capitulation of Yugoslavia |
| April 27 | Germans enter Athens |
| June 22 | German armies invade Russia |
| July 7 | US troops land in Iceland on Icelandic invitation |
| July 13 | Mutual aid pact between Britain and Russia |
| July | Hopkins's first visit to England and Russia |
| August 14 | Atlantic Charter issued on *HMS Prince of Wales*: first FDR-Churchill meeting |
| August 25–29 | Britain and Russia invade and divide Persia |
| September | Harriman-Beaverbrook mission to Moscow |
| October 1 | 1st Soviet Protocol, by which Britain and the US agree to supply essential war material to Russia |
| October 16 | Soviet government and diplomatic corps go to Kuybyshev |
| October 30 | US grant of $1 billion credit to Russia |

| | |
|---|---|
| November 24 | US forces land in Dutch Guiana |
| December 7 | Japanese attack Hawaii and Philippines |
| December 11 | Germany and Italy declare war on US |
| | Sikorski in Moscow |
| December 16 | Eden in Moscow (till 22) |
| December 22 | Second FDR-Churchill meeting (Washington) (till January 20, 1942) |
| December 25 | Fall of Hong Kong to Japan |

## 1942

| | |
|---|---|
| January 1 | Declaration of Washington by United Nations |
| February 15 | Fall of Singapore to Japan |
| March | Japan occupies Burma and Java |
| April 9 | Fall of mainland Philippines to Japan (Corregidor falls May 6) |
| May 26 | Mutual aid pact between Russia and Britain becomes Anglo-Soviet Treaty |
| June | Japan invades Aleutians; Germans drive towards Caucasus. High point of Axis achievement |
| June 20–25 | Churchill in US for third FDR-Churchill meeting |
| October 23 | British victory at El Alamein |
| November 8 | American and British forces land in North Africa |
| November 19 | Furthest German advance into Russia: battle of Stalingrad begins |

## 1943

| | |
|---|---|
| January 14–24 | FDR-Churchill fourth meeting Casablanca |
| March 12 | Eden in Washington |
| April 6 | Polish government-in-exile asks for Red Cross enquiry at Katyn |
| April 27 | Soviet Union breaks relations with Polish government-in-exile |
| May 12 | Churchill in Washington (fifth FDR-Churchill talks) |
| May 12 | End of German resistance in North Africa |
| May late | First British liaison with Partisans in Yugoslavia (Col. Deakin) |

| August 11–24 | Quebec Conference (sixth FDR-Churchill talks) |
| July | Second British liaison with Partisans in Yugoslavia (Brig. Maclean) |
| July 10 | Eisenhower's invasion of Sicily |
| July 25 | Mussolini overthrown |
| September 2 | Allies land in Italy |
| September 3 | Italian armistice |
| October 13 | Portugal grants Azores to allies as base |
| October 19 } | Moscow conference of Foreign Ministers (till |
| November 1 } | Oct 30) 'the Four Nations Declaration' |
| November 9 | UN Relief and Rehabilitation Administration (UNRRA) set up |
| November 28 } | Tehran conference |
| December 1 } | European Advisory Commission set up |

## 1944

| February 20–26 | Major air onslaught on Germany |
| February | Soviet troops reach old Poland and Estonia |
| | West ceases aid to Mihailović (mission withdrawn May) |
| June 4 | US and British enter Rome |
| June 6 | US and British land in Normandy: 'OVERLORD' |
| July 20 | Bomb plot against Hitler |
| July 21 | Chicago convention nominates FDR and Truman |
| July 24 | Last large Russian city (Pskov) liberated |
| August 1 | Polish resistance rises in Warsaw |
| August 12 | US and British enter Florence; Churchill meeting with Tito at Caserta |
| August 21 } September 27 } | Dumbarton Oaks Conference |
| August 24 | Hyde Park meetings of Churchill and FDR |
| September 18 | Tito's secret visit to Moscow |
| October 9–18 | Churchill in Moscow: 'percentages agreement' |
| October 9 | Dumbarton Oaks call for UN |
| October 13 | Fall of Riga to Russians; fall of Athens to British |

| | |
|---|---|
| October 14 | General Scobie lands in Athens |
| October 20 | Belgrade liberated |
| October 28 | Bulgaria capitulates |
| November 6 | Re-election of President Roosevelt in the United States |
| November 27 | Hull resigns; succeeded by Stettinius |
| December 4 | Greek Civil War: General Scobie secures Athens (Dec. 14) |
| December 10 | De Gaulle in Moscow: Soviet Union and France sign treaty |
| December 25 | Churchill and Eden in Athens |

## 1945

| | |
|---|---|
| January 12 | Soviet drive into Poland |
| January 17 | Fall of Warsaw |
| January 19 | Fall of Tarnow, Cracow and Lodz |
| February 4–11 | Yalta Conference |
| February 7 | US 3rd Army enters Germany |
| February 12 | Truce in Greece at Varkiza |
| February 13 | Fall of Budapest after siege |
| March 2 | Groza government in Romania |
| March 3 | Finland declares war on Germany |
| March 7 | US 1st Army crosses Rhine |
| March 27 | Argentina declares war on Germany and Japan (recognised April 9 by US and Britain) |
| April 11 | US 9th Army crosses Elbe |
| April 12 | Death of Roosevelt |
| April 20 | Russians at Berlin |
| April 21 | 20-year Polish-Russian pact agreed |
| April 25 | US and Russians meet at Torgau: Renner government in Vienna |
| April 25 }<br>June 26 } | San Franciso conference |
| April 28 | Mussolini shot |
| April 29 | Germans surrender in Italy |
| April 30 | Hitler's suicide |
| May 1 | Battle of Britain |

| | |
|---|---|
| May 7 | Germans sign armistice at Rheims |
| | Persia requests Russia, US and Britain to withdraw |
| May 10 | Czech government moves to Prague |
| May 14 | Democratic Republic of Austria proclaimed |
| May 26 June 6 | Hopkins's last mission to Moscow |
| June 22 | Preliminary draft of UN Charter submitted to San Francisco Conference by Stettinius |
| June 28 | Government of National Unity in Poland |
| July 17 August | Potsdam conference |
| July 20 | Franco reshuffles government |
| July 26 | Labour victory in British election: Attlee Prime Minister |
| August 3 | Sudeten Germans deprived of Czech citizenship |
| August 6 | Atom bomb on Hiroshima |
| August 8 | Division of Austria, and Vienna, into four zones |
| August 8 | Soviet Union declares war on Japan |
| August 14 | Surrender of Japan |
| September 1 | Western Allies in Vienna |
| September 2 | Formal terms of surrender signed by Japan on *USS Missouri* |
| September 9 | Capitulation of Japanese armies in China London Conference |
| October 14 | Provisional National Assembly, Prague |
| October 21 | French elections |
| October 24 | UN comes into legal existence |
| November 3 | Hungarian elections give Smallholders majority |
| November 6 | Yugoslav election |
| November 8 | Elections in Bulgaria: 'Fatherland Front' wins |
| November 25 | Elections in Vienna: People's Party wins |
| November 30 | De Gasperi Prime Minister in Italy |
| December 2 | Albanian elections give Hoxha victory |
| December 6 | US grants loan of $3.75 billion to Britain |
| December 18 | Dr Figl Prime Minister in Vienna |
| | Moscow Conference of Foreign Ministers |

# 1946

| | |
|---|---|
| January 6 | Polish Government nationalises all industries employing fifty men or over |
| January 11 | People's Republic of Albania proclaimed |
| January 20 | De Gaulle resigns as Provisional President of France |
| January 22 | Félix Gouin Provisional President of France UN General Assembly in London |
| January 31 | New constitution adopted in Yugoslavia |
| February 1 | Hungarian republic proclaimed: Dr Tildy President, Ferenc Nagy Prime Minister |
| February 9 | Stalin's 'election' speech, Moscow |
| February 22 | The 'long telegram' sent from Moscow |
| February 28 | Secretary of State Byrnes's speech in New York |
| March 4 | US, Britain and France appeal to Spain to oust Franco |
| March 5 | Fulton speech by Churchill |
| March 6 | Byrnes's Note to Russia over Azerbaijan |
| March 10 | Mihailović captured (shot July 17) |
| March 15 | Fourth 5-year plan adopted by Supreme Soviet |
| March 19 | Government changes in Soviet Union: Kalinin gives way to Shvernik as President Persia protests to Security Council (UN New York) |
| March 31 | CP-dominated government elected in Bulgaria |

# LIST OF MAPS

# BOOK ONE

# DESPOTISM AND IDEOLOGY

We cannot fail to recognise that now we face an enemy of a new type, more dangerous than the Entente – international revolution. Please look beyond the initial advantages to us. These threatening clouds can only be dispelled by immediately ending the war.

Kaiser Karl to Kaiser Wilhelm, 1917

# ONE

# STALIN'S 'ELECTION'

In the early years of the XXth century, the triumph of Western civilisation seemed to be assured. Representative government by the consent of the majority, well established in Europe and North America, seemed certain to be the usual formula for politics in the next generation. Democratic elections were being tried out in such unpromising places as the Ottoman, Persian, Russian and Chinese empires. It seemed possible, therefore, that Western European standards would conquer in those then apparently decaying realms. Free enterprise, as well as enriching the two Atlantic seaboards, seemed likely to bring a steady increase of prosperity. The decay which capitalism appeared to have left in its train in Europe was being compensated for by a mild taxation which did not yet raise the spectre of an overpowerful state, such as had ruined antiquity. Knowledge, or at least education, promised to make all free. Imperial administrators brought up on the study of Plato, Cicero and the Bible were confident that they could carry respect for law, Christianity and commerce to the vast populations whom they soberly governed before they were given the chance to rule themselves. The United States was conscious of an obligation to inspire the rest of the Americas.

Forty years on, that sunny picture had vanished. The cultivated, art-loving, superior European nations had set about each other in war with astonishing ferocity. The industrialisation of the wars led to the militarisation of industry. Millions died in humiliating circumstances. Men of evil unknown since Nero ruled Rome seized first the imagination of masses, then authority, in states long civilised. Although in the conflicts of the XXth century there were acts of heroism and magnanimity, the revival of torture, murder of civilians, the waging of war without declaration, and the bombing of cities from the air were the marks of a new age of tyrannies.

At the beginning of the second half of the 1940s, however, the storm of open war seemed momentarily to have blown out. It was a truce of exhaustion, attended by numerous half-declared civil wars, themselves the consequence of earlier international conflicts. The only promising sign was that, except in Argentina, the age of the great demagogue, speaking in vast auditoriums to thousands of crazed or thwarted youths, seemed temporarily at an end.


Early in February 1946, Joseph Stalin, the tyrant of Russia, General Secretary of the Communist Party since 1921, President of the Council of Peoples' Commissars since 1941, made a speech in Moscow, at the conclusion of what was described as an election campaign for membership of the Supreme Soviet. There were deceits in this occasion. Stalin's written statement, read out in a 'toneless, slow' voice, familiar to Russians from hearing it during the late war, might not have been reckoned a speech in a more precise, or less exhausted, age. Nor would anyone in any other age have described the series of declarations by Stalin's colleagues, similarly read out from typed scripts, as 'election' addresses, with the element of choice between different persons and policies which that word implies. Stalin, sometimes still spoken of by his foreign allies in the late war by the sentimental nickname 'Uncle Joe', was really called 'Djugashvili'; and even Russia was no longer officially so named by its leaders, who affected to call their country the 'Union of Soviet Socialist Republics', USSR. That combination of words would also once have seemed a misnomer, since 'Union' signifies a voluntary association which the 'prisonhouse of peoples' ruled by Stalin was not; 'Soviet' means the determination of policy by a spontaneous organisation of delegates from factories, such as was embarked on in 1905 on the suggestion of a by then forgotten Menshevik, Paul Akselrod, which had no equivalent in 1946[1]; 'Socialist' suggested an equality which the Russians enjoyed in 1946 less than many other countries, save perhaps for those millions of slave labourers in Russia who were equal before their gaolers; and the 'Republics' were in truth fifteen monocracies each directed by a single tyrant, himself dependent on Moscow, with less concern for the opinion of others than had been usual in absolute monarchies.

Despite these confusions, characteristic of the time, Stalin was widely reported, in his own country as abroad, to have, on February 9, 1946, made his first speech since that of September 2, 1945 (on the occasion of the surrender of the Japanese Empire) and, indeed, the penultimate one of his life to a large audience.*

The Supreme Soviet now about to give way to a new one was the first to have been 'elected', in December 1937, under the new Soviet Constitution of 1936. In theory, it was the highest state authority in Russia. That constitution of 1936 had provided for the Supreme Soviet to have two chambers, each serving a term of four years: the Council of the Union, elected on a basis of one deputy for every 300,000 citizens; and the Council of Nationalities, elected on a basis of twenty-five deputies for every 'union republic', eleven for each 'autonomous republic', five for each autonomous region, and one for each national district. A new 'election' had been postponed year by year because, it was said, of the war which had begun for Russia in 1941.

As in 1937, the deputies in 1946 were to be elected from single lists, ostensibly including non-party candidates, as well as Communists. That device was a fine example of a tribute paid by vice to virtue, since the non-party candidates were nonenti-

* Stalin's last speech was in 1952, to the XIXth Party congress of the Communist Party of the Soviet Union.

ties. This 'preposterous fiction', as the process was described by Mr George Kennan, the Minister at the embassy of the United States in Moscow, and the outstanding Western diplomatist in that capital, was put forward with seriousness. As in 1937 so in 1946, voters would find themselves faced, in polling booths, for all the world the same as those in free countries, with a list of names which, however, had merely to be handed in; if these papers were marked in any way, or mutilated, they would be considered invalid. There had been no 'by-elections' since 1937. Those who had died, and there had been many (including some from natural causes), had been replaced by 'co-opted' members. As in 1937, the list of candidates included a substantial number of police chiefs: in 1937, twenty-six of the thirty-three heads of the provincial secret police forces were elected – of whom nearly all had died with their leader, Yezhov, at the hand of an executioner, a year later.[2]

The influence of this carefully screened body had been, in the years since 1937, nil, though in theory it had enjoyed a number of rights, such as annulling decisions of the Council of Peoples' Commissars (officially the Soviet Government) if they did not conform to law. The Supreme Soviet was in truth an honorary panel of docile if, by Russian standards, distinguished people, who met at rare intervals in order to register unanimous approval of programmes put forward by the Soviet Communist party. The wonder is that so much trouble was taken to make it seem other than it was. From time to time, nevertheless – for example, over entry into the war in the East – Stalin had spoken of it to his Allies as being of critical importance: how could he explain matters to the Supreme Soviet unless certain conditions – for example, the cession to Russia from Japan of South Sakhalin and the Kurile Islands – were met?[3]

The Supreme Soviet had assembled once during the war, in June 1942. The Commissar for Foreign Policies, Molotov, had then made to it a speech about his recent visits to London and Washington. The wartime Soviet propaganda chief, Shcher-bakov, had spoken for Moscow – 'Comrade deputies, you can see your capital intact!' Zhdanov had spoken for Leningrad,

followed by a Lithuanian, an Estonian, a Latvian and others. The
theme had then been the Anglo-Soviet treaty, just signed, a
document which bound the great British Empire to an alliance
with Russia for twenty years and *vice versa*. [4]

The elections of 1946 had been announced without warning,
on January 2. On that day, throughout the winter-bound Soviet
Union, nominations of official candidates began. As in 1937, these
were made in ceremonial meetings of groups and organisations,
some numbering 10,000 people. Unanimous support for the
candidates chosen was usual. These gatherings customarily
began with a spirited speech in praise of Stalin and of the other
members of the Politburo (the word, signifying the Soviet
equivalent of a Western Cabinet, stood for the 'Political Bureau'
of the Central Committee of the Communist Party). Objection
to any name on the list would have been unthinkable. The
outcome of the election was not a matter for doubt, since there
was only one candidate for each position. [5]

There followed what George Kennan described as an 'unprecedented effort of propaganda' to ensure a large percentage of
voters. The purpose of this was to show confidence in the
leadership which had carried the nation through the recent war.
Another motive was to take an informal census of the population.
Yet one more was to combat the weariness, discouragement
and disappointment which marked Russia in 1946, as it did all
countries recently belligerent. An election campaign was, after
all, an opportunity for a vigorous public advocacy of current
policy. Perhaps the election had been decided upon in order to
give an opportunity for this campaign. Finally, and again George
Kennan was a good judge, the Kremlin was determined that,
'without relaxing an iota of its real totalitarian power, it can make
the Soviet people go through motions of democracy with such
impeccable fidelity and enthusiasm as to establish the thesis that
the Soviet system was the most democratic on earth'. [6] One of
Kennan's most prominent debating opponents, the then Soviet
Deputy Commissar for Foreign Policy, Dr Vyshinsky, might
almost have agreed: 'The Soviet election system', he wrote a
year or two later, with presumably this election of 1946 in mind,
'is a mighty instrument for further educating and organizing the

masses politically, for further strengthening the bond between the state mechanism and the masses, and for improving the state mechanism and grubbing out the remains of bureaucratism'.[7]

The candidates in this charade were chiefly people who had already made successful careers in the army, state or party bureaucracies. Industrial workers constituted a little more than ten per cent of the candidates, the 'cultural intelligentsia' about the same, and the 'technical intelligentsia' a little less.

Stalin spoke on February 9 at the Bolshoi Theatre: one of the most famous buildings in Russia since its rebuilding in 1854 after a fire. For many years, it had the reputation of having the largest stage in the world. Beneath the pediment over the Ionic portico surmounted by a colossal group of Phoebus in the Chariot of the Sun, lovers of ballet, and opera, have happily trooped in order, for an hour or two, to escape, in the mellow mood induced by traditional music, their otherwise interminable reflections on the iniquities of the Soviet state. The theatre was also used for large meetings, such as the celebration of anniversaries of the Revolution of 1917. Undamaged by revolution, civil war or world war, never knowing financial difficulties because of its favoured place among Soviet institutions, the theatre constituted, both in its architecture and its performances, a priceless link between past and present, between the age of grace and the age of steel. Within, on February 9, 1946, however, the 4,000 spectators were all Party members, army officers, or officials: the upper class of the first classless nation: similar, indeed, to the candidates in the electionless election to be held next day.

Stalin liked this building: not so much because he enjoyed music but because in it he felt himself an emperor. Seated discreetly in Box A, a picnic of hard-boiled eggs in a bowl in the *avant-loge*, he came often, preferring, for obvious reasons, Glinka's strongly monarchist *A Life for the Tsar* (*Ivan Susanin*, as it had been renamed) to the disturbing *Boris Godunov*, admiring the soprano Schpiller or the mezzo Davidova, and realising that no ruler of old Moscow had ever had more power. Today, of course, there would be no opera: only a 'speech'.[8]

'Comrades', Stalin began, in his 'soft monotone' and strong Georgian accent, with its 'exceedingly hard' 'r'.[9] This accent was the only thing which remained Georgian about Stalin, for otherwise he 'lacked all that was characteristic of a typically Georgian temperament' being, as his daughter put it, 'neither hot-tempered, nor open-hearted, neither emotional nor sentimental'.[10] Those who heard this opening, however, did not especially observe the voice – after all, most had heard it before, not least in that bleak broadcast of July 3, 1941, in which Stalin seemed, after the unexpected German attack on Russia, to be ailing and at the end of his strength. Nor was the audience interested in the fact that Stalin's face was pock-marked, from a childhood case of smallpox; that, though often portrayed as a giant in posters, he was only five feet five inches tall; that his left arm seemed still deformed in consequence of an early injury resulting in blood-poisoning; that he had unusually narrow sloping shoulders and a brow which seemed pithecanthropoid both to old friends and old enemies; that his hair was grey and thinning, contrasting with his black moustache; that his teeth were irregular and yellow; that his eyes too had a yellow hue; that he was scented;[11] that his lower eyelids were higher on his eyeballs than is usually the case with Caucasians, giving him a faintly Chinese appearance; nor indeed even that his square-cut tunic appeared a little too large; and that, despite it all, his head was 'relatively beautiful – like the peasants from Montenegro'.[12] None of this occupied the listeners much.

The comrades in the auditorium were, of course, interested to see how well, or how old, the leader looked: the previous June, he had made an impromptu speech to generals and officials in which he had mentioned his age and suggested that he would retire in two or three years' time.[13] Between August and October 1945, Stalin was said to have been ill. He had become sixty-two in 1945 and his daughter thought that 'the tension and fatigue of the war years were beginning to tell'.[14] All the same, what was important to those used, over so many years, to learn the truth from nuances of expression, and from the order of names in lists, to interpret from a mere intonation where a possible hint of heresies such as 'infantile leftism' or 'right wing opportunism' might lie undetected, was that Stalin used the word 'comrades' as his word of address: not 'brothers', 'sisters', 'my countrymen' nor 'my friends', expressions which he had used in the course of the late war. That change meant surely that the sense of nationhood used by, or forced on, Stalin between 1941 and 1945 was no longer by him considered appropriate for the new days of peace.

That perception was shown to be correct when the audience heard Stalin say that 'our victory means, in the first place, that our Soviet system has won': not 'Russia'; not the Allies. The first impression was further confirmed – in those dangerous days, double or treble guarantees were essential – when the listeners realised that, for the first time since 1941, Stalin made no expression of gratitude to the other Allies, neither to Britain nor to the United States. There was no recognition, for example, of the twelve billion or so dollars sent from the United States to Russia without which the then American ambassador believed the Russians 'would have been pushed back to the Urals and probably beyond'.[15] Indeed, not only were the Allies not mentioned but Stalin specifically distanced himself from any comment which might have suggested that the British and Americans (and other capitalist states too feeble to mention by name) were living on the same planet as the Soviet Union. Early in the speech, Stalin explained that the late war had broken out as 'an inevitable result of the development of world economic and political forces on the basis of modern monopoly capitalism'; after all, 'the development of world capitalism takes place, not as a smooth and even advance, but through crisis and war': that, being translated, signified the same as the view that capitalism and Nazism were at the same 'last stage of capitalism' as Communists had conceived them to be in the early 1930s. Perhaps the 'catastrophes of war could be avoided' if one could now re-distribute periodically raw materials and markets among the countries in accordance with their economic weight. But 'that could not be achieved under present capitalist conditions'. Hence, the First World War; hence, indeed, the Second.

These were all views and expressions which Stalin knew from his study of, and listening to, his predecessor Lenin. They were the things which he had mentioned often in the 1930s. But they had been banished from his talk for five years. Their use now resembled the return of emigrés after a counter-revolution.

He did not mean to suggest, the Vozhd* continued, that the Second World War was an exact replica of the First. The main fascist states – Germany, Japan, Italy – had destroyed all 'the last remnants of bourgeois democratic liberties at home', had established terrorist regimes, had ignored sovereignty and declared that their aim was fascist domination of the world. The Second World War had, at one stage, 'assumed the nature of an anti-fascist war', a war of liberation and one to re-establish democratic liberties. Hence the international anti-fascist coalition. But that was by the way. Stalin believed that, in normal circumstances, Communism could only be established as the inheritor of a bourgeois democratic revolution. The first consequence of the late war was (as earlier indicated) to show that the Soviet social system could win. That was a reproach to the foreign press and others who believed that the Soviet social system was a 'risky experiment, doomed to failure' or a 'house of cards without any roots in life', maintained by the secret police. The war had shown not only that the Soviet system was a 'perfectly viable and stable form of organisation' but that it was 'a form of organisation superior to all others'.

This passage of the speech was delivered in the sing-song repetitive manner reminiscent of litanies of the Orthodox Church, which recalled to his hearers that Stalin, as a young man, had been intended for the Church and had, indeed, passed six years with the monks at the Orthodox monastery at the old Georgian capital of Tiflis (Tbilisi).

Secondly, Stalin continued, 'our victory means that our Soviet state system has won, that our multinational Soviet state has withstood all the trials of war and has proved its viability'. Even the experienced or erudite listener had to strain his attention at

* Vozhd is an ancient Russian word for 'ruler'.

this. To what extent was this, actually, a *second* point? Had it not been said just before? The answer occurred in the next sentences: foreign journalists, prominent foreign journalists, had more than once made statements to the effect that the Soviet multinational *state*, not the *society*, was 'an artificial and non-viable structure', and that, in the event of 'complications', it would collapse; the Soviet Union would share the fate of Austria-Hungary. At all events, the war had refuted those arguments. The war had shown – and here the tone of liturgy could once again be heard – the war had shown that the Soviet multinational state could survive the test. Those 'gentlemen of the foreign press' (whoever they were) failed to understand that the comparison with Austria-Hungary was fallacious, since 'our multinational state' had grown 'on a Soviet foundation and not a bourgeois foundation'. A Soviet foundation cultivated friendship between peoples in a multinational state, whereas a bourgeois foundation stimulated national distrust. This was a harkening back surely to old Soviet ideas that the Soviet state was a prototype for a world Republic.[16]

The third thing proved by the victory, Stalin went on, was that the Red Army, whose capacity had been so doubted by so many, five years before, had withstood the adversities of war. The war had swept away all such doubts as 'groundless' and 'laughable': now 'one cannot help but admit that the Red Army' was an army of the first class from whose achievements much could be learned.

Naturally, such a great victory could not have occurred without a preliminary preparation of the country for active defence. Gallantry alone could not win against an enemy such as Germany. One had to have armaments. One had to have armament factories. That had been possible as a result of the Five Year Plans before 1941. Those Plans had prepared for the victory.

Stalin listed the production in the country of certain items in 1913. He compared the figures to those of 1940. Russia had statistics in the age of Communism even if it did not have happiness. Several of the earlier figures appear to have been wrong. The main point, however, which he made had validity. Thus:[17]

|                | Stalin's<br>Figures for 1913 | Real<br>Figures for 1913 | Figures for 1940<br>(According to Stalin) |
|----------------|------------------------------|--------------------------|-------------------------------------------|
|                | PRODUCTION<br>(All in million tons) | | |
| Pig iron       | 4.2                          | 4.6                      | 15                                        |
| Steel          | 4.2                          | 4.9                      | 18.3                                      |
| Coal           | 29.0                         | 38.0                     | 166.0                                     |
| Oil            | 9.0                          | 10.0                     | 31.0                                      |
| Wheat          | 21.6                         | 28                       | 38.0                                      |
| Raw cotton     | 0.74                         | Not known                | 2.7                                       |

He claimed that this transformation was a unique one. It was principally due, he said, to his policy of industrialisation. Unlike industrialisation in capitalist countries, Russia had begun her efforts in this field of activity with heavy industry. The Party had remembered Lenin's words that 'without heavy industry it is impossible to uphold the country's independence'. Here, as was frequent in the Communist speeches, Stalin left the impression that there had been no industry in Russia before 1913: whereas, in truth, the speed of industrialisation between 1860 and 1913 was often, for good or evil, faster than it had been after 1917.

Stalin also recalled the collectivisation of the land. That, he said, had in Russia avoided 'the ruin of agriculture' so typical of capitalist agricultural developments. It had covered the whole country with collective farms large enough, efficient enough, to use new agricultural machinery, and 'take advantage of all the achievements of agronomic science'. Of course, there had been opponents of it, including people inside the Party, who had 'in every way tried to drag' the Party back towards 'the discredited, unsatisfactory, too slow' and 'unusual' capitalist path. Nor had the Party succumbed to the threats of some (Bukharin, let us imagine), or the blackmail of others (Stalin's own second wife, for example, Nadezhda Alliluyeva), who had advised other courses: 'Did the Communist Party succeed in using correctly the material possibilities thus created, in order to develop war production?'

(Once again, the tone of an Orthodox priest's interrogative.) Stalin answered himself: 'I believe that it *did* succeed in accomplishing that, and it accomplished it with the utmost success'. Stalin then described how, in 'the last three years of the war' – Russia had only been at war for four years – the country had annually built more than 30,000 tanks, self-propelled guns and armoured cars: 40,000 aircraft; 120,000 guns of all calibre; 450,000 light and heavy machine guns; more than 3 million rifles; 28 million tommy guns; 240 million shells; and 7.5 thousand million cartridges. The recital of these figures naturally led to 'thunderous applause'. A pause was necessary; a sip at the glass of water presumably already tested by Stalin's special food and wine taster, his private secretary, to avoid the possibility of poison.

As for the future: there would, Stalin went on, be a new Five Year Plan to restore the districts afflicted by the war to their level of living before 1941. The plan would seek to do in the

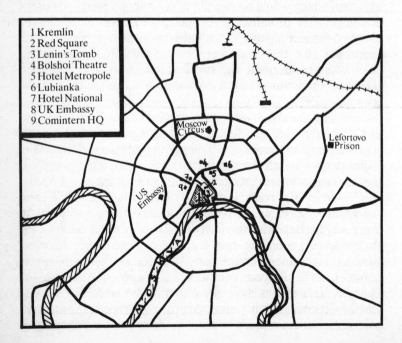

1 Kremlin
2 Red Square
3 Lenin's Tomb
4 Bolshoi Theatre
5 Hotel Metropole
6 Lubianka
7 Hotel National
8 UK Embassy
9 Comintern HQ

next five years, 1946–50, what had once been projected for ten, 1941–50. Rations, however, would soon be abolished. Attention would be given to the production of consumer products, and to raising the standard of living, by a steady reduction of prices, and by the 'extensive construction of scientific research institutes'. 'I have no doubt', Stalin added, 'that, if we give our scientists proper help, they will be able, in the near future, not only to overtake but to surpass the achievements of science beyond the boundaries of our country'. Could he be referring to the new mystery developed so successfully in the West, nuclear energy? Presumably. But how soon in Stalin's Russia was 'the near future'? Ten years, after all, was a short sentence there, where prisons were concerned. That was a passage which should have been pondered over by the intelligence services of the West, had they had their eyes on Moscow.

As for economic development, Stalin went on, 'our Party intends to organise a powerful new upsurge of the national economy which would enable us, for instance, to raise the level of our industry threefold, as compared with the prewar level'; and then the dey sentence, according to many foreigners, in the whole speech, 'only under such conditions can we regard our country as guaranteed against any eventualitities. That will require perhaps three new Five Year Plans, perhaps more'.

Stalin ended with a little ironic play, always difficult to know how to take from him, and some apologetic statements of false modesty: the Communist Party in these elections was, of course, ready to accept the people's verdict. The Party fortunately did not march alone in the election, since it had at its side the 'non-party people'. In conclusion, said Stalin: 'allow me to thank you for the trust you have extended to me [prolonged, "unabated", applause here interrupted the speaker, at least according to the transcript, followed by shouts: "Hurrah for the great captain of all victories, Comrade Stalin"] by nominating me a candidate to the Supreme Soviet. You need not doubt that I shall try to justify your trust'.

At the end of this speech, all, naturally, rose. There was again, according to the Russian press, 'prolonged, unabating applause, turning into an ovation'. From all parts of the great hall, that same press reported, cheers followed: 'Long live our great Stalin!'; 'Hurrah! Hurrah for the great leader of the peoples!'; 'Glory to the great Stalin!'; and 'Glory to Comrade Stalin, the candidate of the entire nation!'; and 'Glory to Comrade Stalin, the creator of all our victories!'[18]

To those who read this report, there must have come into the memory thousands of other such sycophantic eulogies: for example, the poem by the Kazakh poet Djambul in 1939, published in *Pravda* in March 1939, at the time of the last Congress of the Communist Party:

*'Tenderly the sun is shining from above*
*And who cannot but know that this sun is you?*
*The lapping waves of the lake are singing the praises of Stalin!*
*The dazzling snowy peaks are singing the praises of Stalin!*
*The meadow's million flowers are thanking, thanking you.*
*The well-laden table is thanking, thanking you.'*[19]

But those present at the Bolshoi Theatre in 1946 must also have contrasted this speech with another which Stalin made at the end of the war, in May 1945, in which he praised the Russians – 'the most remarkable of all the nations of the Soviet Union' – 'the leading nation, remarkable for its clean mind, its patience and its firm character.' Now the Russians had slipped back, in the mind of the General Secretary, into merely being 'comrades', not distinguished as such, and 'an international vanguard'.

It is idle to speculate how the clapping for Stalin died down on this occasion. The writer, Solzhenitsyn (at that time a short distance away from the Bolshoi Theatre in the Kaluga Gate prison in Moscow), has described how difficult it was to end applause, even at a mere district party conference, about this time when, of course, there was no chance of Stalin being present (except in spirit). At the conclusion of one such conference, a tribute to Stalin was called for. Of course, as in the Bolshoi Theatre, everyone stood up. Of course, there was 'stormy applause rising to an ovation'. Three minutes, four minutes, five minutes the applause continued. The palms were getting sore, the raised arms bending. The older people were becoming exhausted. But who would dare to be the first to stop? The secretary of the district Party committee could have done it. But he was a newcomer. He had taken the place of a man who had been arrested. He was afraid. Secret policemen were standing at the back, watching indeed to see who would stop first. So, in that obscure hall, the applause continued. Eight minutes, nine minutes! With assumed enthusiasm on their faces, the district leaders went on. Then, after eleven minutes, the director of the paper factory put on 'a businesslike expression and sat down'. Everyone else also stopped dead. They had been saved! That night, the factory director was arrested. He received ten years – for something else. But after he had signed the final document of his interrogation, Form 206, his interrogator warned him: 'Don't ever be the first to stop applauding'.[20] Similar events can be found in the history of Rome in the days of Nero: Suetonius has a comparable story.[21]

The careful listener, or reader, would also have noticed three more points made in this speech even if only implicitly.

First, the programme as announced signified that the Party and its ideology were to be reinforced. The late war had really been, as everyone knew in their hearts, a narrow escape for the Soviet system. Party loyalties had broken in areas occupied for a time by Germany. Even the partisans – whom Stalin did not now mention – had often fought well against Germany because they relished the unexpected freedom of the forests of West Russia, not because they loved the Soviet system. Even when Soviet citizens had fought for a cause, that had been Holy Russia: not Communism. Stalin had once admitted as much to the American Ambassador.[22] Despite its appalling hardships, the war had also even brought a habit of freedom of thought which terror had in the past prevented. So the Party organisation, if it were to continue, had to be revived.

Second, there was obviously now to be a diminution of talk of patriotism and of Russia. Those things might still be needed in the battle against encirclement. But Russians would have again to look on themselves, first and foremost, as 'revolutionary vanguard', not as descendants of Alexander Nevsky.

Third, there would be no talk of the great marshals and

generals who had won the war. Armaments, the products of successful industrialisation, yes. Marshal Zhukov, no. Personalities would not be allowed to count. Political officials concerned to guide commanders – every military district had a political member of general rank on its council – such as Nikita Khrushchev, N. A. Bulganin and even Leonid Brezhnev – would, if necessary, be mentioned rather more often than the real commanders.

The international consequences of this speech were less obvious. All the same, they were clear to those who knew the vocabulary of power. Russia would prepare herself, without external help, for any eventuality. The countries nearby would serve as a '*glacis*' to smother any assault. Atomic weapons in the hands of the United States would not divert the Russians from their own enquiries in that line. The Allies? Their shrill, if unexpectedly delayed, anti-Soviet rhetoric might be useful since it could be quoted to remind Russians that they had opponents; that in fact they were still encircled by capitalist hyenas. Otherwise the Allies could be discounted. But they might be, should be, if possible, frightened. They should be reminded of Soviet military might. They should be discouraged by good propaganda from intervening in Eastern Europe. Stalin needed time to recover before any new real test.

Some of the ideas in Stalin's speech had been for years in the public domain. Eighteen months before, for example, he had told Eric Johnston, the president of the United States Chamber of Commerce, that Russia would seek to increase her production of steel from twelve million to sixty million tons a year. But he had also then mentioned all kinds of hopes for trade with the capitalist world. He had said that he had wanted to buy American goods almost without limit. As for Russian exports to the West: 'would you like manganese? We have quantities. We could give you chrome, platinum, copper, oil, tungsten. And then there's timber and pulpwood, and furs. Perhaps you will want gold . . . Most capitalist countries want gold'. Russia's needs were so considerable, and its development as yet so modest, that 'I can foresee no time when we will have enough of anything'. At the end of that discussion, on June 26, 1944, Stalin had added: 'I

like to do business with American businessmen. You fellows
know what you want. Your word is good and, best of all, you
stay in office a long time – just like we do over here. A politician
is here today and gone tomorrow and then you have to make
arrangements with a new set'.[23] There was no hint in February
1946 of those latter views. Businessmen had vanished from
Stalin's mind as if they had been politicians. There was no desire
for, nor expectation of, trade with the West.

The same kind of message as Stalin's in 1946 had been made
in speeches by several of Stalin's colleagues, earlier in the week.
For example, there was the speech on February 6 by the
Commissar for Foreign Relations (or Foreign Minister),
Vyacheslav Molotov. He was a competent but sombre official
christened, by the British ambassador to the United States,
'smiling granite'. This speech was unyielding so far as control of
power by the Communist Party was concerned: 'some people
still dream that it would be well if our country's leadership passed
to some other, non-Communist party. We can answer them with
the simple Russian proverb, "if only beans grew in one's mouth"
. . . There was', said Molotov, 'no need to speak too much
about such people – people, so to say, of the other world'.
Molotov was also anxious to remind his hearers of his belief in
the ideology of Marxism-Leninism and its sense of predesti-
nation: 'the world, my friends, does not just turn round; we
affirm that it turns *purposefully*, and that it has its own forward
course, towards its own better future'. The Soviet people had
matured, together with their Communist Party, and, if some
people abroad did not like that, they could be easily consoled –
a joke – since in those other countries, too, Communists, as
leaders, often enjoyed the confidence of the broad masses of
the people. At the same time, the standing of Russia had
been transformed: 'Important problems of international relations
cannot now be settled without the participation of the Soviet
Union, or without listening to the voice of our Motherland'.

That was a first formulation of a doctrine in foreign affairs of
which the world would subsequently hear a good deal.[24] Molotov
then added that Comrade Stalin's continued participation in
politics was looked upon as the best guarantee for 'the successful

solution of complicated international problems'. Still, the Soviet people needed to be alert: 'Hundreds of thousands of German troops of the routed Hitlerite army' were being preserved in some shape or other in the areas administered by the United States. The Polish 'fascist', General Anders, 'notorious for his hatred of the Soviet Union', and a Russian White Guard infantry colonel, Rogozhin, still held armies in Italy and Austria respectively. There were other dangers. So the Soviet Union had to re-build its economy: 'we shall need a certain time to raise our socialist industry to the level which it had reached before the war. But a couple of years will pass and we shall achieve this'. Then, 'in order finally to accomplish this major task we need a lengthy period of peace and ensured security'. This peace-loving policy was 'no transient phenomenon'. It followed from the 'deep confidence' that the Soviet Union would successfully accomplish all its tasks, provided the 'aggressors' pack' was 'chained'.[25]

Another speech was made that February in this series by Georgi Malenkov who seemed, in 1946, likely to be Stalin's heir. Malenkov had been the planner of the Soviet economy during the world war. More recently he had controlled the Soviet Union's sequestration of all useful German capital equipment. Factories, laboratories, engineers and scientists of all sorts had been exported to Russia, under Malenkov's direction. In Moscow, in the winter of 1946, Malenkov's 'cold, dull gaze', as the poet Naum Korzhavin had put it, was always to be observed in the background at Stalin's appearances.[26] He spoke a fine Russian, was only forty-three and, despite certain well-publicised differences with Andrei Zhdanov, the Communist leader in Leningrad, seemed the most formidable of Stalin's advisers.

Malenkov talked about 'the great Marx' but pointed out that 'creative leadership' meant adapting Marx to everyday practice. 'We have people', he said, 'who have quotations from Marx and Engels ready for every possible occasion. They have only one standard: either "Marx said" or "Marx never said". Daily, comrades, we come across routine and stagnation, of this type.' (This was, perhaps, an echo of that old Jewish joke, known no doubt to Marx if not to Malenkov, about the scholars who counted the commas in the Talmud.) On the harsher questions of international affairs, Malenkov sounded icy: 'There have been cases in history when the fruits of victory have escaped the victors. It is up to us to conduct matters so as to secure the fruits. To do this, we must continue first of all to make secure the Soviet state, created by Lenin and Stalin'. Comrades had to remember that 'the weak are not respected'. Malenkov added, 'it has been frequently demonstrated that the weak are thrashed. We already represent a very great power. Let us not forget that we are strong enough to maintain the interests of our people. If necessary, we can wait till all concerned realise that we have achieved victory for ourselves, and work to safeguard our Motherland against all eventualities. We do not want to pull chestnuts out of the fire for others. If we have chestnuts, let us use them for the benefit of our own glorious people.'[27]

The last image was doubtless a roundabout allusion to the same phrase used by Stalin at the 18th Congress of the Party in March 1939 when he wanted to say how reluctant he was to help Britain and France against the Nazis. It was a sensible thing to recall now that in 1946 Russia had determined to return to being the Soviet Union, the capital of world Communism, not the great ally.

# TWO

# NATIONAL SOVIETISM

The speeches of Stalin and his colleagues in February 1946 suggested that the Soviet successes in 1945, and the uncertainty of the Western allies as to how to deal with them, meant that Russia could risk isolation; but also that the Soviet leaders were too set in their ways, too determined to maintain their own place, and too reliant on Marx and Lenin as prophets and as sources of legitimacy, to put on foot a prolongation of the relative liberalism, the Russian nationalism, the appreciation of capitalist democracies and the recognition of the values of religion which had characterised the years of war. The speeches implied that the Soviet leaders believed that their system could not survive moderation. It needed enemies abroad. Its survival domestically also depended on its menace abroad to others. Russian Imperialism, Marxism-Leninism and internal control were interwoven. The system which Stalin had built up had validity in the minds of those who exercised it only if it aspired to be a world system. The interconnection of all those things was intimate.

When in doubt, Stalin and his colleagues clearly conducted themselves in international affairs as they thought Russian imperialists of the past would have done. Thus in January, Stalin had told Chiang Ching-kuo, son of Chiang K'ai-shek, the Chinese President, that he was trying to strengthen himself everywhere that he could in areas adjacent to Russia and attain as many strategic positions as possible.[1] Nearly a year before, he had told Djilas, the clever young Montenegrin Communist, to whom he was apparently drawn, that the Second World War had not been like the old wars: nowadays, 'whoever occupies a territory imposes on it his own social system. Everyone imposes his own system as far as his army can reach'. He went on to say that, though the war would soon be over, 'we shall recover in fifteen or twenty years, and then we'll have another go at it'.[2] Djilas wondered whether Stalin was thinking of the Russian people's war on behalf of Bolshevism; or Bolshevism's war on behalf of Russian nationalism. He inclined himself to the latter interpretation.

These matters are, however, complicated and, before seeking further explanations, it would be best to inquire into the nature of the political engine which Stalin drove so astutely.

Russia in 1946 – all the Russias – was ruled by the Political Bureau (Politburo) of the Central Committee of the Communist Party of the Soviet Union. There were nine members of that body. These men had in theory been elected at the eighteenth Congress of the Party in 1939. (The first Congress had been before the capture of power, in Minsk, in 1898.) In fact, they had been chosen, as freely as if they had been domestic servants, by Stalin, the General Secretary of the Party since its eleventh Congress in 1922 (Stalin was the first to hold that position). The Politburo of 1946, which had beaten Germany, was much the same as that of 1939, which had signed a pact with that country.

The Politburo itself was a body devised before the Bolshevik *coup d'état*, in October 1917. It had existed, with a gap between then and March 1919, ever since. Its numbers ranged between five and ten. Stalin had been a member from the beginning. Its powerful Secretariat, headed by Stalin, consisted of five men, of whom four were also members of the Politburo. The fifth was a 'candidate' member of it. Including this last, there were four candidate members, all of whom sat with the Politburo on the now rare occasions when it met; these could speak, but formally could not vote. In practice, power was exercised by Stalin, who had used his control of the Secretariat to secure his own nominations for all the posts.[3]

Next to Stalin in importance were those who dined with him either at the Kremlin in Moscow, or at his country house outside (or who stayed with him when he was at a resort on the Black Sea in the summer). These were the influential men, even if they were 'temporary people', as Nikita Khrushchev, the greatest survivor among them, later put it, whatever their formal status. Beria, a 'candidate member', was head of the political police, and so more powerful than Andreyev, Minister for Agriculture, a full member of the Politburo, but who dined with Stalin much less often than Beria did.

Formal meetings of the Politburo seem in 1946 not to have occurred since the late 1920s. Indeed, Stalin had reduced the membership to the position of 'expert consultants'.[4] According to Khrushchev, 'Neither the Central Committee, nor the Politburo nor the Presidium Bureau worked regularly. But Stalin's regular sessions with his inner circle went along like clockwork'.[5] Beneath this Politburo, whose purpose was to decide policy, there was an organisation bureau, *Orgburo*, intended 'to allocate forces'; that is, decide who would do what. It too had a phantom existence in the days of Stalin.

In the war, Stalin set up another committee, the State Committee for Defence (GKO). Created in the dark days of June 1941, its members had, at the beginning, been Stalin, Molotov, Beria, Voroshilov and Malenkov. These men were then at the heart of that 'conspiracy within a conspiracy', to use George Kennan's formulation,[6] which made up government in Russia. All save Voroshilov were, whatever their faults, men of a remarkable capacity for work, management and organisation. During the war, Mikoyan and Voznesensky, a clever Armenian and an economist respectively, joined the committee; later still, the Jewish master-manager, Kaganovich, came in and, in November 1944, Voroshilov gave up his place to an expoliceman, Bulganin. This committee had been formally wound up in September 1945. But the people on it remained intimates of Stalin.

To be a member of the Politburo offered great opportunities for power, houses, food, travel, education for one's children. It was also a serious risk to personal survival. Thus, out of fifteen members 'elected' to it in 1934 (including candidates) at the seventeenth Congress of the Communist Party, four had been executed on charges of conspiracy (Kossior, Chubar, Postyshev and Rudzutak), one killed himself (Ordzhonikidze), and a sixth (Kuibyshev) died of a mysterious heart attack. Only one (Petrovsky) had been happily demoted, to become an assistant director of a museum.

Beneath these men in positions of responsibility, there were the officials of the Communist Party. The General Secretaries of each of the Soviet republics which made up the so-called Union were the Central Committee's men in those places. They were dependent on it and, if the territory were important, were also often members of it. There were similar networks of officials in 'provinces' (*Krai*) and 'counties' (*oblast*). Each of these rungs of power also managed, or were served by, a local politburo, a local secretariat and a local party; an ideological bureaucracy which monopolised power.

There were doubtless divisions of interest and opinion among these leaders and their followers. Western writers sought to decide who were conservatives and who liberals. It was a vain task since, like the Whig Party in England in the days of the Duke of Newcastle, cliques within the Communist Party in Russia grew up according to personal loyalties, as a result of help given in the past, or sometimes relationships by marriage. Stalin himself had noticed this, in a speech in 1937: 'most frequently, workers are selected not according to objective criteria, but according to accidental, subjective, narrow and provincial criteria. Most frequently, so-called acquaintances are chosen, personal friends, fellow townsmen, people who have shown personal devotion, masters of eulogies to their patrons'.[7] But in Russia, as everywhere else, human weakness could not be overcome. Malenkov would complain of the same things in 1952. Stalin and Malenkov themselves practised, and profited from, the same activity. Beria was the greatest practitioner of it since, though chief policeman, he was also the tyrant of the Caucasus, who promoted his local friends wherever he could. The comparison with English Whiggery is only true up to a certain point. An English historian remarked that 'it is the intensity rather than the nature of the Soviet power struggle which is so difficult to envisage'.[8]

The Communists in 1945 constituted three per cent of the population in Russia (including candidate members): there had been 3,965,000 members and 1,794,000 candidates – 5,760,000 in all, in May 1945. The youth movement, *Komsomol*, numbered 15 million in October 1945: half of those eligible for membership.[9] Most of these members were new, having joined since the outbreak of the war in 1941. The figures were higher than they had been in 1939, when Communists, decimated by the massacres of old Bolsheviks, had numbered only a million and a half; and at the end of the civil war in 1921, less than 60,000. In February 1917, the Party may have had as few members as 10,000 and there had been only twenty-two Bolsheviks in 1905.[10]

The Party member was thus an aristocrat in Russia. Russia was 'a galley, a slaveship', its greatest poet of that day Boris Pasternak, had said, and the party members 'were the overseers who whipped the rowers'.[11] Like all aristocrats in a working autocracy, however, the party member had duties, as well as privileges: 'you have to attend meetings, pay dues, go to the Party school, study Stalin's short history of the Party, study the works of Marx, Lenin and Stalin, read the Party newspapers, explain the decisions of the Party to non-Party people, take part in putting up wall newspapers: at the time of an election [such as February 1946], you have to be an agitator . . . I had to be disciplined and behave well, I could not be a drinking man nor engage in hooliganism nor could I have unbecoming behaviour'.[12] 'A Communist has no right to be a detached bystander', Khrushchev said ten years later at the 20th Party Congress.[13] It is not, therefore, surprising that there had been purges in the Party and that, at periodic intervals, 'rascals, bureaucrats, dishonest or wavering Communists' had to be removed, nor that 'Mensheviks who have repainted their "facade" but who have remained Mensheviks at heart', to quote Lenin's characteristically uncharitable phraseology, were expelled.[14]

There were rewards. A party member lived in a private state, as it were, within the state, with his own private shops, free flats and villas in the country, chauffeur-driven cars, sanatoria on the Black Sea, occasional banquets in, say, the Hall of St

George in the Kremlin, the tables heavy with old glass and silver, sturgeons and caviar.

The Secretariat of the Politburo, of which Stalin was the unquestioned director, had a number of departments comparable to a civil service of its own in many countries. Another group of secretaries headed them to form a further board which worked alongside the *Orgburo* in the early days, but was now superimposed on top of it. From this labyrinthine bureaucracy, the future leaders rose. (All the leaders of the Soviet Union in future years until Chernenko were members of one or other of these secretariats in 1946.) The Secretariat employed 3,000, engaged in appointments, the scrutiny of new Party members, and the preparation of briefs for both Politburo and the government. There were departments concerned with ideology, with agriculture, with 'organisational Party questions', as with foreign Communist parties, this last department being new, having been set up on the dissolution of the Comintern in 1943. The small department of the Secretariat known by the unassuming name of *Organisatim* was, however, the most important body in the Soviet government. In 1946, it was managed by General A. N. Poskrebyshev, a small man with a big head, devoted to Stalin, who had begun work for him as long ago as 1922.[15]

Most of the senior Party secretaries in the provinces belonged, as earlier noticed, to the Central Committee of the national Communist Party. In the heroic days of the civil war that Central Committee had numbered between twenty-five and thirty. But it had been increased, on Stalin's suggestion, to forty in 1923, and had numbered seventy-one since 1927. The Central Committee was a no more lively body than the Supreme Soviet. Lenin had prescribed that it should meet every four months. It had, however, come together only twice during the war: in October 1941, when the members had been summoned to Moscow, where they waited for two days before being told that the meeting would not take place;[16] and in 1944. The Central Committee would one day be revived but, under Stalin, it had ceased to be anything. Even the executive committees (*plenum*) of the Central Committee did not meet, though grandiloquent declarations were sometimes issued in their name.

Alongside this highly elaborate political hierarchy, there was also a hierarchy of government. The ministers, or members of that Council of People's Commissars which had been created by Lenin on November 8, 1917, and their senior officials, were all communists. Their standing depended not on their commissariats but on where they stood in the Party. The same applied to those communists in the armed services, municipal government, farm management and trade unions. Party membership was the test of everything. In 1946, the percentage of members of the armed forces who were Party members was high: half the Communist Party had been in the armed services at the end of the war; while almost a quarter of the Red Army were members in 1945, and almost a third of the Navy.[17] During the war, the screening of future Party members, and the training in Party schools which had been insisted upon for ten years or more before 1941, had broken down. Those arrangements were now being re-established. Local and governmental arrangements received a complicated, overdue dose of ideology, discipline and direction. *Oblast* and *Raion*, *Guberniya* and *Uyezd*, returned to the permanent insecurity of peace.[18]

These Party and governmental arrangements bound together a multinational empire. Russia differed from other European empires in its central direction as well as the ruthlessness of its management: as it did in the territorial contiguity of the subjugated nations. The Tsars' empire in Russia had been cemented by railways; the Communists confirmed it by electricity, the telephone and the radio. The bureaucrats, both official and Party, aspired to turn all the population, the Uzbek and Ukrainian peoples, as well as the greater Russians, into a vast hierarchy of public servants. The arrangements, however, often, before the war, at the top as well as at the bottom, were marred by friction caused by the system of dual control. Even politically appointed factory managers resented the time insisted upon for party propaganda. During the war, a serious effort had been made to merge party and government. But it did not seem now that the merger could continue.

The relation between the leaders in Moscow and the Party was defined in two concepts which meant less than their phrasing promised: these were, first, 'democratic centralism', indicating that policy was initiated and decided at the top, in the heart of the Politburo, and passed downwards to the Central Committee, then to secretaries and to other Party members; and, second, 'vanguardism', an idea which meant that the leaders, like the Soviet Union in the world or, indeed, like a Communist Party in a tiny state, could assume that they were the conscious 'vanguard' of a great movement, the Communist movement, and so could take responsibility, as it were, for others' decisions in the knowledge that, in the long run (and it could be a very long run), the world would see that they were right.

'Democratic centralism', a phrase invented in the German Social Democrat movement of the 1860s, had been incorporated in the Party's constitution at the Fourth Congress at Stockholm in 1906. It was mentioned in the twelfth commandment of the Third (Communist) International in 1921, and had to be accepted by all Communist parties which wished to join that body.[19] Lenin said: 'Parties belonging to the Communist International must be based on the principle of "democratic centralism". In the present epoch of acute civil war, the Communist Party will be able to fulfil its duty only if its organisation be as centralised as possible, if iron discipline prevails, if the Party centre, upheld by the Party membership, has strength and authority, and is equipped with the most comprehensive powers'.[20] All had to pursue the 'line' as decided at the centre, whatever the previous 'line' had been, or whatever the real beliefs were of those at the periphery. That was applied to Communist parties whether they were in power, as in Russia (and in 1946, in effect, in most of East Europe, half of China, and of North Korea), or not. 'Democratic centralism', though primarily an internal affair for each party, gave Stalin a technique for imposing discipline not only on Russian Communists but on Communists everywhere.

An anticipation of what 'democratic centralism' might mean in practice was given by Trotsky, in debate with Lenin at the Second Congress of the Party, in 1905 at Brussels: 'the organisation of the Party takes the place of the party itself; the Central Committee takes the place of the organisation;

and finally, the dictator takes the place of the Central Committee'.[21]

The idea of a 'vanguard', on the other hand, occurred in *The Communist Manifesto*, where Communists were described as 'the most conscious part of the proletariat'. The essence of Leninism, that the workers could not themselves develop a revolutionary socialist 'consciousness', but had to receive it from the educated intelligentsia, did not appear till the work of the future 'renegade', the German socialist thinker, Karl Kautsky.

Since 1921, all Communist parties had been run on the basis of these two principles. Indeed, it might have been said that Communist parties only remained such while they practised 'democratic centralism'. Otherwise, they had individually neither separate ideologies nor strategies.[22]

This disciplined system had a purpose; that was the furtherance of the 'ideology' known as Marxism-Leninism, as interpreted for the time being by Stalin, and the preservation of the power of the Soviet communists.

Ideology was a word introduced to political vocabulary, like those other misleading categorisations, 'Left' and 'Right', during the French Revolution. The name 'Ideologists' was given to those who maintained the tradition of the Encyclopedists and was sometimes used by Napoleon, Hegel and Marx. It gradually slipped into international philosophical usage.[23] In 1946, Marxism-Leninism was the ideology which played the determining part in the governance of Russia. This ideology was not simply an adjustment to the system but an 'absolute condition of its existence', in the same way that other states have derived legitimacy from elections, or divine right, or feudalism.[24] Since the ideology was by definition 'totalitarian' (a word invented, but not fully practised, by Mussolini), there was no institution, nor movement, nor private society, which was not to be explained or absorbed by the ideology.

This ideology was introduced to Russia by Lenin immediately after his and his comrades' *coup d'état* in 1917. Stalin, creature of the ideology from long before 1917, as well as conserver of it, was in this respect in Lenin's shadow. Lenin had proclaimed that the Soviet government, which he had founded, embodied the interests of all workers everywhere, that it reflected their 'real' aims, and that it constituted the first step towards the global revolution, which would 'liberate' the masses, wherever they were. The tactics of the Soviet state might not always be theoretical in a particular circumstance; but ideology had always to be available to justify tactics, however unexpected, when necessary. It also had to be far enough away from day-to-day politics to justify any move, however paradoxical: friendship with Hitler, for example; or, alternatively, war with Hitler; intervention in Persia; or, non-intervention in Finland. The essential thing was that all the policies which Stalin decided would have to receive an intellectual justification by reference to the works of Marx, Engels or Lenin. Ideology was the underpinning of the entire construction of 'this half-prison, half-barracks', in Stalin's daughter's words describing the Soviet nation.[25]

Whatever served Soviet interests had to be described, therefore, as 'progressive' and whatever did not as 'reactionary'. Any action outside Soviet borders by the Red Army was automatically 'liberation'. Feudal principalities could be looked upon, temporarily no doubt, as of assistance to the 'progressive cause' if they undermined the 'imperialist front'. Despite its occasional ambiguity, ideology was not something which could be trifled with: Nikita Khrushchev, then the party leader, almost the viceroy, of Ukraine, reflected later: 'To speak of ideological compromise would be to betray the heritage left to us by Marx, Engels and Lenin'.[26]

The Soviet leaders were not Old Testament prophets. There were in Stalin's entourage more men motivated by fear and ambition than by philosophy. But the most fearful and most ambitious man would have to know what the philosophy was. Self-deception was constant among both the philosophers and the ruthless.[27] Ideology, in the words of Solzhenitsyn, was 'what gave the evildoer the necessary steadfastness and determination . . . the social theory which helps to make his acts seem good, instead of bad . . . so that he will receive praise and honours, not reproaches and curses'.[28] In the 1970s, an American news-paperman asked a Russian, with whom he had made one of those unsatisfactory half acquaintanceships so characteristic of the connections between West and East in our time, why people joined the Communist Party. 'They join the ideology', was the Russian's answer; which he defined as 'our promise of a future paradise: a society of equals, with equal opportunity for all'. He added, 'our people see all kinds of mistakes and shortcomings and squabbling going on around them. But they think – after a decade or two – that the real line of the Party will triumph'.[29] In the 1930s and 1940s, shortcomings and squabblings might have been interpreted to read 'murders' and 'injustices'. But the same mixture of innocence, self-deception and longterm optimism was there, all the same.

This ideology dominant in Russia in 1946 was a hundred years old. It had been initiated by Karl Marx, a political exile from a rabbinical family settled at Trier in the Rhineland (Marx's father, born Herschel Levi, had been received as a Christian in 1817). Marx, born in 1818, lived first in Germany, then in France and, after 1848, in England. He died in 1883 when Lenin was thirteen, and Stalin four. Marxism was a theory of human history which derived its method of analysis from the Prussian professor of philosophy, Hegel; and its idealistic picture of the future from French Socialists of the 1840s. Its drive and self-confident tone derived from Marx's own nature, his birth into Romantic Europe and, perhaps, his Jewish ancestry. From Hegel, to whose lectures he had listened at the University of Berlin, Marx had derived the impulse for the most original, and to some, most exciting, side to his thinking: the notion of the inevitable progress of man towards a historically predicated utopian destination. This was the harnessing of Hegel's idea of the 'dialectic' to a specific political programme: what Marx himself called 'standing Hegel on his head'.[30]

In one sense, Marxism implied the use of history for the purpose of prophecy. But Marx aspired to be more than a prophet. He sought to formulate a science of all human life, politics and history combined, whose laws would be accepted as if they were the laws of science. Marx excluded prehistory from his analysis: tribal and hunting man were placed into the limbo of folklore, though the 'clash' between hunters and agriculturalists, with their sharply differentiated interests, seems to the modern mind at least as sharp as any other. Subsequent to the discovery of agriculture, Marx conceived of all historical change as having derived from changes in means of production. There is something to be said for that point of view, though the change from, say, manpower to horsepower, as that from copper to bronze, did not merely occur; individuals played a part. Societies and civilisations were nevertheless determined, for Marx, by their technology. The water mill produced feudalism; the steampowered mill, capitalism. More important still, both production and change were for Marx brought about by the antagonism of classes, deriving from these technologies. When there was no antagonism, there could be no progress. Marx argued that all these changes had a dynamic of their own. There was no dilemma between historical necessity and conscious action. The class consciousness of the proletariat was itself the historical process. There was some uncertainty, admittedly, in Marx's writings as to how exactly Communists should conduct themselves before the revolution began. Should they organise the masses, for example, and educate them to become aware of both their predicament and their opportunity? Or should they be the passive instruments of determinism? That was a point where Marx's greatest follower, Lenin, would have his own views.

The consummation of the historical process would be, for Marx, the establishment of Communism. That would benefit everyone, capitalist and feudal landlord, as well as factory worker and peasant; even though the first group might find the blessings disguised for a time. That stage would be achieved as a result of a final 'clash', in a revolution between capitalists and the proletariat. The 'clash' might be short, as if it were a paroxysm; or, take the form of civil war. It might be followed, in certain circumstances – if, for example, the revolution were to occur in one country and did not immediately spread – by a 'dictatorship of the proletariat', in practice a tyranny exercised by the local Communist Party. But Marx did not expect that that period would last long. Indeed, he used the phrase 'dictatorship of the proletariat' very infrequently.[31] He assumed that the Commune in Paris had given an indication of what conditions in that dictatorship would be like. Nor, in his writing, was there a prediction of a long interim during which humanity would rest, as it were, in a waiting room, before the train of history arrived. No, the paradise of universal Communism, a united world market, presumably, with advanced technology, would be waiting at the next station. At that point, the 'entire state machinery' would vanish into 'the museum of antiquities', next to the spinning wheel and the bronze axe.[32] The state would not even have to be absorbed: it 'withers away'.[33]

The nature of the paradise in store following the world-wide proletarian revolution was not explained so fully by Marx as were the steps towards it. Thus, though the state would have withered away, it was not evident what fate awaited nations. The identity of some would vanish in the 'revolutionary holocaust'.[34] But it was clear that Communism in practice would mean the end of any division in life between public and private. Marriages would be easily dissolved, education would be entirely a social responsibility. Distinctions of race, people and class would also vanish. So would the antithesis between town and country.[35] Individuals would no longer feel 'alienated' from society (an important element). It would be possible for a single man to 'do one thing today and another tomorrow, to hunt in the morning, fish in the afternoon, rear cattle in the evening, criticise after dinner', just as he wished.[36]

Voluntary solidarity would, as in an orchestra, ensure both efficiency and harmony: national distinctions and contrasts, 'already tending to disappear more and more, as the bourgeoisie develops', would be even more effaced.[37] On all these matters, Marx was, except in one or two details (federalism, the role of authority), in agreement with both anarchists and conventional or democratic Socialists; that is, in theory. It was his view of the method with which the aim was to be achieved, and the missionary zeal with which he depicted the 'inevitability of the historic process', that made Marx so singular.

There were some ambiguities: when the proletariat had carried out its revolution globally, would each nation have its own 'dictatorship' during the interim 'period of revolutionary transformation' with separate nations loosely bound by a confederate tie in a World Republic? Or would there be a centralised dictatorship of the proletariat for the world? It seems that Marx would have preferred centralisation. He disliked federalists. His collaborator, the business man Engels, was later more explicit: 'the proletariat can only use the form of the one and indivisible republic'.[38]

Marx did not expect his ideal society to be initiated by Russia. He despised Slavs, especially Russians. He was writing for Western Europe.[39] At one moment, however, in 1877, he thought that Russia might escape Western industrialisation – 'the best opportunity that history has ever offered to a people to escape all the catastrophes of capitalism' – provided revolution there was followed by a Western European upheaval.[40]

Events after 1861 suggested that capitalism in Russia was growing 'with feverish speed';[41] and Marx wrote in 1882, in collaboration with Engels, that 'today . . . Russia forms the vanguard of the revolutionary movement in Europe';[42] Engels had earlier argued that the socialist revolution would not occur in a country where there was no working class, in the special sense of a large number of factory workers as there were in Britain, the United States or Belgium and Northern France. But if the village commune in Russia were to last, it could provide a nucleus of Socialism to stand alongside revolution in Western Europe.[43]

It was less Russian backwardness than the fact that a Western European structure of classes had not developed which made it hard for the ideas of Marx to be acceptable in Russia. As in other Asiatic monarchies, state power was pronounced over all classes, including the aristocracy. Changes in Russia were imposed from above. Totalitarian control could not be impressed on the Russia of the Tsars since that needs modern technology. But the Tsars desired it as much as the Communists. Notions of freedom at a popular level were in the Western sense non-existent.

Marxism, to become either attractive or appropriate in Russia, had to be adapted. That was partly the work of Plekhanov; more importantly, of Lenin. Plekhanov laid the foundations of Russian Marxism. With him, Russian Socialists turned their back on the countryside. The working class, small as it was, could do what the peasants never would. First, a bourgeois revolution was necessary. To achieve it, Plekhanov turned his 'face to the liberals', planning that they, and other intellectuals, would follow the lead of the proletariat.

It was, however, Lenin's interpretation of Marx, as expressed in many articles, books, speeches, long ago collected together in a multi-volume 'complete works', as well as in Lenin's actions, which dominated the mind of Russia in 1946. Soviet Communism seemed by then to be Lenin's achievement, in language, content, and manners.

Lenin was the son of an inspector of schools born in Astrakhan, probably of Kalmyk origin. His family lived at Simbirsk on the Volga. He read, accepted, or rejected, the ideas of a hundred Russian reformers of the XIXth century: from Bakunin to Herzen. He inherited some views from the purist revolutionary, Tkachev; in particular, that dreamer's belief that, in the absence of both 'national bourgeoisie' on the Western European model, and urban proletariat, revolutionaries in Russia, who could only come from a well-organised clique of the intelligentsia, should seize power, establish a revolutionary dictatorship, and use the state machine in their own name: as it was put later by Elie Halévy: 'a group of armed men, moved by a common faith, decreed that they were the state'.[44] The Finnish communist, Otto Kuusinen, defined the Leninist view of the tactics concerned: 'for us this slogan, "a workers' government", is nothing more than a secret name for a dictatorship of the proletariat. We need it in order to gain the support of unripe workers'.[45] 'Unripe' workers would suffer a good deal in consequence.

In Lenin's youth, young Russian progressives were dominated by arguments over the 'peasant question', which divided the Marxists from the Populists. In the course of them, as in most controversies of an ideological nature, each side infected the other. Peasants accounted for a majority of the Russian population; perhaps half were the children of families which before 1861 had been privately owned serfs. Though generally passive, this peasantry had shown itself capable of outbursts of savagery which both intoxicated, and puzzled, city-bred intellectuals.

Lenin adopted Marxism in the 1890s. He assumed that all major questions of theory had been settled by that master. He looked on his task as the application of Marx's principles to Russia. Unlike Plekhanov, he advocated that, in Russia, the proletariat (a still small, though growing, working class in the new factories) should work with the peasants, not the 'bourgeoisie'. (By 1897, 13 per cent of the population of European Russia lived in towns, and 'workers' – factory workers – numbered 2.5 million, out of 130 million).[46]

An innovation of Lenin was that he built up a disciplined party around a core of professional revolutionaries, whose aims were to exploit, and infiltrate, all forms of opposition (Lenin knew, of course, that he would have to destroy some of these 'activists', when circumstances changed). This included opposition to the Tsarist regime by nationalist movements; such as Finns; or Poles.

On returning from exile in 1917, Lenin allowed himself the fictional assumption that 'the bourgeois revolution' in Russia was complete. To those who wondered how that could be so, he quoted, to Kamenev, that useful saying of Goethe that theory was 'grey, but green is the eternal tree of life'. Lenin now argued that Marx had given 'not a dogma, but a guide to action'. That interpretation enabled Lenin to insist on the appropriateness of a Bolshevik revolution in a Russia still mostly rural: and on compressing what Marx had thought of as likely to be two 'stages of history' into one. The consequence was a state of affairs for which there was no theoretical justification, though Lenin's then ally Trotsky had spoken of the idea in 1905 when talking of 'uninterrupted revolution'.[47] Marx would not, perhaps, have approved the seizure of power carried out by one party in the name of Socialism before the conditions for it were ripe. He might surely have described some of the consequences as 'the substitution of one form of oppression for another' – as he accused the Jacobins in the French Revolution of having organised.[48] He might even have been sceptical about Lenin's demand that, after the revolution in Russia but the failure to extend it, the communist workers of the rest of the world had a duty to defend 'the socialist fatherland'.[49]

Had he lived beyond his fifty-fourth birthday, Lenin might perhaps have done something to humanise the state which he had insisted on building: a one-party one in which that party claimed its right to run every aspect of life. Some dissent after all, within the Communist Party, at least, survived until Lenin died. Still, to judge Lenin by his writings and by what he did, it cannot be argued that his death in 1924 prevented a benign amelioration of his system. How angrily he dismissed in 1918 talk of the state then withering away, as a 'violation of the historical perspective'! How realistically he observed that, in the XXth century, 'force does not mean the fist or the club; but troops'![50] How firmly he stated in 1921 that practical men knew the suggestion that every worker could administer the state to be a 'fairy tale'! And, how candidly did he recognise that the 'dictatorship of the proletariat' was the dictatorship for the time being of the 'vanguard', of the proletariat – that is, the Party![51]

Lenin was harsh on traditional morality. That attitude derived from his innermost sentiments. In a speech when in power, he said 'our morality is entirely subordinated to the interests of the proletariat's class struggle . . . To a Communist, all morality lies in this united discipline . . . we do not believe in an eternal morality and we expose the falseness of all the tales about morality'.[52] He acted accordingly, and spoke brutally, or untruthfully, whenever it suited him:[53] 'We have never rejected terror on principle', he said in 1901, 'terror is a form of military operations which may be entirely useful or even essential at a certain moment of combat'.[54] (He disliked 'uncoordinated acts of terror'.) Lenin believed in repression, including 'terror': 'clean all that up by terror, summary procedure, the death penalty with no appeal', he instructed those concerned to deal with those peasants who opposed him in 1920; and, 'it's machine guns for . . . Mensheviks'.[55] He allowed his 'acrimonious' and 'domineering' character full rein.[56] Lenin's favourite reading was the English social realist novelist, Jack London; and he enjoyed in particular the tale *Love of Life* 'in which, in a wilderness of ice where no man had previously set foot, a man dying of hunger fights and eventually eats a dying wolf'.[57] One of Lenin's chief legacies was an insulting, violent and intolerant style of language, which mocked all opponents as pitiful, as well as vile; and which survives among his successors to this day.

Lenin's character, which he imposed on his nation as Bismarck did his on Germany, was one of firmness of purpose and capacity, not only for audacity, but to make audacity seem the right course to his often more hesitant associates. He was candid. He even foretold how he would be deified after his death.[58] In 1922, at the eleventh Congress of his Party, he mercilessly castigated the 4,700 Communists of Russia – 'nearly a whole army division', he commented with his usual partiality for military metaphors – and asked if, in power, they had come under the influence of an alien culture. It might be argued that the vanquished Whites had a high level of culture. But that was not the case; their culture had been 'miserable, insufficient'. Even so, it was 'at a higher level than ours'.[59]

Except in small ways, Stalin did not develop the ideology of the Soviet state. The word 'Stalinism' was not used by his Party in Stalin's day: it would 'have implied a separation of Stalin and Lenin'.[60] The notion of 'Socialism in one country' and the view that the closer the world approaches Socialism, the sharper becomes the character of the class war were Stalin's only original contributions. In 1939, he had argued that, even under Communism, something like the state would have to survive. That sounded like an innovation. Stalin, however, believed that he acted according to Lenin's ideas. He saw himself as a high priest guarding a cult which someone else had created: as, indeed, he said at Lenin's funeral, in terms which were, even more than his speech in February 1946, liturgical in style.[61] Far from distorting Lenin's legacy, Stalin gave it the machinery which it required in order to survive indefinitely, in the circumstances of a dispute between his heirs. 'Marxism-Leninism' as a phrase was invented by Stalin. Stalin's simplified summing-up in his book, *Problems of Leninism*, also, as Djilas put it, 'linked Marxism-Leninism to power and turned it into a guide to action' – for slow-witted bureaucrats and ambitious youth leaders alike.[62] His short history of the Soviet Communist Party was also widely read.

Stalin's phobias about conspiracies, his jealousy and cruelty were, however, a personal mark of his system; and resulted in the deaths of tens of thousands, where perhaps Lenin might only have insisted on thousands. It is improbable that Lenin would have visited the sins of his enemies on their children (or their parents). Many of the grotesqueries of Stalin's day might have been avoided had Lenin lived longer. But it is unlikely even so that, had Lenin lived, the spiritual life of Russia would have avoided the fog of mendacity which marked the 'era of Stalin'. The 'cult of the personality', the name which Soviet Communists later gave to Stalin's day, was not, therefore, anything more than a colossal embroidery on Lenin's examples. (That was why, indeed, 'destalinisation', when an opportunity seemed to open up, in the 1950s, did not occur.) The suggestion that Stalin was unfaithful to Lenin in essential matters – such as the nature, and leading role, of the Party in the revolutionary process, and the maintenance of the proletarian dictatorship – is incorrect.[63] Where Stalin did differ was in tactics: his instinct led him always towards the recovery of imperial assets, no doubt to be expected of the first Georgian, Communist or no, to capture authority in Muscovy. Both Lenin and Stalin deliberately inculcated a mood, or a temperament, within the Party, in which Party members, even those who had suffered from it, habitually suspended all powers of criticism. A follower of Trotsky, Piatakov, who capitulated to Stalin in February 1928, later that year defended himself to old friends now in exile, when visiting Paris, as Soviet trade representative, against accusations of lack of courage and said: 'A true Bolshevik has submerged his personality in the collectivity, the "Party", to such an extent that he can make the necessary effort to break away from his own opinions and convictions and can honestly agree with the Party – that is the test of a true Bolshevik. There could be no life for him outside the ranks of the Party and he would be ready to believe that black was white and white was black if the Party required it'.[64]

These ideas were not confined to the Russian Communists, but were amply shared by all 'paid up party members' throughout the world. Isaiah Berlin describes meeting 'a handsome lady who had been one of Lenin's secretaries' and who told him, in Moscow in 1945, 'we are a scientifically governed society; and if there is no room for free thinking in physics – a man who questioned the laws of motion is obviously ignorant or mad – why should we Marxists who have discovered the laws of history and society permit free thinking in the social sphere?'[65]

In the war just concluded, nevertheless, the ideology of Marx and Lenin (nothing if not international), had been steeped, as it were, in Russian patriotism. The regime sponsored that in order to win the war. The Russian people responded vigorously, after realising the atrocities practised by the invaders. Hence, a great outflow of popular Russian poems, plays, novels, based upon hatred for Germans, as much as affection for the mother country. Alexei Tolstoy, Sholokhov, and Ehrenburg, were the writers of this new dimension to Stalinist Russia. The famous poem of Simonov entitled *Kill Him* may not have been subtle. But it was effective. Marxism-Leninism never fully recovered as an ideology from this wartime marriage with the Russian soul. All the same, that marriage helped to preserve the ideology even when its basic tenets seem increasingly dubious, in the nuclear age.*

These then were the theories which in 1946 dominated the large empire known as the USSR. The fact that the leaders had won the late war in collaboration with other states did not mean that they felt any gratitude to them. Theory prevented that, even if many – even Stalin – may sometimes personally have

---

* The emphasis on patriotism in wartime propaganda had been partially anticipated before 1941 during the Five Year Plans. Stalin had in the 1930s abandoned experimental education and substituted a disciplined system designed to prepare children for their future in a hierarchical society. The authority of the family had been revived, abortion and free love restricted, the state praised almost as if it were Prussia not Russia. An industrial society needed literate, numerate patriots of disciplined manners. The fact that *Pravda*, as early as June 1934, had talked of the Fatherland in glowing terms – a cry which 'kindles the flame of heroism, of creative initiative' – recalls that Mother Russia was brought back to help the Third Revolution, not just the government in the war. But certainly the 'traditionalist' restoration flourished even more in the war, when Tsarist imperialism was rehabilitated.

experienced twinges of sympathy for some of the Western leaders with whom they came into contact. But for a Communist a personal liking for anyone is comparable to a weakness for a special dish: something marginal, which one can abandon on advice. The size of the victory also made it easy for Stalin to revive the party's commitment to the theory by which they had been brought up, and to which they would continue to adhere, even if it seemed among some to be 'kindergarten Marxism':[66] since, without it, their title to rule would be non-existent.

The military opportunities of 1944 and 1945, incidentally, presented a few intellectual difficulties to the Soviet leaders. Marx and Engels had despised the people of the Balkans. They conceived of them as small subject races which had played no part in European history and had no especial right to be independent. Rather less conveniently, in a different way, Marx had looked on Poland as a 'historic' people which should be returned to her boundaries of 1772.

The war also gave birth to some new communist phrases if not ideas. As early as 1945, Marshal Tito in Yugoslavia had been speaking of 'people's democracy' to describe his own version of the dictatorship of the proletariat. In the winter of 1945–46, Communist diplomats, such as Vyshinsky, spent a long time explaining to their bemused Western interlocutors, often unresponsive to questions of ideology, that the world would soon be seeing in Eastern Europe the evolution of a new version of democracy, neither Western nor Russian, but indigenous. Most of the leaders of Communist Eastern Europe would say the same: 'a special form of revolutionary authority' was what Bierut claimed he was setting up in Poland; while some Soviet commentators held that the world was seeing in the Balkans 'new, higher forms of democracy' still not yet Socialist nor proletarian, much less Communist. The fact that these states were held to be at a different stage to the Soviet Union in their development towards Socialism meant that they did not have to be absorbed as such by the same 'dictatorship of the proletariat' as Russia: which country would be a guide, nevertheless, being more advanced.

Neither Lenin nor Marx would have had any use for the

theories of liberty encapsulated in the declarations about freedom between the three great powers at Yalta: 'Should we
subordinate our future policy to certain fundamental democratic
principles and attribute absolute value to them; or should all
democratic principles be exclusively subordinated to the
interests of our Party? I am decidedly in favour of the latter'.[67]
The leaders of 'People's democracies' could echo those words
of Lenin.

Stalin had now also at his disposal the use of certain ideas
which floated, as it were, on the general consciousness of
Western, even world, progressive opinion. These ideas included
concepts as vague as that the part of economics in history had
in the past been neglected; that the trends in capitalism were
leading towards an appreciation of Socialism; that the public
ownership of the means of distribution and exchange were, even
in the temporary stage of the dictatorship of the proletariat,
likely to be more efficient than private enterprise; and that
Socialism was a world cause. By 1945, the idea that technical
progress was the deciding factor in bringing about economic
change was, because of the horrors of war, which had been
influenced by modern technology, less fashionable, though more
true than ever. Another matter which assisted Stalin, and the
reputation of Stalin outside Russia, was that much of the world,
including Churchill and Roosevelt, and including most democratic
Socialists as well as Communists, had chosen to overlook both
the tragedy of the 1930s in Russia and the continuing repression
there. It was not that these things were not known. It was a
global reflection of the fact that in Russia itself there was a dual
consciousness: Professor Kołakowski sums that up very well:
'at public meetings, and even in private conversations, citizens
were obliged to repeat in ritual fashion grotesque falsehoods
about themselves, the world and the Soviet Union and, at the
same time, to keep silent about things which they knew very
well, not only because they were terrorised, but because the
incessant repetition of falsehoods which they knew to be such
made them accomplices in the campaign inculcated by Party and
state'.[68] In the same way, the leaders of the West had been
unable to take in the enormity of the murder of the Jews

by Hitler. Human capacity for recognising evil was shown in 1940–1945 not to be great.

The dominance of the ideology discussed in this chapter had important implications for Russian foreign policy. Lenin had said in 1918: 'we live not only in a state but in a *system of states*; and the existence of the Soviet Republic next to a number of imperialist states for a long time is unthinkable. In the end either the one or the other must triumph. Until that end comes, a series of terrible conflicts between the Soviet Republic and the bourgeois states is inevitable'.[69] Stalin showed that he knew of this formulation when he wrote his letter to Comrade Ivanov in February 1938. Nothing which had occurred between then and 1946, neither the atom bomb nor the long personal conversations with Churchill, Roosevelt and other Western leaders, had caused the Russian leaders to alter the ideas implicit in these views. (Even Stalin's 'humane' successor, Nikita Khrushchev, would later talk of the 'progressive disintegration of the world capitalist system' and 'the irresistible advance of all mankind towards Communism', and say that 'the Soviet people are confident of victory' against capitalism.) That does not mean that all Soviet policy was geared, in the style of Jenghiz Khan, to meaningless, or murderous, expansion. It did mean that Stalin bore in mind Lenin's rule that, when faced with opposition – and the whole non-Soviet world could constitute an enemy to the Soviet Union – 'only the wholesale deportation or internment of the most dangerous and stubborn exploiters could ensure victory'.[70]

There were elements of continuity with the past in this 'revolutionary' Russian government. Herzen, in the middle of the XIXth century, had seen the government of Russia as 'a mixed structure, without architecture, without solidity, without roots, without principles . . . a civil camp, a military chancellery, a state of siege in time of peace, a mixture of reaction and revolution, as likely to endure a long time as to fall into immediate collapse'.[71] Gorki, in his *Life of a Useless Man*, has a character saying that 'everything belongs to the Tsar: the whole earth is God's earth and the whole of Russia belongs to the Tsar'.[72] The Western sense of property and of persons independent of the state developed late and never became deep-rooted.[73] 'The state became swollen while the people shrank' wrote the historian Klyuchevsky, in a judgement about Peter the Great's time which embraced all Tsardom.[74] Though Russia began to industrialise in the XIXth century, particularly after 1861, that derived from the intervention of the already absolutist state, not from the endeavours of an indigenous mercantile class. (Capitalists in Russia before 1914 were often Germans, Englishmen, Welsh, Swedes or Frenchmen.) In the generation before 1917, new methods of communication, such as the railway and, later, the telephone, enabled the state to control opponents more efficiently than in the past. The spread of censorship went hand-in-hand with that of literacy. Industry, as in the time of Peter the Great, continued to serve military purposes.

Then there were the institutions of the state. The conquests of Ivan the Terrible, for example, were confirmed by a much-feared security police, Oprichnina, certainly a state within a state, whose members rode black horses, wore black uniforms and carried the emblem of a broom on their saddles to indicate that their mission was to sweep Russia free of treason.[75] According to one of his biographers, Stalin deliberately re-modelled the CHEKA, which he inherited from Lenin, on that institution.[76] The Oprichnina did not have a continuous life after the death of Ivan. But a political police was usually available to Tsars.

Beneath the veneer of sophistication which the French-speaking upper class, officialdom and bourgeoisie gave to old Russia, the country remained uncivilised. 'The Russians', wrote Souvarine in his *Life of Stalin*, 'may have received a visit from Diderot; they may own Voltaire's library; but they are still living in the age of theology'.[77] The destruction of this 'all-too-thin' veneer, the upper layers of Russian society, by Lenin and Stalin was complete, so that, in 1946, the Soviet government was still 'a government of peasants ruling over a peasant country brutalised by civil war, international war and revolutionary violence'.[78] Throughout Russia, there were very few traces of the old culture by which new men could direct themselves even if only subconsciously.

Peter the Great had, in the early XVIIIth century, cut 'a window into Europe', in Pushkin's words. But, like Stalin, he wanted technology, not philosophy, to come in. Catherine the Great, a real liberal, from a part of Germany which had experienced the Reformation, opened the window wider, but was terrified, first by the rising of Pugachev and then by the French Revolution, into closing it. The Napoleonic Wars signified that Russian patriots often thereafter identified liberalism, as did Spaniards, with anti-patriotism. The defeat of the Decembrists in 1825, and 'the age of the handkerchief' which followed it, caused demand for change. Alexander II's emancipation of the serfs, the beginning of industrialisation, and the increase in population in the late XIXth century which occurred all over the world, were accompanied by a new bureaucratic repression briefly interrupted only by the events of 1905. The short year when a thousand flowers bloomed in 1917 led first to civil war, and then to a revolutionary tyranny more skilful and more effective than that of the Tsarist bureaucracy.

'Marxism', as has been suggested, had not been expected by its proponents to establish itself in Russia. But Russia did turn out to constitute good ground for the doctrine under the direction of Lenin and Stalin. There were paradoxes here: some Russians such as Solzhenitsyn[79] have looked on Marxism as a fatal Western influence – which, in collaboration with certain negative, self-destructive elements in the Russian psyche, had a devastating consequence. His injunction is: 'Get rid of totalitarian Marxist-Leninist ideology so that Russia can be Russia again'.[80] Others speak of the 'cultural Westernisation of Russia' under Communism, asking, 'What was it about Marxism which enabled it to push Russia back, in one terrible blow, to the Tartar tradition, under the name of "Socialism"?',[81] though, under Stalin, Socialism developed into something different from what the old Bolsheviks had thought it in Lenin's day.[82] Whatever it was, the circumstances by which Marxism-Leninism became grafted onto Russian imperialism owed much to Russia: to 'the Russian national ethos, the emulation of the extremist element in Leninism and the personality of Stalin'. In particular, the idea of a disciplined conspiratorial party was Russian in inspiration. So was the use made by Communists in power of that particularly useful concept, the dictatorship of the proletariat. A great Polish diplomatist bitterly pointed out that whereas, under the Tsars, the protection of all Orthodox Christians was made the excuse for Russian expansion now it was the inspiration of communist revolution.[83] Kołakowski wrote: 'although Communism is alien to the strong spiritual component in Russian culture, it has nevertheless taken root in Russia and is nurtured by the missionary, despotic, and imperialist elements in Russian history'[84].

# THREE

# THE VOZHD

The influence of personality in history was a matter much discussed by the last generation of historians. Bertrand Russell believed that the best example of an individual determining events was Bismarck and his deliberate schemes to build the second German Reich.[1] Karl Marx, however, placed no emphasis on individuals, despite his own strong character which transformed Socialism. His view of history was that kings and generals had played little part in the unrolling of events which were principally, he believed, determined by technology. Even technology had in Marx's view little to do with technologists. Marx's views on these matters have affected many who reject his general theories. Personalities have been ignored. That neglect is a mistake when considering Lenin and Stalin.

For events since Marx's day have offered the basis for a new interpretation. The concentration of power in modern states, and habits of subordinating all authority to the state, acquired in war, offer many great opportunities for leaders to impose their will, even their whims, on their peoples, provided that they can bully, or inspire, or bribe, their bureaucracies to do what they ask of them. That applied as much to Churchill's England as to the Russia of his ally.

The influence of Stalin on Russia was profound. Yet 'how', asked the Yugoslav revolutionary, Milovan Djilas, in 1946 a senior Communist official in his own country, could this 'dark, cruel and cunning man have led one of the greatest and most

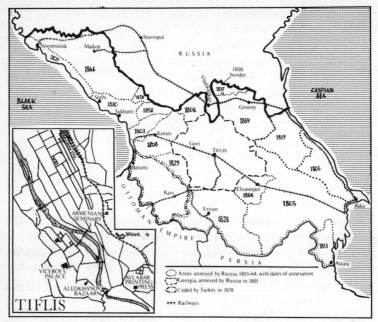

Acknowledgment: This map reflects closely a map in Martin Gilbert's 'Russian History Atlas'

powerful states, not just for a day but for thirty years?'[2] Averell Harriman, the ambassador of the United States to Russia between 1943 and 1946, wrote: 'It is hard for me to reconcile the courtesy and consideration which he showed me personally with the ghastly cruelty of his wholesale liquidations'. He added 'for me, Stalin remains the most inscrutable and contradictory character I have known. I found him better informed than Roosevelt, more realistic than Churchill, in some ways the most effective of the war leaders. At the same time he was, of course, a murderous tyrant'.[3] Solzhenitsyn, his appeal against unjust imprisonment having been sent to the Supreme Soviet about the time of the speech by Stalin previously discussed (it was never answered), wrote that 'we were forever being told that individuals do not mould history . . . but, for a quarter of a century, one such individual twisted our tails as if we were sheep and we didn't even dare to squeal'.[4] 'Whatever standards we use to take his measure, he has the glory of being the greatest criminal in history and, let us hope, for all time to come. For in him was joined the criminal senselessness of a Caligula with the refinement of a Borgia and the brutality of a Tsar Ivan the Terrible': that was a further judgement by Djilas.[5] Yet, as a biographer has pointed out, a comparison of Stalin with even the worst tyrants of the past omits the consideration that 'most of those killed enemies who had actually opposed them: not friends, or colleagues, who had done nothing and constituted no danger to them'.[6] Another biographer described him as one who 'for all the evil which he incarnated, and for all his blunders during the civil war, was nevertheless a man without equal in the art of outwitting political opponents, building up power and preserving it'.[7] At Yalta, Sir Alexander Cadogan, a conventional English official, noted 'in particular "Joe" has been extremely good. He *is* a great man and shows up very impressively, against the background of the other two ageing statesmen'.[8] Roosevelt's beloved friend, Harry Hopkins, described his first interview with him warmly – 'there was no waste of word, gesture, or mannerism. It was like talking to a perfectly co-ordinated machine, an intelligent machine . . . His answers were ready, unequivocal, spoken as if the man had had them on his tongue for years'.[9] Lord Beaverbrook thought him 'a kindly man' who 'practically never shows impatience' – though that press lord was scarcely a connoisseur of patience.[10] Roy Medvedev described him as 'a profound connoisseur of human failings, a brilliant master of bureaucratic psychology'.[11]

As these memories suggest, Stalin, like most successful statesmen, was a good actor. He knew how to behave with foreigners as if he had been hemmed in by others – the Politburo, say, or the Supreme Soviet – who prevented his freedom of action. That myth deceived the most perceptive foreign observers: Churchill, Hopkins, even 'Chip' Bohlen.[12] Churchill thought that behind Stalin sat 'black care': some other dark Politburo individuals who really controlled policy;[13] and, on the first occasion that he went to Moscow, thought that the 'Council of Commissars' had taken against Stalin's interpretation of his visit.[14] Stalin told Churchill once that only he and Molotov were in favour of dealing 'softly' with the Polish democrat Mikołajczyk: others in the Kremlin were more harsh.[15] ('As time went on', Roosevelt and Hopkins 'became more and more aware' of the Politburo as 'an unseen, incomprehensible but potent influence on Stalin'.)[16]

Stalin knew how to appear one day as the jovial 'Uncle Joe', the next as the man of steel, and then as the businesslike manager of a difficult country. To Dr Eduard Táborský, secretary to the Czech Prime Minister, he seemed 'an elderly gentleman with thinning hair, and a lot of wrinkles . . . an old uncle with a pleasant expression'.[17] He knew that it was politically wise to be seen smoking a pipe, rather than a cigarette; even if, during the war, he seemed to Hopkins and to Beaverbrook a chain smoker.[18] He could impress foreign visitors as 'an austere, rugged, determined figure',[19] in a marshal's uniform, with or without decorations; or, with a delegation of miners, he would appear in trousers tucked inside his boots, 'the way that Russian workers had done before 1917',[20] though after 1945 he was almost always the marshal, never the worker.[21] At Potsdam he dressed 'like the Emperor of Austria in a bad musical comedy; cream jacket with gold-braided collar, blue trousers with a red stripe and one jewelled order'.[22] He could seem to James Byrnes a 'very likeable person'[23] or to the British foreign secretary 'very straight, direct and reasonable'.[24] Another British official, usually realistic, found him 'very good-humoured and patient, with no suggestion of doctrinaire opinions'.[25] One of his most intemperate critics, Antonov-Ovseenko, whose father was murdered by him, explained that, whether he 'was playing the role of the straightforward good-hearted fellow or the strict and serious keeper of the Party's values, or the omnipotent leader, Stalin entered into each part so thoroughly that he sincerely began to believe it'.[26] Djilas agreed: 'it seemed he never dissembled but was always truly experiencing each of his roles'. To Djilas, he was also of a 'lively, almost restless, temperament, who always questioned – himself and others; and who argued – with himself – and others':[27] he was 'a very alive person, with very alive, fast reactions – with fast nerves. You could do nothing in the presence of Stalin which he did not notice'.[28] To the United

States Ambassador of the 1930s, Bullitt, Stalin seemed a man of extraordinary intelligence 'and extraordinary intuition . . . when you talk with him he seems to be reaching out all over the room with his mind in a dozen different directions . . . he can follow half a dozen different conversations simultaneously';[29] 'the most hard-boiled realist in the world' and from 'some points of view much more capable than either Roosevelt or Churchill'.[30] With foreign visitors he often doodled wolves – wolves with a red background; just that hint of violence always necessary in dealing with democrats,[31] whom he hated and feared, as the greatest musician at his court, Shostakovich, remarked.[32]

Stalin's ancestors were people of the Caucasus. His mother, Ekaterina Geladze, was born in Gambareuili in Georgia, but moved with her family in 1864, when she was nine, to Gori. Her parents were apparently serfs. Their move to Gori was probably due to the Act of Emancipation of 1861. She was a determined, devout seamstress and laundress, who worked hard, after her husband died in 1890; first, in order to bring up her son; then out of habit. She was barely literate but she had wanted her only surviving child to rise in the world – and so ensured that he went to a seminary, where there was a good general education, after he had shown promise in his first school, at Gori. When Stalin had become master of Russia, she went to live in the Tsar's viceroy's palace in Tiflis. Stalin went to see her shortly before she died. She said 'What a pity you never became a priest'.[33]

Some said that Ekaterina Djugashvili was an Ossete. The Ossetes were a Farsi-speaking people who lived in the north of the Caucasus, were descended from the Alans and had a reputation for both ugliness and brutality: hence Stalin's anger when, in 1935, the poet Osip Mandelstam wrote, and read aloud, a poem with explicit allusions to him as a 'low-browed Ossete', for whom 'every killing was a treat'.[34]

Stalin's father's family, the Djugashvilis, were also peasant in origin. His great-grandfather, Zaza, is said to have been active in an anti-Russian rising in the Caucasus about 1810, not long after the Russian union with Georgia (this Act of Union occurred in 1801). Stalin's grandfather, Vano, is believed to have tended vineyards at Didi-Lilo, near Tiflis (the Caucasus is the region where grapes were both indigenous and first pressed). Vissarion, Stalin's father, was a shoemaker – a 'simple shoemaker' Stalin would assure his colleagues – in Gori. Later, he worked in the Adelkhanov boot factory in Tiflis. There were rumours, endorsed by Khrushchev, that Stalin's father in the end employed nearly forty – or was it ten? – skilled craftsmen in his workshop.[35] That would have given Stalin 'petty bourgeois' origins, by Marxist interpretations; so the story was not much mentioned in his lifetime. Vissarion was a drunkard, treated his wife and son harshly, and died in a brawl in 1890.

The Caucasus has been since time immemorial a place of combat, diversity, intrigue, conspiracy and murder. The fertility of the territory attracted Greek, Jewish, Roman, Persian and, latterly, Genoese colonists. A tranquil stability was achieved in the XIIth century under the Bagratid dynasty. That monarchy, however, was broken by Jenghiz Khan. Several centuries of pillage and war followed. It was known for the Mongols' '*razzias*' of 'human cattle'. Kings of Georgia, however, survived. The last of them, George XIII, gave up his crown to the Tsar since he preferred the 'unenviable but endurable lot of the Russian peoples' to living with the threat of continual invasion from Persia.[36]

In Gori in 1879, where Stalin was born, the population of 20,000 were mostly Georgians. But Tiflis, fifty miles south-east down the River Kura, the seat of the Russian viceroy of the Caucasus, was composed of many different peoples – Armenians, Persians, Jews, Turks, Tartars, Germans, as well as Georgians and Russians, of whom the Armenians were much the most prominent in commerce. The city was growing: it had 100,000 inhabitants in the early 1880s; and 350,000 in 1913. It was high and hot. Baedeker's Guide for Russia in 1914 described it: 'the streets are generally steep and often so narrow that two carriages cannot pass each other. The houses, mostly adorned with balconies, are perched one above the other on the mountain-slopes, like the steps of a staircase. From sunrise to sunset, with the exception of the hot midday hours, the streets are crowded with a motley throng of men and animals, walkers, riders and carts. The most conspicuous elements in the population include the Georgian sellers of vegetables, fruit and fish, with their large wooden trays on their heads; the Persians, with long caftans and high black fur caps, often with red-dyed hair and fingernails; the Tartar seyyids and mullahs in flowing raiment with green and white turbans; the smooth-shaven Tartars, in ragged clothing; the representatives of various mountain tribes in their picturesque tcherkéskas and shaggy fur caps; and the porters carrying heavy burdens on their backs. The Mohammedan women never appear in the street without their veils. Among other features are the lively little donkeys bearing heavy loads or ridden by one or more men and horses carrying water-skins . . .'[37]

Tiflis was the city in which Stalin grew up. It was also where his (second) father-in-law, Alliluyev, was a locksmith, where the writer Gorki worked as a manual labourer and where Kalinin, titular head of the Soviet state in 1946, worked as a lathe-maker.[38] Stalin began his education at the parochial school in Gori. 'Among the best pupils there', he soon passed to the seminary at Tiflis; where, after a few years, his revolutionary career began and where he was expelled for political activities. He had shown himself already to have a 'mechanical memory', a grasp of technical knowledge, and a capacity for intrigue. He began at the seminary the long path towards assumption of a Russian, not a Georgian, character. Also, according to his daughter, 'in a young man who had never for a moment believed in the spirit . . . enforced religious training could have brought out only contrary results': extreme scepticism of everything 'heavenly', of everything 'sublime'. The result was 'total materialism, the cynical realism of an earthly, sombre, practical and low view of life'.[39] 'When young Russians lost their religious faith, they seldom became rationalist sceptics', commented Hugh Seton-Watson, 'but carried into their atheist beliefs and doctrines of social revolution a religious fervour'.[40] The same phenomenon was to be observed at the same time among anarchists in Spain and Southern Italy. But Stalin's eccentricity was to combine revolutionary and millenarian atheism with, as has already been seen, a strong liturgical manner in public speech.

In the twenty years between abandoning the seminary and the Bolshevik Revolution, Stalin organised strikes in the oil refineries in Baku and Batum – where he became a 'practical fighter, and practical leader' – participated in robberies of banks ('expropriations' which Lenin approved and others condemned), in order to gain funds for the Bolshevik cause and became, he later said, a 'journeyman of Revolution'. He rose in the Georgian branch of the Bolshevik Party and represented it in congresses abroad; and spent several years in Siberia in exile – his imprisonment explains why he did not serve in the Tsar's army during the First World War. He met and collaborated with famous revolutionaries in the Caucasus and elsewhere; established an association with Lenin; became a co-opted member of the Party's Central Committee in 1912; and acquired a capacity for espionage, deception, terrorism and the uses of both provocation and mendacity which never left him nor the regime which he dominated. The hoodwinking of enemies at home and abroad, and the mocking of their weakness and credulity, characterised him and Russia ever after.

It was of this period in Stalin's life (and of his rivals, such as S. Shaumian, his competitor for the leadership of the oil workers in Baku in 1907, within the Bolshevik movement) that he was presumably thinking when, in 1923, he described his idea of happiness: 'to choose one's victim, to prepare one's plan minutely, to slake an implacable vengeance and then go to bed . . . There is nothing sweeter'.[41]

One of Stalin's secretaries, Boris Bazhanov, one of the few who both broke with him and succeeded in surviving in exile, later wrote that Stalin, by the time that he came to know him in the 1920s, was a 'vindictive Asiatic with fear, suspicion and revenge deeply embedded in his soul . . . he would recoil from nothing, drive every issue to its absurd extreme, and send men to their deaths in large numbers without the slightest hesitation'.[42] A certain Vereshchek, who had been in prison with Stalin in Vologda, recorded that the future Vozhd admitted there that he had betrayed to the police his comrades in the secret Socialist club while still in the seminary. He noticed – and there were others who recalled that too – that, in Siberia, Stalin made a habit of mixing with common criminals, not with 'politicians'.[43] In exile, Stalin was said to have spread tales of treachery among his opponents, and persuaded others to murder those concerned, on his behalf. He showed, it is said, an extraordinary capacity for secretly urging others to action – rebellion, escape, murder – while himself remaining aloof: or going fishing or shooting in that Siberia whose lonely *taiga* he afterwards said that he loved.

Between the emergence of the relatively unknown '*Koba*' – only 'a grey blur', as he seemed to the diarist Sukhanov in the early days of the Revolution[44] – and his appearance as the great victor of 1946 in the elections to the Supreme Soviet, Stalin did not change much. He just made himself indispensable. He first established himself in Lenin's confidence: so becoming, he said in his autobiographical reflections, a 'master craftsman' in revolution.[45] He was the 'wonderful Georgian' who would do things to which he committed himself, unlike the rhetorical cosmopolitan Jews who rose so far in the first years after the revolution. Then he outmanoeuvred Lenin's heirs and had most of them killed, for all the world as if they had been minor political gangsters in Tiflis instead of intellects known throughout Europe – not only them but their friends, followers and families, to the figure of hundreds of thousands. He had some of the most remarkable of them tortured to confess crimes which no novelist of espionage would have dared to invent. His policemen in the 1930s invented a fiction of a great conspiracy to undermine Soviet power, his enemy Trotsky was made out in court to be the supreme agent of the British secret service, an act of imagination of such surrealism as to rank among the most absurd, as well as the most cruel, charges in history. Hitler killed Jews because they were so. Stalin killed Russians in as great numbers for no reason except that he wished to remove them from the face of the earth. After all, he could comfort himself, had not Engels said that 'without force and an iron ruthlessness nothing is accomplished in history'?[46]

Stalin also carried out the transformation of Soviet agriculture in such a way as to make Nero seem a 'moderate'. He developed a system of preventive imprisonment on a scale unknown in history. He both made friends with Hitler and then, on being attacked, presided over his defeat. He accompanied this last victory with an astonishing series of diplomatic successes which gave him the sort of international position which only Alexander I among Russian rulers had ever surpassed, at the end of the Napoleonic wars. The fact that he reminded Averell Harriman at Potsdam that the Tsar had reached Paris showed that the Tsar's example was on his mind.[47] At the same time, he enjoyed the admiration of communists throughout the world.

In the 1940s Stalin met his Russian or, on occasion, foreign colleagues, principally at dinner. These dinners were the then Soviet equivalent to cabinet meetings. Extraordinary pictures of these occasions have been made available by several of those often present, such as Nikita Khrushchev, and Stalin's daughter, Svetlana; and by one or two visitors, of whom the Yugoslavs Djilas and Popović, and the Polish Jakub Berman were the most perceptive.

As a rule, these dinners were held at Stalin's villa at Kuntsevo, a village used by Muscovites for weekends since the late nineteenth century, about ten miles from the middle of Moscow. Stalin always travelled there by motor car, varying the route. This villa, referred to as the 'near-by' dacha (*Blizhny*), was a single storey one, built especially for Stalin in 1934 by the architect Mirion Ivanovich Merzhanov. It seemed at first, to Stalin's daughter, 'a wonderful, airy, modern' building set in a garden. The roof was a large sun-deck. Stalin lived in one big room and 'made it do for everything. He slept on the sofa which he had made up at night as a bed and had telephones beside it'. There was a large table piled high with papers, newspapers and books. At that table, he dined, whether alone or whether, as he often did, he invited his colleagues. The other rooms in the house were furnished in exactly the same way. That meant that Stalin could change and move into any of them. Around the house, there were terraces and a verandah, woods and some small summer houses. Stalin walked among these woods and, in summer, often sat outside to work.[48] He lived alone, with no companions, no wife since 1930, and customarily went to his office in the Kremlin, in the palace known before 1917 as the

'Nicholas' or 'Yellow' Palace, built in the reign of Catherine for the Metropolitan Plato, to see films or foreign visitors. He had been lonely ever since his wife had killed herself in protest at his policies, fourteen years before. His visitors were usually now Communists who did not dare to speak their mind. Occasionally, he would see the British or the United States ambassadors; no others from the West, except on the occasion of visits by their Prime Ministers. Like Churchill and Hitler, Stalin enjoyed films: particularly Eisenstein's *Ivan the Terrible* or those which, like *Unforgettable 1919*, showed him in a favourable light, for example on the footplate of an armoured train clasping a sabre.

A dinner with Stalin lasted a long time – six or more hours, from ten at night till about four or five in the morning, with many toasts, perhaps with glasses of pertsovka, fiery vodka with a red hot pepper at the bottom of the glass.[49] Djilas described how 'one ate and drank slowly, during a rambling conversation which ranged from stories and anecdotes to the most serious political and even philosophical subjects'.[50] Khrushchev would describe how such evenings might have begun in Stalin's study at the Kremlin or in the Kremlin cinema; and how, after the film, the leaders of Russia would adjourn to Kuntsevo. Thanks to his suspicions, everything that Stalin ate or drank had to be tasted before being eaten – by one or other of the colleagues. These dinners, Khrushchev said, 'were frightful. We would get home early in the morning just in time for breakfast and then we'd have to go to work.'[51]

There was much drinking, even much wild drinking, on these occasions. Khrushchev described how Stalin himself not only drank inordinately, but encouraged all present to do so, since he 'found it entertaining to watch the people round him get themselves into embarrassing and even disgraceful situations'. The quantity of food was also enormous. All helped themselves. Stalin 'usually chose meat, a sign of his mountain origins'.[52] Molotov, Beria and Zhdanov all drank great quantities without enjoyment, while Shcherbakov, who had run Moscow in the war, and controlled all the information and communiqués about it, had apparently drunk himself to death in March 1945. The

Pole, Jakub Berman, describes eating 'a delicious roast of bear meat' and also dancing with Molotov – not Mrs Molotov, who had been sent to a labour camp; secrets passed during a waltz: 'Stalin didn't often dance. He turned the gramophone . . . He would put on records and watch.'[53] (Popović, however, recalls Stalin dancing and the other comrades would call out 'Comrade Josif Vissariovich, how strong you are!'[54] On one occasion at least, he took Tito round the floor.)[55]

It was in such circumstances, at 'these interminable agonising dinners', that the destiny of Russia, and so much of the human race, was decided. Such was the theatre of ideology.

Stalin was an exception to the usual rule that no one who has a sense of humour can be wholly evil. He liked jokes. Harry Hopkins even thought his humour 'keen, penetrating'.[56] A 'rough humour', Djilas noted, 'self-assured, but not entirely without subtlety and depth'.[57] Voroshilov remembered Stalin when young as 'a bundle of energy, gay and full of life'.[58] When he lived in St Petersburg with his in-laws, the Alliluyevs, both in 1912 and 1917, Stalin 'greatly amused those around him with his comic anecdotes'.[59] Alexander Cadogan described Stalin at Yalta: 'The President flapped about and the PM boomed, but "Joe" just sat taking it all in and being rather amused . . . He's obviously got a very good sense of humour'.[60] Stalin naturally changed his jokes to suit the audience; at home, when at table with his 'companions-in-arms', nothing prevented him from 'cracking coarse peasant jokes and telling coarse peasant stories'. When his daughter left the table in dismay, he might send back for her and greet her as a 'Comrade hostess, why have you left us poor unenlightened creatures without giving us some direction? Lead us! Show us the way!'[61] Stalin also enjoyed practical jokes which made the 'comrades-in-arms' seem ridiculous. He liked not only to persuade them to drink too much but to put a tomato on a companion's chair; or salt, or vodka, into a glass of wine.

There were grimmer pleasantries: one of his favourite ones concerned a professor who shared an apartment with a secret policeman. The professor, irritated by the policeman's ignorance, once exploded: 'Oh you, you don't even know who wrote

*Yevgeny Onegin*'. The policeman later arrested the professor and boasted to his friends: 'I've got him to confess: *he* was the author!'[62] He also enjoyed jokes of real brutality: 'one of our men was leading a large group of German prisoners', he told Djilas, 'and he killed all but one. They asked him, when he arrived at his destination: "where are the others?" "I was carrying out the order of the Commander-in-Chief to kill everyone to the last man – and here is the last man!"'[63] Presumably it was with his sharp tongue in his hard cheek that, at the height of the agrarian revolution of the early 1930s, which he himself had inspired, Stalin wrote 'life has become better, life has become merrier'.[64] The suggestion, a little before that, that those who were carrying out those upheavals – the deportation of districts, the arrests and executions of millions, the transportation of infants from temperate to glacial regions – were 'dizzy with success' shows the mark of a master of the macabre.[65] Bierut, the leader of the Polish Communists, would regularly ask Stalin, when he came to Moscow, what had happened to certain party members from Poland, who he thought might not have been killed in the fearful purges of that party in 1938 or 1937. Stalin would turn gravely to Beria and ask 'Lavrenty Pavlovich, don't you know where they are? I told you to look for them, why haven't you found them yet?' He enjoyed playing this scene.[66]

Stalin had left Russia four times in his life, apart from visits to Tehran and Potsdam during the late war. These journeys were: to London in April 1907, for the seventh Congress of the Russian Social Democratic Party; to Cracow and to Vienna in 1910; to Stockholm and then to Germany in 1906. He also visited Finland in 1917 to encourage the Finnish Bolsheviks to try and seize power.[67] These occasions were significant because it was abroad that Stalin met Lenin, Trotsky and Bukharin, Plekhanov and Voroshilov: not because he gained knowledge about non-Russian conditions. He did, however, think that he knew something of Germany, since he was accustomed to recall that 'when I was in Germany before the revolution, a group of Soviet Democrats came late to the Congress because they had to wait to have their tickets punched to enable them to leave the railway station.

When would Russians ever do that? Someone has well said: "in Germany, you cannot have a revolution, because you would have to step on the lawns".'[68]

Stalin had some knowledge of languages. He could read Georgian, though used to say that he had forgotten it. He could read a simple German text with the help of a dictionary. In his old age, he still remembered some of the Greek which he had learnt at the seminary.[69] Stalin did not travel much in Russia. He did not visit a village in Russia after 1928 and only once in the war went to the front line.[70]

Stalin's daughter thought that, by the end of his life, the dictator had lost all touch with theory, ideology and Marxism-Leninism and was a pure pragmatist. That may be so but when younger his talents in this respect could not be utterly dismissed. His work *Problems of Leninism,* of which eighteen million copies had been published by 1948, satisfied a need throughout the Communist world for an easily assimilated compendium, as a guide to action. For example, hundreds of Communists read the following exchanges, with profit:

'Is the thesis that Leninism is the theory and tactics of proletarian revolution correct?'
    'I think it is correct', wrote Stalin.

'Is it possible, in the present phase of Socialist construction, to reach a real and durable agreement with the middle peasant . . . ?'
    'It *is* possible.'

'Did the peasants act wisely in supporting the October Revolution?'
    'Yes, they acted wisely.'

'. . . what is needed is that the government support the collective-farm peasants to the utmost with men and money . . . Have we got such a government?'

'Yes, we have. It is called the Workers' and Peasants' Soviet Government', said Stalin;

and, even:

'Where will the chain break in the near future?'
'. . . where it is weakest', said Stalin, 'it is not precluded that the chain may break let us say in India.'[71]

In 1938, Stalin published his *History of the CPSU: A Short Course*. It was a volume which represented its author in a heroic light. It was inaccurate and vindictive. All the same, it was essential reading for all Communists. Thirty million copies were published during the next ten years. Everyone with a career to make in Russia not only read it but mouthed its platitudes. That book is perhaps the best example ever written of the slogan of Pokrovsky: 'history is politics projected into the past'.[72]

Stalin's use of Russian patriotism in the war came easily to him. Marxist and Georgian he might be, but his recollection of 'our great ancestors', from Alexander Nevsky to Kutuzov, in, say, his speech of November 6, 1941 in the ornate hall of the Mayakovsky underground station, seemed quite natural.[73]

The essence of Stalin was well summed up by one of those few who in the West knew him: he was not immoral; he was simply amoral. He did not understand those elements of Western thought which Churchill and Roosevelt expressed to him during the wartime conferences.[74] That made the chance of his collaboration with them, or their successors, after the emergency of war, unlikely. 'Stalin's school was a very rough school', A. V. Snegov told the All-Union Conference of Historians in 1962, 'beside destroying honourable people, he corrupted live ones'.

There had been difficult moments in the late war for Stalin. He had believed in the durability of the Nazi-Soviet pact. He conducted himself between 1939 and 1941 towards Hitler in a way that made Chamberlain's appeasement seem like resilience. The war with Finland had nearly been a catastrophe. In the early days after the Nazi attack, he was shaken into complete inertia.

All the same, he was able in two weeks to change his approach from speaking of the war as 'a struggle of predatory imperialist nations over the control of world markets' to describing it as 'a great patriotic war of freedom-loving nations against fascism.' The British and French had still been 'fomenters of war' on June 20, 1941; on July 3 they were part of 'a united front of peoples standing for freedom against enslavement'.[75]

Suspicion and secrecy were so much second nature to Stalin that even matters essential to the prosecution of the war were kept private. Thus the elaborate attempts of the Japanese to make peace with the United States before the Russians were in the Far Eastern war (and before the atom bomb had been dropped) were not passed on to the United States. Stalin's reaction to the death of President Roosevelt in April 1945 was to send a cable to Washington requesting that an autopsy be performed to see if FDR had been poisoned.[76] Stalin knew of Hitler's death in Berlin at the end of the war. But he was soon telling his allies that he thought that he might have escaped to Japan by submarine.[77]

Stalin once said: 'You know the Russian people is a Tsarist people. It needs a Tsar'.[78] He provided them with the reproduction of one. Like Tsars in the past, he aspired to veneration. The evils which peasants and industrial workers encountered daily in his Russia could meanwhile be attributed to officials. His caprices, his unpredictable suspicions and mad fears made his time the most terrible in Russian history.

The Soviet empire was saturated with monuments to Stalin: factories called after him, innumerable cities – Stalinsk, Stalino, Stalind and Stalingrad were complemented by Stalinbad, Stalino-vavosh and Stalinnkan. One town in Georgia boasted both a Stalin Street and a Djugashvili Street. Children in schools sang songs to him:

> *'Stalin is our military glory!*
> *Stalin is our youth as it takes flight!*
> *Our people, singing, battling and winning*
> *Follow Stalin to the end of the night!'*

They would also intone: 'Thank you, Comrade Stalin,[79] for our happy childhood'.

Stalin had built a state in which unquestioning obedience to him offered the best hope of survival. He was himself an object of worship. Police, Party, army, state bureaucracy might sometimes differ; he alone could resolve their differences. While they watched each other, they deferred only to him. He could switch all of them towards a quite new line of policy and did so several times. He never gave concessions to those who desired more consumer goods, more freedom, less discipline. While speaking the language of limitless equality and international revolution, he could encourage patriotism, families, and an education which favoured the intelligent and the strong. The forced industrialisation of Russia, and the creation of a modern military power, were his legacies. To assure his success a bitter enmity with the surrounding capitalist states was essential to play upon; and to believe in. Professor E. H. Carr wrote in respect of the early 1920s: 'world revolution was the sole guarantee of national security; but national security was also a condition of the successful promotion of world revolution'.[80] That was no longer so in 1946. It was all the same impossible to abandon the illusion of world revolution. Stalin himself was perfidious and cruel. He was also subtle, intelligent and persistent. His skill as Commander-in-Chief in the war had been evident to his allies.[81] The combination of characteristics made him an individual of unique interest, and a unique problem to his rivals and enemies. The question whether he was, clinically speaking, mad is a matter to which, understandably, given on the one hand his qualities and, on the other hand, the lack of interchange between historians and physicians, little attention has been paid.[82]

# FOUR

# HOMO STALIENS

Lazar Kaganovich, a member of the all-powerful Soviet State Defence Committee (GOKO) during the war, the only man of Jewish origin left in Stalin's inner circle, and one of the most persistent and fortunate of Stalin's followers, was once approached by a relation who asked him to help her husband to leave a concentration camp where he had been unjustly imprisoned for many years. Kaganovich replied that he could not do so. He was powerless: 'you must understand', he said, 'there is only one sun. The rest are all pathetic little planets'.[1]

Kaganovich was a man who knew nearly everything about Stalin. His brother had killed himself just before being arrested on the accusation of having, when Commissar for Air, placed aeroplanes so close to the Polish frontier that they could easily be taken over in the German advance: a sign, in Stalin's argument, that he was preparing himself to be minister of a puppet government in Moscow after Hitler had captured it: an improbable conspiracy for a Jew. He, Lazar Kaganovich, had lent himself, in the 1930s, to the most surreal fancies: as Commissar in charge of Railways he remarked, to a group of railwaymen: 'I cannot name a single line, a single road where there's no Trotskyite-Japanese wrecking'.[2] So Kaganovich knew what he was saying.

That said, there were in the Kremlin a group of men to whom Stalin did speak about foreign policy. They had much in common. Galina Vishnevskaya recalls them as 'gloomy squat idols –

silent and motionless figures, at the centre of a whirling carnival of snivelling toadies'.[3] (She excepted the Armenian Mikoyan from this categorisation thinking he had the 'individuality . . . the lively temperament of a Southerner'.) The poet Mandelstam spoke of them as 'a rabble of thin-necked leaders, fawning half-men for him to play with'. They were indeed mostly small in build, for Stalin, himself short, did not like people taller than himself around him.[4] All of them were motivated by fear. None of them knew, as Khrushchev told Harriman later, 'whether their bodyguards were protecting them or watching them'.[5] 'None,' Roy Medvedev remarked grimly, 'were actually born criminals. But all of them knew that they risked their lives if they were to hesitate about committing crimes'. All worked hard. All intrigued. All were competent in many respects.

Molotov like Stalin had been in one place of authority or another in Russia since the Revolution's first days. In 1917, when still a mature student at the Polytechnic Institute in Petrograd, aged 27, he had been one of the three members of the Central Committee of the Bolshevik Party at liberty. For a month or two, he was a major party leader, until brushed aside after the return of Lenin and Trotsky. After the tenth Congress of the Party in 1921, he had become, with Kuybyshev, one of Stalin's two assistants, when the latter was first General Secretary. Molotov joined the Secretariat and Central Committee, and became a candidate member of the Politburo. In the 1920s, he was always at Stalin's side. In 1926, he carried out the purge of the followers of Zinoviev in Leningrad: merely expulsion from the Party then, not 'liquidation'. It did not surprise anyone that in 1927 Molotov should have become a full member of the Politburo. In 1931 he became Chairman of the Council of Commissars, titular head of government. In 1939, on the breakdown of the ludicrous negotiations with Britain, he took over from Litvinov as Commissar for International Affairs, giving up the chairmanship of the government to Stalin.

Much blood was on Molotov's hands in consequence of these appointments. He had also been, in 1930–31, a special functionary, with unlimited powers throughout Russia, during the agricultural revolution. In 1932, he directed the policies for procurement of grain in the Ukraine, which led indirectly to the worst famine of the century, perhaps of history, a man-made phenomenon in which several millions died. In 1937, Molotov took the lead in Stalin's vicious campaigns against those 'old Bolsheviks', who unwisely had lived on in Russia; and, at the Central Committee's *'plenum'* in February of that terrible year, it had been Molotov who called on the Party to 'reinforce the struggle against saboteurs' – a combat more mythical, as Molotov must have known, than anything in the Norse sagas. By then, cities, towns, streets, and promontories were called after him.[6]

Molotov was a serious Communist. The son of a shop assistant named Scriabin, of Nolunsk in Vyatka province, he was persuaded to join the Bolsheviks in 1906 by a rich friend, Victor Tikhomirnov: an early example of those *gauches de vigne* who have made such a contribution to the growth of Communism in this century. Between then and 1914, he worked on the Party's journal *Pravda* which Tikhomirnov financed. No doubt, all his life, Molotov had been a true believer: that the working class was a revolutionary body; that history was determined by class war; and that Communism would, eventually, triumph over capitalism. Young Scriabin took the name 'Molotov' during the Revolution: it meant 'hammer'. A modest indication of humanity in Molotov's life is that, when he had two days in the United States to spare in 1942, while waiting for his aeroplane to be mended, he went to New York out of curiosity.[7] He also wanted, for the same human reason, to stay in the White House, at least one night, at that time.[8]

Molotov had a Jewish wife, Paulina Zhemchuzhina, a factory worker in Ukraine in her youth, later head of the Soviet perfume and cosmetic industry. As Molotov's wife, she was, Stalin being a widower, the senior government lady in Moscow. She lived in a lavish style. She was in her own right a candidate member of the Central Committee. She was, for a time, Minister of Fisheries, and a deputy to the Supreme Soviet in 1937 (and in 1946 would become one again). Like her husband, Paulina Molotov was a convinced Communist who like him had to pretend to believe that the death, torture or imprisonment in the 1930s of all her and her husband's old comrades had been the necessary treatment of a dangerous fifth column organised in the darkest recess of Whitehall in London.

Molotov drank a good deal – more than Stalin, says Djilas,[9] even though that expert observer of the Soviet upper class, 'Chip' Bohlen, only saw him drunk once, on November 7, 1943. That was the occasion of Molotov's banquet, at the end of the first Foreign Minister's conference of the war, when several ambassadors in full dress were carried out, and home, incapable: including the British one, Sir Archibald Clark Kerr.[10]

Molotov had survived many transformations. But it is astounding that, in 1946, in Soviet Russia of all places, where the slightest slip could lead to death or a lifetime in the Arctic circle, the man who, with Ribbentrop, had given his signature to the Nazi-Soviet pact should still be in power. Did he now recall with mirth, or shame, his remarks in October 1939 when, having talked of Poland as the 'monster child of the Treaty of Versailles', he argued that 'now Germany stands for peace, while Britain and France are in favour of continuing the war'? 'The ideology of Hitlerism', he went on, 'like any other ideological system, can be either accepted or rejected – it is a matter of political view. But everyone will agree that an ideology cannot be destroyed by force . . . Therefore, it is both senseless and criminal to urge a war', for the liquidation of Hitlerism, 'while flourishing above it the false flag of the struggle for democracy'.[11] He had spoken often in the two years of the pact between his country and the Nazis. He had justified the incorporation into Russia of the Baltic states, of Bessarabia and North Bukovina. He had visited Hitler and heard a British air-raid overhead. Then, with the 'correlation of forces' suddenly changed, it had been he who made that first bleak speech, in a faltering, slightly stuttery voice, on the night of June 22, 1941, over the radio (when Stalin could not bring himself to talk at all) indicating that, in its dealings with Germany, the Russians would have made almost any concessions. Molotov was the master of Soviet diplomacy from 1939 until well into the 1950s and earned a grudging respect from Western colleagues in consequence.

Molotov's deputy foreign minister, whom Westerners grew

to know well, was Andrei Vyshinsky. This ruthless man was one of the most loathed individuals in the Soviet regime, 'high-coloured, voluble and satanic-looking'.[12]

He was the son of a rich chemist in Baku, of Polish origin. Harold Macmillan thought that he resembled a chairman of the Conservative Party. Another English observer compared him to 'a prosperous stockbroker accustomed to lunch at Simpson's'.[13] In the early years of the century, he became a Menshevik and engaged, in ways which remain obscure, in terrorism, bank-robbery and political murders in the Caucasus.[14] In 1908, he found himself in the same cell in Bailov prison as Stalin. Perhaps his subsequent career, even his survival, was due to having made available to the future dictator some of the succulent foods that his parents sent to him.[15] Stalin did not as a rule, however, value help in the past as a reason for saving a man's life: rather the contrary.

In the early years of the Revolution, Vyshinsky, still a Menshevik, had written an article about Bolshevik atrocities.[16] In order to erase the memory of that solecism, he had been later more violent in his treatment of opponents than any of Stalin's colleagues. How he made his way 'across the planks of the wreck'[17] of the Russian state to the Bolsheviks is obscure. Sheer cleverness? A good education? Such things were enough to kill, not to preserve, greater men. At all events, Vyshinsky was to be found in 1928 as Rector of the First Moscow University and also Presiding Judge at the first of the truly disgraceful trials of the Stalin era, the Shlachty trial, before a special assize of the Supreme Court of the USSR. In 1934, he became Deputy Procurator of the Soviet Union and, as such, signed, perhaps drafted, a statement 'unmasking' a terrorist 'Leningrad Centre' which had just carried out, so it was said, the murder of Sergei Kirov, Secretary of the Leningrad Communist Party. Vyshinsky said that 'these gangsters' had been given money which had come from Trotsky, through the Latvian Consul, but Khrushchev later hinted that Stalin himself organised this crime to which, therefore, Vyshinsky must be supposed to have been a party.

A year passed. The Chief Procurator of Russia, N. V. Krylenko, stepped down from his invidious post and passed into the limbo whence he would only emerge to be accused of, and himself confess, nameless crimes against his state. Vyshinsky was his successor. As such, it was his voice, virulent, mocking, 'mercilessly pursuing',[18] which would coax so many illustrious Bolshevik leaders to admissions of guilt. 'Here in this dock is not just one anti-Soviet group, not just the agents of one intelligence service. Here in the dock are a number of anti-Soviet groups . . . implicated in the case are at least . . . four foreign intelligence services, the Japanese, the German, the Polish and the British – and, it goes without saying, all the other foreign intelligence services which maintain friendly operative contact with them'.[19]

Vyshinsky's command of all the extraordinary invented detail with which he had to trap the defendants fascinated foreign observers. Thus he ensnared Zelensky:

'Vyshinsky: That is, the public was offered felt boots in the summer and summer shoes in the winter?
Zelensky: Yes.

Vyshinsky: Was this your plan?
Zelensky: Yes.

Vyshinsky: Was this accidental, or was it a plan and a system?
Zelensky: Seeing that it was wrecking work, there can be no question of its having been accidental.'[20]

Only once was Vyshinsky, in those engagements which seemed to sound like an evil parody of a morality play but were, because of the torture made possible by modern technology, one of the most squalid reminders of the humiliation to which men can sink, nearly outmanoeuvred. That was when he was questioning the ex-chief of the GUP, Yagoda, about the death of Gorky's son. Yagoda looked at Vyshinsky with baleful eyes, and said quietly: 'I would not advise the comrade Prosecutor to pursue that line any further'. Vyshinsky moved to another subject. As Charles Bohlen, who was present, in the foreign observers' box, remarked: 'what sensitive nerve had been hit, what aspect of the agreement between Yagoda and Vyshinsky had been touched, we will never know'.[21]

This was the individual to whom Stalin with specially shameless malevolence had now entrusted the task of dealing with foreign governments when Molotov was too busy, as Deputy Foreign Minister of the Soviet Union. His diplomatic career had begun in Cairo in 1943. He then became Ambassador to Rome. In Italy, he had 'laid the foundations for Soviet policy in Western Europe' by arranging the re-establishment of the Communist Party in that country after the war. Later, in Romania, he had been Stalin's emissary in 1945. There he was remembered for having slammed the door, on leaving the King's study, 'so violently that the plaster cracked'.* The consequence was the King's acceptance of the stooge government of Dr Groza. It seems that he had played a similarly determining but perhaps easier part in Poland during the events of 1945.†

By 1946 he was well known among Westerners. Both Robert Murphy, the senior US political adviser in Germany, and Charles Bohlen even ventured to ask him about his life as a prosecutor. To Murphy's question as to how he had secured the confession of so many old Bolsheviks, he smiled, unembarrassed, and replied 'it was simply a matter of careful collection of the evidence, like weaving a fine tapestry. It took patience and tenacity – only that. There was no need of "wonder drugs"'.[22] To Bohlen (whom he knew to have been present in the gallery) he replied, however, with a question: 'How did it look to you?'[23]

Vyshinsky had visited London, for the first time, for the first meeting, in January 1946, of the UN. There, he 'liked the sense of calm and order, the smooth way that everything had seemed to run'. He had liked Hyde Park, he found the English a 'cold and reserved race', even if, 'deep in them, fires burned'.[24] As to his reliability as a Communist, he told Harold Macmillan in Algiers that 'during his professional days, he had tried to read Benedetto Croce's books. He had found them as tedious and obscure as those of Karl Marx'.[25] Harsh and rough in public,

* See page 407 below.
† See page 342 below.

caustic and even humorous in private, Vyshinsky was a clever and cruel cynic caught up in a drama which he could not bring to an end and in which he could only survive by subservience.

The second Deputy Commissar for Foreign Relations in 1946 was a survivor of a different sort, Maxim Litvinov. Litvinov was one of those children of Jewish merchants from Western Russia who might, had his father emigrated rather than prospered, have become either a millionaire or a member of the Communist Party in the United States. His experience was second to none. He had served in the Tsarist army; in a sugar factory in Kiev, as part of the Bolshevik underground; and a year in prison from which he escaped. He assumed the name 'Litvinov' since he admired Turgenev's character of that name in the novel *Smoke*. He worked for Lenin (as 'Papasha') in Paris and was once arrested at the Gare du Nord on being found with twelve of the lost 500 rouble notes stolen by Stalin in a famous raid on the State Bank in Tiflis in 1908. He had travelled, he knew what Flaubert called *'la mélancolie des paquebots'*, he had worked for John Murray in London, and had become the first Soviet representative in that capital after 1917. By that time, he had married an Englishwoman, and had even tutored Rex Leeper (British Ambassador in Athens in 1946) in Russian.

In the interwar years, Litvinov had eventually become chief Commissar for International Affairs. Amiable, articulate, easygoing, he was the ideal spokesman for the idea of Soviet support for collective security in the 1930s. His removal in 1939 just before the pact with the Nazis seemed to mark the end of an era; and, of Litvinov, most people assumed. Thereafter, it seems, like so many others, he always had a suitcase, packed and ready, to take with him to prison if the need should arise.[26] He survived, despite what appears to have been a case mounted against him by Beria personally, including accusations of treachery and espionage.[27] In 1942, after being in 1941 Stalin's interpreter, at wartime discussions with Harry Hopkins, Harriman and Beaverbrook,[28] he became Soviet Ambassador to the United States. Again, he appeared as the benign, would-be friend of the West: candid and confidential. Doubtless, he was encouraged to give this benevolent impression by his chief. All the same, in May 1943, he talked to Mr Sumner Welles of his anxiety about the future of the Alliance. He said that he was unable to talk to Stalin, whose isolation bred a distorted view of the West. He even criticised the 'rigidity of the Soviet system'. When back in Moscow, he would try to improve things.[29]

He did return to Moscow in 1944 and became again, as he had once been under Lenin, Deputy Commissar for Foreign Affairs, Vyshinsky's colleague, concerned with post-war questions, such as the United Nations. It seems that it was his article, signed N. Malinin, in *Zvezda* in July 1944, which argued for the curtailing of the activities of small nations in future. Britain, the US and the USSR should, afterwards, be the determining states. Those were ideas which gave some confidence that President Roosevelt's plans for 'four world policemen' might prosper.[30]

In 1945–46 Litvinov began making new statements to foreigners in his fluent if guttural English. Thus in June 1945, he told Iverach Macdonald of *The Times*, that the 'actual conduct of Soviet diplomacy was so clumsy' that the foreign countries had every right to be suspicious.[31] On November 21, he met Harriman, the American Ambassador, by chance – but does anything happen in Russia 'by chance'? – in the interval at the opera; in that same Bolshoi Theatre where Stalin spoke on February 9. Litvinov said that he was disturbed by the international situation. Neither the Americans nor the Russians knew how to behave to each other. Harriman suggested that time might cool the problems. Litvinov replied that 'however, issues were developing'. 'What, then, could the United States do about the difficulties?' asked Harriman. 'Nothing'. 'What can you do about it?' 'Nothing', replied Litvinov, 'I believe I know what should be done but I am powerless'. 'You are extremely pessimistic?' 'Frankly, between us, yes', said Litvinov.[32] Not long before, Litvinov had gone further, and asked the United States journalist, Edgar Snow, author of that most influential of books, *Red Star over China*, 'Why did you Americans wait until now to begin opposing us in the Balkans and Eastern Europe? . . . You should have done this three years ago. Now it's too late, and your complaints only arouse suspicions here'.[33] In 1946, he would assure Harriman's successor that the 'best the West and the Russians could hope for was "an armed truce"'.[34] Litvinov suggested that Stalin might have acted with more restraint in East Europe if the West had been firmer and less equivocal. These comments were a mystery at the time. They are still a mystery.[35] Was Litvinov acting under the usual controls in so speaking? Was he just taking a risk? Khrushchev said, years later, that plans had been made to murder Litvinov by running him down in the street: they were surprisingly never carried out.[36]

The views of Litvinov appear to have been shared by others: the bleak Soviet ambassador to London in the last years of the war, Gusev, also apparently said that if the West had taken a stronger position, the regimes in Eastern Europe might have been saved from Communism.[37]

One must not omit, in consideration of Soviet makers of policy, Vladimir G. Dekanozov, the secret police's man in the Foreign Ministry. He was a Georgian and had come up to Moscow from there with Lavrenty Beria to be head of the foreign department of the NKVD in December 1938 and then to purge the Foreign Ministry in 1939 after Litvinov's eclipse. He had been a notably unobservant ambassador to Berlin in the days of the Nazi-Soviet Pact but had been promoted, all the same, on his return. His cruel face, solid figure and conscientious service to Beria was as much part of the character of these times as was Litvinov's indiscretion.[38] He 'sat next to Ribbentrop for a year and that's all he knows of Europe', Litvinov said of him to Edgar Snow.[39] Whatever he knew he certainly managed the buildings abroad, embassies, trade commissariats and information offices, which were used by his government to organise Soviet foreign policy.

Stalin may be supposed also sometimes to have listened to the man who was assumed then to be his heir: Georgi Malenkov. Malenkov, as has been seen, had been the manager of the Soviet wartime economy. He had before the war been one of the four secretaries of the Central Committee Secretariat. He entered the Politburo as a candidate member in February 1941. He had been in charge of the Cadres Directorate, which, among other things, decided important appointments. He was looked on as one of the 'new Stalinists' emerging at the eighteenth Party Congress in 1939, along with Beria, Voznesensky and Khrushchev, as opposed to the 'old guard' of Molotov, Kaganovich and Mikoyan. Malenkov was in 1946 supposed, in Party circles, to be the rival of Andrei Zhdanov, the fourth secretary of the Central Committee Secretariat who was then in charge of the often unreliable Leningrad Party.

Georgi Malenkov at the end of the war was Stalin's chief assistant in most matters. Born in 1902, Malenkov was the son of an office worker in Orenburg. What kind of office? What kind of worker? Those were questions no one dared to ask about this omni-competent manager. Malenkov went to the war in 1918. In 1920 he joined the Bolshevik Party. In 1921 he married Valeria Goluttsov who had, at that time, 'a minor job' – as a secretary, as a filing clerk? – in the newly formed Secretariat of the Central Committee under Stalin and Molotov. That was how Malenkov started his 'terrible career'. He was soon asked to vet the loyalties of those students who had been supporters of Trotsky, but who wanted to remain members of the Party. 'Technical Secretary' to the Politburo, Malenkov was the protégé first of Stalin's own long term private secretary, Poskrebyshev, then of Lazar Kaganovich. By the mid-1930s he had been in and out of many party offices and was in charge of the so-called 'Orgburo' of the Moscow Party's Central Committee. Then, on Kaganovich's nomination, he became Deputy Administrator of the 'personnel sector' of the National Central Committee. In that post, he invented the system of 'cadre lists', or detailed biographies (and autobiographies) of all members and candidates of the Party, which was held systematically in Moscow.[40] In this position, he was most useful to Stalin during his major purges. A close associate, and even friend, of Yezhov, the murderous head of the NKVD (who had previously been Malenkov's boss in the personnel section), Malenkov was often present when old party leaders were interrogated under torture.[41] Khrushchev described him as having 'actually helped to promote people from the ranks only to have them eliminated later on'.[42] Malenkov nearly became Yezhov's deputy in 1937 but, fortunately for him, that task went to Beria.[43]

At the beginning of the war, Malenkov's chance came. He became one of the five original members of the Defence Secretariat (GOKO) and a Deputy Chairman of the Council of Commissars. His base remained the Party Secretariat.

Just before Russia entered the war, in February 1941, Malenkov made a famous speech (not unlike that quoted earlier which he had made in 1946*) in which he criticised violently the habit of looking at people's qualities on the basis of their family backgrounds: 'It is time to put an end to the biological approach in the selection of cadres, and to test people in action'. He also appealed for the dismissal of 'business leaders who are ignoramuses' and who boasted of proletarian origin. The Soviet Union had 'no need of talmudists or troglodytes . . . who continued to invoke Marx and Lenin as guides to action in industrial management'.[44]

Throughout the war, Malenkov was one of the two or three most important men in Russia; the manager *par excellence*, specially responsible for all the difficult tasks in turn – carrying the industries of West Russia to beyond the Urals in 1941, building the aircraft and tank industries in 1942, chairman of the committee on the rehabilitation of liberated areas in 1943, dismantling the economy of East Germany in 1945, carrying its industries into Russia, as had been done in 1941 in West Russia, and, finally, a member of all the supreme bodies with any responsibility. But, at the end of the war, his position seemed to be crumbling; or rather, he had apparently (and characteristically) been placed by Stalin in a position where he was bound to quarrel with Zhdanov who, together with his deputy A. A. Kuznetzov, could mount a formidable challenge to him. (Zhdanov returned to Moscow from Leningrad early in 1945.) It appears that a commission headed by Mikoyan urged that Malenkov's arrangements to deprive East Germany of all movable property was misguided: it would be better henceforth to found Soviet corporations there to make goods for Russia.[45]

* See above, page 48.

Malenkov had a round, womanish face and was known to his rival Zhdanov as 'Malanya', a frequent usage among Russian peasant women. In physique, he was small and plump, with a hint of Mongol in his face. He had prominent cheek bones, with a pock-marked skin, and gave the impression of being cautious, withdrawn and 'not very personable'. Djilas thought that, 'under the layers and rolls' of fat, there lurked 'another man, lively and adept, with intelligent and alert black eyes' who just might have fought his way out of the closed world in which he lived if he had had a chance.[46] Stalin said of Malenkov that he was 'a good clerk. He can write out a resolution quickly. He's a good person for allocating responsibilities to but he has no capacity at all for independent thought'.[47] Later on, though, Malenkov seemed to have 'a more Western-orientated mind than other Soviet leaders. He at least seemed to perceive our position and, while he did not agree with it, understood it'.[48] He was more sophisticated in manner than Khrushchev, his future enemy, and his household was an intellectual one, with no luxuries: 'at table, the conversation was always general', recalled Svetlana Stalin, who considered him 'the most reasonable and sagacious member' of the Politburo.[49]

Malenkov's great friend was Lavrenty Beria, General Commissar of State Security since 1941. (From 1941, the People's Commissariat of State Security [NKVD] was turned, under Beria, into two bodies: first the NKVD proper, controlling the police under Beria directly; second, the MVD, the ministry of internal affairs, under V. N. Merkulov.) 'One could always see Beria and Malenkov walking arm in arm. They always moved as a couple', wrote Svetlana Stalin.[50] They had together been in the war members of the State Defence Committee and Beria had become deputy chief of that body.

Beria seemed to Svetlana a 'magnificent specimen of the artful courtier, the embodiment of Oriental perfidy, flattery and hypocrisy' who had succeeded in confounding 'even Stalin, ordinarily difficult to deceive'.[51] He had gold pince-nez, 'somewhat plump, greenish eyes and pale . . . with soft damp hands', and had 'a square-cut mouth and bulging eyes'. In him, there was also 'a certain self-satisfaction and irony mingled with a clerk's obsequiousness and solicitude'.[52] Those who knew him depicted him as a 'man devoid of any feelings'.[53] He was important since he was head of the police in a government which was 'a police regime *par excellence*', in which the police was the essential 'lever by which one man could move a vast country'.[54]

His family, however, was calm, normal and dignified, Nina, his wife, being 'charming and beautiful'. When not quite seventeen, she had appealed to Beria, then head of the GPU (as the NKVD was then known) in Georgia, on behalf of her unjustly arrested brother. Hearing that Beria had arrived in her native village, she entered his train compartment. She never emerged, being carried off to become his wife.[55] They lived in 1946 in an immense dacha outside Moscow, with children who evidently took after their mother. There, Beria would practise firing guns, plan executions, and tell fearful jokes, such as 'listen, let me have him for one night and I'll have him confessing he's king of England'.[56]

By this time, Beria was powerful enough occasionally to speak disrespectfully even of Stalin, though Khrushchev thought it 'probably a provocation designed to pull one into making similar remarks'.[57] There were even occasions when Beria would challenge Stalin himself at those intolerable dinners of the Politburo – at which Beria would insist on eating grass, like Nebuchadnezzar and other men of the Caucasus.

The war had been Beria's opportunity, as it had been Malenkov's. In the few days when Stalin lost control after the, to him, unexpected German invasion, Beria became 'the terror of the Party'. He filled Stalin's personal entourage – cooks, servants, butlers – with Georgians, of his own choice. As a member of the Defence Committee, he had every opportunity for aggrandisement. His NKVD played a large part in the training of the partisans which, after the end of 1941, operated behind German lines. The NKVD had also been effective in preserving morale during the difficult days. Indeed, there were some who argued that it was the only competent ministry in the Soviet system. Beria had deported, swiftly and ruthlessly, those peoples whom Stalin thought potentially threatening. His ministry was responsible for much of the production of weapons. A whole vast sub-economy was run by Beria's men. In 1946, Beria was also engaged in re-establishing police control of Ukraine and Lithuania, where guerrillas were still waging a war against the re-imposition of Soviet rule in some areas. The budget of the MVD-MGB, the ministry which he controlled, seems to have more than doubled in 1946 over 1945.[58] Stalin himself sometimes appeared a little afraid of him, though he had always promoted him. Svetlana Stalin recalls how once, when visiting Beria's wife, she was telephoned by Stalin, who shouted at her: 'come back at once. I don't trust Beria'.[59]

Khrushchev said that, by the 1940s, 'you could not even report to Stalin without getting Beria's support in advance: if you made a report to Stalin in Beria's presence, and you had not cleared it in advance with Beria, he would be sure to tear down the report'. Stalin once complained to Khrushchev (provocatively, surely): 'before Beria arrived, dinner meetings used to be relaxed, productive affairs. Now he's always challenging people to drinking contests and people are getting drunk all over the place'.[60] As a result, Stalin dismissed in early 1946 the Georgians whom Beria had appointed to his kitchens; but, all the same, his entourage continued to be manned by other people whom Beria appointed.

In January 1946, there were some reorganisations in Beria's empire, making it ready for peace. A new Minister for State Security (MGB) was appointed under Beria, a protégé of his, Victor Abakumov, a Cossack apparently of Ossetian origin, who had worked for Beria in a variety of ways before. Another long-standing official under Beria, S. N. Kruglov, became Minister of the Interior (MVD) (he improbably received a knighthood, KBE, from the British Government at Potsdam). But both these men were under the overall direction of Beria, whose power was not diminished. He was now also in control of the Soviet nuclear weapons project.[61] Stalin thought that he had found in Abakumov a bright young man who was dutifully carrying out his orders. Actually, Abakumov reported to Stalin what Beria had told him that Stalin wanted to hear.[62]

As well as being powerful on an 'all union-basis', Beria, in the late 1940s, kept control over the party and police in the Caucasus. It was for that reason that Stalin allowed himself to listen in particular to Beria on foreign policy where Russia's relations with Turkey and Persia were concerned.

The explanation as to why a man who, in all other civilised countries, would have been executed, or in prison for many years, for innumerable crimes was in a position of great power is due to the role of ideology. If to distinguish between right and wrong, tenderness and brutality, is a bourgeois weakness, it was unsurprising that men of criminal violence came to the top of the unusually 'greasy pole' of Russian politics.

Beria rarely spoke in public. But he probably shared the views – indeed, doubtless inspired them – of his subordinates. Nikolai Krasnov, a young Cossack, later described how he was interviewed by Vsevolod Merkulov, Beria's deputy and Minister of internal affairs – one of those Caucasus men (he was a Russified Armenian) who had known Beria in Baku, in the 1920s.[63] Merkulov, a member of the Central Committee of the Soviet Communist party since 1939, began, in his interrogation in August 1945 of Krasnov's father, to talk of the British. 'We know that we have them checkmated and that we have made them dance to our tune like pawns. Sooner or later, there will be a clash between the Communist bear and the Western bulldog. There will then be no mercy for our sugar-coated, honey-dripping, wheedling allies. We'll blow them all to blazes, with all their kings, traditions, lords, castles, heralds, Orders of the Bath and Garter and white wigs. When the Bear's paw strikes, no one will remain to nurse the hope that their gold can rule the world. Our healthy socially strong idea, the idea of Lenin and Stalin, will be the victor. That's how it will be, Colonel . . . I am told that there were Tsars who watered their horses in the Oder. Well, the time will come when we will water Soviet horses in the Thames'.[64]

Another indication of Beria's thinking can be derived from a similar speech by Merkulov's successor, Abakumov, who became Minister of State Security between 1946 and 1951. He said, in 1946, 'it is our good fortune . . . that the British and Americans in their attitudes towards us have still not emerged from the post-war state of calf-love. They dream of lasting peace and building a democratic world for all men. They don't seem to realise that we are the ones who are going to build a new world, and that we shall do it without their liberal democratic recipes. All their slobber plays right into our hands and we shall thank them for this, in the next world, with coals of fire'.[65] The master spy, Leopold Trepper, met Abakumov too, in early 1946. Abakumov said mockingly 'you see, there are only two ways to thank an agent in the intelligence service: either cover his chest with medals, or cut off his head'.[66] (He remarked, *à propos* of the Guzenko case, then developing in Ottawa, 'one of our networks had been broken in Canada. In several North American newspapers, the "experts" have recognised the style of the Big Chief, that is Trepper himself'.\*)[67]

During the course of the war, the NKVD had been able, through its own persistence and the optimism or gullibility of its allies, almost to establish its credibility in the eyes of the world: thus, as a result, a 'Charter' had been arranged between it and the British wartime secret service SOE (Special Operations Executive) providing for collaboration in Europe during the conflict.[68] That meant British agreement to Soviet leadership of the resistance in, for example, Czechoslovakia.[69] Some of the leaders of SOE in Britain even thought that the SOE and NKVD might continue to collaborate after the war.[70]

Beria's task inside Russia was not just to discover potential opponents of the government but to transform everyone into potential informers. Fear was his weapon as much as outright brutality. Stalin described it himself in 1927: 'The GPU or CHEKA . . . is more or less analogous to the Committee of Public Safety, which was formed during the great French Revolution . . . it is something in the nature of a military-political tribunal, set up for the purpose of protecting the interests of the revolution from attacks on the part of the counter-revolutionary bourgeoisie and their agents . . . People advocate a maximum of leniency: the dissolution of the GPU. But we are a country

* The affair of Guzenko, a clerk in the Soviet mission in Ottawa who abandoned his masters in 1945, is discussed in Chapter Eight.

surrounded by capitalist states. The internal enemies of our revolution are the agents of the capitalists of all countries . . . We do not wish to repeat the mistakes of the Parisian Communards. The GPU is necessary for the Revolution and will continue to exist, to the terror of the enemies of the proletariat'.[71] In 1939, he said much the same again, at the 18th Party Congress: 'It is sometimes asked: we have abolished the exploiting classes; there are no longer any hostile classes; there is nobody to suppress; hence there is no more need for the state; it must die away – is it time we relegated the state to the museum of antiquities?' 'These questions', said Stalin, 'not only betray an underestimate of the [character of] capitalist encirclement, but also an underestimate of the role and significance of the bourgeois states and their organs which send spies, assassins and wreckers into our country, and are waiting for a favourable opportunity to attack it with armed force'.[72]

The secret police over which Beria presided so successfully was in all but a few respects the same CHEKA ('all-Russian Extraordinary Commission for the struggle against sabotage and speculation') founded by Lenin in 1918. The first director, a Polish minor nobleman, Felix Dzerzhinsky, had set a tone which none of his successors had any difficulty in following. The chief difference in the early days to what came later was that, to begin with, captives worked merely to satisfy the needs of their own concentration camps; only about 1925 did the regime begin to exploit its prison population, 'former people', Mensheviks, anarchists, or 'White Guards', for nationally significant public works, mining, canal-digging and wood-cutting; tasks which, by the mid-1930s, were carried on by millions of prisoners, for whom the word 'slaves', with its specific responsibilities (and, often, rights), was quite inadequate.

Beria was born the son of a peasant from a village, Merkheuli, near Sukhum, in Georgia. His father had been illiterate, but his mother who came from a tiny tribe, the Karaims, probably of Jewish origin, could both read and write. An intelligent boy, the Russian civil war found him already studying as an engineer at the 'Technikum' in Baku.[73] Beria became a Communist in 1918 at the 'Technikum' and fought on the Romanian front. He then became associated, in that city, with several of those (such as Dekanozov, and Merkulov) who were to be his close collaborators later in the government. After he was arrested in 1953, Beria was accused of having been recruited at that time by the intelligence service of the 'counter-revolutionary' Mussavat Government in Azerbaijan, then, it was said, controlled by Britain. He was also denounced as having allowed himself to be used by 'the Menshevik secret service' – equally a branch, allegedly, of the legendary British service. He was apparently, however, a Bolshevik agent within the Menshevik movement in Tiflis and made his way initially by helping the cause both there and in Baku, assisting such atrocities of the civil war as the murder of the bourgeoisie of Baku on Nargen Island. A protégé of Ordzhonikidze, he joined the CHEKA in Baku in 1921. The same year, he met Stalin for the first time. It may be that he committed some blackmailable indiscretion at this time but if so it has not become evident.*[74]

Beria anyway made his reputation as an utterly ruthless, amoral, unjust and cruel secret policeman in the Caucasus in the 1920s, as Deputy Chairman of the CHEKA in Georgia then in Azerbaijan, later Chairman of the Georgian Communists and of the Transcaucasian GPU. 'The Soviet prison is neither a health resort nor a boarding house', was a favourite phrase, as he pursued the enemies of the people 'with a red hot iron', as Stalin adjured him. In these undertakings, he began to see something of Stalin when on holiday; providing his bodyguard for example. He thus 'wormed his way up' (as it was put in his later indictment)

* Svetlana Stalin's friend, Olga Shatunovskaya, told her that Beria worked during the civil war for the Armenian nationalists and that he was condemned to death by Sergei Kirov, then Communist chief of operations in the Caucasus. A telegram demanding Beria's death was believed in 1946 still to be in existence. A certain H. S. Kedrov, himself a Chekist under the coldhearted Dzerzhinsky, was murdered in the late 1930s, apparently because he knew something of Beria's past. At the plenum of the Communist Party in 1937, at which many extraordinary things were said, Grisha Kaminsky, People's Commissar for Health in the Russian Federation, also accused Beria of working for the English during their occupation of Baku. Kaminsky then disappeared without trace. Others allege that Beria had been an occasional agent of the Okhrana before the Revolution.

to arrive at the job of First Secretary of the Communist party in Georgia. The local communists in Georgia were appalled. Ordzhonikidze said 'for a long time I've been telling Stalin that Beria is a crook but Stalin won't listen'.[75] Stalin's wife also made scenes. She insisted 'this man must not be allowed to set foot in this house'. Stalin would not listen to her: 'I asked her what was wrong with him. Give me facts. I'm not convinced'. The reply from Nadezhda Alliluyeva was 'What facts do you need? I just see he's a scoundrel. I won't have him here'. But Stalin thought Beria 'a good Chekist – he helped us forestall the Mingrelian rising':[76] an occurrence probably invented by Beria.

By 1934 Beria was a member of the party's Central Committee. In June 1938 he went to Moscow to act as deputy to Yezhov when Commissar for Internal Affairs. He succeeded Yezhov in December of that year. Soon he had his predecessor and all his associates dead and buried, and his own men, mostly from Georgia, reigned in their stead. In Moscow, all Stalin's old friends loathed Beria, as well they might, since in the end he destroyed them all; most, literally; the rest in spirit. It is true that he brought an end to the mass brutalities of the so called *Yezhovshchina*. But that was on the orders of Stalin, and Beria was responsible for almost as many atrocious crimes as was Yezhov, such as the massacre of the Polish officers at Katyn.[77] The spell cast by this 'evil genius' lay over Russia in 1946. The 'correlation of forces' played some strange games, none odder than that.

Others in Stalin's dining circle, such as the drunken marshal, Voroshilov, or the artful Armenian, Mikoyan, no doubt passed on impressions which sometimes assisted Stalin's international policy. The promising genuine peasant's son, Khrushchev, knew something of Poland, as well as of the Ukraine, and the hard-working Kaganovich even had absorbed knowledge of American industry. But none of these men had ever lived abroad. Among them, even Stalin's journeys outside Russia before 1914 were quite exceptional. Their time for influencing Soviet policy lay in the future.

The Russians, of course, also maintained by this time a

foreign service. The heady days when Trotsky assumed that the business of diplomacy could be done away with by issuing a 'revolutionary declaration to the peoples of the world and then closing the shop' were far away.[78] But what Soviet diplomatists reported may not have been useful. They had been demoralised by the 1930s. The British Embassy in Moscow thought that 'the Soviet government were extremely badly informed by their representatives of the true situation abroad'.[79] In April 1946, the American Ambassador in Caracas, Venezuela, noticed that his Russian colleague and his Counsellor 'were living in an atmosphere entirely new to them . . . on many of the things about which they and, I suppose, their government would like to know they are starting from scratch'.[80] Still, occasional intercepted telegrams between the Soviet commissariat for foreign affairs and embassies abroad which have become available suggest that the former at least never allowed sentiment to prevent candour. Thus a telegram from Molotov to Tokyo in 1940 spoke of the 'Japanese-American war, which we desire'; and blandly commented that 'a war is required in Europe'.[81]

One survivor of the purges of the 1930s was the wartime ambassador to London, Ivan Maisky, who had an acute brain. He was now back in Moscow. Among new officials were the ambassador to the United Nations Andrei Gromyko, Maisky's successor in London, Gusev, and ambassadors Vinogradov, in Paris, and Bogomolov in Rome. Whatever the immorality of the government, which they served loyally, they were competent men, skilful at taking account of the contradictions and 'manoeuvring' among other countries, which Stalin, in 1921, had described as the 'whole purpose' of the existence of the People's Commissariat for foreign affairs.[82]

In addition, the Soviet Government had at its service for information about, and in, other countries a unique network of foreign Communist parties and secret agents.

The Third Communist International (Comintern), whose secretariat had linked the Communist parties of the world, had, from 1919 to 1943, made out that it served a single world Communist party, temporarily divided for convenience into national parties. This division was conceived as a short term

one for the proletarian takeover of power on a worldwide scale
– a 'gigantic international army' (the military metaphor was
important), national parties constituting just one more detachment assigned to each one of the sectors of 'the revolutionary
front'. Connections between Moscow and these parties were
maintained by a secret '*apparat*', the International Communications Section. The Comintern had, in its heyday, been a large
body, employing several hundred revolutionaries in Moscow,
and several thousand agents all over the world. From at least
1922, it had been fitted into the framework of Soviet foreign
policy instead of Soviet foreign policy being fitted into a frame
of world revolution.[83] Stalin might despise or fear the Comintern
and call it a 'grocer's shop'. It did contain at its peak in the mid-
1930s, however, a large number of extraordinarily daring and
imaginative men and women.[84]

The abolition of this agency occurred in May 1943 with no
warning. Even those who worked in the body itself had no
foreknowledge. The news came as a thunderbolt to those working at the 'Comintern school' at Kushnarenkovo, outside Ufa in
Russia.[85] Stalin took this decision because he wanted to reassure
his partners in the alliance against Hitler that the Russians would
indeed not use their military victories for the promotion of
indiscriminate revolution. The reaction was generally what he
wanted. Senator Connally, Chairman of the Foreign Relations
Committee of the Senate of the United States, for example, said
that Stalin's decision meant that Russian Communism would no
longer interfere in the affairs of other nations.[86] The *Herald
Tribune* in New York argued learnedly that the abolition marked
the climax of the process that began when Stalin won his duel
for leadership in Russia: the organisation of that country into a
national state run on Communist lines, rather than as a centre
of world communism.[87] In Britain, many officials also took the
dissolution seriously. The first doubts about the character of
the event seem only to have occurred in 1945, at the time of
the eclipse of Earl Browder in the US.* The naivety of these
Western perceptions can only be explained by ignorance of

* See below, pages 244–5.

Soviet ideology and by desperate optimism inspired by the war.[88]

It is true that there were one or two changes in Moscow because of this abolition. The above-mentioned Comintern school, for example, was closed. Officials were moved. Periodicals changed their names. But the functions of the Comintern were mostly transferred to the new International Department of the Soviet Communist Party. Russian officials who had worked with the Comintern, such as Boris Ponomarev, moved to the Central Committee's buildings. (Some had already moved in 1937: for example, the Finn Otto Kuusinen.) So did several distinguished foreign Communists, including the signatories of the act of dissolution, such as Maurice Thorez, the French leader; Palmiro Togliatti, the Italian; Dimitrov, the Bulgarian secretary-general of the whole body; Dolores Ibarruri, the rhetorical Spanish leader; and others, such as the Hungarian, Rákosi, and the Romanian, Ana Pauker. These and other leaders continued their work in much the same way in Moscow, still living at the Hotel Lux, in Gorki Street, preparing for what would happen when the Red Army entered their own countries. They were enabled, or made, to collaborate by the joint supervision of old members of the Comintern secretariat, such as the Hungarian Ernö Gerö.[89] Abroad, leaders of parties, in open societies or in clandestinity alike, continued to communicate with Moscow as if they were bishops serving the Roman Pope. They were a little more free in some ways than they had been in the past. The foreign communists who had been the Comintern 'instructors' disappeared. But, all the same, one of the senior persons in the party concerned was always, as it were, Moscow's man. Every Western European Communist party also still had a Soviet type of internal police force built into its organisation.[90] Financial ties bound the parties to Moscow through skilful, if sometimes byzantine, arrangements effected through foreign banks. Stalin continued as a rule to look on foreign parties as intelligence-gathering agencies, or spy recruiters, rather than as institutions to take decisions of their own.[91]

This was to underestimate their capacity. It is true that the communists in opposition throughout the world, as in the 1920s,

1930s and early 1940s, still had in 1946 to make their way, with pathetic attention to detail, through all the accusations of 'adventurism' or 'opportunism', of 'infantile leftism' or 'proletarian defeatism', in search of the welcoming shore of 'bolshevik consistency': only to find that, at one time or another, they could have been exposed themselves to the accusation of 'wavering' or worse *en route*. All the same, the determination of young party members and their courage when faced with torture argues that, here, indeed was a breed of revolutionaries capable of most things, good as well as bad. One cannot read the account of communist activities in Yugoslavia before the war, for example, in Djilas's memoirs, without having the impression that, for all the dogma of these men and women, something radically new was in the air;[92] a force which was able to capture power in both Yugoslavia and Albania without much Russian assistance, and would surely have done so in Greece, had it not been for British, and later American, intervention.

In 1946, the most important Communists were those in Italy, France and Germany.* The Chinese Party was also impossible to ignore, though relations with it were not easy, and though (or because) its leaders already controlled a small empire of their own.†

The larger Communist parties abroad had created, even before 1939, in the countries in which they lived, a kind of 'counter-community' by which the lives of the members were wholly contained. This had its basis in the world of German Social Democrats before 1914. Broken by Nazi occupation, the peace brought chances to extend these states within states. By early 1946, Italy and France, in particular, had revived them. In East Germany, as in most of Eastern Europe, the state and the Communist Party had already intimate relations.‡ These parties all operated as Stalin's ears and eyes. Of course, there were French and Italian Communists, whose loyalties, in the end, might turn out to be towards France and Italy. Patriotism had

* See pages 529, 514–15, 490–1.
† See below, page 577–8.
‡ See below, page 491.

caused great crises of conscience among English Communists in 1939 and 1940. But the institutions of the parties still acted as fifth columns for Soviet intelligence. Thus 'proletarian internationalism' – Lenin's formulation – survived into the post-war world.

Most parties abroad were in 1946 more relaxed than they had been before the late war. It was not considered criminal, for example, to read non-party books or newspapers; or to have non-party friends, as it had once been. But, all the same, most parties continued to insist on strict enquiries into background, views, families and so on, before membership was conceded. The leaders had made their careers at a time when discipline had been insisted upon, and welcomed. Many of the original instructions of Lenin to the Comintern continued to be observed. Thus, parties had been told that, since 'in practically every country . . . the class struggle' was 'entering the stage of civil war', Communists could therefore have no confidence in bourgeois legality. They were still 'obliged everywhere to create a parallel illegal organisation', which, at the decisive moment, 'will help the Party to do its duty to the revolution'. Legal, and illegal, work would have to be combined (this was the third of the twenty-one points of the Comintern).[93] The consequence was that secret 'submarines' were to be found among civil servants, nominally democratic socialist politicians, army officers, actors and writers, even right wing or conservative politicians.[94] In most countries, in West as well as East Europe, there was thus a section of the Communist Party with a deceptive role. These men were not precisely spies, though they could so be activated. They were men (and women) awaiting their moment. In the meantime, they could be 'agents of influence'. Of course, Communists should, if need be, still 'resort to all sorts of stratagems, artifices, illegal methods, to evasions and subterfuges, only so as to get into the trade unions, to remain in them and to carry on Communist work within them at all costs'.[95]

In addition, Stalin had at his disposal a large network of real secret agents. Some of them worked for military intelligence, the GRU; and some for Beria's service, the GPU or NKVD.

Much, often bizarre, has been written about this side of Soviet policy. Many Soviet agents came into the service through their Communist parties or the Comintern. For example, the Soviet spy who told so much about wartime Japan, Dr Richard Sorge, had joined the German Communist party in 1918, became a full-time conspirator in 1919 in Germany, and Soviet military intelligence had claimed him by 1925.[96] Attention paid to Soviet agents in Britain or America should not ignore those who, like General Zaimov, worked effectively in countries such as Bulgaria. The GRU's Red Orchestra operating throughout Western Europe on a large scale after 1936 laid the plans not only for espionage against Germany in the course of the war but for the same activity against the Western allies after it.[97] There were Soviet agents in all the governments-in-exile.[98]

The Anglo-Saxon dimension cannot, however, be dismissed. Igor Guzenko, a member of the GRU, who, in September 1945, had first shown those in Western intelligence, who wanted to hear, that Soviet agents were active on a very large scale, against Western democracies as well as the Nazis, and that there were 'thousands' such in Britain alone.[99] No doubt that was an exaggeration. But it seems that, because of skilful penetration in that country, in the United States and elsewhere, most of the internal workings of the more important governments of the West were known in Moscow – just as, indeed, through intercepts of radio messages, the doings of the Germans had been known to the Allies during the war. All those telegrams carefully graded 'top secret' or, earlier, 'most secret'; the reflective despatches about Soviet policy; the discussions even about Soviet agents – the secret yellow boxes, with material intercepted by radio and decoded by computer; all the information passed to the Soviet Union.[100]

The element of comedy in consequence should not be quite overlooked. In British government papers, we find Guy Burgess, a Soviet agent in the Foreign Office, pondering in 1946 whether reference could be safely allowed, 'on security grounds', in a planned publication of the diaries of the late Italian Foreign Minister Count Ciano, to 'secret sources'.[101] There was an occasion in 1946 in Washington when negotiations on the question of withdrawal of allied troops from Austria was handled by Donald Maclean, a Soviet spy acting head of chancery at the British Embassy in Washington, and Alger Hiss, about whom the evidence for his having been a Soviet agent at least in the 1930s seems powerful.[102] The number of occasions when Maclean's name is mentioned as having been present at meetings of significance in Washington (in the State Department papers) makes it evident that the information he could, and presumably did, give Russia was considerable: 'Maclean of the British Embassy called last night on instructions to request that United States instructions to General Clark be changed' (also about Austria).[103] But the deaths of hundreds of friends, as well as agents, of the West in East Europe and elsewhere because of those agents' work, if nothing else, makes it most inappropriate to linger on the humour of the matter. The details of all policies, American and British alike, in Germany and Austria, throughout the Balkans and in Poland, must have been available to Soviet makers of decisions through the treachery of these and other men. For example, Russia would have learned from Maclean that the British took Churchill's 'percentages agreement' with Stalin seriously.* The Soviet Government would have known exactly how much and how little the British knew, and cared, about Polish independence. They would similarly have known of American attitudes to the various sticking points in the negotiations on the establishment of the United Nations.[104] A conversation between Stalin and Djilas in 1944 showed that the former had seen a copy of a report by Churchill's special envoy to Tito, Fitzroy Maclean, soon after it was written, about how to deal with the partisan movement.[105] The papers regularly obtained till 1940 by Mussolini in Rome through the services of Signor Constantini, a butler at the British Embassy in that city, were also provided to the Russians – how precisely is not clear.[106] The use of these, and other, papers obtained by Mussolini from the British clearly affected Italian policy; it might have so affected Russian too. Throughout the war, the British, as is now well-known, were, thanks to the reconstruction of the

* See Appendix III.

Enigma machine and to brilliant 'decoders', reading German radio messages, including those of the SS. The information so obtained was officially passed on, where appropriate, to the Russians, but not the method by which it was obtained. The secret of that method, however, may have been made available to the Russians through the services of their agents such as Leo Long (then in MI15); John Cairncross, of the Foreign Office; or Harold Philby in the Secret Service (concerned with Spain and Portugal to begin with, subsequently in charge of anti-Soviet espionage and, according to his wartime colleague, Hugh Trevor-Roper, the man favoured to be chief of that service in the 1950s). Given the known pre-war activities of Britain, in this department, Stalin could not have been at all surprised. Many other names have from time to time been hazarded as possible colleagues to these men, often without evidence: doubtless some of the accusations were true, as was the later comment by a British Prime Minister that it might be that the world would never get to the bottom of this particular extraordinary conspiracy of Stalin's.[107]

In Canada, it appeared from Igor Guzenko's revelations, Soviet agents included men or women in the scientific research buildings in Ottawa; the nuclear laboratories in Montreal; the External Affairs Department; the British High Commission; the newspapers; and even Parliament (Fred Rose). There were, of course, also chauffeurs and messengers. Fourteen Canadian civil servants would be arrested in February 1946 as Soviet agents. They included a scientist at the National Research Council, Dr Raymond Boyer; two engineers there; and the Deputy Registrar of the British High Commission.[108] Whether all these persons were worth the investment made in them by Stalin may well be doubtful. All the same, this espionage was on a scale quite unknown in past international affairs. Whether the effort was enough to compensate for the serious damage that knowledge of even a part of it caused must also be open to doubt. The information conveyed by Guzenko, for example, in the autumn of 1945, helped to make President Truman sceptical about the possibilities of collaboration with Russia.*

* See page 628.

In all countries, the line between agents and extravagant sympathisers was often faintly drawn. Thus Harry Dexter White, the main architect of the Bretton Woods agreements, Assistant Secretary of the United States Treasury, and the leading official there,* may have been an innocent, concerned to tip United States economic foreign policy towards friendship with the Soviet Union, to promote Communists in America to places of influence, but perhaps not a communicator of information. The son of Jewish immigrants from Lithuania,[109] White was nevertheless the leading advocate in the United States of a substantial loan to the Soviet Union, as well as the most vigorous supporter of a harsh post-war policy towards Germany. Though Maynard Keynes admired his brain,[110] his motives remain obscure. White's assistants, Frank Coe and Harold Glasser, were probably more close than he was to the Soviet Union. Then Colonel Faymonville, the United States military attaché in Moscow in the 1930s, and during the early part of the war, seems also to have been merely a 'great admirer of the Russian people',[111] though, when he returned to Moscow as Lend Lease Representative, he appeared, to his own successor as military attaché, Major Ivan Yeaton, to have 'ceased to be a soldier of the United States'.[112] General Marshall, not one to exaggerate needlessly, thought Faymonville 'a representative of the Russians' not of the United States,[113] even 'a traitor'.[114] Yet perhaps it really was, as Harrison Salisbury put it, that, like his British colleague Colonel Firebrace, this officer had reported that 'regardless of losses, the Red Army would prevail.'[115]

These ambiguities also affected the press: what were the real loyalties of Peter Smollett (Smolka), wartime member of the Ministry of Information and later correspondent of *The Times* in Austria, his native country? Or of Wilfred Burchett, *The Daily Express*'s correspondent in Germany? With Ralph Parker, *The Times*'s correspondent in Moscow, the situation was more obvious: he was a broken man, suborned by the Soviet Union into becoming an apologist for them.[116] (The Times's man in East Europe, Michael Burn, was, however, merely an enthusiast for

* See page 270.

socialist revolution whose realities soon disillusioned him).

Stalin and Beria in 1946 had agents seeking industrial and scientific secrets as well as military ones: and the gap between the two was not always evident. The Soviet Government had over a thousand employees in their purchasing mission in the United States. All were available for industrial espionage. There were also several agents among scientists working in one department or another of the United States 'Manhattan Project' for atomic energy during 1943 and 1944.

Some of these men were persuaded to act because they were flattered: Abraham Brothman was told by his Soviet contact that his value to Russia was greater than 'two or three brigades' of ordinary men. Others spied because they were believers in Marxism-Leninism; or in Russia. Many were Jewish in origin and were either born in Russia (for example, Nathan Silvermaster, of the 'ring' which bore his name, came from Odessa and came to the United States in 1915) or children of those who were. [117]

To half America the interweaving of the tales of all these people, their wives, their expertise and their Russian connections would be shocking excitements of two or three years ahead. The nation would learn, for example, how at a dinner in New Mexico in February 1945, Julius Rosenberg had asked Ruth Greengrass to meet her 'courier', with a picture of the atom bomb, outside the Albuquerque Safeways Store during the last week in April; and how, in 1943, Jacob Golos, the then chief of Soviet espionage in the United States, had travelled to Norfolk, Virginia, to see some engineers in one of his networks. They would learn too, later, that, as early as the autumn of 1945, Golos's mistress, the 'Red Spy Queen', Elizabeth Bentley, had talked about all these activities to the Federal Bureau of Investigation, just as Guzenko had to the Canadian Mounted Police. Such tales had not been told before in America, not even in fiction. It is understandable that they later caused a national crisis of conscience, easily exploited by demagogues.

This side of Soviet policy is not comprehensible unless it is remembered that Russians had for a long time been troubled by what they took as Western espionage against them: 'these people are agents of foreign governments', a junior policeman is made to remark of intellectuals who criticised the Tsar, in Gorki's *Life of a Useless Man*,[118] 'chiefly of England. They receive huge salaries for stirring up the Russian people to revolt. The English do it so that we shall not take India from them.' Those fancies remained, after 1917, to inform enterprises of espionage on a scale never before even attempted, carried on by a government preoccupied by spying: nearly all Stalin's opponents in the late 1930s were thus persuaded to confess not just to opposition or 'banditry' but to being members of foreign intelligence services.

It is obscure how much attention was paid to incoming advice from those innumerable sources. Because of Stalin's suspicious nature, the reports of many agents were often dismissed as 'provocations'. That is what happened to the evidence, presented by a variety of good agents (above all, Richard Sorge in Japan) about the impending attack of Germany in June 1941. Other despatches by Sorge were left uncoded when he had begun, wrongly, to be suspect.[119] Sometimes also the agents, particularly the ideologically committed ones, probably told their controllers what they wanted to be happening, not what was. Stalin misinterpreted information. Thus, at the end of the war in Europe, a 'friendly source in the British government' seems to have given the impression to Stalin that the Allies' interest in talking to the German Commander-in-Chief in Italy, General Wolff, was the prelude to general negotiations for a separate peace. That report led to the angry exchanges between Stalin and Roosevelt in the last weeks of the latter's life.[120] Perhaps the accurate reports from Berlin about the Germans' lack of attention to the possibility of making an atom bomb may have cancelled out the equally accurate reports from the United States about Western efforts in the 'Manhattan Project'.[121]

The truth of Soviet perceptions of the West will always be hard to disentangle. That was particularly so in 1945–46. The information obtained must have been on so large a scale as to have occupied the attention of thousands. The question of who in Russia received accurate information about the outside world and what happened in consequence is unclear: for example, what use did Soviet scientists make of material about nuclear research in the West and in what form did it reach them? George Kennan, in his famous long telegram,* pointed out that, in the atmosphere of 'oriental secretiveness and conspiracy which pervades this government, the possibilities for distorting or poisoning sources . . . are infinite'. Even more important, 'the very disrespect of Russians for objective truth – indeed, their disbelief in its very existence – leads them to view all stated facts, true or false, as instruments for furtherance of one ulterior purpose or another.'[122]

Soviet secret services abroad were not concerned only with the gathering of intelligence. In the 1930s, they had been able to carry out a number of secret kidnappings (for example, those of General Miller and General Kuteypov in Paris) and murders (for example, Ignace Reiss in Lausanne in 1937, Trotsky in Mexico in 1940; perhaps Krivitsky, the next year, in Washington). Most, if not all, of these actions before 1939 seem to have been carried out against Russian opponents in exile. During the war, the Soviet services moved over, in the cause of 'resistance' or secret war against Germans and their collaborators, to more indiscriminate murder or terrorism. Thus, in Bulgaria in 1942, Metodi Shatarov (alias Atasanov), a Macedonian Communist who had, in the late 1930s been responsible in Paris for helping Bulgarian volunteers for the international Brigades in the Spanish Civil War, set about organising the murder in Sofia of police agents, Nazi-minded generals, and others.

Espionage had certainly been useful to Russia in the course of the late war. For example, when Stalin travelled to Tehran in 1943, a special German commando unit was bent on killing him, along with Churchill and Roosevelt. Stalin knew about this through the remarkable agent 'Schultz' (Svetlov), who was one of his own most reliable men masquerading as a senior German agent in Iran (he had been in Germany since 1930, a storm trooper, and engaged to a German diplomat's daughter).[123] Equally, 'Lucy', at the heart of the German high command, was obviously an invaluable agent. Leopold Trepper's 'Red Orchestra' (*Rote Kapelle*) sent to Moscow, mostly through Lieutenant Colonel

* See page 674.

Schultze-Boysen, plans of the new German T-6 tiger tank; an analysis of production of Messerschmitts; and even German battle plans – 1500 useful despatches in 1940–43.[124] A Soviet agent in the communications department of the Foreign Office in 1939 slowed down the reception in London of the American knowledge of the Nazi-Soviet Pact in 1939.[125] Friends of the Soviet Union in the British Secret Service, or the Special Operations Executive in Bari or Cairo (or both), may have had an influence in the revolutions in Albania and Yugoslavia. Others, in the BBC, may have helped that cause also.[126] Philby, in British Secret Intelligence, was probably instrumental in preventing the head of 'Lucy' from defecting to the West, instead of returning to Russia, and perhaps he helped to prevent Admiral Canaris from pursuing effectively a compromise peace with the West.[127] As controller of counter-espionage, he, on his own admission, certainly ruined the would-be agent Volkov, who had wished to defect to the West in September 1945, and, whatever else he did or did not do, he had every opportunity to destroy both British agents abroad and British files at home.[128] He apparently persuaded his superiors not to pass on to Churchill information gained by the decyphering of radio messages between Moscow and foreign Communist parties in Europe during the last year of the war.[129]

A characteristic of Soviet diplomacy was that the leaders always knew that what seemed to be happening was as important as what actually was happening. Furthermore, in war as in peace – and, with the Soviet Union, there was no substantive difference – the Russian government sought to use public opinion, and the media, to propagate campaigns of publicity second to none. From 1917 till 1933, the British Empire was the chief target of Soviet propaganda. The Soviet press was then full of cartoons depicting fat capitalists and British proconsuls as the arch-enemies of the people. At the first Conference of 'the Toilers of the East', in 1921, at Baku, Zinoviev roused the Moslems gathered there to call for a crusade against the British Empire. After 1933, the Russians turned their attention to the Nazis: an attitude which lasted till 1939. During the totalitarian two years, 1939–41, this propaganda was both more muted and more obscure. The years from 1941 to 1945 were also exceptional. But from 1945 onwards, and particularly after the election speech by Stalin in February 1946, 'the United States became target Number One' for Soviet propaganda, for no other reason than that it was 'the chief source of power left in the non-Communist world'.[130] Thereafter it was impossible, as 'Chip' Bohlen once said, to read 'any worthy or decent sentiments attributed to the United States.' Any action which the United States took, no matter how progressive, was judged on the basic premise that all capitalism was evil, and anything good that might come of it only apparently so.[131]

The Soviet propaganda machine was in 1946 of vast diversity. It operated through press, books, films and pamphlets. What was built up in war was allowed to remain. Nothing was done at the end of it to wind it down. Thus in Tehran the Russian publishing and information department took over in 1945 the buildings – even the radio time – previously filled by the British.[132]

To these activities, conducted through parties abroad, agents and Soviet embassies, Stalin's diplomacy would soon add a network of friendly states nominally independent of Russia, but actually controlled by him.

# FIVE

# RUSSIA IN 1946

The Soviet military achievement in the Second World War was remarkable. The Red Armies fought well. However difficult the conditions, they rarely cracked. Few were disloyal. Their endurance astonished the Germans and disheartened them: Hitler had counted on a *blitzkrieg* victory. They probably surprised Stalin too.

This was a contrast with the First World War. In 1914, much of Russia's population 'lacked an elementary sense of citizenship. Some peasants even wondered in August 1914 whether the declaration of war affected their villages'.[1] In 1941, the Russians knew that they had a state, whatever doubts they may have felt about it. The much extended system of education, the machinery of indoctrinisation, and the Party, as well as the officialdom which now stretched into agriculture, had helped to create these conditions. Had Stalin asked people to fight for Communism, matters might have been different. He asked them to fight for Russia. He gave the impression that patriotism would be the next thrust of the nation which he had recreated. German brutality made even anti-Communists fight for Russia.[2] 'Let the many images of our great ancestors,' Stalin said on November 7, 1941, the anniversary of the Revolution, 'inspire you in this war',[3] and listed Alexander Nevsky, Suvorov and Kutusov, and others who were certainly not forefathers of his own.

The Russian people supported the war not only because they were patriotic but because of the relief it offered: 'When the war broke out, its real horrors, its real dangers, its menace of real death, were a blessing compared with the inhuman power of the lie', Boris Pasternak caused Misha Gordon to remark in *Doctor Zhivago*, 'it was not only felt by men in . . . the concentration camps but by everyone, without exception, at home, and at the front, and they all took a deep breath and flung themselves into the furnace of this deadly liberating struggle, with real joy'.[4]

The war thus loosened the grip of ideology. Marxism-Leninism did not inspire the nation. It almost disappeared: 'It was amazing how quickly the complete transformation of Soviet propaganda had its effect on national feeling about Soviet patriotism and the idea of a patriotic war; and how quickly the ideas of Party and of Socialism and Communism disappeared from the propagandists' vocabulary'.[5] The *Internationale* was replaced as a national anthem by a hymn glorifying Russia. Atheism ceased to be pressed. The leaders of the Orthodox Church, reticent, humiliated, second-rate men though most were, were invited to help to maintain patriotism.[6] Stalin still had portraits of Kutusov, Suvorov and Nevsky in his office in the Kremlin in 1946.[7] He gave his great offensive of 1944 the code-name 'Bagration' after the commander of royal Georgian birth, mortally wounded at Borodino in 1812. The war, as a result, led to something like a Russian cultural revival.

For three years, sixty-five million Russians and about 400,000 square miles of the Soviet Union nevertheless fell under the rule of the German army. About 100,000 collective farms, including forty per cent of the cultivated area of the Soviet Union, were occupied by Germany at one time or another. For another year, over five million Russian prisoners of war were held, or were working, in various parts of the by then diminishing Third Reich. This was, as the historian of that experience says, a unique challenge for Germans, 'militarily, politically, morally, economically'.[8] It was one which they failed utterly to meet. That was because Hitler attacked Russia with no plans for the occupied territory made beforehand except for the provision of 'special detachments' to kill Jews and Communist Party members. That failure in turn prevented the anti-Communist spirit of European

Russians from a collaboration with the invaders which a subtle approach might have ensured.

There were Germans, especially in the army, who realised that the only way to win the war against Russia was to win over the population which they had temporarily conquered. 'Russia can be beaten only by Russians,' said Major Hans von Herwarth, an ex-diplomatist with experience of the Soviet Union, who was a determined opponent of Hitler.[9] But the arguments put forward for the Ukraine by the villainous Koch generally triumphed. 'If the German soldier has conquered the Ukraine', he believed, 'he has done so not in order to make the Ukrainian people happy, but to provide possibilities for settlement for the descendants of the German front line soldier and to provide a market of the first order for Europe.'[10] Colonel von Stauffenberg, famous for his attempt on Hitler's life in 1944, shared von Herwarth's attitude towards the conquered peoples in the Caucasus. So did his Commander-in-Chief, von Kleist. Few else did.

Among all the Russian peoples conquered, the Germans made serious efforts to establish good relations with the Cossacks and with several other minor peoples of the Caucasus. They were in touch with the latter for only two or three months. The Cossacks, as so defined by the individuals themselves, turned out to be the only real allies of the Germans.

Even Goebbels knew that the Reich had made a mistake. 'We have had tremendous military successes but we still have no constructive plan for Russia. We came as conquerors where we should come as liberators'.[11] The different Russian emigré organisations were a hindrance not a help. Clustered about the German foreign ministry, just as they had been in the first world war, there were Said Shamil, the grandson of the last heroic fighter for the independence of the Caucasus; Count Heracles Bagration, pretender to the throne of Georgia; and the last Hetman of the Ukraine, Skoropadski. All three quarrelled, just as did the various German organisations concerned with them. So too did the ministry run by Rosenberg quarrel with the Gestapo; while the economic empire run by Goering fell out with the Nazi Party. All of them quarrelled with the *Reichkomissars*. None of these heirs of past heroes profited from the revival of traditionalism which marked Russia during the war: Shamil, for example, was still treated in propaganda as an Anglo-Turkish agent who tried to resist the 'progressive' and 'necessary' union of Daghestan with the Tsarist empire.[12]

The Russian victory over the German war machine had in the end been a colossal one. Stalin celebrated this triumph. There was a great reception on May 24, 1945. He had then praised the Russians as opposed to the other nations of the Soviet Union. There had been the great parade, on June 24, reviewed by Zhukov, and commanded by Rokossovsky, at which hundreds of German banners had been thrown down at Stalin's feet below the mausoleum to Lenin.

At the reception the latter night, Stalin had, however, spoken pointedly of, among other things, the 'little screws and bolts' without which the machinery of victory, with its marshals and generals, could not function. Soon, too, a poem by Nedogonov, a reliable friend of the regime, appeared, *The Flag over the Village Soviet*, which was given much publicity. It ended ominously: 'And if you don't work hard on the Kolkhoz, we shall spit on all your medals and decorations'.[13] Only a fool could have mistaken the signs foreshadowing a change of policy.

This domestic turn-about was to be interwoven nationally with a similar change in international policy.[14] But at home the most obvious fact was that, by the spring of 1946, the Red Army was in the process of deflation. The war heroes, including Marshal Zhukov, were already being, or were about to be, sent down to junior commands to prevent them from maintaining their status. Of what avail was it that, in 1942, Zhukov had contradicted Stalin himself, had saved Moscow and Stalingrad, and later had captured Berlin? Or that he had established a good understanding with the American General Eisenhower?[15] Zhukov in February 1946 might be still Russian Commander-in-Chief in Berlin. But his days there were numbered. Soon, he would return to a quite minor post in the Ministry of Defence. Stalin later told Khrushchev that Zhukov did not deserve his fame[16] and apparently told Zhukov himself that Beria and Abakumov had accused him of having been 'an agent of British intelligence for more than fifteen years'.[17] The Vozhd later also circulated rumours that Zhukov had made money in Berlin selling captured treasures – while Alexei Antonov, Deputy Chief of the Soviet General Staff, assured Djilas that Zhukov had turned out to be a Jew![18] The fate of Zhukov characterised the fate of most lesser military commanders.

In October 1945, the British Embassy in Moscow reported that 'the morale of the Red Army, and the connected issue of demobilisation' were already the most serious problems faced by the Soviet government. The army was, however, being maintained at greater than its pre-war strength. Wartime privileges were then confirmed or even extended. The troops abroad were homesick. The British chargé d'affaires thought that that mood could be held in check: after all, Russian troops had never been abroad before and the interest of being abroad, even in a ruined Europe, was to many considerable.[19]

From twelve million in 1945, Russian troops would drop to not much more than three million in 1947.[20] Soviet plans nevertheless envisaged 'an armed establishment which far outclassed, in numbers and power of ground forces in particular, anything that existed in the non-Communist world'.[21] That was traditional in Russia, whose rulers have always placed faith in numbers. The policy had the advantage of keeping a substantial proportion of young men well-disciplined.

There were, however, more problems in Russia than those concerned with demobilisation. These were partly political, partly economic and partly psychological. But all revolved round the central fact of the nature of the Revolution – the so-called third Revolution – which had been carried out by Stalin in the 1930s, which had launched the country into the industrialisation which, in turn, had made it into a first-class military power. This success had been achieved at the cost of the death of millions of people and the ruin of thousands of ancient communities. Economic achievement and wanton neglect or murder accompanied one another. In the 1930s, the majority of the Russian peasantry had been disciplined, or transported. Those who remained on the land in 1939 were a quarter of those there in January 1, 1923. Most had been gathered into state or collective farms. The others had been carried into, or ordered to build, the cities which made the industrialisation of Russia possible. If they had resisted, they would have been killed or left to starve. This was far the most elaborate, as well as far the most brutal, act of social engineering in history. The memory of it was the dominant fact of the Soviet empire.

From the point of view of the economy, the achievements of the Five Year Plans, however terrible, can scarcely be gainsaid. Steel production between 1928 and 1940 did increase, from four million metric tons to eighteen; coal from thirty-five to 166; oil from nearly twelve to thirty-one; cement from two million to six; and electricity from five billion kilowatt hours to forty-eight.[22] Other grandiose achievements were an increase in the production of machine tools from 2,000 to 58,000 a year; tractors from 1,300 to 32,000; and leather shoes and boots, 58 million pairs a year to 200 million.[23] The Five Year Plans of 1928–1933, 1934–1939, and 1939 till the war were soon to be emulated in other countries with less brutality, less determination and, it must be said, less effect.

This industrialisation of Russia in the 1930s also meant innumerable opportunities for those with quick wit and a desire to rise. Even the remains of the old intelligentsia were given tasks to perform. Non-Party engineers gained positions of responsibility.[24] Thus Russia at the outbreak of the war – her war began in 1941 – was a major military power. She had, for example, 24,000 tanks against 3,550 German ones on the Russian front.[25] The T34 tank was also heavier than its German equivalent.

The German attack, and the subsequent difficulties attendant on the evacuation of 1,500 industrial plants eastward in late 1941, of course caused a collapse in production.[26] But, by late 1942, Soviet industry had revived. Vast numbers of women had been sent to work. New mines were sunk, new power plants built. A 'second Baku' in the East for the exploitation of oil was established. Though the Soviet engineering industry had lost half its strength because of the German occupation of the Ukraine, it had overcome these difficulties by 1943. In that year, Soviet aircraft and tanks had begun to be competitive with German. It is true that British and, particularly, American military aid made a difference: perhaps ten to fifteen per cent of the total. That was so marked in some respects that Averell Harriman, the American ambassador, could argue at one point that 'almost all the Army's transport equipment and much of its food is supplied by us'.[27] All the same, the Soviet achievement, directed by D. F. Ustinov, Minister of Armaments, was astonishing.* For example, in 1941, in three weeks, 5,800 metal working lathes were carried from the Kirov works in Leningrad to new buildings in the Urals. These began producing tanks there even before the buildings had a roof. Military production exceeded German totals considerably in all essentials: tanks, military aircraft, guns and mortars.†

The lesson which could be drawn from this success achieved by Stalin and his colleagues in industry and war was that brutality paid: trust in international friendship (such as they had had with the Germans for two years and with the West for four years) was an error; humanity did not matter. This was an understandable conclusion, in the circumstances. But it not only made Stalin difficult, if not impossible, to deal with after the war by his allies of 1941–45. It also meant that he continued to rely on slave labour in the economy, and brutality in politics at a time when, given the construction of the new economic base, a lighter hand would probably have produced a more prosperous, as well as a happier, country. This confidence in cruel doings, justified by a return from old patriotism to Marxist-Leninist ideology, was imposed on a people which was already suffering from the consequences of the last ten years of both peace and war.

* Ustinov was subsequently, and for many years, minister of Defence in the Soviet Union. He died, a marshal, in 1984, in office.

†

|                                   | USSR<br>July 1941–July 1945 | Germany<br>1941–1945 |
|-----------------------------------|-----------------------------|----------------------|
| Tanks:                            | 95,099                      | 53,800               |
| Aircraft:                         | 108,028                     | 78,900               |
| Guns: medium and large calibre:   | 188,000                     | 102,000              |
| Mortars:                          | 348,000                     | 68,000               |

Source: Roger Munting *The Economic Development of the USSR* (London, 1982).

The destruction caused by the war in European Russia was great. Noble cities, sleepy towns, tiny villages, all had been fought and refought over. Retreating Germans had had time to destroy almost all that remained in, say, Rostov, Voronezh and Sebastopol. Populations had been cut by three quarters: death in fighting, death from torture, murder, deportation to Germany, flight (during the German withdrawal, of, for example, collaborators). Great literary monuments had been destroyed. In Byelorussia, the Ukraine, the Crimea and much of the Don region, most of the towns had been burned, Jews massacred, agriculture turned into desert zones, not only by the fighting but by deliberate action: special rollers had even been used by the Germans to crush crops, special trains to destroy railway lines.

Russia suffered about eleven million deaths in battle, and about seven million civilian deaths. The population probably declined by twenty-four million between 1941 and 1945. If another two million died in German camps for prisoners, it can easily be seen that Russia would want to make up for this by importing prisoners from Germany or Austria, in compensation.[28]

Between 1941 and 1945, the Germans had captured about five and three quarter million Russian prisoners of war. The majority – 3.8 million – were taken between June and December 1941. No provision had been made by the Germans for these men before the war. Many of them were soon at work, either in Russia or in the greatly expanded territories of Germany. Some were sent back to Russia quietly. But vast numbers were left in neglected camps without food or shelter. The Nazi ideology, of the superiority of the race, gave this cruelty its justification. A million were released in 1944 or 1945. Another million served in collaborator units. As many as a million and three quarters were unaccounted for.* The size of this tragedy was on a scale quite without precedent in previous conflicts.[29]

---

* These figures may be disputed. See, e.g., Heinrich Böll in *A Letter to my Son* where he speaks of 3.3 million dead prisoners of war. Whatever the numbers, one can certainly contrast what happened to them with the 5.4 per cent only of Russian prisoners of war who died in Germany in the First World War.

At the same time, another two and three quarter million Russians were shipped to the Reich as 'Eastern workers' in German factories. Most of these were Ukrainians.[30] Once again, the Germans' official conviction that these men (and women) were *Untermenschen* ensured their ill-treatment.

Stalin distrusted those millions of soldiers of his armies who had been captured by the Germans. No food parcels, no Red Cross aid ever reached them. He had made intercession for none of them, not even for his eldest son Jakob who later died, probably by his own hand, in Oranienburg camp. Solzhenitsyn recalls coming across a camp of such Russian prisoners, recently freed, in East Prussia: in 'a swampy meadow encircled by barbed wire' a multitude of bonfires; and, around the bonfires, 'beings who had once been Russian officers, but had now become beastlike creatures, who gnawed the bones of dead horses, who baked patties from potato rinds, who smoked manure, and who were all swarming with lice'.[31] The Soviet government knew perfectly well of the ill-treatment of Russian prisoners by Germans, as Molotov spoke of the matter to Roosevelt in 1942 in Washington. All the same, they were nearly all sent off to labour camps when liberated. Their real demobilisation took many years.[32]

At the end of the war, the population in the camps maintained by GULAG (the 'main administration of corrective labour camps') were being increased not only by these unfortunates but also by large proportions of people of the provinces which the Germans had overrun, many of whom also were looked upon as likely to be 'wreckers' or spies. Thus Beria, in early 1946, must have had somewhere between seven and twelve million prisoners at his disposal in his concentration camps.*[33]

If one were to ask why this number of the Russian labour force were in concentration camps in 1946, the answers from the authorities would be various: so-and-so had been accused

---

* An official Soviet document, '*State Plan of Development of the National Economy of the USSR for 1941*', captured by the Germans, revealed that, in that year, 18 per cent of total Soviet capital investment was in projects of the NKVD, 12 per cent in lumbering, and a good deal in mining (gold mining was entirely in the hands of the NKVD).

of deliberately selecting spotted horses for the Red Cavalry so that they would spoil the camouflage before the enemy; so-and-so was there because, in a secret agreement with Finland, she had agreed to become Queen of a Finnish-speaking people in the Volga-Ural region, the Mari, after the overthrow of the Soviet Government. There was a cutter from a clothes factory who was accused of fomenting discontent among the people of Minsk because he had designed too narrow pockets in the trousers of the workers. But the truth was more complicated. For there were, in addition, old Bolsheviks; survivors of old parties of the days of the civil war; even now, a few genuine 'White Guards'; anarchists; and an extraordinarily large number of foreigners; men or women who had been foolish, or unlucky, enough to have become drawn into Moscow's web at some time since 1917: German, Italian, Japanese, Romanian and Spanish real prisoners of war (as well as some dissident Spanish Communists). A labour camp in central Asia might be a real United Nations. There were the remains, too, of shattered peoples from within the Soviet Union: Lithuanians and Letts, Georgians and Armenians, hundreds of thousands of slaves scattered in the 'holocaust of history', in Engels' phrase. Those who might complain could indeed be reminded that Engels was not particular about the way that such 'ethnic trash' was dumped into the dustbin of history. Such a thing as a great revolution, he had written, was not accomplished 'without forcibly crushing many a delicate little national flower'.[34]

The existence of the camps hung over Russia like a heavy cloud. In 1946, all Russia remembered that, before 1941, peace had meant purges: there had been an atmosphere so frenetic, incredible, demented, as to make bedlam seem normal. The victims were still in many cases suffering. Even those who were dead had left families whose lives were dominated by the injustice of the past. Children also had been killed and many of them were in prison or camps. Leaving aside how real opponents of the Party were treated between 1924 and 1953 'on the most cautious of estimates,' Roy Medvedev calculates, between 1936 and 1939, 'four to five million people were subjected to repression . . . At least four to five hundred thousand were summarily shot. The rest were given long terms of confinement . . . from which few returned alive. These were not streams, these were rivers of blood . . . not one of the tyrants and despots of the past persecuted so many of his [Stalin's] compatriots.'[35] Though the purges were now over, temporarily, the camps remained.

All those Russian citizens of 1939 who had either collaborated with the Germans, or had taken advantage of the German invasion and Soviet reverses to try and act independently, were, of course, suffering the persecution which they must have expected. This affected, for example, the half million Tartars of the Crimea and the Volga Germans, accused, as peoples, of collaboration in the occupied areas (though the Volga Germans' autonomous republic had never been reached by Hitler's armies); and several small tribes of the Northern Caucasus, such as the Chechen and Karachai, the Balkars and the Kalmyks. Some of these peoples staged rebellions against the Soviet government before the arrival of the Germans. They were subsequently well-treated by the German army (whose commanders also tried to protect the Tats, or mountain Jews, against the Gestapo). As a man from the Caucasus, Stalin probably found great satisfaction afterwards in destroying so many of the one-time neighbours of his ancestors. Khrushchev later said that Stalin would have deported the Ukrainians too had there not been so many of them.[36] (Khrushchev would have had to carry through the deportation himself and done so with his usual bombast, for he was then the Party Secretary, as well as the chief political officer of the Red Army, in the region.)

Within the Soviet Union, no kind of peace had yet come to many provinces of the West. Armed conflict continued in the Baltic states, particularly in Lithuania.[37] The acquisition of Karelia, handed over finally to Russia in 1945, meant the occupation of a zone almost wholly abandoned by Finns. But, in the Ukraine, a civil war which had begun while the Germans were still there seemed to have no end. Ukrainians in the World War had both suffered vastly and behaved atrociously. They had assisted Nazi massacres of Jews, they had been persecuted by both Nazis and Russians. Many spent the last years of the war living like savages. In this confusion, a Ukrainian Insurgent Army (UPA) had come forward to help the Germans in destroying Communist partisans. But they were denied the prospect of a separate state by the Germans; and, from 1943 onwards, fought both Germans and Russians. Their doomed cause was not helped by their own divisions, between the UPA, controlled by Stefan Bandera, and the so-called Ukrainian National Revolutionary Army. Bandera emerged on top and, in the last stages of the German-Russian War, had been able to establish something like an administration generally confining the Germans to the towns. The Ukrainians had been well organised enough to kill at least one senior Russian general, Vatutin, when he diverted from a main road in 1944.[38] In 1945 they had been able to hold up main line trains on railways for days.[39] These guerrillas, who may have numbered 30,000 to 40,000,[40] were well entrenched. In the Carpathians, they were in a position to mount a network capable of stealing arms from government posts and of distributing Ukrainian nationalist propaganda. In south-east Poland, Ukrainian resistance was stronger, better organised and even more active.[41]

The Germans had occupied much of the famous region of Black Earth, the most productive part of the Soviet Union. In the rest of the country, mobilisation had taken nearly half the labouring population off the land. The government sought to compensate for the loss of the first by increasing cultivation in Central Asia and Siberia, and for the second by organising women to take the place of men. Workers living in towns had been encouraged to produce vegetables in their gardens. All the same, many of the casualties of the war had derived from malnutrition.

The war losses were considerable in agriculture. Thus, in 1940, production of grain totalled eighty-three million tons; in 1945, that figure was down to eighty-one. Production of vegetables in the same years had fallen from over fourteen million tons to just over nine. Only the production of meat and potatoes had mildly increased. But the stocks of cattle went down between 1941 and 1945 from fifty-five million to forty-eight. Horses and hogs were also down, by six per cent and sixteen per cent respectively.[42] In 1946 agricultural output was still only eighty-six per cent of what it had been in 1913, without taking into account the substantial increase of population.

One reason for this was undoubtedly psychological. During the agricultural revolution Russians knew that they were being treated abominably: 'We are no longer people, we are animals', the wife of one emissary, a *komsomol* from outside the region, had said in the Roslavl region.[43] 'Don't think of the *kulak*'s hungry children; in "the class struggle", philanthropy is evil,' a certain Litenbrand had remarked in the same region.[44] But on top of this experience in the early 1930s, there had been imposed the German invasion and occupation, the partisan war, and the shock of liberation.

The harvest of 1945 was said in October 1945 to have been 'average', although, as a result of an early winter, much of the potato crop had been frozen into the ground.[45] All the same, the prospects for 1946 were not good and in many provinces in that year Russia was expected to be close to famine – a fact kept as secret as possible.[46]

After liberation, the *kolkhozes* (co-operative farms) had been revived. That was easy, because the Germans, unwisely for their own success, had, as a rule, maintained them, as what seemed a good way of securing deliveries of food to the army. After discovering the intense hostility of the peasants to the collective system,[47] the Germans made some concessions to them: individual plots were not taxed and could be enlarged up to double their previous size; unlimited private cattle-breeding was permitted; and, in 1942, there was an agrarian reform which annulled all Soviet laws about collective farming. Nevertheless, *kolkhozes* were made into village communes no more free than their predecessors. This lack of radicalism in their policies had been one more reason for the German defeat.

In early 1946, a few people in Moscow believed that there might be a new 'charter of freedom' for the Soviet peasantry, and a revision of the old system. The regime seemed to tolerate these rumours which more experienced men distrusted – rightly, as it transpired.[48] The long-serving Commissar for Agriculture, Andreyev, did have something in store for Soviet farmers; but, unwisely, it was not a free market. No one in the Kremlin

believed that that was desirable, or possible without unacceptable political risks.

Not surprisingly, industrial production in general had fallen:
probably 30 per cent in 1946 in comparison with 1940. A fifth of
the capital assets of Soviet industry had also been destroyed in
the war. The Germans had worked the coal mines, the iron and
steel works, and other industrial enterprises in occupied Russia.
But they had had to reconstruct them since, in the main, the
retreating Soviet troops had carried through an effective policy
of destruction. In their turn, the Germans destroyed much in
their withdrawal.

The Soviet Union could, however, from their successful military base, now embark on the new Five Year Plan announced
by Stalin in February 1946 with confidence. It is obvious, from
what happened in the next year or so, that Russia made a
characteristically strenuous effort to develop nuclear power.[49]
She also began the modernisation of her air defence, and a
programme of naval building, which emphasised fast and powerful cruisers, as well as a long-range bomber force.[50] Within
eighteen months, the Russians were, for example, able to display
their copy of the American B-29A, of which four had crash-landed
in Siberia in 1944. This was the TU-4, to be known to the West
as the 'Bull'.[51]

But though the military potential of the Soviet state remained
considerable in peace as in war, it was a state which, because
of the character of its leaders, its ideology and its internal mood,
could not have fitted into any design to create a tranquil world.
Its produce and its commerce were as much outside the world's
markets as its masters were outside the way of thinking of those
who presided over the rest of the globe.[52]

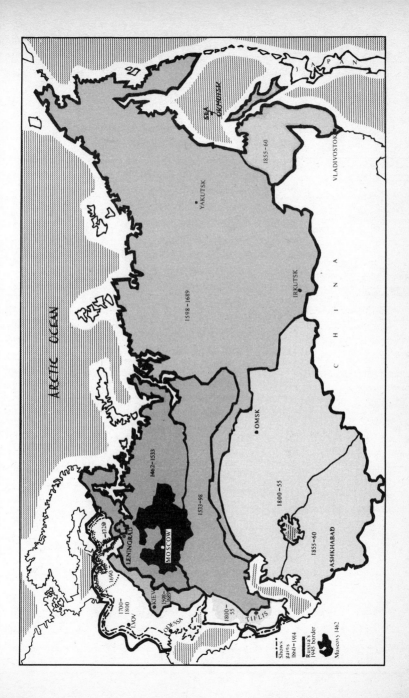

ARCTIC OCEAN

JAPAN

SEA OF OKHOTSK

YAKUTSK

VLADIVOSTOK

1855~60

1598~1689

IRKUTSK

C H I N A

OMSK

1800~55

1462~1533

1855~60

1533~98

ASHKHABAD

LENINGRAD

MOSCOW

1729

1690

1700~
1800

1598~
1688

KIEV

AZOV

ODESSA

1800~
55

TIFLIS

Shows
gains
1860~1914

Russia's
1945 border

Muscovy 1462

# SIX

# RUSSIA'S INTERNATIONAL POLICY

The relation between Soviet Communism and the ghost of Russia past naturally exercises historians. After all, the threat of Russia towards other peoples and cultures had been posed long before 1917. The advance of that country was, for example, a prime preoccupation of Frederick the Great: 'This is a terrible power,' he wrote to his brother Henry in 1769, 'sprung from those Huns and Gepides who destroyed the empire of the East, they could well break into the empire of the West before long. I can see no remedy but to form, when opportunity offers, a league of the greatest rulers to stem this dangerous torrent.'[1] There were, he later thought, two choices: 'either to stop Russia in her headlong career of conquest or – which would be wiser – to try to profit from it'.[2] More recently, Napoleon at Elba, in conversation with his escort, Colonel Neil Campbell, thought that 'if Russia were able to dominate Poland, it would be impossible to foresee or limit the consequences. Hordes of Cossacks and barbarians, having seen the riches of more civilised countries, will be eager to return. They will overrun Europe and some great change will probably result from it, as has been the case in former times from the incursions of barbarians'. Napoleon referred to the subject later: 'I was the only man who could have stopped him [Tsar Alexander] and his flood of Tartars,' he added, 'the menace for the continent of Europe . . . is serious and will endure.'[3] Heine, one of the few good modern prophets, spoke in 1833 of Russia as 'the dreadful giant who now is still sleeping and growing in his slumber, stretching his feet far into the scented gardens of the Orient, touching the North Pole with his head, dreaming of new world empire.'[4] The last Chancellor of the old German Empire, Bethmann Hollweg, was even more gloomy: 'The future lies with Russia,' he wrote to his son on July 7, 1914, 'she grows and grows and lies on us like a nightmare.' He advised against a plan to plant long-growing trees on their property in East Prussia since, when they came to maturity, only the Russians would profit.[5]

The spread of Russia from the XVth century onwards, beginning with the grand-duchy of Muscovy freed from the Tartars, has indeed been as striking a development in the history of the modern world as that of Rome in the ancient; even though, where Rome spread law, the rulers of Moscow not only 'engulfed more and more territory' but 'spread serfdom and tyranny wherever they went'.[6] In the late XVth century, some Russian cities, such as Novgorod (whose independence ended in 1478) or Tver (annexed 1485) enjoyed relatively free, if oligarchic, polities. Those city states were destroyed, as were Pskov (in 1510) and Smolensk (in 1514), and much of Lithuania, along with independent despotisms previously established in Kazan and Astrakhan. Serfdom was established specifically to pin the peasants of these newly-conquered regions to the soil. The peasants concerned fled into Siberia. To recover them the Russian Empire followed them east and south. Was this the constant striving for security of a state with no natural frontiers and surrounded by enemies?[7] Or was it mere imperialism? Or were the two distinguishable? Both served to justify Nicholas I's comment, when his flag was raised on the Yalu River, without his instructions: 'Where the Russian Flag has been run up, it must not be hauled down.'[8] Nor should one forget that the Austrian empire had been saved from dissolution in 1849 by the Tsar: 'an extreme resource, and, in every way, deplorable,' Prince Schwarzenberg admitted. Had it not occurred, Hungary would have become free.[9] Schwarzenberg, alas, preferred to bring the Russians into Europe than to allow such an eventuality. His heirs would bear the brunt of his misjudgment.

The Russian rulers thus, from the beginning of 'early modern history', have domineered over many other peoples. The Russian people themselves, for whom all who know them have affection, if not enthusiasm, complained about these rulers through the brilliant and often moving prose of their writers. But they have not been able to change the conditions in which they themselves suffered.

Even before 1917, the justification for Russian imperialism was pretentious. Engels, for example, complained that: 'There was no land grab, no outrage, no repression on the part of Tsarism, which was not carried out under the pretext of enlightenment, of liberalism, of the liberation of nations.'[10] This confidence in their mission was usually, and uniquely, accompanied by a sense of insecurity, deriving from the memory of invasions in the past, from the lack of natural frontiers, and from fear of other empires (Swedes and British in the XVIIIth and XIXth centuries; Persians, Turks, Mongols before; Chinese afterwards). Rulers of Russia have, therefore, demanded, and obtained, a large army, as well as political tyranny.

Many of these memories lay in 1946 as a residue in the bottom of most Russians' minds; so did recollections of Tsarist unfulfilled imperialism: the 'warm water port' in the south; or the permanent settlement of Port Arthur in the east. That was so even though, for a Marxist-Leninist, the change which occurred in Russia in 1917 was looked upon as an event as determining as that of the birth of Christ to a Christian, or the flight of Muhammad to a Moslem.

These considerations were as important for external policy as for internal. Fear of anarchy – a new 'time of troubles', such as preceded the Romanovs or a renewal of the disorders of the 1770s, of 1905 and of 1917 – was one of these. Doubt as to how to arrange the succession peacefully was another. At least with the Romanovs there was usually a Tsarevitch.

Russia was certain to have been a great power in the twentieth century. Her resources, vast size as a land empire and manpower assured that, once railways had enabled her to industrialise.[11] Russia's greatness, however, depended on dictatorship, either Tsarist or Communist, since, as the events of 1917–18 showed, liberty would lead to disintegration. The Tsarist autocracy had been adequate to hold Poland in 1830 and in 1863, and Finland after 1905. But another regional challenge might not have been met.

In some respects, therefore, the external policy of Russia in 1914 and that of 1946 resembled each other. In the former year, for example, Sazonov, the Foreign Minister of the Tsar, envisaged an Eastern Central Europe, divided into small, nominally independent states, which were essentially Russian clients, not unlike that in Stalin's mind in 1946. Among these states, there might be Poland, to be enlarged by the acquisition of Eastern Pomerania and Silesia at the German expense: an idea which certainly occurred to Stalin in 1941. Other officials in the Russian Foreign Office had envisaged a vassal Czech monarchy, following a dismemberment of Austro-Hungary.[12] These dreamers took most of their ideas from Nicolai Danilevsky and other Pan Slav writers of the 1860s: Danilevsky, in *Russia and Europe* (1869), had proposed a Slav federation in East Europe dependent on Russia.[13] With scarcely a word changed, *Izvestiia* in 1918 talked of a Central and Eastern European Socialist federation following the Soviet re-conquest of the Baltic littoral.[14] Stalin's programme in 1944–1946 was intended not only to increase the military strength of Russia, but also to prevent the formation, in Central and Eastern Europe, of any power or coalition of powers capable of challenging Russia.[15] In the years before 1939, France and the West in general, had tried to create, in that region, a *cordon sanitaire* with which to insulate themselves from the Soviet bacillus. Stalin was happy to have another such *cordon* which he could justify as, perhaps believe to be, one against Germany. A man who had destroyed many thousand-year-old Russian village communities would not mind about the suffering caused in Poland or Hungary.

But he had also a Marxist-Leninist duty to do what he could along these lines. Lenin had explicitly, and often, stated that the task before the Russian workers was to 'maintain the power of the soviets till the working class of all countries revolts and raises aloft the banner of a world working-class republic'.[16] Others had spoken in the 1920s of 'a Russian Soviet republic', to be surrounded by 'daughter and sister republics' which would be the basis for a 'federation first of Europe, and then of the entire world'.[17] Lenin had several times not only spoken of a 'world-wide Soviet Republic' but had even hazarded a date by which it was to be finished. Stalin had frequently alluded to the Soviet Union in speeches during the 1920s as the first step towards a world state, whose next move presumably would be the creation of further such states dependent upon it. Admittedly, there had been a period of retreat in the late 1920s and 1930s. All the same, the *Large Soviet Encyclopaedia*, in 1938, reaffirmed that the Communist International was devoted to a 'world Union of Soviet Socialist republics'.[18]

With the one exception of his blind trust in the Nazis from 1939 until 1941, Stalin conducted Soviet diplomacy skilfully through the shoals of the Second World War. Even in 1939, he benefited from the German desire to have a friend in the East while they turned on France and Britain, in order to secure the Baltic states,* Eastern Poland,† Bessarabia‡ and North Bukovina, and a general understanding of Soviet interests 'towards the Persian Gulf'. Whatever complaints may legitimately be made about Western weakness later, concerning Stalin's activities in these areas, it was Hitler who agreed – temporarily, of course, in his mind – to Soviet expansion in this way, without discussion. These expansions of Russian territory were treated in the Soviet press as 'victories for revolution and for Marxism-Leninism,' of course, not for the great Russian nation. When Molotov told Ribbentrop that the Soviet Union was vitally interested in the fate of all east Central Europe as well as the Persian Gulf, Hitler did not discourage him.[19]

Churchill in 1939 described Soviet policy as a riddle, wrapped in a mystery, concealed within an enigma.[20] That was to over-stress the puzzle. There was nothing confusing, for example, about Stalin's demand of Anthony Eden in December 1941 for

\* See below, pages 450–1.

† See below, page 356.

‡ See below, page 412.

British recognition that Soviet boundaries after the war should be those of six months before. That meant, in particular, the incorporation into Russia of the territory conceded to him by Hitler. Britain rejected this plan, as did the US. All the same, Churchill would have been prepared to accept recognition of some territorial changes in the proposed Anglo-Soviet Treaty of 1942. The Americans argued, however, that all such arrangements should be settled at the peace conference. For a variety of reasons the treaty, in the end, was signed without territorial clauses, in May 1942. There was then little detailed attention given to the post-war world till the Conference of Foreign Ministers at Moscow, in October 1943. In the meantime, Stalin maintained his policy, gained useful understanding for it from British officials, if not from those of the US, and, by his victories at Stalingrad and Kursk, transformed his own diplomatic position; clearly exploiting the persistent postponement of that 'Second Front' in Western Europe which he had been promised for 1942.

East Europe after the war was brought up at a meeting of foreign ministers in Moscow in October 1943 on the initiative of the British Foreign Secretary, Anthony Eden. That statesman suggested a paper entitled *Joint Responsibility for Europe* which would have made possible the establishment of a federation, or federations, in East and Central Europe.[21] Molotov made a guileful speech speaking, as it were, on behalf of such small states (a contrast with Stalin's later comments on such entities). The idea was premature; it might endanger European stability. It also reminded the Soviet people, he said, of the pre-war schemes for a *cordon sanitaire* against them. (It was, in fact, the one thing which Stalin was determined to avoid.) Eden's suggestion was, therefore, dropped. Molotov went on to say that, after the war, Russia would hope to see an independent Poland, not one in a federation with Czechoslovakia, but 'friendly to the Soviet Union'.[22] So Eden soon abandoned his department's long-held opposition to a treaty between Russia and Czechoslovakia; and, within a few weeks, Stalin made just such a treaty with the Czech leader, Dr Beneš. This guaranteed Soviet trade interests in Czechoslovakia and turned the future of that country towards the East.* The Soviet-Czech treaty meant that the Polish-Czech treaty of the previous year would lose its value; one of its purposes had been to encourage a federation in East Europe. Here there were to be seen clear signs that the Soviet Union was hoping for substantial booty after the war to be obtained from East Europe. Meanwhile some very innocent individuals from the United States travelled to Russia (for example Wendell Willkie) and Stalin must have seen from their remarks that American ignorance of his system was remarkable.

By then, Italy had surrendered and had a new anti-fascist government. Molotov, affecting to forgive the British and the Americans for signing a separate armistice there, insisted that the government 'should be made more democratic, by the introduction of representatives of those sections of the Italian people who have always opposed Fascism': that is, Communists – a formula which was later useful throughout Eastern Europe.

The conference at Moscow agreed to establish in London a tripartite committee of officials, the European Advisory Commission (EAC), to suggest how to resolve all problems relating to Europe and make joint recommendations to the three governments: Germany and Austria (to be considered a country to be 'liberated' and not a war criminal country) particularly. Like almost all the ideas for post-war reconstruction this was a Western proposal, which in the end, however, the Soviet Union accepted. Stalin also agreed in general terms to join a new international body.

Soon afterwards, at the end of November 1943, Stalin met Churchill and Roosevelt at Tehran. Stalin had insisted on the site. With his usual cleverness, he persuaded those around Roosevelt, and Roosevelt himself, that he had to be treated sensitively. He surely sensed the vast possibilities open to him because of Roosevelt's evident desire to please, and because of the differences in approach, which could be made to seem important, between the President and Churchill. The delay in establishing the 'Second Front' in France had caused some sense of guilt among the British and the Americans. Stalin skilfully

* See below, pages 379–80.

took advantage of the complicated state of affairs. He did not have to try very hard. Roosevelt* stated that the 'members of the new family' had gathered at Tehran not for discussing the peace but for the purpose of winning the war. This enabled him to avoid serious discussion of the future. Even so, Churchill and, by inference, Roosevelt agreed with Stalin's solution for Poland's borders;† and, in return, Stalin agreed to listen to Roosevelt's still vague ideas for the future United Nations.‡ The Western leaders were impressed by the way that Stalin spoke of himself and his comrades as 'we Russians', not 'we revolutionary communists'.

After another campaigning season in the summer of 1944, it became evident that Stalin was establishing himself and his agents wherever his armies conquered. He did bring himself to salute the long-delayed Second Front handsomely: 'One cannot but acknowledge that the history of warfare knows no similar enterprise that equals it in breadth of conception, enormity of scale and high skill of execution'.[23] Churchill tried to secure a minimum of British influence in the Balkans by negotiating direct with Stalin: suppose Russia were allowed to have a controlling interest in Romania, and Britain the same in Greece? Roosevelt accepted this for a three-month trial period. Then Churchill suggested a similar division of influence affecting Bulgaria and Yugoslavia. The Americans were unenthusiastic. Meantime, the Russian armies occupied both Romania and Bulgaria. Churchill and Eden went to Moscow in October and, in optimistic mood, proposed immediate wartime arrangements, carrying the idea of percentages further: 90 per cent British influence in Greece, 90 per cent Russian in Romania; in Hungary and Yugoslavia 50–50 per cent influence; in Bulgaria 75–25 per cent in Russia's favour.[24] Stalin agreed, also emphasising their temporary nature,§ with a qualification by Stalin (90 per cent, not 75, to Russia in Bulgaria) according to the Foreign Office report.[25] The two heads of government decided to hand over further discussion

* See below, page 258.
† See below, page 352.
‡ See below, page 260.
§ See Appendix III.

on these contentious matters to Eden and Molotov. Some further juggling of figures went on. With a parade of condescension, Molotov proposed also to insert, in Article 18 of the Bulgarian armistice, an arrangement that the Allied Control Commission should after all execute the armistice terms with the participation of Britain and the United States. Churchill saw these things as a success. They certainly suggested that the Russian army would probably not march directly into Greece – a real possibility once they had reached the Bulgarian–Greek frontier; nor, a more difficult task, into Turkey to Istanbul, near which city they soon made evident that they coveted a base. Meantime, though Russia had 'liberated' much of Eastern Poland, she had allowed an army of anti-Nazi – and essentially anti-Communist – Poles to destroy itself, in a vain attack on the Nazi occupiers in Warsaw.

The Soviet Union had been represented at the conference in Dumbarton Oaks, in Washington, for the creation of a new international organisation: 'Nine tenths of the security problems were solved at this conference in a spirit of complete unanimity,' Stalin said happily afterwards.[26] Again, the ideas suggested for a United Nations organisation were not Stalin's. But he believed that he could work within them. The same was true to a lesser extent in respect of the plans for a world economic rearrangement agreed in the United States at Bretton Woods.

Now that the war had been almost won, it was clearly necessary to think ahead. The West thought of post-war world planning. Presumably, Stalin thought of the inter-relation between domestic and international policy, between Communist and Russian aims, between ideology and wartime leniency. In the autumn of 1944, a warning was issued against 'Western' and 'bourgeois' tendencies in the official Party magazine, *Bolshevik*: 'Recently, views have been expressed in various quarters that, after the war, art and literature will follow "the easy road" and will be calculated to entertain . . . Such tendencies must be fought. They are reactionary and in flat contradiction with the Lenin-Stalin view that art is a powerful weapon of agitation and education among the masses.'[27] This warning came after a wave of nostalgic, scarcely revolutionary, often not even patriotic, music and light comedy. One need not read too much into that.

All the same, the identical line was followed in an editorial in that same journal: 'In the complex international situation, the Party member needs a compass and there is no better one than Marxism-Leninism.' So the good Communist should read Stalin's *Short History of the Communist Party*. This return to political education was considered to be specially important in the newly liberated areas, where the enemy had spread 'the poison of racialist theories'. *Zvezda* had said the same: 'The ideological training of members is now more necessary than ever . . . A Communist needs a sound ideological equipment more than ever.'[28]

So it was unsurprising that, in the winter of 1944–45, a stream of decrees should issue from the Central Committee of the Communist party which hammered away at the need to improve 'mass political and ideological work'. A mass lecture programme was organised to correct 'the drift from Marxism-Leninism' and the 'drift to individualism'.[29] On October 17, 1944, *Pravda* recalled that the Party had to devote special attention to reviving 'a socialist attitude' to labour, 'overcoming the private property, anti-collective farm and anti-state tendencies planted by the German occupiers'.[30]

These attitudes had their external resonance. For, in that winter of 1944–45, Stalin was in a strong position in East Europe. In addition to his military successes, he had already a government to his liking in Bulgaria;* one that would probably crumble to his satisfaction, if he were to insist, in Romania;† and puppet governments of Communists were already in both East Poland and East Hungary.‡ A Communist resistance movement was the strongest one in both Yugoslavia and Albania.§ The Czech government in exile, though still in London, was on better terms, it seemed, with Russia than with its hosts. As for Poland, the Red Army occupied Warsaw effortlessly on January 17.

A few weeks later, Stalin received Churchill and Roosevelt at

* See below, page 413.
† See below, page 402.
‡ See below, pages 359 and 394.
§ See below, pages 425 and 439.

Yalta in the Crimea: symbolically, a good place for Stalin, since it was there that the White Russians staged their last stand in 1921. (Stalin's 'doctors' told him he could not travel far, unlike those of FDR, who was much less fit). Roosevelt was also interested in the landscape.[31] Once again, Roosevelt and Churchill had not co-ordinated their policies; and so once again Stalin, who knew approximately what he wanted to do, was able to outmanoeuvre them, even though Roosevelt settled down at Yalta to do some serious planning for the future for the first time.[32] By that time, Stalin's troops had pushed on to occupy Budapest and most of Hungary, and had swept through Poland as far as the River Oder. The Polish provisional government which he had named was in Warsaw. He was in such a strong position militarily that he was able to seem to be generous towards the 'Declaration on Liberated Europe' produced by the Americans. This promised free elections in all the countries occupied by the Germans. Doubtless recalling Lenin's strictures about bourgeois decency, Stalin accepted. American officials at the Department of State had at first thought of proposing an 'emergency High Commission' to ensure the Declaration was carried out.[33] But Roosevelt demurred. He had not much liked the European Advisory Commission in London and thought that another such might perpetuate itself. Instead, at Yalta, various agreements were reached *ad hoc*: the Polish government was to be reorganised, 'on a broader democratic basis', with the inclusion of new leaders from Poland itself and from among the Poles abroad. Roosevelt and Churchill accepted the so-called Curzon line* for the Polish–Soviet frontier. There would be concessions in the West at Germany's expense. In these arrangements, Stalin saw the Western leaders abandoning formally (as they had previously done verbally) their stand in favour of the Atlantic Charter; and Roosevelt at last abandoned his previous insistence that no territorial agreements should be made till after the war.[33A] Stalin accepted the zones for Germany which the European Advisory Commission in London had by then approved. The Soviet Union also agreed to enter the war

* See below, page 352.

in the Far East against Japan, on condition of certain concessions of territory to her there: a plan agreed privately by Roosevelt and Stalin.* Churchill signed the appropriate paper most reluctantly.

After Yalta, Stalin's advance continued. It was his troops who liberated Berlin, Prague and Vienna. In other circumstances, Western armies just might have done the same. But the American generals saw no military advantage in the thrust to Berlin in 1945 and neglected the political significance.† At that time, Roosevelt was in declining health; and only he could have overridden his military advisers.

Red Armies were, therefore, at the end of the war in Europe, in control of all of Poland, as Germany had been in 1941; of the Baltic States; of East Prussia; of the Karelian peninsula; of East Germany, including Berlin, as far as the line from Lübeck to the Thuringer Wald, and then East to the extreme point of the Bohemian quadrilateral; of North and East Austria, including Vienna; of Hungary, Romania and Bulgaria; and, as it seemed, of Yugoslavia and Albania. In all those countries, the Communists such as Ulbricht in East Germany, Ernst Fischer in Austria, Gottwald in Czechoslovakia, Rákosi in Hungary, and Kolarov in Bulgaria, who had been trained as revolutionaries in Moscow, were the dominant men in the country concerned. Gheorghiu-Dej in Romania, Tito-Broz in Yugoslavia and Hoxha in Albania were also in control of their countries but they had experienced less training in Russia. Possibilities for Communism were posed in both France and in Italy, where the presence of Western troops was balanced by Communist parties larger and with deeper roots than any in East Europe, which were also led by well-trained, subservient and clever Moscow men. In the East, meantime, Russian troops were established in both Manchuria and in North Korea, and were taking over South Sakhalin and the Kurile Islands from Japan. These forward movements confirmed Russia as far and away the strongest power on the Asian-European continent. Britain, with her strategic position offshore in Europe, her Indian Army, and her cleverly placed

*  See below, pages 571–2.
†  See below, page 228.

but militarily modest dispositions in the Middle and Far East, was her only rival among the ancient European powers; while the United States, with clamour for withdrawals of troops everywhere, and with her future attitude to international commitments obscure, and not clarified by the new United Nations, was an unknown quantity.

The consequences, as usual, were foreseeable in the way that ideology was presented. Western diplomatists recall being told by informers near Moscow in March 1945 that Party agitators were busy telling their comrades in the provinces that, after the war, there would be a change of attitude to the West, from one of alliance to one of challenge.[34] In April, Jacques Duclos, for many years one of the leaders of the French Communist Party on the Comintern's executive, publicly attacked the American Communists for collaborating with reaction during the war.[35] The American *Daily Worker* soon published a humiliating acceptance of these views by the American Communist Leader, Earl Browder. *Bolshevik*, the Party theoretical journal in Moscow, published an article in April, also arguing that only 'the fundamental reconstruction of the world on genuinely democratic lines' – that is, Bolshevik classless lines – could abolish war; until then, and while classes existed, war was inevitable. The Soviet Union would have to be ready to repel 'imperialist aggression'. Not perhaps what the weary student of world affairs would have desired to read from an ally after four ruinous years of war.[36] Wolfgang Leonhard wrote that on April 29, 1945 he heard an anti-Western joke in Moscow for the first time since 1941.[37] A careful student of the Soviet press over the next few months would also have found criticisms of 'insane anti-Soviet pretensions in the American and British reactionary circles'; many similarly phrased exhortations to return to revolutionary purity; or, 'the study of revolutionary theoretical work or the heightening of its ideological and political level should be demanded of every Communist from the first days of his enrolment'.[38] A certain Feodeseev wrote, in *Bolshevik* in August, that the challenge from predatory capitalism had to be met with determination.[39] The head of the Soviet state, Kalinin, said to a group of party comrades in Leningrad: 'Even now, after the greatest victory known in history, we cannot, for one minute, forget that our country remains the one socialist state in the world . . . the victory does not mean that all dangers to our state structure and social order have disappeared. Only the most concrete, most immediate danger . . . has disappeared'.[40] Shortly after this, the Central Committee of the Party announced the decision to establish a five-year plan to make up for the damage caused by the German invasion. To secure that, Russian people would have to work as hard as they had done in the war. This was one more reason to invoke the capitalist threat.[41]

The same month of August, another Party journal had written: 'In the closing stages of the war, when the Red Army is completing the collapse of Hitlerite Germany, only naive persons can think that the subversive spy activity of the enemy has somehow stopped being a danger. On the contrary. Stalin says, "It is necessary to recall that the nearer we come to victory the greater must be our vigilance".' It continued: 'He who thoroughly understands what capitalist encirclement is – he who takes into account that, as long as capitalist encirclement exists, there will be spies from foreign states in the rear areas of the Soviet Union . . . will not give himself over to complacency or trustfulness.'[42] These remarks, some possibly written by Stalin himself, would have given the signal for the expression of anti-Western sentiments, among all who had read that journal. Since most were written before the dropping of the atom bomb, there is no reason to suppose that matters would have been different, had that weapon not been exploded. Merkulov's speech, mentioned above, to the Krasnov family, in June 1945, no doubt gives a good impression of the true state of affairs.*

These ideas coincided with a new direction in Soviet diplomatic propaganda. The Russians had observed the beginning of discussions between the British and the French for an alliance, as for the creation of a Western European economic unit. That admirable, if long delayed, association caused a good deal of anxiety in Moscow. The idea of such a 'Western bloc' seemed

* See above, page 110.

to some in Moscow to be a genealogical descendant of the *cordon sanitaire* of the time of Munich.[43]

Stalin's attitudes at Potsdam admittedly suggested a wish for some continued collaboration with the West, particularly on his own terms. He denied to Churchill that he wanted to 'sovietise' East Europe.[44] In conversation with President Truman he was at pains to present himself as a statesman concerned with *realpolitik*. His Marxism was still often buried beneath Russian imperialism. Patriotism, for example, was in his mind in September: on the 2nd of that month, he spoke, on the radio, to the Soviet people, about the end of the war in the East, in a way which shocked all Communists. He described the Tsar's defeat in the Russo-Japanese War of 1904 as 'a dark blot on our country. Our people,' he went on, 'trusted, and waited for the day when Japan would be defeated and the blot would be eradicated. We of the older generation have waited forty years for that day. And now that day has come'.[45] What an insult to the Party! For all Marxists, all Socialists, had learned that the defeat of 1904, far from being a blot, was the event which led to the Revolution of 1905: he, 'Koba', as he was then, rejoiced in the Tsar's defeat.[46]

Stalin presumably realised that such double-faced attitudes could not last, even with his hand on the tiller of propaganda. Everything was anyway falling into shape along the lines which he wanted in Eastern Europe. The time when he could exploit Western softness was also past since, the war being over, the Americans no longer needed his help in the Far East. Nor did Britain fear any more a separate Russian peace with Germany. Stalin had squeezed all that he could from that charming wartime temporary gentleman, 'Uncle Joe'. 'Uncle Joe' now could retire. So it was not surprising that, after the Council of Foreign Ministers in London in October, Molotov should give a bleak interview to the Soviet press in which he presented the West as having 'fallen victims' to the 'reactionary wings' of capitalist democracy. George Kennan thought that it would still be difficult for Russia to break off all discussion with the West: 'Soviet failure to come to terms . . . would not only be a direct source of deep disappointment and concern, . . . but would complicate [their] . . . economic problems'.[47] Yet, on October 9, *Bolshevik* published another article by P. Feodoseev, which made three (to the careful reader) tell-tale points: it was 'just propaganda' to suggest that racism or chauvinism could never lead to war; secondly, World War II had begun because of conflicts among imperialists, just as Marx and Lenin had said; and, thirdly, in a paraphrase of that Clausewitz so dear to Lenin, peace should be looked upon by Communists as a time for an extension of the policy carried on in time of war.[48]

The slogans of, or for, the Communist Party of the Soviet Union at its annual celebrations of the birthday of the Revolution in November, studiously did not mention the Anglo–Soviet–American Alliance;[49] and Molotov's speech at that birthday – it was the annual celebratory speech of the nation – was neutral.[50] Presumably, in Stalin's absence from 'illness', no grand decision was made about policy towards the West. Probably, Stalin was using his 'illness' as a time for thought: Harriman met Stalin on October 25 in the Black Sea and found him in good health. (Western officials thought that the Soviet Politburo all visited Stalin during this period of 'illness' to take certain decisions about the 'offensive' line then to be taken.[51]) Nothing suggests that the Soviet mood was altered then by the realisation that the United States were interesting themselves in other Allies' bases – particularly British bases – throughout the world. A sense, however, that new policies were in the making that autumn was confirmed by the strange conversation between Averell Harriman, the American Ambassador, and Maxim Litvinov, then a Deputy Commissar for Foreign Affairs, previously discussed.*

There was evidently communication about the new Soviet attitude from Moscow to the Communist parties of the world. Thus Benoît Frachon, the Communist Secretary General of the main French trade union, the Confederation of Labour, said, in December, that he and his comrades were concerned that, in recent months, the United States had 'changed her policy of refusing to support anti-Soviet moves'. America might encour-

* See above, page 103.

age British 'provocation':[52] Britain being, in Communist eyes, the most dangerous leader of reaction. To accuse the US of such a change was a sure sign that the Russians also had changed.

The extent to which these ideas were widespread was next shown by a review of the year 1945 in another Soviet journal in January 1946. For the first time since the war, a Soviet writer argued that 'the American departure from a policy of isolation' did not mean the establishment of 'democratic peace-loving peoples'. On the contrary, America came out from the war with 'barefaced imperialist predatory ideas, a doctrine of uncontrolled militarism' with 'pretensions . . . to a leading role in world affairs'. A characteristically energetic campaign for the acquisition by America of bases on almost all seas and continents had followed – inspired by naval interests. It was a 'campaign to preserve great armed strength for America in peacetime.' This was creating a new situation. Formerly, the Soviet Union had had few contacts with the Americans. Now there were many such, and every other country had become 'a potential ally or enemy' between them.[53]

Such changes as were underway in late 1945 had precedents. In 1927, Stalin had described a 'period of "peaceful co-existence" receding into the past and giving way to times of imperialist surges and preparation for an intervention against the USSR.'[54] Then, in the 1930s, that hope for 'peaceful co-existence' had been revived, by Stalin as well as Litvinov: 'We can peacefully co-exist if we do not indulge in too much fault-finding about all sorts of petty matters,' the Vozhd had told Roy Howard, the American newspaper publisher, in March 1936.[55] 'Peaceful co-existence' was a phrase used by Molotov to describe the Nazi–Soviet Pact.[56] That too had to be revised, as all the world knows.

The changes in Soviet attitudes to the outside world reflected two things; one institutional, the other theoretical. The first was the recovery of the position of the Communist Party in the state, as opposed to government and army. That was accompanied by a large-scale reorganisation of the main economic enterprises as a result of demobilisation.

The second, theoretical, matter was the discussion in

governmental circles in Russia of the recent work of Eugen Varga, a Hungarian economist, long domiciled in Russia (he had been People's Commissar for Finance in Béla Kun's revolutionary government in Hungary in 1919). The burden of this work was to insist that, since the days of Lenin, the state had assumed a big role in the management of Western economies. Furthermore, Western statistics – and the use of them made by Varga was itself an innovation – showed that, despite the war, capitalism was not about to collapse. This meant only a postponement of the moment of crisis. There was an imbalance between the different capitalist countries. Britain and France had had their entrepreneurial structures ruined by war. Their colonies were exploding. Their difficulties with the newly-rich US made catastrophe in the capitalist world one day inevitable. But it might not happen soon. This view was clearly much discussed even if Soviet journals talked about the coming 'crisis of capitalism' which would eventually fling the United States and Britain into armed conflict.[57] A third view, that the capitalists would make common cause against the Soviet Union, had, however, some support in the Soviet Foreign Ministry.

These discussions influenced the *apparatchiki* abroad as much as those at home concerned with propaganda. It also characterised the 'intelligentsia'.

In the winter, Stalin acted as host in Moscow to the Conference of three Foreign Ministers. The Vozhd on that occasion again conducted himself as if he were interested in *realpolitik* more than ideology: 'The British had India and the Indian Ocean in her sphere of interest; the United States had China and Japan; the Soviet Union had nothing,' he artlessly told the British Foreign Secretary, Ernest Bevin, and then himself asked for a protectorate over Tripolitania.[58] Stalin also laughed about Chinese habits of exaggeration, and joked about Anglo-American rifts.[59] Molotov allowed himself sometimes to smile at these meetings, and the conclusions of Moscow were certainly realistic; acceptance of the United States' idea for a United Nations Atomic Energy Commission;* *impasse* over Iran;† and

* See above, pages 652–3.
† See below, pages 563–4.

a three power 'commission' to go to Romania.* Perhaps it was with these lurches into Machiavellian politics in mind that Stalin, in a curious new introduction to his *Collected Works*, wrote that sometimes a leader might have to take the risk of deceiving even Party insiders about his real ideological position.[60]

This edition of Stalin's *Collected Works*, which would soon begin to appear in many volumes, was an enterprise by which the Party hoped to restore its dominance after the wartime years of patriotic 'liberalism'. Stalin wrote his introduction – or had it written for him – in early 1946. In it, he talked of the occasions when, before 1917, Lenin had spoken of things which, in terms of Stalin's own version of Marxism-Leninism, could now be seen to be incorrect. That was partly because Lenin had then not yet 'discovered' the laws of imperialism. But Lenin knew his Bolshevik 'practical workers', and realised that they could not (yet) be sufficiently equipped to understand and accept the right theory. They had, therefore, sometimes to be tricked by their leader. This explanation gave Stalin a freedom to act as complete as it was theoretically dubious.

One or two other tell-tale signs of Soviet change of interest in the outside world had been evident in the winter of 1945–46. Thus the British Embassy was assured in January that antisemitism had reached 'alarming proportions'. The word 'Yid', which had not been known in Moscow for years, could be heard openly in the cheaper restaurants of Moscow. There appeared to have been 'serious clashes' between Jews and Russians in Kiev.[61]

Historians writing long after, in far-away America, have apparently reached a general agreement on the limited nature of Stalin's objectives in 1946, as opposed to the notion current in the late 1940s that he was preoccupied by world revolution.[62] Both points of view neglect the essential point that the combination of the extreme subtlety of the Marxist-Leninist philosophy with the brute force of Communist methods made for policies which needed the appearance at least of conflict: and, if possible,

* See below, page 409.

conflict blame for which could be attributed to the capitalist or imperialist enemies.

No doubt it was conflict which should not be carried into real war. The class war was never intended by Marx necessarily to imply shooting. Thus, though expansion should be everywhere attempted, it should not come too close to fighting in zones where the United States, and probably Britain, would resort to arms. Stalin, who accepted ideology, must have suspected that neither of his capitalist ex-allies would fight for anything in East Europe. American investment there before the war amounted to a mere $560 million, only 4 per cent of total US investments abroad. United States exports to East Europe at $62 million annually in 1936 to 1938 was only 2.1 per cent of total United States exports. Immediate post-war trade was confined to shipments under UNRRA.[63] True, there were important United States oil interests in Romania and Hungary. But little could be done by the United States, even for Standard Oil of New Jersey's Hungarian subsidiary, MAORT, once responsible for a third of the production of oil in Europe.

In May 1945, Stalin told Harry Hopkins that, so far as he was concerned, the worsening of bad relations between Russia and the West since the conference at Yalta was due to five things: the United States' insistence that Argentina join the United Nations and that France join the proposed German Reparations commissions; the United States' reluctance to accept the existing government of Poland as the 'kernel' of the administration to be reorganised there in accordance with Yalta; the manner in which Lend Lease had been brought to an end; and the question of the disposition of the captured German fleet. The first two matters were debating points. The fourth was one of unwise United States manners, and the fifth was a matter for settlement at the forthcoming conference at Potsdam. The third, Poland, was a substantial concern, on which the Soviet Union, on any fair definition of the terms agreed at Yalta, was in the wrong. This was a list of trumped-up reasons – there could easily, in the aftermath of the war, have been five others – which Stalin believed would appear tactically a good justification for a glum posture. He had decided the attitude before seeking pretexts for it. His own aims were clear: in the far distant future the establishment of a Russified world state; in the middle distance, a Soviet Union surrounded by a network of Communist-inspired republics which would look at his government as the model for a Soviet world republic, [64] and be the cause of 'all progressive mankind'. As for the immediate future: 'don't worry they'll swallow it', he remarked once of 'bourgeois' intelligentsia. [65] For a time, they did.

Some of the attitudes which Stalin took up during the war, and the first years of the 'armed truce' in 1946, were ones which he had tried out before. It has been pointed out how 'peaceful co-existence' had seemed temporarily useful in the 1920s. In 1931 he had been most encouraging about the 'sound and comparatively simple habits in American productive life' in contrast with the 'haughty spirit of the feudal aristocracy' in Europe. [66] In 1934 he had told H. G. Wells that he failed to understand the nature of man: 'You, Mr Wells, apparently assume that all people are good. But I don't forget that many are evil. I do not believe in the goodness of the bourgeoisie'. [67] There were precedents for Stalin's speech of February 1946 in the era of Socialism in one country. In the future all these moods would be tried out, or on, again. History, though on his side, as he believed, would no doubt require many halts on the route to Communism.

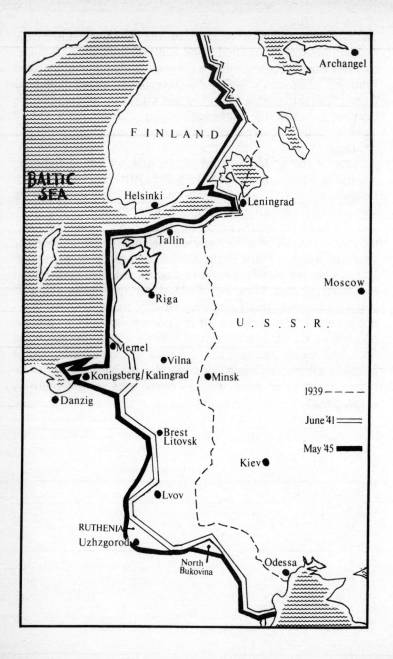

# BOOK TWO

# THE WEST

'Here, where the sword *united nations* drew,
Our countrymen were warring on that day!'
And this is much, and all which will not pass away

Byron *Childe Harold's Pilgrimage*, III, xxxv

The Americanization of the world, in a certain fundamental moral sense, would be a piece of good fortune
for mankind.

Thomas Mann, December 1942

# SEVEN

# THE COMING OF ENTANGLING ALLIANCES

'The West' is an expression which began to be used in place of 'Christendom' when the implications of that word became inappropriate for countries whose leaders were free thinkers. It derived from memory of the old western Roman Empire. There were many advantages in the use of a purely geographical expression supposed to contain the common factors discernible in such disparate concepts as representative government and capitalism, within the frame of ancient custom as well as of the Christian religion. Though the usage was already occasional in the XVIth century, when Shakespeare spoke of 'all the Kingdoms of the West', and though there are certain advantages in modern politicians knowing themselves to be the heirs of Charlemagne, it is, all the same, unsatisfactory.

This confusion was never more obvious than at the time of the Second World War when the leaders of Christendom considered their aims in the war. In a conversation between Winston Churchill and Harry Hopkins, special representative of President Roosevelt, in January 1941 at Chequers (the country house given for the benefit of British prime ministers by Lord Lee of Fareham as a consequence, appropriately, of his wife's American fortune), the Prime Minister said that, when the war was over, 'there would be a short lull, during which we would have the opportunity to establish a few basic principles, of justice, of respect for the rights and property of other nations, and indeed of respect for private property so long as its owner was honest, and its scope moderate. We could', he added, 'find nothing better than Christian ethics on which to build and, the more closely we followed the Sermon on the Mount, the more likely we would succeed'. Hopkins in his turn explained that Roosevelt was 'not much concerned about the future. His pre-occupation was with the next few months. So far as war aims were concerned, there were only a very few people in America, liberal intellectuals, who cared about the matter; and they were nearly all on our side'.[1]

In the following months, Churchill made other occasional efforts to define what he was fighting for (it was obvious what he was fighting against). But these efforts were tentative, in a country which disliked statements of principles in this style, most of whose leaders thought 'the national interest' an adequate description of their motives, and which was about to lose its empire, as it had begun it, 'in a fit of absence of mind.' These efforts seemed unlikely to be welcomed by the leaders of the United States. Not only was that country not yet at war but President Roosevelt continued to make clear that he also would hesitate about making general statements of principles. There was an excellent reason for that. The United States had already a golden treasury of fine axioms about international policy which led in a different direction to the line of his policies.


The tradition of America's international policy had been, from her earliest days, one of celebrating her distance, even escape, from Europe. The most famous early President of Harvard, Increase Mather, said that the original settlers had 'shaken off the dust of Babylon' to come to the New World. The rebellion against Britain in the XVIIIth century owed much to the idea of rejection of participation in 'European politics and wars', as John Adams put it in 1776. Thereafter, a famous series of well-turned sentences, setting an example of how to write English which has not always been followed subsequently by American public men, made evident the views of the founders of the Republic. A resolution of the Continental Congress in 1783 first used the famous word 'entangled' to show the kind of association in which the US should not be concerned. President George Washington's Farewell Address in 1796 asked, in words known to every politically conscious American since, 'why, by inter-weaving our destiny with that of any part of Europe, entangle our peace and prosperity in the toils of European ambition, rivalship, interest, humour or caprice?'[1] His successor Jefferson's policy was one of 'peace, commerce and honest friendship with all nations, entangling alliances with none'.[2]

There were always, from the beginning, two qualifications to these policies. First, President Washington did not wish to insulate himself utterly. He wanted freedom of action: 'temporary alliances, for extraordinary engagements' might be needed.[3] Second, the freedom of the United States from England was, in the minds of all leading Americans, to be looked upon as an inspiration for others: the 'sacred fire of liberty' might have to be preserved by all Americans in the face of, say, an association of European powers such as the Holy Alliance. But both principles seemed for a long time to be combined with the advantages offered by geography. In the 1820s, Senator Daniel Webster thus mocked those who pointed out the thunder rolling 'at a distance; the wide Atlantic is between us and danger'.[4] The doctrine associated with President James Monroe for the relations of the United States with South America warned Europeans in unmistakeable terms to keep out of the New World.

The dilemma posed by the conflict between Washington's two ideas remained throughout the XIXth century. John Quincy Adams in 1821 sought to straddle the gap when he said that, though America 'goes not abroad in search of monsters to destroy', the sympathies of America were engaged wherever 'the standard of freedom was unfurled'. His qualification encapsulated an ambiguity which lasted a long time: the United States 'is the well-wisher to the freedom and independence of all. She is the champion and vindicator only of her own', since enlisting in foreign wars for independence would mean that the United States would be drawn into 'all the wars of interest and intrigue, of individual avarice, envy and ambition which assume the colors and usurp the standard of freedom'.[5] Senator Henry Clay,

Daniel Webster's rival, thought that the American contribution to freedom was merely 'to keep the lamp burning brightly on this Western shore, as a light to all nations';[6] and, a little later, President Fillmore, not otherwise known for eloquence, described his programme as 'to set such an example of national justice, prosperity and true glory as shall teach to all nations the blessings of self-government and the unparalleled enterprise and success of a free people'.[7]

Those were the days when Americans were moving West into empty Indian and Spanish lands alike; driving along the scantily populated territories of the Gulf of Mexico; infiltrating Texas; and, in consequence of the subsequent Mexican War, seizing New Mexico, Arizona and California. This was the age when it certainly seemed that Frederick Jackson Turner, the exponent of the idea of the frontier in American history, was right to argue that American democracy was 'born of no theorist's dream . . . it came out of the forest . . . Not the constitution, but free land and an abundance of national resources open to a fit people made the democratic type of society in America'.[8]

In the years leading up to the Civil War, in the 1860s, the rhetoric of freedom led to heady expectations of what seemed likely to turn out to constitute that intervention, in freedom's name, which John Quincy Adams had feared. It was the era of 'manifest destiny', a phrase devised by the newspaperman, John O'Sullivan, in 1845, to suggest the benefits to all of America's expansion throughout the continent.[9] 'What, speak of "isolation"?' asked Senator Pierre Soulé in 1852, in the first political use of that later famous word, 'have you no markets to secure for your future wealth?'[10] A colleague, Senator Hart Benton, believed that America should 'wake up and reanimate the torpid body of Asia'.[11] Mexico, Central America, Cuba and Brazil were obvious zones for future expansion. Imperial Russia was at that time, after all, moving into the far older civilisations of Central Asia, such as Bokhara and Samarkand.

There were, however, still traditionalists: John C. Calhoun, the conscience of the old South, argued that the US would 'do more to extend liberty by our example, over this continent, and the world generally, than would be done by a thousand victories'.[12] Furthermore, the Civil War in the 1860s consumed within the nation all the energy which had been directed temporarily towards the outside.

For a generation after the Civil War, Americans were reticent, busy with industrialisation, recovery, and the final settlement of the West. Until the 1890s there was no need to warn against 'entangling'. The *New York Sun* suggested the abolition of the American diplomatic service.[13] The greatest of American writers, Henry James, thought that diplomacy was 'no profession for a gentleman'.[14] President Cleveland's (second) inaugural address reiterated Jefferson's old policies of neutrality. The United States navy remained smaller than that of most Latin American countries.

By the turn of the century, old concepts of manifest destiny and encouragement of liberty abroad had, however, been revived. Partly that was because of an appreciation that, as Brooks Adams argued, the British navy would not forever guard the Atlantic; partly, with vast new immigration from the Russian and Austrian empires, there was a renewed awareness that Europe's troubles might one day be America's. President Harrison had seen that, if the United States were not on occasion prepared to act, European empires might absorb all the Pacific islands. Cleveland had taken a strong line against Britain over the frontier of Venezuela. President McKinley seized Hawaii on the ground that it was indeed 'manifest destiny' – he used the phrase again – that the United States (and no one else) should have it. Under the influence of the naval historian Captain Mahan, men like Henry Cabot Lodge and Theodore Roosevelt argued for a large navy; though a later age finds it hard to see, in Mahan's sober prose, the clarion call which it was to his own generation.

The Philippines and Puerto Rico were taken, as dependencies, after the war with Spain in 1898 over Cuba; which herself passed into that ambiguous status of half independence, half protectorate, which later gave so much ground, or excuse, for violent nationalism. McKinley told his cartographer in 1899 'to put the Philippines on the map of the United States',[15] where they would, indeed, stay till 1946. Wake Island, Guam and

Samoa accompanied them there. Secretary Hay's notes to the powers about an 'open door' in China followed the same year.

An increasing sense of responsibility, and the belief of Theodore Roosevelt, when President, that 'American politics is world politics', did not, however, persuade the United States to seek 'entangling alliances'. Roosevelt, one of the most energetic men to have become President of a great country, sought to solve world problems as well as to intervene in them. Hence his chairmanship of the peace conference to end the Russo-Japanese War and his consequent Nobel Prize for Peace: a happily ironic award to one who believed that 'no triumph of peace is quite so great as the supreme triumphs of war';[16] and who also planned the Machiavellian politics which led in turn to the digging of the Panama Canal. His 'corollary' to the Monroe Doctrine, contained in his annual message of 1904, proclaimed that the United States might, 'in flagrant cases of wrongdoing or impotence', have to contemplate 'the exercise of an international police power'[17] which his distant kinsman, and successor but six, Franklin Roosevelt, would echo.

It was, however, equally ironically, the improbable figure of President Woodrow Wilson which took the United States into her first major alliance with extra-American powers. Ironically, because this ex-president of Princeton University had been primarily elected to achieve domestic reforms. His European intervention was preceded by an intervention in Mexico inspired by hatred of the cruelty practised there by General Victoriano Huerta, rather as McKinley had intervened in Cuba fifteen years before.

Pride in the American experiment left room for hope, for, usually, those leaders who looked outwards, that there would be space for others to share in the dream. Between a hope that others would enjoy liberty, and a willingness that they should have the means to achieve it by membership of the union (or the empire), there was only a gentle step.

Henry James studied the relations between the new Americans and the old world. These Americans were in his day, however, people willing to resolve the problems of Europe, not to lead it. It was leadership which, in the end, after 1945, it would need.

President Wilson, to begin with, described the world war which began in 1914 as one 'with which [America should] have nothing to do'. But the warfare in the Atlantic tried that stoic neutralism. When the Germans sank the *Lusitania* in May 1915, 128 Americans drowned. That outrage took the American public close to the Allies. It suggested that a German victory over France and Britain would signal the emergence of a new dominant European power. Wilson sought to maintain peace. Theodore Roosevelt, smarting in inactivity, believed war to be inevitable and thought the sooner that it began, the better it would be for a swift peace. Germany declared that she would wage a programme of unrestricted submarine warfare, in January 1917. Wilson had to choose between an abject surrender to the threat of force and the resolution to challenge it. He broke off diplomatic relations with Germany. The publication of a telegram from Berlin to the German legation in Mexico (obtained by the British through an interception of the German code and circulated in an effective if underhand manner), proposing an alliance between Mexico and Germany and offering Texas, Arizona and New Mexico to Mexico as an inducement, shocked American opinion. On April 2, 1917, Wilson asked Congress for a declaration of war on Germany. The request was granted. The United States sent troops to France. Germany was defeated.

In order to prepare America for war, Wilson had made many promises. Some of them were difficult to fulfil. He, and others, promised that victory would be followed by 'a universal dominion of right', by final settlements that would be holy as well as just; indeed, by 'a new glory' to 'shine in the face of the people'.[18] For this biblical consummation, a permanent 'entanglement' was obviously necessary. Membership of the League of Nations would signify the institutionalisation of American willingness to be permanently concerned in 'global processes'. In 1919, Wilson explained that 'the isolation of the United States is at an end, not because we chose to go into the politics of the world but because, by the sheer genius of this people and the growth of our power, we have become a determining factor in the history of mankind; and, after you have become a determining factor, you cannot remain isolated, whether you want to or no'.[19]

Wilson's prophecy was right. He was the wrong prophet for it. He had aroused enmity through his arrogance. It was easy to criticise the League of Nations since its Covenant was, as it were, tacked onto the end of the imperfect Treaty of Versailles. The Treaty was signed by the President but rejected by Congress. There, Senators Borah and Lodge spoke the language of John Quincy Adams, though their personal distaste for Wilson's character and preaching told more. They persuaded their generation to drop 'the task eternal',* for the time being. President Wilson gave way to President Harding. The American nation for a time preferred President Coolidge's 'good three cent cigar' to Wilson's vision that 'America shall in truth show the way. The light streams upon the path ahead and nowhere else'.[20]

The United States maintained this old, understandable, comfortable, and enviable stand in international affairs for another twenty years. Britain and France were unable, even allied, to act in its stead. Americans breathed for the last time the air of irresponsibility. American manufacturing strength reached record levels. In 1920, the United States was owed over $12.5 billion, produced nearly half the world's manufactures and had that 'navy, second to none', of which the Naval Appropriation Act spoke as desirable. They retained that pre-eminence throughout the 1920s. The great creditor nation also had influence on the world's art – especially cinema and fiction.

Americans were willing to intervene *ad hoc*, as Washington would have liked them to have done, to solve specific problems. Their concern with other nations grew. There was the Washington Naval Conference. There were the Dawes and the Young Plans. There were frequent interventions in Latin America and the Caribbean. There was the world economic conference. There was the Kellogg Pact. An American relief mission distrib-

---

* 'Have the elder nations halted? . . .
We take up the task eternal, and the burden, and the lesson
Pioneers! O Pioneers!' (Whitman)

uted more than $60 million worth of aid to Russia in the 1920s; and President Hoover encouraged businessmen to look on Russia as an 'economic vacuum' to be filled by United States interests.[21] But there was no permanent commitment. Isolation still had determined followers. President Coolidge believed that 'we can best serve our own country and most successfully discharge our obligations to humanity by continuing to be openly and candidly, intensely and scrupulously, American'.[22]

In these circumstances, the Bolsheviks established themselves in Russia, the fascists in Italy, the Nazis in Germany, and military tyrants in Japan. 'All about us rage undeclared wars – military and economic', President Franklin Roosevelt pointed out in his message to Congress in 1939.[23] But, until the new war formally began in 1939, American public opinion opposed commitment. President Roosevelt was an internationalist to the marrow.* But he, like Wilson, had come to power in America to resolve domestic problems. He had to coax his people into a mood of international responsibility, assisted by contemporaries who had earlier been inspired by President Wilson. But he was unable to move fast enough to prevent ruin from reaching Europe and East Asia. The opposition to any form of international commitment grew as it became urgent.

Japan attacked America in 1941 in order to have a free hand to complete her conquest of China. Germany took the opportunity to declare war on America too, for reasons which seem hubristic. By then, Roosevelt had succeeded in persuading his fellow citizens to extend to the opponents of the Nazis 'the material resources of this nation', through the 'Lend Lease Bill', passed in February 1941; to increase military and naval appropriations to $17 billion; to build a navy on two oceans; and to give Britain some old destroyers in return for naval bases throughout the North Atlantic.† The United States was already thus 'the arsenal of democracy'. Soon she would have to provide men. Senator Arthur Vandenberg, leader of the 'isolationists'

* See below, page 253 for a consideration of Roosevelt.
† The bases in Newfoundland and Bermuda as gifts; those in the Bahamas, Jamaica, St Lucia, Trinidad, British Guiana, and Antigua by 99 year lease. See below, page 289.

after the death of Senator Borah, wrote in his diary: 'we have torn up 150 years of traditional foreign policy. We have tossed Washington's Farewell Address into the discard. We have thrown ourselves squarely into the power politics and power wars of Europe, Asia and Africa. We have taken the first step upon a course from which we can never hereafter retreat'. [24] He may have been right, but there were several more steps before the nation, and Vandenberg too, were committed as far as he said.

President Roosevelt was the architect of the necessary changes. 'To-day, in the face of this newest and greatest challenge', he said in a speech even before the Japanese attack, 'we Americans have cleared our decks, and taken our battle stations'. [25] And what was the battle for? To begin with for 'Four Freedoms', announced by Roosevelt in his State of the Union message of January 6, 1941, of speech and expression, of worship, from want and from fear.

The first more detailed general statement of 'war aims' by the West were contained in the eight points known as the Atlantic Charter issued by Roosevelt and Winston Churchill on *HMS Prince of Wales* on August 14, 1941. That was still nearly four months before America was at war. In this document, these two memorable men announced that their countries sought no aggrandisement; desired no territorial changes contrary to the wishes of the peoples concerned: respected the right of all nations to choose their own forms of government; and wished to see self-government, and sovereign rights, restored to peoples who had been deprived of them. Britain and America favoured equality of opportunity with access to essential raw materials for all nations. [26] They would seek to promote friendly collaboration among the peoples of the world, fair standards of labour, social security, freedom from want as from fear, free access to the high seas for all, the abandonment of force as a means of settling disputes, and the disarmament of nations which had been aggressors. The language was unremarkable; the principles were controversial from the beginning.

When it was issued, the Charter seemed to some merely 'an inspired plagiarism of Wilson's fourteen points'.* The *New York Times* was more encouraged: it was 'the beginning of a new era, in which the United States assumes the responsibilities which fall naturally to a great power'.[28] But the difficulties began immediately. Churchill's first draft had spoken of an 'effective international organisation' to guarantee the future peace. Roosevelt thought this proposal inappropriate at that time. He did not want to risk opposition in the United States – at least until, as he put it, there was a new 'international police force' actually functioning. That at first sight even more radical proposal did not figure at this stage in any written document. The duller but more mysterious phrase 'the establishment of a wider and permanent system of general security' was substituted.† Then it was noticed that 'freedom of religion' had been omitted from the Charter. Nor did Churchill seem to have anticipated that there might be consequences for the British Empire as a result of all these pledges. He had later to say, in the House of Commons, that the commitment to the restoration of self-government was 'primarily' for Europe: it was 'quite a separate problem from the progressive evolution of self-governing institutions' in 'the regions' of the British Crown.[29] It was not only the British who had early doubts about the principles so expressed. The Czech government in exile, for example, made evident that they had no intention of letting their German minority express themselves by self-determination, within a month of the issuing of the Charter. Nor was consideration given at the time of its signature as to whether the ideas in the Atlantic Charter could possibly be accepted with any sincerity by the Soviet Union in the form which it had assumed since 1917.[30] Since Britain and the United States were then working out how to assist that nation, much subsequent embarrassment thus ensued.

* The first draft of this document had been written, on Roosevelt's request, by Alexander Cadogan. Sumner Welles, Roosevelt's friend in the Department of State, made some amendments. Roosevelt made further suggestions. So did the British War Cabinet in London, consulted by telegram.[27]

† See below for Roosevelt and the international organisation page 260.

Stalin, however, was entirely happy to accept the Atlantic Charter. He did so, after the United States entered the war in December 1941, on January 1, 1942, when the Charter was re-issued as a declaration of the 'United Nations' (with 'freedom of religion' dutifully included, after some doubts by the Soviet ambassador, and other alterations and improvements). The phrase 'United Nations' was Roosevelt's formulation, a substitute for the previous expression 'Associated Powers'. It was one specially satisfactory to Churchill, after he had established that Byron had used it in *Childe Harold*. The declaration of the United Nations was 'a manifesto of a military alliance', accompanied by a general statement of principles to govern policy after the war.[31]

Like the Atlantic Charter, the declaration was also hastily written. Difficulties over its interpretation began immediately. For Stalin, such documents were useful as long as the 'correlation of forces' obtained. For the West, as Hopkins's biographer said, it was a matter of learning 'that, when you state a moral principle, you are stuck with it, no matter how many fingers you may have crossed at the moment'.[32] In order to keep his hands free for negotiation with Russia, Churchill was soon forced to say that the clauses on self-determination in the Charter did not apply to the territories of enemy states. He also urged Roosevelt in March 1942 that 'the principles of the Atlantic Charter ought not to be construed so as to deny Russia the frontiers which she occupied when Germany attacked her'.[33] Since there was no chance that any British Government led by Churchill would contemplate that this Charter should apply to the territories of allied empires, it became hard to know where indeed he thought that it was applicable. By mid-1943, the British foreign secretary was uneasily admitting that his Polish policy was also 'contrary to the Atlantic Charter', but saying it had to be pursued to secure Soviet collaboration after the war.[34]

With the United States, the fate of the Charter was equally interesting, though different. Roosevelt did not want it to be regarded as a Treaty which would have to pass through Congress. So it was merely released – not inscribed on parchment, not sealed, and not even signed. He himself believed, therefore, that he had kept his hands free for any subsequent negotiation or, if necessary, commitment. But American officials in the Department of State looked on the Charter more seriously. Sumner Welles told Lord Halifax, the British ambassador, during the discussions about recognition of Russia's absorption of the Baltic States, that, 'if we did not build our new world on principles, we would crash again'.[35] American officials believed that they had moral commitments. The President might seek to avoid post-war plans. Churchill might preach *realpolitik*. They would not.

Thus, for the British, the Atlantic Charter lasted scarcely longer than the battleship on which it was signed;* for the United States, it marked the beginning of a series of arguments within the administration, as well as with allies.

For three years after the United States was at war, Roosevelt made no commitment about the kind of world that he would like to see afterwards. He hinted, he speculated, but he did not promise.† His, and British, officials worked on a Charter of the United Nations. Churchill and Roosevelt committed themselves to a policy of unconditional surrender in respect of Germany (never adopted by the Soviet Union).[36] But what would be done with the *tabla rasa* so provided remained obscure. A four-power Declaration was issued after the meeting of Foreign Ministers in October 1943, which Secretary of State Hull looked upon as constituting another long goodbye to the Balance of Power.[37] All officials in the US declined responsibility for detailed discussion of European frontiers. Equally firmly, being essentially 'universalists', they declined to consider anything so Machiavellian as allowing 'spheres of influence' anywhere. Still, at the conference in the Crimea in early 1945 the American delegation produced their new version of the Atlantic Charter, by then limited to Europe, known as 'the Declaration on Liberated Europe'.‡ For the rest of the world, there would be the United Nations (which came into force in October 1945).§ Both committed the United

* *HMS Prince of Wales* was sunk by Japan on December 10, 1941.
† See below, page 260.
‡ See below, page 278.
§ See below, pages 263–4.

States to international action: the first to try in Europe to secure
governments not unlike her own; the second to playing a part
in the world to maintain peace. Though by the first winter after
the war both documents were open to challenge, the United
States had undertaken to play a part very different from that
which she had enjoyed before 1941 or 1914. The United States
had well and truly entered what Sumner Welles, Under-
Secretary at the Department of State, had in November 1941
described as 'the valley of decision'.[38] Washington's Farewell
Address was placed on a high shelf in the libraries of responsible
Americans: accessible but more and more dusty.[39]

# EIGHT

# THE NEW AMERICANS I: TRUMAN, LEAHY AND BYRNES

The President of the United States who faced the strange entanglements of the peace in 1945 was not Roosevelt but Harry Truman. He was ill-prepared. He had been abroad once. He had little knowledge of European history (apart from what a diligent reader could derive from *The Federalist*). He had learned nothing of foreign affairs, nor of the events of the war, from his predecessor. He came from a state, Missouri, in the middle west of the United States, which had never previously produced a President. His background was agricultural; 'just a country boy', he described himself; and, indeed, on both sides of his family his ancestors were farmers. Yet he seemed to have no roots; Truman's parents had moved from farm to farm (though his grandfather had owned a 600 acre farm at Grandview, Missouri). His father had left him no money, having indulged unwisely in speculation in grain. Truman himself had farmed before the First World War for eleven years. In the 1920s he had tried to make money as a haberdasher, but he had been ruined by the sudden price deflation of 1921–22. Though honest, he had made his way to Washington thanks to a corrupt party machine whose parochiality would have made Jane Austen seem cosmopolitan. A county judge, and a junior Senator in 1934, Truman disliked intellectuals and, though he admired the New Deal, hated 'new dealers'; he preferred poker-players. He was sixty years old.

This provincial individual nevertheless made, in the end, a

much more effective President than anyone thought likely and, almost certainly, than any possible rival would have been (such as Alben Barkley, Henry Wallace, Harold Ickes, Jimmy Byrnes or William O. Douglas, other possible vice presidential candidates in 1944). Truman's life as a farmer was a help, not a hindrance. A man who had sown a 160-acre wheatfield in Missouri with four mules, and who 'could plow a straight furrow',[1] had a powerful appeal for a nation which had only recently become primarily industrial. His relations had helped to build Kansas City.[2] His childhood on the farms had been almost as idyllic as Roosevelt's in the mansions of the East. Isaiah Berlin described how, during the war, he had been 'liked by almost everyone for his impeccable honesty, affability and modesty'.[3] He may have made only one journey abroad but that had been to France during the First World War. It lasted for a year, during which time he had been a Captain in the artillery: 'Captain Harry' would say that he gained 'his education in the army'.[4] (Many of his later 'cronies' were ex-alumni of Battery D; or freemasons; or both.)

Truman's ignorance of modern Europe was balanced by a thorough knowledge of both Classical and American history; 'if you were listening in,' he wrote to his daughter in 1941, when he was the successful Chairman of the Senate Special Committee on the National Defense Programme, 'you would understand why Diogenes carried a lantern in the daytime to find an honest man'.[5] Since he had been always short-sighted he had rarely played games as a boy and so read voraciously: his favourite book being the four volumes of Charles Francis Horne's *Great Men and Famous Women*.[6] He played the piano well. Reading history, for Truman, 'was far more than a romantic adventure. It was solid instruction and wise teaching'.[7] *The Federalist* papers, and the other writings of the founders of the United States, meant much to Truman; and, in the writings of those early American statesmen, classical precedents were often cited. A student of Hamilton knows how to avoid 'the perpetual vibration between the extremes of tyranny and anarchy',[8] and realises the importance of philosophical preparation for political initiatives. Truman's humility in 1944 and 1945 may have been more tactical than is sometimes allowed. But he did have remarkable self-knowledge for a politician.

Truman was a quick worker who knew that 'in government there can never be an end to study, improvement and the evaluation of new ideas'.[9] He was good at making decisions. 'You could go into his office with a question and come out with a decision from him more swiftly than any man I have ever known', said Averell Harriman.[10] Many thought that, at the beginning of his presidency, he made decisions too fast – on the basis of inadequate information or because of a conscious desire to seem decisive. That was his style.[11] His short-sight, and shortness of build, made him develop a method of speech in which good humour was combined with an appearance of toughness, assurance and quickness.[12] One assistant, the director of the Budget in 1945, Harold Smith, thought Truman less good as an administrator than Roosevelt.[13] The diplomatists who served Truman disagreed: 'In contrast with Roosevelt', wrote Bohlen, 'Truman studied the files and papers prepared for him and was well prepared on all aspects of a subject when the time came for discussion and decision-making'.[14] A. A. Berle, ambassador and Assistant Secretary, thought Truman 'a very fine, clear-thinking man, who has more head than many around him . . . anyone who worked for him would feel on much more safe ground than anyone who worked for FDR'.[15] Dean Acheson agreed.[16] Truman himself reflected, 'once a decision was made, I did not worry about it afterwards', adding 'I had trained myself to look back into history for precedents, because, instinctively, I sought perspective in the span of history for the decisions I had to make'.[17]

Truman certainly had a more organised method of discussion within his cabinet than had been usual under Roosevelt who had used meetings of that body as a chance for his colleagues to argue. Roosevelt's cabinet after 1941 seemed often to be no more than 'a social gathering at which the President rather subtly indicates the trend of his mind, and the various cabinet members cautiously bring forward different items in an effort to find in which way the wind is blowing'.[18] Roosevelt never delegated to his cabinet; Truman tried to. Truman was direct where

Roosevelt was elusive. Though Truman had before 1945 no knowledge of administration, he knew the Congress well. He was conscientious about detail; and was accustomed to the requirement that, in democratic politics, one must often compromise. Truman soon ensured that he had a cabinet with whom he was in sympathy; and if, intellectually, Fred Vinson was a poor substitute for Henry Morgenthau, at the Treasury, and Robert Patterson for Henry Stimson, at the War Department, there were many benefits in having a cabinet which spoke with one voice. Truman had the economic sense to appreciate that his biggest difficulty at home after the war would be inflation, not unemployment, as many supposed, and had the courage to say so, as early as January 1946.[19]

Truman's attitude to Roosevelt, like that of most of those who had known him, was ambiguous. He spoke of him sometimes as a 'great leader' who, in 1932, had 'rescued the nation from chaos'.[20] But, in a private note, during the presidential campaign of 1948, he remarked 'I don't believe the USA wants any more fakers – Teddy and Franklin are enough.' He thought Roosevelt 'did not develop men. When they developed he shoved them aside'.*[21] Roosevelt, only sixty-three years old in 1945, had not expected to die in office; he believed that his famous luck would hold; and so treated Truman without consideration, as every president had always treated his deputy. He had selected Truman because he was popular in the Senate and so could help him 'when he went up there and asked them to ratify the peace'.[22]

None of this meant that it was easy for Truman to be Roosevelt's successor. To many people, he would remain the 'haberdasher in the King's chair'. To some, the White House under Truman, at the beginning, evoked the 'lounge of the Lion's Club of Independence, Missouri', where 'the odor of the ten cent cigar' competed 'with the easy laughter of a risqué story'.[23]

In international affairs, Truman had been, all the same, convinced, as Theodore Roosevelt had been, but in his case by his

* That is, Theodore and Franklin Roosevelt.

experience in France, of the duty of Americans to play their part in international politics if civilisation were to be preserved. His speech of acceptance as Vice President in 1944 had been an onslaught on isolationists.[24] He believed that the United States should be the 'world's marshal and sheriff'.[25] Now, in 1946, it was clear that, apart from the United States, there was 'no power capable of meeting Russia as an equal'.[26]

Truman had as yet no idea, however, how to cope with Russians. In the course of the war, he had made a casual remark of shocking *realpolitik*: 'If we see that Germany is winning, we ought to help Russia and if Russia is winning we ought to help Germany and that way let them kill as many as possible. Neither of them thinks anything of their pledges'.[27] His qualification that all the same he did not 'want to see Hitler victorious under any circumstances' saved him from political catastrophe. There were other Americans who had seen the conflict on the Eastern front as one 'between Satan and Lucifer'.*[28] Truman's position as president made his perplexity a source of weakness in the early, critical days. But none of his rivals for the vice presidency in 1944 would have brought any serious knowledge of Russia, nor of Communism, to the White House.

Truman was optimistic in 1945 for a time on these matters: 'I had hoped that the Russians would return favour for favour', he remarked in his memoirs.[29] Yet in his first conversation with the Secretary of State, Stettinius, whom he had inherited from Roosevelt (though they had never met before),[30] he had reflected that he thought that Roosevelt's agreements with the Soviet Union so far 'had been a one way street'; and, now, if the Russians did not co-operate, 'they could go to hell'.[31] A fortnight later, on April 23, after the Russians had suddenly signed a treaty with the new Polish provisional government, and after conversations with advisers, he told Molotov that the United States were tired of waiting for the Soviet Union to carry out

* When at a private lunch, at which reporters were present, a British Minister, Lord Brabazon, had said much the same – he hoped that the German and Russian armies would annihilate one another – he had to leave the government, after the remark reached the press.

the agreements into which they had freely entered at Yalta, and which would have given Eastern European nations a chance to establish democratic regimes. Molotov tried to steer the discussion to the, for him, more favourable subject of the Far East. But Truman cut him off: 'That will be all, Mr Molotov. I would appreciate it if you would transmit my views to Marshal Stalin'. Charles Bohlen was asked how he enjoyed interpreting Truman's sentences. He replied: 'They were probably the first sharp words uttered during the war by an American President to a high Soviet official'.[32] Truman himself added, 'I was sure that Russia would understand firm, decisive language and action much better than diplomatic pleasantries'.[33] Doubtless Molotov had been used to such treatment only from Stalin: he had often himself spoken with far greater brutality.

This exchange was used – by the Soviet Union, first and foremost – to argue that there had been a change of policy in America following Truman's accession to power: with Roosevelt alive, the Soviet government had full confidence that differences could be worked out.[34] Some argued that, in this first interview, Truman 'declared the cold war'.[35] Those are Molotovian views. They discount the fact that American policy had been changing since Yalta, even under Roosevelt; that Truman himself, like all concerned in such matters, would alter his views several times as to the right policy, and even the tone, to follow; and that he thought that he was doing what Roosevelt would have done. Truman's methods of work made it inevitable that, fit and well, he would wish to make explicit what Roosevelt, ill and elusive, might have sought to keep vague. There were enough of Roosevelt's remarks during his last weeks to suggest that he might, if he had been physically up to it, have considered what Harriman called 'a policy of much greater firmness';* even if he would scarcely have listened, as Truman had begun to, to the Department of State as represented by Joseph C. Grew or 'Jimmy' Dunn. Roosevelt's final messages to Stalin suggested that a change of policy was coming. 'Averell is right', he remarked at lunch, on March 23, 'we can't do business with Stalin. He has

* See also pages 222–3 below.

broken every one of the promises he made at Yalta'.*[36] There is a hint in a message of Roosevelt's to Churchill on April 6, 1945 that he might later that month have supported the British against Eisenhower on the question of the liberation of Berlin: 'Our armies', he wrote, 'will in a very few days be in a position that will permit us to become "tougher" than has heretofore appeared advantageous to the war effort'.[37] (In 1943, he had once even suggested that it might be desirable to reach Berlin before Russia did.)[38] Such accusations also ignore the entire pattern of Soviet policy itself.

Truman was in fact anxious to carry out Roosevelt's policy in international subjects, providing, that is, that he could discover exactly what it was. On the most important of issues, Poland, the Department of State had the same officials at work in May 1945 as in March, and would have much the same staff in February 1946.[39] Neither Truman nor Roosevelt had the slightest idea of sending American troops to secure any goal in the East of Europe, nor did they organise any combination of economic leverage, propaganda, intimidation, cajolery on a considered basis, to pursue those goals.[40]

In the two weeks following after April 23, Truman seemed convinced that a 'tough method' – the President's words to Joseph Davies – was the right one with Russia.[41] On May 2, he heard a first hand account of Soviet and Communist repression in Romania and Bulgaria from Generals Schuyler and Crane, the United States' military representatives on the Allied Control Commissions in those countries.[42] That week, Truman said that the swift end of Lend Lease aid, to Russia as to other allies, was a 'more realistic policy' and 'right down his alley'.[43] The consequent decision was put into effect by Leo Crowley, the Foreign Economic Administrator, and Joseph Grew, the experienced diplomatist who was acting Secretary of State in Stettinius's absence in San Francisco. So the ships carrying goods to Russia were turned back. But then, after Stettinius had talked to Truman, those ships sailed on, the order being temporarily

* See below, page 279.

rescinded, in order to avoid accusations of tactlessness.* Whatever the legal justification for this policy, and the actions by Russia which made it deserved, it was an ill-considered move. On May 12, Truman also gave firm support to his British allies in their policy of demanding a Yugoslav withdrawal from Trieste: Tito could not be allowed to grab land 'in the style of Hitler or Japan'.[44]

Truman then became abruptly convinced of the benefits of a softer line. One influence here was the president of the War Production Board (previously vice-president of Sears, Roebuck), Donald Nelson, who had hopes of trade with Russia. Another was the ex-ambassador in Moscow, Joseph Davies. After talking at length on May 13 with this self-deceiving but underestimated lawyer, Truman's tone changed markedly.[45] He told Roosevelt's daughter, Anna Boettiger, that he considered his original 'hard' line to have been a mistake.[46] He hesitated over a confirmation of his support to Britain of May 12 in respect of Trieste and said that he was 'unable and unwilling to involve America in war with the Yugoslavs', unless they attacked, even if, in some unexplained way, they had to be expelled from places which they had earlier occupied.[47] He now had less time for those of his advisers who, with Winston Churchill, thought that the Western Allies might stay in the parts of Germany which they had occupied in the closing weeks of the war, regardless of the agreement on zones earlier reached.† 'I'm not afraid of the Russians', he said at this time, 'they've always been friends and I can't see any reason why they shouldn't always be', he confided to his diary.[48] Throughout the early summer, he wanted to avoid giving the Russians the impression that he and Churchill were 'ganging up' on them.[49] Rather ominously, he told his Secretary of Commerce, on May 18, that 'he had no confidence in the State Department whatsoever'.[50] Nothing was done to respond to the continued requests by the United States' representatives in Romania and Bulgaria to take a firmer line in those countries.[51]

* See below for a detailed discussion, page 273.
† See below, page 467.

Truman accepted, too, on the prompting of his Chief of Staff, Admiral Leahy, the idea of a new meeting with Stalin on the lines of those at Tehran and Yalta.[52] Both Grew and Harriman also believed that such a meeting was desirable, while Churchill thought: 'a settlement must be reached on all major issues . . . before the armies of democracy melted'.[53] Why all these men placed such faith in such a meeting is curious: could they have believed that the resolute, but inexperienced, Truman would succeed where the skilful Roosevelt had been outmanoeuvred, at both Tehran and Yalta, by Stalin? No, the fact is that they did not recognise yet that those conferences were most 'unsuitable' (the word is that of Churchill's military secretary Sir Claud Jacob) to deal with major diplomatic problems.[54] Truman wisely procrastinated. To some, he explained that he wanted to deal with the budget (the American financial year ended on June 30). To others, he said that he would be in a stronger position at the conference if he knew by then whether the atom bomb would work. Probably he merely wanted, above all, to get abreast of the task of being President before he faced Stalin and Churchill. The rest of Truman's career shows him to have been wary of such top-level meetings (he never had another one). 'Wish I didn't have to go', was what he wrote to his mother on his way to Potsdam, on July 3, 'it is a chore'.[55]

Truman continued to be reserved in his comments about Russia. This was so even though the early summer of 1945 was a time of argument with both that country and Britain over zones of occupation in Germany and Austria; and, in the end, of a firm line with Tito of Yugoslavia over Trieste.* Truman sent Harry Hopkins to Moscow at the end of May to try 'to straighten things out with Stalin' over Poland.† He told Hopkins of 'his great anxiety at the present situation and also his desire to combine President Roosevelt's policy of working with the Soviet Union'.[56] Hopkins, now ill, had been for a long time Roosevelt's closest counsellor, and had been the first American adviser to go during the war to Moscow, in 1941. The simultaneous despatch of

* See below, page 432.
† See below, page 364.

Joseph Davies to London to soothe Churchill suggests Truman's appreciation of Davies's advice. Davies had the odd task of having to tell Churchill that Truman wanted to see Stalin alone before the conference.[57] Another purpose of this mission was to tell Churchill that Truman planned to keep all the engagements made by Roosevelt but above all to find out what those engagements were.[58] Evidently, that consideration was on Truman's mind: 'I have conferred with all who knew anything about his policy, including the immediate members of his family', he told the Secretary for Commerce.[59]

The advice which Truman received in these weeks from the Secretary of War whom he had inherited from Roosevelt, the experienced Henry Stimson, 'the Colonel', was dourly realistic: since Russia would occupy 'most of the good food lands of Central Europe', it was essential, the 'Colonel' thought, 'to find some way of persuading her to play ball'.[60] Stimson knew that Russia would not give up much in Poland. Some have argued that Stimson persuaded Truman to a policy of strategic delay: not to press Russia over Poland till the bomb was ready.[61] If such an ultra-Machiavellian line had been Stimson's policy, all the more reason why Truman, beset by a hundred problems, should hesitate about meeting Stalin and Churchill. But the evidence suggests that it was not Stimson's policy.[62] Churchill and many of Truman's more explicitly hard-line advisers – Grew, Harriman, Bohlen – were disappointed at the delay in holding a conference. They thought that, bomb or no bomb, a golden moment was being lost, since allied troops would soon 'melt away' in Europe. That is a sustainable view: but so is the argument that it would have been better to have waited till the war in the East was over as well as that in the West before conferring again. The American press was, meantime, criticising Truman for siding with Britain against Russia, and for abandoning Roosevelt's alleged role as a 'mediator' between the two. *Time* talked of the danger of 'World War III' on June 11.[63] But the weeks immediately before Potsdam were effective in reaching certain United States–Soviet understandings: over zones of occupation and withdrawals of troops in Europe; and indeed over Poland. This was, too, the time when the United Nations was being launched. Thus the President delivered the Charter of that organisation formally to the Senate on July 2 at the conclusion of the Conference in San Francisco.

Although worried about Soviet propaganda – 'the Russians distribute lies about us,' he wrote in his diary on June 13 [64] – Truman went 'to Potsdam with the kindliest feelings towards Russia'.[65] He told the American Society of newspaper editors, on June 16, 'I don't give a damn what kind of government the Russians have if they are satisfied; and they seem to be, or some thirty million . . . wouldn't have died for them'.[66] (Also on June 13, Truman said, at a press conference, 'the Russians are just as anxious to get along with us as we are with them'.[67]) In these early months of his presidency, 'Truman, still feeling his way, was puzzled by conflicting advice'. At Potsdam itself, Truman[68] following so many others, had at first liked Stalin: 'he is honest – but smart as hell', he noted in his diary and added, in the style of Roosevelt, 'I can deal with Stalin'.[69] He subsequently likened Stalin to Pendergast, the Missouri political boss who helped Truman reach Washington as Senator;[70] unfortunately for everybody, Stalin had 'a Politburo on his hands like the 80th Congress'.[71] Byrnes, in his memoirs, spoke of the 'very pleasant conversation' which Truman had had with Stalin on July 17, and recalled that 'the President was favourably impressed by Stalin, as I had been at Yalta'.[72] A few days later, with what an official called the 'great poker game' of Potsdam only half over, Truman became angry at Stalin's refusal to talk about the internationalisation of inland waterways – one of his favourite solutions to the problems of the world.[73] This led Truman to reach the conclusion that the Russians really 'were planning world conquest'.[74] In casual conversation, Truman then asked Stalin what had happened to the Polish officers last heard of at Katyn. He elicited the reply: 'they went away'.[75] Then Truman's unyielding but unproductive policies on Eastern Europe, echoing his attitudes of April and early May, made no impact. Stalin expressed the 'hurt' complaint that the United States were demanding changes in the governments of Bulgaria and Romania whilst he was not meddling in Greece.[76]

The failure of Potsdam to achieve a good peace is discussed

where appropriate. But, by the end of the conference, Truman
was convinced that Russian policy was based on the misjudge-
ment that the West was heading for an economic depression, of
which setback the Soviet Union could take advantage;[77] that
force was 'the only thing the Russians understand'; and that,
more surprisingly 'the oligarchy in Russia is no different from
that of the Czars, Louis XIV, Charles I and Cromwell. It is a
Frankenstein monster worse than any of the others, Hitler
included'.[78] Still, at the end of the meetings, Truman told Stalin
that he hoped that they might meet again in Washington. 'May
God grant this', said Stalin, with the odd fervour that he often
showed when he invoked the deity whom he himself had abandoned so long ago in the seminary at Tiflis. Truman wrote to
his mother, however, hoping that he had seen the last of Stalin
and his colleagues.[79] Indeed, he never did see Stalin again.
Stalin reciprocated his adverse verdict; 'he considered Truman
worthless', so Khrushchev reported in his memoirs.[80] Despite these apparent misunderstandings, Truman on his return
to the White House gave a friendly report to his staff about
Stalin: he 'seemed to be favourably impressed . . . and to like
him'.[81]

Truman's own performance at Potsdam was not convincing
to everyone: 'On first contact, Mr Truman made a very good
impression . . . But, as the conference wore on, his vacillations
became rather trying . . . Pretty soon, people stopped taking
his snap judgements seriously'.[82] Thus the British Ambassador
to Moscow, Sir Archibald Clark Kerr. His apparent decisiveness
seemed to Kerr a cloak for continuing uncertainty. That was
probably then a correct interpretation.[83] Over a year later,
Truman was still saying on occasion that 'he had always liked
Stalin and Stalin liked him'.[84]

By the time that General de Gaulle visited the United States
in August, and expressed anxiety over the Russian armies in
Europe, President Truman had collected himself enough to insist
that they presented no threat: if any nation became aggressive,
he said, the United States could use the bomb to stop them.[85]
Matters were, of course, more complicated; the one thing
certain, even then, about the atom bomb being that it could not

be easily used. After the news came, at Potsdam, that the bomb existed and after its subsequent use, Truman's confidence that he could 'deal with' Russia for a time increased.* All the same, neither he nor his administration had set out determinedly to use the non-military means that they could have found to secure the achievement of their policies in East Europe: trade, aid, propaganda, vague threats: all could have been used, quite apart from 'atomic blackmail'.[86]

This was still a period when Truman and his new Secretary of State, Byrnes, saw eye to eye. The President, therefore, gave no specific instructions to that statesman when he left for the Conference of Foreign Ministers in London, on September 5, except 'stick to your guns' and 'give 'em Hell'.[87] He told Byrnes to use his best judgement, in which case he was sure things would come out all right. Byrnes had been successful at Potsdam, particularly over reparations in Germany, and Truman had been pleased.

During the autumn of 1945, Truman's attitude both to Byrnes and to Russia began, however, to wobble. He did not, admittedly, take the failure of the London Conference seriously.† 'This was almost bound to happen at the end of the war', he told Stettinius on October 22; 'it was perhaps better' that it should be 'in the open at this stage'.[88] Truman apparently still thought Stalin 'a moderating influence in the present Soviet government'. It would, he thought, be 'a real catastrophe if Stalin should die at the present time'.[89] Stalin was so 'tired' that he might want 'to retire', he told Henry Wallace. That would be a pity since he was a 'fine man who wanted to do the right thing'; even if often prevented from so doing by Molotov and the 'gang'.[90]

At the same time, Truman was beginning to see that agreement with Russia on atomic matters was likely to prove difficult, if not impossible, short of world government.‡ But he still wanted to please Henry Wallace and 'completely agreed' with that now understandably most confused politician that 'the thing

---

* See Chapter Fifteen.
† See below, page 205.
‡ See page 630.

he most wanted in the world was an understanding with Russia, which would make impossible a third world war'. That was on October 26.[91] Perhaps in order to avoid taking up an attitude of any sort for a time, in his address on Navy Day, October 27, 1945, which listed 'fundamentals' of foreign policy, Truman did not so much as mention the Soviet Union. Even so, four out of his twelve points echoed the 'Declaration on Liberated Europe' of Yalta, and sought to encourage the democrats of East Europe: all peoples ready for self-government should be permitted to choose their own form of it by their own freely elected choice (point four); 'we shall help the defeated enemy states establish peaceful democratic governments' (point five); 'we shall refuse to recognise any government imposed upon any nation by the force of any foreign power' (point six); 'we shall approve no territorial changes in any friendly part of the world unless they accord with the freely expressed wishes of the people concerned' (point three).[92]

These invigorating words in Central Park, New York, with nearly fifty naval vessels anchored significantly in the Hudson River at the time, unfortunately gave false encouragement to King Michael and Dr Maniu in Romania, and to Nikolai Petkov in Bulgaria. It would have been much better had they never been said. Rhetoric without policies always leads to disillusion. Those beleaguered Westerners in the Balkans must also have been confused by their observation of how this trenchant line of the President's was at odds with speeches by Secretary Byrnes who, after being thwarted in London, had begun to talk in favour of a more conciliatory posture towards Russia. On December 4, Truman privately said that, though he was trying to come to an agreement with the Russians, he had no confidence that such an understanding would be lived up to: 'there is no evidence yet that the Russians intend to change their habits, so far as honouring contracts is concerned'.[93] At the time of Byrnes's mission to Moscow, in December, Truman tugged at the coat-tails of the Secretary of State in order to prevent him from telling more 'atomic secrets' to Russia than he or Congressional leaders desired. Truman's disavowals of Byrnes at this time, and Byrnes's continuing pressure to try and achieve something, must also have been confusing, though it may have been entertaining, to the Russians.

When Truman confessed himself 'baffled by it all' in another talk, with Henry Wallace, the Secretary of Commerce, on November 28, he was obviously being honest: for he was then siding with Wallace, in conversation, not only about the iniquity of Britain in Greece, but also about the inadequacies of Secretary Byrnes in dealing with Russia. He comforted Wallace with the reflection that Admiral Leahy's anti-Sovietism, however he might dislike doing so, would soon compel him to 'get into the State Department and straighten it out'.[94] In mid-December, Truman continued in this uncertain mood: Russia had half a million men in Bulgaria, and one day they would move against the Dardanelles. As for the American reaction, 'We cannot send any divisions over', said the President, 'I don't know what we're going to do'.[95]

Some part in the evolution of Truman's thought in late 1945 was probably played by the revelations about Soviet espionage which became available that autumn as a result of the case of Guzenko.

When that official in the Soviet GRU (Soviet military intelligence) deserted in September, making extraordinary allegations, the President seemed at first not to be much interested. But the full report of the Canadian Royal Commission investigating the case established that Soviet spying in Canada had been under way, and had prospered, since 1924; even throughout the late war. The network operated widely. The Canadian prime minister had been much influenced by this report (of which only a bowdlerised version became public); his own attitude to Russia underwent a major reversal. Truman did not go so far. But it did affect him – more than it did his Secretary of State, who probably did not have time to do more than read what his Chief of European Affairs thought that he should see.[96] Another factor in Truman's thought was a conversation with the new ambassador from Persia, Hussein Ala, who described the Soviet intrusion in that country vividly to the President on November 29.[97]

By the end of 1945, Truman had given up hope of reaching

anything like a general agreement with the Russians. In a letter to Byrnes of late December,[98] he wrote: 'At Potsdam we were faced with an accomplished fact and were, by circumstances almost, forced to agree to Russian occupation of Eastern Europe and the Polish occupation of that part of Germany east of the Oder River . . . It was a high-handed outrage . . . When you went to Moscow, you were faced with another accomplished fact in Iran. Another outrage, if I ever saw one . . . There isn't a doubt in my mind that Russia intends an invasion of Turkey and the seizure of the Black Sea Straits . . . Unless Russia is faced with an iron fist, and strong language, another war is in the making. Only one language do they understand: "how many divisions have you?" I do not think we should play compromise any longer . . . I'm tired of babying the Soviets'.[99]

Although this famous letter was never sent – Truman's unsent letters were his main contribution to the epistolary art – Truman used it apparently as an *aide mémoire* from which to speak to the Secretary of State on January 5, 1946. It presumably represents what Truman then really thought. Though he was more pessimistic about Persia than the facts warranted,* it was true that the 500,000 Russian troops still in Bulgaria might easily have driven on to the Bosphorus. (The letter described Truman's complaints about Byrnes's handling of the information about the Moscow conference, but there is nothing to prove that he made those complaints aloud. Truman's accusations were private; just as well, since many of them seem not to have been just.)[100] The President had also realised that public opinion was hostile to any policy approving the abandonment of the small nations of East Europe; and that any similar policy might affect the forthcoming Congressional elections of 1946. He had seen that his Secretary of State was making himself unpopular by an excessive willingness to compromise. But it seems too as if Truman wanted to place the blame for his own inability to formulate a coherent policy on Byrnes.[101] The fault may have lain with the weakness of institutional arrangements between the White House and the Department of State as to where

* See below, page 564.

foreign policy, in those post-Rooseveltian days, really originated.

In early January 1946, meantime, Truman also read the reports of Mark Ethridge, of the *Louisville Courier Journal*, about events in Bulgaria and Romania. He was furious: as much because Byrnes had sent the reports to him late, and casually, as by the bleak news of intimidation and murder that they gave.

These changing moods show that, in dealing with Russia, Truman found it very hard to determine the right line. By early 1946, before Stalin's speech of February 9, Truman seems to have realised that the mere enunciation of principles was not going to be enough in the post-war world; that atomic problems were going to be impossible to resolve; and that they should not anyway be embarked upon till the disputes about East Europe were settled. The complexity, contortion, and unpredictability of the Communist mind, particularly when combined with a Georgian soul such as Stalin's, were as yet beyond his imagination, as they had always been beyond Roosevelt's and even Churchill's. Truman had read the lives of great men. He knew that 'it takes men to make history or there would be no history'.[102] He had led Battery D in battle. He had won political contests in Missouri and in Washington. He had a real vision of the United Nations as a way of ensuring his country's participation in the affairs of the world. But he had not studied the history of Russia nor of Communism. He was a kind, cautious man; one nothing like so intemperate as his unsent letters might suggest. But, as the Alsop brothers suggested, in a fierce article in January, 'Captain Harry' still did not quite know what to do about Russia.[103] That did not mean that the plans which he had inherited from his predecessor were ruined. But it did mean that he was probably living in 'a torment of indecision'.[104] The consequence was that he was still, on the surface, friendly and co-operative to everyone, even to those with whom he disagreed. That was because, as Wallace saw, 'he does *so* like to agree with whoever is with him at the moment'.[105] Truman would become a decisive President. But in February 1946, despite one or two resolute actions, such as the acceptance of Morgenthau's resignation or his approval of dropping the atom bomb, he was so only in appearance.[106]

Truman's closest adviser on international matters was not the
Secretary of State but the seventy-year-old Admiral Leahy, the
chief of staff at the White House. Leahy had been chief of naval
operations in 1937. He had caught Roosevelt's eye during the
first war; and he had been Ambassador to Pétain's France
between 1940 and 1942, where he acquired an admiration for
the old Marshal that had much to do with both his and his chiefs'
suspicions of de Gaulle.[107] Leahy talked almost daily to President
Truman in 1945 and 1946. The staff in the White House was
then never more than thirteen and, with the possible exception
of General Vaughan, none of the President's poker-playing other
advisers there concerned themselves much with international
matters.

Leahy was candid: it was he who at Potsdam told Truman in
a whisper that 'the Bolshies have shot the lot', when Stalin told
the conference that the Germans in Western Poland had fled.
He was unpopular among the English, and disliked them –
Cadogan thought him a 'spiteful old great-aunt'. He thought
Stalin a 'liar and a crook'.[108] In a memorandum in 1944, he had
argued that the only chance of a war in future was one between
Britain and Russia over their respective spheres of interest –
into which the United States might be drawn by mistake.[109]
Leahy has been mocked for thinking that the atom bomb was a
'lemon' which would not work. But, according to his own
account, he was also critical of the idea of the use at all of 'this
barbarous weapon' against defenceless non-combatants, and
thought that it had been of 'no material assistance' in the war
against an already defeated Japan. These doubts had not influenced Truman. It is somewhat unclear if Leahy then expressed
them. Nor did Leahy's (naval) view that Japan would surrender
without the bomb being used make an impression.[110]

Leahy assiduously fed Truman with the view that the
Secretary of State (whom he disliked) was influenced by
'Communistically-inclined advisers in his Department', being
himself influenced by the full text of the report on the Canadian
spy case, which he alone in the White House had seen, apart
from Truman.[111] In these accusations, he was echoing the
charges expressed by the mercurial US Ambassador in China,

General Patrick Hurley, who had just resigned tempestuously, with a flood of unjust accusations directed against John Stewart Service and George Atcheson, who had offended Hurley by their honest reports of the weakness in the *Kuomintang*. Leahy was the captain of Truman's 'palace guard' which Joe Davies had described as plotting Byrnes's downfall, on New Year's Eve 1945, on the Presidential yacht *Williamsburg*. He and his friends urged Truman to tell Byrnes that his accomplishments at the Moscow conference had been 'unreal'.[112] By early 1946, the Admiral had indeed convinced himself that the Department of State had adopted a policy of appeasement of the Soviet government 'reminiscent of Mr Chamberlain's at Munich';[113] and had almost persuaded Truman on the subject. On February 21, he would note that it would be difficult to induce the Secretary of State to admit any fault in his 'present appeasement attitude'.[114] These were early examples of the reckless use of pre-war analogies, in particular the recollection of 'Munich', of 'appeasement' and of the 'lessons' of Hitler and his remilitarisation of the Rhineland, which certainly did not make it easier to understand the politics of that age.[115]

Byrnes was not quite correct when he said that Leahy had become accustomed to the idea of being Secretary of State *de facto* during FDR's day.[116] He was, however, a close confidant. Leahy, for his own part, thought that the behaviour of Russia at Potsdam implied 'serious doubts that any peace treaties could be negotiated'.[117] But he also thought that America herself, through the use of the atom bomb, 'had adopted an ethical standard common to barbarians of the Dark Ages'.[118] Earlier on, though, he had decided that Communism was 'a kind of religion that people were glad to die for' and the United States had always to be ready for the onslaught of such.[119]

James Byrnes, the real Secretary of State after July 1945, 'Jimmy' to almost everyone, including those who did not know him, was formally Truman's chief diplomatic adviser. There was then little that he had not done in American politics. He was the son of an Irish immigrant, an ancestry that made him an aristocrat among non-Anglo-Saxon Americans. He was self-educated, from the age of fourteen, and self-made – other useful quarterings on a political escutcheon. His accent had the charm both of the South and of the Irish. He had begun life as a law clerk. He had been both a Catholic, as a child, and an Episcopalian, after his marriage. He had been a junior Congressman as long ago as 1911, a Senator in 1931 and later a judge of the Supreme Court. He was financially honest. His wants were few: 'two tailor-made suits a year, three meals a day, and a reasonable amount of good liquor'.[120] As a Senator, he had been Roosevelt's 'fair-haired boy' during the early days of the New Deal. During the Second World War, as Director of War Mobilisation, Byrnes had been 'assistant president' for domestic politics (as the press called him, to his own satisfaction), while Roosevelt had concerned himself with strategy. He had expected, and wanted, to be vice-presidential candidate in 1944. But Roosevelt had abandoned him at the Democratic Convention in Chicago. Byrnes thus believed that he should have been President instead of Truman, whom he had ignored as an upstart when, from the hauteur of his long experience in the capital, Truman had first arrived there. Byrnes had nevertheless helped Truman in his career, including arranging money from the financier, Bernard Baruch, in 1940 to assist in his campaign for re-election as Senator. Truman had named Byrnes Secretary of State partly out of guilt but also because he was 'eminently qualified to serve as President';[121] and, in those days, a Vice President who succeeded to the Presidency did not have the power to name his own deputy: the heir was the Secretary of State. (It was a characteristic of the office then that few noticed in 1945–49 that there was no Vice President of the United States.) Truman, to begin with, also revered Byrnes and, indeed, had apparently himself wanted to nominate Byrnes as Vice President at the Democratic Convention at Chicago in 1944.

Before being formally appointed Secretary of State by Truman in July, Byrnes had had some useful experience in international negotiations. He had made the long, dangerous journey with Roosevelt to Yalta where he had made a stenographic record of those proceedings which he had attended (which, however, excluded much, particularly that which discussed the secret protocol in the Far East). He subsequently showed this record to Truman who read it attentively. It seems, however, that Roosevelt invited Byrnes to Yalta less for his stenographic powers than because he afterwards would know what arrangements had been made, and why, and so could help sell them to Congress – a poisoned chalice which later helped to ruin him.[122]

Byrnes did, indeed, return to the United States to tell the American people about the achievements of Yalta, in glowing terms which he later regretted, while Roosevelt was still abroad. After Roosevelt's death, Byrnes had unofficially become Truman's chief adviser on foreign policy even in April 1945, while, in May and June, he had been the President's representative at private meetings with atomic scientists.* He of course did not know Russia and began by believing that dealing with Stalin 'and the gang' was probably like dealing with recalcitrant Senators: 'You build a post office in their state and they'll build one in ours'.[123]

Byrnes had been a clever negotiator in Washington: a 'quiet, middle-of-the-road, extremely tactful liberal', he had seemed to British observers in 1942 to have 'exceptional talents as a compromiser and conciliator'.[124] He worked hard, took decisions easily and disliked verbosity. He also disliked having retinues of advisers. He travelled light. His few communications to the public were terse. He was prepared to travel; out of the 562 days which he served as Secretary of State, he was away from Washington for 350,[125] a first manifestation of the peripatetic Secretaryship subsequently so familiar in the days of Foster Dulles and Henry Kissinger. In private, he was a curious mixture of the affable and the puritanical. He also liked a sing-song round the piano. The 'great cure for discord', in Byrnes's opinion, was 'more free-hearted drinking'. 'When I see Jimmy Byrnes coming, I put one hand on my watch, the other on my wallet, and wish to goodness I knew how to protect my conscience', said Senator McNary.[126]

His weaknesses were, firstly, that he was secretive; thus he did not benefit from the advice which the Department of State, neglected as it had been under Roosevelt, could unquestionably

---

* See below, Chapter Twenty.

provide. He liked cronies, not advisers: in that, comparable to Truman. Yet the lawyers, Benjamin Cohen, sombre and brilliant, Roosevelt's legal friend who had been the drafter of much of the New Deal legislation, and occasional drafter of Roosevelt's speeches, and Donald Russell, a conservative of financial acumen, did help him when they became, respectively, in the Department of State, Counsellor and Assistant Secretary for Administration. Byrnes did not much like to communicate with the President, whom he both despised and envied, even though, to begin with, Truman had looked on him as 'able and conniving', with 'a keen mind' and 'an honest man' who would outmanoeuvre the 'smart boys in the State Department'.[127] Second, he was so quick and clever that he believed that he could go into any discussion without either agenda or preparation. This overconfidence irritated those of his staff who had worked hard on the details of a major problem which they saw brushed aside by Byrnes's approach. Thirdly, he was a man whose 'whole life had been a career of compromise',[128] except over civil rights, where he remained a convinced segregationist till he died. However well Byrnes's conciliatory approach worked in respect of domestic politics with senators and trade union leaders, it was, as Senator Vandenberg complained, a rash policy to adopt with the Soviet Union. The 'horse-trading' which he proposed to Molotov at the Conference of Foreign Ministers in London did not yield results – though something similar had been done at Potsdam over Germany and reparations.* Molotov did not respond to Byrnes's idea for a twenty-five-year guarantee of co-operation against Germany; while the agreements which Byrnes reached with Stalin in Moscow over the recognition of Bulgaria and Romania, in return for Stalin's agreement to broaden the basis of the Bulgarian parliament, and send a commission of ambassadors to Romania, were (as Kennan put it) 'fig leaves of democratic procedure to hide the nakedness of Stalinist dictatorship'.[129] Fourthly, Byrnes was, as his most recent biographer says, 'congenitally uncandid': his 'manipulation of his personal papers goes beyond the normal limits of genteel

---

* See below, page 470.

dishonesty'.[130] Fifthly, Byrnes was inclined to be on his dignity. It must finally be said that he knew nothing of Communism and allowed himself, like so many others, the illusion that Molotov circumvented 'Stalin's genuine desire for peace'. Indeed, he even attempted, when at London, himself to circumvent Molotov by communicating directly with Stalin: who continued to support Molotov.[131] In Moscow he told Stalin, in a private talk alone, one wintry night, that he had been having 'a difficult time with Mr Molotov'. Stalin smiled: that was 'unexpected news'.[132]

By the spring of 1946 Byrnes had learned much. He had, for example, realised the interest that Truman, despicable though he might continue to seem, was going to take in international affairs. Byrnes thus knew that a Secretary of State serving him would have to consult the president. Byrnes had seen from his experience of Soviet behaviour in London that negotiation with Molotov was a quite different, more taxing, matter than dealing with congressmen and New York trade union leaders: the Russians were 'stubborn, obstinate and don't scare'.[133] (Byrnes's attitudes to the atomic bomb between April and December 1945 are discussed in Chapter 20). Byrnes tried several different approaches to Molotov at London, sometimes tough, sometimes conciliatory. Molotov preferred to procrastinate. The Conference broke up over Romania and Bulgaria (elections and recognition, as well as conditions), and on the procedural question as to whether France and China should attend the proposed conferences on peace with the European allies of the Axis.

After the failure of that meeting at London, Byrnes saw, among other things, that the atom bomb could not be a useful diplomatic lever. So, in one of those swift changes so disconcerting in respect of international policy but which might have tactical benefits at home, Byrnes had spoken out, in late October, about how Russia had legitimate interests in East Europe; but that they had not presented them properly before the public. Having been the member of the administration most optimistic that a vague threat based on what Russia was already calling 'atomic blackmail' might cause Stalin to abandon, *inter alia*, Bulgaria and Romania,[134] he was soon found telling the Secretaries of the

Navy and War the old story that the Soviets believed 'that the rest of the world is ganging up on them'. He was now keen to try and co-operate with them. [135] Perhaps this was the influence of Benjamin Cohen or of Leo Pasvolsky – two advisers whom Byrnes had taken over from his predecessor and who, during the war, had been the brains behind the planning of a new international organisation. At all events, there was a change in Byrnes's approach at the very time that his President was girding himself for a tougher attitude. The consequences were seen at the Moscow conference which led to the collapse of Truman's confidence in him.

Byrnes might indeed have considered 'atomic blackmail'. But there is no sign that he tried to. With a continuing political crisis in Romania, where the King was still hoping to establish some kind of independence, and with the American representatives in Bulgaria happy to have secured the postponement of the elections there, the London conference occurred at what seemed a moment of opportunity for the United States – the only one at that time. Byrnes could perhaps have mixed bribes with threats in conversation with Molotov: the possibility of loans, to both Russia and to East Europe, as well as intimidation based on overwhelming atomic strength; a major propaganda campaign in the region; even personal visits by himself; all in order to achieve democracies in East Europe on the principle enshrined in the Declaration at Yalta. Perhaps such a policy would not have been successful. But it was not attempted.

Byrnes's meeting in Moscow was not as unsuccessful as Congress, Truman and some historians have asserted. The arrangements achieved on both atomic matters and the Far East* were promising. The 'surrenders' over Bulgaria and Romania were scarcely more than what Roosevelt had conceded over Poland.† Byrnes's alleged inadequate communication with Truman derived from his distrust of Leahy, possibly of his own Department, as much as from *folie de grandeur*. But what offended both his countrymen and the English was his sickly

* See below, pages 571–2 and 652.
† See above, pages 410 and 423.

manner of attempting to charm the Russians, even Stalin: a dangerous policy at the best of times.

Byrnes might have been an effective Secretary of State in other days. He could draft extremely complicated papers providing for compromises on difficult subjects in a very short time. The settlement of reparations at Potsdam showed that. His use of a skilled journalist, Mark Ethridge, of the *Louisville Courier Journal*, to give him an account of the situation in Bulgaria and Romania, in late 1945, showed that he was, at least, no dull bureaucrat. But anger at being considered by some whom he respected as an appeaser, an incomprehension of the nature of Communism, and an incapacity to deal with his ex-subordinate Truman (also given to disturbing changes of mind at that time), which he never shook off, prevented his being a success in 1946. The record of what occurred between Truman and Byrnes on the presidential yacht *Williamsburg*, on the Potomac, after the latter's return from Moscow at the end of December 1945, is thus most unclear. Probably Truman thought that he would reprimand Byrnes for secrecy, for exaggerating his own success, and for 'babying the Soviets'. But Byrnes, believing the conference to have been a success, did not notice; or at least pretended not to.[137] Anyway, Byrnes had decided to withdraw from public service at some convenient date; and Truman had decided that his successor would be General Marshall, after his return from China.[138] Byrnes later described a bad heart as the reason for leaving the government. But that excuse was false. Disillusion was the explanation.

Byrnes's methods of work were demonstrated by the way that he had decided, during the Thanksgiving weekend in 1945, 'with only the ticking of a grandfather clock for company', to arrange the meeting of foreign ministers in Moscow in December at very short notice, 'against advice of the diplomats and the columnists', as he recalled with relish.[139] On purpose, to allay Russian suspicions of 'ganging up' against them, he did not consult the British (he would not have cared if Bevin had not come). It had been earlier decided to hold conferences of the 'Big Three' foreign ministers every three months but no one had suggested that the next one should be in Moscow. Byrnes did not invite the French, whom Stalin both despised for their current weakness and feared for their intelligence; nor the Chinese, whom Stalin thought should not be allowed to pontificate about Europe.

This was a meeting of the 'conference' of three wartime allies, not of the 'council' of five foreign ministers set up at Potsdam: a nice, but important, difference. (Possibly Byrnes may have thought of the idea earlier, in which case the grandfather clock must have been a myth, but it only assumed solid shape now.)[140] At the conference, Kennan, sitting behind him at the meetings, thought that Byrnes's 'main purpose' was to achieve 'some sort of an agreement, he doesn't much care what'. The realities behind this agreement, 'since they concern only people such as Koreans, Romanians and Iranians, about whom he knows nothing, do not trouble him. He wanted an agreement for its political effect at home'. Byrnes seemed to Kennan to rely 'entirely on his own agility and presence of mind' in negotiations, which, in Roosevelt's style no doubt, he had started upon 'with no clear or fixed plan, with no definite set of objectives or limitations'.[141]

This adverse view of the Secretary was not, however, shared by all. Robert Murphy, for example, a senior official who was not 'soft on Communism', thought Byrnes made a valiant attempt to carry through Roosevelt's dream of a grand design which would tie the Soviet Union into the United Nations. Byrnes seemed to him 'keenly aware that America's foreign affairs were more important than ever before':[142] a simple point, but one which would be underestimated. Bohlen another prominent official thought much the same, though he agreed with Kennan that Byrnes 'ran much of foreign policy from within his head'.[143]

Byrnes in early 1946 was in the unfortunate position of having gained a reputation for trying to appease the Soviet Union during the autumn and winter; and of having earlier tried to wield a big stick against them. His bad personal relations with Truman and Leahy also limited his effectiveness. When the Alsop brothers published their article on January 4, 1946, *We have no Russian Policy*, it was partly against Byrnes that it was directed.[144] Byrnes's unwillingness to communicate with Truman from

Moscow might not be repeated, but the bitterness so caused remained. At the next big meeting, that of the United Nations in London, Byrnes's relations with his Republican critics, such as Senator Vandenberg and John Foster Dulles (both of whom came to London), had if anything worsened. By then, too, he had become that weakest of all public figures: a senior minister who has privately resigned. This weakness was made patent when, in a press conference at the end of January, after returning from London, he became involved, not for the first time, in a tangle over the terms which Roosevelt at Yalta had reached with Russia over the Kurile Islands, in return for Russian help in the Far Eastern war. Byrnes had to admit not only that he had been kept in the dark about the matter by Roosevelt but that he had not known what he had been talking about when he spoke of it in August 1945, when already in charge of foreign policy. In early February 1946, the publication of the Yalta protocol on the Far East made Byrnes's reputation as 'the man who had been at Yalta' seem a dubious one, on several scores.[145]

# NINE

# THE NEW AMERICANS II: OFFICIALS, FRIENDS, CRONIES

The main task of the Secretary of State was, of course, to manage the Department of State, an institution which had a character of its own. Unlike the British Foreign Office, the Department of State was staffed by men and women who considered that their main mission was to serve the American Embassies and legations abroad. Neglected by Presidents (above all by Roosevelt), despite their physical proximity, in the Executive office building, to the White House, American diplomatists, at that time mostly from the great universities of the East Coast, and from the comfortable classes, had a lofty, often critical view of Washington, of Presidents, and even of Secretaries of State. These attitudes led Presidents, of all kinds, including Truman after he had been President for two months, to talk of there being 'not much material to work with'.[1] Roosevelt before him had shared the view of the Department held by his assistant Harry Hopkins: 'a querulous maiden aunt, whose sole function is to do all the worrying for the prosperous family, and cope with the endless importunities of the numerous poor relations'.[2]

In Truman's early days as President, the Under Secretary as has been observed was Joseph Grew. His firm, cautious but informed views influenced Truman in April 1945. He came to symbolise the 'hard' view in the Department of State, which the President for a time later rejected. Grew, then at the end of a long career in the American Foreign Service, had at first been relieved to find that Truman would not stand for 'pussy-footing in foreign relations'.[3] He, with Leo Crowley of the Foreign Aid Administration, had persuaded Truman to cut off Lend Lease on May 11, 1945, personally believing that this action would serve as a political weapon in connection with difficulties with Russia in Central Europe. He had advised Truman, on May 5, 1945, to try to get Eisenhower's armies to hold the line of the Moldau, in order to secure Soviet concessions.[4] Grew had some experience of Russia: he had been in Denmark after the First World War, with the specific task of reporting on the Russian Revolution. He negotiated in Lausanne in 1922–23 with Lenin's Foreign Minister, Chicherin. He had opposed recognition of the Soviet Union by the United States in 1933. In 1945, he believed that 'the most fatal thing' to do was to 'place any confidence whatever in Russia', knowing 'that she will take every opportunity to profit by our own clinging to our own ethical behaviour as a weakness to us, and an asset to her'. Grew believed already that, 'as a war to end wars', the Second World War would prove to have been futile, for the result would be 'merely the transfer of totalitarian dictatorship and power from Germany and Japan to Soviet Russia, which will constitute, in future, as grave a danger to us as did the Axis'.[5] (The fact that he had had to write a despatch in almost the same language in 1941, when ambassador in Tokyo, about the threat of Japan, gave a disagreeable resonance to his words.) He was unable to sleep because of this perception and wrote a personal memorandum, to himself, to that effect.

No one in Washington was more experienced than Grew. He was the Monsieur de Norpois of the United States. He had been Ambassador in Tokyo at the time of Pearl Harbor, and chargé d'affaires in Berlin, when the *Lusitania* was sunk in 1916: a combination of experiences which would have ruined less persistent men. Before 1914, he had been in St Petersburg. He had known Lord Cromer in Cairo, the Archduke Franz Ferdinand in Vienna, and had served Kellogg in Washington. Even more helpful perhaps to him, he had known Roosevelt at Groton and at Harvard. For 166 out of his 240 days as deputy, he acted as Secretary of State.[6] He must have thought, for the first month of Truman's presidency, that he had presided, in his last months in Washington, over a re-birth of, even a creation of, the influence of the Department.

Grew retired in the summer of 1945 as the Under Secretary of State and was succeeded by a liberal conservative, Dean Acheson, a lawyer who had served previously as assistant Secretary of State in charge of economic, then of congressional, affairs. With Byrnes continuing to be away so much, Acheson, like Grew, was often Acting Secretary of State and so sat in at the Cabinet. He would brief the President every evening on foreign affairs and developed a good friendship with him. Acheson was a self-disciplined man, whose appearance suggested the military background of his father: a soldier as well as a bishop. Bishop Acheson had been born in Ulster: one more contribution of Protestant Ireland to American public life. Acheson himself, an Episcopalian, looked an Anglo-Saxon to the ends of his moustache and was then inclined to think that Britain offered more intelligent leadership than the United States did.

Acheson was a product of Groton, Yale and Harvard Law School. He belonged to a golden generation of Edwardian Americans, whose self-confidence was accompanied by optimism.[7] He was a fine representative of the old East Coast of the United States, with a good recollection of the long peace which Britain had maintained in the past and could not do any more. A pupil of Judge Felix Frankfurter, Acheson was subsequently clerk to an equally fine judge in the shape of Louis Brandeis. He left his law firm in 1933 to be Under Secretary at the Treasury, but resigned, in protest against what he considered the unconstitutional action by Roosevelt in reducing the gold content of the dollar. He returned to the administration in 1941, just before the outbreak of war, as Assistant Secretary of State for Economic Affairs. He negotiated the first Lend Lease Agreement with Maynard Keynes. In 1944, he had become responsible for the Department's relations with Congress. There, he had helped to ensure that such new colossi as the

United Nations, UNRRA, the IMF and the World Bank, as well as the new FAO, received a welcome by Congress.*

To begin with, Acheson was impatient with those who thought that a good relationship with the Soviet Union would be impossible after the war. He believed for a time that the United Nations might seem to afford the same guarantee to the Soviet Union as to the United States. In his memoirs, he made the curious observation that, in the Europe of 1945, only in Britain and Russia did men have confidence in government, social or economic organisation, or currencies.[8] A. A. Berle, an old enemy in bureaucratic arguments, had looked on Acheson as one of the leaders of the 'appeasement group' in the Department of State, so far as Russia was concerned.[9] He seemed at first to liberals a welcome change from Grew. But, in November 1945, he was already debating against those who sympathised with the Soviet Union. He thus made a speech in Madison Square Gardens in which he recognised that Russia might not understand that 'friendly governments along its borders should be ensured for the benefit of peace as such, not just for Soviet security': 'the adjustment of interest' should take place 'short of the point where persuasion and firmness became coercion, where a knock at the door at night struck terror'.[10] The boos which greeted those words told Acheson that he had crossed a great divide. A month later, Acheson believed that the conference in Moscow had proved that the 'Soviet diplomatic method was to bargain hard – accept all concessions in the other side's sphere and make no concessions in their own'. Later, he remarked: 'until the Soviet leaders do genuinely accept a live and let live philosophy . . . no approach from the free world . . . and no Trojan horse from the Communist nest will help to resolve our mutual problems'.[11] Looking back, years later, on the events of 1946, Acheson would recall that 'we were slow then to see through the murky methods by which Moscow was extending its control, always under the shadow of the Red Army'.[12] Later still, he wisely remarked about the relations of the United States with Russia, 'there is no formula which will

---

* For these bodies, see below, pages 269–70.

remove the difficulties which confront us. Danger and difficulties are with us, not because the right policy or the right action eludes us, but from the very nature of the situation we face. The idea that there is a right policy, or a right action, which will remove them and make all well, is based upon the unspoken assumption that we could control the present situation if only we knew how'.[13] In 1946, his position, between a President (Truman) and a Secretary of State (Byrnes) who misunderstood one another, was difficult. He even contemplated resignation.

Acheson had a sharp mind though he was perhaps a less strong character than he seemed at first sight. The events of the next few years would give him an immense opportunity. He seized it. No one would impose their personality, for good or evil, on the post-war world more than he. This world was, therefore, framed in large part by the son of an Anglican bishop to whom the Bible was familiar.[14]

The Department of State itself comprised in 1946 men who had mostly spent the years of the war planning, in innumerable neglected committees, for a world at peace in circumstances different from what now seemed available. The variations of view among the assistant secretaries, directors of 'offices' and, beneath them, of 'divisions' were considerable: so much so that, despite the neglect of the department by Roosevelt, by Truman (after July 1945) and even by Byrnes, it is difficult to detect an institutional consensus. They might seem 'cookie-pushers' to Roosevelt, but they were a diverse group. Thus the senior official, James Dunn, Assistant Secretary for 'European, Asian, Near Eastern and African affairs' and as such the man who oversaw all reporting from all posts abroad except Latin America, was a conservative much in the mould of Grew. Roosevelt said that he put in 'Jimmy' just 'to make Cordell Hull "feel good"'.[15] Drew Pearson, a famous columnist, had written in 1943 that Dunn (and others) 'would really like to see Russia bled white – and they know it'.[16] But, to balance Dunn, there was Archibald Macleish, the charming poet and librarian of Congress, who was now Assistant Secretary for public relations: a new dealer to the satisfaction of everyone. Who, in liberal politics, did not remember Macleish's 'Democracy Alcove', in the Library of

Congress, or his wartime battles against 'defeatism', when he headed the 'Office of Facts and Figures'? Macleish had headed the Department of State's remarkable publicity campaign to gain support throughout the nation for the assumption of international responsibilities. The office of European Affairs, under Dunn, was managed by H. Freeman Matthews, nicknamed 'Doc' because of post-graduate work at the *Ecole des Sciences Politiques* in Paris. Matthews was thought to be a 'conservative but by no means a reactionary' by the left-wing journal *PM*. Matthews was optimistic after Yalta: 'it was clear throughout that the Russians genuinely wished to reach agreement,' he wrote. He was still innocent in matters relating to the Soviet Union.[17] Matthews's deputy, John Hickerson, in 1945 thought that the era of Communist expansion was over.[18] But in 1946 he realised 'we are standing at a crossroads. There could be two types of world. The first one is a world built around the United Nations' conception, built on the principle of the sovereign equality of all states. The second is a big power world, with "spheres of interest".'[19] Hickerson still prayed that 'we shall have the privilege of living in a world built on the United Nations'.[20] But he must have known, surely, that there was by then no chance of it.

In the Division of Eastern European Affairs, which included the Soviet Union, supervised by 'Doc' Matthews, the responsible official was Elbridge Durbrow, who had been in Moscow in 1934 to 1937 under the ambassadorship of William Bullitt.[21] He was an able official already 'exceedingly well-informed' on Soviet affairs. But, if several of these men seemed to lean towards the Conservative side in politics, they were balanced by the chief of the section dealing with international co-operation, Alger Hiss, who (whether he was a traitor or merely shielding his wife) was plainly a progressive.[22]

A more resourceful diplomatist headed the office of Near Eastern and African affairs, which included responsibility for three troubled countries: Greece, Turkey and Persia. This was Loy Henderson, a man of outstanding moral courage and determination who was looked on with respect even by those who thought his bleak interpretation of Soviet motives too pessimistic. He had been chargé d'affaires in Moscow before the war and afterwards assistant chief of the division of European Affairs.[23] He was a patient, hard and powerful intellect, who, though not himself a Russian scholar, was responsible for the specialisation in Soviet affairs that had produced such experts in the American Foreign Service as Charles Bohlen and George Kennan. He was married to a Latvian, the tribulations of whose country between 1941 and 1945 he thus knew intimately. His move from the office of European Affairs (after failing to prevent the nomination of Colonel Faymonville as administrator of Lend Lease in Moscow) to look after the affairs of the Near East brought to those countries' affairs a man now disturbed that his government did not yet recognise the strength of Soviet hatred for capitalism, nor the ruthlessness of the communist leaders.[24] Henderson ensured that the President learned directly of the apparent Soviet threats in 1945 to Iran and to Turkey, and secured interviews for the ambassadors of those countries with Truman. After George Kennan, he was the most successful official of his day but some including Acheson discounted his judgements because of his apparent anti-semitism.

Under Roosevelt, the most influential American professional diplomatist had become his interpreter at Tehran and Yalta. Charles, or 'Chip', Bohlen had been since December 1944 Assistant to the Secretary of State for Liaison with the White House. Of German origin, he had, like Henderson, been in the American Embassy in Moscow before the war. With Roosevelt, he had, like Leahy, been an important adviser. With Truman, he was less in tune. Bohlen was a fine man of amiable habits, with a deep, slow voice which many thought 'the most attractive' that they ever heard.[25] He was the only close counsellor of Roosevelt who knew Russia well. He knew, for example, that 'for the United States, the ideological element of Soviet policy was of vital importance', and that 'there can be no harmonious relation with Moscow, in the customary sense of the word'. 'Present-day Bolsheviks,' he went on, 'still insist that they believe that the USSR is surrounded by capitalist nations ready to destroy it . . . the leaders in the Kremlin still regard every government of a non-Communist state as in a transition phase on the way to achieving Soviet status. All settlements with such countries are temporary, to be altered when the "correlation of forces" was more favourable to Moscow'. Soviet ideology, Bohlen believed, 'does not lead to personal enmity of Russians towards Americans. It does not, however, prescribe adherence to any objective standard of morality. Lies are perfectly acceptable if they advance the Soviet cause'. That did not mean that the United States was inherently more moral than the Soviet Union. But one had to recognise that the United States, unlike Russia, operated in a society where good and evil were differentiated. The use of violence in itself produced no tremors in the Bolshevik mind. Indeed, the use of the Red Army in order to promote Soviet regimes, or to prevent their liberation, was a duty, unless the action imperilled the Soviet Union itself. Moscow would continue both to support and control foreign Communist Parties.[26] The United States should 'try to get along with the Soviets'. But Bohlen did not have any illusions that the end of the war would usher in an era of good feeling.[27] Regardless of all that had been agreed to at Yalta, there was nothing that could have prevented the break-up of the victorious coalition and the onset of the cold war, 'once Stalin had set his course'. Yet in these days, after the end of the war, Bohlen found it 'almost impossible to convince others that admiration for the extraordinary valour of the Russian troops . . . was blinding Americans to the dangers of the Bolshevik leaders'.[28] At the same time, in February 1946, he was found arguing that Americans should try to encourage Russia to act in the spirit of the United Nations, and that could come only if conditions inside Russia improved.

The quotations above derive from Bohlen's memoirs. They therefore represent his considered views. In 1945, as he himself admits, he, like so many others, was inclined to believe the prevalent myth that Stalin was a moderate, surrounded by harder, darker, unknown men. There is no evidence as to whether he drew the attention of Roosevelt, Truman and Byrnes to the harsh facts of Marxism-Leninism which he knew well. He was, of course, young, having been brought into Roosevelt's charmed circle at the time of the Cairo conference in 1943, by Averell Harriman, and pushed forward by Harry Hopkins.

American missions abroad were in 1946 not a good reflection of the views in the Department of State. Nearly all, at one time or another, were perplexed by the gap between their Government's rhetoric in favour of democracy and their practical tolerance of inertia. In the critical countries, there were four political appointments: Averell Harriman, in Moscow; Richard Patterson, in Yugoslavia; Laurence Steinhardt, in Prague; and John Winant, in London; of whom the first two seemed to be hard-liners, in relation to the Soviet Union, the third had much insight into these questions having been once ambassador in Moscow, while the fourth still seeming a charming liberal, neglected by the Department and by-passed continuously, as he himself complained, by Roosevelt in his direct communications with Churchill.[28A] (In China, the embassy was vacant, waiting for a successor to the flamboyant General Hurley, whose unexpected resignation had caused such an upheaval in Washington in November 1945.)

The ministers or other representatives in Eastern Europe were mostly career diplomatists whom the previous year's experience had turned into critics of the Soviet Union; though Arthur Bliss Lane, in Warsaw, had always been hostile to the Bolshevik regime, for he had served in Poland as a young man, during the Polish-Russian war of 1920. His subsequent experiences in Riga and Belgrade, between the wars, had deepened this antipathy.[29] Maynard Barnes, in Bulgaria, and Burton Berry, in Romania, both agreed that 'we must match Russian firmness with firmness'.[30] Barnes had taken the administration's commitment to the Yalta Declaration on Liberated Europe seriously and, with his resolute colleague, General Crane, had helped to ensure a delay in the Bulgarian elections, against the instructions of Washington, the previous year.* Edwin Wilson, in Turkey, had been Counsellor in Paris to the anti-Soviet ambassador, Bullitt, before the war, and seemed apprised of Soviet realities. Though Patterson in Belgrade was new to foreign policy, having previously been Chairman of the broadcasting company RKO, he was guided by his counsellor

* See below, page 420.

Harold Shantz, who had served in Moscow with Loy Henderson and who had even been in Helsinki during the Russo-Finnish war. Lincoln MacVeagh in Athens was a whiggish friend of Roosevelt's who, at this time, seemed on the liberal side of United States politics. He was therefore critical of Britain, though he would soon move to the right on Greece.

Averell Harriman in Moscow in early 1946 was the most influential of all American diplomatists. He was about to leave his post after a most successful mission there as Ambassador. The simplicity of his arguments about taking a firm stand towards Russia had carried weight with Truman at the beginning of his presidency. Even so, Stalin had been warm towards him on the two occasions that they had met since the end of the war: in October at Gagra, and, in January, in the Kremlin.[31] Molotov 'deeply regretted' Harriman's departure, he said, since he had done so much for 'the cause of Soviet-American relations'.[32] Khrushchev, in his recollections, described Harriman as a man who had 'conducted policies that were very much to our liking'.[33]

Harriman was an improbable man to be the recipient of appreciation from such quarters, being the son of the great 'capitalist' millionaire who had built the Union Pacific Railroad. His early career had been spent in and out of great gambles, one of which had taken him to Russia and a conversation with Trotsky in 1926 (not the best year for a balanced talk with Trotsky, admittedly). As a young man, Harriman had been to both Oxford and Yale, home of American team spirit. There he had been rowing coach when Acheson had been in the freshman eight. He had in the 1940s a large fortune and used it wisely for his political adventuring, which he had begun as a friend of Harry Hopkins, Roosevelt's closest adviser.* His freedom from financial necessity helped, as is often the case, to give him independence of spirit. He had an immense 'capacity for work';[34] 'unique in his single-mindedness of purpose, it was natural for him to pursue only one interest at a time', wrote his

* See below, page 241.

minister, George Kennan, at a time when that single interest was the American war effort as President Roosevelt understood it.[35] To this, Kennan wrote, Harriman addressed himself with 'a dedication, a patience and an unflagging energy and attention that has no parallel in my experience'. He also had, Bohlen added, an 'enormous capacity' – again that very special word of praise – for assessing 'the tactical nature of the problem and what the Russians were after in a specific situation'. But, Bohlen thought, he probably never 'really understood the nature of the Soviet system [and] . . . did not carry his keen observations to the overall Soviet ideological attitude towards the world and the capitalist nations'.[36] Much of his capacity to deal with Russia derived from George Kennan's advice.[37] Many years later, he discussed the interconnection between the expansion of the Russian state and the advance of Communism: he doubted whether Stalin and his colleagues 'ever stopped to ask themselves which of the two was their principal motivation'.[38] At the time, he said, he personally 'did not give a damn about Stalin's character, or the 1936–38 show trials, or the collectivatisation campaign. I was concerned to get him to do the things we wanted him to do. For me, he was simply the leader of a country we had some very important business with'.[39]

Harriman's attitudes to Russia were thus 'pragmatic'. They also changed backwards and forwards, like those of nearly everyone among the Western leaders.[40] Thus in late 1943 he was exorbitantly enthusiastic at the apparent success of the conference of foreign ministers in Moscow;[41] and, in January 1944, he was to be heard dismissing as mistaken the idea that the Russians were 'desirous of communising Poland or setting up a puppet government, or making it a part of the Soviet Union. The Soviets,' he said rashly, 'have enough racial indigestion'.[42] He favoured post-war loans to Russia, though not for altruistic reasons: for 'leverage'. He seemed ingenuous in his welcome to the Soviet Poles in Moscow, whose cause Stalin promoted in mid-1944. But the Russians' 'insensitivity' – the word is modest enough – to the rising of the Home Army in Warsaw affected him deeply. He recalled later that, as a consequence, he was

'one of the first Americans to face the realities' of Soviet power
and to warn Roosevelt that the Soviet Union might become a
'world bully'.[43] He had pointed out that 'if the policy is accepted
that the Soviet Union has a right to penetrate her immediate
neighbors for security, penetration of the next immediate
neighbors becomes at a certain time equally logical'.[44] In April
1945, just before Roosevelt died, Harriman argued that the
Russians 'considered as a sign of weakness on our part our
combined generous and considerate attitude towards them, in
spite of their disregard for our requests for co-operation'. He
added that he could not discount 'the almost daily affronts and
total disregard which the Soviets evince in matters of interest to
us'. He recommended that 'we make them realise that they
cannot continue their present attitude, except at great cost to
themselves'. Even so, Harriman thought that 'if we deal with
the Soviets on a realistic basis, we can in time attain a workable
basis for our relations'.[45] For Harriman that meant, above all,
personal discussions with Stalin.[46]

Immediately after Roosevelt's death, Harriman returned to
Washington. He had been affected personally by the fruitless-
ness of his efforts to help Poland. He told Truman that the
Russians were mounting a new 'barbarian invasion of Europe'.[47]
He still repeated, though, that a 'workable' relationship could be
found, provided the Americans abandoned their illusions that the
Soviet government would soon act in accordance with accepted
principles of international behaviour. Truman was impressed.
Harriman was the most influential voice with Truman before
his terse conversation with Molotov in April. Harriman spoke
similarly to Forrestal, Secretary of the Navy: 'Using the fear of
Germany as a stalking horse', Russia would 'continue their
programme of setting up states around their borders which
would follow the same ideology as the Russians . . . the outward
thrust of Communism was not dead . . . we might well have to
face an ideological warfare just as vigorous and dangerous as
fascism or Nazism'.[48]

Harriman was irritated at Byrnes's neglect of his advice at
both Potsdam and the Moscow Conference and he continued to
believe that conciliatory moves towards Russia were usually

construed as appeasement rather than as the expression of a
sincere desire to work together.[49]

In November 1945, Ambassador Harriman, in consequence
of these views, had suggested that the United States establish
a powerful radio transmitter somewhere in Europe which would
broadcast the truth in all the appropriate languages to Russia.
The Assistant Secretary of State (William Benton) agreed.
The plan would be to have 'powerful, solid and interesting'
programmes because the Russians had only a vague understanding of the United States. Harriman returned to this theme in
one of his last communications to Washington before he left
Moscow in January 1946. The 'small group of men' who ruled
the USSR had, he said, 'consistently sought to represent to the
Soviet people a distorted and unfavourable picture of the United
States'. The Russians had been told that three million women
and girls in the United States had been discharged from war
work to become housemaids, prostitutes or live mannequins in
shop windows.[50] They were told that the function of the Senate
was to afford the ruling class of the United States protection
against laws contrary to their interests.[51] The Ambassador
wanted a 'vigorous and intelligent American information programme' to redress the balance. How could it be done? The
illustrated magazine *Amerika* was a success – with an influence
exceeding its circulation of 10,000. But it was subject to Soviet
censorship and, anyway, 'reliance on the printed word' was
'likely to prove fundamentally unsatisfactory'. Radio was the
only medium through which Americans could speak freely, and
directly, to the Russian people. The jamming of American broadcasts, he argued, would be 'an admission to their own people'
that it feared outside ideas. Such broadcasts should not attack
the Soviet system nor personalities within it. It would, though,
be the voice of liberty.[52]

Harriman, like almost everyone involved with Stalin and
Russia since 1941, had his moments of pessimism. When leaving
Moscow in January 1946, he told his staff at the United States
embassy: 'I am not discouraged but I think we have a long
slow scrape ahead. So much depends on how much effort
the American people are willing to put forward'. Peace and

accommodation of differences with the Russians depended on American willingness to assume 'world responsibility'.[53]

Harriman's staff in Moscow mostly agreed with him: for example, General John Deane, a Californian, chief of the military mission to Russia, was by now 'nauseated by Russian food, vodka, and protestations of friendship':[54] 'we are . . . at the same time the givers and the supplicants'.[55] He personally longed for much greater official toughness towards his hosts.

Almost all these utterances of Harriman must be presumed to have been influenced by the minister George Kennan, whose words have already been quoted, an outstanding public servant already on the threshold of greatness. He was the nephew of a once famous traveller to Russia with the same name as himself. After Princeton, he had learned Russian at Riga in the company of passionate White Russians, in the 1920s.[56] He had served in the embassy of the United States in Moscow in the 1930s, and was probably influenced there by William Bullitt. He had a deep love of Russia and as deep an antipathy for Marxism-Leninism. He also wondered whether the United States was capable of being a world power.[57]

In 1944 Kennan had predicted that the Russians would seize much of Eastern Europe. In September of that year, he believed that Britain and the United States should have taken action over the issue of the Russians' failure to help the Polish Home Army before Warsaw. Russia should have been told that, unless they went to the help of the Poles, or at least permitted the Western Allies to help them, aid would be cut off.[58] A little later, in February 1945, Kennan had, however, recognised that Russia's war effort, masterful and effective as it was, had to 'find its reward at the expense of other peoples in Eastern and Central Europe'. He thought that the United States and the Soviet Union should, in consequence, 'divide Europe frankly into spheres of influence – keep ourselves out of the Russian sphere and keep the Russians out of ours'. The organisation of the United Nations meantime should be buried as quietly as possible.[59] But, the United States had 'refused to name any limit for Russian expansion' and held onto its meaningless support for the Atlantic Charter, '. . . thereby confusing the Russians'. He believed that it was idle for the West to 'hope that we could have any influence on the course of events in the area to which Russian hegemony had already been effectively extended. So the United States should have no programme of aid, and assume no shadow of responsibility there'.[60]

The idea of spheres of interest seemed, as has been seen, an unpopular concession to *realpolitik* in the Department of State. Because he held those views, and for other reasons, Kennan stood a little to the side of his government's policies in 1946. He made up his mind about the fundamental issues, whereas the administration was feeling its way; and from scratch. But he did not think the Soviet Union desired war immediately; not for fifteen to twenty years. There was too much reconstruction to be done at home.[61]

Among other diplomatists, Adolf A. Berle, grand-son of a German immigrant, now ambassador in Brazil, one of the most influential men in Washington during the war, as Assistant Secretary of State, had moved in 1945 from 'a blank uncertainty' whether 'this Russian business would last forever' to a considered belief that the Russians had embarked on a 'new concept of world empire', with vast intrigues afoot through Communist parties even in Latin America.[62] He sent a memorandum along these lines to Truman in July. Berle thought that Russia's immediate aim was to seize the Middle East and that the 'moral aspects' of the situation were now similar to those in Germany in the 1930s: the 'same tactics are used: violent propaganda, smear accusations, portrayal of other people's patriotism as criminal or reactionary, financing of fifth columns, stimulated disorder, street terrorism, ultimately direct territorial and occupation  demands'.[63]


A President is not influenced only by officials. Both Roosevelt and Truman listened a great deal to outsiders, the latter knowing that a president 'is not well served if he depends upon the agreed recommendations of just a few people around him'.[64] In the early days of his presidency, Truman saw a good deal of Joseph Davies, the rich trust-busting lawyer from Wisconsin whom

Roosevelt had made Ambassador to Moscow. He would have preferred London but served in the Russian capital from January 1937 to June 1938. This gave him his reputation as an expert on the Soviet Union. He went to Potsdam. The reason for Truman's liking for Davies was that they played poker together. Subsequently, Truman thought him a 'crackpot'.[65] But, in 1945, the parting of the ways implicit in that description seemed improbable. Davies was in no way a perceptive observer. He had seen Russia in the 1930s through spectacles for which the adjective 'rose' would seem inadequate. For him, Stalin's 'brown eye' had been 'exceedingly kind and gentle'. A child would 'like to sit in his lap and a dog would sidle up to him'.[66] He was obsequious, and fawning. Churchill said that, after talking to him, he had needed 'a bath to get rid of the slime'.[67] Loy Henderson, Bohlen and Kennan in Moscow had contemplated resignation from the Foreign Service on his appointment as ambassador. They 'doubted his seriousness', saw every evidence that his motives in accepting the post were political, and that 'he had a readiness to bend both the mission and its function to the purposes of personal publicity at home'.[68] It can scarcely be credited, but Roosevelt asked Davies to go back to Moscow as ambassador in the middle of the war before he decided on Harriman: fortunately, he was too ill.[69] He had nevertheless been right to predict – or guess – in 1941 that 'the Soviet Union would surprise the world' by withstanding the Germans.[70] His *Mission to Moscow* owes much of its interest to the fact that the Department of State had allowed him to quote confidential matter in it. Known in the Department as '*Sub*mission to Moscow', it was a long argument to the effect that Russia had changed, for the better. A film version of this book, however, met appalling reviews. All the same, Davies was unabashed. He received a Lenin Prize for his pains in 1945, and for arguing that Russia should always be given the benefit of the doubt. He was busy in 1945 arguing that 'the Russian situation' was deteriorating fast and had to be salvaged.[71] He was skilful at keeping his connections with important people. Davies was essentially a 'lobbyist' – and, at this time, it was as if he had been asked to act by the Russians.[72] Truman confided in him: even telling him about the nuclear weapon, for example, on May 21. It was partly at least because of the long conversation with Davies, on May 13, that Truman took a more friendly tone towards Russia between then and July.[73] Like Harriman, Davies was an advocate of the idea that difficulties with Russia could be solved by meetings with Stalin. In 1946, after the news broke of the Guzenko case, Davies declared that Russia, in self-defence, had a moral right to seek out such secrets if they were excluded from them by their allies:[74] a defence of espionage as unusual as it was candid. By then the influence of Davies on Truman was on the wane. Even so, they still met often.

These sources of advice were supplemented in Truman's administration by a number of soldiers who, by virtue of their rank, had access to the President. Contrary to what is often assumed, these military men were mostly more tolerant in their judgements about the Russians than their civilian colleagues. Many of their ideas reached Truman as the recommendations of the Chiefs of Staff. There was also 'SWNCC' – a committee bringing together officials of the departments of State, War and Navy: a foretaste, on a simpler scale, of the National Security Council.[75] In addition, certain officers saw and influenced Truman privately. First among these was General Marshall, sixty-five in 1945, an able officer, who had managed the transformation of America's tiny army of 140,000 in 1939 into the great well-equipped world one of eight million in 1945. He had had a long, solid, and successful career. He came from what a biographer calls 'a fairly well-to-do family' from Uniontown, Pennsylvania. His 'extraordinary sense of the requirements of global war', and of the logistics of all the services, as of his sense of the relative importance of the different theatres of war, had made him indispensable in wartime Washington.[76] His father had made a modest fortune in coal and was connected with the Marshalls of Virginia, a family which had given a Chief Justice to the nation. The only shortcoming of Marshall – that he had no political sense – was to presidents an advantage. Marshall hated political life. That had been a weakness when, from the time of Roosevelt's return to Washington after the conference at Yalta and his death, Marshall was in virtual control of United States' policy in Europe because of being Chief of Staff. So, when General Eisenhower sent his report, in late March 1945, that 'Berlin itself is no longer a particularly important objective', and entered without authorisation into direct telegraphic communications with Stalin on the matter, Marshall had no hesitation in approving; 'the battle of Germany is now at a point where it is up to the field commander to judge the measures which should be taken'. Marshall and his colleagues, the Chiefs of Staff, anyway considered Eisenhower's strategic concept sound.[77] This angered Churchill as well as disappointing Montgomery, who had hoped to capture Berlin, with his 21st Army Group. Marshall did not see any important psychological consequences in a Western liberation of Berlin. Marshall telegraphed Eisenhower on April 28, 1945: 'I would be loath to hazard American lives for purely political purposes'.[78] They would both have benefited from reading Lenin, who wrote: 'The philistine does not understand that war is a continuation of politics'; and 'to neglect the demands of politics for purely strategic interests is fraught with dangerous consequences'.[79]

Truman considered Marshall 'deeply steeped in democracy'. That meant no more than that he knew that Marshall accepted the principle of civilian supremacy over the military. By later 1945, Marshall was the President's choice to succeed Byrnes as Secretary of State. Truman had known Marshall when on the Senate Investigating Committee on defence expenditure and had, at least once, referred to him as 'the greatest living American'[80] in 1943: a comment which could scarcely have pleased Roosevelt.

Marshall was sent by Truman in late 1945 to try and solve a critical political crisis in China: a strange choice since it gave great political authority to a man who, for all his virtues, did not know the first rule of Clausewitz that war was an extension of politics by 'other means'.

Marshall's great quality was calmness in crisis, a characteristic first noticed by General Pershing, whose protégé he had become, during the dark days in France in 1918 (for years, Marshall was Pershing's friend and correspondent: he had even organised Pershing's funeral in 1939, a feat performed too early since Pershing would live on to 1948). Marshall's personality escapes his biographers. But those who knew him all recognised his charm: even his 'majesty'.[81] Great or no, he was in 1945 'more universally admired in the United States than any other individual, and . . . regarded as a figure of such unimpeachable impartiality, integrity, efficiency and ancient American virtue as to be almost beyond criticism'.[82] His acceptance in 1943 of the nomination of General Eisenhower to the post of Supreme Allied Commander in Europe, which he himself dearly wanted, was a stoic gesture worthy of his great reputation.

General Eisenhower, who was eventually Marshall's successor as Chief of Staff, and victor of the Western front in 1945, appeared to an acute observer to be 'one of the least profound men . . . one of the most pleasantly superficial men of great reputation and achievements I think I have ever listened to'.[83] He seemed as unpolitical as was Marshall. He had described the civilians hovering round his headquarters in Britain as 'locusts' as early as 1942[84] and, in 1945, he apparently believed that, by a concession here, and a compromise there, the United States and Russia could establish, for good and all, those friendly relations which he described as so very desirable in his address to Congress on November 17, 1945.[85] In May of that year, he considered that the American (and British) relationship with Russia was at the same stage of 'arm's length dealing' that had marked the early contacts between Britain and America 'when we first got into the war'.[86] But by then he had been shaken by the vision of the concentration camps – not the extermination camps in Poland – at Ohrdruf-Nord and Buchenwald which he had seen for himself in April 1945: 'The things I saw beggar description', he wrote to his wife, 'I never dreamed that such cruelty, bestiality and savagery could really exist in this world'.[87] The fact that the perpetrators were Germans meant that some could have been remote cousins of the Eisenhowers, who left the Rhineland in the Thirty Years War for Switzerland. The reflection must have been disturbing.

Eisenhower was on bad personal terms with his deputy, the British general Montgomery: 'Ike would not have gone out of his way by 1945 to offer any chance of glory to "Monty"'.[88] But the chief reason why 'Ike' did not wish to capture Berlin was apparently the influence of the commander of his 12th Army Group, General Bradley, who not only was also naively nonpolitical but wanted to end the war leading a thrust to Leipzig.[89] Also 'Ike' wanted to work with the Russians, not compete with them. He believed that co-operation was possible'.[90] His enthusiastic reception in Moscow at the victory celebrations in May 1945 confirmed him in these views. In the latter part of that year his drinking comradeship with Marshal Zhukov suggested to him that the Soviet Union might become a military dictatorship under that officer.[91] When he left Germany, in November 1945, to succeed Marshall as Chief of Staff in Washington, he exchanged letters with Zhukov which were fulsome: 'I truly feel that, if the same type of association that you and I have experienced could be established, and maintained, between large numbers of Soviet and American personnel, we would do much in promoting mutual understanding, confidence and faith between our two peoples. I know that, during the entire period, my own admiration, respect and affection for the Red Army and its great leaders and for the Russian people, all the way up to the Generalissimo himself, considerably increased'. Others wrote like this. Eisenhower apparently believed it.[92] Eisenhower, incidentally, like Leahy, had been against the use of the atom bomb in 1945; and his diary shows that he soon began to think for himself about politics – perhaps because he had already begun to be mentioned as a possible (Democratic) candidate for the Presidency in 1948.

There is an ambiguity in these things: while Marshall and Eisenhower were insisting that they had nothing to do with politics, and were recognising themselves to be bound by civilians' decisions, diplomatists such as Grew admitted that political decisions had sometimes to be made in the light of military reasons; thus, in a memorandum to Truman of May 5, recommending that the American armies go to the River Moldau in Czechoslovakia (to gain 'a strong bargaining position with the Russians'), Grew said that he realised 'that the decisions will no doubt have to be based primarily upon military considerations'.[93]

Apart from General Patton, who considered Russians 'a

scurvy race, Mongolian and permanently drunk',[94] no United States general took in 1945 a view very different from Eisenhower's. Thus General Lucius Clay who became, after Eisenhower, the United States commander in Germany, thought to begin with that there was 'no reason why quadripartite governments should not succeed'.[95] His colleague in Austria, General Mark Clark, was still in 1946 'confident' that he 'would be able to get along with them even though others failed'. As a result of negotiating with Russia in, or over, Austria, he later became one of the most convinced that 'the Communist enemy is a voracious beast. The more he is given, the hungrier he becomes'. But that was later.[96]

There had been, admittedly, by this time, many official papers about future United States' policy towards the Soviet Union. As early as February 1945, General Deane, head of the United States Military Mission in Moscow, had argued that co-operation with Russia should cease and that the United States should wait till the Russians 'came to us'.[97] A JCS paper about the same time, on the other hand, suggested that Soviet concerns for security were legitimate, being induced by 'fear of capitalist encirclement'. A further paper, *US Post-War Military Policy*, finished in August, argued blandly that the peace which all desired depended upon continuing co-operation between the wartime allies, especially the United States and Russia.


There were in 1946 two men who had once been Secretary of State and who were still influential: Cordell Hull, Roosevelt's Secretary of State from 1933 to 1944; and Edward Stettinius, Byrnes's immediate predecessor. Of these two, the first was far the more important since Hull was still, even more than Marshall, 'to the average American, the most distinguished living embodiment of traditional American virtues'. In the long years of his office, he left the impression that it was only his wise and moderating influence that had acted as any kind of break on the 'impulsive extravagances of the New Deal'. He was listened to with almost as much attention as that accorded to Roosevelt. His beliefs, however, were confined to a support

of the principles of free trade. His credulity both before and
during the conference of foreign ministers in Moscow in 1943
indicates an ignorance of Communist behaviour difficult to relate
to his reputation.[98] In retirement, he had little to say. Roosevelt
had seen in Hull a guarantee of keeping conservative opinion in
the Senate in favour of post-war internationalism instead of the
isolationism of 1919. Hull who had retired because of ill-health
retained a store of experience which, however, he now seldom
drew upon.

Edward Stettinius, before 1941 a successful businessman at
General Motors and United States Steel, had ceased to be
Secretary of State soon after President Truman took over.
But, as Ambassador to the United Nations, this handsome and
prematurely white-haired man was in touch with policy. Still
young (he had been only forty-four when he became Secretary
of State in 1944), with a father who had been a partner in
Morgan's as well as Assistant Secretary of War in 1917–18,
energetic, a rich 'wonder boy', protégé of Roosevelt's friend,
Harry Hopkins, successor to Welles as Under Secretary of
State, always smiling, very 'good with people', 'the exemplar of
the glad-handing, back-slapping vigorous American executive',
Stettinius, at this most critical period of United States foreign
policy in history, was scarcely well prepared.[99] The Latin Americans called him 'the teeth' (*los dientes*) because they came to
know his smile too well. Still, Stettinius believed in the United
Nations; he created an easy atmosphere in a previously staid
department;[100] he thought the United States' failure to join the
League of Nations had been a 'blot on our record';[101] and he had
done much to ensure the conclusion of the Charter of the United
Nations. He was convinced that, 'with good will, understanding
and tolerance we could find a solution' to almost any problem.
British officials considered 'Ed . . . completely inexperienced
. . . and very superficial',[102] and Stettinius certainly returned
from Yalta talking of 'every evidence . . . of the Russian desire
to cooperate along all lines with the United States'.[103] 'A decent
man of considerable innocence', wrote 'Chip' Bohlen;[104] while
another, younger, diplomatist, Charles Yost, spoke of him as 'a
great conciliator who would never admit that a difference was

irreconcilable'.[105] To George Ball, who had worked with him when he was administrator of Lend Lease, Stettinius always 'wanted things to look right, no matter how much disarray might lie beneath the surface'.[106] As representative at the United Nations, Stettinius, who had planned the Conference at San Francisco, found it difficult to impose his personality even on his own delegation. More fitted for business than for politics, he would soon resign altogether. In his diaries, he explained that Roosevelt had told him that the reason he had not appointed Byrnes was that he was 'not sure that he and I could act harmoniously as a team'. 'In other words, Jimmy might question who was the boss?' said Stettinius. 'That's exactly it', said FDR.[107]

Yet at the Department of State Stettinius made good appointments. Acheson, Nelson Rockefeller, William Clayton, Julius Holmes, and Archibald MacLeish, his five contrasting nominations for Assistant Secretaryships, were remembered long after he had died.[108] It would be unkind to conclude that the only other contribution which he had made to the Department was the installation of telephones of different hues on the desks of his officials; though he did make a lot of use of the telephone (Cordell Hull's interest in innovations had been limited to the central heating). He had tried in other ways to modernise the Department, but had failed, so he would later say, because of the 'reactionaries' who opposed him.[109] Truman himself gave a different answer: 'Never an idea, new or old' and 'as dumb as they come'.[110]

Henry Wallace, the Secretary of Commerce, often pronounced in those days on foreign policy. As Roosevelt's successful first Secretary for Agriculture, and then Vice President from 1941 to 1945, he would have liked to have been Vice President in 1945 instead of Truman. He would have then been President. In international affairs, he too was an innocent man. It is easy to make fun of him. Dwight Macdonald described Wallace as 'living in a land of perpetual fogs caused by the warm wind of the liberal Gulf Stream coming into contact with the Soviet glacis'.[111] He was saddled with the remark that 'half in fun', he had said that 'the object of this war' was to ensure that everybody in the world has the privilege of drinking a 'quart of milk a day'. He clearly believed that the dissolution of the Comintern had meant the abandonment of revolutionary imperialism. But so did many. He had a veritable obsession about the danger of American diplomacy being dragged in to support Britain and her, as he saw it, crumbling empire. He despised the British upper classes and distrusted Churchill, as having been an evil influence on Roosevelt.

When he visited Russia in 1944 he was introduced to S. A. Goglidze, one of Beria's cronies, a secret police chief with innumerable crimes behind him: Wallace thought him 'a very fine man, very efficient, gentle and understanding with people'.[112] Wallace had a number of seedy associates who may even have been Soviet agents,[113] and was given to sweeping assertions: for example, that the presence of four military men on the proposed Atomic Energy Executive Committee would lead to military dictatorship.* All the same, he did admit that, if 'the Russians had the atom bomb, they would not have the scruples about dropping it that we would have'.[114] He had the advantage of having served Roosevelt as his personal representative when Vice President in 1941 on the mixed scientific and military committee which was first concerned with the decision to go ahead with nuclear bombs.[115] The son and grandson of farmers, he believed that those who worked on the land were the special agents of the Lord on earth. He like others knew 'we failed in our job after World War I . . . But by our very errors, we learned much'. He thought that, after 1945, this knowledge could be put to build a world 'economically, politically and spiritually sound'. His rousing speeches in the war did inspire Americans to believe that they could build 'the Century of the Common Man'. He had been the first member of Roosevelt's administration to state openly, in April 1941, at the Foreign Policy Association, his support for 'an international order sufficiently strong to prevent the rise of aggressor nations'.[116] Of Ulster Scottish origins (his great-grandfather was an immigrant), Wallace's judgements were often shrewd and he had the useful

* See below, page 626.

gift of remaining on good terms with those whose views he disliked.

Another Cabinet member who concerned himself with foreign policy was the Secretary for the Treasury, Fred Vinson, though he did so less than his predecessor, Henry Morgenthau, Junior, dismissed by Truman in July 1945. Vinson was an intimate of Truman's and Byrnes's and owed his appointment to that: he had succeeded Byrnes as Director of Mobilisation in April 1945. On January 22, 1946, Vinson had revived the question of a loan to the Soviet Union for reconstruction. Vinson had suggested that the loan should be granted in return for concessions. But he did not specify what those were.* Vinson seemed genuinely perplexed as to why the Russians were not more co-operative about the International Tariff Conference at Bretton Woods.† Within the Treasury, the senior official Harry Dexter White was less influential with Vinson than he had been with Morgenthau. He might be writing, in November 1945, that 'the only task that has any real value' was 'to devise the means whereby continued peace and friendly relations can be assured between the United States and Russia'.[117] But he no longer counted as a major influence. Indeed, by early 1946, White was being watched by the FBI.

The most powerful member of the Cabinet concerned with international questions was James Forrestal, a 'restless, brooding man',[118] who had been Secretary of the Navy since 1944. He had 'a quiet, animal quality about his apparently physical perfection', the carriage which films gave 'to better gangsters, swift, easy, with the suggestion of possible violence'.[119] His 'hard-nosed' forthright manner was what Truman admired. It was the reason for his success with the President. Forrestal had been President of Dillon Read, the stockbrokers of New York, till, to the outrage of New Dealers, he entered Roosevelt's administration in 1940, first as a Special Administrative Assistant, then as Under Secretary, finally as Secretary of the Navy (1944–47). He was a good administrator and the creator of the new United States navy.[120] Like Kennan, he was a product of

* See below, Chapter Seventeen.
† See below, page 251.

Princeton, 'a boxer, a wide and serious reader', who would visit General Eisenhower in 1945 to counsel alertness in dealing with Russia: 'be courteous and friendly in the effort to develop a satisfactory *modus vivendi*; but never believe that we have changed their basic purpose, which is to destroy representative government'.[121] It had been Forrestal who, at an early meeting of senior advisers with Truman, had argued that 'if the Russians were going to pursue a rigid course, it would be better to force a showdown now, not later'.[122] In May 1945, Forrestal was already thinking in terms of balances of power and calculations of the threat which had not troubled the minds of many Americans during the war.[123] In June 1945, he told a dinner table in Washington that 'it was not inconceivable that the real reactionaries in world politics would be those who now call themselves revolutionaries, because the dynamics of their philosophy all tended towards the concentration of power in the state'.[124] In the autumn of that year he commissioned a special study of relations with Russia from Professor Edward Willett of Smith College, who, in January 1946, concluded that the Russian leaders were committed to a 'global, violent proletarian revolution', which meant that violence between the United States and Russia 'would seem to be inevitable'.[125] Forrestal, a Roman Catholic, sometimes seemed as worried about his own plans for the unification of all the armed services as he was about Russia. In 1946, he was among the most powerful voices in American domestic politics because he saw things clearly and did not entertain doubts.

Several other influential politicians had strong views on the international situation. The Republican candidate in the presidential election of 1944, Thomas Dewey, was not one of these. His early opposition to the United Nations during that election had not struck a popular note. His change of front in October 1944 on that matter had also made him enemies. His attempts to defend the wartime alliance with Russia but, at the same time, to attack the 'Pagan philosophy' of Communism in the United States were not notably effective.[126] In 1946 he was inactive. More important was the Chairman of the Senate's Committee on Foreign Relations, Senator Tom Connally of Texas, quick-tempered, always in a frock coat of old fashioned cut, he appeared a typical southern senator. But he was a 'Wilsonian'. He, like Henry Wallace, had believed in the significance of the abolition of the Comintern in 1943 and had said: 'Russians for years have been changing their economy, and approaching the abandonment of Communism, and the whole Western world will be gratified at the happy climax of their efforts'.[127] His Republican colleague, Senator Vandenberg of Michigan, was the most powerful member of the Senate in those days. He was the archetype of the old Republican isolationist, for whom George Washington's warnings against 'entangling alliances' were second nature. He was charming but pompous, vain and ambitious (to be President, in 1948). He spoke and wrote very well, if often rhetorically, was clear-headed, determined and not too proud to change his mind if necessary.[128] As Dean Acheson said in his memoirs, on those occasions Vandenberg's method was to 'enact publicly his conversion to a proposal, his change of attitude, . . . [as] . . . a kind of political transubstantiation. His method was to go through a period of public doubt and scepticism; then find a comparatively minor flaw . . . pounce on it and make much of it, in due course propose a change, always the "Vandenberg amendment"'.[129] The son of a harness-maker ruined in the crash of 1893, he had made his way to the Senate by means of journalism, editing the *Grand Rapids Herald*. Until 1941, he had believed that the Pacific and the Atlantic were 'moats' which protected the United States from foreign wars. But he had already realised, from observing the conduct of Neville Chamberlain in the 1930s, that, as he put it, appeasement of enemies can turn into 'surrender on the instalment plan' and that the United States in the end could live without trouble only by creating a 'free world of free men'.[130]

Vandenberg saw that 'the United States obviously must be a far greater international co-operator after the war than ever before'.[131] He supported the idea of a United Nations Organisation. But he was suspicious of Roosevelt's methods, had tried to present General MacArthur* as Republican candidate in 1944,

* See below, page 587.

and proposed to Dewey that the Republicans should incorporate in their platform 'the language of the Atlantic Charter, since it was there that Roosevelt was deserting all those Americans who hailed from Poland and the Baltic States'.[132] Vandenberg was pointing to the danger from Russia as early as January 1945: was Stalin in earnest about setting up a workable international security organisation, with justice for all? Or was he out to grab whatever he could for Russia, and try to use the security organisation to protect the spoils?[133] His speech of January 10, 1945 had seemed a turning point in American foreign policy. In it the Senator announced 'we can never again – regardless of collaborations – allow our national defence to deteriorate to anything like the point of impotence'. Given aviation, and recalling Pearl Harbor, 'our oceans have ceased to be moats which automatically protect our ramparts'. The Senator added that the principles behind the Atlantic Charter (Roosevelt had explained that neither he nor Churchill had actually signed that document) could not now be dismissed as 'a mere nautical nimbus', for 'they march with our armies. They sail with our fleets. They fly with our eagles. They sleep with our martyred dead'.[134]

Vandenberg was asked by Roosevelt to go to the Conference of the United Nations at San Francisco as a United States representative. This was a concession to a legislative role in foreign policy which many senators thought should have been made long before. From then on, his mind was made up that 'we should stand our ground against those Russian demands and quit appeasing Stalin and Molotov'.[135] But he avoided precise suggestions as to how that should be done. Vandenberg played as large a part as any in deciding the details of the Charter and subsequently involved himself in the domestic side of nuclear politics. He believed in late 1945 that peace was possible only 'if Russia is made to understand that we can't be pushed around'.[136] In a speech on November 15, 1945, he used the phrase already put into circulation by Churchill in private that an 'iron curtain of secrecy' divided the Russians from the West.* But at that time he was also perturbed at the lack of

* See below, page 699.

consultation, as he thought it, by the executive with the legislative branch, and, like several of his colleagues, was against Byrnes's approach in Moscow to nuclear energy; it seemed a 'give-away'. In January 1946, Vandenberg went to London for the first session of the United Nations General Assembly, partly because he was doubtful whether Byrnes 'could face up to the Russians'.[139]

Vandenberg aspired to, and indeed had almost achieved, a supervisory role in the foreign policy of the United States: the legislature's watchdog over the executive. Byrnes also perhaps knew, from the record of the as yet secret hearings of the Senate Foreign Relations Committee, that Vandenberg must be fully informed of the terrible tangle into which Byrnes had become enmeshed over the concession at Yalta of the Kuriles to Russia,* and therefore might be able to blackmail him.[140]

Other one-time isolationists in the United States were also transforming themselves into ardent opponents of Russia. Senators Burton Wheeler of Montana and James Eastland of Mississippi, for example, had made powerful speeches in the last weeks of 1945. For the first, Russian control of East Europe derived from Western appeasement;[141] for Eastland, as for others, the Russians had embarked on the same road of conquest as that trodden by Hitler.[142] Wheeler's change of position was as significant as Vandenberg's, for he had been the man who had in 1940 attacked Lend Lease as likely to 'plow under every fourth American boy' and before that had led the campaign against Roosevelt's Supreme Court reorganisation bill. The movement known as 'America First' now took a different line. Senator Edwin Johnson thus believed that the possession of 'plenty of atomic bombs' enabled the United States to outlaw wars of aggression.[143] These men were eloquent. But again none of them suggested how their principles could be turned into politics.

Not all Republicans were consistent hardliners. Few were consistent. Thus, John Foster Dulles, the high-minded Wilsonian lawyer who had been grooming himself for years to be Republican

---

* See below, page 572.

Secretary of State, in the tradition of his uncle (Robert Lansing) and his grandfather (John Foster), wrote in early 1945 that both the United States and the USSR had reason to distrust one another. 'The very fact that millions of Americans share your view that we should distrust the Russians,' he wrote to an editor of *Reader's Digest*, 'is, I think, a reason why Russia should distrust us'.[144] Dulles genuinely believed in a universal order laid down by the United States and, at the San Francisco Conference, opposed anything like a great power consortium. As Chairman of the Federal Council of Churches of Christ in America's *Commission to Study the Basis for a Just and Durable Peace*, he had given his name to some inspiring long-term goals; and in 1944 he had influenced Governor Dewey to that end. By September 1945, however, he had become convinced of Soviet ill-will. Byrnes had invited him to the London conference. Dulles believed that he had restrained Byrnes from making dangerous compromises with Molotov on the Balkan treaties.[145] Even so, he was still arguing in October that Russia feared encirclement by the United States.[146] In early 1946, Dulles no longer entertained such tolerance; at a lunch in March 1946, for example, he would be so gloomy about relations with the Russians that all who were with him left the table in a state of depression 'much more extreme than when they sat down'.[147]

A different kind of influence on Truman's administration was that wielded by the Press. That medium was both less excitable and less all-demanding than the television companies which later succeeded it in its control over the American imagination. Rational journalists, such as James Reston, Arthur Krock, and Walter Lippmann, were widely listened to. Lippmann, a long time internationalist, had been partly instrumental in persuading Vandenberg to abandon isolationism. His immensely successful book *US Foreign Policy: Shield of the Republic* in 1943 had stated a bleak argument in favour of permanent alliances, permanent display of power, permanent responsibilities. In its successor, in the middle of 1945, however, Lippmann, characteristically had begun to question whether American internationalism might not lead to imperialism. He was also extraordinarily incensed by the way that the United States had brought Argentina, then under military rule, into the United Nations. Lippmann seems for a time even to have believed (with Stalin) that the behaviour of Russia was 'largely the fault of the naughtily provocative British Lion'[148] and that there might be a deeper conflict of interest between the British and the Russians than there was between the Americans and the Russians.[149] In May 1945, he had put forward the curious view that the death of FDR had robbed the United States of the only man who could maintain a position independent of both Britain and Russia and, therefore, could have been a 'unifying power'.[150] Despite that view, or perhaps because of it, Secretary of State Byrnes had offered Lippmann the task of manager of 'information and propaganda' in the State Department. He refused. He wrote several articles in 1945 and early 1946 warning of the difficulties of exercising world power well. In November, he had talked of the United States as 'drifting towards catastrophe'.[151] He defended Byrnes against those who criticised the 'accord of Moscow'. Still, he remained in close touch with the men who made decisions and probably had as much influence on events as most officials.[152] He was to spend much of the rest of his life suggesting ways whereby democracy and communism could find 'a way of living together' – never to his satisfaction.[153]

Though Hanson Baldwin had, in 1942, written in the *New York Times* that the only argument for a large United States army, after the war, was the need to prevent the spread of Russia and Communism in Europe,[154] friends of the Soviet Union were active in the press. For example, Averell Harriman met the Press during the Conference of San Francisco. His realism about Russia 'was greeted with dismay by the audience' – Lippmann and Raymond Gram Swing were so angry at his opinions that they left the room.[155] For many years the *New York Times* correspondent in Moscow, Walter Duranty, had given the best interpretation of all Soviet actions. But the enemies of the Communists were also active in print. In late 1944, for example, Whittaker Chambers and Willi Schlamm, two ex-Communists, became foreign news editors of *Time* and *Fortune* magazines respectively. Both journals thenceforth took strong anti-Soviet positions. That would have been less surprising had the event not followed a period characterised by the occasion when another publication belonging to Henry Luce, *Life*, had, the previous year, in a famous article, presented the argument that the Russians were 'one hell of a people . . . [who] . . . to a remarkable degree . . . look like Americans, dress like Americans and think like Americans' even if 'The process of integrating our future with the USSR is bound to be a slow one'. Americans 'should not get too excited' about the fact that the Russians lived 'under a system of tight, state-controlled information . . . if the Soviet leaders tell us that the control of information was necessary to get this job done, we can afford to take their word for it' for the time being.[156] Such changes of front in these years were frequent. Few had consistently adopted the realistic tones of the best historian of the Russian Revolution, W. H. Chamberlin, who, during the late war and afterwards, deplored efforts to 'prettify Stalin, whose homicide record is even longer than Hitler's' and who argued that United States policy should be 'frank and candid, based on American national interests and not on insisting on her allies' moral excellence'.[157]

There was one element of American opinion which remained in 1946, as in 1941 or 1943, uncompromising in its view of the Soviet Union. That was the hierarchy of the Catholic Church. Monsignor Fulton Sheen, for example, persistently argued that Communism was an Asiatic form of Fascism. The editor of *Catholic World*, Father James Gillis, wrote in late 1944 that the 'greatest potential menace to permanent peace' was Soviet Russia. Fascism had never been as dangerous as Communism. Archbishops Edward Mooney, Stritch and Spellman wrote to Roosevelt in December 1944 that Stalin had been trained in 'the school of revolutionaries who plot the overthrow of all governments of the world'.[158] William Bullitt, Ambassador to Russia in the thirties before Davies, an intelligent and passionate man whose hatreds ruined his virtues, expressed those views in private to Roosevelt and in print, later, in for example, *Life*.* His article, 'The World from Rome', of September 1944, was a

---

* See below, pages 257–8.

long denunciation of American policy in aiding Stalin without guarantees; for 'Rome again sees approaching from the East a new wave of conquerors'.[159]

Curiously enough, it was 'business opinion' which had been most impressed by the Russians during the war. Innocent of politics, and inexperienced in propaganda, Donald Nelson, director of the War Production Board, but previously Vice President of Sears Roebuck, considered 'that there is, in some ways, more free enterprise in Russia than here in the United States'.[160]

One personality which had characterised Roosevelt's policies was missing in the age of Truman. That was Harry Hopkins, the devoted controversial social worker and ex-Secretary of Commerce who acted as assistant to the late President. He was ill, as Roosevelt had seemed, at Yalta. He went to Moscow on Truman's request in the summer of 1945 but that was all. He died at the end of January 1946, universally regretted at the time, soon to be almost as universally excoriated. It had been Hopkins whom Roosevelt had used to 'act as a burr under the saddle – and get things moving' so far as aid to Russia had been concerned in 1941.[161] Now the burr was needed in another place. Hopkins's general sense had been that 'the common folks of Russia like the system which they have'.[162] His remarks about Stalin and Russia in the middle of the war now sound vain and wrong: 'you will find us lining up with the Russians', he told Churchill's doctor en route to Tehran.[163] Hopkins's judgement after Yalta that here was 'the dawn of the new day we had all been praying for' was soon to sound embarrassing: so, too, increasingly, was his observation that 'the Russians had proved that they could be reasonable and foreseeing and there wasn't any doubt in the minds of the President or any of us that we could live with them, and get along with them, peacefully, for as far into the future as any of us could imagine'.[164] His qualification – that we could not foretell what the results would be if anything should happen to Stalin – was not prescient.

Special difficulties affected the small Communist Party of the United States (as they did that of Britain).[165] The Party had been constructed in the 1920s by men and women most of whom had come to the United States in the early years of the century from the Jewish area of Western Russia. In the 1930s, the Communists gathered to their cause a vast number of well-intentioned liberals, either as Party members or sympathisers, for whom Roosevelt's policies were inadequate. Harry Hopkins told Molotov in 1942 that this Party was composed of 'disgruntled, frustrated, ineffectual and vociferous people – including a comparatively high proportion of distinctly unsympathetic Jews'.[166] All the same, the American communists were then at their most influential, with nearly 100,000 members and many well-established Party supporters in the armed services and the OSS.

The leading American Communist was then Earl Browder, as American as Thorez was French, an accountant from Kansas, a Socialist conscientious objector in 1917 who confessed to having used three false passports since 1921. He had run for President in 1940 from a prison cell. Browder had led the Communists out of the Comintern for tactical reasons in 1940. He soon asserted himself as the spokesman for what sounded like a broadly democratic coalition, Communism which seemed both painful and inexplicable to many old hands. After Tehran, Browder had remarked, 'if J. P. Morgan supports' the Soviet–United States alliance, 'I as a communist am prepared to shake his hand'.[167] The CPUSA was formally dissolved in 1944. Instead there was formed a 'Communist Political Association of the United States', whose members were urged by Browder to 'co-operate' with 'either of the two existing great political parties'. The party had stood in the war for the postponement of agitation for civil rights, and seemed to be against the idea of 'class struggle and for Wall Street'.[168]

In April 1945, however, the French Communist leader, Jacques Duclos, delegated presumably by Moscow, denounced Browder as an 'opportunist and liquidator' in the columns of *Cahiers de Communisme*. Duclos argued that Browder had sown 'dangerous opportunist illusions' in advocating the possibility of class peace in the United States.[169] In July 1945, Browder was condemned for the crime of 'Browderism', and was succeeded as new national chairman of the party by the much older W. Z. Foster (who also had been his predecessor). In late February 1946 he would even be expelled from the Party as a 'social imperialist'.[170]

The tiny organisation which he left behind had lost half its members since 1944. Communists entertained expectations of industrial chaos, and vast unemployment, after demobilisation. The optimistic outlook of American industrialists about favourable commercial opportunities had not been shared by the Kremlin.[171] The disappearance of Browder was interpreted as being the local manifestation of the end of a period of 'collaborationism'.[172]

As well as having to contemplate a world foreign policy, without experience, the United States was hampered by having at the time no serious international centralised intelligence service. Before the war the Presidents of the United States relied on sources of information which 'were not a great deal better than those of the *New York Times* . . . and in some respects shockingly inaccurate'.[173] The administration, in 1945, expected to be dependent on its military and naval intelligence services, which did not venture far into those fields of secret intelligence pursued by allies such as Britain and France, much less Soviet Russia. The war had, admittedly, seen the spectacular development of communications intelligence (COMINT) jointly operated by the departments of War and Navy.* This service, Army Security Agency (ASA), despite its great success, was being run down in 1945. But in a truncated form it did survive and had established working arrangements, illegally it would seem, with the main telegraph companies.[174] It seems not to have been reading Soviet codes in 1945–46. The FBI concerned itself, as was traditional, with Latin America, but its Director made no attempt to pass on the information so gathered to those interested in international problems. Edgar Hoover, its long-

* Itself closely collaborating with the British similar service – see pages 314–5.

serving director, did not believe in giving other agencies any information and disliked the Department of State.

The coming of the European crisis in 1940 had altered some traditional policies. Roosevelt had allowed the FBI to tap the telephones, and open the letters, of those suspected of damaging the nation's security. In May 1940, he had declared 'we know of new methods of attack: the Trojan Horse, the Fifth Column, that betrays a nation unprepared for treachery. Spies, saboteurs, and traitors are the actors in this new strategy'. He spoke of 'dissemination of discord'; of groups encouraged to 'exploit prejudices through false slogans and emotional appeals'.[175] In 1942 he appointed a mercurial hero of the First World War and would-be Republican politician, William J. Donovan, grandson of an Irish immigrant, to set up the 'Office of Strategic Services' (OSS), a special intelligence service on the model of Britain's, with capacity for covert activities as well as the gathering of intelligence*.[176]

The achievements of this famous, ultimately large, organisation were many, complicated and sometimes glorious.[177] But Donovan, a friend of Roosevelt's, could not survive in Truman's Washington. He had suggested to Roosevelt a plan for a central intelligence agency which would report direct to presidents: the plan leaked to an outraged Press. He was dismissed by Truman, on September 20, 1945. Truman disliked Donovan personally and, at that time, did not want a national secret service. He found it irritating that reports reached him 'on the same subject at different times from the various departments, and these reports often conflicted'[178] (Truman also closed down FDR's Communications Room). What remained of Donovan's network of 20,000 agents, their files and their activities, mostly passed either to the Navy or War departments, or into the vacuum of civilian life or to a small new research activities section of the Department of State. This was directed by Colonel Alfred McCormack, Princeton '21, who had once been in the War

* In a presentation to the British War Cabinet on June 16, 1942 Donovan described his OSS as 'corresponding approximately to the British SIS and SOE'.[179]

Department (when his somewhat liberal approach had led him to be regarded as leader of a 'pro-Communist group' in the intelligence division of the General Staff).[180]* A few people in the OSS went to a 'Strategic Services Unit' in the War Department: but its director, General Magruder, had left it by February 1946 and few specialists were left there.[181] During the war, Roosevelt had instructed his intelligence service not to study the Russians. Until late 1943, at least, this instruction seems to have been kept: thus, when the OSS established an agent close to a private secretary of the Soviet Ambassador in Washington, Litvinov, the scheme was discontinued.[182] In 1943, at the time of the conference at Quebec, OSS, as well as the Department of State, began seriously to question Russia's long-term motives. The OSS presented several studies on Russia.[183] There was one entitled *Strategy and Policy: Can America and Russia Cooperate?* This included, among US post-war aims, 'to prevent the domination of Europe in the future by any single power (such as the Soviet Union); or by any group of powers in which we do not have a strong influence'.[184] In September 1943, the OSS briefed a civilian engineering contractor, R. E. McCurdy of Badger and Sons, as to what to try to see in Russia and how to communicate. Some OSS men were working on the Russia-China border, nominally for geological surveys. An OSS representative was in Russia officially from December 1943; and exchange of information about the Germans was agreed between them and the NKVD. But although some information was passed by the OSS to Russia – including German intelligence about Russian cyphers – it does not seem as if much analysis of, much less espionage in, the Soviet Union occurred.[185] An intelligence report entitled 'Russia's position', for instance, apparently of value to Harry Hopkins in 1943, suggested that it was essential to develop and maintain the most friendly relations with Russia after the war because 'without doubt she will dominate Europe on the defeat of the Axis'.[186] It was only when the Russians refused to help

* McCormack himself was apparently tactless, not 'soft on Communism'. Even so, the House Appropriations Committee, in April 1946, rejected finance to McCormack's unit. McCormack resigned on April 23, 1946.

the Polish Home Army in Warsaw, in September 1944, that Donovan embarked on any serious operations in respect of Russia. Even these were modest and not carried through.[187]

The OSS had had, however, some undertakings in parts of Europe controlled by Russia in the winter of 1944–45. In the spring of 1945, for example, they combined with the British to take photographs from the air of Russian-occupied Germany and much of Austria, Yugoslavia, Albania and Bulgaria.[188] One of Donovan's officials, Frank Wisner, was busy reporting on the activities of Romanian Communism in September 1944 and, between then and March 1945, the old Romanian security service, about to be dismantled by the Communists, passed on all it knew of Soviet activities in the Balkans to another OSS officer, Major Bishop.[189] Other OSS men were busy in other Balkan countries. Even so, in the summer of 1945, the OSS was still collaborating with the NKVD over matters arising from German espionage against Russia and, on July 28, Donovan was still exchanging with his 'Soviet counterparts' information about such esoteric matters as Hitler's dentist's report.[190]

Some Americans were far-sighted. Thus Allen Dulles, director of OSS in Switzerland, asked Frank Wisner in April 1945 to talk to Colonel Gehlen, the recently retired German head of *Fremde Heere Ost* (Foreign Armies East, an intelligence unit which concentrated attention on the Soviet Union), who had escaped to Allied lines on the assumption that his services might one day be useful.[191] Gehlen, a master of intelligence, subversion and deception, had played a great role in the German attack on Russia in 1941. He had always opposed the Nazi policy in the East as 'an error of the most grievous kind'.[192] Other American recruitments were less happy. They secured, for example, several officers of Hitler's SS for their own intelligence services apparently exchanging their information for an immunity from prosecution for war crimes which subsequently rebounded against everyone concerned.

During the war, J. Edgar Hoover's Federal Bureau of Investigation, had sometimes concerned itself with Soviet, as well as Nazi, sabotage. But it did so tardily. Perhaps some of the phobia felt, after 1945, for Communists by Hoover derived from the recollection of earlier laxness; for example, Hoover directed one of his officials to investigate Whittaker Chambers's famous charges against Alger Hiss and others in August 1941, but no enquiry was made till May 1942 (although Hoover's informant, Adolf A. Berle, then Roosevelt's Director of Security, had spoken to Chambers about alleged Soviet agents, including Alger Hiss, as long before as September 2, 1939). In May 1944, Averell Harriman had complained, 'is there anything that can be done about the FBI? They are perfectly crazy in the way that they call certain people communists'.[193] But at that time their targets were mostly liberals such as Henry Wallace, or even Harriman himself.

This relative inactivity by the FBI was the more surprising since, in the late 1930s and beginning of the 1940s, intrigues by the Russians had been on the mind of Americans. A general of the GRU, the Soviet military intelligence, Gaik Ovakiminian, had been deported in May 1941 for trying to inspire strikes in the United States defence industry. Another agent, Jacob Golos, had been fined for failing to register as representing a foreign government. Russian assets of $39 million in the United States had been frozen. The Treasury said that they would only be released if assurances were given that they would not be used for anti-United States propaganda. When Germany attacked Russia, there were many who agreed with ex-President Hoover when he declared that aid to Russia would be a 'gargantuan jest'.

Military security was more effective than the FBI was. Although imperfect, its branch at Los Alamos became aware of the attempts by Russians or Communists to find information.[194] In early 1945 nevertheless the files of United States intelligence on Russia as such were empty. Even the most elementary facts – the siting of roads, bridges, factories and airfields – were unknown. There were no maps of Russian cities available.[195] Truman was made aware of these inadequacies by Leahy. In January 1946, Donovan had some discussions with his own staff about the future of foreign intelligence, just after he himself had left Washington. The Army and Navy put forward a scheme. With that, the idea of central intelligence was launched. George Kennan had argued forcibly, in telegrams from Moscow, that a new approach to intelligence was needed to cope simply with the question: 'what are other nations doing in the atomic energy field?'[196] Truman spoke of the need for this in his first State of the Union message, issued an 'Executive Order', on January 22. This set up a 'Central Intelligence Group', under the supervision of the Committee of the Secretaries of State, War and the Navy (SWNCC), with Admiral Leahy representing the White House and with Admiral Souers, who had done the bureaucratic negotiations, as first 'Director of Intelligence'. Truman asked these officers to 'better our foreign relations through more intensive snooping'.[197] This gave Truman a daily summary of all intelligence received at all the different departments.

In practice this new intelligence group (CIG) did not function at all well.[198] Many prominent Americans (for example, Dean Acheson and Admiral King) opposed the idea of a single agency to collect intelligence. Even Forrestal, no enemy to military efficiency, thought that 'over a long period of time such an agency might acquire' monstrous power, inconsistent 'with our ideas of government'.[199] Souers had neither much imagination, nor money, nor even many people of his own. The National Intelligence Authority sat above him, the Intelligence Advisory Board housed him, and all his staff were on temporary loan to him.[200] He had been assigned a staff of 165 people, of whom only seventy-one had joined by the time that he retired, as he had desired from the start, to New Orleans, in June 1946.[201] It was the launching of this new group under Admiral Souers, nevertheless, that led to a party at which Truman gave his guests a cloak, a dagger and a pirate's hat. Though everything was small-scale and amateurish in this organisation, it began the country on a long and controversial bureaucratic innovation.

The FBI in the winter of 1945–1946 seemed to be less sleepy than it had been during the war. It was on November 8, 1945, for example, following (and inspired by) the Canadian police's report on Guzenko, that the FBI sent to the White House accusations based on testimony from the ex-Communist Elizabeth Bentley, which, for the first time, implicated, among others, Harry Dexter White, Assistant Secretary of the Treasury.[202]

But the FBI's action, under the White House's direction, was at first muted. Bentley's evidence, being circumstantial, could not lead to prosecution. It was as if no one could bring themselves to deal with such extraordinary charges. After all, White had devised the very organisation at Bretton Woods which was the linchpin of capitalism. On February 4, a more detailed summary of White's alleged malpractices was given to the White House.[203] Truman, even so, went ahead to approve White as American Executive Director of the International Monetary Fund. After all, nothing against him had been proved, and Truman wanted to avoid cancelling a plan already sent to the Senate for approval.[204] He must have felt in dealing with this case that he was on the edge of a precipice.

In considering American attitudes to Russia, the size of the American population of Eastern European origin should be remembered. In the years 1900 to 1914, the number of Central European immigrants to the United States had never been less than 100,000 a year, and in 1914 reached 278,000 (with 35,000 Germans).[205] Immigration from Russia, which had then included the Baltic states and East Poland, was of the same dimension: between 1901 and 1914 never less than 100,000, once as high as 258,000. Roosevelt told Stalin at Tehran that there were six or seven million Americans of Polish origin.[206] It is certainly clear that in Detroit, Chicago and Buffalo there were very large Polish settlements – and those Poles might hold the balance of power in votes in Illinois, Ohio and New York State. Senator McMahon in Connecticut talked of the 'heat on the back of his neck' because of his Polish-American electorate.[207] Such judgements affected many in high places. Thus Samuel Zemurray, the President of the United Fruit Company, had been born a Bessarabian fruit pedlar;[208] while the chief of the United States signal intelligence service, William Friedman, had been born in Kishinev, in what had just again become Russian Moldavia. Leo Pasvolsky, Byrnes's special adviser on international organisation as he had been Cordell Hull's, had also been born in Russia before the turn of the century. Ely Culbertson, the bridge expert who had written a famous wartime book arguing for world federation, had been born in Romania, of a father who had extensive oil holdings in southern Russia. The list could be endlessly extended. This meant that there was an informed public opinion on these matters even if it was not always alert, if it was not always prudent, and if it was frequently less insistent than political leaders feared that it might be.

# TEN

# THE LEGACY OF ROOSEVELT

Over all Truman's advisers, associates and thoughts there lay
– fatally, for several of them – the shadow of Roosevelt, the
memory of whose charm, optimism and ebullience long survived
his death. They linger still. That great American political voice,
the first to become nationally well known through the invention
of the radio, still reassures when it is heard even on an old
record on the gramophone. Roosevelt had an instinctive grasp
of how to conduct himself successfully in domestic politics. 'He
played upon the ambitions of men as an artist would play upon
the strings of an instrument', remarked Jimmy Byrnes, who
suffered in consequence.[1] Though ingenious to the point of
near-mendacity, FDR remarkably combined this quality with
fearlessness. 'A conjuror, skilfully juggling with balls of dyna-
mite,' was Anthony Eden's judgement of him.[2] He triumphed
extraordinarily over his physical disabilities.[3] He had a genius
for improvisation.

In foreign policy, this genius also worked as well, to begin
with, as it had in domestic. In Latin America, the 'good neighbour
policy' was, indeed, almost an international equivalent of the
domestic New Deal. Roosevelt saw the significance of Hitler for
the new world before most Americans did. He realised the
importance, for the future of America as well as for that of
Europe, of keeping Britain free. The countless statements on
international matters which he made between 1939 and 1941
were a fine mixture of generosity and realism. 'If France and

England should be defeated,' he said, in November 1939, 'the United States will have to watch its step'. In June 1940, he described the isolationist dream as a delusion. Could a lone island survive in a world dominated by force? 'We too have a stake in world affairs', he said, in April of that year. He led the United States first to become 'the arsenal of democracy', then away from isolationism.

In his early days as President, he had original ideas by the score even in international affairs: 'England, France, Italy, Belgium, Holland, Poland and possibly Russia should get together and agree on a ten year disarmament programme which would look forward to doing away with all methods of warfare'. If Germany were to refuse to collaborate, a blockade might be imposed on her to which the United States would contribute.[4] His policy of 'Germany First' as a war target was neither popular nor obvious but it had been successful. In 1943, he was contemplating trying to achieve a customs union for all Europe.[5]

Still, during the last years of his majestic life, the combination of Roosevelt's characteristic methods of improvisation, his determination to avoid post-war commitments, his worsening physical condition and his weakness for procrastination lay this great man open to a hundred accusations. His interpreter thought that a 'deeper knowledge of history and a better understanding of the reaction of foreign peoples would have been useful'; not to speak of more study of the papers.[6] Kennan recalls that Roosevelt 'was one of the many who could not easily distinguish World War II from World War I' and still inaccurately pictured 'the Prussian *Junkertum* as a mainstay of Hitler's power, just as it had been . . . the mainstay of the power of the Kaiser'.[7] As to Russia, according to Harriman, FDR failed to understand that Stalin 'would not be as anxious to have our help in the post-war period as he had been during the war. He did not realise how tough-minded the Russians would be and with what determination they would stick to the long term goal of world revolution . . . [he] . . . was mostly optimistic about what he could achieve personally'.[8] He probably believed seriously that 'the sources of international brutality, wherever they exist' could 'be absolutely and finally broken down'[9] – an echo of 'the lovely world' of his Victorian childhood.[10] Roosevelt explained away his dealings with the French Admiral Darlan with a quotation from an Orthodox priest: 'My children, it is permitted you in time of great danger to walk with the devil until you have crossed the bridge'.[11] But FDR did not seem to look on Stalin as a devil comparable at least to Darlan. He hoped instead, by consistent generosity, and by restraining himself from criticising Russian actions, to convince Stalin that the United States could be trusted. Being a religious man, Roosevelt thought that atheistic Communism would not be able 'to suppress permanently the religious tradition of the Russian people'.[12] He was thus fond of telling how he had persuaded Litvinov, then the Soviet Ambassador in Washington, to accept religious freedom: 'every man in his deepest heart knows the existence of God . . . you know, Max, that your good old father and mother, good old pious Jewish people, always said their prayers. I know they must have taught you to say your prayers. Now, you may think you're an atheist . . . but, I tell you, Max, when you come to die . . . you're going to be thinking about what your mother taught you'.[13] The idea that Communism, as an ideology, might have become, for some, a metamorphosis for religion was a philosophic idea apparently beyond FDR, the master tactician. Doubtless, this radiant man found it difficult, too, to see not only that his enemies were evil and had to be defeated; but that one of his allies had at least to be faced. He did not see, and seems not to have been told by, for example, Bohlen (who knew), that for communists trust and love are mere commodities.

In addition to his incapacity for coming to grips with Communist ideology, Roosevelt's reluctance to deal in details affected policy. His 'lack of precision',[14] and his confidence in his own intuition, worked so well in domestic politics that it is understandable that he should have had the same belief in himself in international affairs. But when negotiating with another man of genius, such as Stalin, who was fitter than he was, and who clearly did master his briefs, this reluctance of Roosevelt's was a disadvantage. He never gave precise instructions to his subordinates and while some, such as Harriman, were stimulated by this, many were frustrated.[15] His insistence on a lack of formality, combined with an equal insistence on respect for him in his office as President, was perhaps not important – but his pleasure in other people's discomfiture, including that of close allies or friends, such as even Churchill, was unfortunate.[16] It might be acceptable, in the Cabinet, when Roosevelt, who always affected to look on politics as the 'great game', encouraged Hopkins to attack Ickes; or Ickes, Hopkins. But to watch Churchill and Stalin fall out at Tehran was altogether different. Was this 'a boundless faith that he could bring order out of conflict'? Or was it a capacity to enjoy himself in all circumstances?

Roosevelt's actions in some things, such as, above all, nudging the United States towards war in 1941, came close to deviousness: 'The fact that Roosevelt and Truman were substantially right in their assessment of the national interest in no way diminishes the blamefulness of the precedents that they set', Senator Fulbright wrote censoriously in 1971, the horses of a later apocalypse thundering in his ears.[17] Roosevelt thus cleverly manipulated the press over the incident of the *Greer*.[18] Even so, in 1941, there were, too, many who thought that Roosevelt's propaganda to persuade public opinion that the Nazis were more dangerous opponents of religion than Communism was unnecessary: 'Let's not pretend there's anything sweet-smelling about the "Commies"', one editorial proclaimed, 'give them guns, tanks, planes – but don't keep on saying "Call me brother"'.[19]

The late war years were thus full of ambiguities, even if they were accompanied by the military triumph of the armies of which Roosevelt was commander-in-chief. He did not concentrate his mind on the problem of atomic energy after the war and, though he had good ideas for zonal boundaries in Germany, did not press them.[20] He believed that a commitment to any specific post-war plan would generate both domestic and international controversies. But, given the way that Stalin used the Red Army, that procrastination made it more difficult to obtain satisfactory settlements later. FDR and his beloved aide, Harry Hopkins, kept the rest of those concerned with the foreign policy of the United States at arm's length. Robert Murphy, a devoted official, asked the President's Chief of Staff, Admiral Leahy, whether the State Department had agreed with Roosevelt's decision to land troops in North Africa. The Admiral explained that the Department had not been consulted: 'We decided what to do in twenty-five minutes. If we had referred this to the State Department, it would have taken twenty-five days.'[21] Robert Murphy also told the Secretary of State, Cordell Hull, himself, that the operation of the Foreign Service would be improved if its members could be told what transpired at secret conversations between Roosevelt and Stalin. To which Hull replied that his own activities, as Secretary, would have been improved if he had only known anything of what had happened at the conference at Tehran.[22] The very existence of the Communications Room in the White House, through which Roosevelt maintained touch with the war, was a secret kept from the Department of State.[23] Roosevelt acted thus since, as he once explained to Marriner Eccles, Chairman of the Federal Reserve Board, 'you should go through the experience of trying to get any changes in the thinking, policy, and action of the career diplomats and then you'd know what a real problem was'.[24] Roosevelt allowed himself illusions. He believed that he could bring Stalin into the club of world leaders which he was now hoping to found, and lead. In 1942, Roosevelt told Churchill: 'I know you will not mind my being brutally frank when I tell you that I think I can personally handle Stalin better than either the Foreign Office or my State Department. Stalin hates the guts of all your top people. He thinks he likes me better'.[25] No doubt Stalin thought Roosevelt's friendliness towards him the height of deviousness. Perhaps he in consequence stepped up his espionage to find the truth behind the innocence. Still 'I can handle Stalin' remained a frequent phrase on Roosevelt's lips.[26] In 1943, William Bullitt who had been Roosevelt's ambassador to Russia in the 1930s (and who was doubtless the only American to have been kissed by Stalin 'full on the mouth')[27] had told Roosevelt many home truths about Stalin and Russia in colourful language. But FDR became disillusioned with that passionate ex-ambassador because of his role in the ruin of Sumner Welles.

Admiral Standley, ambassador to Moscow from 1942 to 1943, had advised Roosevelt to 'treat Stalin like an adult, keep any promises we make to him but insist that he keep his promises too . . . hold out till he does'. But Standley had been dismissed to make way for Harriman when he expressed anger that 'the Russians seem to want to cover up the fact that they receive outside help'.*[28]

Roosevelt found Stalin at the conference at Tehran easy: 'he is truly representative of the heart and soul of Russia', he reported to the nation on the radio, 'and I believe we are going to get along very well with him and the Russian people – very well indeed'.[29] When asked by a reporter what Stalin was like, he replied, 'I would call him something like me – a realist'.[30] Such remarks – and how many of them there were! – need to be studied with reserve.[31] This was no doubt what Roosevelt wanted the world and Stalin to think then that he thought. Roosevelt believed, in his 'heavily forested interior',[32] that there was no point in a fuss about matters, particularly details, which he could not affect one way or another. Roosevelt was a master of loquacious ambiguity. As an actor, he was happy to play the part of the innocent. But under the 'surface impression of casual, even frivolous, superficiality,' it seems certain, as a modern scholar has written, that 'darker, more cynical but more perceptive instincts' lay hidden.[33] Even so, and despite (it is worth repeating) the presence of 'Chip' Bohlen at his side, Roosevelt did often seem to trust Stalin: he was surely talking from his heart when he told Henry Wallace in 1942 that 'The United States and Russia are young powers and . . . England is a tired old power'.[34] He was also presumably doing so when he told the American people, after Yalta, how 'at the end, on every point,

* Bullitt continued his advice in public. Thus, in a speech in Philadelphia in March 1943, Bullitt said that United States policy to Russia should be like the method used with an obstinate donkey: 'a real carrot' should be held before its nose, and 'a real club (which this country possesses) behind its tail'. After a violent article in *Life* in September 1944, the British Embassy in Washington described Bullitt as a 'victim of unrequited love for the USSR, for France and for FDR, by all of whom he was in turn scorned and against whom he . . . turned'.

unanimous agreement was reached. And more important even
. . . I may say, we achieved a unity of thought and a way of
getting along together'.[35]

Roosevelt went to the first wartime conference with Stalin,
at Tehran, with no clear arrangements for the discussions. He
avoided a good opportunity of tying Stalin to concessions over
Poland.[36] In order to please Stalin at one point, Roosevelt even
told him that the best solution for India after the war was 'reform
from the bottom, somewhat on the Soviet line'.[37] Roosevelt
allowed Stalin to accuse Churchill of harbouring a secret affection
for Germany.[38] Stalin must have come out from his discussion
with Roosevelt about the Baltic states supposing that the President's concern was to present Russian policy to the American
public in the most favourable manner, rather than to secure
literal compliance with the principles of the Atlantic Charter.[39]
Even taking into account the guile necessary for wartime diplomacy, the 'unquenchable vitality' which was such a mark of
Roosevelt in the past was undoubtedly diminishing by then under
the strain of the war, as was obvious when he gave Mikołajczyk
assurances about Polish independence which he must have
known that he could not fulfil.[40]

Even so, Roosevelt had a rational policy: to avoid arguments
with Russia on the basis of the belief that, by being well treated,
both by him and Churchill, Stalin would not only continue to fight
in the West until the end, but would participate in the East
against Japan and collaborate in his plans for a better world after
the war. That was why he wanted, as he put it in his last
message of April 11, 1945 to Churchill, to 'minimize the general
Soviet problem'.[41] He sought to the end to prevent Soviet
suspicions that the British and Americans were acting in collaboration, just as he had when in 1943 he had said: 'It would be a
terrible mistake if "UJ" thought we had ganged up on him on
military action'.[42] The United States and Britain accepted that
they could not have defeated Hitler without Russia's help, and
Russian sacrifices of men, on a large scale. Roosevelt, who had
been much affected by the First World War (which he had seen
at close range), had a horror of committing American troops to
a long war in Europe again.[43] Of course, FDR did not know that

the atom bomb, or even the threat of it, might have brought
Germany to her knees in 1945, even without Russian assistance.
But nor is it certain that he would have approved its use in
Europe.

These approaches coincided with Roosevelt's desire to impro-
vise on the spot. He fended off criticism of his Polish policy by
saying casuistically that neither he nor Churchill had themselves
really signed the Atlantic Charter. They had, of course, issued
it; and he and his government, as well as those of all his major
allies, had subscribed to the principles therein enshrined. [44]

There was still in 1945 in Roosevelt's mind the hope that the
United Nations – the name, as has been seen, was his – could
function as a guarantee of the post-war peace. It was worth
making several, at first sight, unpleasant sacrifices to achieve
that: certainly a Russian-owned railway in Manchuria; and why
not the Kurile islands?

At the conference in Tehran Roosevelt sketched out to Stalin
privately his concept of an organisation for the preservation of
peace in future. It was to be an undertaking in three tiers: first,
an assembly of all the members of the United Nations – perhaps
forty nations – which would meet at various places at regular
intervals to discuss world problems and suggest ways to resolve
them; second, an executive Committee which would consist of
the 'Big Four' plus two Europeans, one South American, one
Middle Eastern, or Far Eastern State and a British dominion.
(This would deal with non-military questions such as Health,
Agriculture and Food.) Third, there would be the 'Four policemen', the 'Big Four' alone, who would deal with any sudden
emergency, such as the Italian attack on Ethiopia in 1935. [45]

Stalin made a number of suggestions: for example, for regional
committees; and extracted the admission from Roosevelt that
he did not foresee any maintenance of American troops in Europe
after the end of the war: a most unwise admission. Stalin agreed
with FDR that the United Nations, in which there would, of
course, be a Russian contribution, should have permanent bases
throughout the world. But he did not think that China would be
strong enough after the war to be a member of the 'Big
Four'. [46] Despite other minor differences, Roosevelt was encour-

aged. Earlier he had been sustained by a large majority in the Senate in favour of Senator Connally's resolution supporting a new international organisation to take the place of the League (the vote on November 5 had been 85 to 5). On Christmas Eve 1943, on his return to the United States, he told millions of Americans that, subsequently, there would be no 'pious hopes' that aggressors would learn and understand 'the doctrine of purely voluntary peace'. No, 'the well-intentioned, but ill-fated experiments of former years' would not be repeated. He wanted the post-war world to be led by great powers acting much as 'policemen' (or 'trustees', or 'sheriffs', he also sometimes put it), with special police stations, and special responsibility for their own geographical spheres.[47] 'The Council of the United Nations', he had explained in 1944 during one of his few election speeches that year, 'must have the power to act quickly and decisively to keep the peace by force, if necessary. A policeman would not be a very effective policeman if, when he saw a felon break into a house, he had to go to the town hall and call a meeting before the felon could be arrested. If we do not catch the international felon when we have our hands on him . . . then we are not doing our share to prevent another world war.'[48]

Roosevelt's plans were thus subtle. They were aimed at making possible a realistic intervention to keep the peace. They did not seek to provide a mere international debating society. They combined that concept, consciously, with the idea behind 'Concert of Europe' of the nineteenth century: The idealism would draw in the New Dealers. The *realpolitik* would soothe the conservatives, both the men of 'America First' and the isolationists. FDR had to remember that the Congress elected in 1942 had given him his smallest majority ever and, though the elections of 1944 had brought him gains in the Senate, a conservative coalition held the balance on Capitol Hill.[49]

In this skilful craftsmanship, Roosevelt was living up to his past. Roosevelt was an internationalist by birth. His parents had habitually lived abroad. He himself had visited Europe first in 1885, at the age of three. His first memory was that of a jumping jack – a toy figure – which was swept away by seawater, flowing into his cabin, on a return journey from England that year.[50]

Between seven and fifteen, Roosevelt spent several months annually in Britain or on the European Continent, while his parents were shooting or hunting in England, taking the cure at Bad Nauheim, or bicycling, in the Black Forest. His family might have served as an inspiration for a novel of Henry James's early period. His own character had, indeed, a blend of generosity, cynicism and subtlety which would have fascinated that novelist.

It was unsurprising, therefore, that it should have been Roosevelt's personality which, in the 1940s, imposed the idea of the United Nations on a nation still isolationist in many of its reactions, and which inspired such a deeply Mid-west politician as Truman. With what skill, for example, did the sick Roosevelt deploy his vision in his speech to both Houses of Congress after Yalta, announcing 'the end of the system of unilateral action, the exclusive alliances, the spheres of influence, the balances of power and all the other expedients that have been tried for centuries'. The phrasing owed much to Wilson; for, for Roosevelt, the ghost of Wilson 'was always somewhere within the rim of his consciousness', Robert Sherwood recalled. [51] These words sound either highly ambitious; or foolishly unrealistic. The point was, however, that Roosevelt knew already that the Soviet pursuit of *realpolitik* in Eastern Europe might give trump cards to his domestic enemies, the critics of all international organisations – just as Wilson's departure from his Fourteen Points had helped the isolationists of 1919. [52] That was one reason more why he sought to win over Russia, not challenge her. Old opponents of internationalism such as Senators Hiram Johnson and Robert Taft were still very active, as were Colonel McCormick's *Chicago Tribune* and the Hearst newspapers.

The English had worked on similar ideas, though even the first of the many papers on the subject, 'the Four Power plan' in November 1942, had begun with a summary of known American views. The English differed from the United States in being doubtful about the capacity of China, determined to bring back France as a great power, and more dubious about Russian willingness to collaborate. As to Britain, she 'could not relapse into isolation . . . We must have powerful allies or cease to be a great power; we could not expect to have powerful allies, unless we were powerful ourselves'. Churchill also really wanted a world-wide body supported by regional councils.[53] The British prepared a long analysis of possibilities for a peace settlement: a revised version of which, taking in American suggestions, was ready in July. It contained a skilful tying-together of Roosevelt's and the British ideas and contained an outline of what became the Charter of the United Nations. Thus, in the end, the new world organisation was an Anglo-Saxon production. Neither Russia, nor China, nor indeed France made any contribution to the drafts even though the former made many amendments at both Dumbarton Oaks and San Francisco.[54] Arguments about voting procedures, regional pacts and the proposed military presence were the most important problems raised.

The Charter of the United Nations, as it emerged from preliminary meetings between the Allies, was still untarnished in early 1946. Roosevelt's idea of having the great powers as policemen had been enshrined in their permanent membership of the Security Council. The anxieties of those who remembered the inadequacies of the covenant of the League were met by the provision of a veto in that new body. The Executive Committee had vanished but the General Assembly was there, all right. The principle of universality was respected by the invitation to all sovereign states which had joined the Allied war effort, including, to the well-assumed disgust of Stalin, Argentina, considered to be fascist, which had only declared war on Germany, late, in 1945. The strength of the world's largest nation had been respected by giving the Soviet Union three votes (though not sixteen as Stalin had at first proposed); including the fiction of independent membership for the Ukraine; and, for that much fought over territory, White Russia (Byelorussia). These provisions had caused the first major public outcry over Yalta in the United States, particularly since Roosevelt had not mentioned them straight away: 'The bargain was bad enough, the deceit was worse'.[55] The commitment of the United States was guaranteed by the agreement that the permanent site of the United Nations should be in New York (the Russians also wanted it there perhaps in order to have an extra mission in the United States, for the purpose of espionage), though the first,

temporary, site had been in London.[56] The first Secretary-
General was to be Trygve Lie, for many years Foreign Minister
of Norway. Though Norway had fought, and been occupied by,
Germany, Scandinavia had already assumed the role of honorary
neutral in the world's troubles. All the difficulties raised in 1945
by the Russians – what right the United Nations had to intervene
in internal affairs 'essentially' within the jurisdiction of states;
what voting powers the great nations should have in a range of
disputes – had been settled, as a result of the patience of
American and British officials and, to be fair, some capacity for
compromise by the Russians. The Charter also gave effect, in
its Article 52, to states' desires, if necessary, to establish
regional pacts. It made possible the United States idea of establishing 'bases' on a global scale in order, such was the fiction,
to enable the United Nations to operate effectively against
aggressors. The recruitment of a secretariat was begun without
difficulty. The Charter was not a perfect document. But it
seemed workable. It still represented not only the idealism of
both Britain and the United States, but, at least in rhetoric,
the mainstay of their policies. Roosevelt died between the
conferences of Dumbarton Oaks in Washington in 1944, and San
Francisco, in the early summer of 1945. But he would not have
been discouraged by the latter's conclusions.[57]

Until his death, Roosevelt was still apparently thinking that
there could be a world in which there would be no 'mutual
discord, no minor misunderstandings'.[58] He thought to the end
that American troops would not stay in Europe 'much more
than two years . . .' He could obtain support in Congress and
throughout the country for any reasonable measures designed
to safeguard the future peace but he still did not believe that
that would extend to the maintenance of an appreciable American
force in Europe.[59] He did not think that the British Empire could
be maintained as a major power and was, therefore, happy to
contemplate economic pressure to hasten the dismantlement.[60]

In these attitudes the policies pursued by Truman had their
roots.

The Charter had been presented by Truman to the Senate of
the United States in July 1945. Unlike that body's treatment in

1919 of the Charter's predecessor, the Covenant of the League of Nations, the Senate gave consent to ratification by 89 to 2 on July 28. The American Legislature, in particular the Republicans, had been consulted throughout: one of Cordell Hull's (and then Dean Acheson's) great achievements. 'I have seldom worked harder on any project', Hull had said later, of his successful effort to keep the issue of the United Nations out of the Presidential campaign of 1944.[61] Roosevelt had insisted on bringing in the senators, including Republican senators, at every stage. There must, he insisted, be multi-party support for this coalition policy: that is, he would proclaim his own policy to be that of a coalition and work to ensure the support of his opponents. Because of Roosevelt's work on these foundations, President Truman could sign the document by which the United States ratified the Charter on August 8, 1945. The United States was the first nation to complete the action necessary to bring the Charter into being. The Charter came into legal force on October 24, 1945, after instruments of ratification had been deposited by the required number of states; and so became a part of 'the law of nations': whatever that phrase would mean in the post-war world.

There had already been regrettable quarrels over the United Nations between the West and the Russians. The two extra seats for the Soviet Union (Ukraine and White Russia) caused trouble inside the United States, not with Stalin. But at the conference of San Francisco, Molotov had first refused to accept the custom that the representative of the nation acting as host should be the chairman. He tried also to insist that the Poles of Lublin should be seated there and then, as Poland's representatives, while that matter remained a major dispute at the level of heads of governments. Voting arrangements at the United Nations, however, were finally agreed by Stalin during Hopkins's visit to Moscow. In August, the Russians showed themselves unenthusiastic about establishing a military staff committee and about contemplating any collective action to enforce the Charter. There were similar arguments over appointments in the Preparatory Commission, its committees and eventually in the General Assembly. The Russians had made clear by the end of

1945 that their prime concerns were the Security Council, its secretariat and its operations. Nevertheless the new institution – and again Roosevelt would not have been disconcerted by its final shape – did exist by the end of 1945.

The first meeting of the Security Council, in London in January 1946, had been dominated, unfortunately, by Persia's complaints against Russia. The Soviet representatives, who included both Molotov and Vyshinsky, had conducted themselves roughly, though just within the acceptable bounds of diplomatic behaviour. The United States permanent representative, ex-Secretary of State Stettinius, behaved in a conciliatory fashion and was plainly well served by his chief adviser, Alger Hiss. All those, even the Republicans, on the United States delegation seemed to breathe the air of Roosevelt's wartime messages: 'it is useless to win a war unless it stays won'; or, the United Nations 'can and must remain united for the maintenance of peace'.[62]

Some of the inadequacies of the United Nations had, however, been already seen. An international institution cannot take the place of a foreign policy. Furthermore, by the nature of things, an international body is a static one, concerned to preserve the *status quo*. The United Nations was, as George Kennan said, scarcely different from the Holy Alliance. All the same, the United Nations in 1946 represented for countless Americans and Englishmen the best hope for mankind. Even generals and admirals took it seriously. Of course, the United States, if it maintained its responsible mood, would need bases, bombs and intelligence. But these were to be at the service of the United Nations. The United Nations would be what Wilson, as well as Roosevelt, had dreamed of. It would enable the United States to use her power on a global scale, surely, without incurring the accusations of imperialism. Here would be the frame of a world society, with neither the bureaucracy nor the doubtless repressive centralisation which might be inevitable in a world state.

The communiqué at the conference in Tehran in 1943 ended: 'We recognise fully the supreme responsibility resting upon us and all the United Nations to make a peace which will command the overwhelming mass of the peoples of the world . . . we look with confidence to the day when all people may live free lives untouched by tyranny, and according to various desires and their own consciences'.[63] These reflections were idealistic but they were not foolish. Without such ideals, even hardened warriors like Churchill or Roosevelt might not have been able to continue their efforts. Even great men need illusions. Truman, when the two armies of Russia and the United States met at Torgau on the Elbe, in April 1945, said: 'Nations which can plan and fight together, shoulder to shoulder, in the face of such obstacles of distance, and of language, and of communication, as we have overcome, can live together, and can work together, in the common labour of the organisation of the world for peace'.[64] He too needed to believe. Both Roosevelt and Truman also knew that the 'fellow Americans' to whom they addressed their speeches and fireside chats would only support international responsibility if it were given an idealistic explanation: Americans would not exert themselves for 'spheres of interest'.

In January 1946, support for the United Nations, as for the guarantee of peace arranged within it, was still one of the pillars of United States foreign policy: 'we are convinced that the preservation of peace between nations requires a United Nations organisation composed of all the peace-loving nations . . . who are willing to use force if necessary to ensure peace' – thus Truman, in the twelfth point of his address on Navy Day 1945. 'We believe that the Charter constitutes a solid structure upon which the United Nations can build a better world. With all our might we intend to back our obligations . . . under the Charter' – thus categorically the Department of State in a general review of policy dated December 1, 1945, intended for its own staff not for publication. Internationalism so phrased would surely keep isolationists at bay.[66]

The war had also, certainly, if surely unfortunately, given a fillip to the idea of international meetings at the 'summit'. Churchill liked such discussions: in respect of Greece in 1944, he wrote to Roosevelt, 'why is all this effective direction to be broken into a committee of mediocre officials . . . why cannot you and I keep this in our own hands?'[67] This was not an original idea. Tsar Alexander and Castlereagh had thought that periodic meetings of rulers would serve peace, just as Henry VIII and

Francis I had believed that good would flow from the Field of the Cloth of Gold. After the collapse of the Holy Alliance in the 1820s, the idea temporarily vanished. But railways stimulated anew the notion of such meetings. The Congress of Berlin in 1878 heralded the age of conferences at the 'summit'. Neither the peacemaking at Paris in 1919, nor Chamberlain's conferences with Hitler, discredited this idea. The grand meetings between the foreign ministers (Moscow 1943) and the 'principals' (Cairo and Tehran 1943, Yalta 1945, Potsdam 1945) as well as Churchill's many special meetings with Roosevelt (*HMS Prince of Wales*; Washington; Quebec; Hyde Park; Casablanca; Ottawa) and with Stalin in Moscow twice, as well as Roosevelt's and Churchill's discussions at Cairo with Chiang Kai Shek, stimulated the idea. Another great illusion was created that, 'at the summit', personal relations could overcome national differences. The fact that all those war meetings were badly organised and, from the British and American point of view, unsuccessful (except perhaps for the foreign ministers' conference in Moscow in 1943) was overlooked. So was the fact that all the meetings were arranged at the West's request, but held at places to suit Stalin.

The legacy of these occasions was that presidents, secretaries-general and prime ministers have, since that time, been tempted to look at the possibilities of making 'a decisive breakthrough to peace' by 'a well publicised summit'.[68] The truth is, as Kennan would put it in his last despatch from Moscow, at the end of March 1946, the view 'that Soviet "suspicions" are of such a nature that they could be altered by personal contacts, rational arguments or official assurances . . . constitutes . . . the most insidious and dangerous single error which Americans can make'.[69]

A less dangerous legacy of the war was the Council of Foreign Ministers. This plan for a continuation of the war-time meetings had been made at Potsdam on Truman's suggestion, principally to work on the peace treaties. (An idea for such a council had been proposed by the Department of State in 1944.) Membership would be the same as the permanent members of the Security Council of the UN.[70] China and France had been added, to meet, curiously, possible complaints from the small nations that the 'Big Three' were dictating peace to the world. Stalin did not see why China, scarcely a good representative of small nations, should deal with European peacemaking and would have liked to have excluded France. At the same time, Churchill also wanted to be able to maintain 'periodical consultation' among the 'Big Three'.[71] Thus, while the London Conference in September was one of the new 'Council of Foreign Ministers', the Moscow Conference in December was a 'conference' of foreign ministers of the old Big Three. At it, Secretary of State Byrnes achieved one important, characteristic, concession: the peace treaties would be worked out by the Conference of the Three, as Russia desired: and reviewed by the Council of Five, as he had wished.


The United Nations was not the only institution with which Americans of Roosevelt's way of thinking hoped to bind the post-war world into co-operation and liberty. There was, also, first, UNRRA (Relief and Rehabilitation Agency) for the relief of refugees, which had been set up in 1943. It would have distributed $4 billion worth of essential goods between then and 1947 to war victims (contributed by forty-four nations, though three-quarters of it from the United States; Americans controlled the central organisation but not the local distribution of the aid). Long before February 1946, though, this service had become a matter of controversy in Central Europe and the Balkans, where Soviet-backed governments accused the United States of using the agency for espionage; and where the United States reported misuse of goods for political purposes. All the same, it was American deliveries, of American food, even if internationally made available, which provided the margin of survival during 1945–1946 in much of Europe and East Asia. There was also the Food and Agricultural Organisation (FAO) founded in March 1943 in Hot Springs, Virginia, whose first meeting was described by Roosevelt as an 'epoch-making demonstration that free peoples all over the world could decide on a common machinery of action'. There were too the International

Labour and World Health Organisations (ILO and WHO) which were survivors from pre-war attempts at idealist or at least statistical collaboration, which lingered on into these new gaunt years, and would now be re-born. The leaders of the United States also believed at the end of the war that an economic policy towards the rest of the world was necessary. They realised, as they or their fathers in 1919 had not, that the international economy of effortless exchange of commerce, capital investment, and modest governmental intervention, could not, given the breakdown between 1929 and 1945, be revived without work by governments in the background. Americans, officials and business leaders alike, looked now on the interwar years as a time when Roosevelt had drawn out of the World Economic Conference in London; when the administration had refused to cancel war debts; and when Congress had damaged trade, by the Smoot-Hartley tariff of 1930, and other measures.

The first move in this new policy had been the assembly at Bretton Woods, in New Hampshire, in July 1944, of delegates from forty-four nations. Roosevelt, in a characteristic message, welcomed these men and urged co-operation because 'economic diseases are highly communicable'.[72] The Russians present were warmly greeted by the American leading representatives, Henry Morgenthau and Harry White. The main issue of the conference, the fight against protectionism and preference, was a special concern, even an obsession, of the then Secretary of State, Cordell Hull, so that for once there seemed to be no differences of principle between the Treasury and the Department of State. The conference, therefore, was easily persuaded to endorse a plan, devised in the Treasury by White, whereby each nation represented would subscribe a small amount of its currency to an international monetary fund (IMF) and an international bank, for Reconstruction and Development (IBRD). These agencies would regulate currencies and distribute loans to those in need. They would operate without regard to whether the country receiving the loan was capitalist or socialist, democratic or authoritarian. The United States' economic position gave her dominance in both institutions, but that, White and Morgenthau

believed, was the best way of ensuring her responsible participation. The Soviet Union was offered the third largest subscrip-
tion in the IMF after Britain, in terms of voting powers as well
as contributions. The United States accepted the Soviet request
for a near doubling of her contribution to the fund ($800 million
instead of $1200 million) and even arranged to make up the
Russian share to the World Bank when the Soviet delegation
hesitated about their payments. Morgenthau wound up the
conference by claiming that it marked the death of the 'economic
nationalism' which had caused such ruin in the 1930s and, he
argued, had led to dictatorship and war.[73]

Though Roosevelt had taken care to arrange for both American political parties to be represented in the United States
delegation at Bretton Woods, conservative congressmen fought
it on the grounds that it was 'an international New Deal'. Senator
Taft did not want to pour dollars 'down a rat-hole'. But the
Allied victory in Europe, the death of Roosevelt and various
concessions to the critics (for example, a National Advisory
Council to oversee the institutions of Bretton Woods) ensured
the ratification of the agreements in the United States by the
end of July. Other countries followed. Yet the Soviet Union did
not ratify and allowed the deadline of December 31 to pass with
no more communications. This naturally worried Americans not
only because a self-imposed isolation would favour repression,
but because it might encourage the formation of other closed
economic blocks elsewhere.[74]

Instead, Americans turned towards Western, as opposed to
Eastern, Europe. True, officials still believed, as late as April
1946, that the 'rehabilitation and stabilization of Europe, like that
of any other region of the world' was the primary responsibility of
the United Nations. But, all the same, United States aid to
Western Europe (which included all the countries which one day
would receive Marshall Aid, and excluded Spain) would total
$2752 million in 1946 or 48 per cent of total foreign aid (in place
of $554 and 28 per cent in 1945). This undoubtedly helped the
rise in European productivity already beginning to be observed
in the spring of 1946. It may even have given the impression
that Europe's economic problems were within sight of solution,

a view which the harsh winter to come, and the shortage of coal
the following year, would show to be premature.


In late 1943 Averell Harriman had told President Roosevelt that,
after the war, Russia would need United States help for the
reconstruction of her economy and society. Harriman supported
this idea partly because, as has been seen, he believed in its
'leverage' as the best way of influencing Soviet policy; partly,
to help the United States avoid the unemployment which had
marked its economy after the First World War. These views, or
varieties of them, were widely held among leaders of American
opinion. Donald Nelson, Chairman of the War Production Board,
had predicted in 1943 'a great future' for United States–Soviet
trade. Cordell Hull told Molotov at the Conference of Foreign
Ministers in Moscow that year that the Americans desired to
collaborate in the rehabilitation of his country. Harriman told
Mikoyan of his interest in helping Soviet 'rehabilitation'.[75] Late
in December 1943, Molotov picked up these suggestions and
asked what kind of post-war credit might be possible. A month
later, Anastas Mikoyan, the artful Soviet Commissioner for
Foreign Trade, suggested to Harriman that the United States
might like to lend Russia a billion dollars, at a rate of interest of
one and a half per cent, repayment to begin only sixteen years
after the loan was made and to be complete after twenty-five
years.[76]

By then, the United States had already been sending vast
consignments to Russia for two and a half years. Something like
eleven billion dollars' worth of war material had been despatched
between June 1941 and June 1943. Repayment for it was to
begin, without interest, five years after the war, for the first six
months' worth. Repayment was to be indefinitely delayed for
the rest. These deliveries were, however, not to continue 'one
minute . . . into the post-war period', according to Senator
Vandenberg's insistent phrasing.

Harriman from Moscow supported Mikoyan's request for a
loan – but a loan of $500 million, he thought, would be right –
for reconstruction. But the administration judged that a new bill

in Congress would be necessary for that. They argued that money for Soviet reconstruction should come out of an extension of the old Lend Lease arrangements. The plans were approved: the scheme was that the US would contract to sell the Soviet Union those items that were both ready for shipment and were of postwar use. Payment would be stretched over many years, on easy terms. Harriman continued to argue that the Russians were then planning a reconstruction programme stretching fifteen years. They needed long-term loans or nothing. He repeated his earlier arguments. Not only would a loan give the United States a chance of influencing Soviet behaviour. It would help United States industry if Russia placed orders there. Russia negotiated with what Dean Acheson recalled as 'exasperating tediousness'.[77] Many officials in Washington, remembering the low level of United States trade with Russia before 1939, maintained their criticisms of Harriman's ideas. Harriman received most support from the Treasury: there, Dexter White was optimistic that the land of his fathers would be able to produce manganese, chromium and mercury to exchange for American agricultural products – and from private business. In the winter of 1944–45, many businessmen did agree with *Fortune* magazine when, in January 1945, that journal named Russia 'without doubt the richest potential export market for American industrial equipment and products in the immediate and future post-war period'.[78] Harriman and Stalin, it must be said, both expected an economic depression in post-war America, for different reasons; and Harriman thought that American trade with Russia might prevent it.[79]

Little transpired in respect of Soviet economic relations with the United States till January 1945, when Molotov said that if the United States would extend to the Soviet Union a $6 billion loan at 2.25 per cent interest, Russia would place orders for capital equipment in America. Harriman thought this 'offer' extraordinary. All the same, he supported it in principle.[80] Molotov wanted the credit to run for thirty years, with repayment to begin at the end of the ninth year. The Treasury revived their previous proposals: this time, Morgenthau suggested a loan of $10 billion at 2 per cent interest, to purchase American products, the loan to last for thirty-five years. It would be repaid mainly by export of gold and strategic materials.

Roosevelt, however, decided to do nothing about these ideas till he had talked to Stalin at Yalta. Stettinius held off Morgenthau. The Department of State, all the same, more and more thought that the loan could be a useful political weapon. 'Hard line' men and 'soft line' men could agree on the matter. Junior officials unwisely leaked the idea to the press. Even so, Stalin never raised the matter at Yalta.[81] Nor did Roosevelt. The Department of State was by this time becoming angry with the Treasury's interference and busy fighting it on the issue of the Morgenthau Plan for Germany.[82] Essentially, the decision not to act, at any rate with any speed, had been made by February.[83]

In March 1945, after months of controversy within departments in the United States, the annual bill dealing with Lend Lease came to the House of Representatives. Representative John Vory, the Republican congressman for Ohio, introduced an amendment prohibiting the use of any Lend Lease aid for any post-war relief, or for reconstruction. The Republicans did not want the United States to be 'world suckers' and pay for 'the reconstruction of the world'. So, in the worsening political climate following Yalta, Representative Vory's amendment was accepted. A further amendment, however, forbade the use of Lend Lease for reconstruction, but permitted countries to receive what they had already contracted for, provided that they paid for it. After a debate, this bill, as amended, was passed, by both the House of Representatives and the Senate (on April 10) and then signed by the new President, Truman (on April 17). Thus the administration did not go ahead with a loan. It refused to let Russian reconstruction be financed through Lend Lease. But it kept open the door for purchases of equipment to be paid for on terms to be negotiated. These decisions on policy were made in Roosevelt's time. President Truman had to carry them out.

After the German surrender, Harriman suggested that the time had come to begin the end of Russia's Lend Lease shipments. Supplies for possible military use by Russia against Japan might be sent. The administration should be firm, but should avoid any implication of a threat or even of 'political bargaining'.[84] Truman approved, without realising the significance of his action. This decision was then put into practice, as has been seen, by the Foreign Economic Administrator, Leo Crowley, and Under Secretary of State Joseph Grew. They would allow supplies to be sent to Russia if they were necessary to complete plants already begun. Otherwise, there should be a cut-off as soon as practicable. Crowley was more a legalist than a Russophobe. Grew was keen to use the economic weapon suggested by Harriman. Crowley anticipated difficulties with Russia and did not want them 'to be running all over town looking for help'. All the same, once he gained Truman's support, he ordered the ships which were not intended for use in Russia's war in the Far East to turn round. Harriman said that he was 'taken aback' by this; it is always hard to see one's own policy tactlessly enacted. Truman countermanded the order to turn the ships round. These actions nevertheless were a godsend to the Russians looking for further arguments in propaganda against the United States. Stalin complained to Hopkins on May 27, that the abruptness had been 'unfortunate and even brutal':[85] words whose meaning, it must be said, he knew. Stalin continued to appear to be bitter. He made Hopkins feel guilty. Harriman was, however, logical in his debating reply in June to Molotov: Russia had had a year to decide whether they wanted to buy non-military items arranged under Lend Lease for post-war reconstruction, and had done nothing.[86]

The administration now ensured that, if necessary, a loan to Russia could be offered. Not $6 billion, but anyway $1 billion. The bill enabling this was signed by Truman on July 31: though not without Representative Everett Dirksen trying to secure that it should be written down firmly that credits should not be given to nations which refused to accept the principles of the Charter.[87] Congress also approved a request by the White House that the assets of the Export-Import Bank (an institution founded in 1934 to help to increase United States exports) should be increased greatly, to cover loans of this sort, from $700 million to £3.5 billion. At the same time, Russia was allocated substantial supplies, under Lend Lease, to fulfil her supposed war needs in the Far East, as well as what was termed a 'pipe-line agreement' for post-war Lend Lease purchases.[88] These arrangements came to another abrupt and confused end after the victory in the Far East. Once more there were complaints from Russia, whose officials plainly did not understand the Truman administration's incapacity to act without congressional approval.

The next contact between the United States and Russia on this matter occurred in September. Seven members of the House of Representatives went to Moscow, and several other capitals, to discuss post-war loans. They were received by Stalin on September 14. Their leader, Representative William Colmer, from Mississippi, Chairman of the House's Select Committee on Post-war Economic Policy and Planning, raised the question of a loan. Stalin recalled that Molotov had asked for a loan of $6 billion earlier in the year. But he had heard nothing about the matter recently. The loan would be useful, he said, for Russia to buy United States industrial equipment to help reconstruction. It would be paid for by gold and other materials. Stalin was irritated, it seemed, about the Congressmen's questions about repayment, particularly since the United States was known to be making easier loans to China.[89] Kennan accompanied this group of legislators. Much to his relief, one drunken Congressman did not carry out his previously announced threat to 'biff the old codger on the nose'; instead he merely leered and winked at the General Secretary, whose experience of drunken politicians was, of course, second to none.[90]

On their return to the United States, Colmer and his colleagues did recommend a loan to Russia; but on the condition that Russia disclose what proportion of her economy she devoted to armaments; that non-Russian statisticians would be allowed to check the accuracy of those figures; that Russia abandon political disbursements in East Europe and publish what their new trade treaties with the countries there were; that American books, magazines, films and newspapers were allowed to circulate freely in Russia; and that the Soviet government guarantee freedom of religion and free elections, withdraw troops from East Europe, and promise to carry out political obligations on the same terms as those of other governments.[91] 'Leverage' was thus wheeled into the centre of the stage. As previously provided for, an agreement for the Soviet Union to buy Lend Lease supplies under contract in the US was in fact concluded to cover shipments worth $400 million. After this, discussion of a loan to Russia came to an end. The Department of State suspended all consideration of further credits for Russia at the end of 1945. In January 1946, the NAC (National Advisory Council) discussed moving the $1 billion earmarked for Russia to other uses. That was not done. Acheson assured a Russian interlocutor that the money was still available, in May 1946.[93] Nevertheless, by then, Russian diplomatists had begun to imply to their American counterparts that repayment of debts contracted for industrial items sent under Lend Lease had already been done: in Russian blood.[94] Similarly, American businessmen began to find that, contrary to their earlier fears, their domestic demand was so good that fear of depression vanished, as did the need for new external markets in Russia, and elsewhere. The Soviet Union could easily have obtained a loan of $1 billion through the Export-Import Bank in 1945 if they had only been ready like other recipients of Land Lease to give an inventory of those supplies which had survived the war.

There have been suggestions that the purpose of the United States in its relation with the Soviet Union and East Europe was that the former's policy was based on the economics of an 'open door' for American trade. Leaving aside that 'dollar diplomacy' has rarely counted for much in United States policy, the fact should be evident from this narrative that neither the United States, nor her allies, had the capacity for integrating economic and political programmes so well as that would imply. Even political programmes were hard to establish.[95]

The conduct of Roosevelt at the conference at Yalta has come in for much criticism. Not all of it is fair-minded, not all is wrong. He was there at last ready to bargain, and to discuss details.[96] In the circumstances of the Soviet Army's occupation of most of East Europe, except Czechoslovakia, Yugoslavia, Albania and Greece, he was prepared to barter strategic territories in China for Soviet participation in the war against Japan and to abandon the idea of postponing settlements till the peace in order to secure Soviet support for the United Nations. He wanted first, a new international order; second, the swift withdrawal after the victory of all United States military forces from Europe. A case can be made on FDR's behalf that all the preceding years of discussion about post-war circumstances had no point. Only now in the Crimea, in those ex-Tsarist palaces in a territory so recently fought upon, was it even possible to plan on the assumption that the war was won, and that, even if better decisions might have been made before about, say, the future status of Poland, or of Ruthenia, Riga or Bessarabia, they would then have been discountable, because of the Red Army's occupation of the territories concerned.

At Yalta, Roosevelt also proposed that the Allies essentially put into effect the Atlantic Charter in the limited area of 'liberated Europe'. Both the Russians and the British agreed. The new document concluded as a result meant that both countries need not apply the principles to their own empires.[97] Thus a 'Declaration' on 'Liberated Europe' was issued. This recalled the Atlantic Charter's principles – 'the right of all peoples to choose the form of government under which they will live' – as well as 'the restoration of sovereign rights and self government' to the peoples forcibly deprived of them by the 'aggressor nations'. The 'Yalta powers' agreed jointly to assist the people in 'any European liberated state', or 'former Axis satellite state', in four ways: to establish conditions of internal peace; to relieve distress; to form 'interim governmental authorities broadly representative of all democratic elements in the population'. They also pledged the 'earliest possible establishment through free elections' of responsible governments; and to help such elections where needed.[98] But there was no institutional arrangement to put these ideas into effect. Roosevelt rejected the Department of State's ideas for a High Commission to deal with the matter.[99] He instead accepted Molotov's draft phrasing that the three great powers would 'immediately take measures to put those things into practice'.[100]

Roosevelt regarded the achievement of this Declaration as a

success. He told Americans so.[101] It was the guiding instrument of American foreign policy in the region throughout in 1945. The United States government would thus refuse to recognise the administrations in Bulgaria, Romania and Hungary till the Declaration could be said to apply there. British officials were more realistic. They could see that the political conditions of near civil war throughout East Europe made nonsense of the Declaration almost from the beginning. The Americans held onto their principles till Potsdam. There, Truman presented a paper discussing the application of the 'Declaration' to Romania and Bulgaria (Hungary was temporarily forgotten). But the issue became confused in charges and counter-charges, and comparisons between these countries and Greece and Italy. In the end, the issue was postponed to another conference, as part of Secretary Byrnes's 'package deal' involving all outstanding issues. The communiqué at the end of the conference at Potsdam did speak of peace treaties with 'recognised democratic governments'. No one discussed the meaning of the word 'democratic'. The genuinely democratic leaders in East Europe interpreted the inclusion of it as meaning to indicate that the Allies stood by the Declaration at Yalta on Liberated Europe.[102] But that document itself was not mentioned in the final communiqué at Potsdam.

Still, Truman spoke afterwards as if he still considered himself as bound by it. 'That responsibility still stands,' he said, speaking of the commitment to establish democratic governments in Europe.[103] This message was widely broadcast in Russia and in East Europe. King Michael of Romania took it seriously.[104] Much the same occurred in Bulgaria that summer, less dramatically. (Maynard Barnes, the United States political representative there, understood the President's statement after Potsdam, and the Department of State's repeated commitment to the Declaration, as an encouragement to forceful action.) At the Council of Foreign Ministers in London, Byrnes spoke as if the Declaration was something in which he still believed. Britain by that time was ready to accept the Soviet possession of a sphere of influence in East Europe not only because of Churchill's 'percentages deal' but because they could not see anything to do about it. The United States never considered themselves bound by the 'percentages deal' and anyway considered the Declaration at Yalta superceded it.[105] President Truman supported the ideas in the Declaration in a speech on Navy Day 1945; and, at the end of the year, officials were repeating their support for the Declaration 'even if we have been unable to bring the Soviet Government to line up for it'.[106] They continued to do so. They did not devise initiatives to secure the success of their policies. But they held to them all the same.

Despite all these uncertainties most wise Americans in 1945 knew, with the freshman Senator J. W. Fulbright, that their turn for something like the leadership of 'Christian civilisation' – Churchill's expression in 1940 – had come. The only serious differences were as to how this leadership would be exercised. Henry Luce, founder of *Time*, *Life* and *Fortune*, held, if his leading article 'The American Century' is to be believed, that there would be a peaceful world, dominated by American power and missionary Christianity.[107] Henry Wallace thought that it could be the 'Century of the Common Man'.[108] The American Trade Unions, the Churches, of all varieties, and countless private bodies had pronounced overwhelmingly in favour of some kind of international organisation.[109] Some have thought that the 'primary' and 'essential' aim of Washington in 1945 was 'to restructure the world so that American business could trade, operate and profit without restrictions' everywhere.[110] Perhaps some did so think, though it was far from being a consensus even among businessmen, much less in Washington. But, at all events, few Americans expected to return to the *status quo ante* December 7, 1941. In 1945, the annual convention of the American Legion, a reliable indication of opinion, had pronounced in favour of United States participation, on a permanent basis, in an 'association of free and sovereign nations, implemented with whatever force may be necessary to maintain world peace.'[111] Harry Hopkins explicitly told Stalin in May 1945 that 'now the interests of the United States were world-wide, and not confined to North and South America and the Pacific'.[112]

Three and a half years of war following eight and a half years of the New Deal had also transformed the United States economy. The state was thus both internationally and domestically unrecognisable to those who had known it in, say, 1930. True, there was a strong current in the United States of reaction against wartime controls, high taxes and 'government from Washington'. That had 'demobilisation fever' as its first symptom. Nevertheless there was scarcely any sense of that judgement so evident in the 1920s that commitment in the First World War had been a mistake; or that Wilson's freedom (and therefore Roosevelt's) to take unneutral steps had pushed the country into war and that only limitations on presidential discretion could prevent it from happening again.[113] For many, the change was realised, at the time. Roosevelt had written to Ambassador Bullitt in Moscow, then still a friend, in 1936, 'these may be the last days of peace before a long chaos'.[114] Most realised that when Roosevelt, in his 'quarantine speech' in 1937, at Chicago, talked of America 'actively engaging in the search for peace' he had opened the gates to a new era. Civilisation, Americans knew, would not survive if United States influence remained 'about zero', as Roosevelt admitted it to have been in 1940. Innumerable Americans must be supposed to have read with approval the well-intentioned book of the good-hearted Republican candidate in 1940, Wendell Willkie, *One World*. It sold two million copies and told those who read it in simple language not only that the age of power politics was over, but that America was part of the world community. Like its author, it was naive about Russia but comforting about the world as a whole.[115]

The success of American industry in the war underpinned the new mood. In the five years from 1940 to 1945 the United States built nearly 300,000 aircraft, 86,000 tanks, nearly 70,000 ships, and over 5,000 large vessels and produced 17.5 million small arms.[116] The United States had in 1946 a fleet larger than that of the combined fleets of the rest of the world put together, Britain included. Twelve million men had been armed and employed in numerous conflicts across the globe. It seemed as if the United States was in the same position relatively speaking to the rest of the world as Britain had been in 1815. The United

States had in addition suffered no bombing, and no wartime damage to its industry or population. Her deaths in the war numbered about 290,000[117] – against Britain's 244,000, much less than Russia's millions. By the end of the war, the United States was producing 45 per cent of the world's war equipment and munitions. War had strengthened, not weakened, America. Between 1940 and 1944, industrial output had increased in the United States by 90 per cent; agricultural production by 20 per cent; total production by 60 per cent. Employment was at a peak at 52 million; unemployment was a mere 1.5 million. The efficiency of agriculture was such that one family working on the land could produce enough to feed eight living in the city. Although not exhilarated by the prospect of a long period of international responsibility, the United States was ready for it.

But this sense of success had its inevitable consequences for the armies and so for foreign policy. In August 1945, one and a half million United States troops were still in Europe (another one and a half million had already been carried since May either back to the United States or to the Far East). These Americans – in Germany, Italy, France, Austria and even England – longed for home. Politicians backed them: 'bring the boys home'. Wives sent photographs of their children to Congressmen with 'I want my Daddy' written below. There was unrest, even rioting, among the troops who remained. The 'points system', introduced to release those soldiers who had served longest, or longest abroad, or had families, or who had 'superior' records in particular battles, did nothing to soothe this agitation.[118] Unmarried veterans, in particular, were furious. By the end of 1945, the consequent confusion was almost turning into chaos.[119] In November, the new Secretary of War in the United States, Robert Patterson, the successor to Henry Stimson, wrote to Byrnes telling him that, by April 1946, United States troops in Europe would have been reduced to 400,000 and total United States armed forces to 1.6 million, having been eight million in August 1945; could the United States sustain any foreign policy at all with such nugatory levels?[120]

Secretary Byrnes was disturbed: 'I am deeply concerned,' he wrote, 'at the rate at which we are losing our military strength'.

In reply to questions put to him by Patterson about future policy requirements in Germany, Byrnes said that 'it is conceivable that a police-type force of occupation would be sufficient'. But, even so, some forces might continue to be needed even in 1947. Byrnes hoped that all forces might be withdrawn from Austria by January 1, 1947. In Japan, however, occupation forces would be needed into 1947. Korea might be on its own by mid-1946 but only if it were under an international trusteeship: that presumably would need some troops. Men would be required, too, in Italy and Venezia Giulia, for an indefinite period. Byrnes believed that 'Our country must have sufficient military strength at home and abroad to give evidence of a determination to back up the policies of our government anywhere that may be necessary'.[121] To show that this was no personal view of Byrnes's, Acheson said to Forrestal, in January 1946, that demobilisation was a 'great embarrassment and concern' to him.[122] General Marshall proposed universal military training as an alternative to a large standing army. The idea was unpopular. It sounded un-American. (The draft – 'muster' Roosevelt had called it – was to be extended a year, in April 1946; but Congress was most reluctant to approve.)


To have lived in the United States during the Second World War had been intellectually the most stimulating time. One might have made fun of Wendell Willkie or Henry Wallace, one might have preferred the schemes of Clarence Streit (*Union Now*) or Ely Culbertson (*Total Peace*) to those of Sumner Welles (*Time for Decision*), one might have been enraged by Walter Lippmann's reminder, in *US War Aims*, that 'we are not Gods . . . we are mere mortals with limited power and little universal wisdom', one might have disliked Roosevelt's apparent move away from the New Deal or welcomed it; but ideas then seemed to matter in the US; just as the idea of the US now counted in the world.

# ELEVEN

# ANGLO-SAXON RELATIONS

Britain and America were less linked in 1946 by alliance than divided by the sudden end of Lend Lease, and by arguments over the economic conditions for the loan which the former desired from the latter; by Bretton Woods; by uncertainty over the right policy to follow towards both the Soviet Union and the atom bomb; and by the United States' judgement that the British Empire was at the end of its useful life – a view decided partly because of Roosevelt's hostility to empires as such, partly because of the realisation of British economic weakness. Since 1939, Britain and the United States had been bound together by commentators such as Ed Murrow and Raymond Gram Swing. Up till 1941, Britain had been the acknowledged outrider in the battle for liberty, even on equal terms up till 1944. But Churchill's defeat and Roosevelt's death had snapped the old cords. True, Roosevelt had given Churchill undertakings of unprecedented generosity to help re-build the British economy after the war but then Lend Lease had dried up. The war in the Pacific had been an exclusively American affair at the end, and so had Potsdam. Now the two nations seemed jointly preoccupied only about the consequences of demobilisation.

That was everywhere criticised as too slow; and it usually seemed to lead to as many difficulties as it solved. A mutiny in the Royal Air Force in India had an American echo in the demonstration of United States troops outside the headquarters of General McNarney in Frankfurt. Both countries were also concerned about the black markets allegedly run by their troops in Germany. British and United States generals and administrators met in Germany and in Austria, in China and in Japan, in Italy and to some extent in Hungary. But the 'two Anglo-Saxon powers', as de Gaulle had begun to call them, did not have an alliance. In most ways, relations between them towards the end of President Truman's first year in office were worse than they had been since 1938; or than they would ever be since.[1]

Thus, at the Conference of Foreign Ministers in London in September 1945, no common Western position had been sought beforehand, much less arrived at. For example, Britain, France and the United States each had had their different ideas for the disposition of the Italian colonies and for the Italian frontier with Yugoslavia. At that conference, 'no one really knew what was the point of view of any of the other delegates, except through the endless open meetings'.[2] Relations at the smaller conference at Moscow in December had been worse. As has been seen, Byrnes arranged the meeting without consulting Britain. Byrnes showed himself negligent of British feelings; indeed 'quite unconcerned about Anglo-American relations'.[3] Byrnes's new paper about atomic energy had been shown to neither Britain nor Canada before he reached Moscow. It was given to the Russians before Bevin had had time to consult his own government about it. In the field, so to speak, British and United States representatives sometimes concurred as to how to treat the Soviet Union, as in Bulgaria; often differed, as in Romania. In general, British officials were disposed to allocate Russia a 'sphere of influence' in East Europe since they believed by mid-1945 that the 'Declaration on Liberated Europe' of Yalta could not be applied except for Greece: and there it might be a close-run thing. British politicians and officials alike were haunted by their knowledge of President Roosevelt's reluctance to avoid committing United States forces to a long stay in Europe; and believed that Britain might one day find herself alone in a ruined continent to face Russia.

During 1945, sensing the divisions, Russian propaganda, and instructions to its friends abroad, had emphasised that the British had a more combative posture than the United States towards the Soviet Union. Americans were sometimes warned by Russians not to be dragged into 'adventurous' policies by following the British lead. Communist parties, throughout the world, and Soviet officials in remote embassies repeated the same message: 'The USSR now understands the United States. Soon Americans will understand Russians. There is no hope whatsoever that the Russians and British will ever understand each other . . . Americans and Russians should stick together and solve the problem without British interference'.[4] The facts, however, do not support such a picture of United States tranquillity and British forcefulness. Churchill, if out of power, was unpredictable.[5] Kennan described how, in December 1945, he and Bohlen 'shook Cadogan's composure with our observations on the technique of dealing with the Soviet government'.[6] The British influenced the Americans to carry out the exact terms of repatriation of Soviet prisoners of war or kidnapped labourers.[7] Nor is there anywhere in United States papers of this time anything comparable to the desire of the British wartime agency, SOE, to have a private post-war treaty with the NKVD.[8] Henry Wallace and his friends on the progressive American Left denounced the British, whenever they could, for imperialism and accused the Department of State for its 'pro-British game'. But to some Englishmen (or Scotsmen) the British policies had been too unclear or too weak.*

Any construction of fundamental differences of approach between the British and United States on any of these matters is illusory. Both Britain and the United States, before and during the war, did their 'best not to notice the GULAG' as Shostakovitch complained.[9] Although the British were the first to abandon the Atlantic Charter, and to accept frontiers for Poland, as elsewhere, based on *realpolitik*, the British in 1945 seemed in respect of Poland tougher than the United States.[10] Britain was more anti-Soviet in some countries (in Greece, Bulgaria, at least superficially in Germany), but more compliant elsewhere (Hungary, Romania, even Iran). Whereas, in the

* For example, Lord Dunglass (Sir Alec Douglas-Home) who had spoken against Yalta in the House of Commons in February 1945.

autumn of 1945, the Russians directed their 'irritation' against Britain, and even suggested that the new 'Western bloc', or 'Western European bloc', was directed against America as much as against the Soviet Union, a Soviet diplomatist in May had been asking a British colleague 'why we worked so closely with Americans . . . [since] we had much more to gain by working with the Russians'.[11] The Russians and the Americans quarrelled in London at the level of foreign minister while Soviet junior officials were attacking the British, and praising the Americans. Of course, the British were more experienced in diplomacy than the United States and were firm when their own perceived interests, in Greece above all, seemed seriously threatened. Stalin showed too, in a farewell discussion with the departing British Ambassador, Sir Archibald Clark Kerr, on January 29, 1946, that he was prepared to pretend that he valued friendship with Britain. He regretted, for example, that he had not established 'a good official and personal relationship' with Bevin when the latter had been in Moscow in December. Both he and Russian 'public opinion' alike had been distressed by certain of Bevin's recent remarks: 'All he wanted was to be trusted as an ally'.[12]

Britain in 1945 was in an ambiguous position – never more so than in its attitude to the United States. Lord Coleraine, a junior minister in the Foreign Office, whom Roosevelt liked, told Freeman Matthews, head of the Western European division in the Department of State, in January 1945, that 'we do not want you to go back to isolationism. On the other hand, we do not seem to want you to have independent policies of your own . . . so many of our people would like to have your influence and prestige and material strength utilised to support British policies'.[13] But all the same, few Englishmen had 'heretofore wasted much time on what the United States might be thinking or doing', Matthews accurately wrote later; and Stettinius, on January 2, 1945, had told Roosevelt of what he took to be the 'emotional difficulty which . . . any Englishman has in adjusting himself to a secondary role, after having always accepted a leading one as his natural right. The British have an unhappy sense of unprecedented and unrepayable obligation to us'.[14] But some Americans, such as the President of Johns Hopkins University, Isaiah Bowman, thought that when 'perhaps the inevitable struggle came between Russia and ourselves' it would be useful to have the support of Britain.[15]

There were also differences between Britain and the United States over the survival after the war of United States and British military participation in the Joint Chiefs of Staff Committee in Washington. The British desired a continuation of this committee which, set up in January 1942, had been a success. In September 1945, the British mission to that committee argued that 'it would be a mistake to create the impression that all collaboration is at an end, or to cut too severely those staffs which may be required if the Americans agree to carry collaboration into the post-war period'. They hoped that, despite the United Nations, Anglo-American 'collaboration will continue in the fields of intelligence, communications, scientific development and training. Even if the Joint Chiefs were to be dismantled, this collaboration should continue, under cover of the British Embassy: a detachment from the Chiefs of Staff in London should be seconded to the Embassy, and have its own communications'.[16]

The Americans were much more concerned in extending their interest in the bases in British territory which they had been allowed by Britain to take, rent-free, in 1941 for ninety-nine years, as part of an exchange for destroyers (the bases were in Newfoundland, Bermuda, the Bahamas, Jamaica, Trinidad, Antigua and British Guiana). They wanted to add to these, to include Ascension Island and Christmas Island, in the South Atlantic and Pacific respectively.[17] Air and naval bases would also be retained in the Philippines after the (imminent) independence of that country. A base at Okinawa, acquired from Japan, would control the Yellow Sea. United States bases on the old Japanese mandated islands, which had been so hard fought over in 1943–44, would also be retained: on the Marshall, Mariana, and Caroline islands. The United States administration began making known this grand design for what Roosevelt called a 'permanent system of intervention' in 1942. It was to be intervention on behalf of the United Nations. It was also thought that, where these bases were on British islands, their acquisition might be linked by the Americans to the negotiation of a loan or repayment of debts incurred under Lend Lease.[18]

Soon the United States made clear that they were going to ask Denmark if they could have a permanent base in Iceland, and Portugal for a similar permanence on the Azores: perhaps to be shared with Britain, Portugal's oldest ally. (Roosevelt had sent troops to Iceland in July 1941 – the first overt American action in the war, five months before Pearl Harbor.) The United States also revealed that they were interested in the island of Manus, in the Admiralty Islands, an Australian mandated territory in the Pacific, where they had had in the war a naval repair and air staging base; in the island of Tarawa, also in the Pacific, where other fighting against Japan had occurred; and even in the desolate French island of Clipperton, off Mexico, some 600 miles into the North Pacific. The United States air force wanted to be able to maintain continuously 'a transcontinental transportation service of about a hundred planes'. That seemed to General 'Hap' Arnold, the air force commander, specially important between Greenland and Alaska. He already feared 'raids from Moscow via the North Pole'.[19]

Britain was unenthusiastic. Ascension Island had an important cable station. Christmas Island could take settlers. Nor did Britain want the negotiations on the bases to be linked to the discussions of a loan.[20] The suggestion that the existing bases in the West Indies, leased to the United States for ninety-nine years, might be converted into leases of 999 years was discussed.[21] The Chiefs of Staff in London were reluctant. The Cabinet, however, authorised more detailed discussions.[22] American officials generally agreed with Stimson that these bases, 'which must belong to the United States with absolute power to rule and fortify them', would not be colonies but be 'out-posts' to maintain access to Asia and to Europe. There were European officials who could have argued that the difference often seemed a narrow one.[23]

Finally, between Britain and the United States, there was a difference over the future role of the British Empire. President Roosevelt and most of the officials whom he appointed (and whom Truman inherited) believed the Empire to be an anachronism. Roosevelt thought that the world would subsequently be dominated by two non-imperialist powers who would liberate subject nations from the West European empires. He overlooked Russia's character as an immense empire. The profound differences on imperial policy between Britain and the United States may have been hidden throughout the war. But they were there. They continued after the war, though the new British Government had already committed herself to carry through a major act of withdrawal – the major act as it turned out – from India, and anticipated other such radical moves. Even this policy did not, however, make for an end, or even a suspension, of anti-imperial attitudes in the United States. The British decision in March 1946 to give India her freedom was not mentioned in the diary of Henry Wallace, even though Wallace's anti-imperialism was a determining element in his imagination.

Despite these gaps in understanding, President Truman received from the British, as from the prime ministers of the Commonwealth, a good deal of advice, mostly unasked for. Mackenzie King, the long-serving Prime Minister of Canada, for example, went to the United States in September 1945 to discuss the implications of the scandal over the Guzenko spy ring. That event, as has been said, had much affected him, though Truman had at first discounted its significance. King had often talked with American Presidents. But he was not taken seriously in Washington, since a 'host of unseen witnesses', presumably angels, were believed by him to hover round him and to guide 'his conduct in emergencies'.[24] Yet Canada was the United States' nearest neighbour. In addition, Canadian citizens had been involved in, and her government had early known the secrets of, the manufacture of the atom bomb. Canada also had rich deposits of uranium. She had, too, been the home of a team of Anglo-French scientists working on chain reactions by slow neutrons, leading to the birth of plutonium, the basic material for thermonuclear weapons. The project established at Montreal and then at Chalk River had become an Anglo-Canadian one, and would give Canada a 'flying start into the nuclear age'.[25]

The Guzenko case needs some attention, since Mackenzie King's experience in 1945 had constituted such an unpleasant course of further education in Soviet studies. Igor Guzenko, a Soviet intelligence expert in the GRU, in the Russian Embassy in Ottawa, had come to the Royal Canadian Mounted Police to explain the reality of Soviet espionage above all in Canada, but also in the United States and in Britain. He brought documents proving his case. King learned therefore for the first time of the 'vast espionage system' established in Ottawa and how 'the abolishing of the Comintern' had been 'nonsense'. He thereupon changed his mind from thinking that the Russians should be given all the secrets of the atom bomb, as he remembered Roosevelt had argued, to the determination that they should not. King saw that the Soviet Union was concerned in intrigue on a vaster scale than Germany, Italy or Japan had ever been. He was very deeply shocked to know that, while Canada had been helping Russia during the war, and 'doing all we can to foment Canada-Russian friendship', there should have been such subversion. [26]

King's conversation with Truman on September 30 about Guzenko was also probably important in making up Truman's mind about the character of espionage. It was then that the President first heard that 'an Assistant Secretary' in the Department of State, 'close to Edward Stettinius' earlier on, was a Russian agent. [27] By November, King was convinced that the Russians did not intend to co-operate but desired to become a 'vast power in the Orient', set against all Western powers. [28] What had been disclosed signified no less than a conflict as to whether Russia or the United States should control the world. Thereafter Mackenzie King looked upon himself as 'an instrument on the part of unseen forces' to bring about the exposure of the conspiracy. [29]

King had also experienced a disagreeable education in inter-imperial relations. Attlee's new British government took decisions affecting the future of nuclear energy without consulting Canada. King's minister of munitions, in charge of atomic energy, Clarence Howe, found himself ignored by Britain but then asked to help on Britain's relations with the United States.

Sir John Anderson who, though he had worked with Churchill, continued to be the British official responsible, offended Howe. On all these matters, Britain, it seemed to King, sought to behave as the leader of an Empire which it could not afford; indeed, whose future it had not planned.[30] Joseph Chamberlain's exhilarating vision of a permanent global empire based on imperial preference had been abandoned. Nothing had replaced it.

The main foreign contributions in these months from abroad to President Truman's thinking might have been supposed to come from the British. But, as earlier suggested, one can spend a long time in the archives of both countries for 1945 or 1946 before finding much common understanding between the two nations. Truman had a sentimental affection for Winston Churchill. But he had not known quite how to deal with him and before Potsdam had not wanted to give Stalin the impression that he was 'ganging up' with England. Anyway Churchill had lost power, an event which left the Russian leaders 'gibbering with astonishment' on July 27.[31]

The new Prime Minister of Britain, Clement Attlee, was nevertheless at sixty-three years old, a realistic statesman with, because above all of his membership of the War Cabinet, a clear knowledge of the facts of power in Europe. He had been concerned with post-war planning in Germany as chairman of the British cabinet's Armistice and Post-war Committee (which framed British policy for the European Advisory Commission). As such, the lines of the zones in Germany owed much to him. He had once seemed to have had an innocent attitude to Russia: when he had been there in 1936. A biographer wrote that then 'he admired the Russians, who seemed to him to be building up their own society, not working for landlords or capitalists'.[32] By 1945, however, he recognised that 'without the stopping power of the Americans, the Russians might have easily tried sweeping right forward . . . it is no good thinking that moral sentiments have any sway with the Russians; there's a good deal of old-fashioned imperialism in their make-up'.[33] For him, the Russians were 'ideological imperialists'.[34] Attlee thought that the Americans had insufficient appreciation of this.[35] True, Attlee knew, with all Englishmen, that had it not been for the Russian alliance, Britain would probably have been defeated by Germany. He therefore went through the motions of trying to keep the memory of wartime friendship as warm as he could, and wrote in late October to Stalin to tell him that he was going to Washington to discuss 'the problems to which the discovery of atomic energy have given rise'.[36] But, as all members of the left of his party in Britain ruefully recalled, Attlee had had no sympathy whatever for, or even understanding of, Communism in the 1930s – despite some blurring of the lines between democratic and totalitarian Socialism in his own unreadable articles or books. He had never read Marx.[37] By October 1945, too, the Guzenko case had suggested to Attlee, as it had convinced King, that 'the time had come when there must be a showdown with the Russians'.[38]

In the course of the war, the historian Arnold Toynbee (then in the Foreign Office research department) had influenced Attlee towards a vague sympathy for world government but those ideas vanished under the burden of office.[39] Attlee was, however, hard in his attitude to the Germans and to anyone, such as Mihailović, who had collaborated with them. In March 1945, he had remarked, of the beaten Germans, 'they have broken down the old barriers and, therefore, I say that they cannot appeal to the old Europe. If they have to yield to make restitution, they are not entitled to appeal on the basis of the moral laws that they have disregarded or the pity and mercy that they have never extended to others.'[40]

There were, as with all nations in 1945, ambiguities in Britain's public policies. Thus Attlee and his government formally believed that they had been elected (according at least to their manifesto of July 1945) to 'consolidate in peace the great wartime association of the British Commonwealth with the US and the USSR'. 'Let it not be forgotten', the manifesto continued, 'that in the years leading up to the war, the Tories were so scared of Russia that they missed the chance to establish a partnership' which might 'have prevented the war'. Now the British had to be 'brave and constructive leaders' in international affairs.[41] In practice, at the beginning, Attlee conducted foreign policy on the assumption that Britain still had an alliance with the United States. When that soon turned out to be less than evident, he was flummoxed. The end of Lend Lease in mid-August was a serious blow and 'for some time it was almost impossible to fathom what the Americans would do', wrote a recent biographer.[42] By the time that Attlee left power in 1951 the alliance had been recreated. It was one of his government's greatest achievements. But little sign of that recreation existed in 1945.

Attlee's Foreign Secretary, Ernest Bevin, illegitimate son of a housemaid in Somerset, a man who never knew his father, was of a similar frame of mind to his leader in respect of Communism and 'our gallant Soviet ally'. In public, he paid lip service to the idea of collaboration with Russia: in a debate in the House of Commons in February 1946, he described how he had told Stalin at the recent conference at Moscow 'that, if we kept the ball bearings well oiled, all our difficulties would vanish eventually'. He also sometimes talked of himself as 'a member of the proletariat', as were the Russian leaders, according to him.[43] At the conference of the Labour party in May, Bevin had permitted himself the famous if even then largely rhetorical statement: 'Left understands Left, but the Right does not'.[44]

In reality, as a negotiator on behalf of his trade union, this 'heavy ugly man with extraordinary charm' who did not want 'to have Britain banged about'[45] knew perfectly well the persistence, and obstinacy, of Communists. He also knew 'you can never . . . deal with the Russians if you lie down and let them walk over you'.[46] He had been a member of the Cabinet and its committees throughout the years 1940 to 1945 and had often taken part in decisions on foreign policy. He was a patriot. He said: 'I believed [that] the development of Socialism meant the absolute crushing of liberty, then I should plump for liberty, because the advance of human development depends entirely on the right to think, to speak, and to use reason'.[47] He knew foreigners, he told his private secretaries, since he had had 'a good deal of negotiation with ships' captains of all nationalities'.[48]

In 1945, he thought that Russia, having carried out two five year plans and won the war, was returning to its 'original Lenin idea';[49] and that any hope of a new style of diplomacy of 'cards on the table, face upwards' was inconceivable.[50] He had made a forceful attack at Potsdam on the new frontiers between Poland and Germany demanded by Russia.[51] The *Times*'s correspondent in Moscow, Ralph Parker, told the British minister in Moscow in March 1946 that the Russians now looked on Bevin as they did Trotsky: 'a very important but dangerous and hostile personality'.[52] At the first meeting of the Security Council in London, Bevin had said, 'the danger to the peace of the world has been the incessant propaganda from Moscow against the British Commonwealth, as a means to attack the British . . . as if no friendship existed between us'.[53] He told Byrnes that the Soviet Government, 'if they saw a piece of land instinctively wanted to grab it'. Earlier, at the London Conference of Foreign Ministers, he had made a famous comparison between Molotov's line of argument and that of Hitler.[54] When Molotov began to walk out, he had apologised.[55] Even so, at a dinner in January 1946 in London, with Foster Dulles and Senator Vandenberg, he again argued that Russia's policy in Persia and Turkey was reminiscent of Hitler's.[56] On January 26, he complained to Vyshinsky in clear terms about the habit of the Soviet authorities in Berlin of making allegations against the British commanders, and protested that 'it seemed to have become the practice for the Soviet Government to make every important international conference the occasion for vindictive attacks on British policy and British interests'.[57]

Bevin's general view in 1946 was that the world was 'drifting into spheres of influence or what can be described as the three great Monroes'. By that, he (and the officials in the Foreign Office who had presumably first thought of the concept) meant that, while the United States had long held, with British support, to the Monroe doctrine for the Western Hemisphere, they were now seeking to extend it to China and to Japan; the Russians wanted their area to stretch from Lübeck to Port Arthur; and the British stood between the two.[58] Bevin, for all his blunt ways, and his reliance on clever officials for papers on strategy, was an original mind and would have as large an effect on policy as any Western statesman in the next four years, except perhaps for Dean Acheson. Britain's predicament was that, though she was no longer one of the great powers, she had to act like one. Bevin was a great enough man to manage this challenge.[59] Bevin was vain and sometimes rather jealous of Churchill, though he was also fond of him. Churchill, on the other hand, looked on Bevin as 'far the most distinguished man the Labour Party have thrown up in my time'.[60] Bevin was prejudiced, disliked 'catholics, intellectuals, Jews and the lower middle class'.[61] He looked on Secretary Byrnes as 'only another cocky and unreliable Irishman, similar to ones whom he had known in his experience as docker and Labour leader'.[62] 'A big bumble bee caught in a web who thinks he's the spider,' remarked his critical colleague in the Cabinet, the brilliant if mercurial Aneurin Bevan.[63] Truman at the beginning disliked Bevin and thought him a 'boor'; even Stalin and Molotov at least knew the 'common courtesies'.[64] Yet Bevin had 'character', that mixture of eccentricity, self-confidence and simplicity which alone enables great work to be performed. His work as Minister of Labour during the war had told him how governments can operate in times of crisis.[65] Much of Bevin's time was to be spent speculating on the chance of new arrangements in the Middle East whereby Russia would be prevented from establishing a position there and a new British Empire set up.[66] On Russia itself he was consistent and candid. He was in person affectionate and impulsive, good-hearted and a lover of food and drink. He believed that 'Britain could capture the moral leadership of the world' even if she had lost her power.[67]

Almost all Attlee's Cabinet had views about foreign policy. But most were more concerned with the Empire than with Russia. The Chancellor of the Exchequer, Hugh Dalton, who had expected to be Foreign Secretary instead of Bevin, was a strong anti-communist. But in 1946, Britain's weak economic position, and the difficulties of arranging a good loan in the United States, would convince him that the country could not play a part forever in, for example, holding the line in Greece.[68] Lord Addison, the seventy-six-year old Secretary of State for the Commonwealth and probably Attlee's closest confidant,[69] thought the situation 'as bad as, if not worse than, the situation which the world was faced with before Hitler declared war'.[70] On the other hand, Bevan, Minister for Health, the most attractive public man on the Left, was at heart half a Marxist. Nor did Sir Stafford Cripps, the influential President of the Board of Trade, appear to have much faith in the future of capitalism. On the strength of having been the ambassador of rapprochement with Russia in 1940, Cripps had used a slogan in the election of 1945, that 'with a Labour government, we should have much better relations with Russia'.[71]

One minister soon concerned in relations with the Soviet Union was Harold Wilson, the young President of the Board of Trade. His first indication of the nature of power politics came early in his time in office when the Soviet Union wished to buy jet aircraft engines which had strategic uses – the turbine blades were made of a secret steel called 'Mnemonic 80'. The Foreign office 'fought like cats' to prevent this, but the Board of Trade believed that exports were more important than ideology. The minister approved the idea in the absence of Ernest Bevin in Moscow. These engines were subsequently copied in the new MIG fighters used by Russia all over the world.[72] It was one of the most valuable exploitations by the Soviet Union of the interval between war and open realisation of a 'cold war'.

For all the Labour Cabinet the late war had constituted an education. The example of Roosevelt and the contributions of the United States glowed in the minds of forward-looking members of the Government as brightly as did the optimism of Maynard Keynes that capitalism and democratic socialism could work together. Keynes appeared to be a kind of Roosevelt of the mind. Lend Lease, totalling $46 billion, of which nearly 70 per cent had gone to Britain (even taking into account reverse Lend Lease of £4 billion), had been an intellectual lever, as well as an essential tool to win the war.[73] Among younger socialists, the influential young economist, Evan Durbin, had as early as 1943 seen that 'our post-war problems will be with the Russians. They will want, soon if not at once, to expand, like every other great and growing power . . .' He doubted whether 'talking to them will be any easier than talking to other lunatics such as Hitler'.[74]

As to the British Foreign Office, that famous institution was then led by men of fine character and great experience: a 'civilian regiment of cultivated men'.[75] Most, however, were conditioned by their backgrounds. It was thus as difficult for them to judge Stalin as it had been Hitler for, in both of those men's motives, ideology, a most uncertain element (and scarcely considered in English public schools) played a real part. Not knowing how to cope with it, many of these men (particularly those who had come to maturity before the Russian revolution) fell back on the habit of looking at the regimes of those modern tyrants as if the traditional German and Russian were the skulls behind the propaganda skins. Since a traditional nation did lurk beneath both systems, and since that fact did affect policy, there is a sense in which these able men were right. In a marsh, it is as well to stand on the few tussocks that one can identify. Yet this marsh needed long boats for it to be crossed at all. Sir Reader Bullard, the British ambassador in Persia, had then had many years of contact with Russia, including four years in the embassy in Moscow. Yet he complained in March 1946, in almost his last despatch before retirement, that the Russians 'have never provided us with a *Mein Kampf*': which, in the sense of having a programme, was one thing which Marx and Lenin certainly had done.[76]

These shortcomings were much less obvious among the new generation entering official life in 1945. All the same, a disinclination to consider the ideological element endured. That meant that the Soviet Union remained ahead of Britain, as of the United States, in the recognition that the struggle 'was for the world', as in 'the concentration to win it';[77] as it had meant that, during the war, the Foreign Office had thought that 'every possible effort (which meant in practice every possible concession) should be made to convince the Soviet Government of the sincerity of the British desire for collaboration.' Many British officials, like their political leaders, thought between 1941 and 1945 that 'nothing would be lost, and a great deal might be gained, by assuming Russian sincerity'.[78]

There were other difficulties. The industry of Britain had been in decline since the 1890s. That had an effect on British diplomacy, however much it might be masked. The lack in particular of Russian specialists of the calibre of Llewellyn Thompson, Kennan and Bohlen (whom the, to many Englishmen, upstart United States had before the war trained at Riga) was marked. It was twenty years before Britain sent an ambassador to Moscow who could speak Russian well. Before 1939 in the British Embassy in Moscow only one or two officials spoke Russian: as a rule, they relied on translators hired on the spot. In 1936, a senior official had had to write to deny that there could be 'any great danger' in learning Russian, 'since all those who go to Russia full of enthusiasm return very much the reverse'. The trouble was, he added, 'that Russian was a difficult language and people hesitated to study it'.*[79] Moscow was 'just another unpopular posting' in the 1930s. It is clear all the same that some realistic reports were written in those days by British officials in Moscow.[79A] But that seems to have ceased in 1941. The outstanding British diplomatist of his generation, the resourceful and brilliant Lord Vansittart, instinctively right about Russia as about the Nazis, had been promoted into impotence out of political jealousy of his long vision. Robert Bruce Lockhart, the wartime head of the Political Warfare Executive, had been a brilliant Russianist. But certain weaknesses of character seem to have prevented him playing the part in policy-making for which his splendid capacities entitled him.

These shortcomings were partly, it is true, compensated for after July 1945 by the Labour Cabinet's (specially Ernest Bevin's) knowledge of domestic Communism: 'ever been to the Communist Club in Maiden Lane?' Bevin asked his most senior official the day that he took office. Sir Alec Cadogan replied 'No', as if 'suddenly charged with murder'.[80]

The British Ambassador to Moscow since 1942 perhaps symbolised Britain's problems. Sir Archibald Clark Kerr was elegant, cynical, aesthetical, charming, possibly homosexual, with the 'weather-beaten face of a sheep farmer'.[81] He mastered his briefs quickly. He wrote with quill pens on stiff paper and dusted

---

* It was easier to get a high mark in Russian than in other languages.

his letters with sand to dry the rich black ink. He liked to make provocative remarks out of boredom. He had inherited from Sir Stafford Cripps an embassy inclined to take the Russian line on such matters as the Second Front or the Baltic States.[82] His embassy in China had been a conspicuous success.[83] He set out to charm statesmen and largely succeeded. He was often perceptive about personalities.[84] He was also good with newspapermen, of whom one, usually difficult to please, called him 'Moscow's saving grace – a totally cultivated man'. Clark Kerr knew in 1945 that, in Russia, 'policy is going to change. We don't want anyone in Moscow who remembers what was said and done in the war. That would be just an embarrassment'.[85] Clark Kerr was not always so prescient. Unlike Churchill, he was not much disturbed by the harsh sentences on the leaders of the Polish Home Army in 1945.[86] When talking to Molotov before leaving for Washington, in January 1946, he described, with the same *dégagé* gaiety that he would have once described as Oxford fashion, how, in Romania, he had encountered an 'apparently universal fear' that that country was 'destined to become the seventeenth (Soviet) republic'. He had 'done his best to allay such fears, and had pointed out how ridiculous they were'. Molotov agreed, 'with a smile'.[87] Alas, Molotov's smiles on such occasions were like other men's grimaces and poor Romania had already by then been sucked into the whirlpool. During the war, Clark Kerr told the Labour minister, Hugh Dalton, that he was convinced that if once the Russians trusted 'us they will be tremendously keen to play with us on everything'.[88] The 'chief contact' of this strange ambassador was believed to be Dr Fierlinger, the Czech envoy, who had been suborned by the Russians; and who, as Prime Minister of Czechoslovakia, would help to betray that country to them.

Deserted by his beautiful Chilean wife, whom he had treated as a toy, living in an isolated fashion, devoted to gardening, Kerr is a difficult man to judge. When leaving Moscow in January for the embassy in Washington, Stalin (whom Clark Kerr also flattered as if he had been a duchess) asked him whether he had any requests. Clark Kerr requested to be allowed to take with him a valet, Evgeny Yost, a Volga German whose presence disturbed Washington but who may not have been of use to his old government in Moscow.[89]

Clark Kerr might fairly be judged by a despatch sent to London on March 2, 1945, summing up Soviet policy since Yalta. Despite the setbacks, he still did not think that the Soviet Government had given up all intention of collaborating with the West after the war. Despite Soviet 'recalcitrance' over Poland (and Clark Kerr had been sometimes weak in those negotiations in Moscow with Molotov and Harriman over a 'reorganised' Polish government), their 'relationship with us' would remain 'considerably closer than that which existed between Britain and Tsarist Russia between 1907 and 1914'. 'We need not meanwhile be "nice" to the Russians. Indeed, we should discourage the "gush of propaganda" in Britain eulogising not only the Soviet war effort, but their system'. That might merely indicate that 'our attitude was motivated by fear and inferiority'. Their need for British help in reconstruction might give a solid basis for Anglo-Soviet co-operation: 'We need not allow recent events to lead us to fear the worst'. The Anglo-Soviet alliance, he concluded, would probably 'pay a steady, though not spectacular, dividend'.[90] The ambassador's new, young and able minister, Frank Roberts, wrote, most unusually, a comment on the despatch, of a more robust kind: unlike his ambassador, he believed that 'we had to show that there was a limit beyond which the Russians could not safely go'.[91]

The most important diplomatic official in Britain in 1945–46, was Alexander Cadogan, Permanent Under Secretary at the Foreign Office from 1938 to February 1946. Dry, resourceful, lucid, able (if limited, '*borné*', his private secretary put it in 1940)[92] but hard-working, and knowledgeable, he exuded confidence. Beneath, as his waspish diary (published after his death against his intentions) revealed years later, he was troubled, and irritable, save when looking at flowers and birds. He disliked most people except Lord Halifax, the ambassador in Washington, and loathed all 'planning'. In February 1939, he wrote, 'I abominate both Communism (as practised in Russia) and Fascism or Nazism. I don't like oysters or oatmeal biscuits, but it has never occurred to me that it would be profitable to devote any of my time to discussing which of them I dislike more'.[93] Like Grew in Washington, he had had a varied life, having been British Chargé d'Affaires in Vienna in 1914 when the Archduke had been murdered. He had been through the crises of 1938, with Chamberlain; and all the great dramas of the war, with Churchill. But he had served in neither Russia nor the United States and knew little of either at the time. For the next few years, from 1946, he would be Britain's representative at the United Nations. He had written the first draft of the Atlantic Charter,[94] even if he had had, on occasion, to forget it.

Cadogan's successor as head of the Foreign Office was the tall, charming, thoughtful Sir Orme Sargent, a bachelor, 'a philosopher strayed into Whitehall',[95] who had been a firm opponent of appeasing Hitler: a factor which was enough to endear him to Churchill. 'He knew all the answers', wrote his pre-war chief; 'when politicians did not want them, he went out to lunch'.[96] But his knowledge of the countries in which the 'world's game', in Pope Julius II's phrase, was now played was modest: an unknown complaint – 'perhaps claustrophobia' hazards a biographer – 'made travelling difficult for him'.[97] 'Very clever, but very sick, nervy and malicious', one of his juniors described him.[98] 'Moley' was believed to have 'the best brain' in the office: also to be, 'in spite of feeble health, and a cynicism born of long experience of politicians, the only man of action'.[99] During the war, he had toyed with the idea of a Balkan federation as 'a nucleus against Russian attempts to Sovietise all Central and South Eastern Europe'.[100] But the Soviet Union made plain that such a new *cordon sanitaire* against them was unacceptable. By June 1944, he thought, with Churchill and Eden, that the plan to give Romania to Russia as 'a sphere of influence', and allow Britain the same with Greece, was probably a 'promising arrangement'.[101] To save Greece by losing the rest of the Balkans was Sargent's policy. It became Britain's. Sargent realised by then that the country which he served with devotion had become 'a mere Lepidus, in a three-power triumvirate' (in which he did not know yet whether Russia would take the part of Antony or Augustus).[102] The notion of 'spheres of influence,' leading to divisions of interest with Russia, was not outrageous to him since, after all, it dated from the early part of the century at least, when the British and the Tsar so divided Persia. Sargent thought that, having, as he admitted, appeased Russia for so long, Britain would find it hard to change to a 'tough line', without being misunderstood. In May 1945, he had succumbed, like so many, to the illusion that the 'hardening' of the Soviet attitude in a whole host of things might be due to the 'mysterious influence' of the victorious Soviet Marshals.[103] At the time of the London meeting of the Council of Foreign Ministers, he had, however, urged co-ordination of Anglo-American policy in Eastern Europe and the joint avoidance of 'promises, express or implied, to the peoples of these areas which it might be found could not be carried out.'[104] That wise advice was not followed by the Americans.

While the Russians, meantime, were at this time pretending that the Nazi-Soviet pact had never occurred, the British also had something which they wisely preferred to forget: the fact that only the collapse of Finnish resistance in March 1939 had restrained them, and France, from going to war with Russia to help Finland in the early part of that year.[*105]

The officials who dealt directly with Russian problems during the Second World War in the Foreign Office had been, of course, overshadowed by their Prime Minister and Foreign Secretary who throughout the war were consumed by the difficulty of dealing with Stalin and the frequent need, as it seemed to them, to placate him.[†106] All the same, the officials lacked vision. The head of the northern department, the section responsible, was Christopher Warner, whom the historian of the Foreign Office describes as 'having no personal knowledge of the USSR' and being therefore 'inclined to submit, without comment, memoranda written by junior members of his staff'.[107] He worried more about the placing of his commas in drafts than he should have done. The only member of his staff who knew Russia was Geoffrey Wilson, a clever Quaker lawyer who had served in Moscow with Stafford Cripps and who strongly believed Russia

* See page 448 below.
† For Churchill see below page 695.

to be entitled to guarantee her Western frontiers. Another temporary official in the northern department who knew both Russian and ideology was Christopher Hill, a communist from Oxford, a historian of promise, whose post-war volume, *Lenin and the Russian Revolution*, scarcely suggests an objective view of Soviet policy.[108] Matters changed after the war, with the coming of men who knew Russia and her real character better. In the circumstances of the war, however, the Northern department believed that it was right, as a popular phrase then was, for Britain 'to cast its bread upon the waters' for Russia to pick up and to give 'the least unfavourable view of Russian lack of co-operation'.[109] In August 1944 a Foreign Office memorandum, prepared in the northern department, suggested that Stalin belonged to the 'collaborationist school of thought', in the Soviet government as opposed to the 'dogmatic' obstructionist one.[110]

Still, what characterised one department, important as it was, did not mark the Office as a whole. The southern department, for example, which dealt with Yugoslavia, had a consistently realistic attitude towards the risks of Communism there: more so, it would seem, than Churchill had. (Churchill had tried to persuade the Yugoslav leader Tito to declare that he renounce Communism; such declarations did not count for much with men who were Marxist-Leninists.) On August 31, 1944, Churchill had written to Anthony Eden, reminding him of the likely difficulty that would arise, after the war, when all the arms in Yugoslavia would be in the hands of Tito: Tito would be able to subjugate the country with weapons supplied by Britain. The Foreign Secretary tartly noted that his Department did not need reminding of that, for it had been the Prime Minister who had persistently 'pushed Tito'. On March 5, 1945 Churchill chided the Foreign Office for its criticisms of Soviet policy in Romania, 'in this extraordinary vigorous manner'.[111]

Naturally, the times being what they were, the southern department did from time to time entertain fancies. Thus, no doubt knowing of Churchill's weakness for Tito, they allowed their Secretary of State not only to complain that the communists behaved 'ungratefully and ungracefully' (words which have also little meaning for Marxists) towards Britain, but also to rest his policy in Yugoslavia, in March 1945, on hoping to 'keep the Marshal on the right lines': a wholly improbable scheme.[112]

It can be argued that it was inevitable that Britain's policy towards Russia since 1939 should be inconsistent. Following the unsuccessful effort, just before the war, to reach an agreement with her, there had been a year of hostility which, during the Finnish war, had come close to conflict.* In 1940, Sir Stafford Cripps's mission, and subsequent ambassadorship, had articulated a desire for *rapprochement*, a design intended to distance Russia from Germany: if only because of the economic help given by Stalin to Hitler, in accord with the Nazi-Soviet Pact of 1939. In 1941, Britain had extended these policies: a British military mission had gone to Moscow a week after the German attack on Soviet territory. But, for the first year after that, relations were uneasy. Russia made innumerable claims. Britain tried, with lavish American help, to maintain Russian assistance by military shipments. When Stalin talked of his views of a post-war settlement in Eastern Europe, the British listened, torn between their need to keep Russia in the war and their knowledge that Stalin's schemes conflicted with the principles of liberty and democracy for which they themselves were fighting. Stalin urged the British to open a 'Second Front' in France – an argument heard continuously in his messages to Churchill from July 1941 onwards. Britain knew that such a thing could be ruinous if launched too soon or inadequately. Still, Stalin's requests were supported by Cripps from Moscow and, after his own visit to Russia, by Churchill's friend and colleague Lord Beaverbrook. When Churchill continued to delay over the 'Second Front' in France, Stalin suggested Britain send twenty-five or thirty divisions to help Russia on the Eastern Front.[113] When this idea in turn seemed unwelcome, Cripps telegraphed to say that the Russians were 'obsessed by the view that we were sitting back and watching them'.[114] German propaganda that Britain was prepared to 'fight to the last drop of Russian blood' was being successful. Churchill offered to relieve the Russians in Persia or send a small force to the Caucasus. Those

* See page 448.

artful ideas were rejected by Stalin. Churchill continued to argue that Russia's problems were partly of her own making, through the Nazi-Soviet Pact; and that a symbolic sacrifice of British troops on the Russian front was a less satisfactory contribution than the provision of British and American arms to the 'millions of trained soldiers' which Russia could put in the field.

Anthony Eden, the Foreign Secretary, went to Moscow in December 1941 'to remove the Russian suspicions that we wished to make an "Anglo-American" peace excluding Russia.' Stalin immediately ventured onto discussion of post-war frontiers: 'the Americans have asked us not to agree to any altered boundaries in Europe', said Eden.[115]

Eden was bullied mercilessly, and cleverly, by Stalin over the Baltic States.* Eden just survived this with difficulty, but it became evident that the Russians were going to use their territorial demands as a threat: 'support us over these concessions as a condition for continuing to fight your battles'. Then, Eden recalled, 'We . . . need to maintain collaboration with Russia, after the war, since otherwise she might turn to Germany'. So Britain had to think of ways whereby the Soviet Union would find it to her advantage to maintain friendship. A concession over the Baltic States was one possibility. But such a concession clashed with the Atlantic Charter.† Churchill sought with embarrassment to escape from the dilemma. Forced to choose in the spring of 1942 between, on the one hand, President Roosevelt's reluctance to make any commitment and, on the other, the apparent political need to please Stalin, the British decided to satisfy the Russians.[116] They went ahead with plans to make an Anglo-Soviet Treaty on the understanding that the Baltic states would be abandoned.

This policy was decided upon for good reason: because of the anxiety that Russia might make a separate peace; the hope for future Russian collaboration after the war against, among other things, a revival of German strength: and because Russia might anyway occupy the territories which she claimed.

* See page 451.
† See Appendix IV.

Nevertheless, as the official historian of British foreign policy, Llewellyn Woodward, put it, this was 'a surrender of principle' which implied that 'the Soviet use of democratic terms could be allowed to cover acts which were in fact contrary to the theory and practice of free states'.[117] The consequences of this surrender were soon evident, even though the intransigence (and further demands) of the Russians prevented, in the end, the Anglo-Soviet Treaty from including any territorial questions: it was, however, not the moral question of the Baltic States which caused this. It was the Polish frontier. The Anglo-Soviet Treaty was signed on May 26, 1942. It was for twenty years and pledged mutual help. The avoidance of territorial concessions was 'a miracle', according to Sumner Welles. It indeed did seem in the end a most successful negotiation by Eden.[118]

Disputes between Britain and Russia continued, despite the Treaty: over the temporary suspension of British convoys to Russia, over the flight of Hess to England, over the continued postponement of a 'Second Front'. Churchill visited Moscow in August 1942, but did not dispel distrust. Nor did Stalin look on the Anglo-American landing in North Africa in December 1942 as a 'Second Front' worthy of the name. His followers in Britain made evident their support for these complaints in a series of pamphlets and other propaganda. Stalin's communications to Churchill became 'offensive' in the summer of 1943. Such disputes continued, even at the conference at Tehran, where Churchill, previously the advocate of *realpolitik* towards Stalin, suddenly seemed, in the minds of Americans, to be the 'obstructionist', on such matters at the Italian settlement and Turkish belligerency, as well as the 'Second Front'; which last was definitely promised at Tehran, for 1944.

By the time that the event occurred in June 1944, Russia had already reoccupied nearly all of what had been Russian territory in 1939. It was obvious that the war would soon end, with the Red Army entrenched well inside old Europe. The question as to what policy to follow in consequence exercised the British government most of 1944 and 1945. In an atmosphere of considerable perplexity, the Foreign Secretary had probably been right, in April 1944, if scarcely profound, in saying that he thought that we should 'let matters drift a little longer before we have a showdown with Stalin'; even though he personally was disposed to agree to all the territorial demands made by Russia earlier in the war (the Baltic States, the Polish frontier, Poland, Bessarabia and northern Bukovina).[119] Argument followed argument, paper followed paper. The northern department believed that the foundation of post-war European policy would have to be the Anglo-Soviet alliance. There was, they argued, no sign of a desire to impose Communism on any of the Central European countries: an assessment scarcely valid even at the time it was written. Russia would be unlikely to work for any combination with German communists. In Poland, there were signs that the Russians were ready to welcome a new regime in Poland based on the democratic and socialist parties. What signs, one wonders, were these?[120] Geoffrey Wilson, writing in the northern department, predicted in the summer of 1944 that Russia would probably be 'genuinely worried about the state of affairs that they find in Europe when they come in. So long as any good administration is not hostile to them, I think the chances are that they will tend to support it, rather than otherwise'.[121] A little later, the same official had complained that 'the military' in Whitehall had identified Russia as the only likely danger in future and that the way to meet that was to 'organise against it now, largely by preparing to build up Germany against Russia'. Wilson thought that such an assumption would make inevitable the danger which they were all trying to avoid.[122] There was also anxiety lest the military apprehension just noticed would be communicated (as usual with British military recommendations) to the Commonwealth and thus leaked to the Russians at an inconvenient moment.[123]

The 'Post Hostilities Planning Sub-Committee', composed of representatives of the three services, with a chairman from the Foreign Office, also produced an analysis in 1944. It had been instructed by the Cabinet to plan on 'the assumption that it remained the policy of HMG to foster and maintain the friendliest possible relations with the USSR'.[124] They could not therefore challenge that unrealisable conclusion. This Sub-Committee recommended that Britain should not 'oppose any reasonable demands of the USSR where they do not conflict with our vital strategic interests'. Those interests were: (i) threats to Middle Eastern oil; (ii) the Mediterranean; (iii) 'vital sea communications'; and (iv) maintenance of the concentrated industrial areas of Britain.[125] Eastern Europe did not figure in this list. Another paper, by the Joint Intelligence Committee in December 1944,[126] described the potential threat of Russia as that of a 'land empire' comprising 'nearly all the raw materials essential for an adequate war economy' and 'an industry capable of supporting, in the field, armies substantially larger than those of any other power in Europe', with good dispersal of economically important targets and a 'large, youthful and rapidly expanding population'. The main aim of Russia after the war would be to seek the improvement of the standards of living of her people. To do that, she would 'not be prepared to take any chances' internationally and would 'seek to build up a system of security outside her frontiers, in order to make sure that she is left in peace'. Russia would be expected to experiment in collaboration with Britain and the United States but, all the same, would build up buffer states as a protective screen. That screen would consist, the Committee accepted, not only of Poland, Czechoslovakia, Hungary, Romania, and Bulgaria but also of Finland and, to a lesser extent, perhaps, Yugoslavia, 'Northern Persia', control of the Straits of Gallipoli, Japanese Sakhalin, the Kuriles, Korea and Manchuria. Russia would allow independence to these countries only so long as they pursued policies which protected her own strategic interests.

This paper did not mention the role of revolutionary Communism and, like a United States paper produced a year later by an American committee of the same name, thought chiefly in terms of power politics directed by Stalin. The authors, it will be seen, by envisaging the 'loss' of Finland and all Korea, as well as part of Persia, went further than seemed likely even to Russians in 1945. It appears, however, that these and other post-war schemes were 'never properly discussed in the Cabinet'.[127] It was difficult enough to win the war. Whatever allowance must be made for British diplomatists and statesmen concerned indeed to win a terrible conflict, it must remain surely a matter of curiosity, at the least, that nobody within Whitehall seems to have appreciated, from, say, his reading of Souvarine's *Life of Stalin* (1939), Arthur Koestler's *Darkness at Noon* (1941) or Krivitsky's *I was Stalin's Agent* (1939) that George Orwell and Victor Serge might be right when they predicted in January 1944 (as Serge did) that 'Stalinist hegemony over Europe would be a new nightmare'.[128]

By 1945, English officials often were realistic, it is true. Thus Bevin's private secretary thought 'the main objective of the Russians is access to, and a base in, the Mediterranean'.[129] The inspiration of much of the British post-war planning, Gladwyn Jebb, soon to be one of Ernest Bevin's closest advisers, wrote that no doubt 'we shall find it advisable and necessary to abandon many positions, in order to defer to Russian views: but there is presumably a point beyond which we could not go'. He added, only too correctly: 'At the moment, only the Russians seem to have a clearly defined national policy. The absence of such a policy in England and America, more than any other single factor, is likely to give rise to misunderstandings and difficulties which, if they are allowed to continue, may darken the prospects of the world organisation we are seeking to create'.[130] As for Cadogan, he noted when at the Conference of San Francisco, that he 'really did not know' how to cure 'Russian suspicions and unwillingness to cooperate. And I don't know whether it's better to have a good showdown with the Russians or to attempt to go on coaxing them. I am inclined to think the former'. The next day he wrote: 'No one will face up to the problem presented to us by the Russians'.[131] Some officials, meantime, took Communist manners at face value: thus Adrian Holman in Paris wrote that the Communist party should be treated 'on its merits, like any other political party in France'.[132]

One qualification might sensibly be made: the realistic support for such concessions to Russia as 'a sphere of influence' in Eastern Europe, generally accepted among British diplomatists with various justifications (Russia's need for security, for example), was at least a policy: it did not feed Eastern European democrats with false hopes, which the Americans continued to do during 1945.

One man always willing to face these intractable questions had been the Prime Minister of South Africa, General Smuts, whose influence in those days was great. Charming, talkative, cultivating the impression of a philosopher-king, 'very old, very wise, very convinced that, in the end, it is conduct and principle which decide events, not ingenuity', no one was more listened to than he was.[133] On March 20, 1944, he was the first, within the circle of Commonwealth leaders, to suggest that a paper on Russian policy should be written: 'There is already much in present Russian actions which is obscure and disquieting', he wrote, 'and, with the immense power that Russia is likely to wield in the post-war world, the whole field of her foreign policy has to be surveyed with great circumspection'. Not only would the idea of a regional grouping of Western Europe around Britain have to be discussed. So also would the possibility of a broken, and perhaps communised, Germany falling willingly within the Russian orbit – an eventuality more to be dreaded than anything else.[134]

One difficulty in considering these matters was that there was in Britain, as in the United States, little serious attention paid by intelligence officers to Russia. In 1941, following the German attack on Russia, Churchill had apparently told the Chief of his Secret Service to concentrate all his resources on the Axis: the Soviet Union was an ally.[135] Intercepts of Soviet radio messages nevertheless continued, though given scant attention by a British officialdom disinclined to eavesdrop on a friend. Officials collaborated with Russia where they could: nothing indicates the character of the era more than the suggestion of the head of the northern department, Christopher Warner, that, in respect of British (SOE) operations in Bulgaria in 1944, 'it would be best for the SOE representative in Moscow to raise the matter with the NKVD'.[136]

The decision not to consider Russia as worth studying was revised in 1944. A special unit, Section IX, of MI6, was then re-vitalised to concern itself exclusively with Russia. It employed several able students of Soviet society: such as the political analyst Carew Hunt, author of *The Theory and Practice of Bolshevism*; and Jane Archer, late of the Security Service. Its head, however, by one of the most bizarre paradoxes in history, was, from late 1944 to early 1947, the bibulous but clever agent of the Soviet Union, H. A. R. Philby.[137] Counter-espionage in MI5, on the other hand, always kept an eye on the Soviet Union.[138] It does not seem, however, to have been very effective, considering how easy it was for the Soviet agent and naturalised Englishman, Dr Klaus Fuchs to work on atomic matters, when the 'British authorities had been informed by the Germans prior to the war that he was a communist'. 'For some reason', said the American General Groves, in charge of the development in the United States of the atomic weapon, 'they ignored this and did not even record the information where they would find it'.[139] A paper by MI5 written in 1947 later explained how, early in the war, 'government departments had become less inclined to exclude Communists from secret work and, in fact, members of the Communist Party are known to have been placed in positions where they had access to information of great secrecy. Many . . . are known to have volunteered to the Communist headquarters information about British war production, with the intention that this information should be passed on to the Russians'.[140] Later on, Britain had become more steely: 'I suppose you know that we are weeding out remorselessly every single known Communist from all our secret organisations', Cadogan wrote to Churchill in 1944; 'we did this after having had to sentence two quite high grade people to long terms of penal servitude for their betrayal, in accordance with Communist faith, of important military secrets'.[141]

Both in consequence of Philby's extraordinary position, and for other reasons, it is hard to believe that the British Secret Service (SIS or MI6, as it was known) constituted a formidable challenge to the Soviet Union in 1946, despite its fame. The senior members of the institution were 'fanatically anti-communist', even 'lunatic in their anti-communism' but they misunderstood Marxism. They were lax.[142] The director of those services, the legendary 'C', Sir Stuart Menzies, was a popular chief, a considerate, honest, humane and relaxed gentleman, a fine rider with the Beaufort Hunt but without the depth of intellect for his daunting task.[143] 'He was a bad judge

of men,' wrote a wartime member of his staff, 'and drew
his personal advisers from a painfully limited social circle . . .
incapable of giving him the support he needed'.[144] His successes
– photo-reconnaissance by air, and sabotage – had become
independent operations. Shortage of resources prevented the
institution from concentrating on Nazism and Communism at the
same time. Even before the war, there appears to have been
little attention paid to the Comintern, neither its policies nor its
personnel, which so greatly influenced events in the 1940s (and
which because of the peripatetic lives of the leaders, especially
during the 1930s, could surely have easily been penetrated).
The old 'Passport Control Offices' had not survived into the war
and that loss was not compensated for by new relations with
allied secret services, except for the emigré Polish and Czech
ones. Such papers as are available for 1945–46 suggest modest
ambitions, modestly pursued. The service, for example,
decided not to send any agents into Austria 'for a month or so'
after the arrival of the official British Mission there. Yet that
was a country at the heart of the world's dramas (see Appendix
VII). One of the service's senior officers wrote that 'serious
intelligence coverage of Soviet intentions did not get under way
until the Soviet take-over of Czechoslovakia'; up till then, 'the
services were still restrained by the concept of Russia as a
wartime ally. We were obviously suspicious';[145] nevertheless,
one of their representatives in Washington, Wing-commander
Roald Dahl, did believe that a combined Anglo-American secret
service was necessary 'to prevent Russia from blowing up
Anglo-Saxon civilisation'.[146] The idea was not pursued.

The Special Operations Executive, the often brilliantly successful wartime agency for setting 'Europe ablaze', was meantime being wound up, and even its archives destroyed: 'I know
that the SOE have done good work in the past but I am confident
that their time for useful work is over,' wrote Oliver Harvey on
July 16, 1945. 'Their contacts can only be dangerous,'[147] he
added, inexplicably. All through 1945, indeed, the Foreign Office
was working to ensure that (despite suggestions by both
Churchill and Eden that SOE might survive after the war) 'all
activities abroad in time of peace' would be 'under the control

and approval of the Foreign Office', and that SOE would be terminated.[148] Given the belief of some senior officials in SOE (for example, Henry Sporborg) that the organisation might usefully collaborate with the Soviet NKVD after the war (as well as its bad relations with the old secret service), this decision seems to have been wise, even if it was taken for reasons of bureaucratic politics ('we think it most unwise to tell the Russians that we cannot enter into any commitments as to working with the NKVD without prior approval from London', Sporborg had written to Warner in the Foreign Office, in April 1945).[149] Similarly, the Political Warfare Executive, the propaganda organisation directed during the war by Bruce Lockhart, was ended. It was supposed that peace would not need publicity.

The exception to these economies was the British code and cypher service which had been successfully set up in the First World War.[150] In the 1920s, Britain read the codes of many countries, particularly those of Russia, employing exiled code-breaking Russians. Until well into the 1930s, the chief target of the Secret Intelligence Service, with their network of Passport Control officers in over twenty European places, had been Russia. But the surveillance of Russian codes was unfortunately revealed by Baldwin when prime minister, and by several members of his Cabinet, in the House of Commons in 1927, in a debate after the so-called Arcos raid by MI5 on the Soviet Trade mission.[151] The Soviet government then changed their codes and so little of importance could thereafter be looked at. Still, these operations continued, and were fully shared, by an agreement (BRUSA) in 1943, with the United States, in which Britain remained the senior partner. Australia, Canada and New Zealand were also integrated in the business.

Britain was then a country deeply bruised by the world war in which it had fought from beginning to end. The recent six years of conflict, and the previous four and a quarter years a generation before, had transformed the political apparatus. The Conservative Party, shaken into passivity, for the moment, by its electoral defeat, and in the process of being reformed under the influence of Winston Churchill, had little independent contribution to make. Ernest Bevin's first speech on foreign policy in August 1945 had seemed to do no more than show 'the importance of being Anthony' – Anthony Eden was his predecessor – and to do so authoritatively and powerfully. Britain was 'virtually bankrupt'. On August 21, after Lend Lease from America had been cancelled, almost with the abruptness that had characterised the cancellation of the Russian aid in May, Lord Keynes, the most gifted English intellectual of his day, ill but still resourceful, had told the Cabinet that, without a loan from the United States, immediate economies abroad, and an intense effort to increase exports, Britain faced an 'industrial Dunkirk'.[152] During the war, Britain had lost a quarter of her pre-war wealth (£7,300 million). She was now the world's largest debtor nation. Capital assets abroad of £1,300 million ($8 billion) had been sold, cutting income from this source by a half. Britain's losses in merchant ships totalled 11.5 million tons. That fleet was down to 70 per cent of its figure for 1939. In December 1945, a loan from the United States of $3.75 billion at a low interest had been agreed by Keynes with the United States Treasury. But that agreement had not yet been through Congress. Perhaps it would be made conditional on unacceptable new demands, even though the British had accepted Bretton Woods in 1944 only on the understanding that a loan would be made. As it was, the United States extracted numerous humiliating conditions even in the original agreement.*

The Labour Party had captured power in a nation which war had accustomed to state power, exercised by men and women whose collectivism might be coldly bureaucratic and ideology-less, but which certainly represented a step on the road to socialism. In addition, the relief which most British citizens had felt after the alliance which had been thankfully made with Stalin

---

* Britain had to end, by December 31, 1946, the sterling area dollar pool and quantitative import controls; to restore sterling convertibility in mid-1947; and to scale down the sterling balances accumulated by other countries during the war. In return Britain got not only her loan but the United States wiped out the Lend Lease account of $20 billion and sold over $6 billion worth of surplus post-war Lend Lease property for $650 billion.

following Hitler's invasion accustomed people to give Russia the benefit of the doubt. The British knew from 1941 that Russia was bearing the brunt of the struggle against Germany and that Russia needed help. The high intentions of the Atlantic Charter gave way to an emphasis, in the mind of the public (as well as the Ministry of Information), on the unity of the 'Big Three': which phrase became a euphemism for power politics. As Djilas put the matter years later, the Soviet Union became 'a much lauded ally whose government' they, the British, 'had for many years considered to be essentially no different from their own. The British did not realise . . . that the Soviet Union was no normal, no legitimate state by any accepted standard'.[153] Stalin was called 'Uncle Joe' (or 'UJ') half mockingly, but also half affectionately, by the Prime Minister, the head of the Foreign Office, the Foreign Secretary, and millions of humbler men. Many of the Labour members of Parliament elected in 1945 had been friendly to Communism in the 1930s. One of them, John Strachey, now a Junior Minister (for the Air Force), published a pamphlet on Labour policy in 1945 in a form almost unchanged from the version of it which he had first published in 1938 when he had been a Communist.[154] The Left of the Labour party believed in the possibility, and desirability, of a real 'socialist foreign policy' based on friendship with Russia and her friends in East Europe and a decisive break with capitalism and the United States, its protector. 'Most English left-wingers', Orwell thought, favoured 'a niggling policy of "getting along with Russia" by being strong enough to prevent an attack and weak enough to disown suspicion'.[155]

There were many examples of men who had become accustomed, by hatred of Nazism, to smile at Russian threats, without being themselves Communist. They believed – because they wanted to believe it – that the abolition of the Comintern had meant something genuine. It had been T. S. Eliot, the poet who would be looked upon as a major conservative sage, who, on behalf of a well-established publishing house, Faber and Faber, had in 1944 rejected George Orwell's *Animal Farm*, a satire eventually published in August 1945.[156]

Despite the great alliance (or because of it) most people lived

in ignorance about the nature of Russian society. Even the
brilliant men in the 'Economic and Reconstruction Department'
of the Foreign Office seemed, in their well-written state paper
'The Four Power Plan', above mentioned, to have thought that
Britain could one day play off Russia against the United States;
'the suggestion was that, in dealing with America, we should,
while doing our best to induce them to participate in the scheme
[of four power world control] not fail to hint that, if they made
their terms too stiff, we might be obliged by the force of things
to make a close working alliance with Soviet Russia'. It remained
for the liberal economist, Lionel Robbins, to point out that the
chances of any agreement which relied on economic collaboration
with Russia were modest.[157] The consequence of these attitudes, coupled with the pledges in the Labour Party's manifesto
in 1945 to extend the welfare state begun before the First World
War by Lloyd George, and broadened during the second by
Sir William Beveridge's report on social services, made a bad
impression among the American legislators, who, in early 1946,
were being asked to approve such a large loan to Britain.

Both the Foreign Office and the Ministry of Information had
been concerned in 1941 lest public enthusiasm for the Russian
alliance might cause 'the British public to forget the dangers of
Communism' (Churchill's words to the latter ministry). The
Foreign Office helped to found an 'Anglo-Soviet public relations
committee', which reflected these hesitations. But the effort
to distinguish in propaganda the military, and patriotic, side
of Russian life from the economic, and political, one was
difficult to achieve. The first anniversary of the Anglo-Russian
alliance was thus marked by a pageant at the Empress Hall, Earls
Court, at which Communists, or fellow travellers, dominated the
organising committees. The Ministry of Information then sought
to 'get in ahead of the Communist Party' to celebrate the 25th
anniversary of the founding of the Red Army. These efforts
became blurred with the agitation in favour of an early 'Second
Front' supported by Lord Beaverbrook who, though evidently
a capitalist and an imperialist, had never published much about
the purges of the 1930s and denied the fact of religious persecution whoever exercised it. He had always admired power.

One consequence was to help the Labour Party: it seemed that, in Russia, Socialism had organised industry; so perhaps, in England, nationalisation could prosper.[158]

In Britain, as in the United States, the myth of the victory achieved by the Red Army was a powerful influence; 'there can be no question', George Orwell wrote, in 1945, of 'the poisonous effect of the Russian myths on English intellectual life. Because of it, known facts are suppressed and distorted to such an extent as to make it doubtful whether a true history of our times can ever be written'.[159] Such a history would have to take account of how the Socialist Archbishop of Canterbury, William Temple, in his treatise *Christianity and Social Order* (1942), had argued that Marx 'was not far wrong' in saying that the victory of the bourgeoisie had left 'naked self interest' and 'callous cash payment' as the only bond between men. It would not forget how the influential Chairman of the Labour Party, Professor Harold Laski, argued in 1942 that the age of competitive capitalism was over, nor how the most successful English writer of the day, J. B. Priestley, had written, in *Letter to a Returning Serviceman*, that 'whatever their faults, the Bolsheviks had put their hand to the great task, and were trying to lift the load of want, ignorance, fear and misery from their dumb millions'. One of the most influential political philosophers of the Labour Party, G. D. H. Cole, Professor of Politics at Oxford, would write, in the *Intelligent Man's Guide to the Postwar World*, to be published in 1947, that he accepted 'Soviet democracy as a legitimate form of democracy'. He rejected altogether 'the notion that it is merely autocracy in disguise'.[160] The intellectual inspiration of the Labour party, Harold Laski, believed that the first consequence of Labour's electoral victory in July 1945 was that, 'at long last, we have made possible full friendship with the Soviet Union'.[161] Lord Beveridge, the father of the new Welfare State introduced during the war, showed his ignorance of Soviet conditions when in an article in the evening newspaper, the *Star*, published in August 1945, he said of the Russians, 'if they are content with repression, or do not feel strongly enough to get rid of these things, that is their funeral'.[162] As for America, the best known of the younger historians in England, A. J. P. Taylor, told a radio audience in December 1945 that 'nobody in Europe believes in the American way of life, that is, in private enterprise: or rather, those who believe in it are a defeated party, which seems to have no more future than the Jacobites in England after 1688'.

Both *The Times* and the *Sunday Times* had as their correspondents in Moscow men, Ralph Parker and Alexander Werth, who usually gave a favourable interpretation of Stalin's policies, domestic and international. Ralph Parker, a tragic failure, was also for a time correspondent for the *New York Times*. He had worked for *The Times* of London in Prague before the war and afterwards in the Albanian section of SOE. He was seduced by Russian agents and became gradually a Soviet mouthpiece. For example, he described the determined Polish Communist Gomułka in 1945 as 'a quiet-spoken, reserved middle-aged . . . oil worker from south Poland, who remained in Poland throughout the occupation'.[163] He married a Russian, Valentina, later left *The Times* for the *Daily Worker*, lived in Moscow, tormented, trusted by nobody, till he died years later.[164] 'Alex' Werth, a more complicated man, was a Chekovian dreamer, born in St Petersburg, son of a Jewish industrialist, who sometimes spent whole days playing Chopin on his piano in his room at the Metropole Hotel. Though a serious individual and an admirable writer, nevertheless he often found it essential to 'curry favour with the Soviet officials'.[165] The most influential weekly of Britain was the *New Statesman*, whose mercurial editor, Kingsley Martin, took a line which, from the start of the Labour government, distanced itself from both Bevin and the United States, and had no fears about the consequences of Soviet policies being pursued in east Europe for the peoples of the countries concerned.[166]

*The Times* itself had not supported either of the main parties in the election of 1945. Its editor, Robin Barrington-Ward, too clever for quick decisions, preferred a coalition. But his leader writers gave support to the Labour government in power: victory makes friends. In its attitude to foreign policy, the influence of Edward Carr, ex-diplomatist and future historian of the Bolshevik Revolution, was dominant: above all, as far as interpretation of Russia was concerned. Carr believed strongly in 'spheres of influence'. Author of a book, *The Twenty Years' Crisis*, which had been an apology for the appeasement of Hitler, he was now impatient about complaints about Soviet predatoriness. Sympathy for Eastern European peoples was to him mere sentiment. East Europe was the Russian zone of influence. It seemed absurd to Carr, and so to *The Times*, that 'questions of recognising, or not recognising, regimes within the Soviet zone should be allowed any longer to cloud relations between the major powers'.[166] The Foreign Office complained. Bevin talked to Barrington Ward. But Carr, cold and determined, maintained his production of lucid articles, and his personality influenced others around him. Barrington-Ward himself pressed the idea of agreement with Russia with the same missionary zeal and earnestness with which he had earlier supported appeasement with the Nazis. He even included among the instructions of his correspondent in Moscow, Ralph Parker, the goal of 'creating understanding' with Russia. The determination of this dedicated editor to maintain friendship with a country which could not respond led to his early death, as unrequited passions have often done.[167]

The lack of knowledge by most Western people of the real Russia had some tragic immediate consequences. The British Cabinet in September 1944 took a decision to return to Russia all Soviet citizens found in German combat uniforms. In the circumstances of the war, this decision, harsh as it certainly seems now, was comprehensible. Any Soviet soldier who took up arms against the Soviet Union, such as General Vlasov and his corps, could not have been in much doubt as to their future fates if Stalin should win the war. Much more agonising was the position of those Soviet soldiers who had been forced to join labour battalions after their capture by the Germans, in order to remain alive. Still more distressing was the plight of the hundreds of thousands of Russian citizens who had been conscripted or kidnapped to work in German factories as slaves. In October 1944, Anthony Eden was asked by Molotov about what policy he had towards these categories of unfortunate men and women. He may have been surprised by the question. Molotov

pressed: would he have any objection to the return of all Soviet
citizens to Russia, on the condition that all British citizens were
returned to Britain. 'I have no objection', Eden said.[168] Thus
policy was decided. Britain took it up because they wanted their
own prisoners of war freed by the Red Army, and because,
previously, they had worried lest Russia would refuse to take
back these people, and so leave in Europe a colossal problem
of refugees: there were several million involved. The Cabinet
made these decisions. The officials, some of whom knew that
the consequences would be atrocious, were not the men responsible.[169]

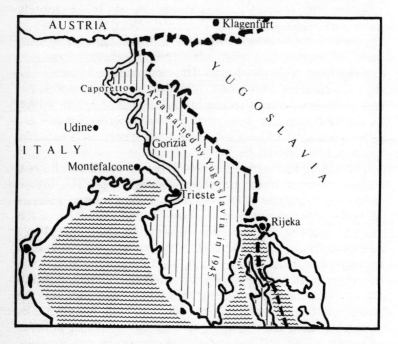

The Americans took up much the same position. Thus General
Deane, negotiating with the Russians for an exchange of American prisoners in German camps liberated by Russian troops,
with Russian prisoners freed by the Western Allies, despite his
dislike of the Soviet system, had 'no reason to suspect that the

Soviet state would treat as deserters all soldiers who had surrendered to the Germans'. An agreement was signed by Generals Deane, for the United States, and Gryzlov, for the Russians, at Yalta, on February 11, 1945. Harriman said later that 'we had no idea that hundreds of thousands of Soviet citizens would refuse, because we had reason to suspect that they would be sent to their deaths'.[170] Yet, from the first week of March 1945, beginning with a cargo sent in *The Duchess of Bedford* from Liverpool, thousands of unfortunate Russians strongly resisted when they were dispatched home.[171] In the confusion at the end of the war, in addition, a small fourth category of men and women were also returned who, although White Russian exiles of the 1920s, had been specifically excluded in those years from being Soviet citizens and whom even the Russians were surprised to receive. The reason why this tragedy occurred remains unclear.*

The consequences were appalling. In June 1945, Averell Harriman had told the State Department that 'the Embassy knows of only a single instance in which a repatriated prisoner has returned to his home and family in Moscow . . . Repatriates [generally] are met at ports of entry by police guard and marched off . . . to unknown destinations. Trainloads of repatriates are passing through Moscow and continuing east, the passengers being held incommunicado while trains stand in Moscow yards'.[172] They usually went to the concentration camps north of the Arctic Circle. The numbers who died must have been a very large proportion of those who were returned.

These 'transfers' were still going on in January 1946. There is a painful account in the files of the State Department describing the handover of 399 Russians (who had served in Vlasov's army) to their Soviet compatriots on the 19th of that month. The men had been held in the ex-Nazi camp of Dachau. They refused to move. They begged to be shot rather than handed back. The embarrassed American soldiers turned tear gas on the huts and drove the unfortunates into the snow. Nine men

---

* A fifth category – that of Yugoslav citizens returned to Tito – is discussed on page 431. See too the footnote to that page.

hanged themselves, two stabbed themselves to death, six men escaped en route, and twenty lingered in hospital from self-inflicted wounds.[173] The events concerned were among the most brutal aftermaths of the war. The numbers handed back exceeded two million in all, of whom several hundred thousand may have escaped and became absorbed in Western countries in the end.

These activities continued on a more modest scale (since most of the possible victims had already gone) throughout 1946. Bevin might have ended the policy; and since the Americans were, on this matter, influenced by the British, that might have been an end to the matter. He did not, however, wish to do so without knowledge of where Russian refugees would go in the West. After the Americans introduced a regulation, whereby those who resisted were not handed back, the British did the same, pending a decision by the Cabinet. That, however, led to much unpleasant subterfuges hated by those called on to carry them through in practice.

One unhappily typical instance at that time was to be seen in the discussions in January 1946 at Brück, on the Mur, in Austria, between British officers discussing how to send home Russian civilians then in camps for displaced persons in the British zone of that country. The British officers argued that Austrian civilian police should not be used to round up the Russians. That would cause alarm, 'whereas British troops were trusted'. 'Low subterfuge would have to be resorted to': such as, for example, 'persuading these persons that Austria was unable to accommodate them any longer and that they would be taken to some brave, but unspecified, new world . . . Since any movement towards the Soviet boundary was regarded with suspicion by displaced persons, some other form of repatriation' had to be found 'such as by sea or by direct train to the Soviet Union from some collecting area farther west.'[174] A devious policy was thus pursued. It is painful to read of these acts. Let the reader be reminded that it was a Cabinet policy, not one decided by the officers, that it was an all-party decision, that the willingness to accept refugees was then modest in all countries of the West, and that the officers concerned hated their task which often left them to have to commit actions which were out of keeping with British traditions.

Given the American and British lead, it is scarcely surprising that lesser states should also hand back to Russia all Soviet citizens who might, by guile, chance, courage or imagination, have reached them. Thus the Swedish government handed over 'their' Russians, mostly citizens of the Baltic States before 1940, on January 25, 1946.[175] The Grand Duke of Liechtenstein, in a more favourable geographical position, however, took a different line; he refused; and the Russians accepted it.[176]

The British army in Austria also returned, in May 1945, to their onetime home perhaps 25,000 Croat, Slovene and Chetnik refugees who had fled at the end of the war from Yugoslavia. Many were either members of, or sympathisers with, the defeated faction in the Yugoslav Civil War, which had grown out of the war with Germany. Others were merely fearful of communism in a general sense. The Croats fled to save their lives; having spent the war killing Serbs, they had no illusion about their chance of life in Yugoslavia. Tito executed most of these after their return, because, wrote Djilas, years later 'in Yugoslavia, there was no civil administration. There were no properly constituted courts. There was no way in which the cases of twenty to thirty thousand people could have been reliably investigated. So the easy way out was to have them all shot'. Djilas remarked, 'we didn't at all understand why the British insisted on returning these people. We believed, in the ideological context prevailing at the time, that the British would have a good deal of sympathy with these refugees, seeing that they had fled Communism'.[177] They did not. These Yugoslavs seemed a burden to the overworked British command in Carinthia, which was a maelstrom of overcrowded and under-fed displaced persons from all over Europe. In addition, Field Marshal Alexander, the commander responsible, thought that he might be called upon to fight Yugoslavia* and he wanted 'a clear front'.[178] War with Yugoslavia could, he and his command

* The Carinthian and Trieste crisis of May to June 1945 discussed on pages 431–2.

realised, become something much more unpleasant: even war
with Russia.


The Communist Party of Great Britain was still tiny but, as in
the United States, it was more influential than its membership
and its one MP suggested. Despite widespread disillusion over
the Nazi-Soviet pact, and the subsequent era of 'revolutionary
defeatism', not to speak of the publication of Arthur Koestler's
*Darkness at Noon* in March 1941, the Red Army's victories in
the war had made, or confirmed, many friends. These remained
an intellectual gathering of communists, headed by the half-
Swedish, half-Indian editor of *Labour Monthly*, Raji Palme Dutt,
and Professor J. B. S. Haldane. The Party had also succeeded
in capturing the leadership of several important unions (for
example, Arthur Horner in the Miners' Union). There were
perhaps twenty 'underground' Communist MPs: MPs elected
as Labour politicians but secretly Communist members or
friendly to the party, as the Comintern's arrangements laid down
by Lenin twenty years before had provided. Communism in
Britain would unfortunately remain a conspiracy within the
Labour movement; but one to be reckoned with, nonetheless.
  Britain's overall strategic position was deceptively strong.
She was all-powerful, with the eclipse of Italy, in the Mediterranean. She still controlled the 'five strategic keys' which the
late Admiral Fisher had believed 'locked up the globe' (Dover,
Gibraltar, Singapore, the Cape – Simonstown – and Alexandria).
Greece was in 1946 as much a British protectorate as was
Egypt. Britain's control of the Western European seaboard was
also absolute. Even under a Labour government, she had leaders
with a will to use that power. But seapower was no longer
decisive. Ever since the building of strategic railways, and since
railways had been supplemented by roads, the importance of
land empires – such as Russia and the United States – had
grown. With aviation, Britain could no longer be 'the great sea
serpent always able to crawl back into its watery lair', which she
had appeared to Heine in 1842. The 'crisis in the British global
position' had coincided with the German challenge in the late

1930s.[180] The prospect of a war against Germany, Japan and Italy, in combination, had been alarming when, as was the case in 1938, the United States had been toying with isolation, and when the Soviet Union was hostile. There seemed, even in the 1930s, no chance of a blockade being effective ever again as a weapon. Such considerations made for a policy of conciliation, rather than challenge. About a quarter of the human race, it is true, still lived in the British Commonwealth or Empire, and no such previous enterprise had ever had such responsibility. There was also the 'informal empire', which still might be said to include the sterling area, Argentina, half Persia and several prosperous points in China. But the Empire was now a responsibility, not a source of strength, as the United States, heirs of the first British Empire, knew and which the Labour government recognised after Keynes's negotiations for the American loan.

In his editorial for the September 1945 issue of *Horizon*, the most interesting literary journal of the time, the critic Cyril Connolly wrote: 'Morally and economically Europe has lost the war. The great marquee of European civilization in whose yellow light we all grew up, and read, or wrote, or loved, or travelled has fallen down; the side-ropes are frayed, the centre-pole is broken, the chairs and tables are all in pieces, the tent is empty, the roses are withered on their stands . . . '[181] The question for Britain was whether she was a visitor to this marquee or an inhabitant of it. It was not until the edifice had been restored that hesitantly she made her choice.

Britain had had in the first winter since the war one experience which was denied to her allies; a visit from a Russian football team, the Moscow Dynamos. They played four matches. In two of these games, there was bad feeling. The Dynamos ended their tour early apparently in order to avoid playing an all-England team. The games, as so often on sporting occasions between national teams, created ill will.[182]

# BOOK THREE

# DISPUTED LANDS

Wild gloomy times are roaring towards us and a prophet wishing to write a new apocalypse would have to invent entirely new beasts – beasts so terrible that St John's older animals would be like gentle doves and cupids in comparison . . . The future smells of Russian leather, blood, godlessness, and many whippings. I should advise our grandchildren to be born with very thick skins on their backs

Heine, July 12, 1842.

Freedom with its pert vauntings shall
No more be heard

Gessler, the Emperor's agent, just before being shot
by William Tell. Schiller, William Tell

*Atrocities*: a British definition
The difference between an atrocity and a war crime, depends upon the nationality of the victim. If the victim were a member of one of the Allied Nations, the offence would be a war crime. If the victim were a member of the Enemy nations or a neutral, it would be an atrocity.        FO 1020/2063

# TWELVE

# FAR AWAY COUNTRIES: EASTERN EUROPE; POLAND AND CZECHOSLOVAKIA

In Eastern Europe – in countries which achieved independence from the Russian, Ottoman and Habsburg multinational empires in the sixty years between 1860 and 1920 – the nature of authority seemed in 1946 to vary greatly. In Poland, governmental power had been handed by the Red Army to a group of Communists and Russophils. In Hungary, a coalition government was led by the neutral, almost non-political, Smallholders' Party, elected the previous November; in the coalition, there were Communists but, to the outsider, they did not seem very well established. Bulgaria and Romania were still monarchies, the first with a regency for a child King; in the second, the King was merely an influence. For Bulgaria had a government led by Colonel Georgiev, a well-known politician of the old days, under whom determined Communists served in key positions. This too was an administration which had been sponsored by the Red Army on arrival in September 1944. The Romanian government was of a similar type, led by the less well-known, equally pliant, Dr Groza. In Yugoslavia and Albania, Communist parties had won power outright by directing a successful resistance against the Germans: and by winning a civil war against those who sought to return their countries, after the war, to the politics of the past. Czechoslovakia had a government headed by the cultivated Dr Beneš. There were several Communists in his government. That was also the case in Western France and Italy. The future of this prized democracy of the inter-war years seemed at least as promising.

In Hungary, Bulgaria and Romania, allies of Germany in the late war, an Inter-Allied Control Commission had formal authority over the governments. In these organs, the Russian generals did much as they wished; the armistice arrangements of 1944 rendered the British and American representatives powerless. Nevertheless, the Western allies, as has been seen, believed that they had a specific responsibility to them under the Declaration on Liberated Europe, signed at Yalta, to guarantee free elections. But their influence was modest. The Americans might have the atom bomb. Some had seen that as a possible source of pressure. But it pressed nothing. Almost the only occasion that the 'decisive weapon' had been spoken of in Central Europe since August appears to have been when, in September, a war memorial was raised in Vienna to the 'heroic Red Army' and a few elderly, disorientated, Communists carried a banner thanking the Soviet Union for saving the city from the atom bomb.[1] President Truman had said, the previous year, that he was determined to remove the 'Soviet blackout' in Eastern Europe.[2] But the Declaration on Liberated Europe was a rhetorical document. It pledged the allies to consult about matters within the countries concerned, not to act. Nor did it say what would happen if there were disputes about the meaning of the word 'democratic'.

In four countries of East Europe, there had indeed by February 1946 been elections since the end of the war: Hungary in November 1945, where the Smallholders gained their good majority; and Bulgaria, Yugoslavia and Albania, where elections in November, and December, 1945, had led to coalitions dominated by Communists. Elections were planned for Poland, Czechoslovakia and Romania in the coming months: even though Russian officials represented to Western diplomats that 'our [i.e. Western] standards of democracy were entirely unsuited to Eastern Europe'.[3] A 'third form of democracy', different from that of the Soviet Union and of the West, was 'growing up in those countries'. For all these countries, the word 'satellite', to describe their relation to the sun of Moscow, was already in use, as it had been towards those of them which had been dependencies of Germany a short time before.[4]

The character of each of these countries in Eastern European centres was, of course, different, just as the circumstances of their release from Nazi rule, and of their original independence, were different. Thus in Poland and, to a lesser extent, Albania and Yugoslavia, something close to civil war between the governments and the anti-Communists continued, in remote regions. The all-consuming activity in Czechoslovakia, in the winter of 1945–46, was the expulsion of the Sudeten Germans;* the expulsion of *Volksdeutsche* from all over East Europe was on a lesser scale in the other countries. Hungary as well as Czechoslovakia seemed on paper to have almost as good a chance as France and Italy to escape Communist domination. In Poland, Romania, Bulgaria, Yugoslavia, and Albania, a reign of terror had begun at the moment of the entry of Communists into the government. In Czechoslovakia, the Red Army had withdrawn, but elsewhere it was mostly evident, though the numbers varied: a few thousand in Poland, a hundred thousand in Bulgaria. Apart from the intimidation which it exerted everywhere, it consumed substantial, scarce, quantities of food and resources. Stalin had anticipated this opportunity: in 1925 he had told a meeting of officials of the Comintern: 'Europe is in decay, no revolution can succeed unless the Red Army brings it there'.[5]

In Hungary and Romania, the Allied Commissions of Control had failed to agree on a reform of the currency: so inflation was rampant. Elsewhere, the governments concerned had carried out just such a reform, with beneficial consequences. In both Poland and Yugoslavia, a skilful student might just already have detected, in the Communist parties, a certain reserve towards the Russians and not only because of Stalin's massacres of the old leaderships of those parties before the war. No such doubts were detectable in the parties of Bulgaria, Romania, Albania and Czechoslovakia. The Soviet Union was helping herself to what had previously been German property everywhere, particularly

* See below, pages 381–2.

in Hungary, Romania and Bulgaria. These self-justifying seizures were explained as 'reparations'. Religious differences remained, as in the past: Poland, Czechoslovakia and Hungary (like Lithuania and Austria) were mostly Catholic; Bulgaria, Romania and Yugoslavia were mostly Orthodox; and Albania was mostly Moslem. The approach to communism of these cults varied: combative in Hungarian catholicism; conciliatory in the Bulgarian orthodox church.

Despite their differences, these nations had much in common. None of them was well known in the West: Neville Chamberlain's remark in 1938 that Czechoslovakia was 'a far away country of whose quarrels we know nothing' was as accurate in 1945. The British Chiefs of Staff had never been asked to prepare a paper on the military significance of Central Europe.[6] Geography determined their fates. Though there were many ancient peoples in Eastern Europe, the states were new, even if, in Poland and Hungary, the nation was old. All had memories of generations when their territory had been part of empires; the Turks had withdrawn from Albania and Macedonia only in 1912. Most of these peoples had more distant memories, comforting to pride, if evanescent on examination, of great days: Poland, in 'early modern history'; Bulgaria and Serbia, in the middle ages; the Hungarians, in the dark ages; while Romania had been the core of Roman Dacia. Another element in common was that the Soviet secret police (NKVD) was, through dependent agencies modelled on it or through the use of 'special advisers', or even directors such as the sinister General Belkin in Hungary,[7] entrenching itself everywhere – even if it was meeting national Communist resistance in Yugoslavia. But, alas, all the peoples of Austria-Hungary had become accustomed to secret police, since the fatal day when the Emperor Leopold II had brought the idea back from Tuscany, where, as Grand Duke, he had found them effective. Stalin treated the Communists in the governments of East Europe in 1946 much as he had when those same people were penniless refugees before 1939, on rungs in a 'ladder of cults', where he, Stalin, stood at the top, while 'those who stood on lower rungs bowed their heads before him but, in turn, donned the robes of infallibility to address those below them'; as Gomułka, the Polish leader, later described it.[8] All the countries were, in 1946, short of food, especially the cities; as they were of medicines, fuel and anaesthetics. All the governments, Communist or no, knew that the prevailing wind in their politics was one which blew from the East, just as in the 1930s the wind was from Germany. Almost everywhere the old political class was submerged (Czechoslovakia was an exception, as to most other rules). Some of its members had withdrawn with the German army, with whom, in the cruelly ambiguous days of 1944, they had fatally compromised themselves; or others had been killed by either the German army or the communists. Some of those who remained had equally for a time believed, like Bishop Mikes of Szombathely in Hungary, that 'Russian communism had changed and no longer threatened the people and the church':[9] he was killed by Russian troops whilst trying to prevent them raping the girls in the village where he lived. The population in these countries except Czechoslovakia lived from the land and most of the territory had abolished serfdom only a generation or two before (Austria-Hungary in 1848, the Ottoman Empire in 1858, the Russians in 1861). Everywhere, new versions of land reform, initiated sporadically in the 1920s, were under way (here Bulgaria was an exception since, in the absence of large land holdings, a co-operative approach to agriculture had been earlier established). Also everywhere German actions had undermined the middle class and, at the least, ruined the Jews. German financial takeovers of the early 1940s assisted what would in the late 1940s be a relatively painless nationalisation:[10] just as the Germans' ruthless policies on resettlement of populations (Germans of the Baltic to West Poland; Poles, in hundreds of thousands, into Russia; as well as Jews, into camps) made more acceptable in the public mind the idea of new transfers of peoples. Nowhere, not even in Czechoslovakia, did the idea of representative democracy seem exhilarating. It had been tried nearly everywhere in one form or another before 1939 but had not functioned well. The ninety-two parties of old Poland's 'sejmocray' did not constitute, for example, a happy memory.[11] Whether democracy had a future would seem to depend on the actions, not the ideals, of the two Anglo-Saxon nations: of whom, the British, preoccupied by a hundred imperial problems, were largely indifferent; while the Americans had few interests.[12]

As noticed earlier, the Polish, Yugoslav and, to a lesser extent, the Bulgarian Communist parties had been cut to ribbons in Stalin's purges which had decimated foreign, as much as Russian, Communists, where the former had been foolish enough to go in the 1930s to the third Rome for inspiration or sanctuary. Equally, many East European Communists had been recruited by the secretaries of the Third (Communist) International (Comintern) and had worked within it. So, many had, in consequence, attended the Comintern schools for revolutionary activity, such as the famous one near Ufa at Kushnarenkovo, the Lenin School in Moscow, the 'N. Krupskaya Academy for Communist Education' in the same city, or perhaps the Communist University for the National Minorities of the West (KUNMZ).[13]

Thousands more East European Communists had also fought, or at least directed fighting, in the Spanish Civil War. Communist leaders in the later 1930s had thought, as did Tito in Yugoslavia, that 'Spain could serve as an excellent training ground for party military and political cadres'.[14] Collaboration between East European Communists was thus in many cases old. How often, in reading of those Communists, who had fought the Nazis and were now establishing their messianic creed in their own country, does one find, as in Artur London's sad testimony, *L'Aveu*, phrases such as '*Nous sommes restés très amis depuis l'Espagne*';[15] or 'As a young man, Kamy had . . . gone to fight in Spain, like so many other members of the Red Orchestra'; or 'Margulies [a Communist police chief in Vienna] earned the name of "*Fels*" ("rock"), during the Spanish Civil War'. Memories of tragic deaths beneath Spanish ilexes – as much as in the slave camps of Kolyma or Karaganda – enveloped their subsequently intricate destinies. Some too had later been members of that 'International Regiment' composed of foreign political emigrés in Russia which, founded in 1941, formed part of a 'Brigade of Special Assignments' which fought for the Soviet Union in the battle of Moscow, subsequently behind German lines in occupied Russia, and later still acted as the organisation behind the small groups of Czechs, Austrians, Yugoslavs, Bulgarians and others who in the last years of the war returned to their own countries as partisans. ('Spain' had also been a place of recruitment for Soviet agents: from Ramón Mercader, the murderer of Trotsky, to Alexander Foote, the senior Englishman in the war in the 'Red Orchestra'.)[16]

Among new Communists who flocked to join an apparently successful new International in 1945 there were in all countries many ex-Nazis or ex-Fascists; some psychopaths; some young men who sought safety from enquiries about the past in a new totalitarian creed to which they could give loyalty in return for protection. The prominence of Jews was also remarkable: particularly in Hungary, where the leaders of the Communists in 1945 were nearly all Jewish, but, as in the Russian social democratic party before 1914, that origin was also noticeable elsewhere in East Europe: the ironic conclusion of that brilliant era of flowering of Austro-Jewish culture which made the Vienna of the early XXth century so creative. It was symbolic that the director of the Comintern school at Kushnarenkovo should have been Ruben Levi, known in his native Bulgaria as 'Ruben Abramov' (when minister of culture in the 1950s). Ana Pauker, daughter of a rabbi in Romania, Moša Pijade in Yugoslavia, Jakub Berman from Galicia in Poland were all among the theoretical guides in their respective countries. This new Jewish contribution to the history of Europe followed a familiar pattern: initiation of a new idea; followed by prejudice; then, persecution.

Many Communist leaders had been not only imprisoned for years, but tortured, by the police of the old regime. The police chiefs in particular of the new era in East Europe were, therefore, only too well informed of degrading techniques of interrogation which they themselves did not hesitate to use. A good example was Alexander Ranković, the police chief in Yugoslavia in 1946, 'brutally beaten' in the 1930s before being imprisoned for five years; another was his Bulgarian equivalent Yugov.[17]

An original decision had been reached by the Allies as to how to treat those countries of East Europe, along with Italy, which in the late war had been Germany's allies. The plan was to conclude peace treaties with the lesser enemies first, postponing the treaties with Japan and Germany herself. The idea was that failures of peace-making after the First World War had derived from a misguided attempt to settle everything simultaneously at the Conference of Paris.[18] This peace-making all the same promised to be slow. Poor nations, drawn by sheer chance or weakness of their leaders, on the wrong side perhaps for the second time, into a conflict not of their making, whose peoples had had little to do with their own belligerence![19] Yet Hungary, Bulgaria and Finland were not really, under their Allied Control Commissions, in positions different from Poland and Romania, which had fought against Germany – indeed Romania had fought against Russia as well. The Conference at London in September 1945 had been supposed to settle these problems. It had broken up partly because of the desire of Britain and the United States to have France present at the discussions; both those democracies having as one of their main aims the revival of France. The Conference of Moscow in December 1945 had done better: conferences on the subject of peace with the European enemies, except Germany, were planned for 1946. But the effect of both meetings had been to delay the actual peace: a postponement which did not inconvenience Russia, since it enabled her to consolidate her territorial acquisitions.[20]

The Communists who led these revolutions in East Europe were men and women who saw themselves as the reincarnation of Lenin and his colleagues in 1917. They shared Lenin's sense of historic mission. They had the same fanatical belief, as he had had, in their own destiny as agents chosen to carry into effect a programme of social reconstruction. They believed themselves on the brink of the promised land. They could inspire young men, such as the peasant Andras Hegedus, Secretary of the Communist Youth Movement in Hungary, to look on the opportunity in 1944 'to do illegal Party work . . . as a slice of bread would strike a man on the brink of starvation'.[21] (They also offered young men the chance of approving violence without being present: 'Hanging, yes, but I don't want to be there', as Hegedus agreed was his attitude in 1945, when two Hungarian

Nazis were being executed). In future, the fate that overtook Lenin's heirs might overtake these Communists: 'the retention of power dwarfed all their objectives', wrote Merle Fainsod of the first Bolsheviks, as 'the party of revolution was transformed into the party of order'.[22] Even those Eastern European Communists who suspected, or even knew, that, somewhere, since 1917, Communism in Russia had lost its way – Tito, Rákosi, Bierut, Gottwald, Dimitrov, and Ana Pauker, had all spent enough time at the disposal of the 'master' in Moscow at least to suspect as much – were being re-charged, if only by the dedication of their followers. These Communist leaders were 'ready, indeed zealous to be led, and deceived, under the auspices of an ideology which they did not always understand', but which nevertheless they fervently embraced since 'it enabled them to blow up a hated order, to punish their enemies, and to assert themselves in the name of history'.[23] When, later, it seemed that their revolution would not be different from the Russian one, in its tragic consequences, the rise of a new patriotism would alter the dimension within which Eastern Europeans saw their regimes. But the peoples of those countries would have to cross many a sullen marsh before their masters so much as glimpsed that.

The Soviet position seemed in East Europe in 1946 to be promising. Stalin might hope that, within a brief period, Communist power might be extended from the East of Europe, already mostly subservient, to the West of that continent: 'the preponderance of military-industrial strength in the world would [then] be assembled under Soviet control. England would represent at best an isolated industrial slum, extensively dependent on the Communist-controlled Continent across the Channel'. The Communist campaign in China for 'expelling the imperialists' seemed also to be progressing almost unbelievably well, with no effort at all on Moscow's part.[24] The Americans, with their army every day dwindling more rapidly, could not be expected to live up to their rhetoric. One could not imagine them using an atom bomb on Russia, whatever a few senators might say. The Communists themselves in East Europe were seeking control over power in all the countries concerned. Accustomed during their years of apprenticeship, in universities, in exile, in Spain, in prison, to look upon themselves as agents of a world movement of which the Soviet Union was the vanguard, they could now look on the Soviet Union as the ultimate guarantor of their revolution – a power which would prevent, or withstand, Western intervention. Their only doubt seemed whether or no their capture of power should be looked upon as the first step towards that full integration into the USSR that many still desired: the Executive Committee of the Comintern had to send a message to Tito in 1941 warning that such an application for inclusion should not be made till the necessary instructions had been received from that Executive.[25]

Some of the programmes advocated by the Communists were attractive to many groups in all these countries. The Communists were wooing the intelligentsia; a factor not to be ignored, since the Nazis had hounded it. They were also wooing the peasants, with the bait of land reform which would ruin great landowners but was vague as to how it would cope with small proprietors. Workers and industrial engineers were interested in getting their factories going again. Some kind of state planning seemed essential.[26] Work for the people could be made to seem more important than formal freedoms.

Everywhere, the Communists of Eastern Europe were able to devise a state of affairs in which those who opposed their policies could be represented as being against the national interest. The opponents of Communism were everywhere ill-organised. Many could be destroyed by exaggerated claims of their collaboration with the Nazis or fascists: that kind of destruction of reputation was one of the techniques of Communists learned in 1917–1921. Those who took to armed resistance had little hope unless there was war between the Americans and the Russians. Those who sought to protest only by the ballot box were outmanoeuvred by electoral frauds of the sort which the old regimes had themselves often effectively used. Most members of the Eastern European opposition believed that the West had placed their prestige on the gamble of free elections. They entertained hopes that even Communist governments would not challenge such great nations as Britain or the

United States. When this hope was not fulfilled, many joined those Socialists who thought that the best course was to accept the system – in the hope not only of saving their lives, but of ameliorating the regime. Nearly all Socialist parties in Eastern Europe had wings within them who took that course. So, more surprisingly, did most Agrarian or Peasant parties.[27]

These countries were not large. Poland with a population in 1945 of a little under 24 million (in place of 32 million in 1931) was the biggest. The others (Romania and Yugoslavia about 15.5 million each, Czechoslovakia 12, Hungary 9, Bulgaria 7, and Albania 1.5 million respectively) brought the total of the region to about 85 million. Estonia (1.1 million in 1934), Latvia (1.95 million in 1935) and Lithuania (2 million in 1923), made the new population dominated by the Soviet Union (taking into account also her direct gains in East Prussia, Bessarabia and Bukovina) to nearly a 100 million. Such a labour force could not be ignored in future.

These figures conceal three things: first, the increase of population since 1900 in almost all the countries concerned. That was surely one reason for the attraction of the new faith, Communism, among young village boys seeking an opportunity for their talents in countries where there was no land; second, there was, at the same time as heavy losses in the war, a fall in rates of birth between 1940 and 1945 which promised a certain stability later (such as East Europe has indeed experienced);[28] and, third, the large number of places where, because of treaties after both Balkan wars and the first world war, there were large settlements of disgruntled minorities, from Bulgarian repatriates in Greece to Hungarians in Transylvania. This whole region was in 1946 a maelstrom of resentment, on which international Communism was being introduced as a successor to nineteenth-century imperial ideas. As for Russia, few in Eastern Europe had observed that the Soviet Empire had established a 'satellite' dependency in the 1920s in Outer Mongolia, a model which surely was in the minds of policy-makers in Moscow in 1945.[29]

It should not be supposed that this history has no heroes: Iuliu Maniu in Romania, Nikola Petkov in Bulgaria, Cardinal Mindszenty in Hungary, Dr Grol in Yugoslavia, as well as

Mikołajczyk in Poland, and perhaps Jan Masaryk in Czechoslovakia, were men after whom great avenues in their capitals will surely one day be named.


Of all these countries, Poland was geographically furthest from, but spiritually closest to, the West. Britain and France had gone to war in 1939 as a result of the German invasion of that country. Poland had been the dearest creation of the peacemakers at Paris in 1919. The country had an ancient history, recently revived, of friendship with France. In France, the United States and even Britain, there were Polish minorities, deriving from recent immigrations. Senator Vandenberg had a large Polish element in his constituency in Michigan. President Roosevelt had, as has been seen, often talked of his own Polish vote. A Polish army, numbering 170,000 men, under General Władysław Anders had fought well, in 1942–45, as part of the British armies.[30] Their contribution to the victory at Monte Cassino had been considerable. The Polish provision to British intelligence of the German code-making Enigma machines had been a fundamental contribution to the winning of the war. Polish pilots, skilfully smuggled out of Romania, had been among the heroes of the Battle of Britain. The Polish emigré government under its first leader, General Władysław Sikorski, an independent officer of good name, and composed of men who had been in opposition to the discredited Polish Government of 1939, had been popular in wartime Britain, particularly when, in 1940, the Poles and the British had alone been at war with Germany: a time when Russia, having herself shared in the new partition of Poland of 1939, was then still delivering militarily valuable raw material to the Nazis and otherwise acting almost as a German ally. The Poles had by 1941 established the largest resistance movement in occupied Europe, with which all the four most important parties of the old Parliament collaborated and which had a considerable education service as well as an army.[31]

In 1946, however, Poland was virtually a Communist state: or rather, the 'kernel', to use one of Stalin's favourite words (he had used it often during discussions with Churchill, Truman and

Roosevelt over the precise position to be filled in the Polish government after the war by the 'Lublin Committee' which he had himself promoted), the kernel was a Communist administration, and the trappings Socialist, Liberal, 'Peasant' or non-party. This arrangement was a favourite one with Stalin. He had established an old Communist, one of the few to survive his own purges of the Polish Party, Bolesław Bierut, as President. An agent of the Comintern for a long time, son of a farmer, a founder member of the Communist Party in 1918, Bierut was a survivor of the short-lived 'Revkom', set up by the Russians at Białystok, during the Soviet occupation of East Poland in the Russo-Polish War of 1920.[32] Fortunately for him, during the critical time for the Polish Party (when the Party was disbanded, and its leaders murdered in Soviet prisons) Bierut was in gaol in Poland, not in freedom in Russia. Bierut in February 1946 was still attending church and concealing the fact of his long-time Party membership, though privately 'consulting' with the Soviet ambassador about everything. Suave as well as shifty, agreeable as well as treacherous, he lived in a palace spared from the war in which the Gestapo had been quartered: the beginning of a well documented craze for living in fine villas throughout his country.[33] One Vice Premier was Władysław Gomułka, leader of the few Polish Communists who had played any part in the national resistance against Germany. Gomułka, an active Communist trade unionist in the 1930s, a good orator (if a poor conversationalist, as Western diplomatists observed), was in addition Secretary-General of the newly formed Polish Workers' Party (*Polska Partia Robotnicza*, PPR), the body formed in 1941 secretly, to articulate Communism in Poland without using the unpopular word 'Communist'. It was a post which he had held since November 1943. He was further, since November 1945, Minister for the 60,000 square miles of 'Recovered' Territories: the newly acquired ex-German lands in the West. In 1946, Gomułka affected a modesty beneath which lay a craving for power.[34] He had been by trade a locksmith's apprentice, from the South, born a citizen of Austria-Hungary in 1905, at Krosno in Galicia, the son of a worker in the oil industry who had once emigrated to America and worked in New York slaughterhouses and coal mines in Pennsylvania.[35] Gomułka, married to a Jewess, had been a Communist since 1926 when he was twenty-one. He was capable of thinking, and talking, for himself, as events were to show in 1956. But there was little public sign of that in 1946.[36]

The Minister for Public Security, Stanisław Radkiewicz, had been, like Bierut, in Moscow during the war. Like Bierut, Radkiewicz was at first sight plausible, good-looking with a keen, mobile aesthetic face. He directed a security police staffed by Communists or by persons who had decided to make their peace with them (those whom the British ambassador, William Cavendish-Bentinck, called 'corner boys, pimps and thimble-riggers').[37] These security organs were controlled by the Russians. A British official called to account for his movements in Silesia by a young Polish policeman recalls a Soviet colonel sitting in the background of the discussion.[38] Asked years later why he had brought in Russian security advisers, the leading ideologist of the regime (Jakub Berman) answered, 'We didn't bring anyone in; they came by themselves . . .' 'But you agreed to have them there?' 'But, my dear lady, we couldn't refuse to have them . . .' 'What about blocking their access to information?' Berman answered: 'These people were quite cunning and experienced: after all, they were not just "advisers". They were security men. They could smell deceit'.[39]

A favourite technique of 'security' in the cities was the so-called 'blockade', whereby they settled on 'a suspicious character', sent their agents to his home and arrested everyone who called on him for the next few weeks.[40] In the countryside, the security forces killed, tortured, intimidated and imprisoned with impunity.[41]

Several of the ministers, such as the 'Socialist' Prime Minister, Edward Osóbka-Morawski; the Minister of Defence, 'Marshal' Michał Rola Zymierski; and the Foreign Minister, Wincenty Rzymowski, were not formally Communists. They were minor survivors from pre-war Polish politics willing to serve the Communists to save their lives. (The smug Marshal, an old friend of Piłsudski's compromised by risky dealings with the pre-war army, privately now claimed to be a Party member.)[42] His only known military exploit had been the unauthorised occupation of the Czech city of Teschen on June 19, 1945, without a shot fired. Most of these opportunists had Communist deputies. That stratagem had been worked out in Russia during the war.[43] The economics Ministry was directed, however, by Hilary Minc, an able Communist who had worked in the Ministry of Finance before the war as a civil servant.

Marshal Roła Zymierski directed an army whose core was those Polish exiles in Russia who had attached themselves, in 1941, under Major-General Zygmunt Berling, to the Soviet army. (Berling, a colonel in the old Polish army, had been captured by the Russians in 1939, at Vilno; he assumed his critical wartime role without, it would seem, any pre-war preparation whatever for such a part). This *Kosciuszko* Division had given a good account of itself in battle. Now expanded, and in the process of 'Bolshevisation', it found itself, in 1946, the target for direct attacks by the remnants of the old non-Communist resistance Home Army (*Armia Krajowa* or AK), which had dissolved itself, in January 1945, to become WRN (*Wolność-Równość-Niepodległość* or 'Freedom Equality Independence'). Another armed opposition to the regime was the NSZ (*Narodowe Siły Zbrojne*), an independent right-wing nationalist group which had collaborated fitfully with the Germans, particularly towards the end of the world war, when the prospects of Soviet invasion had become evident.

An important part was played in these developments by the Polish Socialists. The best men of this large pre-war Party had been killed – either by the Nazis (Dubois and Niedzialkowski) or the Russians (Pajak, Erlich, and Alter). The left of the Party (Cyrankiewicz, and Ósóbka-Morawski) now favoured collaboration with the Communist programmes just as they had supported a Russian alliance during the war. Fear and opportunism, as well as some degree of ideological affinity, led them into connivance with a government which would eventually destroy their self-respect, independence and, in some cases, sanity. To these, one should add a number of independents or men who had split away from the other parties such as the Peasants, for similar motives.

The only man of any independence in the Polish government was Sikorski's successor as leader of the 'London Poles', Stanisław Mikołajczyk, now a Vice Prime Minister along with Gomua, and leader of that new Polish Peasant Party (PSL) which he had founded the previous August (the old Peasant Party, SL, had become a Communist puppet: the split continued, and weakened, the opposition). Mikołajczyk was also Minister of Agriculture. A farmer from the west of the country, he represented the real Poland in the government, along with one or two of his friends, such as Stanisław Grabski. But of these, Dr Władysław Kiernik, Minister of Public Administration, was weakened in will by a spell in an NKVD prison and was also so 'ambitious as to put his name down for any job including that of a bishop'.[44] Czesław Wycech, Minister of Education, was suspected of communist sympathies: accurately, as it turned out. The Secretary-General of Mikołajczyk's party, Bolesław Scibiorek, was murdered in Lodz by security police in December 1945. The Prime Minister promised a commission of enquiry and the PSL remained in the government. But nothing transpired.

These democrats and their subordinates were in a difficult position. They had believed that, by joining the government of Bierut, they might just be able to keep alive the dream of an independent Poland on the Finnish model – friendly possibly to Russia, but ultimately free of Communists. They were criticised by landowners, ex-fascists, and survivors of the old right wing parties, as placing ambition before everything, and as soft; and, by the Communists, as 'reactionaries'. Their continuing faith in Britain and the United States was derided by many of their own followers, who believed that the only way that Poland could now be saved was by war between Russia and the West. Their presence in the government, however, helped to maintain that faith in the rest of the world, in particular among Polish exiles in the United States. They had support, especially in the south-west of Poland, where Cracow was one of the few great cities of Central Europe to have escaped destruction during the late war. They had mildly liberal, democratic socialist policies: Mikołajczyk was also perhaps too mild for the role which, through accident, he had assumed. They all also knew that they were operating in conditions where a vast number of the natural leaders of society – army officers, civil servants, university professors, teachers – had died in the war. (Six million Polish citizens, including Polish Jews, had died between 1939 and 1945: for every 1,000 citizens in 1939, 220 had died – higher than even in the Soviet Union (40 per 1,000) or Yugoslavia (108 per 1,000).)[45] The democrats' movements were controlled. Scarcely a day passed without one or other of them telling the American, or the British, Ambassador that their followers were being murdered, their meetings banned on some spurious excuse, or their newspapers seized by the security police.

The American Ambassador, Arthur Bliss Lane, knew something of Russia, having been in Riga during the 1930s and in Belgrade in 1941. He had tried the previous autumn, unsuccessfully, to use economic aid as a lever to secure a government in Poland elected fairly. Mikołajczyk agreed with the approach. (Poland was the biggest recipient of UNRRA aid except China.) The Department of State had, however, independently encouraged Polish applications for surplus property and credits from the Export-Import bank.[46] In the end, to Lane's disgust, several credits totalling $180 million were forthcoming, without any concession by the Poles. Cavendish-Bentinck, the British Ambassador, one of the ablest British officials,[47] who had been the successful Chairman of the Joint Intelligence Sub-Committee of the Chiefs of Staff during most of the war, used his private aeroplane as a 'peering machine', to ensure that he was well-informed and to visit the estates of landowners whom he had known in Poland, during an earlier posting, in the 1920s. But there was little that he could do when faced with the Russian army. His deputy, Robin Hankey, told Gomułka to his face that he should be ashamed of himself in establishing a reign of terror in Poland. But nothing resulted.[48]

Mikołajczyk believed that he represented the hopes of perhaps nine-tenths of the adult Polish population.[49] That was no doubt an exaggeration. But he certainly could count on vast crowds of supporters whenever he spoke in public. He was strongly supported in 1945–46 in the universities, even by many professors who, before 1939, had been leftist in sentiment. The

Catholic Church supported him, though its position had been weakened by the Vatican's opposition to the Polish acquisition of the new provinces, and though the government had hitherto taken care not to antagonise it: church lands had not been seized as part of the agrarian reform, and the government had given help to the rebuilding of churches destroyed in the war.[50] Despite a successful congress of the PSL, in January 1946, Mikołajcyzk's capacity to fulfil the hopes placed in him were circumscribed from the moment of his return to Poland the previous summer from London. Even if the security forces were inadequate, there was a Russian army in the country and substantial farming land was given over to it.[51] Although Minister of Agriculture, Mikołajczyk had had no hand in the Land Reform and his colleague Gomułka controlled the newly acquired provinces.

The government presided over a nation in near-civil war. The reason was that, ever since the coming of the Red Army in January 1944, the Russian secret police had treated all those who, in the Home Army (*Armia Krajowa* AK) or other bodies, had fought, and were fighting, the Germans, with contempt and cruelty. Survivors of those movements were still being arrested in 1946. Though at first disposed to collaborate with the Russians, and ordered to do so by Mikołajczyk then in London, the Home Army, the largest European resistance movement, had thus had to fight the Russians if they wanted merely to survive. The Home Army became quickly aware that partisans, directed by the NKVD, had received orders to kill the more patriotic or aggressive of the Polish resistance leaders.

The centuries-long hatred of Russia, never far beneath the surface, had thus been re-aroused. Poles had often in the past seen themselves as the last bastion of Christian civilisation: which, with the Lithuanians, they were, if 'civilisation' be equated with the Roman Church. Marshal Piłsudski, the only man of strength in Poland to come forward in her first twenty years of new independence after 1919, had always looked on Russia as Poland's enemy more than Germany: Russia for him was an 'Asiatic monster, covered with European veneer'.[52] Mikołajczyk might not have gone so far. But many of his followers had felt obliged to take to the forests since they believed that the only political debate now could be guerrilla war. Many remained there, even after the amnesty of August 1945 of which 50,000 to 60,000 people had taken advantage.[53] Ukrainian nationalism confused the issue in the south-east. The Polish Communist Party would later report that they lost 3,427 security men and Party members killed in 1945, and another 30,000 between then and 1948, in their struggle against the armed opposition. The real figure may have run into tens of thousands.[54] The end of the world war in Poland was thus not in any way a time of recuperation. The violence, however, suited the Communists since they could, sometimes with reason, argue that Mikołajczyk's followers were in league with bandits. This was an essential theme in their propaganda in 1946. The American Embassy estimated that over 100,000 people were being held in prison or in camps for alleged political offences in 1946. This figure did not cover the million or more Poles who were to remain in the Soviet Union as one of the most persecuted minority groups there.

Poland had by 1946 lived in conflict for seven years. First, there had been the German invasion, then the Russian, in 1939. Both Germans and Russians abducted colossal numbers of Poles, including many landowners, merchants, officials, and police, and most of the army. Much of the officer corps of the Polish army had then been murdered in 1940 at Katyn Forest, and several other places, in one of Beria's 'grave mistakes'. (Beria, when asked in 1940 by Colonels Berling, Bukojemsk and Gorczynski about the possibility of securing these officers to fight for Russia, or the other Allies, against Germany, said, 'No, not those, we made a big mistake concerning them. A grave mistake . . .'.)[55]

The Nazis established in Poland their major camps for the extermination of the European Jews. There followed the tragedies of the Jewish rising in the ghetto of Warsaw in 1943, and of the Home Army in the same city in 1944. In reprisal for resistance by the Poles, the Germans destroyed many towns and villages, shot innumerable hostages, burned countless civilians alive. Then came the Soviet 'liberation'. Further violence was committed by the Germans in retreat. So-called 'labour units' were carried off to factories in the West. The Russians, it is true,

conducted themselves better in liberated Poland than they did
in conquered territories though a British SOE report described
the Soviet army in February 1945 as 'plundering the population
in an alarming manner . . . stripping the people of provisions,
taking watches and valuables, and raping women', just as they
had done in East Prussia.[56] Another British report, in March
1945, described 'the position of the Poles after the entry of the
Russians' as 'far worse than before'. In that area of operations,
'the Red Army completely devastated the countryside, looting
absolutely everything movable . . .'[57] Danzig, Allerstein and
some other towns were destroyed by the Russians after the
Germans had withdrawn. But the worst of it was that the NKVD
had *carte blanche* and, as early as the summer of 1944, were
using some of the Nazi concentration camps, including that
atrocious centre of murder, Maidanek, to house captured members of the Polish Home Army.[58] In January 1945, a British
officer in SOE reported that the NKVD was still the only real
authority in Soviet-occupied Poland: 'the rest is fiction'.[59] Whole
districts were also dominated in 1945 by neutral, but ruthless,
ruffians, such as Captain 'Ogien', of Zakopane. Poland in the
winter of 1945–46 was in frenzy, not peace, with thousands
living in the forest much as hunting man had done eight thousand
years before but in even less tranquillity.

It is difficult however, to see, given the geography of
Poland, the character of Russia under Stalin, and the desire of
the Western leaders to keep the Russian armies in the war
against both Germany and Japan until they were defeated, as
well as their wish for general collaboration with Russia in the
post-war world, how matters could have been very different.
Power in Poland passed from the German army directly to the
Soviet army, whose commanders handed authority to the picked
Committee of Soviet nominees. Perhaps, had Mikołajczyk had
an overpowering personality, or had had the prestige and wit of
his predecessor General Sikorski (whose sense of humour had
impressed Stalin in Moscow in 1941), Stalin might just have
offered him a chance of directing a coalition of his own: the two
were in negotiation in early 1944. But the facts of geography as
well as of Marxism-Leninism and history would still have surely

ensured that Stalin would have sought through him, if not against him, to have made of post-war Poland a Soviet puppet.[60]

That said, Western illusions and disunity during the late war must have amused, as well as encouraged, Stalin. Both Roosevelt and Churchill sought a balance between Russia and the Polish government in exile. It did not seem an impossible dream: the two had signed a Treaty in July 1941. By that, the Russians had accepted that the Soviet-German agreement of 1939 with regard to Poland was invalid and had granted an amnesty to Poles detained in Russia as prisoners of war or on other grounds. But Britain and the United States did not find that balance and ended up by antagonising both the Russians and the Poles. There was never any considered attempt by the British and American governments to work out together, during the war, what might have been done on Poland's behalf by, say, a judicious mixture of economic pressure, hints or threats of an end to Lend Lease, publicity, and then tough diplomacy. Neither Britain nor the United States gave the Russians the impression that they cared deeply for Polish independence. This neglect was presumably noticed in Moscow at the time of the visit of Harriman and Beaverbrook in 1941; and Stalin surely drew the appropriate conclusions.[61]

The issues about which there was so much fruitless discussion had been: the Eastern frontier of Poland; the Western frontier; and the character of the post-war regime. On all three questions, the Western Allies were in the end outmanoeuvred.

The question of the frontiers came up first and that of the nature of post-war Poland last. Had the issues been considered with a different priority, the outcome just possibly might have been more beneficial to Poland. As to the first issue: General Sikorski visited Moscow in December 1941. At that time, he hoped to form a confederation after the war between Poland and Czechoslovakia, as had been agreed by the two governments in exile in November 1940, before Russia was at war. With the artillery of the German armies audible in the Kremlin, Stalin had spoken of arranging that both East Prussia and Germany east of the River Oder should after the war go to Poland.[62] By mid-December, with the German threat less acute, he was

speaking to Anthony Eden of giving the north of East Prussia
to (Soviet) Lithuania.[63] On both occasions, Stalin also suggested
that Poland should 'make very slight alterations' along its pre-war
Eastern frontier a little more than a hundred and fifty miles wide,
in which, before 1939, the White Russians and Ukrainians had
outnumbered Poles. The territory comprised 70,000 square
miles of pre-war Poland – approximately the provinces known
in Tsarist Russia before 1917 as Vilna, Grodno and Volhynia. On
the first occasion of his talk with Sikorski, Stalin had apparently
admitted that the city of Lvóv (Lemberg), and its surrounding
oil wells, was Polish: a concession which he never repeated.
When Anthony Eden talked to Stalin about the idea of an
Anglo-Soviet treaty, the latter was talking of a Soviet frontier
along the line which it had lain when the Germans invaded: he
also spoke of, but 'did not press for', the old 'Curzon line', the
border casually invented by Lloyd George (and put forward by
his Foreign Secretary, Lord Curzon). In 1919 on reasonable
ethnic grounds, Stalin said: 'generally our idea is to keep to the
Curzon line with certain modifications'.[64]

There was little detailed discussion about these matters for
eighteen months. Both Churchill and Roosevelt, particularly the
latter, wanted to avoid discussion of all post-war frontiers for as
long as possible so as to escape causing arguments among the
allies.[65] The Russians were fighting for their lives. The disputed
territory had, as everyone knew, been brutally occupied by the
Soviet Union in 1939. 'Elections' had even been held. Not only
the recalcitrant but the potentially recalcitrant peasants as well
as landowners, probably a million and a half people, had been
deported to Russia.[66] The Poles, meantime, considered that the
Anglo-Polish Treaty of 1939 guaranteed their old frontiers.

By 1943, and despite certain controversial correspondence
between the Polish government in exile and Britain, at the time
of the Anglo-Soviet Treaty, the Foreign Office were insisting
that: 'No British Government could guarantee that, in no circumstances, should Poland lose territory either to Russia or Germany'.[67] Roosevelt confined himself to the expression of support
for the re-establishment of an independent Poland.[68] In March
1943, he and Eden in Washington tentatively agreed that, after

the war, Poland should have East Prussia.[69] Between Poland
and Russia, there was growing bad blood: over the slow release
of Poles from Russia to join Western armies and over Stalin's
reluctance to look on the inhabitants of the part of Poland which
he had occupied in 1939, and deported to Russia, as Polish.

Next month, everything was transformed by the German
discovery of the graves of 4,510 Polish officers murdered by
the Russians at Katyn in 1940. The exiled Polish government
in London asked the International Red Cross to investigate.
The Soviet government, accusing the 'London Poles' of 'fascist
slander', and persuaded the Red Cross to desist. The London
Poles' refusal to accept the Soviet accusation of German guilt in
the matter led to a break in relations between themselves and
Stalin's government, just when the Soviet victories in the war
made the question of the future of Poland again a live issue.
Stalin's motives in this murder had been presumably to decapi-
tate the Polish upper class: 'they were simply shooting a category'.[70] When asked where these, and another 9,000 Polish
officers and NCOs, were, by the Western allies or the London
Poles, the Russians lied: 'perhaps they fled across the Manchurian border?' they suggested.[71]

Later that year, with the prospect growing of a German
defeat, the Poles in London appealed to Britain and America for
help against the likely Russian claims. General Sikorski had still
been thinking, in 1942, of 'a federate bloc', which might include
Lithuania, Poland, Czechoslovakia 'and possibly Hungary, in
close alliance with another Balkan bloc extending to, and including, Greece'. When Eden read of this, in a memorandum, he
circled the word 'Lithuania' and noted, 'Sikorski is wiser than
most Poles, but doesn't learn much, all the same'.[72] All such
Polish ideas presented a serious difficulty to the British, who
could not afford to quarrel with Russia, indeed, had no intention
of so doing, but had gone to war in 1939 for Poland.

The Foreign Office decided, by mid-1943, to support the
Curzon line as the Polish-Russian frontier with an adjustment to
include Lvóv in Poland. In return, they hoped that Poland should
receive as compensation East Prussia, Danzig and the Oppeln
region of Upper Silesia. (Lvóv, before 1918 had been part of

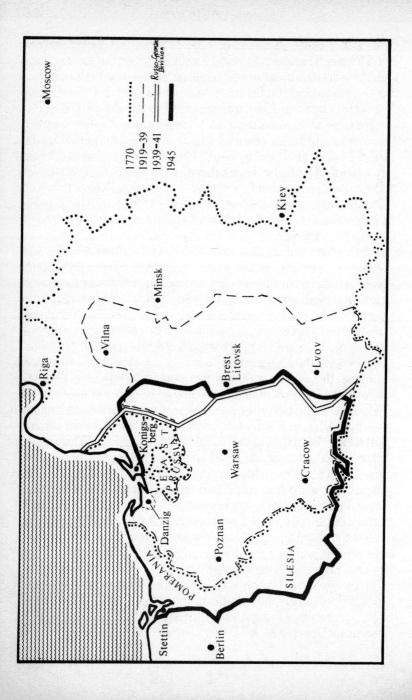

| | |
|---|---|
| · · · · · | 1770 |
| – – – – – | 1919–39 |
| —··—··— | *Russo-German Division* 1939–41 |
| ▬▬▬▬ | 1945 |

• Moscow

• Kiev

• Minsk

• Vilna

• Riga

• Brest Litovsk

• Lvov

Konigsberg

E A S T P R U S S I A

Danzig

POMERANIA

Stettin

• Poznan

• Warsaw

• Cracow

SILESIA

• Berlin

Austro-Hungary.)* Meantime, the Soviet press began to argue that the Poles had 'imperialistic intentions to Soviet territories'.[73] The British and Americans made an attempt to resolve Soviet difficulties with the 'London Poles', to no avail. The Soviet government made no secret of their hostility to any kind of East European Confederation. Not much more was heard of it.[74]

By accident, deriving from the exigencies of war, the frontiers, and fate, of Poland were determined in the oriental capital of Tehran. On the first night of the conference there, there was a discussion in which Stalin said that he would help the Poles establish their frontier on the River Oder, but he was not specific about the Eastern frontier.[75] Then, after dinner, Roosevelt went to bed. Churchill stayed up to chat to Stalin. He returned to the question of post-war Poland. Stalin repeated that he thought it premature to discuss the matter in detail. Churchill thought a 'strong independent Poland' was a 'necessary instrument in the European Orchestra'.[76] He would be happy to see 'Poland moved westward in the same manner as soldiers at drill execute the movement "left close"'. He illustrated the point with three matches representing Russia, Poland and Germany.[77]

There was another discussion about Poland later. Roosevelt told Stalin beforehand, however, that he would prefer not to play much part in it, since there were six or seven million Americans of Polish origin. He might need their votes in the election of November 1944.[78] (Bohlen believed that this was the first time anyone knew that FDR might run for a fourth term.) But he by now agreed with Churchill's position: 'I am sick and tired' of the Poles, he would say later. For him, 'those 1941 frontiers are as just as any'.[79] Later, Churchill and Stalin resumed their talk. (The American contribution was the provision of good maps. Churchill and Stalin only had a map torn out of *The Times*.)[80] Stalin did not insist on the frontier of 1941, as he had

* Baedeker's guide to Austria-Hungary 1914, offers a good indication of the matter: in 1913 'Lemberg', as it was known in German, was the seat of Roman Catholic, Armenian and Greek Catholic Archbishops. With a quarter of the population Jewish, it had 14 Roman Catholic churches, a Greek, Armenian, and Protestant church, as well as two synagogues and several convents.

requested during the discussions of the previous year about the Baltic states in respect of the Anglo-Soviet Treaty: he would be quite happy with the 'Curzon Line' for the Eastern frontier, with a few modifications: that was not identical with the frontier of 1941, which was generally a little to the West.[81] He wanted Lvóv: the loss of which city, Churchill said, 'would not break his heart'.[82] In the West, the Polish frontier should lie along the rivers Oder and Neisse. That concession led to confusion later since there were two rivers named Neisse, both flowing into the Oder in Silesia. But between the two of them there was much rich land, the city of Breslau, and other fine towns of Silesia founded by Germans in the XIIIth century. There was no demographic justification for these plans: in 1939 the formally Polish population in German Silesia and Pomerania was nearly nil (though many Prussians had Slav blood).

The Allies were thus agreeing to the establishment of a Poland which surely could not be other than a protectorate of Russia. A border so unhistoric as the rivers Oder and Neisse – whichever Neisse it might be – could presumably only be defended by force on a scale larger than Poland could hope to muster. Poland had learned not to rely on the West. So she would have to rely on Russia.[83] Roosevelt had given the impression to Stalin that he had conceded all the essential points on the Polish issue.[84] He had probably sought to leave Stalin thinking that he did not want the matter to be a major stumbling block between them.[85] Though he had not made any final concessions, he had indicated that he would not resist Stalin on these matters.

This understanding at Tehran was also likely to determine the question of the German surrender. No German opposition to Hitler could hope to retain credibility at home if it had shown itself ready to surrender so much German territory as this envisaged. So no compromise peace could be contemplated. Similarly, the arrival of eight and a quarter million German refugees from lands annexed by Poland would surely throw Germany into economic chaos.[86]

The British afterwards sought to persuade the Poles of London to accept these roughly decided frontiers. Mikołajczyk, the pre-war leader of the Peasant Party (SL – Stronnictwo Ludowe), and Sikorski's successor, said that no Polish leader could give away either Lvòv or Vilno.* A series of bitter exchanges followed between Stalin, Churchill and the Poles in London. Stalin demanded that the Polish government-in-exile change their cabinet. Churchill tried hard to change the minds of the Poles in London. He told Stalin that the government could be revised so as to exclude men opposed to all understanding with Russia. Roosevelt was beginning to find the Polish Americans restless; he believed that the Polish Ambassador in Washington, Jan Ciechanowski, was trying to stir their emotions.[87] In addition, Russo-Polish relations had been further exacerbated by the arrival in Poland from Russia of numerous Communist Poles, who sought to undermine public support for the indigenous Polish resistance and who betrayed some of those leaders to the Gestapo. Churchill, however, by now was convinced that the compensation offered Poland in the West, at the expense of Germany, would make up for the proposed losses to Russia in the East.†[88] In hard-headed terms of reason, he was right. No conqueror would have hesitated before the choice of, on the one hand, Silesia and Pomerania, and, on the other, Grodno and Vilna. But emotions, not calculations, were involved. Stefan Batory, King of Poland, died in Grodno. Władisław Jagiello introduced Christianity to Vilna. Poland had ruled neither Pomerania nor Silesia for seven centuries.

During 1944, the matter of the future government of Poland became entangled with that of her frontiers. The London Poles' refusal to entertain the Curzon Line, and Stalin's refusal to talk with them till they did – and until they had changed their government – led to a deadlock which Churchill's best efforts could not break. In January 1944, the Red Army crossed the line of 1939 between old Poland and Russia. In a few weeks, they occupied most of the territory that Stalin now claimed as Russian. Some basis for a new administration would be needed

* Sikorski had been tragically killed in an air crash in 1943.
† Poland stood to lose 180,000 square kilometres in the East. After the compensation in the West, up to the Oder and Western Neisse, the total area of Poland would be reduced from 388,000 to 309,000 square kilometres.

in Poland itself. Though Stalin had already accused the Polish Home Army (AK) of collaboration with Germany, he might still just have settled for Mikołajczyk for this task. He liked a 'bourgeois' front to regimes which he supported. But Mikołajczyk would not have been easy to manipulate, and the London Poles refused to negotiate on Stalin's terms. They were resistant to the pressure brought on them by Churchill. Mikołajczyk had been much cheered by a visit to Roosevelt in June, since the President at his most optimistic had then misled him (and possibly himself) by saying that the Poles' eastern frontiers should run east of Lvóv and that they should absorb all East Prussia, including Königsberg and upper Silesia.[89]

Stalin toyed with the idea of bringing in Professor Oscar Lange, a socialist Polish exile economist in Chicago, as an amenable prime minister; even bringing in that strange innocent, Father Stanislaus Orlemanski, of Springfield, Massachussetts. The Father was scarcely representative of the vociferous Polish Americans who were organising themselves to protest against any 'fourth partition of Poland'. But Stalin's invitation to him to go to Russia was a clever move.

It is easy to understand Stalin's hesitations. The Communist party of Poland had before the war never been favoured by Stalin. Its roots might go back to 1918 when it had been formed out of a union of Social democrats from old Russian Poland and some Socialists from old German Poland. They occasionally elected a few members to the old *Sejm*, the Parliament, before Piłsudski's coup closed down democracy. They polled 8 per cent of the vote in 1928. They infiltrated certain social and cultural institutions. Several Communists (such as Henryk Wałecki, or Adolf Warski-Warszawski) played important roles in the international Communist movement. Nevertheless, the activities of the party before 1939, even their support for a subsequently much-discussed strike of peasants in 1937, amounted to little. Stalin ordered the party closed in 1938. Many of the leaders who chanced to be in Russia at that time suffered the same fate as the Polish officers experienced at Katyn two years later. The war subsequently had not increased the prestige of the party, which, as has been suggested, had not participated in the resistance with the commitment either of the Socialists or the Peasant Party.[90]

It is true that after the German invasion of Russia the Comintern placed certain people from what remained of the Polish Communist party in a special 'Initiative Group', in the Comintern School at Pushkino near Moscow. Here, Polish Communists, for despatch into occupied Poland, were trained. A new party was founded: the PPR (Polish Workers' Party). It developed a large network of contacts, including some with other parties, in wartime Warsaw. Nevertheless, it did not gain much popularity because of memories of the Soviet stab in the back of 1939, of Katyn, of the mass expulsion of Poles towards the Soviet Union.[91] Gomułka, like Stalin, in the summer of 1944 was still keeping in touch with Mikołajczyk. Stalin was almost as irritated by 'his' Poles, Polish Communists included, as was Roosevelt with the West's.

By early June 1944, Stalin decided to ask the nondescript group of Communists and fellow travellers whom Gomułka had assembled around himself in Warsaw to become, with some additions, the provisional administration of Poland, after its liberation. In Washington, Roosevelt told Mikołajczyk that he was sure Stalin had no intention of extinguishing Polish liberty, since he could not want to alienate American public opinion. But there were five times as many Russians as Poles and, 'in this political year, I cannot approach Stalin with a new initiative about Poland'.[92] In mid-June, representatives of Gomułka's group met Ambassador Harriman in Moscow. Harriman considered them 'earnest . . . not simply Soviet agents'.[93] By July, these Moscow-directed Poles began to pronounce on the frontier questions. They accepted the Curzon Line, which Mikołajczyk still would not; but they made some clever play with their desire to acquire Königsberg for Poland, as well as to retain the Białowieza forest. They were presented to the world by Stalin as the 'Polish Committee for National Liberation', and as such set up first at Chelm, on the river Ucherka, and then at Lublin, the first large town captured by the Red Army (on July 24) beyond the Curzon Line. About the same time, the Red Army's capture of Lvóv put paid to any more discussion about the fate of that city. The Red Army soon handed over responsibility for Poland to 'the Lublin Committee' in 'matters of civil government'.

At that time there could not have been more than 30,000 Polish Communists – against 4,000 in 1942, 8,000 in 1943.[94] Most of those were new, fair-weather Party members who were joining what they took to be the winning side. A report by SOE in March 1945, however, thought that, by then, most Polish villages had a cell of one or two Communists. These were from 'the poorest peasants who were attracted by promises of land and, drawn, generally speaking, from the dregs of the population, who had everything to gain by any sort of change'.[95]

Thus before the tragic rising of the Home Army in Warsaw on August 1, and before anything like half of Poland had been liberated, Stalin had settled, to his own satisfaction, the question both of the eastern frontiers and of government. That should have been evident, as George Kennan wrote later, when the Soviet Union refused the use of the Russian 'shuttle' bases* in the Ukraine to Britain or the United States to help the dropping of arms and other supplies in Warsaw to the beleaguered Home Army.[96] Stalin considered those heroic fighters to be a 'handful of power-hungry adventurers and criminals'.[97] The rising, therefore, met its doom. The Red Army waited on the other side of the Vistula. The flower of the Polish underground, perhaps 200,000 people, were killed by the Germans; and Stalin allowed only one United States aircraft which was concerned with helping the Poles to land in Russian territory.[98] The losses in aircraft despatched by the Allied Command in the Mediterranean were substantial; 35 out of 182, up till September 5, while only about 10 per cent of the supplies dropped reached the Poles.[99] Most of the Allied pilots were Polish emigré volunteers. Though Stalin's motives have been much discussed, and the Soviet army was not ready for a new offensive, the abandonment of the Home Army was without question a convenient way of securing the destruction of many people who would have opposed Communism.

* The 'shuttle' bases had been allowed by Stalin at Tehran to enable heavy bombing by the United States of Germany. They were set up in February 1944.

George Kennan later argued that it was then, in late 1944, that there should have been 'a fully-fledged and realistic show-down' by the West with Stalin over both the Polish frontiers and the government.[100] The Vozhd should have been faced with a choice between, on the one hand, changing his policy and agreeing to collaborate in the establishment of independent countries in Eastern Europe; or, on the other hand, forfeiting Western Allied support during the last stage of the war. The second front in Normandy had then been established. Western armies were in Europe in force. Soviet territory had been liberated. What was then at stake was the future of the non-Soviet territories previously occupied by the Germans. The cause – 'aid to the brave Home Army' – was one which Western public opinion might have been persuaded to understand. It might even, perhaps, as Churchill considered, have been possible to have halted the convoys carrying Land Lease help to Russia.

The case for that policy seems deeply appealing with hind-sight. At the time, however, Churchill and Roosevelt both believed that the Home Army's commander had been rash in timing his rising for August 1. He had not been able to tell the Soviet government of his plans, though Moscow Radio gave every encouragement to the rising beforehand. In the minds of both Roosevelt and Churchill, who did all what they could to help, the question uppermost was still that of ensuring that Russia would maintain her armies in combat until the end of the war in Europe and afterwards send them against Japan: what Roosevelt called the 'long range general war prospect'.[101]

True, Russia was then enjoying great prestige in both America and Britain as a result of her military triumphs. Nevertheless, until January 1945, half Poland was in German hands (Warsaw included) 'and, in that area, the Polish Home Army, despite what happened at Warsaw the preceding autumn, constituted a real authority', as British SOE reports make clear.[102] Meantime, no meeting of minds occurred, despite arguments between Churchill, Stalin and Mikołajczyk in October in Moscow, and despite some concessions by the latter after some rough talk.[103] In the end, Mikołajczyk did accept a declaration based on the Polish acceptance of the Curzon Line. His colleagues in London could not. He accordingly resigned from that government though he remained active.

On January 17, 1945, the Red Army at last entered Warsaw. They found only ruins. Most of the city's population had been deported by the Germans, in some cases to Auschwitz, a final punishment on a people who had already suffered more than any other in the war. The Russians formally established relations with the Lublin Committee, which moved to Warsaw, and which assumed the name of Provisional Government of Poland. At the same time, the remains of the shattered Home Army (AK) dissolved itself. The civilian resistance remained clandestine, under Russian occupation, much as previously it had been under German. Kennan is correct to say that the subsequent wrangles which occupied so many hours of the time between so many statesmen at Yalta and Potsdam were unreal. At Yalta, Churchill became apprised of the size of the problem of moving Germans in millions out of a Poland which itself had been moved to the west, as he himself had conceded at Tehran. British opinion would be shocked. He might not be. All the same, 'it would be a pity to stuff the Polish goose' too full of German food. Millions of German refugees might be difficult to feed in the West.[104] That argument did not move Stalin.

At Yalta, Poland was discussed at seven out of the eight plenary meetings. As a result, Churchill and Roosevelt formally accepted the Curzon Line as the basis for the eastern frontier of Poland, with some minor adjustments to Poland's advantage. These did not include the much-talked of Lvóv, which was left to Russia. The three great men also agreed to postpone a decision about Poland's western frontier till the final peace conference with Germany. It was, however, understood that the agreement at Tehran about compensation for the loss of territory in the East by gains in the West would be fulfilled. Roosevelt believed that he had persuaded Stalin to agree that the government of Poland would be a 'new one', made up of both 'Lublin' and 'London' Poles. Then there would be free elections, as envisaged by the new Declaration on Liberated Europe. This was the occasion for a famous exchange. Roosevelt said: 'I want this election [in Poland] to be . . . beyond question.

It should be like Caesar's wife . . . pure'. Stalin replied, 'They said that about her, but in fact she had certain sins'. There was a good deal of hair-splitting discussion as to whether the existing Lublin government in Poland should be 'reorganised' or 're-established'. The communiqué blurred the issue: the government would be both 'new' and 'reorganised'. [105]

Roosevelt, and even Sir Alexander Cadogan, thought that they had thus worked out 'a decent settlement' for Poland. [106] So did Bohlen. [107] Their optimism was misplaced. A 'commission' of Harriman, Clark Kerr, and Molotov was, however, set up to work out the details of the more representative 'Polish Provisional Government of National Unity'.

This body made no progress. Despite conciliatory behaviour by Harriman and Clark Kerr, Molotov, 'rigid and at times frivolous', [108] seemed to be concerned principally to 'drag things out till his stooges consolidated their position'. [109] There were many hours of argument as to how to invite leaders from Poland to Moscow; over the desirability of this Commission defining the powers of the Polish Provisional Presidency; the necessity for Britain and the United States to send observers into Poland; how to prevent the Lublin Poles murdering the opposition; and what guarantee to give the Poles who came to Moscow. [110] Roosevelt and Churchill both wrote long letters to Stalin about the failure of the discussions. Stalin replied, defending himself and the Polish provisional Government. [111] In April, Mikołajczyk was prevailed upon under renewed pressure from Churchill, to accept 'the Crimean decision' about the character of the government. But the new Polish government in exile did not do so.

Molotov at first signalled his disapproval of Churchill's talks with Mikołajczyk by saying that he would withdraw from the conference, setting up the United Nations, planned at San Francisco. In the face of what appeared to be an attempt at blackmail, the United States and Britain then prevailed upon that conference not to recognise the provisional cabinet in Warsaw as the government of Poland. Meantime, Roosevelt died and Molotov came to San Francisco, after all, with the intention of meeting Truman on the way: which he did. Against a background of many reports that ex-members of the Home Army and other anti-communists were being arrested, deported to Russia or shot,[112] Truman gave a tough lecture to Molotov in April 1945, specifically about the Polish question.

After further exchanges with Stalin, by telegram, and the somewhat provocative signature of a treaty between the un-recognised Polish Government and the Soviet Union, Harry Hopkins went to Moscow, on President Truman's request, to talk to Stalin about Poland (and the United Nations) at the end of May. Stalin made various minor complaints about United States policy since April, saying that the chief reason for the bad relations over Poland was Britain's desire 'to revive the system of "*cordon sanitaire*" on the Soviet borders' (a charge for which there was then no evidence). He accepted that free elections required free parties and a free press. He also agreed that the Polish government should be broadened to include ministers from outside the Lublin committee: say, two from London (including Mikołajczyk) and two from Poland itself. It was then that Stalin made his comment that he did not believe that a 'country is virtuous because it is small': small nations had made a 'good deal of trouble in this world' such as the two world wars.[113] During the discussion, Stalin said in addition that Poland would live under the parliamentary system.[114] Russia only wanted that 'Poland should not be able to open the gates to Germany'. Russia, he had earlier said, had the right to aim at a government in Poland friendly to it, not hostile.[115] He made comparisons between Poland and Greece or Belgium, where there had also been as yet no elections since liberation: 'the Soviet Government did not . . . interfere in these matters because it understands the full significance of Belgium and Greece for the security of Britain'.[116] Stalin's phrases were so clever that Hopkins believed that he was being honest.

No sooner had Hopkins left than Stalin staged, between June 18 and 21, a most unjust trial of sixteen Polish leaders (headed by the last commander of the Home Army, General Leopold Okulicki, and including leaders of four Polish political parties) who had been tricked at the end of March into a discussion at Pruszkow, outside Warsaw, and then kidnapped by the Red

Army. Nearly all of these were condemned to various terms of imprisonment for 'offences against the Red Army', though the 'crime' of several had been no more than communicating with London by radio. This kidnapping broke the back of the resistance to the Russians in Poland itself. The trial was public, attended by the Western press and some officials. *The Times* described the sentences as an example of Soviet 'forbearance'[117] (an example, in its turn, perhaps of the leader-writer's tolerance of Soviet injustice). The British Ambassador in Moscow was also satisfied; Churchill was not. [118]

A final discussion between London Poles and Lublin Poles was nevertheless held in Moscow. The 'new' government was formed. Poles not part of the old Lublin committee received in the end five ministerial places. Mikołajczyk, with reluctance, but thinking even now that his acceptance of a seat in the cabinet might just give him, and his vision of a 'free and independent' Poland, a chance, accepted: 'the train will not always stand waiting for the passenger to get in', he was told. [119] In early July, Britain and the United States both recognised this government, modestly improved, as it seemed, after weeks of painstaking negotiations. Much of the orthodox Western press was enthusiastic at this 'proof of allied concord', as *The Times* put it. [120] The United States and Britain both maintained their demands for 'free and unfettered elections', as agreed at Yalta, but were not able to do anything to ensure that it happened. [121]

At Potsdam, the discussions about Poland centred upon that country's rights in the large territory of old Germany which it had just occupied, and which had been formally, if still illegally (in the West's eyes), incorporated into Poland, ceremonially, at the end of March: four new Polish provinces being created. [122] But nothing in the end could be done to prevent the cession to Poland of Swinemunde as well as of Stettin. Another wrangle occurred over the question of which Neisse was the right one for the frontier. Churchill in his memoirs says that he would never have accepted the Western Neisse, a decision which was reached after he had left, following his electoral defeat. [123] All the same the Poles were already on that river's banks. There was also discussion about the numbers of Germans to be expelled from the new Poland. Stalin said that they had all fled. Admiral Leahy then whispered to Truman that the 'Bolshies' had killed them all. In fact, there were apparently 3.5 million Germans in 'Poland' in November, according to the Allied Control Commission in Berlin.[124] About a million eventually chose, and were allowed, Polish nationality.[125] The rest were absorbed in Germany, principally the West.

The new Polish government, including the already unhappy Mikołajczyk and the deceiving Bierut, called on the three great men at Potsdam. The former tried to persuade his cabinet colleagues, as they now were, that the British and the Americans might accept the Western Neisse as the Polish frontier if he and the Peasant Party were to receive a bigger share in the government. Gomułka accused him of 'unpatriotic behaviour.'[126] Bierut told Churchill explicitly that Poland 'did not wish to copy the Russian system' and would 'develop on the principles of Western democracy'.[127] At the end, the Western powers accepted Poland's control of the former German territories of Pomerania and Silesia as part of their acceptance of Byrnes' compromise over German reparations. A permanent settlement of the issue would await the final peace treaty with Germany. The leaders of the Polish government went home happy: all save Mikołajczyk. His cause was not helped by a speech in London by the Minister of Economics of the still-surviving government in exile there in which he proclaimed 'we do not want Szczecin, we do not want Wrocław' (Stettin and Breslau). Gomułka would quote the remark often afterwards.[128]

Poland seemed to Stalin, as to any Russian imperialist, Pan Slav as well as Communist, to represent the foreign invaders' route to Moscow (the point was often made by Stalin to Harriman). That it might also be the Russians' path to invasion of the West was ignored in 1945 by a world which believed that Germany would constitute the main problem of the future, as well as of the past.[129] Half Poland had been Russian before 1914. The rebellions of Poles in 1831 and 1863 had been regarded by even liberal Russians with no sympathy.[130] Most Tsarist Russians in exile thought that the frontiers of 1919–39 had been biased in Poland's favour. Stalin may have considered that he was making a concession to Western sentimentality in permitting the existence of an even nominally independent Poland. Certainly he did 'not and never will understand our [Western] interest in a free Poland, as a matter of principle . . . He cannot understand our interests in a country so important to Russia's security, unless we have some ulterior motive'.[131]

Marx and Engels, however, had considered the partitions of Poland in the XVIIIth century to have been acts of aggression. The liberation of Poland would have seemed for them a step towards the overthrow of reaction everywhere.[132] Stalin had told Mikołajczyk that the introduction of Communism to Poland would be like 'putting a saddle on a cow'.[133] Now, in 1946, Mikołajczyk was in turn telling the British Ambassador that 'the critical moment is rapidly approaching which will decide whether reasonably free elections are to be held on the basis of the Constitution of 1921; or whether Communist predominance is to be perpetuated either by the passing of a new electoral law and the use of terrorist tactics against the Polish Peasant Party or by the passage of a new constitution through a Constituent Assembly elected with Mikołajczyk's consent on the basis of a single list'. That would mean the 'establishment of the same type of government as that in the rest of East Europe'.[134] Bierut, meantime, merely maintained that elections would be held 'early in 1946': presumably that would be when he knew that the Communists would win. The fact that he did not act now was a sign of caution. After all, the Communists – or the PPR, the Polish Workers' Party – had grown fast: from 30,000 in January 1945 to 235,000 in December. (This was, however, not as large a figure as Mikołajczyk claimed for himself in January 1946).

The Polish government in 1946 stood for (as well as Communism) agrarian reform and nationalisation of industry. These policies had begun before the end of the war. In September 1944, for example, landholdings over a hundred hectares in the West, or fifty hectares in the Centre and East, were proscribed. There was to be no compensation. Estates owned by Germans, or by 'traitors', were seized whatever the size. In former German territories, land reform was less applicable, since the farms had been mostly smaller than twenty-five hectares in size. The consequence of these measures, however, was, in the first instance, to create a large class of mostly Communist rural bureaucrats, concerned to carry through the reform; but also, paradoxically, to create a resilient class of small peasant who, though initially grateful, was, before long, anti-Communist, even if its standards of living were often improved. The government plans, however, had astuteness since they were in some ways less radical than the land reform put out by the Peasant Party and socialists in March 1944.[135] The Communists were, therefore, able, in the short term, to gain popularity from a measure which their opponents would also have carried through. But both the Communists and the Peasants Party supported policies which took no account of agricultural needs: fifty hectares is large for a pig farm, small for one of wheat. On January 3, 1946, a law also decreed the nationalisation, this time with compensation, of mines, oil fields, power, gas, and water works, as well as numerous other undertakings 'capable of employing over fifty workers a shift'.

These reforms were imposed upon a country which since the German invasion of 1939 had undergone a baffling series of agrarian rearrangements. The Germans had sought to plant a strong German peasantry in their new border regions. As a result, the small Polish holdings in the centre and east of the country (which before 1918 had been part of Russia) had been either given to German settlers, or used to enlarge existing larger farms and given to German administrators. The larger estates in the West (of the old Poland) were, in many cases, either given back to the German families which had owned them before 1914 (when the country had been part of Germany), or given to new German settlers, or managed by the German government, through one agency or another. German settlers had also been brought in from the Baltic states, Bessarabia, the Dobrudja and Galicia, and, later, from elsewhere in the Balkans. In some parts, Polish peasants were evicted *en masse*. There had been some forced consolidation into larger enterprises of small Polish farms, some laxness towards large estates. None of these arrangements prevented a severe shortage of grain in

Poland in February 1946 on a scale such as really to threaten famine.[136]

There was some support for government policies among the younger intellectuals in the country for whom the old pre-war society was discredited. Such young people saw Communism as 'a continuation of the revolutionary humanist socialist tradition – of the spirit of the enlightenment'. To these, Communism was 'the most effective force in opposing the barbarity to which Europe had fallen prey' and these reforms were an earnest of that.[137] On the other hand, peasants who had hoped to profit from the reform were less enthusiastic: 'the hectares which we have been given are no good to us. Take them back and give us work', was one reaction.[138]

The land reform in old Poland was complete by October 1945. The settlement in Western Poland – old Pomerania and Silesia – was only arranged during 1946. Meantime, the Germans who had lived there previously were in February 1946 leaving at the rate of 5,000 a day, usually suffering treatment scarcely better than that which the Germans themselves had visited on those whom they had conquered. Many Germans spent months in horrible camps, such as Lamsdorf, in what was – and still seemed – Upper Silesia. Several thousand died of disease, starvation or murder by officials. The brutality was compounded by real doubt in many cases as to who was or who was not a German. Did name, or ancestor, or language determine it? Did the Kleist family count as German? Of course. But their name, and ancestry, like that of so many Prussians, was Slav. The new settlers, mostly themselves transferred from old East Poland, or Lvóv, or Vilna, arrived slowly. Most came with no possessions, but they soon struck root in the fertile depopulated territory. (Some also came from areas threatened by Ukrainian terrorism.) These movements were not controlled and results were haphazard. The harvest of 1945 was brought in only with the help of Soviet troops. It looked as if they would have to be used in 1946.[139] Famous Junker estates in Pomerania would lie uncultivated for several years.

Poland was the occasion for the world war which began in 1939. The disputes over it in 1944 and 1945 provided the main reason for the collapse of trust between the Allies which led to the cold war. Subsequently, the world forgot it. Indeed, there were signs that the West was beginning to forget Poland by the end of 1945, despite the continuing rhetoric about 'free and unfettered elections' for which the Declaration on Liberated Europe had provided.[140]

The communist control was never in Poland so thorough as in other countries of East Europe. The Church was never broken, as it was broken in Czechoslovakia and Hungary. The peasants continued to hold their farms without the nationalisation of land. Although the takeover of power was brutal, its subsequent exercise was also less demented than it proved to be with some of Poland's neighbours.

Several times during the war the question of a long-term association between Poland and Czechoslovakia was suggested: by English officials, by General Sikorski, even by Czechs. Such an idea would not have been entertained by the Soviet Union. Small, weak states are easier to control than large federations. Still, the government of Czechoslovakia in 1946 was headed by a President of impeccable credentials, so far as the West was concerned: Dr Eduard Beneš, who had been Foreign Minister throughout the 1920s and 1930s during the golden days of the first Czechoslovak Republic. He was the heir, and follower, of the much-loved Dr Masaryk, founder of the Republic. Beneš had been President in exile after 1940, and had lived in England, mostly at Aston Abbots, near Aylesbury, in Buckinghamshire. No one now questioned Beneš's right to govern by decree, till elections were held, as if he were a constitutional dictator (a provisional national assembly of 300 was nominated in October 1945: forty seats for each of the six main parties, another sixty for organisations, such as the trade unions, or appointed by Beneš). The Prime Minister was a diplomat, Dr Zdeněk Fierlinger, who had been Minister in Moscow since 1937. He might be supposed to have known Moscow's wiles from within. The Foreign Minister was the jovial Jan Masaryk, son of the founder of the Republic whose warm voice on the Czech service of the

BBC throughout the war had been so inspiring to Czechs under Nazi rule. There were numerous respectable ministers such as Dr Prokop Drtina, in charge of justice, and Dr Hubert Ripka, in charge of trade (an outstanding journalist, expected to be the next Prime Minister). It was true that the Chairman of the Czech Communist Party, the Moravian peasant's son Klement Gottwald, was a Deputy Prime Minister; but he was thought to be incapable, because he was drunken (always an unwise assumption in politics). The Minister of the Interior, Václav Nosek, was also a Communist, but he seemed humane, he had a conciliatory smile and, an official of the miners' union, he had surely been tamed since he had spent the war in London. Four other ministers were Communists: Education, Dr Mejedly; Information, Václav Kopecký; Agriculture, Julius Duris; and Labour, Josef Soltesz. None was famous. Only Kopecký was well-known in the international Communist movement: editor of the official Party newspaper, *Rudé Prado* (Red Right), after 1929, he was remembered for his contemptuous attitude to Masaryk's republic: which, he said, in 1934, was manifesting itself as 'the same fascism, the same reaction, the same danger' as the Nazi one next door.[141] Those prepared to debate with the Communists could show that Marx and Engels had never believed in an independent Czechoslovakia: 'the Austrian Slavs' were for Engels in every way dependent on Germans and Magyars.[142]

It seemed as if this collaboration with Communism might turn out well for the democrats and that the next government would be indeed elected according to those principles in the Declaration on Liberated Europe, which had eluded the Western allies elsewhere. Eight Communists among twenty-five ministers was a poor minority, and they were divided: four Czechs, four Slovaks. The old London government in exile had six members of the new administration. The army too had been equipped in Britain: and seventy per cent of Czech army officers in 1946 had been in the pre-1939 army.[143] One Communist minister, Kopecký, had even shown himself subornable by the OSS: in return for a gift of medicines, Kopecký had in the summer of 1945 warned an officer of that agency of his impending arrest.[144]

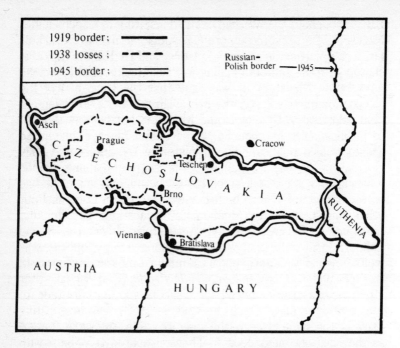

| 1919 border : | ——— |
| 1938 losses : | - - - - |
| 1945 border : | ═══ |

Russian-
Polish border —— 1945 →

Asch

C
Prague                    Cracow

Z E C H O S                Teschen

L O V A K I A              RUTHENIA

Brno

Vienna    Bratislava

AUSTRIA

HUNGARY

Should one be surprised at these promising signs? Bohemia,
after all, had been the most prosperous part of the old Austria-
Hungarian Empire, of whose industrial production it had
accounted for seven-tenths. By the 1930s, because of a thorough
land reform, there had been few large estates; few landowners
owned farms of more than five hectares. Czechoslovak democracy had been one of the few successes of the Treaty of
Versailles. The memory remained. It had not been internal
problems so much as the apparent desire of Britain and France
to force Dr Beneš to capitulate to the Nazis which ruined the
First Republic. Gottwald, the Communist leader, had seemed
to realise that, when he now spoke of the need for a 'national
democratic revolution', of a 'secular, specifically Czechoslovak
type'.[145] A Foreign Ministry official thought that the war must
have done something favourable to the Soviet Union as to the
Communist Party . . . what we would be facing in 1945 would
not be the Communist Party of the purges but a "nationalised

Communism" . . . "the Czech way".[146] The Communists had not had a good war in Czechoslovakia. Between 1939 and 1941, they were said to have 'methodically betrayed democratic partisans to the Gestapo'.[147] The Red Army's behaviour in May and June 1945 – raping, stealing cattle, breaking up furniture, seizing wrist watches, sometimes murdering too – might have been expected to make most of the adult population look westwards.[148]

But Czech independence in 1946 was a dream. The people were disillusioned. They had faith neither in Britain, nor in the United States, nor in Western democracy. The shadow of the West's betrayal at Munich was too long. Many Czechs saw confirmation of this in the fact that the British had done so little to help the Czech resistance;[149] only a few, well-informed people realised that the British SOE had accepted that 'a general rising [in Czechoslovakia], as distinct from resistance, can only be set in motion on the instructions of the Soviet Government . . . because the necessary support for such a rising can only be at present supplied by the Red Armies'.[150] Then, though the Communists might constitute a minority in the Czechoslovak Cabinet, they already controlled the police, through Nosek, at the Ministry of the Interior. Nosek's smile was no safeguard against the cold-hearted determination of his subordinates. Old policemen of the old regime worked with, or for, Communists, without protest.[151] A secret political police had also been formed out of the Communist elements among resistance partisans. Some elements of the Russian secret police, operating from their embassy, had been left behind when the Russian army departed in November 1945. (A case in point was Cicajev, the Soviet link with Czech intelligence in London during the war and, in 1945, 'Counsellor' in the Soviet embassy in Prague.) Communists were already in a majority of the commanding posts in the national police. The Minister of Defence, and ex-commander of the First Czechoslovak Corps in the Red Army, General Ludvik Svoboda, a man of modest intelligence from an infantry regiment, had become to all intents and purposes a Communist during the war, and never changed it.[152] The Prime Minister, Dr Fierlinger, was not what he seemed;

his years in Moscow had not disgusted him at all. Long ago
'bitten by the sentimental bug of Bolshevism, he believed the
best of everything they do'.[153] The turning point for him had
been Munich when the Russians claimed that they would have
helped the Czechs if only the French had done so also. He was
for them now a loyal collaborator. The Minister of Industry,
Lausmann, formally a Social Democrat from East Bohemia, was,
through laziness or through weakness, also an advocate of close
collaboration with the Communists.[154] He had, in January, been
to Moscow to negotiate an economic treaty with Russia. Even
the Foreign Minister, Masaryk, though charming, was not a
strong character: 'as a Czech patriot', he said to Pietro Nenni
in January 1946, 'I know that my country can only exist under
the protection of Moscow. As a liberal, I fear the difficulties of
collaboration with Communists. *Che fare?*'[155] He had anyway an
experienced, and able, Slovak Communist as Under-Secretary,
Vladimir Clementis. The banning of the two main political parties
from pre-war Czechoslovakia, the Agrarian Party and the Catholic Peoples' Party in Slovakia, was an unwise act of Beneš's,
which removed invaluable centres of loyalty and organised men
and women from the political scene: even though the Agrarians
had been treacherous in 1938, and the Peoples' Party later
worse – if no more so than the Communists between 1939 and
1941. The Communists had also had experience of secret work
inside the Czech army: many NCOs in 1946 derived from the
Czechoslovak Corps formed of exiles inside the Soviet Union
during the war.[157] Prominent anti-Communists in the army, such
as Generals Ingr, Neumann and Moravec, had been removed
by Svoboda just before the liberation. The new Chief of Staff, a
conventional man, General Boček, had been suborned and was
beginning to show an unexpected enthusiasm for the Communist
ministers. Then the trade unions had Communists at their head;
for example, Antonin Zápotocký, a stone mason from Kladno
who had dominated the left trade unions before the war, while
the mass organisations being built up to control or plan the
economy were usually directed by either Communist, or philo-
Communist, managers.

The measures of nationalisation carried out by the Czech

government in October 1945 threatened good relations with the
United States, since these affected American investments. The
United States ambassador, Laurence Steinhardt, had persuaded
the Export-Import Bank to withhold a loan of $300 million to
Czechoslovakia until the Czechs agreed not to discriminate
against United States trade. Secretary of State Byrnes wanted
to give a loan to prop up the moderate parties. Steinhardt
counselled against the idea.[158] By the end of 1945 all banking,
insurance and finance, and sixty per cent of manufacturing, was
in government hands: a recipe for economic stagnation, if not
immediately servitude.

Communism was further encouraged in Czechoslovakia by
more elusive factors. The 'moderates' in the Cabinet, as
Steinhardt called them in his despatches, believed that their
Communist colleagues could count on Russia whatever happened – including personal reprisals against those who did not
agree with them. The charge of past collaboration with the
Nazis was also very easy to make, difficult to disprove.
Thousands of suspected collaborators lingered in prison without
having been accorded a preliminary hearing. The courts were
functioning only to the extent permitted by pro-Communist
police.[159] At the same time, the Czechs, before 1945, had
had little knowledge of Russia, despite the elder Masaryk's
scholarly work on that country. Thus many Czechs had
developed an exalted picture in their minds of a benign Slav
brother. The 'correct' attitude of Russia at the time of Munich
– never tested – had left an 'indelible' impression with more
people in Czechoslovakia than just Dr Fierlinger. That was
particularly true of the Communists. 'I simply believed that a
Marxist country can't do what a non-Marxist does. It . . .
can't be imperialist,' recalled Eugene Loebl, many years
later.[160] Then plans already laid for the 8th Congress of the
Czech Communist Party would skilfully, even convincingly to
many people, emphasise the 'non-Socialist character' of the
Party.[161] The press adopted a self-censoring attitude of neutral
apology for Russia, denouncing the memory of Germany as
a substitute for real news.

Not only the memory of 1938, but the reluctance of the West

to redeem that failure in 1945 by liberating Prague, still rankled. The Czechs had admittedly always supposed the Russians would arrive in Prague before the Americans. That had been the expectation of Dr Beneš and his ministers in exile who, in April, had established themselves at the ancient royal free town of Košice in Slovakia, by courtesy of the Russians. But then there had come General Patton's splendid sweep through Southern Germany. By the end of the month, it became evident that Patton could advance to Prague. Churchill and Eden in London, as well as Joseph Grew, the senior career official in the State Department, urged President Truman to allow Patton to move on.[162] But Truman, new in office, deferred on this matter to Eisenhower, the Supreme Commander, who saw no military reason to risk the lives of his men in the advance. As has been seen, his instructions had not included anything about thwarting the Russians at Prague, or anywhere else.[163]

In early May, at almost the last minute of the war, another opportunity arose. Patton was by then actually inside Bohemia. His headquarters, like those of Wallenstein in Schiller's play, lay at Pilsen. His troops had halted along a line stretching from Budweis to Carlsbad, with Pilsen in the centre. Eisenhower would now have let Patton go to Prague. But his Russian colleague, General Antonov, objected.[164] On May 5, a rising against the Germans occurred in Prague. It was a spontaneous affair. The Soviet inspired partisans, the Czech underground, linked with London and the Special Operations Executive (SOE), and the Czech Communists knew nothing about it beforehand, though a regular Czech officer, Captain Mechansky, who was in touch with London, directed operations.[165] There was heavy fighting. A 'National Council of Czechoslovakia' was formed and, in a series of obscure moves, assumed command. The Council was multi-party. Unfortunately, a young Communist student, Josef Smrkovsky, was the driving force. To complicate matters, General Vlasov's anti-communist Russian troops, then in Northern Bohemia, offered their services to the Czechs, and urged the Germans to surrender (seeking mercy for themselves at the hands of the Western Allies). Smrkovsky refused the offer. Vlasov's division withdrew in search of other succour.

The Czech resistance appealed for Allied air support. They got a message to Patton. He despatched three tanks to Prague as a reconnaissance. Their officers said that Patton could reach Prague next day, May 8, at 4 am, provided, however, that the Council made a specific request.

The Czech Council would probably have accepted that offer but Smrkovsky, on his own decision, disregarded it. As the good Communist that he then was, he wanted the Red Army to arrive in Prague first.[166]

The fighting continued. Calls for help continued to reach London, supported by an enterprising British SOE representative, Colonel Perkins. The Germans' conduct in Prague on the night of May 7 to 8 was among their worst offences in the war. As many as 2,000 Czechs were killed. Many were murdered in prison. On May 8, there was further delay. Stalin postponed his acceptance of the general German surrender specifically since the Red Army still had not reached Prague. The local German commander, General Toussaint, meantime, offered to withdraw all his troops, with their arms, if he were permitted to surrender to the Americans. Smrkovsky accepted that, an action for which he was subsequently reprimanded by his Party. When at last the Red Army arrived, on May 9, the Germans had gone. The Czech insurgents had gone home.[167]

The Russian behaviour on their arrival was 'extremely abrupt' to the Czech resistance leaders; they behaved as if they were conquerors, reported SOE's Colonel Perkins, who was present, unnoticed, at the first meeting of the two sides: '"you will", he reported, was the tone of the discussion'.[168]

Had Patton freed Prague, the symbolic effect would have been considerable. Beneš thought so and later said that he was surprised it had not been done.[169] But whether the lasting consequences would have been great is a matter of doubt. Some cities in Germany freed by the United States were later handed to the Soviet commanders. Vienna, liberated in April 1945 by the Russians, is free today. Yet the memory of the West's abandonment of Czechoslovakia in 1938 was so strong that the purely military decision not to liberate Prague added something to the attitude of the Czechs to the balance between the West and Russia. The further decision not to help the rising on May 7 and 8 again led Czechs to believe Communists who proclaimed 'the West turned a deaf ear'.[170] An official of the Foreign Ministry, Ducháček, recently arrived as liaison officer with the United States Third Army, recalls, a few days later in Prague, meeting an old friend, a jeweller, who said to him: 'if Generals Eisenhower and Patton don't dare to displease the Russians, why should I? The East wind is going to blow through Prague'.[171] This mood further limited the efficacy of the American ambassador Laurence Steinhardt; as of his cultivated British colleague, Philip Nichols, whose government, it would appear, had consigned Czechoslovakia, in their minds, to a Soviet sphere of interest.[172]

The second point to consider in respect of the outcome in Czechoslovakia is the personality of Dr Beneš. According to General Moravec, his wartime intelligence chief, he was ill, having contracted spinal tuberculosis, high blood pressure and arteriosclerosis.[173] Beneš, like his countrymen, had been affected by Munich. His Chef de Cabinet, Dr Smutný, remarked, ironically, that, in London during the war, Dr Beneš, Dr Ripka and their colleagues could not 'swallow a spoonful of soup without crying "Munich" if they think the British didn't put salt in it'.[174] Beneš and his friends, all middle class, well-educated in France or Germany before 1914, were real admirers of the power of Russia. They were scornful of Britain, their host. They were apprehensive of the abiding nature of the German evil.

While seething with impatience in the English countryside during the early part of the war, Beneš conceived for his country and himself the post-war role of an intermediary between the West, which would afford capital, and Russia, which would give military backing against any revived Germany. Dr Beneš also became enthusiastic for the idea of the forced deportation of the German population of Czechoslovakia: a new and more brutal use of the experiment carried out in a much poorer part of the world by Greece and Turkey in the late 1920s, after the Treaty of Lausanne – 'successfully' as it is fashionable to assume, though with destructive consequences in both countries. In this way,

Beneš would, Atlantic Charter or no, solve 'the German question'.*

Dr Beneš went to Moscow in 1943 to negotiate a treaty which he hoped would govern the relations of his country with Russia after the war. Just as Chamberlain in 1938 had first broached with Germany the subject of German claims against the Czechs before Hitler had been ready to think of them, so, ironically, Beneš made suggestions to Stalin and Molotov which must surely have surprised them; even though they must have known of his lectures in America earlier in the year in which he had stressed the benign nature of Soviet power; had explained that the perception of hostility of the Soviet Union in the past derived from lack of understanding of the real ideals of the Bolshevik Revolution; and had argued that Russian influence, in Western as well as Central Europe was necessary, since they were a great power.[175] It was obvious from these utterances that he was no longer hoping for anything in the way of a confederation with Poland such as he had earlier supported along with several other even more ambitious ideas.[176]

In Moscow, Dr Beneš said that Czechoslovakia would 'always speak and act in a fashion agreeable to the Soviet Union'. He promised 'loyal collaboration and concerted action in all future negotiations'. He spoke of the benefits of a reorientation of Czech trade towards Russia. He invited the Russians to secure punishment of all who in Slovakia, a formally independent state in 1939–45, had been responsible for making war against the Soviet Union. He would himself press for the 'expropriation of big Czech capitalists'. He agreed with the Czech Communists in Moscow that their compatriots in London were 'a terrible lot'; and predicted that the Communists would, after the war, be the largest party. Dr Beneš also explained his 'blueprint' for the 'transfer' of the German population; 'that's a trifle. That's easy', Molotov replied. Beneš made no requests for changes of border save for the strengthening of his

* It may be recalled that the Czechoslovak government in exile reserved its attitude to the Atlantic Charter from the beginning on this score.

northern border at the small frontier post of Glatz. He also
made the major concession that the poor territory of Ruthenia,
at the far eastern end of Czechoslovakia between 1919 and
1938 (before that no doubt happier to have been part of
Hungary), could be absorbed by Russia and so join its 'ancient
fatherland Ukraine' – without, however, any test of the wishes
of the population.[177]

Dr Beneš assumed in these conversations that he would
ensure for Czechoslovakia a special relationship with Russia.
Perhaps he thought that he could deceive Stalin and, a master
of diplomacy, play off West against East, as the Dukes of Savoy
had so often done in history between France and the Empire,
by the exertion of intelligence and the weight of experience.
But both the talks and the treaty (which gave the Russians a
definite capability for at least economic intervention)[178] had
the effect, four years before the so-called 'coup' of Prague
in 1948, of making it likely that Czechoslovakia would end
as a Soviet 'satellite' state. Perhaps Stalin had not expected
that Czechoslovakia could be fully within his *cordon sanitaire*.
But Beneš's concessions must have decided Stalin that,
if necessary, he could indeed implicate that country in his
design.

By the time that Beneš saw Stalin again, in March 1945,
he had had misgivings, following a realisation of what Soviet
policy in Poland was turning out to be. But all the same, he then
agreed to include Communists in his cabinet and to return to
his country in the wake of the Red Army. He believed in
Stalin when he assured him that he did not intend to interfere in her allies' internal affairs.[179] Beneš realised, before
he died, that Stalin cynically lied to him. But it was then too
late.

Beneš conducted himself in the post-war era as if he were a
great European statesman. He was a real internationalist, spoke
Russian and English well, and talked of liberty in cultivated
tones, and often in moving language. Gentle, thoughtful in small
things, Beneš was, however, out of his depth in dealing with
the facts of power, despite his long experience. It is true that
he had the excuse that President Roosevelt had assured him in

1943 that 'it was necessary to trust Russia'. But a man born in Central Europe should have known better.*

The third matter which affected the colouring of the post-war regime also derived partly from the conversations in Moscow. That was Dr Beneš's plan, to deport the German population, which had by now been welcomed by the Russians and accepted by the British. The number of persons concerned may have approached 2.8 million. Of these, a few had certainly been murderous Nazis. Most naturally had not been. They were the descendants of that powerful German bourgeoisie, and those prosperous farmers, who, along with many German-speaking aristocrats (whose loyalties were above national origins), had made Bohemia the most successful part of the old Empire. Contrary to the statement that the matter had been 'much discussed', it was one scarcely mentioned either at Tehran, Yalta or Potsdam. Dr Beneš and Dr Ripka had conceived the plan under the intellectual influence of ultra-Slav Czech national-ist poets, such as Jaroslav Seifert or Karel Toman. Beneš had before 1941 been a moderate on this matter. It seems as if it was the Nazi crimes at Lidice that changed his mind. Then in May 1945 the last fling of the German army in Prague had understandably inflamed the passions of most Czechs. The sadistic 'pacification' of Slovakia, after the mismanaged rising there of 1944,† had also removed many people's hesitations about the German contribution to barbarism as well as civilisa-tion. After May 9, many Germans were attacked. Those who had served in the SS were naturally shot. Many others active in administering the wartime protectorate then fled, to wherever they could, often to Vienna. Chaos and terror reigned for weeks

* The extent to which his brain was working oddly is shown by the exchange which he had had in November 1942 with Alex Easterman, one of the secretaries of the London branch of the World Jewish Congress. Beneš told Easterman that, in Czechoslovakia, the Germans were not preparing any plan for the extermination of the Jews there. Actually, the deportation of Jews from Bohemia-Moravia had occurred a year before. Nearly all the Jews of Czechoslovakia were dead.[180]

† The two Slovak risings of August 1944 were led by, 1), Communists only partly under Party direction, and, 2), a mutinous section of the Slovak army. Stalin did what he could to prevent the success of both.

among the farms of the Sudeten lands. All Germans' houses were liable to be plundered. Germans were henceforth to receive rations of food smaller than those of the Czechs. They were not allowed to use the post or the telephones and were supposed to shop only at certain hours. They were not permitted officially to go to the cinemas, concerts or theatres which were then opening up again. German schools were closed. Trials began in which over 700 Germans were sentenced to death; nearly 20,000 to many years of imprisonment from which some did not reappear. Numerous Germans, especially those in farms in that part of Czechoslovakia bordering on the Soviet zone of Germany, were told to leave hours only before their prescribed departure. The expulsion of the Germans from the ancient city of Brno was especially peremptory: a quarter of an hour only was the notice given to 25,000 people.[181] The same was true of Bodenbach, where 24,000 people were apparently 'driven like cattle into Saxony': scarcely a very receptive new home.[182] There was a massacre of Germans at Aussig, a little further on into Bohemia: many hundreds of Germans were murdered there on July 31, 1945. The Germans later believed that nearly 240,000 Germans died in one way or another during these expulsions:[183] or ten per cent of the number expelled. It is not impossible.

The American forces in the Western part of the Sudeten territory were in no position to help: 'the majority of the senior United States officials appear never to have heard of the problem'. Even American interpreters with good German could not cope with the Egerland, and other local, dialects.[185] Even so, the United States lost prestige with Czechs because they seemed to be, or were caused to seem, the protectors of Germans; while the Russians were seen to be hastening the expropriations.

This brutal time came generally to an end in July 1945 when 'humane and orderly' treatment was determined at Potsdam. Thereafter, there were rules: Czech citizenship for Germans of before 1938 was allowed if the people concerned could prove themselves anti-Nazi. Germans who had moved to Czechoslovakia after 1938 were expelled. By the end of the year, a general programme for expulsion had been adopted. But the difficulties of organising the export, and the reception in starving Germany of over two and a half million people delayed the conclusion of this calvary. It was not till January 1946 that methodical arrangements were in any way possible. By then, the Czechoslovak Ministry of the Interior had organised district committees, whose task was to list Germans and organise both assembly camps and trains. By February 1946, one train a day was running from Czechoslovakia into the Western zone of Germany, carrying 1,200 each from out of the 1,750,000 who were eventually to go there. The other 750,000 went into the Soviet zone. These fleeing Germans were as a rule allowed 1000 Reichsmarks and 60 to 100 pounds of personal belongings. Thus the entire population of the Sudetenland suffered because of Hitler's rantings about their suffering in 1938: 'three hundred killed,' he shouted to Chamberlain[186] when there could not have been a tenth of that after an anti-German riot. Among those expelled from their holdings a substantial, though incalculable, number were imprisoned, some for several years. Others found the only place to live in the Germany of 1946 was a concentration camp: including, indeed, Dachau, employed for many displaced persons in those disillusioning months of the new peace.[187]

Into the place of these farmers moved, as a priority, those Czechs who had served with the small legion of exiles formed in the Soviet Union. The collaboration of Communist Ministers of the Interior and of Agriculture next gave preference to landless labourers who supported that Party. These arrangements handed over thousands of well-kept and well-equipped farms, untouched by the war for the most part, to Czechs whose gratitude would be expressed in votes and support at a critical time.

The 'Sudeten' Germans in 1919 had not desired to be part of Czechoslovakia. Many voted in consequence for Henlein's Sudeten German party in elections in the 1930s – a party which in 1935 gained the largest number of votes in all Czechoslovakia. Henlein's party became Nazified, because previous efforts to establish Sudeten autonomy had been unsuccessful. Henlein personally became carried away, as did so many, by the Nazi dream. This eclipse had the consequence of weakening Czech individualism; if so many could be displaced by *fiat*, what else

could not be done? It came on top of the Nazis' suppression
of the Jewish community of Prague and Moravia which, because its members were above quarrels between Czechs and
Germans, had been able to draw upon and integrate both
peoples.

The Czech government pursued a similar policy with the
smaller minority of 600,000 Hungarians who had lived for an
equal number of generations in Southern Slovakia (Slovakia had
been part of Hungary till 1919; and a Slovak in the *Oxford English
Dictionary* was described as 'a person belonging to a Slavonic
race dwelling in the north-western part of Hungary'), and who
had also for five years been part of post-Munich Hungary.
Hungarians too were deprived of citizenship, sent to camps, lost
their jobs and schools, saw their newspapers and publishing
houses abolished – and plans made for their transfer. Yet the
Hungarian party in old Slovakia had been anti-Nazi. This question
grumbled on for many months more, though, in the end, a more
equable solution was arrived at. The fact was that the Czech
government was by implication in 1946 seeking to create a Slav
state with the same preoccupation with purity of race as more
famous, if less reputable, administrations.

The skill with which the Communists moved into a dominant
position in Czechoslovakia in 1945 must excite some admiration
among students of the political art. Gottwald told his followers
in Košice they had to be 'seen to be the most active and most
capable', they should concern themselves with the restoration
of electricity and water supply, with the supply of food, and of
course with the arrest of collaborators. 'Our Party,' he said,
'must be the first to prevent chaos, and to thwart attempts by
anyone but the revolutionary committees to seize power . . .
Our Party must be the mainspring of revolutionary development.
It must spread everywhere, into every factory, workshop, office
and community . . .'.[188] These activities, under a President so
ambiguous in his relations to the West, caused the country to
be closer to Russia in 1946 than many of its Western friends
supposed.

Communist propaganda was also effective. It dwelt continuously on the memory of 'martyred' members, such as the writer

Julius Fučík, hanged by the Gestapo in 1942. It created, in the minds of the Czechs, the illusion that the Red Army had won the late war single-handed. It naturally sought too to build the picture of a glorious new society only a little in the future. Many Czech Communists, who had conspired against the Nazis in the 1930s, had fought in the Civil War in Spain or the French resistance, and had served terrible years in the Austrian concentration camp at Mauthausen, had around them the allure of supermen, grand survivors of the century. The fact that it was this class of Communist – the loyal believer, the experienced fighter, often Jewish in origin – who, within a few years, would be ruined by Stalin's megalomania, is in no way to diminish their effectiveness as revolutionaries in the immediate post-war years in creating a state which their fellow-countryman Kafka would have recognised as a harsher version of that implied in his novel *The Trial*.

The Communist Party of Czechoslovakia, more than that of Poland, had played a part in the history of the country as a democracy between 1919 and 1938. Founded by the left wing of the Social democrats, who had themselves had a history of activity in Bohemia and Moravia before 1914, they had been the second most popular party in the elections of 1925, with forty-one seats and nearly a million votes. Their subversive activities had led them to be reduced to semi-legal status in the 1930s, by which time the dogmatic Gottwald had taken over from the more enlightened Bohumír Šmeral (who left to work in the Comintern in Moscow and elsewhere). They had come close to staging a *coup d'état* in 1921. Gottwald had undertaken the 'Bolshevisation' of the Communist Party in the 1930s and cheerfully told his non-Communist colleagues in parliament in 1929 that 'we go to Moscow to learn from the Russian Bolsheviks how to wring your necks'. In 1934, he stood against Masaryk for the presidency of the Republic under the unappealing slogan 'Not Masaryk – but Lenin'.[189] In 1938, as has been said the Communists had let it be known that Stalin would have come to the help of Czechoslovakia if France would also: a factor which they emphasised when, later, the Nazi-Soviet pact of 1939 made such policies totally implausible. Between 1939 and 1941, their role as elsewhere in Nazi Europe was as negative as between 1942 and 1945 it was exemplary.

A word should be devoted to Ruthenia. This tiny territory, 4,000 square miles in size, also known as 'Sub-Carpathian Ukraine' and 'Little Russia' had been like Slovakia part of Hungary before 1919. Ruthenes – closer to Ukrainians than to Slovaks – lived in the North, Hungarians in the South. Romanians, Slovaks, Germans and Jews had completed the old population. The dominant church was Uniate (Greek Catholic) which had prevented early absorption by the Russians or Ukrainians in the past. As a result of the Treaty of Saint Germain, the territory had gone in 1919 to Czechoslovakia. Independent for a day in 1938, Ruthenia was then reabsorbed by Hungary. Reached by the Red Army in April 1944, Ruthenia, as a result of a declaration by Stalin, was handed over to Russia in July 1945. Its possession gave Russia a border with Hungary. The Hungarians complained about their own people living there, but received no reply. Once, later, the Soviet army moved inexplicably from there, for a few days into Hungary, and seemed to be about to occupy a slice of farmland between the new border and the river Tisza. Then, as silently and as inexplicably, they returned.[190] As Harriman pointed out in 1945 in a telegram from Moscow, the Ruthenes had not been ruled by their 'fatherland', Ukraine, since at least 1200. Nor were they consulted. Small in number though they were, they would, as in 1919, probably have chosen independence. Smaller states exist in the United Nations of 1986, whose representatives cast their votes in New York, with cheerful confidence. But the idea of Ruthenia as a nucleus for a greater Ukraine had been used consistently, if ineffectively, by the Nazis. As in so many other ways, the Soviet Union now built where the Nazis had begun. No Western representative was present to salute this transfer of 'people and provinces'; nor, indeed, to observe the ritual drawing of the new Czechoslovak frontier with Russia by 'Slovak and Ukrainian officials'. Beneš, with an idle hope that his silence would later benefit him (and so save Slovakia from a similar fate), said: 'We will never make it any matter of public controversy'.[191] The transfer of Ruthenia to Russia in

1945 passed as unnoticed as its transfer to Czechoslovakia had in 1919.[192]

There had been, admittedly, by February 1946, one development favourable to the maintenance or the creation of free institutions in Czechoslovakia: the withdrawal of the 400,000 troops of the Soviet army, as well as the smaller American detachment, of about 40,000, before December 1, 1945. This strengthened the Czech economy. It obviated the necessity of feeding Russians. It removed obstreperous foreign soldiers, including the unpopular Mongolians who had been quartered at Bratislava, and those who had raped so many women in Brno (4,000 cases requiring medical treatment) and elsewhere, in the first days.[193]

Soviet policy towards Czechoslovakia may have had practical motives. The idea of absorbing Slovakia into the Soviet Union itself had admittedly quickly vanished from the imagination of the Soviet leaders. Nevertheless, they plainly remembered the uranium in the mines at Jachymov and Pribram (so long known for silver)[194] from which the Russians made an official request to receive the mineral in November 1945;[195] and where, in the 1950s, some of the Communists who took over the state in 1945–48 would find themselves in penal work, on account of invented crimes, and count themselves happy that they were there, not in the grave.[196] The word 'thaler' – hence 'dollar' – derives from the coins ('Joachimsthaler') struck in silver found at Jachymov, once Joachimsthal, by Count Schlik in the XVIth century. Soviet management of the place which gave its name to the most distinguished word in capitalism was thus also assured.

One thing stood out in 1946 in Czechoslovakia: the survival of Prague, the capital of Central Europe least damaged in the war. The restaurants and coffee houses remained open. The beautiful squares seemed unchanged since the days of Mozart. A visitor from Vienna observed the old upper class in evening dress in the streets in January 1946.[197] Such intimations of continuity were, however, an illusion. It was said that Jan Masaryk was so witty a raconteur that he had once made King George VI of England late for a reception. But in Prague the day of such storytellers was nearly over. Gottwald might often be drunk. But he was a clever politician as well as a dissembler and philistine.

Thus a new ruin began in a country already once before set back two hundred years by forced exile, confiscations, executions, and the imposition of a 'foreign aristocracy'. That disaster was the prelude to the Thirty Years' War. This new one was at the conclusion of what was for Europe an even more tortured thirty years.

# THIRTEEN

# NATIONS OF THE DANUBE:
# HUNGARY, ROMANIA AND BULGARIA

Churchill in 1944 had suggested in Moscow that, after the war, Soviet influence in Hungary should be 75 per cent and Western influence 25 per cent.* The state of that country in 1946 gave some grounds for greater confidence than those figures betokened among those who believed in the future there of Western influence. Dr Zoltán Tildy, of the Smallholders party, was the new President of the new Republic (declared as such on February 1). Dr Ferenc Nagy, also a Smallholder, was Prime Minister. He had first come to public notice in 1941, as a member of the Committee for Historical Commemoration, an all-party body designed to protest, in the name of Hungary's past, against the war and Hungary's dependence on the Nazis. The Smallholders had won a great victory in the election for the National Assembly on November 4. As a result of a pre-election inter-party arrangement, the Smallholders had the largest number of ministries, though there were also four Communist ministers and four Social Democrats. The Communists had polled a mere 16.95 per cent of the vote (70 seats in parliament) against the Smallholders' 57 per cent (246 seats), and the Socialists' 17.41 per cent (69 seats): one of the most substantial victories for an anti-Left party in Europe. Of the 800,000 votes gained by the Communists, less than a quarter came from Budapest. The Communist strength was among some parts of the urban pro-

* See Appendix III.

letariat in small towns, the radical peasantry in poor regions and an important part of the shattered Jewish electorate.[1] In equally fair municipal elections, in Budapest, in October, the Smallholders had also won. Hungary was a country which had experienced Communist revolution once, in 1919, and might be expected to eschew it in future.[2] The United States and Britain recognised this Government immediately after the elections.

The Communist Party, too, were divided about tactics: László Rajk, a popular leader who had been in Hungary all the war, believed that they could, and should, seize power soon; whereas the leader of the Party (and Deputy Prime Minister), Mátyás Rákosi, who had been in Moscow thought that co-operation for a long time with the Smallholders might be necessary,[3] even though he considered half of them to be 'reactionary' and, therefore, to be discounted.[4] Another leading Communist, Imre Nagy, thought that collectivisation would take twenty years.[5] The population of Hungary had a traditional dislike of Russia, whose role in crushing the Liberal revolution of Kossuth in 1849 was remembered by all. The 800,000 Russian troops established in Hungary a hundred years later in 1946 were making themselves unpopular by eating the scant supplies of food in the country.

The world of the spirit seemed also to be reviving in the spring of 1946. When novenas for penance were held throughout Hungary, between February 1 and 9, 1946, these churches were often too full to contain the numbers of faithful. The Hungarian catholics were led by a brave, powerful personality, Archbishop Mindszenty, recently appointed to Esztergom and, therefore, Primate. The Bishops had played a part in preventing some Jews in Budapest from being sent to Auschwitz. After the war, they had inspired much large-scale relief and charity as well as grand processions. They defended the Hungarian Germans, whom the Allied Commissions expected to be returned to Germany despite their hundreds of years' residence there. Then, the new constitution of January 31, 1946 had provided for a President on the Western model and a parliamentary system. Hungary had enjoyed, for many generations, a constitution which distinguished, explicitly, monarch from people: even if the last had been represented by nobles. Parliamentary institutions of a limited sort had survived until 1944.

Yet the odds were already against the survival of real freedom. Geography partly decided this. Hungary had no outlet to the West, since Eastern Austria was occupied by the Red Army. The Russian annexation of Ruthenia gave Hungary a frontier, short but not insignificant, with the Soviet Union itself. The Russians dominated the Allied Control Commission (Article 18 of the armistice had given Russia the chairmanship of this body till the formal end of hostilities), while the British and American representatives on it were powerless, even though both the British and United States ambassadors to Moscow had joined with Russians to draft the terms of surrender in October 1944.[6] As in other places, Roosevelt at Yalta had refused to interest himself in the rights of his representatives on this body.[7] Truman did no better at Potsdam. The Commission had no secretariat. Only from their intelligence sources did the Western allies even receive copies of communications from the provisional government to the Commission: on one occasion, the Americans so received a copy of a note submitted by the Hungarians to the Russians, and returned with marginal notes by the same Soviet official who had denied that it existed.[8] Then the country had, by the armistice arrangements of 1945, to return to the 'Trianon frontiers' of 1920 and to abandon again northern Transylvania, the ancient centre of Magyar Hungary. That territory had been returned to Romania.[9] The destruction of so much of the wonderfully creative Hungarian Jewish community by the Nazis at the end of the war, and the emigration of many of the survivors, robbed the country of much of its entrepreneurial class. The non-Communist governing parties were inexperienced. Kept in opposition during the time of Admiral Horthy, the 'monarch without a king', both President Tildy and the Prime Minister, Ferenc Nagy, were politically innocent and the former vulnerable because of favourable remarks which he had once made about Horthy. The outstanding member of their Party, Endre Bajcsy-Zsilinsky, had been shot by the Nazis in 1944, along with the most resilient of the Social Democrats, Dr Monus. The Smallholders had anyway no ideology except vague support for

Ottoman Empire 1900-14
Habsburg land until 1918
Borders 1944 & percentages

HUNGARY
USSR 80%
UK 20%

ROMANIA
USSR 90%
UK 10%

YUGOSLAVIA
USSR 50%
UK 50%

BULGARIA
USSR 80%
UK 20%

ALBANIA

GREECE
USSR 10%
UK 90%

TURKEY

Hungarian independence. The Foreign Minister, Janos Gyon-gyosi, might be a Smallholder, but he, like his deputy, the ex-priest Istvan Balogh, 'recognised the importance of Soviet interests' in the country; and, in every important division in his ministry, there was now a Communist, and usually a secret police section, whose loyalties were to that Party.[10] The Communist defeat in the election meant little, since Rákosi had ensured that his party would receive ministries.

The 'Liberation' of Hungary by the Russian army, and the ferocious seven-week siege in Budapest of the winter of 1944–45, had left all democrats with their wills frozen in the face of a determined Communist drive to power, and of the memory of the barbarism committed by the Red Army.[11] The continuing trials by 'peoples' courts', of collaborators with the Germans and the Hungarian fascists, the Arrow Cross movement, and the revelations of atrocious murders committed during the war even by monks (such as Father Andras Kun), transfixed Hungary with fear. Since the Germans had occupied Hungary in March 1944, and taken over the state under the direction of General Szotaj, the number of potentially blackmailable collaborators was legion.[12] The Primate, Cardinal Mindszenty, tireless, dynamic, determined, and iron in temperament, was a possible rallying point. Imprisoned by the Nazis, appalled by the new conditions, he had in November issued a pastoral letter calling on catholics to vote only for 'candidates who represent law, morality, order and justice'.[13] But Mindszenty could not prevent the infiltration of the Church by Communists. The agrarian reform removed the material basis which supported many ecclesiastical institutions, since compensation, though promised, was never paid. The subsidies paid instead to priests damaged their independence. The Catholic press received parlous treatment from the Russian Commander-in-Chief who, alleging a shortage of paper, permitted only two catholic weeklies, whereas Communist papers flourished. The provisional government had already introduced a law making divorce easy. There were numerous impediments placed in the way of those who wished to refound the old 'Christian party', along the lines of those established in the West. Marxism, not Christianity, characterised education. No country which had been at war with the Soviet Union since 1941, as Hungary had been, could expect sympathy from the Allies.[14]

The critical factor, however, was that, from the beginning of the new era, with the formation in October 1944 of the provisional government in Debrecen (under the prime ministership of General Miklos, an army commander who had surrendered his troops to the Russians a few months before), the then tiny Communist Party – did it have then as many as a hundred members? – had, as elsewhere in East Europe, made a special point of controlling the police. The Red Army's occupation of east Hungary in 1944 determined what happened in the country afterwards: a small group of 'Muscovites' which included József Révai, Mihály Farkas, Imre Nagy and Ernö Gerö drove round the east of the country, collecting hand-picked leaders, including some non-Communists, and took them to Szeged.[15] This group formed a Provisional Central Committee of the Hungarian Communist Party, convoked a national assembly and set up a provisional government, in that town, on November 5, 1944. The latter moved to Debrecen in December, and to Budapest in April 1945. But though the opposition were always given a share (in appearance a controlling share: in the provisional assembly of 230 members, there had been 38 social democrats, 55 smallholders, 19 trade unionists, 47 others and only 71 communists) Communist 'partisans' – returning prisoners of war with new politics, Russians of Hungarian origin, outright NKVD agents – formed the only organised body and had the only authority in the municipalities. In theory, towns were run by 'National Committees' on which all parties had a voice. In practice, the Committees were established by Communists who selected, from all parties, docile fellow-travellers as members. Another Communist Central Committee was later formed in Budapest out of 'militants', who came out of hiding. These Central Committees merged and Rákosi became the Secretary of the new body. Both committees hoped to manipulate progressive opinion through multi-party 'Fronts' – the Hungarian Front and the 'National Front for Independence'. These too were soon merged as the Patriotic Popular Front. This 'Front' continued to be valuable to the Communists till 1948. But, in every sense, it was a facade.

The Communist task in Hungary was made even more easy by the fact that the first post-war Minister of the Interior, Ferenc Erdei, formally a member of the small National Peasants' Party, was one of those secret collaborators with the Communists such as Svoboda or Fierlinger in Czechoslovakia who, out of fear or opportunism, or both, helped so much to hand over East Europe to Russia. The consequent Communist control of the police meant, as an American diplomatist reported in September 1945, that 'the national leaders of the people, if suspected of a non-Communist view-point are held and imprisoned on minor charges. The resulting terror is described . . . as more acute than anything experienced under the Germans or Arrow Cross regimes'. As in Poland, people were kidnapped and disappeared for life, or returned from a Soviet camp after years – for no reason other than that they might have become prominent non-Communists. Such actions were carried out both to frighten the population and to weaken its morale. An observer said: 'The Soviets did not care for popularity. They wanted servile submission. This creation of fear and absolute personal insecurity was a necessary precondition . . . for subsequent Soviet political action in support of the Communists'. In the village of Gyomro, the police shot twenty-six people without trial during the summer of 1945. The Minister of Justice's attempt to discipline those responsible failed. Already a political police had been established in Budapest – later called AVO – in a large building in Andrassy Street in which the Arrow Cross party had formerly had its headquarters. Gabor Péter, the deputy head, then head of the AVO, worked directly under Rákosi's orders. A former tailor, unintelligent, weak and brutal, he surrounded himself by a staff of lower-class Jewish interrogators whose ruthlessness served, alas, to exacerbate an underlying antisemitism among Hungarian conservatives.

The efforts of the Social Democratic Minister of Justice, Valentiny, to capture control of the police for his ministry the previous summer failed. Then in November, the Communist, Imre Nagy took over the Ministry of the Interior. The presence of Mátyás Rákosi, a survivor of the previous Communist regime of 1919, in Tildy's government as Deputy Premier indicated his party's real influence.[16] Other Communists in the government included Ernö Gerö, one of the original four 'Muscovites' of Szeged, known everywhere, in the 1920s and 1930s, from Paris to Barcelona, under a variety of names, as a Comintern agent. He was now Minister of Commerce and Communications and, as such, able to interfere with all contacts with abroad, including the despatch of aid from Christian organisations in America sent in response to the appeals of the Primate. It may be that this experienced revolutionary had as much power as, perhaps even more than, Rákosi. The Communist Party for its part was believed to be receiving substantial payments from Moscow, 600,000,000 pengös a month it was said as well as cars and other things useful for winning elections, when the Smallholders had poor material.[17] The Communists, despite their modest showing in the election, had already embarked on that skilful 'salami' process, cutting up one's enemies one by one, of which Rákosi would boast in 1952[18] – (an obvious echo of Vittorio Amadeo's remark about Italy after 1713: 'Italy is like an artichoke, to be eaten leaf by leaf'). Rajk, a handsome man who had never been to Moscow, had spent the war in Hungary and had a real constituency among radical peasants and students, had similarly adjured his followers to learn from Lenin: 'If you have five enemies, ally yourself with them. Arrange to incite four of them against the fifth, then three against the fourth, and so on until you have only one enemy left in the alliance. You can then liquidate him and kick him out' (Rajk, bombastic if attractive was a 'veteran of Spain').[19] Another Communist leader, József Révai, responsible for cultural and propaganda affairs, and another of the four 'Muscovites' to return in 1944, pointed out, retrospectively, 'we were a minority in Parliament, and in the Government, but, at the same time, we represented the leading force. We had decisive control over the police. Our force, that of our Party and working class, was multiplied by the fact that the Soviet Union and the Soviet Army were always there ready to support us'.[20]

'Salami tactics' entailed Communist alliances with the Social Democrats and smaller parties, as well as the manipulation of frightened, or disgruntled, minor members of the Smallholders'

Party. These persons would argue that, since Russia would anyway dominate Hungary, it was best to make peace with Communism as soon as possible to secure good treatment. A good Catholic historian, Gyula Szefkü, thus agreed to be ambassador to Moscow, became intellectually overwhelmed and in the end wrote a book glorifying Russia.[21] The National Peasants' Party, formally still independent, would soon be served by a Secretary who was in reality a Communist: indeed, of that party's two ministers in the Cabinet, one would be a secret Communist, fifteen out of its thirty-two deputies were open Communists, while another eight were sympathisers.[22] The Socialist leader, Arpad Szakasits on the left of his party, intoxicated by the very idea of close association with Russia, was also painfully eager to accept Communist suggestions when he refounded his movement. The only other survivor among the pre-war socialist leaders, Charles Peyer, had been broken by his experiences in the concentration camp at Mauthausen and never regained his authority. Moderate Socialists were soon easily declared 'traitors to the idea of working class unity'. The Smallholders were also under assault. About eighty of their members of parliament, headed by Dezsö Sulyok, were described regularly in the Communist press as 'reactionaries', though Sulyok himself had already flirted with the Communists the year before, when they had dangled the idea of the prime ministership before him. The Communists also controlled the recently revived trade unions. Rákosi, therefore, could argue that 'strikes for the improvement of working conditions or higher wages were not permissible in Hungary: they were a luxury which only the American economy could afford'.[23]

The Communists included many men of quite remarkable experience. Consider the new Chief of Police in Budapest, Ferenz Münnich, son of a Jewish vet, who had established himself as a lawyer before 1914. Drafted into the Austro-Hungarian army, he was sent in 1915 to the Russian front, was captured and, as a prisoner of war, sided with the Bolsheviks in 1917. He fought with them at Tomsk, in Siberia and in the Urals. In 1919, he was back in Budapest, serving as a political commissar in Béla Kun's Red Army. In the 1920s, he served the Comintern, in a variety of tasks and, after long service in Russia, became a commander in the International Brigade during the Spanish Civil War. In the Second World War, he was back in Russia where he fought as a Soviet officer. Even Münnich's young deputy, János Kadár, had experienced several years of conspiratorial activity in pre-war Budapest. Rákosi was even cleverer than Münnich, he came from the same kind of lower middle class Jewish background and had the same experience as a prisoner of war in Russia in 1917. He too had played a minor part in Kun's government. By 1924 he was one of the secretaries to the Executive Committee of the Comintern in Moscow, as well as a leader of the Hungarian Communist Party in exile.[24] He had spent no less than fifteen years in one of Admiral Horthy's prisons. He could, when required, appear 'very mild, very restrained';[25] but the American political representative in Hungary, Schoenfeld (there could be no minister or legation till the signature of a treaty of peace), thought Rákosi forceful and intelligent when he met him in August.[26] Rákosi talked English well, having studied in London before 1914. His connections with Stalin were good, despite being Jewish. Khrushchev described an unsuccessful attempt by Stalin to make Rákosi incapably drunk one summer on the Black Sea.[27] As elsewhere in East Europe, the Communists included skilful opportunists: one memoir recalls how a young doctor who, in a Christmas speech in 1944 had fervently denounced Russians and Communists, had become within months the spokesman of the Communist Party in his own hospital.[28]

Though experienced, however, the Hungarian Communist Party was no more prepared for power than the Romanian or the Polish before 1944. They had created a revolutionary government in 1919. But, during the long years of Admiral Horthy's rule, they had barely maintained a party at all, either in Hungary itself or in exile. No Communist Party had been dissolved and reformed more often. After various successful persecutions, it seems that only ten or twelve party members in Hungary were actually in touch with one another in 1942; from 1941 to 1944 there was no communication at all between the party in Hungary and Moscow.[29] Neither the Communist

Party nor anyone else had done much in the way of resistance. As to Hungarian exiles, several thousand must have vanished in the Stalinist purges; or, should one say, 'in 193– he became victim of the illegalities of the Stalinist period?'[30] After 1944, some Hungarian Communists based in Russia organised guerrilla operations behind the German lines. But this was modest and late and did not occur till there was already a Communist presence in the east of the country.

The remarkable role played by persons of Jewish descent in the Hungarian Communist Party deserves notice. The 'Muscovites' who were the leaders in 1945 were mostly Jews, while the Communists who had survived the war in Budapest were Magyars. The political tension between these groups was exacerbated by the racial aspect. The Jewish leaders, however, were Stalin's men and relied on by him. Magyars like Rajk were the followers, and sometimes reluctant followers, supporting policies they disliked.[31]

In 1945–46, Hungary was hungry. Supplies through UNRRA (the United Nations Relief and Recovery Administration) had had some effect. But Budapest suffered famine that winter. A sophisticated, large, urban middle class had grown up in the late XIXth century with the expectation that good communications and regular sowing by responsible farmers on well-maintained estates would provide by railway all the food that was necessary in the city, at the right time. Those days were over. A bulletin of the 'Save Europe Now' Committee, in January 1946, suggested that a million people would die from starvation in Budapest that winter. The town was said to contain 30,000 homeless children, of whom some had formed into wild bands.[32] The system of transport was broken. The neighbouring estates had been fought over and pillaged by both Soviet and German armies. For a time, in early 1945, East Hungary had been split into ruthless little semi-independent revolutionary republics. Much of Budapest was in ruins. In addition, the armistice with Russia on January 20, 1945 had imposed on Hungary crippling reparations which had begun to be handed over in late 1945: commodities worth $200 million were to go over five years to the Soviet Union, $100 million to Yugoslavia and Czechoslovakia. The Russians, by a bilateral agreement, and by bullying officials, wrung out of Hungary estimates of exchange rates in such a way that, in the end, the original reparations almost tripled in value. Russian soldiers under the command of Marshal Voroshilov, Stalin's onetime drinking companion, seized, in a spontaneous manner, almost everything that they fancied and rarely accounted for it. Machinery was often loaded onto trains and carried off to the Soviet Union as booty. Much of it remained to rust in sidings: while in practice few of the confiscated factories could be reassembled in Russia. The Hungarian foreign ministry submitted, in early 1946, a list of the plants so treated, and asked that their value be assessed and counted against the reparation payments. Discussion of such matters was, however, impossible with either the Russians or the Hungarian Communists.[33] There were never replies. The Russians also seized, without negotiation, all German assets in Hungary, regardless of whether they had been seized by the Germans during the war or had been German before 1939. 800,000 Russian soldiers were still living off the land and Russia, ably represented by her minister, Georgi Pushkin, was also demanding a fifty per cent share in all major Hungarian industries.[34] Through such enterprises, the Soviet Union would control Hungarian railways, river transport, crude oil and petroleum refining, as well as the bauxite mines. At the same time, a State Department official reported: 'private American traders are unable to operate on a normal basis . . . because of lack of exchange rates, or banking facilities, poor communications, inadequate facilities and the rupture of pre-war trade relationships'.[35]

Since successful enterprises were looted, and so many factories dismantled, economic activity did not easily revive. On the contrary: on February 15, 1946, the United States Minister in Hungary reported that 'the financial deterioration' was proceeding 'at a runaway pace'. In that week alone the exchange with the dollar changed from 800,000 pengös to 1,800,000.[36] People were busy bartering their belongings for their existence. The prospects were that 'Hungarian currency will cease entirely to be acceptable as a medium of exchange'.[37] That part of the urban population which depended on income in money might soon be driven to rioting. If that were to happen, only the Russian army of occupation could do anything about it since the Hungarian army was in the process of disintegration. Perhaps the aim of Soviet policy now was to establish an economic colony in Hungary from which Western trade would be excluded, and in which all chance of Western investment would be lost. 'The manifest possibility of . . . engulfment of the Hungarian economy' in the Soviet Union seemed on the cards.

Early in 1946, Stephen Kertesz, a senior official in the foreign ministry, called on the British representative, Alvary Gascoigne. The latter asked the foreign ministry formally to send Britain a note about Hungary's economic plight. The Hungarian suggested that the annulment of the ruling by the Soviet-dominated Allied Control Commission, which prevented direct communications between the Hungarian government and the British (or the Americans), should precede the Hungarian note. Mr Gascoigne 'almost lost his temper' at hearing such logic. By this time, both he and his American colleague were protesting regularly against abuses by the political police and over other shortcomings of Hungarian democracy. But the authorities were powerless and neither of these two could give real help in time of crisis. The West had done little, even in terms of adding morale, to assist the Smallholders at the time of the election in November.

The Communists by now were even purging the libraries. The general provision that fascist books should be destroyed was widely interpreted; and it was common for all books by German authors, even on erudite subjects, even long ago published, to be removed from public libraries. On one occasion, zealous Soviet officers even destroyed books on 'horticulture' since they appeared next to the entry for 'Horthy, admiral' in the catalogue. Guilt by association was thus given a new meaning.

On February 9, 1946, the same day that Stalin spoke in Moscow, Archbishop Mindszenty was preaching in the Church of Eternal Worship in Budapest, at the conclusion of nine days calling for penance in Hungary. 'Only a praying humanity', he said, 'can build a better world. I am not now thinking merely of such external things as houses, bridges, streets, cables and the like, but I am thinking of relations with our fellow men and our own inner selves.' This great priest shortly received his nomination as a cardinal and his consequent summons to Rome. The authorities delayed his passport. He arrived late, on February 18, for the consistory. There were thirty-two new cardinals. The Pope, placing the cardinal's hat on his head, remarked, 'Among the thirty-two you will be the first to suffer the martyrdom, whose symbol this red colour is.'[38] The Pope showed himself a good prophet. Mindszenty's subsequent trials encapsulated those of his country.

Conditions in Romania, with its 15.5 million people in 1946, seemed much as they were in the other seven states which now lay between Russia and Germany: there was a coalition government, nominally run by the 'National Democratic Front', which had been established in 1944 as an amorphous, large, progressive organisation designed by the Communists to establish themselves throughout the professions. The coalition was headed by a rich and amiable timeserver, Dr Petru Groza – chairman of a party called the Ploughmens' Front, which had been founded in 1933, and had achieved a following in Transylvania in the 1930s. Groza had some standing, since he had figured as a minor (if discredited) minister in governments of the 1930s. The coalition was managed by the Communist Party and had been essentially introduced by the Soviet Union a year before. Thus the police was in the hands of a Communist Minister of the Interior, Teohari Georgescu. Seventeen Communists controlled all the important ministries, though an opportunist ex-premier, Gheorghe Tatarescu, well-known to Western chancelleries before the war, was Foreign Minister. A liberal, a clever man, a good speaker, but experienced in other activities, in restricting civil liberties, as well as being an anti-semite, and a onetime friend of the unscrupulous ex-King Carol, he had no reputation to save: but he was a useful, internationally known, survivor. Other such men, essential in the first year of a totalitarian government, were Mihai Ralea, at the Ministry of Culture, a member of the National Peasant Party, who had not only also served King Carol but had collaborated with the Nazis; Father Burducea, an anti-semitic ex-member of the Fascist Iron Guard, who was now Minister of Religion; and Lotar Radaceanu formally still a Socialist who had also had a questionable war record and who was Minister of Labour (his pre-war anti-Communism forgotten). Such men as these were to be found in 1946 in other countries of East Europe, but rarely was service to the Communists so combined with such disreputable pasts. They were men of parts caught up in a whirlwind. All the same, it is hard to explain the obvious enthusiasm shown by, for example, Stefan Voitec, the Socialist Minister of Education, who in February 1945 set about bolshevising the schools of Romania by purges of teachers, by imposing new Marxist Leninist textbooks and organising pro-Communist rallies of children. Doubtless his deputy, General Vasilichi, a Communist veteran of the civil war in Spain, kept his mind concentrated. The novelist, Mihai Sadoveanu, another ex-collaborator with the old regime, had organised an equally pernicious writers' union: he must have had many awkward conversations with his conscience.

The Communists in power represented a reasonably effective alliance between those party members who, like the railway workers' leader, Gheorghiu-Dej, had been in Romania, in prison, during the war; and those who, like Ana Pauker and Vasile Luca, had been in Moscow in exile for some years. Perhaps the most powerful man in the government was its 'Secretary General', and head of the Security Service, Emil Bodnaras, a Communist ex-artillery subaltern who had fled to Russia before the war, in unexplained circumstances, and was now plainly one of Moscow's most reliable agents.[39]

The Red Army quartered in the country numbered in early 1946 to something between 600,000 and 900,000 men. The British believed that Russia would keep some troops there indefinitely.[40] The Allied Control Commission in 1946 was also, as in Hungary, effectively a Russian agency. The armistice had been intended to provide for Soviet control of Romania's economic life till the formal conclusion of peace. It had not explicitly mentioned the need for British and American partici-

pation in the Commission's work. The Commission helped the
Communists, therefore, with transport and secretarial help.
From early 1944, the Western allies had recognised that the
war in Romania, and hence the peace, was 'Russia's business'.[41]
Harriman had also agreed in September 1944 that the United
States had 'a tacit understanding that Romania was an area of
predominant Soviet interest in which we should not interfere'.[42]
Roosevelt had refused to listen at Yalta to the Department of
State's expression of hope that the status of the United States
representatives in the Commission should be made clear.[43] The
issue was not faced at Potsdam. Romania, meanwhile, was also
bound to Russia by the imposition of heavy reparations, by the
transfer to them of property which the Russians claimed to have
been German-owned – a familiar experience in East Europe –
and through the surrender of industrial equipment as trophies
of war, including 40,000 tons of equipment from the American
and British holdings in Romanian oil enterprises.[44] The Russians
had control of all banks which were previously German while
there were Russian engineers in many Romanian factories.
Romanian trade was restricted, since an agreement of May 1945
enabled Russia virtually to monopolise Romanian commerce.[45]
Visits by Romanians to British or American missions – even the
representatives on the Control Commission – were looked on
as crimes.[46] Land reform had been embarked upon in March
1945, on the argument that the reforms of 1918–21 had been
ineffective. There was also fear, repression, midnight arrests,
secret police, beatings and disappearances.[47] Barbu Niculescu,
secretary to the late Prime Minister, General Radescu, later
escaped to the United States to testify to having experienced a
horrifying series of tortures and beatings in prison during the
summer of 1945, and to the presence of Russians during these
procedures.[48] The leaders of those who had collaborated with
the Germans, including Marshal Ion Antonescu and his brother,
were awaiting trial in prison. Some of their underlings were
(again as elsewhere in East Europe) as often as not seeking
membership of the expanding Communist Party.

This bleak state of affairs was primarily the consequence of
geography, even though the political developments of the war

and the years immediately before it had been marked by foolish conduct, by the King, Carol II, the Fascists (the 'Iron Guard'), the generals (above all, Marshal Antonescu) and other politicians. A place between two totalitarian empires, the German Nazi one and the Soviet Russian, is unenviable, as the example of Poland showed. All the same, until 1944, the Romanian leaders did not face the trials of the age with finesse.

Romanians had fought Russia, with enthusiasm, between 1941 and 1944, having fought each other, with even greater dedication, during the years of brawling with the Iron Guard. A Romanian army had been on the German flank at Stalingrad. After the Russian invasion in 1944, and the consequent *coup d'état*, on August 23, 1945, the country had been made by its new government to fight Germany; which it did, with less interest. The consequence had been the loss in battle of a further million Romanians.

In 1944, with the Russian army about to invade, the Romanians had made their first serious attempt to face their tragic predicament. The leaders of the old democratic parties, Iuliu Maniu and Constantin Bratianu, who had been out of power during the fascist and military years, conspired with the King and the small Communist Party to overthrow Marshal Antonescu. Antonescu was imprisoned (by the Communists) and held for trial.[49] A series of coalition governments followed. But with the Red Army in Bucharest, as a result of the subsequent armistice, these administrations found it hard to keep their heads. A small number of Communists were invited to collaborate with them. But that did not satisfy the Russians. In February 1945, just after Yalta, Andrei Vyshinsky, the deputy commissar for foreign affairs of the Soviet Union, came to Bucharest to make plain his demands. In the meantime, the Communists made substantial gains in the countryside. Vyshinsky told King Michael to appoint Dr Groza Prime Minister in March 1945. He probably acted when he did because the American representative on the Central Commission, General van R. Schuyler, had demanded that the Commission announce its intention to put into effect the Declaration on Liberated Europe signed in Yalta (to the annoyance of the War Department in Washington, who did not like such

Borders 1945
·········· Romanian gains 1918 — 45
Bulgarian gains from Turkey
– – – 1883 ; —·—·— 1913

to Hungary 1940—44

TRANSYLVANIA

BESSARABIA

Jassy

ROMANIA

Bucharest

DOBRUJA

Romanian 1913—40

BULGARIA

Sofia

Burgas

TURKEY

THRACE to Greece 1918

explicit suggestions, but to the satisfaction of the Department of State).[50] Vyshinsky, in a second meeting, told the King that, unless he accepted Dr Groza as Prime Minister, he could not guarantee the continuance of Romania as an independent state. He left, and slammed the door on leaving the King's office, to make the intimidation more obvious. The plaster round the door cracked. The Russians blithely explained their action to the Americans by saying that the Red Army needed order in its rearguard while a new government was necessary to rid the country of the last vestiges of Nazism. To the British, they did not think that they had need of saying anything, since Churchill had the previous October conceded Stalin a ninety per cent interest in the country.[51]

That crisis in early 1945, as it now appears, had been the decisive one of the country's history. It had been skilfully managed by the Russians and the Communists: they had brought armed Communists into Bucharest from the country; Gheorghiu-Dej, as Minister for Communications, had placed trains at their disposal; and there had been other familiar preparations. The Russian *démarche* had been preceded by well-managed demonstrations, well-publicised brawls, the seizures of town halls, law courts and police stations, the closing of schools 'in protest', and denunciations in the press of the government of the honest General Radescu as 'friends of the landlords', as well as special broadcasts in Romanian from Moscow which encouraged chaos and intimidated officials.[52] Printers were bullied into refusing to print articles or books which in any way distanced Romania from Russia. Papers were suppressed. Radescu, a brave man, tried to fight back, dismissed his Communist ministers (but the Communist under-secretary in the Ministry of the Interior refused to leave his office), and spoke forcefully to the nation over the radio. But in the subsequent demonstrations eight men were killed. Though it is obscure how that happened (Radescu asserted that the Communists had shot them) the event gave the opportunity for lavish funerals, more speeches, more marches, more protests.[53] The Romanian army was, meantime, away at the front; while the Russian army was available, to back Vyshinsky.[54] The King gave way, believing that he could fight another day.

Equally significant, however, in the winter of 1944 to 1945, both Britain and the Americans had distanced themselves from Iuliu Maniu, the only possible strong man of the opposition even though he was in his seventies. They discounted him as certain to make trouble between them and Russia in the last days of the war: and Eden also distrusted Maniu from pre-war days. Britain, her eyes on Greece, wanted to keep her part of the 'percentages agreement' and so even passed on to Moscow messages from their agents in Bucharest reporting conversations with democratic politicians.[55] Maniu told the United States representative that, without the assurance of Anglo-American support, he would not provoke 'open rebellion' against the Russian authority; though he believed an 'insurrection against the quisling government' of Dr Groza desirable; even essential.[56] Earlier, he had, to no avail, asked the Americans to tell him if 'spheres of influence' existed so that he could make the best possible arrangement for the country with Russia.[57] They could give no reply. Churchill who wavered on this subject, had for a time, in March 1945, wanted to make an issue out of Romania and to try and prevent the destruction of the opposition.[58] But Roosevelt demurred.

The main attempt to challenge Communism in 1945 was made by the King. The personality of King Michael was attractive. He was young. He was not associated with past failure. He could give a real focus to patriotism. The Constitution of 1866 had given him great authority, even if Michael's self-indulgent father, King Carol, had abused it. Michael had managed the overthrow of Antonescu skilfully, even if he had had to give way to intimidation in February. Democrats wore badges with the royal coat of arms, an attitude unthinkable in King Carol's day.[59] The first United States political representative, Burton Berry, who had arrived in November 1944, found in June 1945 that 'enthusiasm for the King dwarfs all others' and that nearly every conversation which he had included the question 'When will the Russians leave?'[60]

In August 1945, the King read the declaration in favour of

liberty which was issued after the Conference at Potsdam and subsequent comments by Truman.[61] With support from the British and American representatives, he therefore decided to dismiss Dr Groza. When Groza refused to leave office, the King, invoking the Declaration on Liberated Europe, appealed to the Allied Control Commission. The Soviet Union was hostile, Britain and the United States powerless. The King retired to a palace at Sinaia.[62] Molotov in Moscow accused the United States of inspiring the crisis. He and Byrnes discussed Romania acrimoniously at the London Council of Foreign Ministers. Bevin offered a compromise: a Commission to examine the whole problem on the spot.[63] Bidault suggested collaboration between the allied diplomats in Bucharest. Molotov insisted that the Romanian government was 'liked by Romanians'. It was more popular, more representative, he said, than those of Greece and Italy, let alone Spain. Meantime, in Bucharest, Dr Groza continued in office, and the King continued not to recognise him. Groza, Tatarescu and Gheorghiu-Dej went to Russia in the autumn. They returned enraptured with Stalin, and told the press in Bucharest so. 'We talked as a small pupil to an old teacher', the artful prime minister reported, while the 'old teacher' had assured his pupil that, so long as he remained in the Kremlin, Groza could remain in power in Bucharest. The King, thereafter, refused to sign papers, and the cabinet continued without him. A great demonstration for the King was organised in November in front of his palace on his birthday but it was broken up by the police: many were killed, the 'monarchists' disappearing into prison, in some cases for ever.[64] The monarchy survived but its contact with the government almost ceased. In November, Mark Ethridge, of the *Louisville Courier-Journal*, in a report for Secretary Byrnes, noted: 'The position of the Western democracies is disintegrating fast. The Russian position is becoming stronger . . . unless we can take firm action and effective action . . . it will be too late.'[65]

This report led to a reaffirmation of the United States' desire to help by restating its Yalta principles. But, the Romanians asked, was this intended to arouse opinion in Bucharest or merely to comfort readers of newspapers in Chicago? There were discussions about Romania at the Conference of Foreign Ministers in Moscow. They led to Vyshinsky's, Harriman's and Clark Kerr's visit to Bucharest in January,[66] and to the later enlargement of the government to include one representative of Maniu's Peasant Party (Emil Hatieganu) and one of Bratianu's Liberals (Mihai Romniceanu). It was no more than a gesture, comparable to that made in Poland to Mikołajczyk. The British, believing themselves still bound by Churchill's 'percentages' concession in 1944, and hoping understandably for Russian inactivity in Greece, had been wanting formally to recognise Dr Groza's government and so be done with an awkward issue. Reluctantly, the United States agreed (Byrnes grossly overestimated the value of the concession made to him over the enlargement of the Romanian government).[67] In Bucharest, the American mission contemplated a general resignation at the news of Allied recognition.[68] They did not believe that the proposed elections would be fair, even if they were held. Maniu told them that the Red Army were allocating to all the Peasants Party newspapers two rolls of newsprint a day; while the Communist daily, *Scinteia*, was alone receiving twenty. All the same, on February 4, 1946, the governments of the United States and Britain went ahead and recognised Dr Groza's government. The Americans appended to their declaration a formidable list of qualifications relating to liberty which were swiftly accepted by the Romanian administration. A breeze of hope, despite everything, blew through the country that spring; open anti-Communist political activity revived; but equally open state-sponsored political violence continued, with meetings broken up and democrats murdered.[69]

Perhaps all was not lost. Two large political parties, the National Peasants and the Liberals, had survived the years both of royal dictatorship and of war. Nowhere else was this true in East Europe. Their leaders, Iuliu Maniu and Constantin Bratianu, were men of substance. Democracies in modern conditions need parties as much as they need constitutions and systems of law. Maniu, who had been a deputy in the old Austro-Hungarian diet, and Prime Minister from 1928 till 1931, and who stood for an improvement in the lot of those who worked on the land, represented the best hopes for constitutional reform. He had been in touch with the British throughout the war, even though he was now old and had seemed indecisive in 1944.[70] His deputy, Ion Mihalache, was also a man of substance. Bratianu was bearer of a great name in Romanian history (he was son of the grand old man of his party, Ion Bratianu), while the Liberal party had a history of activity over the three generations since Romania had gained independence of the Ottoman Empire as a consequence of the Crimean War. There was a strong anti-Russian tradition in the country and there had been free elections in the country several times.

At the same time, the Communist party before 1939 had made little impact. Its membership had never risen to more than 5,000. It never achieved as many as two per cent of the votes cast in the 1920s when it campaigned alone. In 1931, five Communists were elected to Parliament, but that had been in alliance with others. In 1937, it again did badly. The only effective action between the world wars by the Communist party was its management of a rail strike in 1933. Footloose young intellectuals had then been drawn to the Iron Guard – 'the Legion of the Archangel Michael' – more than to Communism. The divided Romania which emerged so successfully from the First World War had also discouraged Communist revolutionaries. So did the Soviet Union's claim to Bessarabia.

The Communist party's appeal was above all to the new minorities (or to minorities within a minority) – Bulgarians in the Dobrudja, Jews among the Hungarians or Germans in Transylvania. It is true that the Communists had gathered over 250,000 members by October 1945, and may have had close to 400,000 by the spring of 1946.[71] But most of these were 'fair weather Communists', with a sizeable number of ex-members of the Iron Guard.

Another good sign for the opposition was that the peasants had 'not shown much enthusiasm' for the land reform: 'Only when government agents threaten a village with the import of people from neighbouring villages to take up land from adjoining estates have villagers shown any alacrity in occupying large estates'.[72] The British Minister wrote, in November 1945, of the 'anti-Communist and anti-Russian bias of the vast majority of the Romanian population'.[73] So the opposition believed that, in a fair election, they would win. But Dr Groza made skilful evasions on this subject: May would be inappropriate because of food shortages; June, because of the harvest; voters in Transylvania needed to be counted before they could be put on the electoral roll; and so on.

The changes in Romania's frontiers, and hence population, during the last two generations created additional uncertainty in the country. In 1913, the original two provinces of historic Romania were expanded, at the end of the Balkan Wars, by the acquisition of Southern Dobrudja from Bulgaria. In 1919, they additionally gained the large territory of Transylvania, with its big Hungarian population, as well as the rich wheat-growing territory of Bessarabia lying between the rivers Dniester and Prut: the first from historical Hungary, the second from Russia. In 1919, they also acquired the small, wooded but strategically valuable one-time duchy of North Bukovina from Austria-Hungary. In 1940 the Russians had re-acquired Bessarabia: Hitler had agreed. But, a year later, it was returned to Romania by the Nazis, in return for help to Germany in the war against Russia, along with Bukovina and even the Russian province of Odessa, which became, for three years, capital of a new Romanian province known as 'Transnistria'. At the same time, Romania lost northern Transylvania to Hungary; and Bulgaria regained the South Dobrudja. In 1945, these arrangements were upturned: Bessarabia and North Bukovina went to Russia, while Transylvania and the South Dobrudja returned to Romania. There were perfectly good ethnic grounds for some of these transfers but it was *realpolitik*, not reason, which determined them. They were events which received no attention in the West. Nor did the Soviet pursuit of the thousands of Bessarabians who, in 1944, fled from the Red Army, or the Soviet regime, across the river Prut. These, among the most wretched of the millions of refugees in Europe, were still being hunted by the Soviet army in 1946; most were carried back to Russia, along with other Romanians swept with even less reason into forced service in Soviet labour camps. The Germans of Romania had been the first to be exported to those camps: an industrious minority for several hundred years, the majority of adults between the ages of seventeen and forty-five vanished by train into Siberia in 1944 or 1945. Their treatment could in no way be justified on the grounds that other Germans, from Germany proper, had been responsible for the deportation and murder during the war of a million Romanian Jews.[74]

The significance of these changes can be most easily imagined if it is noticed that, of the political leaders in 1946, not only Maniu and Groza but Gheorghiu-Dej and Luca had been born in Transylvania when it had been part of the Austria-Hungarian empire; Bodnaras was son of a Ukrainian and a German, born in Bukovina (also then part of Austria-Hungary);[75] Ana Pauker was Jewish, daughter of a rabbi in Moldavia; and numerous prominent Communists were Bulgarians, either from the Dobrudja or, even, from Bulgaria itself.


Bulgaria, known for its Russophil traditions, and revived as an independent state as a result of intervention by Russia only in 1877–78, seemed even more under Soviet tutelage than Romania. Throughout the war, a Soviet legation had been in Sofia, while the Bulgarian Communist Party was also active – as a shadow party, like most parties in the country under the autocratic monarchy, but, all the same, with greater freedom than communist parties in the territory of other allies of Nazi Germany, until 1941. After that, the party was virtually broken, most local party chiefs being in prison or dead. But the best-known leaders in 1946, such as the famous Georgi Dimitrov, general secretary of the Comintern, Vulko Chervenkov, and Vasil Kolarov had, with several thousand other Bulgarian Communists, spent most of the years since 1923 in Russia.[76]

Bulgaria was at war with Russia only for two days in 1944. The royal government had, however, joined Germany and Italy in the Tripartite Pact, in 1941, and fought in Yugoslavia. They declared war on Britain and the United States, receiving, in consequence, heavy bombing which had destroyed nearly half the capital.[77] Though about 20,000 German troops had been in

Sofia with Bulgarian agreement, the government always retained control over the administration. The Bulgarian Jews survived: exceptionally and despite considerable German pressure. Bulgaria's only belligerent action had been their occupation of those tracts of Yugoslav Macedonia and Thrace which they had held before the First World War and considered to be theirs, and where they helped Germany to fight Tito. This half-neutrality had been skilfully managed by King Boris, until his sudden, but probably natural, death, in 1943. The Regency Council, acting on behalf of the infant heir, King Simeon, was less effective. It was inspired by King Boris's last Prime Minister, a supposedly apolitical professor of archaeology, Bogdan Filov, who showed that agnosticism can be as brutal as commitment.

The Bulgarian occupation of land previously Yugoslav and Greek was carried out with cruelty in territory where previously there had been only a few Bulgarians. Two hundred thousand Greeks are said to have been deported from Thrace, and Bulgarian settlers sent in. Eleven thousand Jews were despatched thence to Auschwitz.[77] These actions caused confusion in the Communist Party since their import was that the government which had persecuted them had nevertheless fulfilled a long-held national ambition, the absorption of the whole of Macedonia, a most awkward territory for all of those countries which, like Greece and Yugoslavia, as well as Bulgaria, had, before 1940, shared it.

In 1944, the Russian armies had swept into Romania. The consequence in Bulgaria was that the pro-German government of Dobri Bozhilov fell. His successor, Ivan Bagrianov, sought to negotiate, and received a Communist delegation, as well as appointing a Soviet-educated agronomist as Minister of Agriculture (Doncho Kostov). A subsequent pro-Western government, led by an Agrarian politician, Konstantin Muraviev, did much the same. A sudden Soviet declaration of war, and a *coup d'état*, by pro-allied ex-officers led to a government more fitting for the time, under the direction of the so-called 'Fatherland Front'; one of those convenient, multi-party boards, so liked by Stalin, in which upper class patriots and conventional generals sat next to Communist professors. No matter that this particular name had been used for his party of national regeneration by Dr Dolfuss in Austria. Memory is short.

Had Muraviev's government been formed earlier, something might have been saved in Bulgaria for the West. After all, Churchill allocated to Britain, in his (subsequent) 'percentages agreement' with Stalin, a twenty per cent interest in the country.* Bagrianov had also set in train negotiations with the Western allies in Cairo. But since Muraviev's opportunity came so late, all he could carry out, following the ruthless Soviet declaration of war, with the Red Armies already on his northern border, was a declaration of war on Germany, the ally of the preceding governments in Sofia. To be at war with both Russia and Germany was a tragic fate for a country whose leaders had done their best to keep out of the conflict which had begun in 1939: a policy which undoubtedly had had the enthusiastic support of the vast majority of the population.[79]

The Fatherland Front, which had come into being in 1943, organised about 12,000 to 15,000 'partisans'[80] during the last part of the war. With the exception of several Communist groups on the Yugoslav frontier (which became engaged in the war in Serbia), they had done little save terrorise villages, blow up trains carrying supplies to Germany, and provoke harsh reprisals by the authorities; thereby creating, as they wished, division in the country, from which the Communists could later benefit. In 1944 the multiparty committees of the Fatherland Front had assumed local control, organised welcomes for the Red Army and, largely through its Communist members, had taken over local policing.

As in other Eastern European governments, the Bulgarian police continued under Communist control, direction being exercised by ex-leaders of the 'partisans'. The Minister of the Interior in command of the police was Anton Yugov, a quick-witted, tough and able son of a farmer from Greek Macedonia, whose father had been repatriated in 1919. He had begun life in the tobacco industry. (Among these repatriates, unwelcome in the new country, and always on the move, all extreme creeds were

* See Appendix III.

attractive). Like other instigators of Communist revolution in East Europe, Yugov had also been trained at the Lenin school in Moscow. Implicated in the attempted Communist *coup* in Sofia in 1925 when still a Socialist, he had been in and out of prison and, during the war, had been the most prominent party leader still at large in Sofia. The Minister of Justice, and the organiser of 'People's Courts', Dr Mincho Neichev, had similarly been a Party member since 1923. So had Dobri Terpeshev, the slothful and dull-witted Deputy Prime Minister, and commander-in-chief of the Communist partisans, who had recently taken to appearing in the uniform of a lieutenant general.[81] Another old Communist, Traicho Kostov, Secretary-General of the Bulgarian party from September 1944 to November 1945, was an intense and studious Marxist, who epitomised the intellectual turned professional revolutionary. Crippled from trying to kill himself during a police interrogation in the 1920s, and subsequently deputy Prime Minister concerned with economic matters, he would in 1949, most surprisingly, be accused of, and confess to, being among other things a British agent: an accusation which, unfortunately for Britain, appears to be without foundation.[83] (He had already been condemned to death in 1942 and saved on the intervention of King Boris, who had been persuaded that Kostov was a brilliant intellectual whose life should not be wasted.)[84] A fourth Communist minister, Dr Racho Angelov, in charge of public health, was well known in progressive medical circles in Sofia for many years, being a mild-mannered man in his early seventies. It had been he who had made contact with the other opposition parties in 1942.

By the time that the world war ended, the Communist direction of the regime in Bulgaria was thus already almost complete. The Prime Minister, Colonel Kimon Georgiev, the two non-Communist Regents, the non-Communist ministers in the Fatherland Front, even the Exarch Stefan of the Orthodox Church, remained where they were only because they feared to resign. They no longer sought to persuade themselves, like so many others in such conditions, that, in the face of evidence, they could still influence events for the best. Colonel Georgiev had anyway little real influence since he was not the leader of a political party but of a pro-Western faction of retired or cashiered officers known as the 'Link' (*Zveno*). The fact that he had briefly led the government after Zveno's *coup d'état* in 1934 meant nothing. (Zveno received its name from a publication of that name. Despite its position in 1945–46, it had begun in the late 1920s closely associated with the neo-fascism of Professor Alexander Tsankov and its members had been associated with both the *coups d'état* of 1923 and of 1934.) In the 1930s, Georgiev had denounced the Bulgarian Communist party for being directed by Moscow and for spreading anarchy.[85] His new ministry was equally ineffective, in that it merely gave a front – and in this case a scarcely respectable one – to a Communist regime. The association of Zveno with the Communists had begun in 1936.[86] But such continuity did not make for trust. The association was renewed in 1942, when the Fatherland Front was thought of.

The Ministers of Finance (Professor Stoianov) and War (Major General Damyan Velchev, the real leader of Zveno), and the Foreign Minister (Petko Staikov, an independent) were in the same position. They were unable to prevent the murder, torture or imprisonment by the Communist police even of their own staff. Even Velchev, famous before the war for his military intrigues, was powerless: as powerless before the Communists as he had been before the Macedonians in 1923, when he had organised a coup against Stamboliski, the agrarian leader, which had led to the murder of that statesman, against his orders. The monarchy, it is true, survived but the King was a child, and the new Regency council powerless: one of its three members indeed was a Communist, Dr Pavlov.*

Western influence in Bulgaria was modest: two missions from SOE, for instance, had been lost there[87] and there had been a failure there in respect of activity by the other British Secret Service, the SIS. American influence through OSS may have been greater, to the British annoyance; for Britain considered

* Pavlov, a member of the party central committee from 1924, was in and out of prison in the 1920s, dean of the Faculty of Philosophy in the Moscow Institute in the 1930s and made his best-known contribution to Leninist aesthetics with his *Theory of Reflections*.

the Balkans their own preserve.[88] Joint Anglo-Saxon deliveries
of weapons, clothing and munitions had been received by Communist partisans: they gave profuse thanks, and then forgot
about the matter. By early 1946, the British and American
representatives, Generals Oxley and Crane, on the Allied Control Commission were treated almost as if they were captives,
even though the Armistice had given this Commission more
authority than that in Romania: in Bulgaria, as in Hungary, there
was a stipulation for the Western allies to be on the body, even
if Russia were to be chairman till the formal end of hostilities
against Germany. Neither the status, size, functions nor financing of these Western missions had been fixed: which gave Russia
an excuse for refusing reasonable facilities to them, on the model
of the Soviet exclusion from the ACC in Italy. The United States
had interested themselves in the terms of the armistice more
than they had done in Romania; but, even so, in the end, the
Department of State had left actual negotiations to Eden.[89] As
in respect of Romania, Roosevelt had never pressed at Yalta for
a definition of the rights of the American and British representatives.[90] Nor had Truman at Potsdam.[91] General Crane had, as
early as February 27, 1945, suggested that the United States
announce to the world either that the Declaration on Liberated
Europe did not apply to Bulgaria; or, that she take action to
ensure full United States participation in the Control Commission
and to arrange free elections.[92] He got some support from the
Department of State, but nothing transpired. Like General
Schuyler in Bucharest, Crane found the conditions intolerable.
The Bulgarians had had imposed on them the previous May a
trade agreement comparable to that imposed on the Romanians,
which effectively prevented the establishment of fair and normal
commerce with the West.

The Secretary General of the Bulgarian National Agrarian
Union, Dr G. M. ('Gemeto') Dimitrov, in Cairo during the war
with the British SOE[92], took refuge with the United States
representative in May 1945 (having had at 2.30 in the morning
to leave his sanctuary with the latter's British colleague). Several
hundred 'militiamen' surrounded the house of Maynard Barnes
and held him, as it were, hostage.[93] His secretary was shortly

tortured to death. The Russian army commander and deputy chairman of the Control Commission General Biryuzov and his 150,000–200,000 Russian troops were now the real authorities in the country. New Communist arrivals from Moscow, such as the spiteful, heavy-handed, if experienced, Vasil Kolarov, and Georgi Dimitrov (no relation to his democratic namesake), the two leaders of the party best known since the 1920s, despite periods of disgrace in the early 1930s, later gave a fraudulent Bulgarian colour to the Soviet-sponsored regime. Kolarov had, however, been so close to Russia that he had even headed a special commission in Moscow in 1922 which dismissed an appeal from the farm workers' opposition in Russia as groundless.[95] Dimitrov, hero of the Reichstag trial in 1933, at a time when paradoxically he had been out of favour in Moscow, was general secretary of the Comintern from 1935 to its dissolution in 1943: on the surface one of the great successes of the international Communist system, he was a broken man, in bad health, his first wife dead by her own hand in Germany, his only child dead in Kuibyshev (he had returned to Sofia in November 1946).

The personal cost of this Soviet control was high. In September 1945, the American journalist Reuben Markham of *the Christian Science Monitor* estimated that 200,000 Bulgarians had been killed during the preceding year (chiefly as acts of vengeance in the country against the old authorities, who had sought to stamp out the partisans), with many thousands also in prison, including nearly all the ministers and officials of the wartime government who had been executed in February 1945. The British gave a figure of 40,000 or 50,000 killed between January and July 1945.[96] At all events, the figure was high; the sort of numbers which should have evoked an international outcry of the first importance. Not only the bourgeoisie, Markham thought, were subject to this terror. Most Bulgarians were peasants. Their villages were now terrorised 'by armed, organised Communist bands who wilfully dispose of life and property'. The majority in Bulgaria seemed to consider themselves as living in a 'totalitarian prison'.[97] Hostility was not entirely passive. But it was successfully crushed. The Red Army did not have to intervene directly. Yet its presence gave the

Communists an overwhelming advantage.[98] Most peasants would doubtless have preferred a radical agrarian government such as that offered by Stamboliski in the 1920s. But when the Communists talked persuasively of social justice, a large minority of disillusioned, underemployed and undernourished peasants were prepared to give them the benefit of the doubt; and so support them.

Given the atmosphere of intimidation, it was not surprising that, in national elections held on November 18, 1945, the Fatherland Front should have won a great victory: they won all 276 seats.[99] Maynard Barnes, the United States representative, in close association with the agrarian leader, Nikola Petkov, had pressed unsuccessfully for a postponement of that test of opinion until he could look on them as fair 'in the Yalta sense'. He had in August called for allied intervention to avoid what he called a 'Hitlerite plebiscite'.[100] That call had been effective, though probably thanks only to the personal intervention of Stalin, who had wanted the election campaign to be open enough for the opposition to expose itself. (Barnes's démarche in August had been against the wishes of the Department of State.)[101] In the preparations for the new election, the press had been anything but free. For example, Communist typesetters refused to publish articles in Petkov's newspapers which criticised the recently returned Communist General Secretary, Georgi Dimitrov: 'Even in Sofia, there is hardly a house that has not already been visited by representatives of the Fatherland Front', reported Barnes to Washington, 'conveying menacing indications as to how occupants must conduct themselves on November 18 if they do not wish a second "visitation" in the days immediately following the election'.[102] Barnes was unable to postpone the elections twice. In the event, the Fatherland Front gained 88 per cent of the votes cast, or 76 per cent of the electorate. No precise voting figures became available. The opposition privately claimed that the real percentage of support for the government was less than 40 per cent.[103] There was no way of testing the claim. Early in November the special representative of Secretary Byrnes, Mark Ethridge, estimated that 'the Communists have overreached themselves'.[104] All the same, Maynard Barnes in

December thought that 'all eyes in Bulgaria today are turned toward Moscow'.[105]

Ethridge, publisher of *the Louisville Courier-Journal*, was associated with the New Deal and so was well qualified in principle for the report required of him by Byrnes. He believed specially in the possibility of 'co-existence'. So his adverse, painstaking document had an impact in Washington and, also, at the Council of Foreign Ministers, in Moscow. He persuaded the Department of State to allow him to present his observations about Bulgaria direct to Vyshinsky.[106] The consequent discussion in Moscow led the Soviet government to make an effort to gain greater approval for their policies in Bulgaria, both there and abroad. They did this by agreeing to broaden the base of the government in Sofia by including politicians from the National Liberal and the National Peasant parties. Byrnes, with his usual eye for a quick advantage, seized on this concession as a possible way of breaking out from an ugly impasse. Vyshinsky went to Sofia in January to try and persuade the leaders of the opposition to join Georgiev's coalition. Kosta Lulchev, leader of the Social Democrats, and Nikola Petkov, both refused this invitation unless the National Assembly, which they believed to have been elected on false pretences, were dissolved, new elections held and the Cabinet reorganised, with above all the odious Yugov removed from the Ministry of the Interior. These 'impossible and insulting demands distressed' the Russians. They attributed them to the 'intrusive' activities of Barnes who no doubt had fortified Petkov's courage.

The United States member of the Allied Control Commission, General Crane, leaving Sofia for a medical examination from which he would not return, sent back a despatch on February 4, 1946 to Washington describing the 'most humiliating position' in which he had had to live since his arrival fourteen months before. He had never as much as met his Soviet colleague, Marshal Tolbukhin who indeed had only once attended the Commission. The restrictions placed on him had made him (and so the United States) a laughing stock. Despite the agreement at Potsdam that members of the Allied Control Commission should be able to go where they liked, without previous notice, the Russians had reserved to themselves the right to deny him entry into any place where there were Russian troops: a big restriction, for there were 'Russian troops everywhere'. Those troops talked 'as if they were here for an indefinite stay, especially their wives'. An officers' club of unexampled magnificence had, for example, been opened in Sofia.[107]

During the 'time of actual hostilities', continued General Crane, 'I realised that everything must be sacrificed to keeping Russia in the war, and I bore the indignities to which we were constantly subjected with the thought that, after the war, we could hold up our heads'. He concluded: 'Orders are issued by the ACC unknown to us, yet we share responsibility for such orders. Is not our country of sufficient strength to demand and enforce its demand for reasonable treatment of such a mission as this? . . . I am afraid we are following the policy of appeasement of the late Mr Chamberlain'.[108] Maynard Barnes did not differ very much. He would write, on February 18, 1946: 'I can assure the Department that no member of the United States delegation or Mission staffs has ever arrived in this post disposed not to get on with the Russians. I may even go so far as to say that all arrived convinced that a way could be found to establish effective and satisfactory relations with them. I can report with equal assurance that not one has retained original faith in the fundamental decency of Russians, after the experience of direct contact with them: that in fact there is to-day not a single member of staff, delegation and Mission who retains a shred of belief in Russian objectivity or good faith. They are the instruments of an implacable system that makes no allowances for human decency'.[109]

There were still in Bulgaria opposition leaders of character and courage. Petkov, leader of the wing of the Agrarians called *Pladne* (Noon) from their newspaper, in particular, could have become a statesman of stature. But his divided party was easily subverted: as early as the 1920s, the Agrarians were said to have 'wings, winglets and feathers'.[110] His colleague, 'Gemeto' Dimitrov, was a strong personality, an eloquent physician: he was a real man of the people, twice sentenced to death by the old regime, and twice reprieved.[111] But faced with the police in the hands of Yugov, and the railways, posts, telephones and telegraph service in those of Major General Markov, courage and stature were not enough.

Bulgaria was the only country in Eastern Europe where Communists might perhaps have won power in a free election. In 1919, they had won over a fifth of the seats to the then parliament and, until outlawed, a year or two later, had been for a time the second largest party. It was, with that of Italy and Norway, one of the only three old socialist parties which fully joined the Comintern in 1919. Under the disguise of 'Independent Workers' Party', the Bulgarian party had won thirty-one seats (out of 274) in 1931. Their actions were carried out against a background of some social reform already achieved since there had been an effective land reform in the 1920s, while industrialisation was modest. The estimated membership of 6,000 in mid-1944 ignores the party members in prison who were able to return to swell numbers over the next eighteen months. The party's relations with Moscow had, at the same time, always been excellent. A large number of Bulgarian Communists had been assimilated into exile to Russian life and stayed there for good.[112] Their aptitude for international revolution was no less remarkable. Before 1939, it was said, Bulgaria 'among the most backward of European countries, . . . produced international Communism's best Bolsheviks'.[113]

It has been sometimes argued by historians, determined to place the blame for the 'cold war' on the United States, that that nation wanted to establish democratic governments in Eastern Europe in order to expand trade there. It might have been a good aim. But the evidence from both Romania and Bulgaria suggests the opposite. General Schuyler and Maynard Barnes in Bulgaria both proposed, in May and March 1945, respectively, that the United States open trade relations as a means of assisting the economic, and perhaps eventually political, independence of those countries.[114] The Department of State not only did nothing but did not reply to the suggestion and made no protest against the Soviet trade agreements in either country.[115]

# FOURTEEN

# HEIRS OF THE TURKISH EMPIRE: YUGOSLAVIA AND ALBANIA

Yugoslavia was in 1946 a country as sated with bloodshed as any. About 1.7 million Yugoslavs out of 15 or so million had died in the war.[1] The diversity of its territories, religions and cultures, over which the Austrians, Hungarians and Turks had fought for so long, had left to the modern nation, created in 1919 around the core of Serbia, a legacy of hatred, vendetta and cruelty to which the international war of 1941 to 1945 had given full opportunity.* Two-thirds of the livestock, one quarter of the vineyards and most of the reserves of timber had been lost, as well as much of the railway system and the roads.

Yugoslavia had a Communist government which, to its domestic opponents and to its American ex-allies, appeared one of dictatorship and terror.[2] No party other than Communist had by now any chance of power though, for some months, the government had included twelve representatives from the all-party assembly, AVNOJ (Anti-Fascist Council of National Liberation) – founded in December 1942 – and six from the government in exile, along the lines of an agreement reached in December 1944 between 'Marshal' Tito, President of the Parti-

* The complexity of the national question in 1946 can be seen from statistics of population in 1948. Out of a total of 15.7 million, 6.5 million were Serbs, 3.8 million Croats, 1.4 million Slovenes, 400,000 Montenegrins, 800,000 Moslems, 750,000 Albanians, 496,000 Hungarians, 800,000 Macedonians, 100,000 Vlachs. Peoples with less than 100,000 included Bulgarians, Czechs, Germans, Gypsies, Turks, Rossini, Romanians and Russians.

san Committee of Liberation, and Dr Ivan Šubašić, Prime Minister of the King's Yugoslav government in London. But AVNOJ was dominated by the 'partisans', the name taken by Tito for his guerrillas, apparently in deference to the memory of Russian 'partisans' against Napoleon. Roosevelt had shown at Yalta that he was bored by Churchill's efforts to promote a genuine coalition;[3] just as the Department of State affected to know nothing of Churchill's understanding with Stalin in October 1944 by which they each had a fifty per cent interest in Yugoslavia. All the Communist leaders, Marshal Tito at their head, were men who had triumphed in a civil war of unspeakable brutality. They had for that reason no truck with coalitions such as other Eastern European Communists favoured. They believed, unlike them, that they had already achieved the 'dictatorship of the proletariat' in their country.

In November 1945, this government, like its comrades in Albania and Bulgaria, had felt confident enough to stage an election. Ninety per cent of the electorate voted, 81.53 per cent of them for the government, the people in general being 'sufficiently terrorised by polling time to make extraordinary measures unnecessary'.[4] Both American and British representatives thought that, had the election been free, the overwhelming majority would have been against Communism.[5] So did the Czech ambassador.[6] The last opposition newspapers were published, and that on a tiny scale, during the approach to the election campaign. Subsequently, the United States had, gingerly, recognised the Yugoslav government but held back any financial help.

The consequences of the election were twofold: the formal abolition of the monarchy (an institution which, during the previous two generations, had, for all its inadequacies in the 1930s, created the Yugoslav state out of the 'union of Serbs, Croats and Slovenes'); and the end of the former pretence of playing with the opposition, and allowing it rights, such as the occasional publication of independent newspapers. After interminable negotiations, stretching back to 1942, the King had been abandoned by Churchill and Roosevelt early in 1945. King Peter was in 1946 still in London, bitter, short of money, but dignified.[7] The leader of the opposition in Yugoslavia, Dr Grol, an ex-deputy premier, who had resigned from that shadowy role in the government the previous summer, was 'little better than a prisoner in his own house, for he is afraid to go out after dark and many of his friends are afraid to go and see him'.[8] 'This isn't a state, it's a slaughterhouse', he had remarked, when still in the government.[9] Leader of the Democratic Party before the war, honest, brave, taciturn, a European intellectual of a high order, Dr Grol was respected, left alone, but not allowed to seek supporters. Dr Šubašíc-Ban (viceroy) of Croatia from 1939 to 1941, prime minister of the King, and foreign minister till October 1945, had resigned as a protest against the unsatisfactory political state of affairs but had not made any kind of real stand. The only other active opposition leader, the left-wing 'Agrarian' Dragoljub Jovanović, remained, it is true, in parliament; eloquent, fearless and incorruptible, he hated the Communists, who hated him and probably regretted that they had not murdered him with so many others, in the confused time of Belgrade's liberation. His moment of trial would soon come.[10]

The regime was inexperienced in government. None of the leaders knew much of administration, despite the swiftness with which they took over royal palaces, or aristocratic villas, in the exclusive suburb of Dedinje outside Belgrade, for themselves, and began to behave in a regal manner. (Tito had even taken over the royal custom of becoming automatically the godfather of a family's ninth son.)[11] Most had simple visions of a Utopia directed by Tito. Their Marxism was of the sort which made them recall phrases of Marx in moments of danger; 'the defensive is the death of an armed uprising', a phrase occasioned by the Paris Commune, they had often murmured, as the Nazi troops stumbled on towards them. They had studied *Problems of Leninism* by Stalin and so believed that they themselves had no problems left. Some of them had been fighting for nearly ten years, first as volunteers in the Civil War in Spain, then in their own country between 1941 and 1944.* They were men who had

---

* Fifteen out of sixty-six partisan generals in 1945 were ex-volunteers in Spain. Chetnik is a word from 'Ceta' an armed band, an organisation built up to provide a guerrilla militia, before 1941, for use in time of war. They were mainly Serbs.

much blood on their hands, both during and after the war; now they could start enjoying, as well as using, power, not to speak of the hunting of game which characterised it, always, in Yugoslavia.

The Communists had liberated Serbia and Belgrade (after heavy fighting) from Germans by the end of 1944. They had spent the next winter killing supporters of the old regime, as well as those who, often after hesitation, had collaborated with the Germans, the Italians and General Nedić's puppet government, in order to defeat the Communists: particularly, but not only, the Chetniks, followers of the royalist General Draža Mihailović, once the favoured protégé of the United States and Britain, with whom Tito and the partisans had fought a war, after some ineffective attempts at coalition. The complexity of the war in Yugoslavia is indicated, though far from summed up, in Djilas' characterisation of the Chetniks as, in the beginning, 'standing in Bosnia and Croatia for Serbian self-defence against extermination; in Serbia, for restoration of the monarchy, and hegemony over other peoples; in Montenegro, for counter-revolution'. Given this complexity, Tito and the Communists determined to introduce the simplicity of Marxism-Leninism. Judges, civil servants, merchants, priests, small tradesmen and railwaymen, teachers and landlords, died in thousands, in consequence. Bodies continued to be thrown into ravines to avoid the inconvenience of funerals, as during the war. Those who suffered included not only the Croats, Chetniks and supporters of the old regime but the Hungarian minority in the North. There, in 1941, a Hungarian army had entered the country, nominally to protect the Hungarian population. They committed atrocities, killing Jews and Serbs. They withdrew. At the end of the war, their sins were visited on the Hungarians whom they had sought to protect – and on a scale which exceeded the original crimes.[12]

The Western allies' final switch from support of General Mihailović (minister of war in the Royal Government based in London from January 1942) to that of Tito in February 1944 derived primarily from a simple if brutal estimate by Churchill that Tito would do more damage to the Germans than the former: Tito's partisans were ruthless, whilst Mihailović became inactive when he saw the reprisals visited on the civilian population by German commanders in return for attacks on them. A third reason was that the British government had 'irrefutable proof' – Churchill's words – from, in particular, intercepted radio messages between German SS units in the Balkans, which proved earlier charges, first levied by the partisans in August 1942, that Mihailović was hand-in-glove with not only the Italians[13] but probably also the Germans, the Croats and the Serbian government as well.[14] Mihailović for his part had denounced the English 'perfidy' in a speech to his commanders in February 1943, because of their concurrent help to the partisans (a British liaison officer heard this remarkable speech).[15] He had also rejected suggestions that he confine his activities to Serbia where he was strong and leave Croatia to Tito. He publicly admitted that his enemies were the partisans who he said would establish Communism if they were to win; not the Italians. At much the same time, the British government received encouraging reports from Churchills emissary, Brigadier Maclean, that the Partisans not only constituted a formidable force of 200,000 and so would be certain to play a large part after the war,[16] but that their 'success would be in accordance with our interests, i.e. the establishment of a strong, democratic and independent Yugoslavia'.[17] The Foreign Office had thought the report somewhat optimistic but, like all Maclean's despatches, it carried weight with Churchill. The only way of achieving such an ideal Yugoslavia after the war (and that was most improbable, considering the bloodshed) would have been an Anglo-American allied expedition there: that had been, however, rejected late 1943 by Roosevelt and General Marshall.[18] Had it occurred it would certainly have met the same kind of hostile greeting that the British received from the communists in Greece:[19] and a long civil war might have followed. It could not have been maintained by the Anglo-Saxons without the same kind of support from Stalin that he gave over Greece: his *quid pro quo* would have been considerable.

The war of liberation in Yugoslavia is a legend. Yet, despite the endurance of the partisans, half of the country was in the end not liberated so much as abandoned, first by the Italians, then by the Germans, who were in control of much of the north even in May 1945. Still, much of Western Bosnia and Dalmatia was genuinely freed in 1942. Slovenia was largely so for a time in 1943. Croatia, maintained since 1941 by Germany and Italy as a separate puppet state, directed by the Ustash, a fascist party of great brutality founded in the 1920s, fell in 1945 without a struggle. The partisans' occupation of that territory, for which Serbia had always had a cordial detestation – Croatia had been part of Hungary till 1919 – was attended by further killings. Given the scale of the Ustash efforts to murder the Serbs in their territory, and the extent to which this desire had been fulfilled, the post-war Serbian reprisals were unsurprising. The Communist victory was followed by a major rising in the south of the country by the Albanian minority, whose leader Imer Berisa sought the secession of the region of Kossovo-Metohija to Albania.[20]

It was natural that this victory should be followed by mass-acres, summary trials, and the flight, into Austria, of thousands of peasants and others who feared Communism. Most of these refugees were handed back, as has been seen, by the British army who were unready to look after them, and whose officers, bred in a world of law, could not suppose that, since these refugees were innocent of crimes, they would not survive in their own country. 'The unarmed lot were shepherded onto trains and told they were going to Italy; they crowded on in the best of spirits and were driven off under a British guard to the entrance of a tunnel at the frontier; there, the guard left them and the train drove off into the tunnel'.* Most of the returned refugees were murdered, after terrible forced marches.[21] At the same time, the German population of Yugoslavia numbering some half million, were all deported – most eventually to the West, about 50,000 at least to the Soviet Union.[22]

The refugees in Austria were returned to relieve the pressure on the British administration and because of the risk of conflict between Britain and the United States with Yugoslavia (and perhaps even Russia), over the Yugoslav occupation, at the end of the war, of Klagenfurt and other parts of Carinthia, as well as of Trieste and some places in Venezia Giulia, the extreme north-east province of Italy. This crisis in May and June 1945 had been a grave one. The partisans moved up in the closing stages of the war in the wake of the German withdrawal to occupy not only their own (pre-1941) northern province of Slovenia (half of which had been occupied by Germany, half by Italy, during the war) but also parts of southern Carinthia, where there had been a minority of Slovenes before 1919, the Istrian peninsula and the city of Trieste, a largely Italian city which was surrounded by a Slav countryside. The Yugoslavs reached Klagenfurt, reserved by agreement of the great powers as part of the British zone of Austria, on May 2, a few hours after the British got there; while that day, in Trieste, a New Zealand division accepted a German surrender, only to find Yugoslav

---

* Diary of Anthony Crosland, who added that was 'the most nauseating and cold-blooded act of war I have ever taken part in'.

forces already there too.[23] In both places the partisans busied themselves executing middle class opponents, stealing property, and both requisitioning property and deporting many people.

Britain, determined to force the Yugoslavs out of both places, deemed support to be essential. They received it from President Truman on May 12, though he wavered over the idea a day later. All the same, on May 19, Tito gave orders for withdrawal from Klagenfurt and South Austria, and that was complete by the end of May.[24] The crisis in Trieste was longer and more severe. Churchill was resolute, however, and, after some sharp exchanges with Tito, which he copied to Stalin, he gave the message formally on June 2 to the Yugoslav government that, unless Britain had a satisfactory answer within three days, Field Marshal Alexander would be asked to take matters into his own hands in order to secure Trieste and its neighbourhood for Italy. Churchill told Truman that he did not expect to 'get through this matter by bluff', and the British and United States ambassadors in Belgrade were specifically told not to bargain. The Americans were unenthusiastic but, in the end, Tito conceded, on June 9, and began to withdraw. Stalin complained, but only on June 21. The long-term arrangement and decision on Trieste was left to the peace conference but, in the short term, the Western allies had triumphed.[25] (Henceforward the Americans and the British held in 'trust' the city of Trieste and the land to the west of it, while the Yugoslavs controlled the peninsula of Istria and the land as far as the city).[26]

The brutalities after the surrender of the refugees were explained not only by the Ustash atrocities aforementioned but by a German inhumanity in Yugoslavia comparable to that which was practised in Russia. The American ambassador Richard Patterson, a New York broadcasting executive by profession, reported these post-war crimes. But the Department of State were incredulous: they thought Patterson 'green in the country'.[27]

Mihailović was, meantime, still free and in hiding in the hills of Bosnia. He was not alone: 'The forests were still teeming with "renegades" from pro-fascist units or counter-revolutionaries' in the winter of 1945–46. Chetnik bands known as the White

Eagles, the Movement of National Rebirth, the Crusaders (chiefly Croat ex-Ustash) killed Communist officials where they could – allegedly 3,000 police were killed between 1945 and 1955, not including party officers and secretaries.[28] But, apart from Mihailović, the best-known commanders of these forces had already been caught and executed.

Those few in the West who took the trouble to reflect on the matter thought that the chief difference between Tito's regime and those of his colleagues in East Europe to be that it was more ruthless. But Tito had won power for himself, even if the arrival of the Red Army on Yugoslav soil on September 4, 1944 had been an important point in the war. The Russian propaganda that the Soviet help had been decisive was already infuriating Tito and his friends. The raping, bullying and casual killing by Soviet soldiers in Belgrade also provoked protests by Yugoslav Communists. Nor, in the war, had the Russians seemed to be interested that the partisans were carrying out a social revolution while they went along. Russian intrigues with Mihailović, and with the puppet government of General Nedić in Belgrade had early caused bad blood between them and with the Yugoslav Communists. Stalin had wished to satisfy Churchill and so to allow King Peter to return. Tito had refused, even when Stalin told him that 'you can slip a knife in his back at a suitable moment'.[29] The memory of the purge of the pre-war Yugoslav Communist Party, when it had been directed by Milan Gorkić, also perturbed those many who remembered how he and even his wife Betty Glane (once director of the Park of Culture in Moscow) had been executed by Stalin's police in 1937 without any good cause, apart from a mismanagement (understandable, since he was in Russia) of a large shipment of volunteers for the Spanish Civil War in a boat from Dalmatia.

Those who in the West knew anything of Yugoslavia were aware, however, that the Communist Party in the interwar years was not negligible. During the 1920s, it was always represented in the federal parliament and, in 1919, gained over fifty seats. In those days, the party had included men like Sima Marcović who came from Serb social democracy, and had real roots in the people. During the era of the royal dictatorship (imposed in 1929, because of the threat of Croatian secession) the party had kept the police busy, particularly in the universities, with their 'deep dissatisfaction with existing conditions and an irrepressible desire to change life, not to accept a hopeless monotony'.[30] Although subsequently managed by Milan Gorkić from exile in the ex-imperial capital in Vienna, the party continued to flourish in clandestinity. It sent hundreds of its members for revolutionary education in the Spanish Civil War. Although certainly a minority party in pre-war Yugoslavia, the Communists had had the advantage even then of having become the first national party in the history of the country[31] (*pace* Rebecca West, who in a famous book thought Communism 'not attractive to a nation of peasant proprietors'.)[32]

The fact that Tito had received more help at a crucial time from Britain than from Russia (though Russia had sent many arms in late 1944), and that even the first Russian officers to reach partisan headquarters in 1944 were flown in by the RAF,[33] made a window to the West more easy for Tito to contemplate than was the case with, say, Rákosi or Bierut. Tito had impressed most of the British liaison officers (Brigadier Maclean, William Deakin, Randolph Churchill) as well as the OSS representative (Richard Weil) as a man who would choose country rather than creed if a choice were essential.[34] (In a report dated April 4, 1944, Weil spoke of Tito as being regarded by Serbs as 'first as a patriot and secondarily as a Communist'.) As has been seen, Maclean forecast that Tito's movement would establish an independent government. In consequence he gave Tito every encouragement to carry his organisation into Serbia, against the advice of the Foreign Office. In the end, but not till 1948, his judgement turned out to be right. In the long term, Tito wove a web of deception over his Soviet friends as complete as he did in the short term over his Western ones who, in 1944, believed him when he repeatedly said that he had no political ambitions.[35]

There were already secret disputes in Yugoslavia during the winter of 1945–46 over Soviet policies of trying to recruit soldiers, actors, civil servants and even party leaders for their own intelligence services, particularly when they used blackmail.

When challenged, Colonel Ivan Stepanov, of the Soviet military mission, would explain that Yugoslav Communism was immature, and needed guidance. But both that activity, and the Soviet efforts to flood the Belgrade press, Communist though it was, with dull articles about the Soviet homeland, were already having a bad effect on relations, particularly since the NKVD tried to recruit White Russians and Chetniks as well as Communists, railwaymen as well as cypher clerks.[36]

Nor for their part were the Yugoslavs happy with Stalin's failure to show enthusiasm for their territorial ambitions in Austria and Italy. The Soviet failure to back Tito fully in 1945 over Trieste had seemed almost sacrilegious. Nor did Russians support the Yugoslavs when they requested a zone of occupation in Austria.

The possible opportunities which this distancing between Yugoslavia and Russia might open up for the West were concealed in 1946. Few in London or Washington had even noticed Tito's speech, at Ljubljana, the capital of Slovenia, on May 27, 1945, in which he asserted 'we will not be dependent on anyone ever again': much to the anger of the Soviet Union whose ambassador, Sadchikov, sent a protest: 'We regard Comrade Tito's speech as unfriendly' (that speech was made in the middle of the crisis over Trieste).[37] Nor was it appreciated in the West that Tito had refused to have Soviet staff (secret policemen) at Yugoslav airports. Even the fact that Tito had asked to visit the United States in January 1946 made no impact on Western administrations:[38] the idea was rejected. Tito sent a further conciliatory message to Truman on February 19. It was similarly not followed up.[39] Truman had shown little interest in the fate of Yugoslavia at Potsdam and the neglect continued.[40]

Tito himself was still obscure in the minds of most of his Western allies. As Josip Broz, son of Croat peasants from the village of Kumrovec in the district of Zagorje in north-west Croatia when it had been part of Austria-Hungary, he had had a long career: waiter, apprentice locksmith, factory worker in Wiener Neustadt, Mannheim and Vienna, conscripted in the Austro-Hungarian army, fighting both the Serbs and then the Tsarist army, taken prisoner by the latter, active in the Russian

Revolution like Rákosi, back in newly independent Yugoslavia as a trade union organiser in the metalworkers' union in Zagreb, a worker in the shipyards at Kraljevo, Tito was converted to Communism by a Croatian ex-officer in the army, Stevo Šabić. Tito's imprisonment in Lepoglava and Maribor for five years as a revolutionary, his activities with the Balkan secretariat of the Comintern in the 1930s, and in Paris as an organiser of Yugoslav recruits for the International Brigade in Spain, were, still, both to the West, and to his own countrymen, hidden chapters in his biography. He was a good linguist, who combined charm with ruthlessness: a dangerous man for Stalin whom he in some ways resembled, though he lacked the Georgian's insane suspiciousness.[41] (Where Truman read Plutarch, as a child, Tito nevertheless read Sherlock Holmes.)

The brutalities coldly organised by the methodical new Minister of the Interior, Aleksandar Ranković, gave a dark colour to Yugoslav Communism. Ranković came from a peasant family who lived in a village near Belgrade. He had been tortured and imprisoned for years as a young man in the 1930s. Now he was to have his revenge in full on the old regime. His State Security police, ONZA (Bureau of the People's Protection), had had the power of both judgement and execution up till December 1945. Then the regime tried to bring such spontaneous action to an end. But it continued under different auspices.

Tito was known to have designs on Northern Albania, to be willing to 'play the Macedonian card' against Greece, and to have dreams of a Slav federation to embrace Bulgaria and other Balkan peoples. The future policy of Yugoslavia thus looked menacing to eastern Europe.

Tito would make a visit to Moscow for the funeral of President Kalinin in the late spring of 1946 and relations between himself and Stalin then 'appeared to be more than cordial'. Stalin embraced Tito, referred to his role as of European importance and openly belittled both the Bulgars and Dimitrov.[42] There was then some discussion of the idea of a new Comintern, to coordinate views among the Communists.

Hundreds of well-meaning Yugoslav progressives and intellectuals without political convictions but with the ambition to remain free were in 1946 moving towards the Communist cause. Typical of these people was Miroslav Krleža, intellectual *par excellence*, editor and novelist, ex-Communist and for a time anti-Communist. Silent in the war which he spent in a sanatorium run by a friend of the Ustash leader, Pavelić, he was on his way to becoming the conformist spokesman for a regime of which he had a poor opinion: a frequent literary phenomenon in these circumstances.

The connections with Moscow seemed substantial. Thus Svetislav-Ceca Stefanović, Ranković's chief assistant in the police, had worked with the Soviet secret police and was a graduate of the Party school in Moscow. Andrija Hebrang, leader of the partisans in Croatia during the war and now Minister of Industry, busy preparing a five-year plan, on the Soviet model, for Yugoslavia was a Soviet agent more than a Yugoslav: apparently, he had been trapped by the NKVD who had come to know that, under torture by the Gestapo, he had revealed the names of comrades.[43] The Minister of Finance, Sreten Žujović, despite (or perhaps because of) his youthful membership of the French Communist Party in the 1920s, took the Russian view in all disputes. Tito himself had certain unexplained connections with Soviet intelligence, while Stalin spoke of him as his chief lieutenant in Europe.[44] Arso Jovanović, an ex-officer of the Royal Army who had headed the high command in the war, would soon set off to the Voroshilov Military Institute in Moscow, there to be easily drawn into the pro-Soviet loyalties which would eventually ruin him.[45] In addition, the new constitution of January 1946 seemed a copy of the Soviet one of 1936.

Some elements in the new regime suggested stability, if not justice. The party remained the only Yugoslav national movement. Most of the Communists were Serbs. Yet Tito himself was born a Croat. So was Hebrang. Edvard Kardelj, Vice President, the administrative father of the Communist capture of power, and drafter of the constitution of 1946, was a Slovene. He was trained to be a village schoolmaster as his father was, before his real education in Moscow.[46] Djilas, the most intelligent of the younger leaders, and director of 'Agitation and Propaganda' for the Party, was a Montenegrin. The Vice

President, Moša Pijade, Tito's intellectual mentor in the Lepoglava prison, in the 1930s, much respected though old, was, if
a Serb, of Sephardic Jewish origin.[47] Although there were no
Macedonians among the Yugoslav Communist leadership, it
seemed possible that, in the end the forging of a real Yugoslav
consciousness, embarked upon by King Alexander after the
royal *coup* of 1930, would be achieved by men of these diverse
origins who considered monarchy an outmoded tyrannical institution. In a country where both the royal family and the aristocracy had been of peasant origin, perhaps egalitarianism could be
made to spell unity. Communism had taken control of a nation,
after all, whose recent and ineffective social structure had been
destroyed by the German invasion of 1941, and which had in
the war reverted to tribal or religious loyalties.

In 1946 the most disturbing element to the new men in
power was the Catholic Church. The Croatian Catholics had
collaborated in the war with the fascist regime there directed
by Pavelić, whom the Archbishop of Zagreb, Archbishop Alojz
Stepinac, had encouraged to try to force conversion on the
Serbs. But, unlike some Croatian bishops, Stepinac had remained aloof from the excesses. Tito in 1945 had sought
accommodation with him, suggesting some kind of 'national
Catholic church', though in fact the Catholic Church (unlike the
orthodox one) had begun to be persecuted, as noticed by the
English novelist Evelyn Waugh, a wartime British officer, in an
unwelcome report to the Foreign Office of early 1945. Stepinac
refused Tito's approach and attacked the new government during
the autumn of 1945, in a pastoral letter. Tito responded with a
hostile article in his own Party newspaper, *Borba*, on October
25. In January 1946, the Croatian Communist press began to
publish articles about Stepinac's past association with Pavelić.
The grounds were thus here being laid for a serious clash.[48] The
fact that that did not occur earlier was perhaps due to the need
which Yugoslavia had of aid from UNRRA – which totalled $400
million, mostly in food; and to the Yugoslav suspicion that
American catholics might count in the formation of United States
opinion.[49]

At least it can be said of Yugoslavia in 1946 that it was a fully constituted state. The German partition of 1941, however else it had failed, had stimulated rather than dulled the sense of nationhood. Roosevelt was thus wise not to have pressed his occasional support for Croatian independence.[50]

The Communist party of Yugoslavia would surely have resisted any attempt by Britain to impose a fifty per cent interest in Yugoslavia, however it was defined.[51] They might have anticipated their revolt of 1948 against Stalin if the Soviet Union had implicitly sided with Britain. Britain alone would not have been able to manage a Yugoslav civil war as well as a Greek one. Marshal Tito was a more formidable leader than anyone on the Greek left. The Germans had destroyed the old regime more completely in Yugoslavia than they had in Greece. Very skilful diplomacy by Britain might have secured King Peter and Ivan Šubašić a year's restoration in Belgrade. It is most difficult to believe that it could have done more.

The regime in the tiny, and relatively new, country of Albania was, like that of Yugoslavia, a brutal one led by successful Communist warriors. Most of the leaders had become Communists during some form of higher education abroad in the 1930s: in Italy or in France, while Albania was a monarchy under the indigenous King Zog and in the economic zone of Italy. In those foreign universities, the Communist leaders had learned the rudiments of political craft but none of the moderate virtues. The Prime Minister, son of a Moslem landowner, was Enver Hoxha, aged thirty-six, who before 1941 had taught French in a school in Tirana. Unpretentious, handsome, modest, eager to learn, he had been partly educated in Belgium, as well as in France.[52] With Yugoslav guidance, and apparently quite independently of Moscow, he had helped to found the Communist Party of Albania in 1941, as well as a coalition of Albanian resistance, the National Liberation Movement – subsequently 'Front'. A year later, he became Secretary-General of the Party. A year after that this intellectual of bourgeois origin was greeting visitors as a 'Colonel General' in the Albanian army of the resistance.

His 'bourgeois' origins gave occasional moments of doubt to Stalin but, in the end, he proved a reliable convert to the cause, and for the time being he was content to be looked upon as a Yugoslav apprentice.[53] Albania, occupied by Italy in 1939 and, thereafter, run by her as a colony, had been, however, a not unwilling part of 'Mussolini's Roman Empire'. Most of the middle class collaborated. It had only required organisation by Hoxha to carry off the patriots into his revolutionary camp.

In 1946, Hoxha's government included a number of time-serving, theoretically independent patriotic intellectuals (so familiar in neighbouring countries) such as Omer Nishani, President of the Presidium. But power was in his hands, or those of his army, his police and his Communist Party. A few royalist, tribal or pro-Western democratic groups were holding out in the north of the country. No doubt they would have both lasted longer and been more responsible had they received help from the Americans or the British; and they could have had that more easily than those opponents of communism whose countries had no sea or land frontier with the open world. An emissary told the American representative as much in June 1945, though both he and the British General Hodgson thought that the idea might be a provocation.[54]

The Communist revolution in Albania had already been far-reaching. When later a Czech intelligence officer asked an Albanian whether they had had 'any trouble with the Kulaks' in 1945, his interlocutor replied, 'No, we killed them all'.[55] A security police, *Sigurimi*, had been established out of men personally loyal to Hoxha. The regime was busy controlling all religious activities, expelling all Italians (except those whose expertise they required), arresting employees in foreign missions, confiscating Italian private property and welcoming Russians. Members of the British and United States missions found the same difficulties in travelling in Albania as elsewhere in the Communist world: the British Press Attaché was arrested while walking outside Tirana in February 1946 and told 'not to go walking out of the city again'.[56] Albanians friendly to the United States or Britain had begun to avoid their missions for fear of reprisals. The government had, meantime, carried out a general election in December, which it believed ought to have satisfied the West, and which most Westerners indeed thought reasonably fair.[57] But no serious opposition had dared to challenge Hoxha. In consequence, Hoxha had achieved recognition not only by the Soviet Union but by Britain and the United States. The subsequent constituent assembly had abolished the monarchy and proclaimed the 'Peoples' Republic of Albania'. This regime busied itself by demanding the British and Americans to deliver to them over one hundred Albanians whom they accused of having been in collaboration with Italy or Germany. Those exiles were then in the custody of the Western allies' armies in Italy.

The regime was close to that of Yugoslavia. It needed Yugoslav help to maintain its campaign against the surviving rebels in the north. Its new constitution of 1946, like that of Yugoslavia, echoed the Russian one of 1936. Koçi Xoxe, the Minister of the Interior, successfully played on this association. He was both Yugoslavia's man in Albania and the second most powerful man in the country. Coarse-featured, short of stature, brave but ignorant, he was, in origin, a tinsmith. A rising star was General Mehmet Shehu, the son of a Moslem ecclesiastic, who had had a wider experience than his colleagues. He had gone in 1935 to Naples as a student with a scholarship to Mussolini's military academy there, being later expelled in circumstances not at all clear. He then joined the volunteers to fight in the International Brigade in Spain and was a veteran of the XIIth of those famous units. Like so many others, he joined the Communist Party in Spain.[58] In 1939, with other Brigade members, he was interned in France. Only in 1942 did he manage to return to Albania. There, his Spanish experience made him the best choice for the command of the Communists' first partisan brigade which liberated Tirana. In 1945, he went to Moscow and, after his return, in 1946, already a member of the Central Committee, he became chief of the headquarters of the Albanian army 'to take care of various Albanian officers and students proceeding to Moscow for indoctrination'. Shehu made the way easy for the rapid growth at the end of 1945 of a Soviet military mission to which 'security advisers' – dull euphemism for torturers before whose expertise Baron Scarpia would have paled – were already attached.[59] The desire of Shehu and others to draw Albania closer to Soviet direction apparently caused disturbances, even protests, and hence arrests, among so-called moderate radicals in the Communist Party. But that is an obscure story, like most things in the country at that time.[60]

Within a few months the exposed position and strategic significance of Albania, and its connections with Greek Communists, would persuade the British to begin to build on contacts with Albanian emigrés, such as King Zog, and others who had fled the country. Their plan was to try and establish a royalist, anti-Communist group in Central Albania, with a guerrilla movement strong enough to start a civil war against the Hoxha government. But nothing had as yet come of this.[61]

How Hoxha and the Communists (who in 1941 had been as isolated as they were few) won in 1945 is not clear. Few arms from Britain or America reached Northern Albania, where there were anti-Communist guerrillas among the Gheg tribesmen, led by men such as Abas Kupi or Mustafa Gjinishi; and much reached Southern Albania, where Hoxha and his Communist partisans were established among the Tosk tribes. No Russian arms reached the Communists until 1944, only British ones. Here British Communists or possibly their sympathisers inside the Special Operations Executive – such as James Klugman, subsequently a member of the central committee of the British communists, in Cairo – may have extended a helping hand.[62] There were, however, also officials among the Western allies, who merely knew that, in Albania, as in Yugoslavia, the Communists were better fighters than anyone else and who neglected all long-term political implications. Churchill and Roosevelt would have agreed with them. The war leaders of the West mostly neglected this corner of the battlefield: 'Winston, we forgot Zog', was Roosevelt's comment to his English guest when framing the declaration of the United Nations to be signed by all the Allies in January 1942.[63] He was quite right.

The guerrilla war in Albania had been small-scale: an affair of groups of hundreds, not of thousands. Sides were often taken because of family feuds. Before 1939, Albania had been scarcely a state. It was more a congeries of tribes who happened to speak one dialect or another of Albanian. The revolution owed more to lack of patriotism of the beys and merchants who formed the upper class than to foreign repression in the past, because there had been little of it. Few of the Fascist buildings Mussolini planned in marble had been built. But a great many Albanians had profited from the Italian and the German occupations.[65] They could not hope to survive when the Italian administrators had left, and abandoned the country where they could. As usual their followers paid the penalty in the circumstances.[66]

FIFTEEN

# BALTIC HARBOURS: FINLAND, THE BALTIC STATES, EAST PRUSSIA

In the spring of 1946, the future of Finland appeared most uncertain. That country, an increasingly reluctant part of the Russian empire before 1917, previously Swedish, had been independent since the Russian Revolution. A civil war had followed between Finnish Bolsheviks and Finnish Whites. The latter, helped by the Germans, won. In a period of Russian weakness, the new independent Finland stretched nearly to Leningrad. In 1939, Stalin made demands on Finland comparable to those enforced by Russia on the Baltic States,* though with the greater justification that Stalin had reason to fear the Finns' easy access to Leningrad. The Finns resisted. A brutal war, the 'Winter War', ensued. The Soviet Union was expelled from the League of Nations: virtually that body's last action. The Russians secured their demands at great cost, in the end, by the peace of March 1940. Had the Finns held out longer, Britain and France would probably have supported them, even at the cost of expanding their war with Germany to one with Russia.

The Finns later collaborated in the German attack on Russia of 1941 and moved twenty-four divisions against the common foe. Their contribution to the siege of Leningrad was helpful to Germany. Finland occupied Eastern Karelia, whose population was Finnish-speaking and which they had claimed since 1919,

* See below, page 450.

as well as other territory ceded in 1940. They also participated in the German defeats of 1944. In this 'continuation war', as they called it, the Finns fought Russians with real determination, some hoping for a 'Greater Finland', others for an end to communism.

Finland sought afterwards to save herself. She conducted the diplomacy of withdrawing from her German alliance, and avoiding an armistice on unconditional terms, with great skill and agility. In September 1944, an armistice was achieved: essentially the Peace Treaty of 1940 was revived, with some additions.[1] Petsamo on the Barents Sea was ceded. This cut off Finland from access to the Arctic. The peninsula of Porkkala, close to Helsinki, was to be, for fifty years, a Soviet base. Finland had to pay reparations of $300 million worth of goods in pre-war dollars. All German assets would go to Russia. Persons accused of war crimes would be tried. 'Fascist' organisations would be banned. An Allied Control Commission would be installed at Helsinki, as in Budapest, Bucharest and Sofia.

The Finnish merchant fleet would be handed over. In addition, Finland ceded the entire province of Viipuri, all her islands in the Gulf of Finland, and certain parts of the districts of Salla and Kuusamo in the north. Finland would on Russia's behalf build a railway from the new border at Salla to Kemijärvi where it could link with the line going to Sweden.[2]

Few believed that Finland would survive these punitive conditions or that, if she did, she would be given a chance by Russia. Finland had lost 90,000 dead, over a tenth of her territory, and much of her industrial capacity. Trade was at a standstill. The Allied Control Commission was as much a Soviet sounding board as were the comparable bodies in Hungary and Romania, with the difference that a senior Soviet leader, Andrei Zhdanov, the party's chief in Leningrad, was chairman. At the same time, the newly-legalised, and long-isolated, Communist party became, at the national elections of March 17–18, 1945, the largest single party and did well in the municipal elections of December 1945.[3] As often elsewhere, the Communists ran under an umbrella organisation, here called the SKDL (the Finnish People's Defence League) which won 23.5 per cent of the votes (398,000) and 49 seats. When two Socialists joined them, they had 51 seats, more than any other party.

Further, in February 1946, the Russians, through the Allied Control Commission, had brought influence to bear to secure the substitution of the lion-hearted but sick President, Marshal Mannerheim, ex-officer of the Tsar, strategist of Finnish independence in 1918 and commander-in-chief in 1940, by his Prime Minister, Juho Paasikivi. Paasikivi, an immensely experienced banker, had been a leading Finnish conservative before 1914, and one opposed to taunting Tsarist imperialism; and he had also been Finland's negotiator with Russia in 1919, 1940 and 1944.

His aim now was to convince Stalin of the possibilities of real coexistence, and assure him that Finland would never attack Russia but that there was a line beyond which Russia for her own good should not go.[4] The new Prime Minister, Mauno Pekkala, an experienced social democrat who was also conciliatory where Russia was concerned, would include six Communist ministers in his cabinet – with, as usual in such circumstances, the ministry of the Interior among their posts – together with five Socialists and Agrarians. The political police founded in the past to protect the country against the subversion from Russia was reorganised and soon between forty and sixty per cent of them were Communists or their friends. A perilous position!

Though Finland thus seemed close to reintegration into the Russian system, there were some favourable elements to be taken into account. First, despite the results of the election, the overwhelming feeling among Finns was anti-Russian. When part of the Tsar's dominions, in consequence of an arrangement made over their heads in the Napoleonic Wars, they for nearly a century governed themselves and considered the Tsar their Grand Duke. The Russian connection in 1809 was looked upon by Finns as a step towards independence. When, early in the XXth century, the great Russian centralising prime minister, Stolypin, had sought to introduce discipline into these arrangements, he had been opposed. When Finland was reduced to the status of a province, after 1910, the Finns had resisted: 'the once loyal Finns were driven into hostility'.[5] The Russian Governor General was murdered.

The years of independence between 1917 and 1939 had also been a triumph for Finland. Not even Czechoslovakia had been a more worthy new democracy. The 'Winter War', on the other hand, had been a fearful struggle, with a Russian near-humiliation. Russian soldiers made it known that they had no wish to fight the Finns again.

Stalin, in conversation with Churchill at Yalta, conceded the essential point of independence. He thought that the Finns had been just as cruel towards the Russian population as any of the German units. He said, however, that any country which fought with such courage for its independence deserved consideration.[6] Of course, Stalin did not as a rule have such hesitations. He meant that he did not want his forces to take on the Finns at that time. He also knew that the United States had in 1939–40 done all that they could for the Finns without intervention. Roosevelt had even put it thus in a speech on December 22 of that year.[7] Roosevelt was dead. But his spirit lived. The Finns had been admired for their modernity in 1940 – 'there are no slums in Helsinki' – as well as for their stubborn courage: '*sisu*', the Finnish for that quality, had almost entered the English language. The Finnish relief operation in 1941 had been chaired by ex-President Hoover.[8] Was there not a chance that the United States might if necessary intervene in 1945 to secure Finnish liberty?

Britain too had interested herself greatly in Finland in 1940. She had even decided to send an expeditionary force to Finland, an enterprise which was only abandoned because of the Finns' decision to accept an armistice. Paul Reynaud, the French prime minister, had even proposed to bomb Russian oil fields in the Caucasus.[9] If Stalin had heard of this through espionage, he might well have hesitated to risk a new war in 1946. If the Russians had seen the minutes of the War Cabinet of March 12, 1940, they would have seen that body's decision that 'it was not in our interest to declare war on Russia'. All the same the idea was discussed. It must be one of the wonders of 1940 that the French prime minister pressed hard for an attack on the Russian oil wells: 'he thought it might be possible to destroy the whole Baku region'. The aircraft would have flown from Syria (Chamberlain, then British prime minister, asked 'whether it was in our interests that the war should spread to Russia').[10]

Despite the successes of the Communists in 1946, their patriotic opponents were also agile, farsighted, and experienced. The planned purges and nationalisations embarked upon by the Communists in Pekkala's coalition were blocked by the Agrarian ministers, acting with the backing of the resourceful, anti-Russian and obstinate public opinion. This could not prevent the arrest and preparation for trial of the main war leaders, such as ex-President Risto Ryti. But it could prevent their execution (and, in the end, it did ensure the amendment of their sentences).

Finally, the strongest man of the Finnish Communist Party, Yrjö Leino, was far from an orthodox supporter of Stalin. He had spent nine years in prison, 1935-44, but it had been a Finnish prison, and he thought and acted for himself, even as Minister of the Interior. He was an almost unique case in 1945 of a man being a substantial enough personality to be a patriot as well as a Marxist. Nor did Zhdanov, a far from astute politician, trust his colleague, Otto Kuusinen, the experienced Communist who had headed the puppet government of Terijoki in 1939-1940, whom he knew well. He did not know Leino, who outmanoeuvred him, and who served Finland before he served international revolution.

Finland's independence in 1946 was far from secure. But the Finns had a chance of liberty. Geography helped them. Finland was not on the main route between Germany and Russia, nor indeed between the United States and Russia. Strength of character also counted. The Finns had cards in the hand which were not available to some other threatened peoples further away geographically from Russia. The Finns 'are a serious, stubborn, blunt people', Stalin told Harriman, and 'sense must be hammered into them'.[11] The Americans and British friends of Finland had in truth almost dismissed Finland: 'We will not fight [Russia] . . . to give Finland the port of Petsamo', wrote a member of the Department of State's post-war planning committee, Isaiah Bowman (president of Johns Hopkins University),

in March 1943.[12] All the same, Finland remained what she had
been throughout: defeated, but neither occupied nor conquered.
Her parliamentary system had never ceased to function. The
unbending Mannerheim was matched by the skilful Paasikivi and
Pekkala. Mannerheim was right in arguing that had not Finnish
strength been exerted to the utmost in 1940, the country would
have been absorbed by Russia: Paasikivi and Pekkala were
equally right to negotiate in 1944.[13]

Russia renewed her iron control of Latvia, Lithuania and Estonia
(all three independent in 1919 for the first time for several
hundred years) in 1939. Stalin had used the excuse of an escape
of a Polish submarine from the harbour of Tallin to argue
that Estonia was incapable of protecting the coastline. Russia
demanded an immediate military alliance, including the use of
Estonian bases by Soviet troops. When that was agreed, similar
stratagems were practised on Latvia and Lithuania. All was
attributed to German pressure. Soviet troops moved into appropriate places, and behaved correctly, a reminder that such a
thing could occur when it seemed necessary.[14]

Nine months passed. Finland was defeated. Pressure was
then applied again, first to Lithuania. All the states were accused
of being pro-Allies – then a sin in Soviet eyes – and of conniving
at the abduction of Soviet troops. The Russians suddenly
demanded, in June 1940, the formation of 'governments capable
of fulfilling their pacts' with them, and willing to accept an
unspecified number of Soviet troops. There were hesitations,
resignations, ultimatums. More Soviet troops moved in without
being requested. New governments were formed in all the
countries, comprised of 'progressive intellectuals' with, as usual,
a Communist as Minister of the Interior. 'Elections' were held
a month later. Attempts to present opposition lists were vain.
All these countries voted for slates, or parties, willing, or even
anxious, to support annexation to the Soviet Union. There was
some genuine support for that, especially among the Jewish and
even the Russian communities.[15] The Russian Deputy Foreign
Ministers, Vyshinsky and Beria's appointee, Dekanozov, with

Zhdanov, the Party leader in Leningrad, held out some hope for the survival of these states' independence. Those hopes were fraudulent. 'Mass demonstrations' were held in favour of annexation to Russia. The Supreme Soviet in Moscow voted, in one of its rare actions of any sort, to accept the request of the three countries to join in the great crusade of Bolshevik construction. Some two million people are said to have been subsequently deported from these lands and 're-settled' in Siberia. [16]

The people in these states had belonged to the Russian Empire after 1721 (Estonia and Latvia) or 1795 (Lithuania) till 1919. But they were Russian neither in religion (Lithuania was principally Catholic and the other two principally Lutheran), nor in language, nor in history. Riga had enjoyed several affluent centuries with a dominant German middle class. Like most cities of the Baltic, it had been founded by German merchants in the XIIth century. The Baltic States were not small by the stand-ards of the United Nations membership: Lithuania was as large as Belgium and the Netherlands together. But, once the Russians have absorbed a state, it is a herculean task to escape again.

Stalin and his colleagues in the 1920s considered these states had been 'snatched' from Russia, with German help, though Russian relations with these polyglot and initially constitutional regimes had at first been normal. [17] During the Second World War, Stalin never wavered from his position that these states were Russian, even when German armies were many miles to the East of them: he made that evident, very strongly, in his first discussion with Anthony Eden, in December 1941. [18] Both Britain and the United States had earlier reacted strongly to these high-handed attitudes: Lord Halifax at a cabinet meeting had compared Russia's action to the German conquests of Austria and Czechoslovakia. Roosevelt told a delegation of Lithuanian Americans in 1940 that 'Independence has only been provisionally suspended . . . Lithuania will again be free and much sooner than you suppose'. [19] Sir Stafford Cripps, the then ambassador in Russia, urged British recognition of the absorption in the interests of good relations. The British government left the issue undecided, the legations of the states concerned in London remaining in limbo.[20]

Stalin's views were regularly made evident on this matter to Russia's Western allies in 1942 and 1943 while the territories concerned were, of course, occupied by Germany. Britain soon agreed to concede to Russia control over the Baltic States. In the first draft of the Anglo-Soviet treaty of 1942, for example, Churchill accepted the Soviet frontiers as they were at the time of the German attack in 1941. That meant the abandonment of the Baltic States. The Americans, further away, less concerned about the future German threat, and basically more principled, took a more robust view. Secretary of State Hull wrote to Eden that acceptance of the Soviet claim 'would destroy the meaning of one of the most important clauses of the Atlantic Charter, and would tend to undermine the force of the whole document'. On the suggestion of Sumner Welles, Roosevelt wondered whether there could not be a compromise whereby the territories were absorbed into Russia, and the inhabitants allowed to leave.[21] Assistant Secretary of State Berle criticised that idea as a 'Baltic Munich'.[22] When Molotov went to London in May 1942, he rejected the idea of mass emigration, while Anthony Eden, in turn, refused a Russian draft which would have implied that Britain would have nothing to say about the future Soviet-Polish border.[23] In the end, as has been explained, a military treaty was signed and no mention was made of any future frontier.

During 1942, the Americans came close to accepting the British position. At a meeting of the post-war 'political sub-committee' in the Department of State in July 1942, Sumner Welles conceded that the United States had 'no vital interest in opposing their union' (of the Baltic States with the Soviet Union).[24] Next year, Roosevelt admitted, in talks with Eden, that 'the Russian armies would be in the Baltic States at the time of the downfall of Germany, and none of us can use force to get them out'.[25] But he then thought that the British and United States should 'urge Russia not to take them into the USSR without a new plebiscite'. Eden thought that Stalin would not agree and, in the end, Roosevelt thought that a concession over

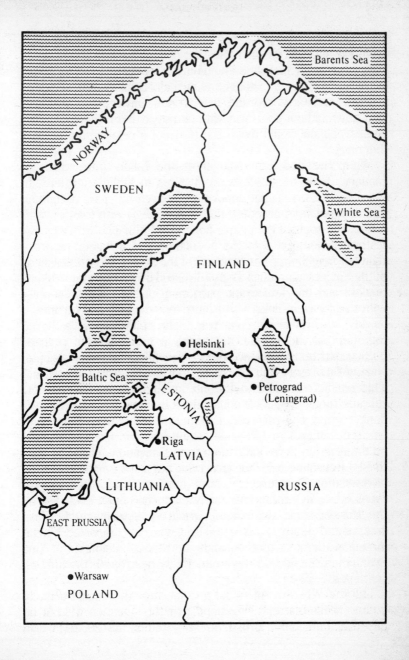

this might be made, in order to secure other understandings from Russia.[26] Even so, FDR kept coming back to the possible difficulties with his public opinion if a concession of principle were made.[27] In fact, though, he virtually conceded these states to Stalin at Tehran and said, in a curious conversation, jokingly, that he would not go to war with him over them, though United States opinion would make the issue of a referendum there a 'big one'.[28]

When the Red Army did enter the Baltic States again in January 1944, there were no changes in Stalin's attitude. In Latvia and Estonia, the population, soured by years of fighting and depopulation, accepted the Soviet *diktat* with calm even if, inside, the souls of the people boiled. In Lithuania, with a longer historical memory, a larger population and a bigger territory than her neighbours, the brutality of the police, the ruthlessness of the Soviet Communist Party (directed by a rising star, Mikhail Suslov) and the democratic patriotism of the Catholic people, with their ancient links with Rome, led to a long and terrible, if largely unchronicled, civil war. The Lithuanians gathered together as 'the Forest Brethren', a movement of perhaps 50,000 patriots, an alliance of rich peasants and simple people, Nazi collaborators and resistance partisans against the Nazis. This conflict spread into Estonia and Latvia and gained new recruits there in tens of thousands.[29] In November 1945 President Truman had received a desperate letter from a group of one-time officials of Lithuania asking him not so much to hold off the Russians as to save them from starvation. The Russians, these Lithuanians said, were carrying out a systematic spoliation of the national resources. A large number of patriots, many of them active in fighting against Nazism, had been encircled by the Russians and were being gradually exterminated. Mass arrests and deportations to Siberia were accompanied by the forced settlement of thousands of Russian colonists.[30] Yet, even when the 50,000 were effectively destroyed, the fighting continued.

Still the Western Allies did not see how they could usefully go into these matters: 'We hope that this question will not be raised' at Potsdam, a British official noted on July 20, 1945.[31] In a brief for the Foreign Ministers' Conference in 1946, the same gifted official, Valentine Lawford, would make the curious reflection that, because in 1942 'we had accepted the above-mentioned clause agreeing support for the Soviet claim', even if it were not included in the relevant treaty's final draft, 'we are undoubtedly under a moral obligation not to go back on the understanding then reached'.[32] Thus the twenty-five years of liberty since 1919 for three independent peoples, with long histories, came, temporarily perhaps, to a cruel end. The three-storied Statue of Liberty in Riga was soon to find one of Lenin beside it, while the guildhalls commemorating a mercantile past became entrepôts of an oriental empire. By early 1946, the Baltic States were remembered, if at all, as a place which proved that Russia would probably never give warning of a step which might lead to hostilities.[33] All that can be said of the Western position is that the Soviet absorption was recognised formally by neither the United States nor Britain.

The events down the Baltic coast at the end of the war in East Prussia should also be considered for an understanding of the international position of the Soviet Union in 1946. East Prussia had been part of the German world since the XIIIth century. The city of Königsberg, birthplace of Immanuel Kant, had been founded in 1255. The Teutonic Knights' conquest of these and other parts of the Baltic coast had constituted one of the great crusades of medieval Christianity. It had been the seat of the old Dukedom of Prussia. Up till the Second World War, no one questioned its Teutonic nature. But in the widespread passion against Germany, itself aroused by Hitler's insane cravings, such considerations were not unnaturally forgotten.

There was discussion of the future of the province early in the war. Stalin, for example, suggested to Eden in December 1941 that in the peace, then far away, East Prussia should be given to Poland except for Tilsit which should go to the 'Lithuanian Republic of the Soviet Union'.[34] Eden had to swallow hard since he had no authority to recognise that latter entity. Still, the idea of the cession of East Prussia to Poland became generally accepted, though not formally so, by Britain and the United States, over the next year or so. Roosevelt, however, told Eden in March 1943 that 'we should make some arrangement to move the Prussians out of East Prussia the same way as the Greeks were moved out of Turkey after the last war'.[35] After he sensed that Britain, and probably America, would accept the transfer of Tilsit, Stalin added at Tehran that Russia 'wanted Königsberg'.[36] That great German city was to the south of both the Neman and the Tilsit.

When the Red Army entered the territory in October 1944, many of their soldiers delivered themselves over to a coldly calculated order of murder and atrocity. This ferocity was encouraged by the propaganda of Ilya Ehrenburg the writer, who not only should have known, but did know, better. Ehrenburg told Russians that the Germans were subhuman. It was probably too the design of the supreme Soviet command to persuade as many Germans as possible to flee. It was the first piece of German territory to fall to Russia.

The truth of what happened would have been difficult to establish had it not been for a modest setback, by which the Russians, having occupied the little town of Nemmersdorf on October 19, 1944, withdrew from it on November 5. That enabled the returning Germans to catalogue the crimes which they encountered: men crucified, women raped, babies with their heads broken, and so on.[37] The Soviet order, when there was another attack on this town, in January 1945, was still, nevertheless, that all could take such revenge on any German that they saw fit.

The consequence was that East Prussia was 'swept clean in a manner that had no parallel since the days of the Asiatic hordes'.[38] Solzhenitsyn served on this front: indeed, he was arrested there in February 1945 (at Wormdit near Königsberg): and in *Prussian Nights* he describes his ambiguous feelings about these events. Königsberg was almost destroyed during the attack in early April 1945. Many thousands of Germans fled: and many, despite the bombardment from the air of refugees both on roads and sea, did reach the salvation of the West. Many able-bodied Germans were, however, swiftly deported to labour camps in Siberia where a half may be supposed to have died.[39] Thousands too must have been killed outright. Stalin declared with apparent pride at both Yalta and Potsdam that 'no single German remained' in the whole area to be given to Poland.[40] That was not true of Silesia and Pomerania. But it could have been nearly so in respect of East Prussia.

This province in late 1945 seemed to George Kennan, who flew over it, low, shortly after the conference of Potsdam, to be 'a totally ruined and deserted country: scarcely a sign of life from one end of it to the other'. In addition to the extinction of much of the human population, the million and a half cattle, the two million pigs, the 500,000 horses (the great product in the past) which had once been there, were nowhere to be seen. The region had been an important agricultural province, with a production of almost four million tons of wheat, fifteen of rye, and forty of potatoes. The harvest of 1945 was negligible. 'I fear terrible things have happened during the Russian advance through Germany to the Elbe', wrote Churchill in May 1945.[41] He was correct.

East Prussia was formally divided in 1945: that had been understood at Tehran. Stalin had said then that all ports of the Baltic froze in winter. The Russians had suffered so much that they believed that they should have 'some piece of German territory so as to give a little satisfaction to the tens of millions of their inhabitants who had suffered'. Thus Marx gave way, not for the first time, to Mars. President Roosevelt and Churchill agreed, though, earlier, the European division in the Department of State had specifically opposed such a concession.[42] Roosevelt had characterised British policy as 'provincial' on this matter.[43] The fact that Russia had, through its absorption of the Baltic States, at least three ports which were substantially ice-free, and that Königsberg was not so, had escaped the West. (Königsberg, indeed, lay at the end of a canal which took only moderate-sized ships.) 'These territorial changes', Kennan wrote, 'seemed to . . . be doubly pernicious, and the casual American acquiesence to them all the less forgiveable, because . . . they served, like the other territorial concessions to the Russians, simply to extract great productive areas from the economy of Europe'.

The 'casualness' with which such decisions were made must have given Stalin and his colleagues the impression that there were substantial areas, and substantial numbers of people, to which and to whom the Western politicians were indifferent.

Few apart from the unpredictable George Orwell thought the expulsion of the Germans from East Prussia a 'crime': one which doubtless 'we could not prevent but might have at least protested against'.[44] The future Nobel prizewinner for literature, the Chilean poet Pablo Neruda (who had assumed a Czech name as well as a Communist faith), in his poem on the unpromising topic of the Russian entry into East Prussia spoke in language which sounded similar to that of Ehrenburg: 'Do not raise tomorrow the flag of pardon'.[45] He was more in keeping with the age. Roosevelt was more naive than usual when he told the Poles in exile in January 1944 that Stalin would probably be willing to retain Königsberg as a 'shrine for the world'.[46]

As for the Baltic States, tiny though, relatively speaking, they were, their cities had had for many generations special qualities which were not those of the comic opera which they seemed to Anglo-Saxons. There were many too, and they were not only foreigners, who always recalled the brief twenty years of independence of these states as a 'paradise'.[47]

# SIXTEEN

# THE HEART OF EUROPE: GERMANY AND AUSTRIA

The tragedy of Germany lay at the heart of the world's problems in 1946. Here was a great nation, united two generations before, whose industry had been the most successful in Europe, and whose people had been the best-educated in the world, now ruined in both reputation and economy. The capital, Berlin, seemed 'more like the face of the moon than any city'.[1] In the unheated cellars of once-fine buildings, a fearful, diminished and indigent population lived the lives of troglodytes. They counted themselves fortunate not to have been murdered during Himmler's terror in the last nine months of the war; nor to have been deported to work in Siberia, as several hundred thousand Germans had been: now making bricks, or working in stone quarries, coal mines, or lumber camps. (Many had died *en route* in cold and overcrowded trains.) If women, they might have been raped in the spring of 1945 by drunken Russians: 90,000 out of a total of 1,400,000 women in Berlin asked for medical help in the weeks following the fall of the city.[2]

The sacking of towns and villages, the indiscriminate violation of women of all ages, as well as the spontaneous shooting of Nazi officials such as mayors, had given to the end of the war the quality of nightmare. That was accompanied by a horrible realisation: the great nation which had created so much great music, and had given birth to Goethe and Schiller, had been seduced into a pursuit of world power, first by the Kaiser, then by the Nazis; and, though Germany had dominated Europe in

1916–18, and conquered most of it in 1940–41, it had, in the end, utterly failed. The senior German officers riding on cows to escape the Red Army in Prussia, observed by the French politician Edouard Herriot in May 1945, were a fittingly symbolic conclusion to the crusade.[3] The bicycle, as a method of communication, and the cigarette, as a unit of currency, alone seemed to represent elements of continuity with the past.

At the end of the war, 15 per cent of houses in Germany had been destroyed, and a quarter partially so, either by bombing or in fighting. Nearly 95 per cent of urban Berlin was in ruins. In what became the British zone of Germany, 3.5 million out of 5.5 million dwellings had been destroyed. Bridges, roads, railways, sewers, tram rails, gas pipes, airports, water pipes, electrical installations, even rivers had been wrecked by the massed attacks of thousands of aircraft.[4] Nearly all the cities of Germany seemed the 'abomination of desolation' (a remark of Sir William Strang, chief civilian assistant to the British Commander-in-Chief),[5] even if the countryside was mostly untouched and if the harvest of 1945 had been reasonable. Twenty million people were homeless. About four and a half million Germans had died fighting. Two million cripples were to be found in the Western zones alone. All German assets abroad were lost – most of the East European ones having been already seized by the Russians. The central administrative bodies had ceased to function. Monetary values had been mostly replaced by barter, ancient monuments by rubble. Internationally, Germany had become a more extreme version of what it had been in 1813: a vacuum between France and Russia. The experience was no less uncomfortable for being faintly familiar.

Quite unfamiliar was the barely conceivable fact that 1945 signified not merely a new defeat for Germany but the broadcasting of the knowledge that the Nazis had directed the murder of an as yet uncounted number of European Jews, in circumstances beyond all belief, as well as many others, including Germans who had opposed the Nazis; while more Russians had died in prisoner of war camps between 1939 and 1945 than in the whole of the First World War. The business of forcing the German nation to come to terms with the Nazi atrocities was everywhere given priority by the conquerors in the West: citizens of towns near concentration camps were ordered to clear the bodies and clear the places of execution.

Hitler's refusal to admit defeat in 1944 had exhausted reserves of food, medicine and other essentials. In addition to the sixty-four million Germans who survived – forty-six million in the zones occupied by the democratic Allies, eighteen in the Soviet zone – there were, in the territory, a high proportion of the ten million men and women transported in the war to Germany as virtual slaves, of whom a large number, from Russia or Poland, Romania or the Baltic States, though starving and sick, did not want to go home. A report by John McCloy, of the United States Control Commission, accurately concluded in 1945 that there was 'complete economic, social and political collapse . . . in Central Europe, the extent of which is unparalleled in history unless one goes back to the collapse of the Roman Empire'.[6]

The destruction of people and of private property had been on a larger scale than of industry. Thus only 20 per cent of German industrial plant had been destroyed, only 10 per cent of the mines and steel industry. The Ruhr, though subjected to heavy bombing for years, lost a mere 30 per cent of plant and machinery:[7] yet the Ruhr's coal production in the winter of 1945–1946 was only 25,000 tons a day in place of 400,000.[8] When later, in the spring of 1946, the Coordinating Committee of the Allied Kommandatura debated the level of industry for Germany, they would plan for 40 per cent of the chemicals produced in 1936, 30 per cent of heavy engineering, and agricultural equipment up to 80 per cent of 1938.[9]


The problems of post-war Germany were compounded by a series of arrangements made by the Allies in the last year or so of the war. In theory, the plan was reasonable: the Allies would govern the country in common until a German government (or governments) acceptable to all four powers could be elected. Germany, in the meantime, would make compensation for the ills which she had visited on her old enemies. But territorial arrangements prevented the new central government from being

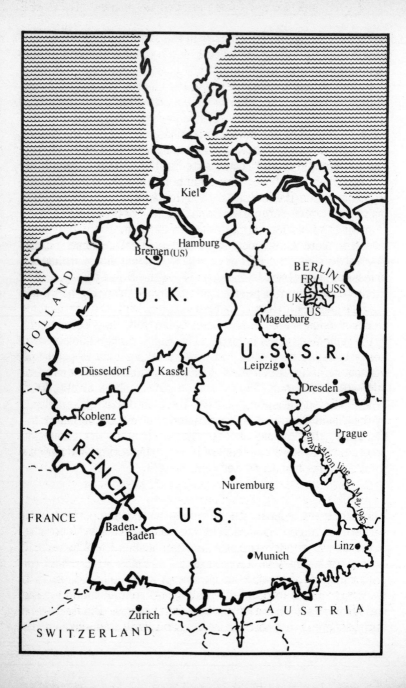

formed. 'During the . . . occupation Germany shall be treated as a single unit'. Thus Article 14 of the Potsdam agreement. It never was. Even in 1945, there was no consultation between the four powers on such an important matter as the production and export of German coal.[10] The reason for this failure was that, in 1943, on the advice of Harry Hopkins,[11] of Norman Davis,[12] and of a committee of the British cabinet chaired by Clement Attlee,[13] Churchill and Roosevelt at Quebec, in 1943, had proposed that, after the war, Germany would temporarily, until the Treaty of Peace, be divided into zones of 'occupation'. Forty per cent of what was left to Germany (after the truncations in the East previously noticed) would be administered by Russia; and sixty per cent by Britain and the United States, with a zone eventually cut out of this sixty per cent for France, on the insistence of Britain, and the eventual agreement of Roosevelt and then Stalin. General Eisenhower would also have preferred mixed military contingents in each zone; fortunately, the Russians were then opposed.[14] Churchill and Roosevelt also, for a time, disputed which of them would have the North and which the South of their Western zone. But essentially this plan was adopted. It was commonly said to have given the British, the industry; the Russians, the agriculture; and the Americans, the scenery.

The decisions about zones were accepted a year after Quebec, 'rather hastily', as Churchill later put it (not wholly accurately),[15] on the basis of detailed recommendations by the so-called European Advisory Commission (composed of British, Russian and American officials) meeting in London.[16] Berlin, an enclave within the proposed Russian zone, would be jointly run by all four Allies, and be the administrative centre. This centre was, among other things, intended to ensure that the industrial West of Germany largely under the English would receive food from the Russian zone; and that the Russian zone would receive industrial products from the West.

The original proposals for the zones had been made in 1943 (that is, before the successful landings in France) at a time when the Western Allies feared that Russia might cease to fight when she had freed her own country; or might then conclude a separate peace with Germany; or alternatively might have driven to the Atlantic and occupied all Europe. A previous arrangement to divide Germany might have helped the Western allies in those circumstances.[17]

The United States accepted the European Advisory Commission's plan for zones on May 1, 1944. Two American senior officials, Robert Murphy and James Riddleberger, suggested that the zones should be arranged to make Berlin the apex of a series of triangles to guarantee freedom of access to it. This intelligent idea, which owed something to an earlier idea of Roosevelt, was dismissed by Winant, the United States Ambassador to London, the American leader in these talks, on the grounds that it would suggest distrust of the Soviet Union; and so have adverse consequences for subsequent Allied cooperation.[18] Murphy and Riddleberger were thereafter not among those who believed that Winant's Lincoln-like profile, and patent liberalism, always compensated for his lack of foresight.

Roosevelt and Churchill endorsed their officials' recommendations. Subsequently, Stalin agreed with them also. At that time, 'it was not foreseen that General Eisenhower's armies would make such a mighty inroad into Germany'.[19]

These ideas were temporary arrangements to last until a Treaty of Peace. For that grand parley there would be many possibilities; for example Secretary of the Treasury Henry Morgenthau's plan, in various versions, for 'converting Germany into a country primarily agricultural and pastoral in character'. These ideas (influenced by his senior official, Harry Dexter White) interested Roosevelt, who had earlier told Morgenthau 'we either have to castrate the German people or . . . treat them in such a manner . . . that they just can't go on reproducing people who want to continue in the way they have in the past'.[20] (The President said much the same once about Japan.)[21] Afterwards, Roosevelt went back on his approval of these ideas. All the same, they later influenced events, as will be seen. Like, paradoxically, the Nazis, Morgenthau had unbounded faith in the feudal idea that the countryside is the embodiment of good living; and the town, of evil. He fully realised that pastoralisation might cause colossal unemployment: the very conditions which had led to Nazism. 'I am for destroying the Ruhr first and we will worry about the population second', he once remarked to Dexter White.[22] He thought that 'Nazi-inculcated' Germans should be transported to central Africa for a 'big TVA* project'. There was also much talk among the Allies of 'dismemberment' which might mean the eventual division of Germany into several – perhaps three or five – states. One, a South German confederation might include Austria, Bavaria, and Württemberg, with Vienna as the centre. Churchill had been in favour of that in 1943.[23] The idea of an independent Ruhr, under international control, was similarly discussed. The Labour members of the British War Cabinet were still in favour of 'dismemberment' in 1945. So was Stalin.[24]

Later still, in April 1945, when Eisenhower's armies had driven 150 miles into what had been agreed as the future Soviet region, Churchill suggested the designation of what he called 'tactical zones'; by which he meant the lines of demarcation as reached at the end of the war. The United States, in the last months of the European war, had sent into Germany seventy divisions. Being equipped with lorries and motor cars, they had moved faster than the Red Army, whose millions of men moved on foot, or on horse-drawn or even camel-drawn vehicles.[25] These tactical zones should, Churchill thought, be pressed as far to the East as possible, for psychological reasons affecting post-war politics. But, as has been seen,† Eisenhower wanted to reach a line which would prevent accidental clashes between his and the Red Army. His instructions from the joint chiefs of staff were to destroy the German armies, not to capture geographical points, however politically important. He thought that a single thrust to Berlin might have exposed his flanks to the Germans; who might thus be able to escape to the 'National Redoubt' which Hitler was said to be planning in Southern Germany and Austria. That was a myth but a compelling one, all the same.

* Tennessee Valley Authority: a famous development scheme of the New Deal.

† See above, page 229 for Eisenhower.

When Eisenhower made his decisions, too, Roosevelt was near death; and Truman, President after April 12, did not yet have any feel for the situation. All the same, at the end of March and beginning of April, the road to Berlin had been wide open to Western armies: just as has been seen, when dealing with Czechoslovakia, Patton's road to Prague was open from Pilsen at the beginning of May. It is difficult not to hanker over lost possibilities. But some restraining words have already appeared in this book doubting whether the American President would have gone back on the zonal frontiers pre-arranged either for Germany or, more recently, for Austria.

After VE day, Churchill again urged Truman to let the British and Americans hold the 'tactical zones' in Germany until they were satisfied about Russian policies in Poland, Germany and the Danube basin.[28] A British aide-mémoire even suggested that no withdrawals of troops in Germany should occur until 'the whole question of the future relations in Europe of the two Governments with the Soviet Government' had been resolved.[29] (Churchill had also tried to encourage Eisenhower to liberate Prague, as has been seen.)* But again the British, themselves converted late to these ideas, were unsuccessful.

The commitments made at Tehran by Roosevelt and Churchill about the Polish-German frontier, as well as Roosevelt and Churchill's commitment at Casablanca to a demand for unconditional surrender, had made it difficult for the Allies to entertain any hopes in 1944 of the German conspirators against Hitler, whose plans were passed to the OSS in Switzerland by the agent Gisevius. Allen Dulles, European director of the OSS, reported from Switzerland that the German conspirators had finally only taken action because they believed 'that the last hope of avoiding Communism in Germany' was 'the occupation of as large a section of Europe as possible by the Americans and the British'.[30] For in 1945 there was no trace whatever of a coherent German opposition save among leaders coming out of concentration camps.

* See above, page 381.

On June 5, 1945, Generals Eisenhower, Montgomery, and de Lattre de Tassigny, representing the United States, Britain and France, confirmed all the previous arrangements with Marshal Zhukov, including the withdrawals of troops from the 'tactical zones' of which Churchill disapproved. A proclamation also formally dissolved the old German government. It gave supreme authority in the country to the Allied Commanders-in-Chief. A second proclamation stated that, until Germany was again a single unit, unanimous agreement would be needed on policies among the Allied commanders. That provision gave each occupying power, even France, a veto; and it became the basis for the indefinite division of Germany. A third and final proclamation confirmed the boundaries of the zones, and the divisions of Berlin into sectors, each with separate garrisons.[31]

The various military administrations, including the Inter-Allied Kommandatura in Berlin, were established soon after. Averell Harriman suggested that the Allied Control Commission should be established at a point where all the zones met (for example, Magdeburg), but Secretary Byrnes thought it too late to consider such a new idea, however good.

So it was without guarantees over the route to Berlin that American troops withdrew from those parts of old Pomerania, Saxony and Thuringia which they had reached in the spring. British troops withdrew from Mecklenburg and parts of Brandenburg. Leipzig was 're-liberated' by the Red Army. Truman needed many of his troops in the East; and, at this point, he believed the United States should maintain their agreements, in the hope that Russia would do so too. Churchill drily commented: 'I sincerely hope that your action will in the long run make for a lasting peace in Europe'.[32]

Truman also separately asked for access to Berlin to be guaranteed for Western troops and civilians to Berlin across the territory of the Soviet zone by air, road and railway. Stalin did not reply to this. Generals Marshall, Eisenhower and Clay assumed that such a guarantee was implicit in the arrangements for the administration of Germany and Berlin: 'since Zhukov was so reasonable about everything, it seemed best to assume . . .

that all the occupying powers would have unrestricted access to Berlin as soon as the zonal areas were completed'. This 'technicality' appeared 'one of those things which would fall into place'.[33] The Russians thought perhaps that, sooner or later, the Western garrisons would be voluntarily withdrawn from the artificial, if psychologically important, position in which they seemed to be in Berlin.[34] As it was, as so often in politics, long-term arrangements were concluded for short-term reasons. For example, both the Americans and British would have liked the exclusive use of a number of roads and railways to Berlin. But General Zhukov explained that his own 'transport difficulties' were too considerable to allow that. Generals Clay and Montgomery then agreed to limit themselves to one railway and one big road on which they presumed they would have the right of unimpeded travel.[35]

Stalin may not have expected an American withdrawal from the 'tactical zones'. Eugen Varga, the Hungarian-born economist then fashionable in Moscow, had made plans for the provisioning of the Russian zone of Germany which excluded Saxony and Thuringia. When told that the Americans had withdrawn from their positions in those ancient provinces the previous month, Varga was 'incredulous'. He had calculated on the assumption that the Americans would remain in those districts of the Soviet zone which they had conquered.[36] Nevertheless, as has been earlier suggested, had Saxony and Thuringia been held as part of the West, Vienna and Lower Austria might well have remained part of the Soviet Empire. (The Russians themselves soon withdrew from 'tactical zones' which they had reached in Austria, to their zonal lines, as they did later from the Danish island of Bornholm.)*

The arrangements of 1945 transferred about a quarter of Germany as it had been in 1937, either to Poland or to Russia. The absorption of Königsberg by Russia meant the Slav conquest of a city which, as has been seen, had been founded by Germans in 1255.† The Poles possessed themselves of territory in Silesia

---

* See above, page 161.
† See map on page 495.

colonised by Germans even earlier. If the Soviet zone of Germany be reckoned as a Russian protectorate, the line dividing the west from the east lay close to that which separated Charlemagne's empire from the Slav 'barbarians' in 814 AD. Yet, even in 814, the East German cities of Magdeburg and Erfurt were Christian. There was, as earlier suggested, neither moral nor ethnic justification for these acts. They were based on Soviet demands accepted by Western governments and not much commented upon in Western papers.

During the war there had been many arguments in Washington, and in London, as to whether the Germany of the future would be best pacified by repression or rehabilitation. The War Department and the Treasury in Washington believed the first, the Department of State the second.[37] Roosevelt lent support to both sides of the argument and left the matter unresolved. In Britain, the government lent towards repression as did, more heavily still, that of the Soviet Union, whose government left the impression that they were primarily concerned with reparations.

That last matter seemed by 1946 less of a problem than it had promised to become at Yalta when Molotov had been demanding $20 billion in reparations from Germany, for all the allies. Half would go to Russia, Molotov insisted not unreasonably (he also had sought to insist that reparations would have first priority over all other considerations, and that nothing should be done to maintain Germany's standard of living. The American point of view was the reverse).[38]

The solution of the difficulty was ultimately one of the achievements of Secretary Byrnes. At Potsdam (in the absence of the British, during their vote-counting, following the general election), he linked the question of German reparations to that of that country's temporary border with Poland. The arbitrary transfer, he said, of so much of old Germany to Poland would cause many difficulties in connection with reparations. Nor could the United States finance these payments, as she had done after the previous war. This was the one principle on which all

American departments of state, otherwise divided over Germany, were agreed.[39] Could not each occupying country take reparations in the form of existing assets from its own zone? (Russia, he knew when he spoke, had already done so on a vast scale.) If Russia desired industrial material from the British or American zones, it could do so in exchange for food or fuel which it would send in from the East. Molotov procrastinated. He argued that Secretary Byrnes's idea might undermine the principle of a united Germany, which even the United States still in theory advocated. Molotov also wanted something more than what had been suggested for the Ruhr – preferably four-power control. But the final agreement on reparations would be much as Byrnes had suggested, with 10 per cent of such industrial equipment as was unnecessary for the 'German peace economy' to go to Russia from the Anglo-American zones. In addition, Russia would be able to get 15 per cent of this in exchange for an equal value of goods such as coal or food sent from their zone.[40] The agreement was somewhat unreal since the total figures on which the percentages were calculated were unclear. It also meant that the British would be handing over more industrial plant and production than the Americans, because of the character of Britain's zone. All the same, it was an agreement which also led to acceptance by the United States and Britain of Polish administration of Germany east of the Oder-Neisse line, on a temporary basis, 'until the Treaty of Peace'.

One element in reparations from Germany was the availability of what remained of her population for forced labour. That too had been agreed by the Western leaders at Potsdam. The length of the Germans' detention in the allied countries would be at the discretion of the victors. Many Germans carried off to Russia thus came back either only after ten years, or never. The Hague Convention on Treatment of Prisoners of War was specifically held not to apply. This was 'punishment not war', as the colonel put it, in Kipling's *Kim*. Nevertheless, the thousands of German prisoners who found themselves in the United States or Britain mostly returned home quickly, having been treated humanely.

Long before the other Allies could take up their sectors in

Berlin, the Soviet troops had in fact been emptying that city and their zone of Germany of everything that caught their interest – in effect, de-industrialising what remained of Saxony, Brandenburg and Mecklenburg with a zest which in practice would have shocked Morgenthau at his most pastoral.[41] What they took from Berlin included much from those parts of the city which would become Western zones. Altogether they apparently carried off $1.6 billion worth (pre-war value) of industrial plant from Berlin together with $600 million in raw timber and a great deal more in other goods, agricultural products and railway equipment.[42] The Russians knew from their own experience in 1941 that whole factories could be shipped more easily than might be supposed. They had done it, from west to east Russia; and, in 1945, as in 1941, the administrative skills of Georgi Malenkov were brought in to manage the transfer. The meeting at Potsdam took no account of this reality, nor of the major shift westwards of the German populations, nor yet of the likely need of neighbouring countries for German-manufactured goods and coal.

In the winter of 1945 over 14 million Germans – *flüchtlinge* – were also being uprooted from countries where in many cases they had lived for hundreds of years.[43] This occurred under the authority of Article 13 of the Potsdam Protocol which stated that the 'transfer to Germany of German populations . . . remaining in Poland, Czechoslovakia and Hungary will have to be undertaken'. There were also innumerable Germans (*Volksdeutsche*) in the Balkans. A far cry from the Atlantic Charter or even President Wilson's Fourteen Points, it might be said. But the great powers had 'considered the question in all its aspects', the Protocol added.[44] This meant, as has been seen when discussing Poland and Czechoslovakia,[45] that revenge was taken on the simple German peasant in Silesia or East Prussia, as in the Sudetenland of Czechoslovakia, as if all had been Nazis. Thus the homes of Kant and Herder in East Prussia, of Kleist in Pomerania and of Schopenhauer in Danzig were handed over to Poles or Russians. All the same, the issue had continent-wide implications, because there was no country in East or Central Europe which did not have a sizeable minority of usually hard-working and politically innocent Germans. The measures were inspired in the long run by the 'successful' transfer of the Greeks and Turks after the Treaty of Lausanne (1923).

The arrangements at Potsdam announced that this 'transfer' of population – dull euphemism devised by bureaucrats to describe the forced removal of an ancient civilisation – was to be 'effected in an orderly and humane manner'. The stipulation, Golo Mann later wrote, was 'reminiscent of the request of the Holy Inquisition that its victims should be put to death "as gently as possible and without bloodshed"'.[46] The British official Committee which earlier considered the matter admittedly thought that the 'transfers could not and should not begin for a year after the end of the war and then should be spread out over five years'. That was not carried into policy.[47]

These ideas for 'transfers' of population had been discussed in the course of the war by the British government. As early as January 1943, the War Cabinet had decided on them 'where they seem necessary and desirable'.[48] The Czechs Beneš and Ripka had become enthusiastic. Others imitated them.

The numbers here were large. The total, as has been said, was of the order of 14 million: 7 million from what had been Silesia, Pomerania or East Prussia; nearly 3 million from Czechoslovakia; 1.8 million from Poland or Russia; 2.7 million *Volksdeutsche* from elsewhere in the Balkans. The deaths may have been anything between 2 and 3 million (over 250,000 whilst leaving Czechoslovakia, 1.25 million in Poland or Russia, 600,000 in the rest of East Europe).[49] Perhaps a million remained where they were, by various means. The consequence was that, by early 1946, there were nearly 10 million extra mouths to feed in Germany, of whom about seven were in the West. Other millions followed. Resented by the indigenous Germans, these newcomers, 'displaced persons' as they were christened with characteristic insensitivity by officials, constituted a financial burden on their reluctant hosts for a generation.

An accurate picture of life in Central and Eastern Europe in the winter of 1945–46 should thus include the sight of hundreds of trains, themselves in bad condition, carrying thousands of victims of international conflict to places where neither they nor their immediate ancestors had ever been, each refugee clutching a sack or two only of possessions, cold, hungry, ill, bewildered. One or two trains a day left Prague in February 1946 for Germany with 1,200 Sudetens on board. Back in their ancient farms, Polish or Czech, Romanian or Serbian, or Soviet, soldiers would be making fires of pianos, grandfather clocks, and kitchen tables. The tragedy of the Germans travelling West in early 1946 was in no way reduced by the recollection that, along those same railway lines, there had travelled in the other direction, four years before, the Jews whom Heydrich had decided would be deported to the East; or that the opportunity for the tragedy had been made by Hitler.

These comparisons were made in the *New York Times* on February 4, 1946: 'as everyone knows who has seen the awful sights at the reception centres in Berlin and Munich, this exodus takes place under nightmarish conditions, without any international supervision, or any pretence of humane treatment. We share responsibility for horrors only comparable to the Nazi cruelties'.[50] Bertrand Russell had made the same unpopular point in a letter to *The Times* in London the preceding autumn: 'apparently a deliberate attempt is being made to exterminate many millions of Germans not by gas but by depriving them of their homes and of food, leaving them to die by slow and agonising starvation . . . as part of a deliberate policy of "peace"'.[51] He said the same in the House of Lords, on December 5: the Poles, with Russian encouragement, had 'committed atrocities very much on the same scale . . . as those of which the Nazis were guilty'.[52] Unlike what happened in 1919, there were no plebiscites, statutes protecting minorities, no serious disputes over frontiers. Nor was there much comment in the press. This was the age of brutal simplicities.

The tragedy is, of course, explained by the conduct of the Germans themselves between 1939 and 1945. They had shown how populations could be moved about without consideration of historical or other rights. Men in the XVIIIth century could afford to refuse to draw up an 'indictment against an whole people'; those of the XXth century had no such qualms, despite a few enlightened reflections that, once the impact of defeat had been received, the concept of punishment should have been abandoned.[53] To win the war, even the national democratic governments had needed to rally the minds of millions. When the at first unbelievable news of the concentration camps began to be broadcast, the sense of outrage was considerable. Among many, those feelings lasted for years. That made the business of treating Germany as a political problem capable of rational measures difficult.

The politicians of the West here followed popular emotions. Truman would have liked to soothe things: 'while we have no desire to be unduly cruel to Germany, I cannot feel any great sympathy for those who caused the death of so many human beings', he wrote to Senator Hawke on December 21, 1945, adding, 'I admit that there are many people in Germany who had little to do with the Nazi terror. However, the administrative burden of trying to locate those people and treat them differently from the rest is almost insuperable'.[54]

Many British were unyielding: 'One must hope that the British public will be made, and kept, aware that the responsibility for all this lies at the door not merely of the Nazi leaders, but of the whole German population'. Thus John Troutbeck in a minute to the Cabinet on the Foreign Office's brief for the Potsdam Conference.[55] (That was an echo of Roosevelt's own remark on the same theme.)[56] Few in 1945 knew or could bring themselves to remember that there had been a brave anti-Nazi resistance in Germany; nor that many of the essential elements in Nazism were taken from other movements in other countries; nor that the Nazi experience was a riposte to the threat of Communism; nor that the nuclear weapon had owed much to Otto Hahn who, in the Kaiser Wilhelm Institute for Chemistry in Berlin in 1938, had, with Fritz Strassmann, found the radioactive-bearing isotope among the products resulting from the bombardment of uranium with neutrons – and who, instead of proclaiming the matter, had communicated his discovery to Lise Meitner, a

Jewish Austrian who had fled because of the Nazi racial laws; nor that in the war itself German scientists had not gone ahead with the manufacture of the bomb.[57]

The best hope for Germany in 1945 was for it to be embedded in some kind of a federal Europe. Dr Adenauer, the new leader of the German Right as it became,* had hoped for that in the 1920s. He believed it even more in 1945.[58] Not only were the old European empires overseas then in decline or rebellion, but Hitler had accomplished 'the technical task of the unification of Europe . . . central authorities in a whole series of areas; in transport, in banking, in procurement . . . why', George Kennan wondered in Moscow, 'could not this situation be usefully exploited after an Allied victory?' Kennan had tried unsuccessfully to win understanding for this idea in the Department of State. He came up against Roosevelt's aversion to anything which resembled a discussion of post-war problems. There was no one in Washington prepared then to 'consider schemes which would be in conflict with Russian wishes; and the Russians desired to exploit the economic potential and the political weakness of West Europe'.[59] 'I dislike making detailed plans for a country which we do not yet occupy', Roosevelt told Hull on October 20, 1944.[60] So, unfortunately, much had to happen before the idea of a Europe united in a new way could be broached.

Then there were the trials of German 'war criminals' and 'denazification'. There was to be no escape from these much-pondered arrangements, as there had been in 1919, after the previous war. Provision for it affected all the defeated and was specifically mentioned in the communiqué after Potsdam.[61] 'Denazification' meant the filling in of a questionnaire containing 130 questions – *Fragebogen* – by all Germans over the age of eighteen. It implied the removal of Nazis from public service and from senior ranks of private institutions or companies. There

* See below, pages 483-4.

were degrees of penalties. For serious criminals, the trials would be regular. But problems began immediately.

In the United States zone, 140,000 Germans had lost their jobs by December 1945: including 80 per cent of school teachers, 50 per cent of doctors.[62] Many of those waiting for trial did so in conditions almost as bad as those in Nazi Germany. Many of the subsequent accusations that the accused were treated brutally turn out to have been true.[63] That was in itself scarcely surprising. But in the event 'denazification', however desirable, could not be carried out. People with special qualifications could not be excluded permanently from their occupations. Each of the occupying powers had need of people who had special skills. Golo Mann remarked: 'As things worked out, it was chance whether a person ended up in the dock or on an intimate footing with the military government'.[64] Thus General Gehlen, the intelligence chief of Germany on the Russian front, was already working in 1946 for the Americans; his former deputy, Heinz Felfe, an officer of the SS, was working for the English (and, since he was later unmasked as a Soviet agent, doubtless for the Russians too).

As for the trials of the Nazis, George Kennan observed: 'To admit to such a procedure a Soviet judge as the representative of a regime which had on its conscience the vast cruelties of the Russian Revolution, of collectivisation and of the purges of the 1930s, as well as the manifold brutalities and atrocities perpetuated against the Poles and the peoples of the Baltic countries during the War, was to make a mockery of the purpose of repudiating mass crimes of every sort . . .'. It was not possible, Kennan wrote, 'to accept the proposition that our governmental leaders were excusably ignorant of what had been done in the name of the Soviet state'.[65]

Still, the international trials of the war criminals began. The first such was the trial of those responsible for the Belsen concentration camp in September 1945. 'Major' trials before international tribunals occupied most of the winter of 1945–46; indeed, until October 1, 1946. In addition, at innumerable prisons and camps, 'minor' Nazis awaited their turn before German courts. Every day, readers of newspapers saw atrocious, extra-ordinary, events recalled in a dull air of tranquillity. Men before whom the world had trembled humbled themselves to recall details of minor military operations.

The difficulties consequent upon this policy in the Western zones were without end. Appeals, successful defence lawyers, incompetent witnesses, sudden and mysterious escapes, all discredited the process. A part of the discussions at Potsdam had been devoted to the need for a psychological campaign in Germany. Whatever the results of the *Fragebogen*, and the trials, the Germans were to be made to feel that they suffered defeat because of their own mistakes and that they could not escape responsibility by, for example, a revival of the myth of a stab in the back. Not only were all Nazi institutions to be destroyed, but 'demilitarisation' and 'denazification', specifically designated at Potsdam, were to be positive policies, as were 'decentralisation' and 'democratisation'. These might be the words of 'slogan-makers', said Robert Murphy, but they were intended to be more than that. At the first meeting, of for example, the new town council of Cologne, on October 1, 1945, the representative of the British Military Government, Major Prior, spoke of kindling the 'flame of democratic responsibility'.

These undertakings were immensely difficult, to begin with, in a nation which had passed twelve years absorbing often brilliantly conceived propaganda which, in the end, by concen-trating on the evils of Russian invasion, had foretold – both in respect of the conduct of Russian soldiery and the extent of Soviet aggrandisement – what did indeed occur. There was also the realisation by a people which had been spellbound by the Nazis for so long, just how brutally their leaders had behaved and to just how humiliating a defeat they had been led. Naturally, these observations delayed the moment of seeing the intentions of the Soviet regime clearly.

By the beginning of 1946, it was clear that the three Western zones of Germany were developing in one direction and the Eastern in another. Within the Western zones, free movement was permitted. The Russians permitted no easy access to their zone. The Western Allies had also become conscious that their access to Berlin by a single rail, road or air route was a limited one. The Western zones maintained liaison with each other of a sort; little with the Russians.

The American zone by early 1946 was beginning to be an effective economy. The docility of the Germans and their eagerness to get back to work made things easy. So did the dispassionate attitude of the occupying Americans, who had neither been occupied, as the Russians and the French had been, nor bombed, as the British had been. Some Americans sought to loot in the early days, but the head of OMGUS (Office of the Military Government of the United States in Germany), General Lucius Clay, recalling the depredations suffered by pillage in Georgia after the American Civil War (he was son of a Southern Senator of the era of reconstruction), made an on the whole successful effort to stop that anyway infrequent practice.[66] Clay's work, however, and that of Americans generally was made more difficult first by a directive, JCS 1067 (the letters indicating the Joint Chiefs of Staff), which had been approved, in an early form, in September 1944. This contained a series of mostly unrealisable prohibitions about 'fraternisation' between the occupants and German civilians, and on production.[67] It included so many elements of Morgenthau's plan for the 'pastoralisation' of Germany that Morgenthau himself remarked, 'I hope somebody doesn't recognise it as "the Morgenthau plan" when Truman signed a final version'.[68] In JCS 1067, 'no steps looking forward to the rehabilitation of Germany, or designed to maintain or strengthen the German economy', were to be taken. The military government was to 'prohibit and prevent' production in a long list of industries.

The inadequacies of JCS 1067 became obvious as soon as, in May 1945, the authorities tried to put it into effect. Lewis Douglas, financial adviser to General Clay, the United States military governor, resigned since it made 'no sense to forbid the most skilled workers in Europe from producing as much as they can for a continent which was short of everything'. (Douglas, a man of principle, had resigned as Director of the United States

Budget in 1934, on the subject of spending for relief.) Truman might be encouraged to adopt a policy of rehabilitation, instead of repression, by Secretaries Stimson and Forrestal. Even so, the joint Chiefs expected Germany to be occupied, 'not for the purpose of liberation but as a defeated enemy'. Kindness even to German children was at first formally held to be wrong. These and other provisions sought to create a gulf between conquerors and conquered as had never existed before in Europe – save, indeed, under the Nazis in the East.

When the American command realised that all their allies, the Russians included, employed ex-Nazis, where necessary, Clay went back on his instructions, in many minor ways. American soldiers usually conducted themselves with generosity. They could talk to Germans in public places after July 14, 1945. But all the Allies, the Russians and the French included, wanted to limit German production – of steel, chemicals, iron, electrical equipment, motor cars, and other industrial products – with the consequence that it seemed that German exports would never be able to begin to pay for imports. The task of running down enterprises, as well as arranging for their transport to the Soviet Union, seemed to be the most important business in Germany in the winter of 1945–1946. General Clay complained that those who had written the policies in 1944 were utterly ignorant of the conditions which prevailed in Germany. They could not envisage the consequences of the retribution (for example, by bombing) already effected. Living a 'cloistered and academic life', he suggested, they had not got out into the 'mud' – of disease, and shortages of food and of shelter.[69]

United States policy in Germany was here affected by numerous competing interests. The occupation might be 'an artificial revolution on behalf of democracy'. But the Department of State and the War Department quarrelled over principles as well as details. 'Re-orientation', 'democratisation', and 're-education' were interchangeable themes to which such things as 'demilitarisation' and 'denazification' were subordinate. In practice, General Clay, in the not negligible tradition of United States proconsular activity, of General Wood in Cuba, or General Pershing in the Philippines, conducted himself as an autocrat, doing 'more or less as he pleased', not only looking 'like a Roman Emperor' but acting like one, according to a British colleague;[70] even if he observed the formalities and accepted JCS 1067 as the general guide.[71] He and those beneath him in Germany, like those above him in the Army in Washington, wanted to end the occupation as soon as they could, providing they could leave behind a nation basically peaceful and with an economy based on free enterprise.

The United States was also limited by the fact that her zone could never be self-sufficient. For example, that territory had only two per cent of German coal. The ideal course would have been to persuade all the Allied partners to consider Germany a single unit. But the Soviet treatment of Germany east of the Oder (and Western Neisse) as part of Poland, their stripping of their zone of all moveable objects, and their reluctance from the beginning to collaborate with their erstwhile allies at any managerial level, made that unrealisable. The United States therefore understood that they would have to finance imports in order to feed Germans; as well as immediately to seek ways, despite JCS 1067, to invigorate Germany industry. But this too was specially difficult for the United States zone. Clay needed to import coal and machinery from the Ruhr, in the British zone, and agricultural produce from the Soviet zone. The lack of a central authority with a policy on transport, power, postal communications thus hit the Americans more than it did the others.

There were many discussions among Americans on these things in late 1945. Clay and Murphy, respectively the chief United States military and political personages in Germany, consulted Washington. Reports were written by Calvin Hoover and Byron Price which argued that further industrial disarmament and the maintenance of minimum standards of living in Germany could not be combined. Nor could creative policies towards the other zones be applied unless the other allies agreed to collaborate. Russia was not the only stumbling block. France suspected that any agreement on an all-German policy would lead one day to a new German central government and she was determined to avoid that if possible (the fact that there had been a declaration at Potsdam on the subject was of no significance to France, since her representatives had not been present).

Eventually, after much inter-departmental argument in Washington, the United States agreed on a new formula for the future: the United States would not seek to limit the German economy forever. They would seek to enable Germans, under a democratic German government, to develop a higher level of living, subject to certain as yet undefined restrictions on production and on armaments. Germany's civilian industries would not be destroyed to gain selfish advantages for the United States. If possible, there would be a minimum standard of life for Germans. The United States would also help to rebuild buildings, roads and bridges.[72]

The consequence was a conference organised at Stuttgart by Clay on October 17, 1945 between the occupiers and newly appointed ministers-president of the zone (Hogner, of Bavaria; Geiler, of Hesse; Maier, of Württemberg-Baden; and Senate President Kaisen, of Bremen). Clay asked these men to establish a co-ordinating agency in Stuttgart to manage 'denazification', refugees, food, and all economic problems. The result, the *Landesrat*, with its United States agency of liaison, was soon functioning well. It had a General Secretary, a staff and appropriate committees. These agencies, established by Clay to make up for French hostility to a central German government, as well as for a general unwillingness to collaborate by the Soviet Union, was henceforth the core of the US-German administration.[73] Administration at the level of the district (*kreis*) was now in German hands again.

Despite these initiatives, however, the state of affairs in respect of food in Germany still seemed bad in February 1946. Direct imports of food into the country only began in January. It seemed improbable that even the low rations could be maintained.

Clay did not abandon hope of collaboration between zones. It even happened, surreptitiously. Thus Hesse, in the American zone, and Thuringia, in the Russian, established a trade agreement in January 1946: a scheme disapproved of by Clay since it could give the Russians (or the French) an excuse for saying that central administration was not necessary. One of his assistants, Professor James Pollock, serving as director of the United States link with the *Landesrat*, proposed a discussion with the equivalent body of the British zone. That was held on February 6, 1946. Subsequent talks were planned, resolutions passed, but, for the moment, nothing substantial was done.

Policy-makers in Washington, on whom so much depended, for all Germany as well as for the American zone, were slow to realise that all Western Europe's recovery depended upon Germany recovery. The conflict between those who wished to neutralise Germany forever and those who wished for its reconstruction was not resolved till 1947. Trade understandably revived slowly. New investment from the United States in Germany was modest. The Department of State even prevented the International Telephone and Telegraph Corporation from re-establishing itself in Germany. (The founder of IT & T, Colonel Sosthenes Behn, said in February 1946 that he was 'going to liquidate every foreign property as fast as he could,' such was the uncertainty in Europe.)[74] Even so, in the spring of 1946, General Clay was considering certain cold decisions of his own which were to be the first steps towards a 'dismemberment' on a permanent basis, if not the type discussed a year or two before during the course of the war.


The British zone of Germany was first managed by Field Marshal Montgomery, a man of energy, imagination and originality. His instructions included one to 'work in line with the Americans' as far as possible. Like Clay, Montgomery had colonial experience to guide him: his father had been bishop of Tasmania, his grandfather governor of the Punjab. He had a civilian adviser, the same Sir William Strang who had led so unsuccessful a mission to Russia in 1939, but an able official and a good student of German affairs.

Montgomery's announcements were characteristically personal. He considered that Nazism had been caused by 'idleness, boredom and fear of the future'; he was now ready to help the Germans to eradicate such things. He was quick to relax the rules about fraternisation: 'members of the British forces' were, from August, 'allowed to engage in conversation with the German people in streets and in public places'. By November, Montgomery had published plans for the swift 'civilianisation' of administration, a process which, when complete, would mean that 'the Germans govern themselves, subject to control and supervision by us'.[75] Montgomery had magnanimous views about subjects which so disturbed his American colleagues. Thus he realised immediately that the level of industry would have to be so fixed that 'there would be a decent standard of living, with the minimum unemployment'. He knew that 1946 would be a difficult time, when so many of the industries which had survived the war would have been taken away as reparations for Russia.[76]

Alongside Montgomery, there was a minister responsible to the British Cabinet, John Hynd. He was named Chancellor of the Duchy of Lancaster, but his responsibilities included the British zone of Austria as well as that of Germany. He was notably moderate over Germany. At the Labour Party's Conference in May 1945, he had criticised the idea of the collective responsibility of the entire German nation for the Nazi atrocities. If that was to be said of the Germans, could not people say the same of the British in India?[77] He had no intention of feeling so responsible.[78]

The British zone, the richest part of old Germany, had been the site of 85 per cent of pre-war German industry. It was also clear already that it would be the most expensive of the four zones to run: costing $400 million in 1946 alone.[79] The relations between the 20 million or so Germans and the occupiers, despite Montgomery's personal inclinations, were bad. The British had suffered too much from the war, for too long a time, to make friends in Germany easily. The re-established Lord Mayor of Cologne, Dr Konrad Adenauer, essentially a conservative, also detected an ideological socialism among the officers in the British army with whom he had to deal.[80] That, he thought, prejudiced them against him. The atmosphere of a British mess was colonial. Many senior officers knew the Empire. Whereas the socialism of the British officers offended Dr Adenauer, the colonial attitude distressed the Socialists: 'We are not blacks', the Socialist leader, Dr Schumacher, told a British colonel indignantly.[81] Some British officers distrusted anyone who sought to employ even minor Nazis, forgetting that the weaknesses of human nature had led many – there had been 8 million Nazis in January 1945 – who did not have the courage to oppose the Nazis to give them, against their better judgement, at least formal support. Here the attitudes of the Prime Minister could be found, since Attlee, a veteran of the Kaiser's war, believed that the facts of defeat had to be impressed on all Germans.

The British might have preferred to have run Germany indefinitely, on the model of India: sensible officials could have managed the Germans with firmness for a generation. After all, the Indian Empire would probably soon end and there would be administrators looking for work. But the Russians and then the Americans quickly permitted German political parties to organise.[82] True, as has been seen, the American permission was at first limited to the *Kreis* or district level; but in November these activities were allowed at the *Land*, or provincial, level. (In the French zone, parties were not allowed till December 1945, and they did not get under way till the spring of 1946.) The British therefore also permitted 'zonal political operations'. It was in the territory for which they were responsible that political life revived soonest.

The Social Democrats made the quickest recovery among political parties. The victory of the Labour Party in Britain in July had given heart to Dr Schumacher, the gifted but obstinate leader of the Party, who had spent most of the Nazi years in concentration camps. Schumacher knew that the victors had nothing to teach him about to how to behave. A Prussian Socialist of integrity and convictions, Schumacher believed that his hour had come: patriotic and democratic Socialism, he thought, would take over throughout the Reich, as it had in Britain. He believed firmly in natural unity.

In October the other surviving party of old Germany, the *Zentrum*, also regrouped. Two months later, many who had survived from that party met at Bad Godesberg. They formed a new group, the Christian Democratic Union. This had, from the beginning, the aim to draw in all who believed in Christian values, not merely the Catholics, who had constituted the core of the *Zentrum* (the old Catholic party of the past). Another such party was founded in Bavaria, the Christian Social Union. These meetings responded to a demand for a new movement based on the Christian limitation to the claims of that state power which, the Christian Democrats accepted, had led the previous generation of Germans from such a splendid eminence of achievement to such now unpitied destruction.

Dr Konrad Adenauer, peremptorily dismissed by the British in October from his chief burgomastership in Cologne, quickly became the national director of this latter movement. His sombre, strange, disdainful features became speedily a characteristic of all pictures of the new Germany. Though seventy, Adenauer's brain was quick. A child of the middle class, a member of the Prussian upper house before 1914, his years as chief burgomaster in Cologne under the Weimar Republic as in 1945 represented continuity. Patient, agile, hard-working, a man of uncontestable integrity like Schumacher, and possessed of real capacity for authority, this patriarchal German would be, already, at the zonal committee in Neuheim-Hüsten in late February 1946, the formative influence among conservative Germans. He was the right man to give substance to the evolving political philosophy of a revived, broad, non-sectarian Christianity which did not dwell on the recent past, and which had links with other such movements abroad.

The winter of 1946 was, however, more concerned with the problems of food than those of philosophy. In January 1946, Montgomery had told the Government that the British zone would be faced by starvation as well as epidemics if an emergency supply of wheat was not sent. Attlee would soon divert supplies of that commodity, which the United States had intended for Britain, to Germany.[83] He, ironically enough, as a victor, soon found himself contemplating the rationing of bread at home.

France represented a problem for all, Germans as well as Allies. Excluded from attendance at either Yalta or Potsdam but, in respect of her part in the Allied Control Commission and occu-

pation zones in both Austria and Germany, a beneficiary of both
– thanks largely to Churchill – France was from the beginning
able to use her position cleverly.* She was not bound by
the Protocol of Potsdam. She was thus able to use her veto
(frequently, in the autumn of 1945, or so it seemed to her allies)
against decisions of the other Allied commanders and seek, by
mere intransigence, to place herself and her interests on the
world scene. Russia, which had opposed her very membership
of the arrangements for Germany, in the end profited.[84] General
Koenig, the French commander, was in early 1946 a more
frequent target for 'Anglo-Saxon' fury than Zhukov was. Byrnes
and Truman both tried to convince de Gaulle and Bidault that,
if confined to matters of transport, currency and food supply,
a centralised administration need not lead to an all-German
government.[85] But de Gaulle argued that any centralised railway
system might revive the German military potential. He feared
that it would, in those circumstances, soon pass to Russian
hands. At the Conference of Foreign Ministers in London,
Bidault opposed any consideration of a German authority, until
a decision had been made to ensure the separation of the Ruhr
from Germany and its internationalisation. Bidault did not want
the Russians to share in an international administration of the
Ruhr. He wanted it to be French. The Americans discussed
among themselves, but decided against, the idea of tying
cooperation in Germany to their willingness to keep France
financially: the strength of democracy in Paris was too frail for
that, the Communist party too strong.[86]

Out of French hostility to centralisation came justification of
Russian intransigence. France also used her small and impoverished zone as a direct benefit to her own economy. They, like
the Russians, took home nearly everything of value. They ran
a huge deficit. French occupation officers lived well and charged
expenses to government as 'occupation costs'.

Even so, it was General de Gaulle who, first among Allied
statesmen, spoke in terms of conciliation. His speech at Saar-

---

* De Gaulle was not welcomed by Truman at Potsdam for having arbitrarily
disregarded a battle order by General Eisenhower.

brücken in August 1945, in which he appealed for Frenchmen and Germans to let bygones be bygones, and to remember that they were Europeans, was heard by most Germans with gratitude.[87]

Whether for good or evil, French policy in these first months of the peace was effective. In the absence of a centralised administration, Germany divided. The Rhineland and Bavaria looked west, Prussia and Saxony east. Germany's policies between 1870 and 1945 may have been revenge for the domination of France since the XVIth century. But France was now playing a final, and a trump, card.

The Russian zone of Germany already seemed a western redoubt of the Soviet Empire so far as Stalin was concerned. Marshal Zhukov, hero of Moscow and of Leningrad, one of the few who had been known to interrupt and even contradict Stalin, was the first Soviet viceroy. But a decisive part was here played by the German Communists. Perhaps, indeed, in the absence of a clear lead by Stalin as to exactly what he wanted to achieve in Germany, they may even have initiated policy.

Most of the leaders of the old Communist Party of Germany had spent the war in Moscow. They returned on April 30, 1945, by air and, taking over the party which they had not seen for twelve years, immediately set about finding mayors, deputy mayors and officials to run the Soviet zone. They were often happy to have Social Democrats in the top posts; but, if that were so, they would arrange that the senior deputy mayor in charge of appointments and the official responsible for education were Communists.[88] This was usually achieved, though the choices were often restricted. 'It's quite clear – it's got to look democratic', the Communist leader Walter Ulbricht instructed his comrades, 'but we must have everything in our control'. Thus it was that a respectable bourgeois, Dr Werner, became Lord Mayor of Berlin; while a Communist, Karl Maron, in Moscow during the war, became his first deputy.[89] Other Communists held key positions in the city (Arthur Pick, chief of personnel; and Otto Winzer, chief of education). The many

genuine 'anti-Fascist Committees' which were founded at the
end of the war by independent anti-Nazis, usually without politics, were closed down on Communist insistence: 'orders' would
be an altogether unsubtle way of describing how intimidation
functions in such circumstances.

Marshal Zhukov permitted the revival of political parties in
the Soviet zone in June 1945. So the Communist Party of
Germany presented themselves in Berlin on June 12, 1945, the
Socialists on the 15th, and a few determined Christian Democrats (including Andreas Hermes, an ex-Centrist Minister of
Finance; Jakob Kaiser, of the Centrist trade union; and Heinrich
Kröne, once a Centrist Reichstag member) on June 17. The
Liberals made an appearance on July 5. These last groups were
new ones. They found establishment difficult. The Russian
military authorities, both in Berlin and their own zone, went
out of their way to help the Communists. Much fundamental
legislation had been decided by the Communists before any of
the parties had much of a being outside Berlin, partly because,
in what was on the face of it a well-intentioned effort to prevent
the emergence of a large number of parties on the scale which,
it was assumed, had ruined Weimar, a specific minimum of
members had to have been signed up as members before a local
party branch could be formed.

By the end of December 1945, the Christian Democrats had
become a continuous target for attacks from the Communists.
Their meetings were even broken up by Communist gangs.
Communists prevented Dr Hermes from attending a meeting of
Christian Democrats in the West, while he and his deputy,
Walter Schreiber (Prussian Minister of Trade before 1933),
were soon persuaded to resign by Marshal Zhukov, in person:
Hermes was told that his son, a prisoner of war in Russia, would
never be released unless he agreed. A British official in Berlin,
Ivor Pink, drily commented that 'the average German may be
terrified to see a certain similarity between Soviet practice and
those which the Allies are pledged to destroy in his country'.[90]

In the months between Potsdam and February 1946, the
Communists consolidated their control over the East zone and
East Berlin. Nothing, short of a renewed war, or an order from

Stalin, could have done anything to prevent this from happening. The Communists had had the advantage of controlling all Berlin for several months (between May and July) before the other Allies had arrived to take up their responsibilities in their enclave. Stalin had also cleverly prepared the way for collaboration with younger Nazis by recalling, in a speech in March 1945, that 'Hitlers come and go, but the German people, and the German state go on for ever.' This slogan was perhaps designed to restrain the Red Army from brutality. But it was displayed on notice boards in Berlin by June 1945 to persuade Germans to collaborate. The Russians also distributed food among the population of Berlin. Probably, the Germans had expected to receive worse treatment.

'Denazification' and 'demilitarisation' were concepts used by the Russians to seize factories and other enterprises useful to them. Where these were not carried off physically to Russia, they were handed over to German local authorities which by then were dominated by the Communists. 'The Communist Party . . . obtained the lead in the Russian zone by being permitted to capture the administrative machinery and by the superior facilities which they enjoy,' reported Colonel Noël Annan, in December.[91] Their prepared 'cadres' dominated the press and radio. Russians often controlled those bodies in Berlin.[92] 'Party schools' already met regularly in confiscated castles, and training programmes for young Communists were being distributed in hundreds of thousands of copies.

By February 1946, as a result of requisition and decree the nationalised share of the East German economy was nearly fifty per cent of industrial production. An agrarian reform had had much the same consequence in the countryside – first being introduced in Saxony, then elsewhere. Property belonging to Nazis, and then all estates over 100 hectares whosoever owned them, were redistributed. The animator of those hastily imposed innovations was a now elderly founder member of the German Communist Party, Edwin Hoernle. He was another man who had passed the war in Russia, having been in the Reichstag in the 1920s and for a long time laboured in the Secretariat of the Comintern. Like so many of the first generation of Communists, including Stalin, he had begun life as a student of theology. He paid no attention to the pleas of proven anti-Nazi landholders, nor to the different needs of different crops, nor even to the farmers' desires for fertiliser from plants being dismantled. No compensation was paid. The courts of East Germany were meantime full of newly appointed 'Peoples' Judges', while the system of education was being reorganised by Otto Winzer, on both Marxist and philo-Russian lines. The change as early as June 1945 of gauge of the German railways in the Soviet zone from the narrow West European one to the broad Russian one was symbolically as well as economically significant.[93]

The German Communists also had a presence of a sort in the West. But, in January 1946, they did badly in the local elections held in the American zone: gaining only 3.5 per cent of the votes. This setback, along with the news of the defeat of the Communists in Austria,* determined the Communists in the Soviet zone to press for a merger between themselves and the Socialists, thus taking advantage of a disposition to favour unity of working class parties against any revival of a Nazi threat, and of guilt because of pre-war divisions between Socialists and Communists (which had helped the Nazi capture of power). The fact that the Communists had opposed unification, and had backed the idea of a separate Socialist Party, in June 1945, in no way affected their new enthusiasm for this policy. Optimism among Communists about this cause was enhanced by the promulgation of a new 'line' by one of their ideologues, Anton Ackermann, who argued persuasively, in a much-distributed pamphlet, that Germany's 'way to Socialism' would not be the same as Russia's.

In December 1945, leaders of both Communist and Socialist parties in the eastern zone, Ulbricht, Dahrendorf and Grotewohl, and some others, were summoned to Marshal Zhukov's headquarters. They were told by that officer that the Soviet Government, which frequently desired to see the unification of their parties, would withdraw most, or even all, of their occupying forces once that had occurred.[94] To this, Gustav Dahrendorf, a

* See below, page 505.

fine Social Democratic leader supposed to be among those in his party furthest to the left, replied that he could contemplate union with the Communists only if they were to support the Social Democrats in condemning the recent atrocities committed by the Red Army.[95] The conversation did not then proceed well. On December 21, the Socialists and Communists all the same declared that they hoped that unification might be possible: a manoeuvre looked upon by many Socialists as an action to gain time, but by the Communists as the justification for a campaign up and down their zone, in factories and in the few other public buildings which were open, demanding the merger at an early date. The Socialists of East Germany, at a zonal trade union conference on February 9 to 11, were subjected to crude but heavy pressure by the Russians to support this. Two Socialists complained to the British that 'their Soviet military government political officer had ordered them to agitate for unification on penalty of being arrested on return if they did not. Some who refused had already been placed in Sachsenhausen prison', previously one of the most evil of the Nazi camps near Berlin.[96]

This pressure had the effect not of breaking, but of dividing, the Socialists, who were stronger in numbers than the Communists. Otto Grotewohl, Chairman of the Socialist Central Committee in Berlin, was bribed or bullied to make him pronounce in favour of unity. Schumacher, leader of the SPD in the British zone, criticised him. To the Americans, however, Grotewohl seemed to have by now 'pretty well discarded democratic methods, in . . . [his] strong desire to achieve a Socialist State in north eastern Germany to begin with'.[97] British interpretations of his conduct were more charitable: he seemed to them to resemble 'a skater gliding round a hole in the ice in ever decreasing circles'.[98]

By mid-February 1946, it seemed likely that the planned Convention of Socialists to discuss unification with the Communists would be attended only by those who favoured it; it was assumed that those Socialists in Berlin or the East zone, such as Germer or Gustav Dahrendorf, who opposed it would go to the West.[99] Grotewohl admitted to Ivor Pink on February 4 that there had been every kind of pressure on his Socialist colleagues, 'from offers of jobs to plain abduction' to support unity. But his nominal leader, Schumacher, was still telling the Communists the unpopular truth that, because they had collaborated twelve years previously with the Nazis in destroying the Weimar Republic, part of the blame for the Third Reich and hence the world war lay with them.[100]

The Communists who were managing these tactics, and this transformation, throughout East Germany were led by old, tough and experienced men. They had been the leaders of the most powerful Communist party between the wars outside Russia. Despite its factional disputes, its purges, its sudden changes of policy at the Soviet behest, and its defeat in the street fighting of 1930–1933 by the Nazis, the Communists had gathered around their standard, men with a capacity for endurance and courage second to none, including endurance of Stalin's policies.[101] Their commander, as has been indicated, was Walter Ulbricht, a tailor's son from Leipzig, a joiner by trade, still only fifty-two in 1945, a man with a strong Saxon accent, who had been in Moscow since 1938.* He had been a Deputy to the Reichstag, and between 1929 and 1933, the Communist leader in Berlin, including eight months of clandestine operations, from January to October 1933. He had apparently been for a time in Spain (responsible for the 'liquidation of anti-Stalinist revolutionary combatants'),[102] Czechoslovakia, and France. His skill at implanting Communists within different enterprises had then given him the nickname 'Zelle' (cell). Like most of his colleagues in East Europe, he had worked in the Secretariat of the Comintern, as, in his case, a most disciplined official. Very hard working, without emotions, 'innocent of theoretical ideas or personal feelings', meticulous, and ruthless, Ulbricht successfully outmanoeuvred the 'anti-Fascist committees', in the name of the re-establishment of the old parties, which he began successfully also to manipulate. A comrade of the old days, Gustav Regler, in 1946 an exile in Mexico, described him as

---

* Ulbricht's group who returned in a Douglas aircraft on April 30, 1945 included, besides himself, Richard Gypner, Otto Winzer ('Lorenz' in Moscow), Hans Mahle, Gustav Gundelach, Karl Maron, Walter Koppe, Fritz Erpenbeck and Wolfgang Leonhard.

having 'a face stiff with a malice that was conscious of its own ugliness. He sought to relieve it with a symbolical Lenin-beard round the plump chin, a hairy appendage that did not, however, rid his faun-like mouth of any of its petty bourgeois arrogance. His eyes, the right sharply observant and the left half-closed, were hidden behind a schoolmaster's glasses. He had the look of a lapsed priest who visits shady houses'.[103]

Ulbricht's principle colleague was Wilhelm Pieck, once an apprentice carpenter, a generation older than Ulbricht, now nearly seventy years old, and the one survivor of the two chairmen of the first meeting of the German Communist Party in 1918. He had taken part in Berlin in the famous rising of the German Communists (Spartacists) in 1919; and, like Ulbricht, had been a Deputy to the Reichstag between 1928 and 1933. In 1933, he had become the President of the Communist Party, worked in the Comintern as head of its Balkan section, and lived in Russia between 1933 and 1945. In July 1945, still the Communist 'President', he had been observed putting his past experience as a carpenter to good use in his own new offices, in the Wallstrasse. Stalin underestimated him when he spoke of him as 'having grown so old' that he had become a 'Grandpa', capable only of slapping people on the back and 'ignorant of how to lead them to a definite goal'.[104] His seventieth birthday, celebrated in Berlin in January 1946 at the State Opera House, one of the few such buildings to have survived, was one of the only public occasions of any interest during this winter. Franz Dahlem, number three on the list of the German Communist Central Committee in 1945, had also been a carpenter. A Lorrainer, he had, unlike his two superiors, spent the war in a concentration camp, having been arrested in France where he had taken refuge after service in the Civil War in Spain as part of the Political Directorate of the International Brigades, in which he had impressed people as an ideal representation of 'the Communist NCO'.[105] Dahlem had been a most useful international revolutionary in the 1920s and 1930s. Also a Deputy between 1928 and 1933, he too had worked with Ulbricht in the Communist underground in Berlin, and only left in 1936.

The Communist leaders in Germany in 1945 included other Spanish veterans: Wilhelm Zaisser, known in Spain as 'General Gómez', commander of the XIIIth International Brigade, but always a member of the intelligence service of the Soviet army (GRU) – he had in 1945 set about the establishment of an East German security police;[106] Richard Staimer, once chief of the military side of 'Red Front' in Bavaria, later 'General Hoffman' of the XIth International Brigade in Spain and now, in 1946, director of the police of East Berlin;[107] and a real Hoffman, Karl Heinz Hoffman, who had also been in the XIth International Brigade as Commissar (as 'Heinz Roth'). At the Comintern school in Russia during the war, Hoffman became personal assistant to Ulbricht in 1945 as the first step upwards in a career of continuous success.* The only prominent Communist apart from Dahlem who had served a long time in prisons in Nazi Germany was Erich Honneker, who in 1946 was organising the revival of the Communist youth movement.

Many ordinary German Communists had been killed by Hitler. Among them was the old party leader of the early 1930s, Ernst Thaelmann, who had died in a concentration camp in 1944. Others had broken with the Party and were now living in England, the United States, even Cuba. But the new team which ran East Germany under the Soviet military command was a strong one. The old Communist centres had in the past been in the Rhineland. The Communists there and in West Germany generally, headed by Max Reinmann, were now less powerful personalities, save in the Ruhr. The Communists placed their best men in the East, wherever they had originated.

In the face of these difficulties, it is understandable that Allied policy should have been tentative. Secretary Byrnes hoped that the problems between the United States and the Soviet Union might be soothed by a 25-year treaty between the four occupying powers which would guarantee demilitarisation of Germany, on the lines of the control by the Allies during the 1920s, with the

* Hoffman was Minister of Defence in East Germany for years.

difference that both the Americans and the Russians would withdraw their forces. Stalin said at first that he thought it a good idea, and would support it. Byrnes's idea was backed in the Senate by a resolution of Senators Vandenberg and Connally.

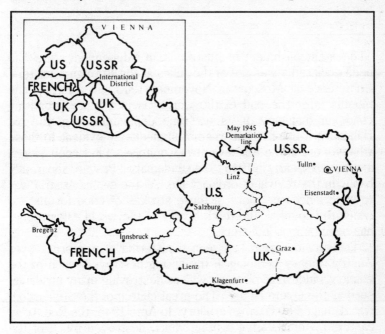

The British and the French accepted. The Russians soon began to hedge. They at first said that the time span was not long enough. Byrnes extended the proposal to one for forty years. The Russians then brought up other obstructions of 'an obviously contrived character'. [108] Evidently, the Russians thought it possible then that all Germany could one day be made Communist.

Communism in East Germany was assisted by old memories of Prussian respect for the state. Take the case of Willy Berg, a policeman under the Kaiser as well as under both Weimar and Hitler. He told Leopold Trepper, the 'Big Chief' of the Soviet spy-ring called the 'Red Orchestra', when in prison, that he could as easily serve a Communist regime as the Kaiser. It appears that he later did so. [109] Prussian and totalitarian Socialism might not be brothers: but there was a family connection, although the memory of the old days of the Kaiser would soon seem, to all but *apparatchiki*, men even the Soviet leader, Mikoyan described as 'Soviet colonists', an intolerably beguiling one.


The 're-establishment of Austria as an independent state' had been declared a war aim of the Allies at the Foreign Ministers' Conference in Moscow in November 1943. So Austria, nine months after the end of the war, was in a more promising condition than any of its one-time dependencies in the old Habsburg Empire. That was not immediately evident to those who worked in the Allied Control Commission in ruined Vienna and travelled early in 1946 to see undamaged Prague, apparently happy in the revival of ordinary life. All the same, Austria was to experience one more of those strokes of good fortune for which the country, the torch bearer of the world catastrophe, had been famous in history.

The previous year had seen the storms of war break over Austria. Heavy bombing in the spring destroyed much of the country's industrial plant, as well as destroying many buildings, such as the Opera House. The great church of the Stefansdom was damaged by German artillery. In April 1945, the Red Army captured Vienna, after fighting which destroyed much of the suburbs. Rape, looting, desecration, and murder followed, if on a smaller scale than in Budapest. Russian occupation began in half Austria. French, British and American divisions closed in on what was believed to be likely to become the last redoubt of the German armies. The Allied armies were followed by refugees: *Volksdeutsche*, with wagons from all over East Europe; Hungarian troops; Cossacks and Russians, fleeing from the Soviet Union; Croats and Chetniks, escaping from Tito. There were also a million foreign workers and ex-prisoners of war of the Germans in Austria in 1945.[110] The country seemed an immense, if impoverished, caravanserai of suffering tribes from the world's most civilised continent.

These experiences were the basis for the reconstruction of

Austria's independence. Austria was, of course, lucky to secure a friendly Allied manner towards them. The toleration was specially fortunate since so many Austrians (for a mixture of reasons) had supported the forced unification (*Anschluss*) with Germany in 1938; and since it had been Austria which had originally inspired Hitler on to his ferocious crusade. A higher proportion of the population of Austria in the 1930s were enthusiastic Nazis than of Germany's. Thirty-five German divisions had been formed chiefly of Austrian conscripts, and had taken part in Hitler's invasion of Russia. Yet the Allies treated the country not, like Germany or Hungary, as a defeated nation, but one to be 'liberated', a victim of Nazi aggression, rather than an integral part of Germany: 'from the American side, there is the fullest understanding that the Austrian matter is entirely separate from the German', a United States official reported after talking to those preparing for military occupation in January 1945.[111] Many Austrians (including pre-*Anschluss* Austrian Nazis) had, in the end, come to hate, or to despise, the German Nazis. But most of them had kept more quiet than their German equivalents.

The key to Austria's good fortune was that the Soviet liberation of Vienna in 1945 was followed by the proclamation of a provisional government, a coalition between the old parties of Austria of the 1920s, to act for the whole country. It was led by the elderly Socialist, Dr Karl Renner. The Soviet army established this statesman, with no consultation of their Western Allies, as Prime Minister.[112] Dr Renner was not only old but experienced. He had been the leader of the Austrian delegation to the treaty-making in Paris in 1919 and, once before, the 'nation-saving Chancellor' of a new Austria ('what is left over', as Clemenceau put it). He had also been President of the lower house of parliament between 1929 and 1934. Dr Renner was seventy-five years old in 1945. Known once before 1914 as one of the leading 'Austro-Marxists' – they had hoped, wisely, to preserve the Habsburg Empire by concessions to cultural nationalism – Renner was now the leader of the Right of the Socialist Party. He seemed, like so many Austrian Socialists, compromised by his one-time support for the idea of union with Germany. Surely, therefore, it must have seemed in Moscow, he was a good prospect for manipulation by the determined leaders of the Communist Party: another Georgiev, as in Bulgaria, or a Tatarescu, as in Romania – a man who would serve the Soviet purpose and then vanish into limbo; or, if necessary, prison. 'What, that old traitor still alive?' Stalin is supposed to have said, recalling events in the days of the Russian revolution, 'he is exactly the man we need'.[113] The western Allies were horrified when Stalin put him in power: 'a fast one', noted that rich English radical, Oliver Harvey, a senior under-secretary in the Foreign Office, in his diary.[114]

The Austrian Communists knew Renner better than so to misjudge him. But Stalin, it seems, did not consult them. Renner believed that he could manipulate the Communists. In the end, and despite hostility from the Americans and the British,[115] it turned out that he was right.

At the beginning of the peace, Renner did seem the prisoner of the Communists. He had a Russian military escort. A detachment of Austrian Communist 'partisans', trained in Yugoslavia, their leaders being Moscow-men, were 'guarding' the Chancellery in Vienna. The Ministers of the Interior and of Education, Franz Honner and Ernst Fischer, were both Communists, the voice of the latter being well-known for his wartime broadcasts from Moscow. The former was at first able to establish Communist police chiefs in many parts of Vienna, as his colleagues had been able to elsewhere, in other parts of the one-time Habsburg empire. All the same, there were some good signs: though the Western Allies did not at first notice this (at least from their written commentaries), the divide between Socialists and Catholics (Christian Social Party) which had prevented the achievement of a viable republic in the 1920s, had been skilfully, and quickly, bridged by Dr Renner's government. Otto Bauer's municipal Socialism, so mocked in the 1920s by the country people as 'Red Vienna', no longer seemed offensive to conservative countrymen; while the imprisonment by the Nazis of so many Conservatives of the old regime created a healing mood among Socialists. Many Socialists and Communists had, also, met in the concentration camps of Mauthausen and Dachau. Socialism in Austria no longer aspired in 1945 to be that complete, exclusive, all-pervasive, way of life that it had been in the previous generation. Finally, for a few months, there was real sympathy between Communists and Socialists, which for once benefited the latter without ruining them, as was occurring in East Germany. Vienna, like Africa, is always ready to surprise.

The eclipse of so many Jewish leaders in the Austrian Socialist Party (men such as Otto Bauer himself who died abroad; Robert Dannenberg, who had been executed; Friedrich Adler and Julius Deutsch, now both old) had in turn also extinguished the great men of the revolutionary left in the Socialist Party. It left authority in the Party to men such as Renner himself, Adolf Shaerf (now Vice-Chancellor) and Oskar Helmer (to become Minister of the Interior in 1945). Shaerf became the plausible architect of a new pragmatic Socialism. In his memoirs, he describes how he suddenly realised that the idea of *Anschluss* with Germany had no appeal for him any more, during a discussion in 1944 with a German conspirator against Hitler, who had expected to secure agreement to maintain the frontiers of 1939 after the war.[116] The only surviving revolutionary Socialists of the old days (Erwin Scharf, Hilda Krones and Theodore Körner) either discredited themselves by their oleaginous support of the Communists; or became, in power, moderate, as Körner did, as Mayor of Vienna.

The old Christian Social or Catholic (or Conservative) Party of the 1920s was, like the *Zentrum* in Germany, meantime, wound up in name, and the Peoples' Party founded (*Oesterreichische Volkspartei* – OVP). The first leaders of this party, Leopald Figl, Raoul Bumballa, Karl Gruber and Lois Weinberger, were men who had avoided collaboration with Dollfuss and Schuschnigg, as well as with Hitler.

In addition to the collaboration in the government, there was also, from the beginning, cooperation between trade union leaders. Thus survivors of pre-1934 unions met together at the Westbahnhof, while fighting between Germany and Russia was still going on in the East of the city. Here Communists, led by Gottlieb Fiala, seemed for a time to wish to work with Socialists and the Peoples' Party.

The Communist Party, it should be said, was in Austria, as

elsewhere, a child which benefited from conflict. Before Dollfuss suspended the constitutional democracy in 1933, the Communists, though influential, never managed to send a representative to parliament. But the period of autocratic conservatism, under Dollfuss and Schuschnigg, between 1934 and 1938, afforded the Communists an opportunity. Their membership rose from 3,000 to 16,000, including some who, like indeed Ernst Fischer, had once been left-wing Socialists but then had despaired of this divided and broken Party.

The establishment of the new Republic was a victory for the politicians of the years before 1938; and of before 1934. The expectations or ambitions of the men of the Austrian resistance, such as the valiant '05', vanished. These resistance groups were not as negligible as is sometimes supposed. They had not been supported by the Allies until 1944. Brave men and women had met, planned, were betrayed, suffered terrible tortures and died nobly in Austria as in other countries dominated by the Nazis. (The resistance lost 2,700 executed, 16,493 died in concentration camps, and 9,687 died in German jails.)[117] Perhaps 100,000 Austrians were in some way 'resisters' if people who worked in factories 'as slowly as possible' or who supplied drugs to those wishing to render themselves unfit for the army are included.[118] It was their actions which saved the treasures of the sacked museums of Europe from being blown up in the salt mine of Alt Aussee by August Eigruber, the Nazi *gauleiter* of Upper Austria.[119] The resistance, from March 1938 onwards, had been the engine which articulated a desire for an independent Austria. Those who died at Nazi hands did so with thoughts of a 'new, free Austria' in their minds.[120] The idea of post-war Austrian independence found its greatest strength in the concentration camps; and the camps inspired the resistance. But the men of the resistance had, mostly, inadequate experience of the guile needed for success in democratic politics. The only exception was Dr Karl Gruber, an able leader of the resistance among Austrians living in Germany proper, who became Foreign Minister in December 1945. Gruber liberated Innsbruck in 1945.

The Communists in Austria were, also, in a less good position than they seemed. True, many of them had conducted a brave war. About 1,400 Communists had been murdered by the Nazis, including no less than thirteen members of their Central Committee of 1938. The Communists had been for much of the war the largest secret opposition in Austria,[121] though they had been nearly destroyed by the Gestapo in 1944. On the other hand, the Party leaders of 1945 had spent most of the war in Moscow. Only in June 1944 did Fritz Honner, and a small group of Austrian Communists, including, as was usual with Communists of that day, survivors of the Spanish Civil War, fly into Yugoslavia from Russia, and there organise two 'freedom battalions'. In 1945, they were so out of touch that it was with the surprise that they discovered that the Austrian resistance had included many who would never have dreamed of voting for the Left.

Dr Renner devised in 1945 a scheme whereby the Communist cabinet ministers would each have two under-secretaries from the other parties as 'watchdogs'. This limited the opportunities even of the determined Honner and the eloquent Fischer. Thus, in the Ministry of the Interior, Honner was observed by Under-Secretaries Helmer and Bumballa, of the Socialist and the Peoples' Party respectively. This was a setback to communist hopes in no way made up for by disingenuous assertions, during the November elections, of their acceptance of national pride, of bourgeois values and even of Christian tradition, made by such unconvincing advocates as the ex-Catholic Communist, Dr Viktor Matejka (Director of Education in Vienna); or Laurenz Genner, (Under-Secretary of Agriculture). The Russians gave a large, prudent donation to help to restore the bombed Opera House; but they overestimated their appeal, and also underestimated both the shock which had been caused by the knowledge, borne from word of mouth, of Communist behaviour in the lost eastern territories of the old Habsburg empire; and by the Russian army's entry into Vienna.

The Red Army on their arrival in April had, it is important to recall, unleashed a wave of rape and looting which terrified a population which had been used to a highly cultivated life, in secure conditions, and which had been willing to greet the Russians as liberators. Among those who so suffered at the hands of drunken Russian soldiers was the sister-in-law of Oskar

Helmer, the provincial Socialist Under-Secretary at the Interior Ministry. She was repeatedly assaulted by Russian troops. Her husband, Helmer's brother, was murdered trying to help her. She herself died a terrible slow death after taking poison.[122] An SOE report alleged that 87,000 women were raped in Vienna in the first three weeks; that being the number of those who reported to clinics or doctors.[123]

There had been other outrages. In the summer of 1945, the Russians had been kidnapping people for work not only in their zone of Austria but in Russia itself. Near Graz, for example (before the Soviet withdrawal from what Churchill in the case of Germany called their 'tactical zone'), all able-bodied Austrians between sixteen and sixty were liable to be called up and sent to Russia, sometimes for months on end. Many households' goods – one knife, spoon, and chair were allowed – were also sent to Russia. Occasional passers-by in Vienna were rounded up for forced labour in Siberian camps. One Russian tried to buy the small boy of the Austrian on whom he was billetted in Vienna for 2,000 schillings.[124] A landowner in the Soviet zone, Prince Karl Croy, described how 'the Russians only took horses, carriages, fruit crops and vegetables [from him], but they say, everywhere else, the Russians have taken literally *everything* – making no discrimination between rich and poor – taking furniture, clothes, harvest, flour, vegetables, farm machinery, horses – in fact have devastated the country, as the Germans devastated Russia. As Austria is supposed to be a "liberated country" this is a little difficult to understand'.[125]

Russian troops, estimated confidently, if variously, in early 1946, at between 150,000 and 800,000, were still, in early 1946, preoccupied by stripping their zone in Vienna, and in the country, of everything moveable that might be useful. Eighty per cent of oilfield equipment, British observers reported in August 1946, had been removed before the other Allies came in.[126] The Russian troops now wanted to requisition 40,000 hectares – perhaps 50,000 – of good farmland in Lower Austria and Burgenland for themselves, including a substantial slice off which they were already living.[127] The justification for this, in the end, was that the estates had been German. The West denied that, because they had been confiscated after the *Anschluss*. The matter continued a subject of dispute. Russian soldiers also continued to steal whatever they could, particularly watches, even in the streets. A correspondent of the (left wing) *Tribune* in London described Russian troops' behaviour as monstrous: a comment complained about by several readers in letters as a 'slander on the Red Army'. George Orwell reflected that these readers implied that the facts ought not to be published even if true; on the assumption that 'Anglo-Russian relations are more likely to prosper if inconvenient facts are kept in the dark'.[128]

In the winter of 1945–46, Vienna was close to ruin. The city had, after all, been bombed, and fought over for eight days in April; and, if the results had been less severe than in Budapest, Berlin or Königsberg, much destruction had occurred; sewers and water mains were damaged, and even lorries for cleaning streets had been stolen by the retreating Germans. Much typhoid and dysentery had thus been caused. All but one of the five bridges across the Danube had been blown up.

Many Communists returned to Vienna in 1945 with no sense of disillusion about the Soviet Union. One of them, recalling those days, said, thirty years later: 'We were concerned that we were called upon to build an authentic form of Austrian democracy – Socialism – and that it was precisely the victory of the Red Army which made it possible for us to do so. Nothing could have been further from our thoughts than to imagine that the Soviet Union represented an oppressive policy. I had no doubt whatever about the merits of Socialist democracy as exemplified by the Soviet Union . . . In spite of my English background . . . I was, I'm afraid, a born believer. The brakes built into my system – if any – just didn't work'.[129] Other Communists, as elsewhere, were refugees from Nazism: copying the Nazis, there were even instances of former Nazis being offered identification papers certifying that the holder had been a long-term Communist – a technique which echoed what the Nazis had done for Socialists, for a bribe in 1938.[130]

The European Advisory Committee in London had in 1944 at

first thought in terms of an occupation of Austria shared only between Russia and Britain. The United States had assumed, in the beginning, that they would not have to provide occupation forces in any country of Southern Europe.[131] It had been the Soviet Ambassador to London, Gusev, who had argued for a United States zone. Roosevelt agreed in June 1944 but at first only to a zone of Vienna.[132] It was Winant in London who successfully pressed for an American zone of Austria of a size comparable to the British and Russian zones: a most fortunate action for Austria.[133] After the meeting of Yalta, on the suggestion of Britain, a French zone was accepted. Vienna was to be quadripartite, like Berlin. The Russians, however, delayed their final agreement to the dimensions of zones until Austria was liberated in May. (The Zones were: for the United States – Salzburg Province and Upper Austria; for the British – Carinthia and Styria; for the French, Tyrol and Vorarlberg; for the Russians, the Burgenland and Lower Austria.) Just after liberation was complete, Russia demanded (and obtained), from their then conciliatory allies, a lavish enlargement of her zone to include all Upper Austria north of the Danube, giving her a share in the management of that river as far as the German border and cutting the Americans off from access to Czechoslovakia through Austria. All the territory of Austria which had boundaries with Czechoslovakia and Hungary was indeed in Soviet hands. In addition, the Soviet zone, being agricultural, was well supplied with food.[134] (The Yugoslavs made a bid for a share in Allied control in Austria and asked for Carinthia:[135] they were for a time unenthusiastically supported by Russia.)[136]

An Allied Commission was then established with headquarters in Vienna, very much on the model of what obtained in Berlin. Power was vested in the hands of this Committee, headed by famous soldiers such as Marshal Tolbukhin (and later Marshal Konev), for the Russians; General McCreery, for Britain; General Béthouart, for France; and General Mark Clark, for the United States. Arrangements for the British, French and American zones for the capital were also made.[137] The famous if now damaged Inner City within the boulevards of the Ring, would be an international zone (in this, unlike the centre of Berlin). The

Americans in Vienna would use the airport at Tulln, the British and French that at Schwechat: both were within the Russian zone. The Western Allies' assumption of their responsibilities in Vienna was delayed until September 1. The British and Americans, responsible for 500,000 people and 375,000 in Vienna respectively, were seriously perturbed since their traditional 'feeding grounds', as Churchill put it, lay to the East, in the Russian zone. Stalin then promised to send food to Vienna. The consequent questions were, however, slow to be resolved.[138]

Yet all the same, despite the Russian presence and despite the near famine, Dr Renner had re-established the old democratic constitution. In November 1945, he had even felt strong enough to hold an election and to believe that it would be fair. Though the Russians ominously guarded places where meetings were held and listed those who attended,[139] the consequences was a substantial majority for the new Peoples' Party headed by Leopold Figl, who before the war had been director of the Christian Social Peasants' Union and had been in Dachau between 1938 and 1942.[140] The Socialists came second. Figl became Chancellor, and Renner, therefore, somewhat reluctantly, gave up that office to become the first President of the new nation, an honorary position. The Communists, 'stunned and disillusioned', gained only five per cent of the vote and so only four seats. (The political advisor to General Clark had predicted 'no party is expected to obtain a plurality and Communists will hold balance of power'.[141] But G. E. R. Gedye, the experienced correspondent of the *Daily Herald*, made an accurate estimate on August 1,[142] as did Martin Herz of the American military mission.)[143] Renner must have known that there would be no large 'intimidation vote'; and that the Austrians had determined to turn their back on their past mistakes and to vote bravely for a creative national solution.[144]

In the coalition formed by Figl, the Communists received a small number of lesser portfolios, none important. Figl soon became a popular hero; though in no sense an intellectual, and so somewhat looked down upon by some members of his cabinet, it had already been observed that he was capable of the useful art of drinking Russians under the table. He was also astute in his efforts to gain for his government the main keys of Austrian administration. He was tactful, determined, far-sighted and discreet. He accepted, for instance, some Russian ('Allied') objections to the first nominations for his Cabinet: even though those objected to included his best friend and intellectual adviser, Julius Raab (a minister with Renner), a powerful personality and serious thinker, who, a builder from St Polten, had committed the imprudence of accepting the Ministry of Trade under Dr Kurt Schuschnigg for a short time in 1938.[145]

Figl's Socialist deputy, Adolf Schaerf, was almost as significant as he. The Socialist Minister of the Interior, Oskar Helmer, the former Deputy Provincial Governor of Lower Austria, and under-secretary in the ministry of which he was now minister, was, however, the most important influence after Figl. When his nomination as a minister was published, the Soviet High Command sent an officer to apologise for the 'incident' affecting his brother and sister-in-law. The apology was not accepted. Tough, cheerful, and as determined as Figl was, that Austria should not be Communist, Helmer as the nominal head of the police with his conservative deputy Graf, set about resolving the problems caused by Communist appointments in the police set on foot by his Communist predecessor.

The main issue in Austrian politics, apart from food, was the question of South Tyrol. The Austrians claimed that the two Tyrols, one on the north side of the Alps, one on the south, like Savoy, had been a single political entity for a thousand years and had been 'stolen' by Italy at the Treaty of St Germain in 1919. Hitler had never demanded this territory from his ally Mussolini. All the same, much of the population of South Tyrol was German speaking. They had been bullied under Mussolini, many being expelled, the remainder forced to change their German names to Italian ones, as well as to speak Italian. All Austrian politicians, Communists and Peoples' Party, Socialists and even ex-Nazis, agreed with each another about this matter. It was more critical than other minor frontier questions which some tried to raise, such as Austria's claim to the enclave of Berchtesgarden; and it received more international attention than Yugoslavia's unconvincing if continued demand for the Klagenfurt basin on the grounds that several thousand Slovenes lived there.

Though in 1945 the Department of State favoured the cession of the South Tyrol to Austria, by 1946 they were divided on the subject.[146] By then the head of the Central European division (now James Riddleberger) and the Southern European division (Samuel Reber) in the Department disagreed precisely as the countries for which they were responsible disagreed. In Britain, Ernest Bevin, out of regard for old Socialist Austrian friends, also supported the Austrian cause. But, in the end, he was swayed by concern lest further losses by Italy might help the Communists there.*

A second large question in Austria was that of Soviet economic activity. The Russian stake in the economy derived from their policy over industry and farms which they claimed to be theirs because of German ownership in the past. But there were other German assets. These included property in German ownership before 1938; German firms founded after 1938, either from scratch or with an Austrian base; and, property seized by Germany, after 1938, often from Jewish Austrians. In all, there were 454 concerns, mostly in 1946 run by USIA: the initials stood not for 'United States Information Agency', as might be assumed, but for the Administration of Soviet Property in Austria. They were separately administered. They paid no tax. Hence their products were cheaper than those of Austrian firms. The shops run by USIA were of importance in the Austrian economy and so a source of fury. The Soviet concerns linked with the Danube river – boats, docks, hotels – had, also, some strategic significance. The chief Soviet consideration, however, derived from her exploitation of the oilfields. At that time, the Russians were short of oil.[148]. There was, in Austria as in Germany, the issue of 'denazification'. The new government was primarily concerned to prevent senior Nazis from holding major positions in business or in government. They hoped to ignore minor Nazis. Criminals, among whom the SS and SD

* See below, page 529.

were initially included, were to be punished; major criminals to be tried and executed. [149] Books, posters, pamphlets and other artefacts were to be confiscated too, if Nazi or 'anti-Allied', save for one copy for 'purposes of scientific studies'. [150]

The Communists and the Russians were not prepared to leave the matter thus. In early 1946, they were seeking to use 'denazification' as a means of eradicating everything directed against the 'Allies' – then a useful euphemism for the Soviet Union and Communism. [151]

By then, about 6,400 arrests of Nazis had been carried out by the British, 9,462 by the United States, and 6–7,000 by the French. No figure is available for Russian arrests but it could not have been less than 10,000. (Already, however, by that time the accusations that pre-war Nazis had been admitted into Communist ranks were 'too numerous to be dismissed as mere vilification'. [152]) Whatever the Russian figures were, these statistics were a small percentage of the ex-Nazis in Austria; 150,000 Austrians had served with the SS in the war; there had been 127,000 paying Nazi members in 1938; and a total of over 500,000 at the end of the war (8.5 per cent of the population[153]). With families, the numbers affected by 'denazification' must have been close to two million. Hence the authorities in Renner's day, as in Figl's, could not look on all former Nazis as below contempt. How should they judge Karajan, the great conductor, who had played so often before Goering and had succeeded Furtwängler as director of the Berlin Philharmonic Orchestra in 1934? Renner decided explicitly that the government had to stretch out a hand of friendship to all 'who, scientists, businessmen, and artists who rarely went in for politics at all, or workers who were threatened with unemployment or concentration camps' and had taken up adhesion to a Party 'which dominated the public opinion of the century, with so much zest and such astonishing initial success'. [154] The figures disturbed everyone. After all, no re-established or new Austrian political party could boast anything like this number of supporters.

The failure of the Communists to establish an ideological police in the capital was the most remarkable event of 1946. The previous April, the old city police and fire-fighting units had been withdrawn from Vienna, since they had become progressively both military and German. After the liberation of Vienna there was, for a time, therefore, no police at all. With broken water-pipes and no telephones, a general breakdown threatened. On Communist advice, the Russians chose a young Communist ex-Socialist, a pre-war member of the (Socialist) *Schutzbund*, Rudolf Hautmann, as police chief in the capital. He appointed as many Communists as he could to be police commissioners: seventeen out of twenty-six.[155] These events occurred the day before the installation of Renner's Cabinet, which included a Communist Minister of the Interior, Honner (and so the minister in charge of the police). Two weeks later, the 'Austrian Freedom Battalion', previously led by Honner, reached Vienna from Yugoslavia. It was chiefly composed of Communists, though it also included a heterogeneous group of deserters, escapers from concentration camps and scattered members of the resistance. It paraded in the Hofburgplatz on May 15. Honner integrated these men into the police, either as frontier police or in Vienna in a special sub-unit, with their own uniforms and personal weapons. Other Communists with no particular experience were soon also drawn into this force.

A few days later, Honner appointed Hautmann as Police President in Vienna. The Socialists opposed this: as Schaerf put it 'under the Communists, the police thought of themselves, in the first place, as the executive of the occupying power; in the second place, as that of the Communists; and only last, as Austrian'.[156] Helmer, then Under-Secretary, argued that the police chief should be a professional. He proposed the name of Ignaz Pamer, then aged seventy-eight, who had joined the police in 1892 and had retired in 1930. Honner accepted, thinking that Pamer would be as pliant as Stalin had thought Renner would be. One or two Communists – including Hautmann, Othmar Strohel and Heinrich Duermayer (ex-Socialist, ex-veteran of Spain and survivor of Mauthausen) – were made respectively head of the administrative division, Vice President and Director of the State Police. Another Communist, Moritz Margulies, became head of the police trade union. The new President of Police carried out numerous measures of centralisation, all supported by Honner in the expectation that his Party would be the beneficiary. Then Helmer succeeded him, after the unexpected election of November.

The first step of Helmer was to open a police academy in Vienna, in January 1946. It was directed by another survivor of the pre-1938 police, Heinrich Huettl. Helmer then set on foot a bitter struggle, the consequence of which would last many months, with Duermayer, the Communist director of the State police. Although the battle was not won for many months it was clear that, in Austria, the Communists were meeting Socialist enemies as tough and as self-confident as their predecessors met in Berlin in 1918–19, in the person of Gustav Noske. The danger of Duermayer can be seen from the fact that, without orders from his police superiors, he established a network of detention camps outside Vienna (*Anhalteläger*) not only for war criminals but for others whom he and his party considered undesirable. Neither this crisis in the police, nor the elections, represented the end of Communist attempts to capture power in Austria. But here were setbacks for them early in a campaign which they had expected to win.


Austria in 1946, like Germany, was beginning to recover from a nightmare which had lasted over thirty years since 1914. The First World War had been followed by poverty, hunger and civil violence: Nazi-, Fascist-, Socialist- and Communist-inspired gangs had terrorised the country before it was forcibly acquired by Hitler in 1938. A further intensity of brutality followed. Much of the Jewish community had been deported or murdered. Probably 372,000 Austrians had lost their lives violently since 1939: 5.6 per cent of the population. The country seemed itself to be like a victim of one of the concentration camps who miraculously had limped home: property and Empire no doubt gone, but life just saved. Too much had happened to Austria since the withdrawal of the Emperor Karl. Anyone in his fifties in 1946 had lived through the collapse of a world as well as of both the Empire and the Third Reich. All that remained was one new national desire, articulated by both Renner and Figl, and supported by many ex-Nazis and Socialists who had once dreamed of one German Reich of Goethe-loving musicians: independence from Germany – a desire not much felt anywhere before 1938 – as much as from Russia. The wild orator from Braunau-am-Inn, Adolf Hitler, had thus in the end prepared the way for the very thing which he least desired. The frontier at Passau which his father, a customs official, was concerned to mark in a way so offensive to him was thus re-established in the minds of Austrians, as much as it was on the ground.

The survivors of the age of intolerance, meantime, if they were fortunate enough to be free, kept to themselves. If they had helped to burn the books by 'Jewish and other politico-clerical writers' on top of that pile of wood in the Residenzplatz in Salzburg in April 1938 – or, indeed, had given a book to be burned – they tried to avoid the 'denazification' procedures. If they had been instrumental in sending the giant fir tree to Berlin to celebrate the 'festival of the German people' instead of May Day, 1939, on behalf of *'Gross Deutschland'*, they were silent. If they thought the figure, on the top of the Russian war memorial unveiled in September 1945, in what had once been Schwarzenbergplatz, was the 'Unknown Plunderer', they kept that also to themselves. At long last, perhaps, Austrians were beginning to see the wisdom of Adalbert Stifter's remarks in *Nachsommer* (Indian Summer): 'Distrust those hotspurs who promise to overwhelm you with immeasurable freedom and eternal gifts of gold . . .'

Dr Renner, in a speech in Salzburg, in November 1945, had described Austria as 'a rowboat in a stormy sea, the oarsmen being elephants [the occupiers] pulling in four directions'. The boat already knew where it was directed, despite the elephants. Those same occupiers, meantime, exhibited, through the four military policemen who patrolled the inner city of Vienna in a jeep, a higher level of collaboration than that seen in Berlin; though to Austrians who had to put up with the headquarters of the NKVD in the delightful spa of Baden-bei-Wien, once beloved by Beethoven and by the Kaiser Franz, that was not in itself an adequate reassurance.

# SEVENTEEN

# GARDENS OF THE WEST: FRANCE, ITALY AND SPAIN

The opportunity offered in 1946 to Communism in the capital of European culture, France, would have seemed intoxicating to a man less cautious than Stalin; one of the few major revolutionaries of the XXth, or any other, century never to visit Paris. The government there was now no longer presided over by General de Gaulle, a personality without parallel, who, suffering from the inconvenience of possessing no party, could not find the mechanism for giving France the leadership in peace which he had offered in the course of the late war. The unhappy position of France in 1946 was symbolised by the stopping of the clock in the Assembly to prolong the year 1945 artificially so as to enable the passage of the budget. It was doubtless the first time, even in the turbulent history of Europe, that a new year had begun at 8.30 pm on January 1. This was characteristic, so it seemed, of a country where standards of living were still lower than they had been during the German occupation: and whose political structure seemed at the mercy of a large, ebullient Communist party.

At the election, the previous October, for a Constituent Assembly whose chief purpose was to prepare the deeds of a new, fourth, Republic, the Communists had become the biggest single party: 151 seats, five million votes, 26 per cent of the votes cast. These achievements were approached by both the Socialists and a new party, the offspring of the non-Socialist and non-Communist *résistants*, the popular Republicans (*Mouvement*

*Républican Populaire*, MRP). Thus there was, as it were, a three-party system. The Communist victories had not generally been won by physical intimidation at a national level; even if, locally, there were instances where party members, during the previous eighteen months, had bullied their way to undeserved authority in town councils (and worse: in the region of Toulouse there were instances of Communists settling scores against old enemies, for example the Socialists). The achievements of the Red Army could be gloried in, since that body was separated from France by the American and British, as well as the French, armies in Germany.

The real victor of the elections, though, was the MRP, none of whose leaders (not even the ambitious leader of the Resistance, Georges Bidault) had anticipated so great a triumph; the loser, the Radical Socialists; and the most disappointed, the Socialists, who had expected to win outright.[1] Others curiously thought that parliamentary democracy had been the loser: but 20 millions voted when the electorate had constituted 24.68 million. An abstention of twenty per cent was surprising, particularly when women were voting in France for the first time. The modest setback to Communist hopes had probably been caused by gruesome stories of ill treatment of French prisoners of war from Russian administration:[2] and also because of rumours of disorders in the provinces committed by undisciplined Communist '*résistants*'. All the same: no Communist was downhearted. After all, in the municipal elections the previous May, the party had gained control of 1,413 councils, compared to 310 in 1935.[3]

A three-party government seemed in 1946 inevitable. In the cabinet crisis in January, the Communist Secretary-General, Maurice Thorez, had first offered to be provisional President and then, tactfully, or tactically, had agreed to be Vice-President to the ex-President of the National Assembly, a Socialist lawyer and resistance organiser, Félix Gouin: a man with moderate ambitions and a moderate sense of his own capacity: he once said that he would have preferred to be French ambassador in a South American country to being head of government. There was, however, a Communist Minister of Armaments, Charles

Tillon, though his authority was controlled, though not neutral-
ised as the Communist ministers had been in Vienna, by three
determined Socialist Under-Secretaries (Tillon, a brave resistance leader, had been previously Minister of Air where he had
been successful in appointing Communists throughout the French
aviation industry).

There were other Communist Ministers in key positions: for
example, the fanatical autodidact, Marcel Paul, at Industrial
Production, with many young Communist members in his private
cabinet; Ambroise Croizat, at Labour and Social Security; François Billoux, at Reconstruction and 'Urbanism'; and Laurent
Casanova, who, with Tillon, had commanded the 70,000 (mainly
Communist) *Francs Tireurs Populaires* (FTP), and was
now responsible for War Veterans and Victims of the War.
There were also some important communist Under-Secretaries: particularly Marius Palinaad, at Labour; and Auguste
Lecoeur, at Industrial Production, who, with Marcel Paul,
had established the Communists' control over the nationalised
coalfields.

It also seemed, in those days, as if the French Socialist Party,
like many of its equivalents in central Europe, had a majority of
members in favour of collaboration with Communism: de Gaulle
had compared the attitude of Socialists to Communists as being
like that of a rabbit before a snake: 'fascinated and paralysed'.[4]
Even in the police, there was a substantial Communist participation in some sections. De Gaulle's Minister of the Interior,
the Socialist, Adrien Tixier, had introduced Communists into
the new riot police, CRS (*Compagnies Républicaines de Sécurité*),
thus 'hoping to neutralise them'.[5] But his successor, also a
Socialist, Edouard Dépreux, had done nothing about that neu-
tralisation. The other Socialist ministers (André Philip, Finance;
Tanguy-Prigent, at Agriculture; Jules Moch, at Public Works;
Marcel-Edmond Naegelen, at Education; Marius Moutet,
at France Overseas) were as hostile to Communism as were
the five members of the MRP in the government (Georges
Bidault, at the Quai d'Orsay; Pierre-Henri Teitgen, at Justice;
Michelet, at Armed Forces; Jean Letourneau, Posts and Tele-
graphs; Robert Prigent, Population and Public Health; together

with a vice-premier, Francisque Gay). But the Socialist party members, many of them young and enthusiastic, mostly supported a close Communist alliance. Even the members of the MRP were young men and women who, interested in national 'renewal', 'repudiated liberal capitalism as much as they did totalitarian collectivism', condemned 'the dictatorship of money' as much as that of the state, 'rejected clericalism as a purely negative anti-Communism' and, indeed, though mostly Catholic, did include, even among deputies, an atheist and a practising Jew.[6] The Communists meantime looked on the idea of unity with the Socialists as a stepping-stone, as their German comrades did, on the way to power.

This tripartite government was supported by a mass Communist Party which consisted of men and women who had played a great part in the resistance against the Nazis between 1941 and 1944. Before that, between 1939 and 1941, it is true, the Communists had followed the extraordinary and discreditable policy of 'revolutionary defeatism': when, particularly between June 1940, the surrender of France, and June 1941, the date of the German attack on Russia, the Communists were in effect collaborators with the Nazis. That era was caused to be forgotten, and was omitted in all versions of the Party's revised history.[7] By 1945, the Party had marketed itself successfully as a patriotic institution, and one which seemed cleverly to fuse 1792, 1871, 1917 and 1944 in a continuing process; for the Communists, France was 'the country of the revolution',[8] even though Thorez had been insisting, as in a speech at the Mairie d'Ivry, a year before, that the Party was not making any revolutionary demands.[9]

Most of the young men and women who became Party members in 1942–45 had no personal memory of the contradictions of 1939–41. Their leaders had infiltrated the organising committees even of those sections of the resistance which they had not organised. Thus, the 'sub-committee of action', of the supreme Council of the Resistance (COMAC – Comité d'Action Militaire), was headed by three members, of whom two were Communists.[10] They had cleverly manipulated a *Front National* of the great and the good (François Mauriac, and Monseigneur

Chevrot, as well as Georges Bidault). They would have liked to create a larger monolithic 'front organisation', such as had been achieved in Yugoslavia and Bulgaria, which would have been strong enough to dominate not only the resistance but perhaps the nation. Thanks to the lack of organisation on the part of the Gaullists, they came close to achieving the first of these aims. Crypto-Communists, as usual in these circumstances, were helpful. De Gaulle's personal resourcefulness (for example, by creating the FFI – *Forces françaises de l'Intérieur* – and giving the command to his reliable ally, General Koenig) was probably the determining factor in preventing an outright Communist victory in the battle for control of the Resistance. [11] This achievement of de Gaulle's was accomplished by a deft domestic diplomacy which in return gave the Communists, for the first time, cabinet responsibility in de Gaulle's provisional cabinet in Algiers. The most balanced historian of the war in France, Robert Aron, was to say that 'De Gaulle and his colleagues prevented a Communist insurrection' in the winter of 1944–45. [12] It may be said that, had it not been for the success of the Allied landing in 1944, Russian armies might have reached France. One defector from Soviet intelligence stated that plans had been made for that eventuality. [13]

Maurice Thorez, the Secretary General of the Communists, controlled the Party with consummate ease. He was Moscow's favourite son, as well as being genuinely a *fils du peuple*, the title of his autobiography. A miner, son and grandson of miners, he had educated himself, teaching himself German in prison in order to read Goethe, not just Engels; Latin, as well as Russian. These interests led his admirers sometimes to forget his ruthlessness, his appetite for power, his capacity instantly to abandon, if necessary, comrades of a lifetime, and his intellectual subservience to Moscow. 'How can such a healthy man be a Communist?' Senator Vandenberg asked the *chef de protocole* at the Quai d'Orsay, Jacques Dumaine. [14] His good health was, perhaps, the consequence of office. Though condemned in 1939 to six years of prison by the military tribunal at Amiens for desertion, and deprived of French nationality in February 1940, he benefited from an amnesty in November 1944 and had returned with his family from six far from arduous years in Russia at the end of that month.

Thorez presided over a Party which, in many ways, sought to combine conformity with revolutionary aims; nationalism in the Jacobin sense, with internationalism. In the 1920s and 1930s, the Party was known for the 'alternative society' which, like the old German and Austrian Communist and Socialist parties, it had created; the organisation of every side of life, from social security to recreation. This was nevertheless claimed to be supremely French; and for the working class leaders whom the many party artists and intellectuals followed, as if they were gods, it was, in the words of the poet Aragon, *'une famille'*.[15] It seemed that, even if less disciplined, the working class party organisation was still expanding: the Communist leaders, Benoît Frachon, Louis Saillant and Ambroise Croizat, dominated the most important trade union organisation, the CGT (*Confédération Générale du Travail*), even though Léon Jouhaux remained Secretary-General, with its 5.4 million members. 'A party ought to be controlled by the millions', Thorez had said in 1944. Hence the creation, in the winter of 1944–45, of new organisations, such as the *Comités de défense et d'action paysanne* (CDAP), hence the efforts to re-write embarrassing history. The consequence was a party of 600,000 members in April 1945, and of about a million in early 1946.[16]

Thorez seemed realistic: even to de Gaulle. In early 1945, he had followed the orders of the General in dissolving the potentially destructive *gardes politiques*, the para-military formations of the Communist wing of the resistance. That annoyed many of the rank and file, as well as some of Thorez's more senior colleagues, such as André Marty and Charles Tillon. Had it been for this that they had braved Nazi tortures, while Thorez had lived in comfort in the Hotel Lux in Moscow? (He said that he would have preferred to have returned to have led the Resistance: but 'Moscow refused in order to avoid complications with the Allies'.)[17] Soon, some of these critics would be charged with '*blanquisme* and revolutionary romanticism':[18] Communists were 'revolutionaries not adventurers'. Nor did Thorez and other party leaders support nationalisation *à outrance*. For

Thorez wanted government, not a liberation committee, for his Party. The astute Director of de Gaulle's cabinet, Gaston Palewski, toyed with the idea that the great novelist, André Malraux, might be induced to lead a 'nationalist CP without allegiance to Russia'. The idea could not have worked,[19] since the party agreed with Thorez, who had, so de Gaulle said, 'a sense of what the State meant'. The British Ambassador, Duff Cooper, who was busy trying to establish a new, lasting alliance between his country and France,[20] believed that, if the Communists were to form the government of France, 'they would throw off entirely their subservience to Russia and become Frenchmen first': few others would have been so optimistic.[21] All other evidence suggests indeed that, slowly but surely, the Communists, supported inadequately no doubt, and clumsily, by the Soviet Union, were aiming at the establishment of a 'people's democracy' in France, with a pro-Soviet foreign policy and strict adhesion in domestic politics to the Marxism-Leninism in which they believed. The unquestioning support for 'democratic centralism' within the Party does not suggest that they would have been tolerant to those without it had they reached power. Duff Cooper might find Thorez 'charming' and Ambroise Croizat 'distinguished'.[22] Those qualities are ephemeral. More enduring were the discreet influences over Thorez: old Comintern hands such as the Pole Michel Feintuch, known as Jean Jérôme the financier of the party, and the *Izvestiia* correspondent in Paris, a certain Boris Mihailovich, who had been famous in the 1930s as 'Williams' in the United States and Latin America.[23]

The French Communists were assisted by a tide of opinion in which general sympathy for Russia for her war victories merged with the remains of the spirit of Vichy to assist the growth of a frame of mind essentially anti-American. Was it Vichy or was it Moscow which had so seductively sold the concept of 'American imperialism'? The idea was scarcely known in Europe before 1939. Like syphilis, tobacco and the potato, it is a product of Latin America. But neither nations nor individuals forgive their benefactors. The American liberation of France had been preceded by what seemed insults to Frenchmen. Both the British bombardment of Oran in 1940, and the American landing in North Africa in 1942, killed Frenchmen, and opened rifts slow to close. Cordell Hull and the Department of State were furious with de Gaulle when, in 1942, his Free French, without consultation, liberated Saint Pierre Miquelon from the control of Vichy. Other Frenchmen asked why Britain had not committed her air force in 1940 to save France; and why the United States had delayed two months after the liberation of Paris before recognising the government of General de Gaulle which, previously, was already exercising the functions of legal administration.[24]

The concept of the 'Anglo-Saxon' menace had thus been born. The idea that the Anglo-Saxons had a secret understanding, and that the French had to resist it, derives from French writers of the monarchist Right, such as Charles Maurras. De Gaulle was using the language by 1941, even in conversations with Russians.[25] The knowledge that Roosevelt disliked de Gaulle was no secret; it was one of the few subjects over which FDR and Cordell Hull always saw eye to eye; while de Gaulle had seen Roosevelt as 'that artist, that seducer', with whom it was extraordinarily difficult for ordinary humans to treat. Every time that either the United States or Britain questioned the wisdom of France's return to Indo-China, or Syria, or other parts of their old Empire, phobia about the 'Anglo-Saxons' revived. At a more banal level, French public opinion thought that the Americans everywhere 'are feeding vast quantities of oranges to German prisoners', that 'Americans treat us like children' and that 'Americans refuse to believe stories of Gestapo atrocities'.[26] The American Ambassador, Jefferson Caffery, a career diplomat of considerable experience in difficult countries (including Cuba), predicted wisely that here were grievances 'that hold the germ of prolonged discord'.[27] Most Frenchmen neglected, seemed contemptuous of, or ignorant of, the great efforts made by England, headed by Churchill, to secure for France a place in 'our general system of consultations' in 1944 and 1945, against both Stalin's and Roosevelt's wishes, though with American support afterwards.[28] ('Winston and Anthony . . . fought like tigers for France,' reported Hopkins, of the Yalta discussions).[29] The sentence deserves translation. Nor did the French take much notice of the commitment in 1946 of $550 million to cover (pipe-line) Lend Lease shipments to France; perhaps because of the condition that France in return should reduce trade barriers, restore trade to merchants and lessen governmental interference generally.[30] United States exports to France, $472 million in 1945, were, however, growing while anti-Americanism flourished.

Many Frenchmen, while not going so far as to be anti-American, hoped that they could create 'a Western bloc in order to avoid being crushed between the two giants of East and West', as Paul Reynaud, back from a concentration camp, put it to Duff Cooper.[31] Essentially, de Gaulle was demanding that also. He had told the French that they were 'between two great powers' in several speeches in November and December (for example, his broadcasts on November 17 and December 12, 1945). Where Britain fitted into this picture was obscure.

The occupation had naturally had 'a terrible crushing effect' on France. George Orwell gained 'the impression that hardly anyone cares about the freedom of the press'. He thought that French publishers were now 'commanded' by the Communist poet, Louis Aragon, and other writers sympathetic to Communism, not to publish 'undesirable' books, such as his own *Animal Farm* or Hemingway's *For Whom the Bell Tolls*: 'the Communists have no actual jurisdiction in the matter but it would be in their power e.g. to set fire to a publisher's building with the connivance of the police'.[32] Orwell had reason to be cynical at that time: the French publisher who had signed a contract to translate his *Animal Farm* had 'got cold feet' and said 'it is impossible for political reasons'.[33] This subservience to the Communists, following defeat and occupation, themselves following a generation of accepting British leadership, had left the proudest European nation in a mood for national revival. But for the moment sales of the Communist journals were thus greater than those of the Right; in October 1945, *L'Humanité* sold 456,000 a day, its equivalent in the evening 419,000; the conservative *Le Figaro* sold only 382,000 and *L'Aurore* 101,000.[34]

Many Frenchmen had conducted themselves with courage and ingenuity in the Resistance. They had withstood torture.

They had helped Jews and Allied airmen to escape deportation and capture. They had blown up German troop trains. Unexpected men had survived iniquities, just as people supposed to be strong had given way. On the wings of the courage of these men and women, the Fourth Republic, and ultimately the regeneration of France, was born.

The Communist opportunity in 1946 was in the short term made easier by the tactics of the hero of the late war, Charles de Gaulle. In the long run, de Gaulle calculated correctly. The gamble that he took in 1946 paid off. He was a man on whom fortune smiled. In the short run, he took a great risk. For, on January 20, 1946, at a special cabinet dramatically summoned in the Armour Room of the Ministry of Defence, hung with tapestries to cover the cracks in the wall, '*écœuré*' by the first meeting of the National Assembly, and for over a year disgusted by what he had seen of internal politics in Paris, he abandoned his post as head of government – Provisional President – which, under one form or another, he had enjoyed since the days of Algiers. (As early as December 1944, the *Chef de Cabinet* to de Gaulle, Gaston Palewski, had told Duff Cooper that the General was disgusted 'with the attitude of the French people, their lack of gratitude, their lack of courage and their inability to understand the realities of the situation. He frequently declared that he had done his work and that he was now prepared to throw in his hand'.)[35] '*Voici, un départ qui ne manque pas de grandeur,*' remarked Thorez as the General peremptorily left his own government.[36]

De Gaulle had acted thus since, in a 'republic of parties', he had no party and hence like Lloyd George in 1922, or Pitt in 1762, no base. He had no control over the course of events. It had become clear that the Communists and Socialists, for different motives, were taking steps to ensure that the office of President of France – and de Gaulle would accept no other – would be largely honorific, as it had been in the Third Republic.[37] The events of 1940 had proved, the General believed, that a country needed a single leader in time of trouble. De Gaulle had felt that, to head a government which, in the current economic position, would have to borrow money from America (negotiations for that loan had begun), would ruin his national reputation. He dreamt too of that presidential republic which would later be his political masterpiece. The British Ambassador commented that de Gaulle 'never seems to tire of slighting the Assembly'.[38] He believed that de Gaulle thought that the proposed new constitution would prove unworkable, that the activities of the parties in the Chamber 'were not compatible with effective government', and that matters would soon move towards a crisis involving disorder, at which point he expected to receive a call to unite and lead the anti-Marxists.[39] Yet, though his close supporters knew this, he himself did not speak. André Malraux, his Minister of Information for the last two months, spoke of the 'necessity of Caesarism', even apparently advocating political assassination as a means to it, according to one source of the British Embassy.[40]

This state of affairs had offered Maurice Thorez, the Communist Secretary General, a new chance of the presidency. But the French Socialists, inspired by their older leaders rather than their younger members, opposed the idea, though only after hesitation. They did not wish to serve in a coalition limited to themselves and the Communists. Perhaps, too, they were influenced by the explicit intervention of General Billotte, of the French General Staff, who apparently told the leaders of the MRP how hostile the army would be to a government directed by Communists.[41] Whoever influenced them, these democratic socialists took a decision in January 1946 which was a turning point in the history of France and of Europe. Had they decided otherwise, the country and continent might soon have become a new dependency of Stalin's empire.

De Gaulle, grand, patriotic, eloquent, independent and obstinate, had been to his Allied colleagues a difficult partner. He believed, his Foreign Minister Bidault had said, that 'Frenchmen always try to please the man to whom they are talking. He thinks they overdo it and he adopts a different attitude. He makes no effort to please'.[42] (He certainly made no effort to please Bidault, since he despised him and showed him that he did so.) He sought by such behaviour to open the way to the revival of France. Certainly, there had been occasions when

Americans had given way to de Gaulle because they did not wish another argument with him: 'for God's sake let's not have another row with de Gaulle' was their attitude.[43] De Gaulle himself complained to Harry Hopkins in 1945 thus: 'the United States has done an enormous number of very helpful things for us . . . [for example] equipped our troops . . . but you always seem to do it under pressure, and grudgingly . . . Perhaps you are right to do things for us only at the last minute and grudgingly: and you are right if France is herself incapable of rising again, of standing on her own feet eventually, of resuming her place in the great nations; but you are wrong if she does rise again . . . '[44] De Gaulle appears, however, to have been oblivious of the fact that the Department of State was characterised in its European policy by 'a single-minded determination to restore and accommodate France'.[45] De Gaulle had tried hard in 1945 to secure what Clemenceau had failed to achieve in 1919, a Rhineland independent of Germany.[46] He wished to secure the return of Syria and Lebanon to France, especially if Britain were to maintain her vast dominions in the Middle East.[47] He had been thwarted in both instances. He remained angry not to have been present on behalf of France at Yalta, Potsdam and Moscow, though, as has been seen,* that had been convenient in respect of his freedom of action in Germany. That was understandable since, at those conferences, decisions were taken – for example, the tactless decision over the future of Indo-China† – which affected France. Such intransigence as de Gaulle's was no doubt necessary if Frenchmen were ever to look again at such monuments as Les Invalides or Versailles with pride; but it made it hard to deal with de Gaulle, all the same. Now, in February 1946, the General expected to be called back to power very soon. His departure was 'pure tactics'.[48] '*Mais, voyons, avant huit jours en délégation, ils me demanderont de revenir et, cette fois-ci, je reviendrai à mes conditions*'. He looked on Félix Gouin's administration as '*même plus le gouvernement d'Assemblée; c'est le gouvernement de brasserie*'.[49]

* See above, page 486.
† See below, page 598.

The only possible rival of de Gaulle on the Right in 1946 was Georges Bidault, the leader of the MRP and both de Gaulle's and Gouin's Foreign Minister. A young teacher of history before the war, a Catholic who disliked the Catholic hierarchy, an advocate of discipline with a disorganised personal life, Bidault had been a brave leader of the non-Communist resistance, and had ended the war as presiding over the entire movement. Ambitious to be another de Gaulle, but despised by the object of his admiration, Bidault's new party was one of the wonders of those days. Yet the MRP had no more capacity in the long run than its leader. Even in the spring of 1946, Bidault would find himself scarcely master of his own house. He thus excluded any member of the MRP apart from himself from even discussing international affairs: his chief interest was to prevent a united Germany. But he soon found out that the Prime Minister had sent the veteran Socialist leader Léon Blum to Washington to discuss the idea of an American loan without consulting him.

The industrial leaders of France had been weakened by the war almost as much as those in East Europe had been. Many had collaborated with Vichy or with the Germans. It had been hard not to do so in modest ways, if one wanted to live; as even Communists had found, at the beginning. Even more damaging was the economic collapse due to the war: two thirds of the merchant fleet gone, an ageing population, the industrial output in 1945 at sixty per cent that of 1938, the harvest at a level of a half that of the 1930s, high inflation, the black market worse now than during the war. The country was ruined. Even the vintage of 1945 had been the worst in living memory: 24 million hectolitres when the country needed 32 million. France was even having to have recourse to Algerian wine.

The shootings of 1944–45 had also been enough to terrify a great many; probably 30,000 collaborators had been summarily shot in France in 1944 as opposed to the same number of Frenchmen shot by the Germans.[50] The latter figure was systematically increased by propaganda to heighten the moral horror of collaboration. The Communists thus spoke of '75,000 Communist martyrs' shot by the Germans or by Vichy; a figure which probably should read nearer 200.[51] Some 700 collaborators were executed after sentencing and 40,000 imprisoned – though not more than 1,500 served as many as seven years.[52] (The figures for the occupation mentioned exclude those killed in the maquis; those who died as a result of deportation; and those who died under German torture in prison.)

Finally, there was the French government's attitude to Russia. De Gaulle had sought an alliance with Stalin of the same character as that achieved by Britain, partly to increase his standing with the United States and Britain, partly to establish a direct relationship with Russia over the heads of his ministers. Stalin played on the idea and flattered de Gaulle. He passed on the news of the request to the United States.

Despite such realities, nearly all Frenchmen gave Russia the benefit of most doubts. Maurice Schumann, spokesman of Free France on the radio from London, once announced in *L'Aube* that Russia had no intention of bolshevising Europe: the Soviet armies had left free, totally or partially, he wrote, 'several' of the countries between Germany and Russia.[53] Léon Blum the socialist was perhaps more preoccupied by the threat of Russia than was Bidault the Christian democrat.

Stalin disliked what he knew of France. He spoke, for example, with bitterness to Churchill and Roosevelt against France both at Tehran and at Yalta. The French deserved no consideration. It would be wrong to leave them their former empire. De Gaulle might behave as if he were head of a great power; but he was representative of a symbolic, and not a real, France.[54] These reflections, of presumably the real Stalin, coincided with his flattery of de Gaulle, and with mendacious assurances that it had been the Soviet Union which had sought to bring in France to high-level discussions: Vyshinsky told de Gaulle in November 1943 that Stalin thought that no European question could be settled without France.[55] Two weeks later, Stalin was telling Churchill and Roosevelt that it 'would be not only unjust but dangerous to leave in French hands any important strategic point after the war.'[56]

The situation in France seemed dangerous to democrats. British officials wondered 'what we should do if the French went Communist at the next election'. Should Britain help, out of socialist solidarity, the Socialist Minister of Finance by increasing coal deliveries from the Ruhr (which Britain controlled)? Could the Americans be encouraged to show 'marked generosity' in their economic negotiations with France?* There were also alarming developments in the French Civil Service. Thus the communist Tillon might have, as Minister of Armaments, no armed men under his command; but, when he had been Minister of Air, he had appointed a Communist, Marcel Weil, to be director-general of Gnome-et-Rhône, and the French Air Ministry was full of Communists. Another of his appointments was Commandant Teulery as chief of the Security Services: he was already handing over documents to the Yugoslav military attaché, himself an ex-agent of the Comintern.[57] Communist *préfets* filled local government with their own men, and Communist ministers, in the gas and electricity supply industries, did the same.[58]

The French had also the problems of their Empire. Indo-China constituted one such.[59] North Africa was another. These troubles were less serious in 1946 than they might have been, since the Communists believed that they might soon control France.[60] Nor did they support an early abandonment of the French African Empire.

Two final factors in French politics in 1945 should not be forgotten: firstly, the eminence of the nuclear physicists. Dilapidated though French politics might have been in the 1930s, their science was nearly as remarkable as was their literature. Professors Joliot-Curie, Halban, and Kowarski might be as distrusted by Americans as they were by Churchill. They were not indeed told anything by their Allies. But they were able scientists, who told de Gaulle what they knew about nuclear physics: which was a good deal. After the war, this knowledge, as well as the belief by the scientists themselves that they possessed patents in certain of the early discoveries, made France a potential atomic power.[61]

The second factor was the personality of de Gaulle. Though

* These questions were raised at a meeting briefing the new British ambassador-designate to Russia on March 18; see below, page 734.

now out of power, he brooded: first at Marly, in the uncomfortable and neglected official residence of the old prime ministers – 'One might have believed oneself at Longwood', he once said. Then, at his own house at Colombey-les-Deux-Eglises (restored after the German sacking of it), where he gazed towards the valley of the Aube, towards the forest, and then towards the village. He speculated both how '*à mesure que l'âge m'envahit, la nature me devient plus proche*'; and how to prepare himself for the next grand role which he had chosen for himself.[62]

Conditions in Italy, newly freed from fascism, were at first sight not dissimilar to those in France: a large Communist Party, with a reputation earned in a long resistance; an upper class damaged by collaboration with fascists (in the Italian case, for twenty years); a constitutional position whose provisional nature was exploited by the parties of the Left; a coalition government which included all parties, and permitted the Communists to establish friendly civil servants within the fabric of the state. The proudest achievement of nineteenth-century liberalism, united Italy, appeared in a dangerously demoralised state. The economic condition of Italy was parlous. In 1945, industrial production was down 29 per cent from the level of 1938, agricultural production by no less than 63 per cent. Italy had also lost at least 8 per cent of her industrial capacity. As an ex-enemy, Italy had a low place on the list of countries receiving American aid.[63]

Appearances were deceptive. Italy is usually stronger than she seems. The Western Allies had permitted the government of Italy (first of Marshal Badoglio, then of Ivanoe Bonomi) to compensate, as it were, for the three terrible years, 1940–43, when Italy, under Mussolini, had been Germany's ally. The old bureaucracy, though tarnished, had not been divided by an experience such as that of Vichy. It successfully represented continuity. The chaos of 1945 – the factory committees under the guise of committees of liberation; the roving bands of 'red *squadristi*' in the provinces killing farmers, landlords and small business people – had come to an end.[64] Alcide de Gasperi, the

Christian Democrat from the Trentino who had served before 1919 in the Austrian Diet (with Iuliu Maniu), and who had formed his administration on November 30, 1945, was showing himself already one of the most skilful politicians. The Allied Control Commission was managed by the Americans and the British: a fact about which the Russians, present only on an 'advisory council', complained, and realistically used as a justification for their own domination of the ACCs in Bulgaria, Romania and Hungary.

The Western powers did not abuse the provisions of the Armistice agreement. By January 1945, the political section of the ACC had been abolished. The remaining sections had only advisory significance. The presence of British and American troops in Italy, not as occupying forces, but as a guarantee of order, counterbalanced the evident threats of the still armed Communist Party and of neighbouring Yugoslavia, and had, indeed, been the determining factor in preventing the extension of Tito's authority to Trieste. Trieste, chief seaport of Austria-Hungary before 1919, had only passed to Italy at the Treaty of Saint Germain. The Anglo-American stand over Trieste had been salutary and, together with economic assistance from America, had convinced Italians that the 'Anglo-Saxons' were likely to be better friends than the Russians.[65] They did not surrender to the anti-American phobias of France. On January 1, 1946, the Allied Military Government restored the administration of Northern Italy (and economic responsibilities) to the Italian government, as they had previously done in the South. Police and prefects appointed by the Committees of National Liberation were invited to enter the regular administrations. Those who refused, and most did, were replaced by career officials.[66] Further, though the Communists were well-organised, it was not clear, perhaps not to themselves, what Soviet policy was towards Italy. The Italian ambassador in Russia thought that they were 'groping', not knowing quite what line to follow, realising that they had to keep their friendships with the Yugoslavs, but divided by the issue of Trieste: to help Tito would harm the Italians, Italian Communists included.[67]

The first problem in Italy was the so-called 'institutional' question. That meant the future of the monarchy. By 1946, the old King, Victor Emmanuel, who had permitted the capture of power by Mussolini in 1922, had withdrawn. His son was acting as *Luogotenente*, 'lieutenant' of the realm. Provided the Allies agreed (which they probably would), it seemed that the question as to whether Italy would remain a monarchy would be put to a referendum in the course of 1946. In the meantime, both Socialists and Communists believed that the lieutenant should be replaced by a Council of (three) Regents, at least one of which might be expected to be favourable to the Communist Party: not perhaps a Communist himself but one more of those courteous, sensitive, infinitely patient, progressive professors who were convinced that, like it or not (and one might not), Communism represented the wave of the future. The other two might be the historian Croce and the Liberal leader Carlo Sforza: even though the latter was an object of special disdain for Churchill who looked on him as a 'foolish and crooked old man'.[68] There would also soon be, it was again presumed during 1946, a general election which would create a 'constituent assembly', whose task would not only be to prepare a new constitution but which both Communists and Socialists hoped, in the short term, would govern the country.[69] This would take the place of the *Consulta*, arbitrarily chosen by nomination, like the Czech parliament, which had first met in September 1945, and which it was hoped would work out the method of election to the assembly.

Two other problems related to reparations, and to the former Italian colonies. The first matter constituted the biggest dispute arising from Italy between the Russians and the West. The Allies had agreed at London in the Council of Foreign Ministers to allocate $100 million worth of Italian reparations to Russia. So it was difficult to exclude all questions of reparations for smaller allied countries which also made claims. The issue was thus unsettled. It was disturbing for de Gasperi. But he was well supported by the Americans who, as Truman had told Stalin at Potsdam, had no intention of lending money to Italy to pay reparations, especially considering the contributions of $500 million which they had already made for food.[70]

The second issue, the Italian colonies, now entailed Libya and the Dodecanese only. For Ethiopia was now once more 'free', and that ramshackle, if ancient, empire had absorbed the former Italian colony of Eritrea, even though it had been held by Italy since the 1890s. Why it should have been thought virtuous in London and Washington to prop up the Emperor Haile Selassie in 1945 and overthrow the Habsburgs in 1919 is a question which may be left to the historians of the future. At Potsdam, Stalin and Molotov had surprised Churchill and Truman by making a claim for Libya or anyway 'a large tract of the African shore'.[71] Molotov had returned to the subject at the Council of Foreign Ministers in London. Molotov's explanation was simple: the Soviet Union had a sea outlet in the North and, 'in view of its vast territory, should also have one in the South'.[72] Molotov believed that Russia should have bases in the Mediterranean, for their merchant fleet. In addition, the Russians curried favour with the Italians over their claim to hold onto the South Tyrol, just as they were hesitating over Trieste.

A more profound difficulty in Italy was that Fascism had been overthrown not by its own failure so much as by the war. In the twenty years since 1922, Fascism had implied an atrophy of political life. Thus there was a real danger of a new unfamiliar authoritarianism, Communism, taking its place. This was the more likely since the Communists were as well led as was the government, by Palmiro Togliatti, an immensely experienced Communist of middle class origins who had passed years in exile, mostly in Moscow, and whose native intelligence and cunning were matched by his wide reading. He had been for eighteen months the dominant personality in the Communist Party during the Civil War in Spain. Togliatti had been one of the directors of the Comintern. His skill at negotiating his own survival in Moscow during the purges was as legendary as his competence as an adviser to the Spanish Communists during their Civil War.[73] To Churchill he had seemed 'a small man with bright eyes' and 'a very animated manner and rather dissipated appearance.'[74] Stalin did not seem to appreciate him so much. He described him as 'a professor who could write a good article but did not know how to rally the people and head them to a goal.'[75] Togliatti had set out all the same in 1944, in the so-called *Svolta di Salerno*, to transform his Communist Party into 'a great national Party . . . we are no longer a sect of agitators . . . the goal which we shall propose to the Italian people . . . will be the creation of a democratic and progressive regime'.[76]

The latter could have meant as little in Italy as it did in Central Europe. In practice, it immediately heralded a dispute in the Italian Communist Party between those who believed that the country could be driven into revolution, such as had nearly occurred in 1920–22, and those who supported Togliatti's more conciliatory, open line. (Here there was a similarity with the state of affairs in France after Thorez's critique of the Resistance.) Togliatti had spent much of 1944 and 1945 warning the rank and file of his Party that revolution implied no 'simple period of violence'; it would take a long time, in the course of which a party such as theirs had to be made into a mass party, capable of winning democratic elections or, at least, of securing a 'hegemonic' position – to use the language of his brilliant and original predecessor, Antonio Gramsci, who had died in a Fascist prison in 1938. Despite this, there were many in 1946, particularly among the young, who thought that the so-called Committees of National Liberation should have taken over the institutions of the new Italian state. Italian Socialists, more pure in motive as they themselves supposed, thought that the Communist leaders were too much involved in *politica* and too dependent on the Russians: for money as well as for ideas.

The restoration of the Communists in Italy on such a sure foundation was due not to the Red Army but to the activities of a Soviet representative, the same Deputy Foreign Minister, Andrei Vyshinsky, who had later been so brutally successful in Romania. He had passed five months in Italy in 1944–45 and negotiated the exchange of diplomatic relations and the return of Togliatti.[77] What else he did remains a matter for speculation.[78] He certainly conducted himself cleverly with the British minister in the Mediterranean, Harold Macmillan.[79] Doubtless he made possible the establishment of solid financial links between the Communist Party of Italy and the international department of the Communist Party of the Soviet Union. No less important in

1946 was the fact that the main Socialist Party, which had split from the Communists in a spectacular fashion in 1920 at the famous conference of Livorno, was now their close ally. Its leader, Pietro Nenni, had passed the years of Fascism in intimate collaboration with the Communists. He too had served in Spain in the International Brigades, and felt no inhibition about serving under Communist direction. In December he had been at the Fifth Congress of the Communist Party. He had found that occasion '*magnifico, giovanile, ardente*'. He wondered '*come mantenere sul terreno socialista un partito al quale i comunisti hanno strappato la direzione della classe operaria?*'[80] Nenni underestimated in 1946 the strength of his own Party and overestimated that of the Communists. But his own dilemma was one which summed up the problem of Italy well.

The opportunity offered to the Communists was so obvious, however, that, in the course of 1946, Alcide de Gasperi was able to create, out of the rank and file of Fascists and the small middle class, a national party, the Christian Democrats. Fascists adopted his noble philosophy as quickly as they forgot their own ignoble past under Mussolini. The future lay with them, as it happened. But with Americans unenthusiastic about his government's request for a loan (of $940 million), that was far from evident in February 1946.

If one were to read the Russian or even the French press, opportunities also existed in Spain for international Communism. The international reputation of the authoritarian Conservative regime of General Franco was at bottom. General Franco had won the civil war which began ten years before in what was now, inaccurately, looked upon as 'a rehearsal' to the world war. He looked upon himself as the last 'sentinel' of the West, to quote from a speech of his in March 1946.* Stalin had told

* 'Yo soy el centinela que nunca se releva, el que recibe les telegramas ingratos y dicta las soluciones; el que vigila mientras los otros duermen' (speech by Franco to officers in the Military Museum, March 7, 1946): a direct echo of an article of José Antonio Primo de Rivera's in 1935 about Mussolini.

President Truman that the Russian agenda for the conference at Potsdam had included the overthrow of Franco.[81] No one in Europe was more unpopular than Franco, though no one was so little known. No one, according to his own lights, was more successful.

Columns of guerrilla forces made up of Spanish exiles – ex-Republicans of the civil war – who had fought in the French resistance against Germany were nevertheless said in the French press to have been advancing through the Pyrenees. In Spain itself, roads were described in those same newspapers to have been cut, police and army barracks to have been destroyed. General Franco's regime itself was believed to be divided; between fascists and monarchists.

In Paris, a coalition government in exile, headed by Francisco Giral, a liberal survivor from the Civil War (in the course of which he had been both Prime Minister and Foreign Minister), had been allowed to establish itself. The French Foreign Minister, Bidault, was known to favour a 'Liberal, Catholic, republican government' in Spain, with 'limited separatism' agreed for the Basques, though General de Gaulle, who knew little of the matter, had been convinced that a pro-monarchist army was the determining factor.[82] At the end of February 1946, the French government would suggest to its friends among other nations a break in diplomatic relations with Franco.[83] The French National Assembly had already called for the closure of the Franco-Spanish frontier. Another ex-Prime Minister of the Republic in the Civil War, the infinitely more formidable, infinitely fascinating, infinitely elusive, Dr Juan Negrín, was busy in England talking to prominent United States officials – and inviting French Socialists, such as Vincent Auriol, over to stay with him.[84] Negrín had been known to have favoured collaboration with Spanish Communists in the past. No one doubted that, were the regime of Hitler's old ally, Franco, to be overthrown, the Communists, founded in 1919 but transformed into a major force by the Civil War, would play a large part in that action and hence, no doubt, in the successor regime. The United States Ambassador to Madrid, Norman Armour, had been withdrawn; for the declaration of Potsdam had distanced the Allies from the regime of Franco. The 'question of Spain' had been raised at the first meeting of the United Nations.

The Spanish participation in the German attack on Russia had, of course, aroused Soviet hatred; and, not only in the Soviet Union. The Spanish Blue Division of volunteers, mostly Falangistas, but led by one of Franco's best generals, Agustín Múñoz Grandes, had been responsible for wrecking the Empress Catherine's palace at Tsarskoye Selo;[85] the Spaniards were believed to have quartered their horses in the ruins of the ballroom.* In consequence, the Russians had devoted considerable attention to 'the Spanish question'. In addition to their help to the Communist Party of Spain, newly and handsomely quartered in Paris in the Rue Kléber, there was, in the same city, a Soviet military mission directed by a certain Colonel Lapkin, and an active Soviet embassy. Prudent Spanish officials, such as the busy Ambassador in Washington, Juan Cárdenas, argued that these moves prefigured a Franco-Soviet attack, or, at least, some kind of Soviet attempt to stir up Spain. The British Chargé d'Affaires in Moscow, Frank Roberts, reported a conversation with ex-ambassador Maisky, now in the Soviet foreign ministry, in which the latter had said that 'a small civil war in Spain would do no harm . . . it was probably the only way of bringing about a really democratic régime'.[86] The closing of the Franco-Spanish frontier on February 27 as a result of a vote in the French Chamber of Deputies suggested that that would not be impossible to arrange.

Most of these rumours were fanciful. General Franco, a statesman who combined artfulness and ruthlessness, had remade his government in 1945 to include a prominent Christian Democrat intellectual, Alberto Martín Artajo. Franco's diplomacy in the course of the late war had been masterly. The explicitly 'Fascist' character to his government was now confined to five ministers out of thirteen. Generals or businessmen, often known as 'technicians', now dominated the administration. The previous summer, too, Franco had introduced a new consti-

---

* The Falange had been the Spanish equivalent of a Fascist party, founded in the 1930s.

tution, the *Fuero de los Españoles*, which, if neglected abroad, had had a good effect in Spain. The Fascist salute had ceased to be obligatory in greeting officials, in September, while a law enabling opinion to be tested by referendum had been promulgated in October. These moves caused a definite, if modest, change to public attitudes within Spain. Since the country had been living in penury, in economic conditions worse than they had been in the Civil War, and also suffering from the iron control of all political activity, any relaxation of any sort was greeted with enthusiasm. Franco still spoke of his government as concerned with a national 'revolution'; 'the more we seek to create, the more we are combated from abroad, the more our actions are discussed, the more we must affirm our revolution'. So he spoke on February 9 (the same day that Stalin spoke to the Supreme Soviet in Moscow) while opening a new electric railway line:[87] symbolic of the new achievements that, he believed, would transform his country. Lenin had in a famous remark said that Communism equals Soviet power plus electricity; Franco believed that electricity plus Francoism spelled national revival.

Though, at the end of the world war, there had been a real attempt by Spanish Communists from France at an invasion of Spain, through the Pyrenees, helped by some Soviet officers, it had not done well at all. 'General operations' by these columns, led by officers active in the Civil War, had begun in October 1944, but the aim – to provoke a 'general insurrection' – had failed. The operations became quickly known to the Ministry of War in Madrid and the resilient General Yagüe, one of the most able generals of the Civil War, destroyed most of the invaders in a short time.[88] Santiago Carrillo, the still youthful Communist ex-socialist youth leader, explained that his men had been received with enthusiasm and flowers in the Valle de Arán. (Carrillo was the leader of the Communists but the best-known spokesman was the famous 'Pasionaria', Dolores Ibarruri, actually Secretary General, at that time in Moscow: a great orator but no organiser. Carrillo had at this point never met Stalin, and Pasionaria only once.)[89]

In fact these *guerrilleros* had met as much indifference as hostility. In early 1946, another 'offensive' had begun. Its intention had been to establish contact with those many like-minded groups who had been in the hills since the Civil War. Then, after Dr Negrín had appealed for *'cinq petits kilomètres carrées'* on which to establish republican institutions, about 6,000 guerrillas entered Spain across the Pyrenees under the Communist General Enrique Lister, another veteran of the Civil War. The most important thrust was in the region of Luchon. But again the Spanish army, led by General Moscardó, police and civil guard, were too much for the invaders. According to the French police, all such operations had come to an end by the spring of 1946.[90]

If this activity exercised the Spanish army, it was never a serious threat. A more serious one to the regime of General Franco at the end of the world war was posed by numerous monarchist generals and their many high-placed sympathisers; among them, even the Foreign Minister, Alberto Martín Artajo.[91] The monarchists, among whom the air force General Kindelán and the Infante Alfonso de Orléans were prominent, and General Antonio Aranda, famed for his stand against the 'revolutionary horde' in 1936 in Oviedo, no less important, were in touch with surviving members of the Anarchist movement within Spain, but not, it appears, with the Communists.[92] The anarchists, including their most popular commander of the Civil War, Cipriano Mera, found themselves assisted, even though they were in prison.[93] The monarchist generals were restless for that change in the character of the regime for which they had been fighting in the Civil War. Others no doubt desired an opportunity for satisfying their ambition. Others still, including the Infante Alfonso, thought a constitutional monarchy the best way to approach Spain's problems in the future, and had organised a substantial party in support. Franco was, however, artful enough to outmanoeuvre these men and to manipulate the different strands in Spanish opinion cleverly.

Other European peoples, it is true, were concerned again with the level of political repression in Spain. The liberal conscience in England and France awoke for the first time since 1939 to the executions of Communists or Anarchists. But, though the Communists were far the best-organised of the opposition parties within Spain, their standing was generally low. Many, even on the Left, recalled their arrogance during the Civil War and their many fair-weather friends had ceased to give them the benefit of the doubt once it had been shown that they were not invincible.

EIGHTEEN

# THE 'NORTHERN TIER': GREECE, TURKEY AND IRAN

In 1946, Greece free from Turkey for over a hundred years, but not from her memory of Turkish rule, seemed a major British cause for anxiety. On the other hand, the Americans seemed then 'a somewhat distant third party, trying to smooth over, or rather gloss over, Anglo-Soviet differences'.[1] For it was Britain, the major external influence in the country since 1914, which, in the winter of 1945–46, had 40,000 troops in Greece. These had been denounced by Vyshinsky, in an attempt to shift attention from Iran,* at the first meeting of the Security Council in London, as 'a threat to the peace', under Article 39 of the Charter of the United Nations. The accusation infuriated Bevin.[2] He insisted, as was true, that the British were in Greece on the invitation of the government in Athens. The Greek representative in London supported him in this claim. Bevin also argued that the British presence was the main force for moderation in Greece. Vyshinsky laughed and went on to make numerous further complaints about the unrepresentative nature of the Greek government. Bevin replied that the British presence was important for the guaranteeing of a fair election, such as that then expected on March 31, and subsequently for the planned plebiscite on the future of the monarchy. Vyshinsky did not pretend to be convinced. But he relished debates of that kind, particularly where the lives of millions were at stake.

* See below, page 565.

These disputes concerned a country which like others in Europe seemed to be sinking into misery. Half a million people (out of seven million) were believed to have been killed or died in violence during the war, 70,000 executed by the occupying Germans, Italians and Bulgarians, many in reprisal for attacks on them. Communications had been as badly broken as those in Germany. The bad roads and railways had been wrecked. A quarter of the buildings had been ruined, two-thirds of the merchant marine lost, a third of the forests burned, the cultivated area cut by a quarter.[3] Inflation was rampant. There was a large black market. There was much brigandage. Agriculture was at a standstill, for the Germans and Italians, who had occupied the country from 1941 until 1944, had stolen the livestock, and everything moveable, during their withdrawal in the summer of the latter year.

As well as these unpromising circumstances, memories were bitter. Divisions of opinion were the only binding forces of the people. The monarchy had little appeal for Greeks who lived in the territory gained in the 1920s; the idea of a republic had none for those who had been born in the Greece of before the Balkan wars. Those Greeks who returned in the 1920s from Anatolia, blamed the monarchy for their expulsion from their old homes. The monarchy was the symbol of an old and, to many, bad order which had collaborated not only with Germany but with Greece's version of national Fascism under General Metaxas. The prospect was thus one of resumed civil war. Violence was already endemic, when the two sides discovered, in this temporary peace, the graves of people killed during the civil war. The Germans, the Press constantly reminded everyone, had conducted themselves in Greece with brutality. Those who had collaborated with them in order to carry on a semblance of normal life were now naturally condemned by all those others who had with courage challenged them.

The constitutional position was this: a constitution had been written in 1911. It had been set aside by the Republicans in 1927 but revived in 1935. A year later the King, himself restored, suspended illegally eight articles of the constitution of 1911 and gave dictatorial power to General Metaxas. In 1940, the Italians invaded, and were subsequently supplanted in 1941 by the Germans, who occupied the country. Metaxas died, the King and the royal family fled to Crete, then to England. Soon after, the King decreed the restoration of the constitution of 1911 and hence of the country's democratic rights. Still, the question of the nature of the regime remained open, since Republican politicians refused to accept the monarchy. The British set about a process of reconciliation, much as they had sought to do in Yugoslavia, both among exiles in Cairo and London, and among resistance groups in Greece.

The resistance had been, from the beginning, in 1942, divided: the major resistance group, ELAS (National Popular Liberation Army), which was the 'armed wing of EAM' (the National Liberation Front), was directed by the secret Greek Communist Party (KKE). Other groups such as EDES (the Greek Democratic National Union) of Napoleon Zervas, an ex-regular officer of the Greek army, had fought ELAS as early as in 1942 as fiercely as they did the Germans.* The situation resembled that in Yugoslavia between Mihailović and Tito. But ELAS was not wholly Communist, since it contained patriotic Greeks, including priests, who were progressive and anti-monarchist, not Marxist. The name ELAS had been chosen to echo Hellas, the usual name of the country which the English call 'Greece'. Some Communists, too, were idealists. Many of Zervas's men were brigands. All ELAS's men were republican, since they blamed the monarchy for the dictatorship of the late General Metaxas. Most of Zervas's followers, though not all, by the end of the war supported a revived monarchy, as did the British. The Communists lacked a leader of Tito's magnetism and Zervas was more worldly and probably tougher than Mihailović. There were probably not more than fifty Moscow-trained Communists in Greece but these occupied every position in KKE's politburo and dominated the policies of ELAS/EAM.[4]

As in Yugoslavia, confusion had exacerbated the violence. The British had secured one wartime armistice between Left

---

* It was thought unnecessary in this general narrative to give the Greek names of these parties and organisations.

and Right which had made possible one of the European resistance's best (if, as usual, controversial) achievements: the destruction, in 1942, of the viaduct at Gorgopotamos, on the railway between Athens and Salonika, by a combined group of ELAS and EDES, which delayed German reinforcements for three weeks to Rommel in North Africa. But even the arrival of gifted British agents from SOE (Brigadier Myers, Colonel Woodhouse) had not made matters clearer to begin with: partly because of disputes between the two often competing British intelligence services, SOE and SIS, as well as between the Foreign Office and the American OSS.[5] The SOE gave arms and golden sovereigns – 'the cavalry of Saint George', as such subsidies had been known in Greece a century and half before – to both ELAS and their opponents, backing ELAS to begin with and never quite cutting off relations with it, even when their Communist affiliations became evident to them, because of their courage and widespread backing: a policy which alarmed the Foreign Office in London.

The 'first round' of the Greek Civil War had lasted between October 1943 and February 1944. It was one fought between ELAS and an agglomeration of opponents – Republican, Monarchist, right wing. The Germans were hardly involved. But the subsequent pause, after the 'agreement of Plaka' designating the respective zones of ELAS and EDES seemed scarcely more than an interval in the internecine activities. The three-sided conflict had been marked by torture, mutilation, killing of hostages, and kidnapping.

Had it not been for an orthodox British military intervention, the Communists might at the end of 1944 have captured power in Athens. For, at that time, ELAS had 70,000 men under arms, many modern weapons captured from Italians, and already constituted an 'alternative state' in the mountains; taxes, laws, education, and social insurance were all managed by it. Peasants had believed ELAS's propaganda that, for instance, Russian aircraft would sow their fields from the air so that they would not need to work again (even if they were also tempted to believe that, if they supported the King, the British would divert the mayor's water mill stream to irrigate their crops).[6] But the

British troops held Athens, having landed 13,000 of their soldiers in Greece in October. This force was asked to sustain a Council of Regency, headed by the Archbishop Damaskinos of Athens. A veteran politican of the past, George Papandreou, earlier brought out of Greece to Cairo by the British, organised a national government, with EAM ministers. Churchill in October gained his understanding with Stalin whereby in theory Russia accepted a ninety per cent British role in Greece in exchange for a similar free hand in Romania and Bulgaria;*[7] and the Soviet officers who had gone to Greece in the summer of 1944 clearly had explicit instructions to accept, anyway until the end of the war in Europe, the British position. When the ministers who had been named by EAM refused to give up their weapons unless the monarchists did likewise, they were forced out of the government. In December 1944, ELAS made what seemed at the time and seems now to have been a serious bid for power, attacking police stations. The British held firm and kept Papandreou in power. They crushed the rising. The Americans held back, some disapproving and articulate, others sympathetic and silent. Churchill himself visited Athens, telling his General, General Scobie, in a famous communication, to conduct himself as if he were in command 'of a conquered city'.[8] Stalin confirmed to Churchill at Yalta that he 'had no intention of criticising British policy in Greece'.[9] Churchill was delighted. It seemed as if Soviet policy in Greece was showing itself constructive. The Yugoslav Communists had supported the EAM's rising to begin with but, probably on Moscow's insistence, afterwards withdrew.

Several further Greek governments, one liberal, the others strongly conservative, took shape under the auspices of the Archbishop. By the end of 1945 these controlled most of the country. The mountains remained mostly in the hands of ELAS. The revived Right was now also inspired by extremist groups bent on revenge for the deaths of their own supporters in the past. The ceasefire of 1944, based on an amnesty, a surrender of all weapons, and purges of collaborators with the Germans in both the civil and security services, was breaking down. At least

* See Appendix III.

one leader of ELAS hoped openly that 'the next round', 'Round Three' of the Civil War, would begin immediately.[10] Communist guerrillas were known to be receiving training in Yugoslavia, Bulgaria and Albania. Anti-Communist groups, such as the Khi, led by Colonel Grivas, seemed equally out of control, driving through the countryside attacking left-wing editors, killing printers, much like the Fascist gangs in Italy, before they captured power.

So it was not surprising that it should have been thought (probably wrongly) that the 2nd Plenum of the Greek Communist Party in February 1946 took a decision to resume Civil War.

Frontier problems, as usual in the Balkans, confused the situation further. Greece, Yugoslavia and Bulgaria each had claims to a share of Macedon that lay in each other's territory. There was, therefore, a Macedonian problem in each country and a source of unrest on each country's Macedonian frontier. The Greek Communists had strong support among the Macedonians of Greece. So they encouraged the idea of nationalism there when convenient.

British public opinion too was divided. The Left of the Labour party, and *The Times*, assumed that Churchill had gone mad when he had sent troops into Athens in 1944. Others believed that the colonial role assumed by Britain, in the interests of saving Greece from the Communists, was hated by a majority of the Greeks. Nevertheless, Bevin's policy in power remained the same as Churchill's. It seems certain that had these policies not been pursued ELAS would have triumphed; and that given the communist position within that body, that would have meant a communist Greece with all that that would have entailed for Greeks, for Britain and 'Europe'.

The Americans watched these developments with concern. They had not been a party to Churchill's percentages deal with Stalin. Indeed, they 'did not much like' it. An OSS mission had been in Greece in the war. It had seemed to some of their British colleagues to be actually 'crusading for EAM-ELAS': too close to the Communists for their own chief's comfort.[11] Those activities led to a quarrel between Churchill and Donovan, the

OSS director, much the worst that they had during the war. In 1945, the United States stood militarily aside but gave a credit of $20 million to Greece in July. Loy Henderson, whose Office of Near Eastern and African Affairs in the Department of State covered Greece, told Byrnes, on November 10, 1945, that 'present conditions in Greece' were 'so alarming' that the British military wanted America to share their responsibilities.[12] The *USS Providence* visited Athens in December.[13] A little earlier, Britain, nearly bankrupt herself, had suggested more United States financial help to Greece.[14] So, in January 1946, the United States offered more funds, and more advisers, on the condition that Greece adopted a programme of economic stabilisation. They also granted a credit of $25 million from the Export-Import Bank to support the economic programme of the governor of the Bank of Greece, Kyviakos Varvaressos.[15] (There was much contact between Greece and the United States, since, between 1890 and 1931, over 500,000 Greeks had gone to the United States as immigrants.)[16] In January 1946, the American Ambassador in Athens gave it as his considered opinion that American aid as well as British was needed if political chaos and famine were to be averted.[17]

In the winter of 1945–46, the British were not only the most influential foreign power but, in effect, the rulers of the country, appointing and dismissing prime ministers, dictating all departments of state from defence to employment, even arranging for the Secretary General of the British Trade Union Congress, Sir Walter Citrine (fresh from similar lectures in Germany), to suggest how to revive the Greek unions. Police, army and education were supervised by British experts. 'Is Greece a British colony?' asked the Communist paper *Rizospastis* in May 1945. The answer was not exactly 'yes', but Greece was all the same close to a British protectorate whose officials believed in monarchy. As for the Greek officials and police, many used the opportunity offered by the continuing presence of the British troops to wreak vengeance on the parties of the Left. That was not at all the intention of the new Prime Minister, the liberal Themistocles Sophoulis, but, at eighty-three years old, patronised by the British, despised by the Right as well as the Left, he was not in a good position to control his civil servants and army. Elections, as has been said, were planned for March 31, 1946. Official international observers had been appointed.

Among the Greek Communists, independence of Russia seemed their outstanding, and most appealing, characteristic. Stalin's neglect of their interests, at least until the spring of 1944, was matched by their poor contact with him. There were some accusations of financial contacts between Russia and the KKE in 1945–46 but as yet none of arms trading.[18] As in the 1920s and 1930s Communist declarations in Greece were more patriotic than revolutionary. In those years, as a result, they had won ten seats and 42,000 votes in the elections of 1926; and fifteen seats in 1936, with 73,000 votes. In the last year, they had held the balance between the two main parties. That had not availed them much since their general strike of August 1936 had led to the proclamation of General Metaxas's emergency powers, and to their temporary eclipse. Even so, here was a past as respectable as any in the country.

In the 1930s, the dominant influence in the Party had been the slow, decisive, solid, pro-Russian, Secretary-General Nikos Zakariades, a Greek returned from Asia Minor after the exchange of populations there, a well-educated teacher by profession. But Zakariades had been captured by the Nazis and spent the war as a prisoner in Dachau. The most powerful Communist during the war and immediately afterwards was instead a more flexible, and imaginative, ex-tobacco worker, George Siantos. Though he handed back authority to Zakariades in May 1945, Communist policy remained formally Siantos's: a propagandistical support of the idea of 'national unity'. All the same, there had grown up in the party or close to it, a school of revolutionary guerrilla leaders of whom 'Markos Vafiadis' was outstanding. These men were fighters, not theorists; Greek fighters above all, despite logistical help, arms and training from Tito's Yugoslavia. They were clever enough to deal with, and benefit from, the circumstances of the Civil War in which many of their followers, including some of those who fought and died, did not know their officers to be members of a Communist party. All seemed in the winter of 1945–46 to be waiting for the opportunity to rise again. They might be restrained by their leadership but not for long.[19]

In a report sent to Byrnes in January 1946, the Assistant Military Attaché of the United States, Captain W. H. McNeil (the future historian of *The Rise of the West*), predicted that, if elections in Greece did not produce a 'visible' government, the most likely eventuality there would be a dictatorship of the Left; 'which in turn would infallibly place Greece, like all the other Balkan countries, . . . under the predominating influence of Russia'. The able Ambassador of the United States, Lincoln MacVeagh, a friend of Roosevelt, agreed and commented: 'persons interested in world politics and the future maintenance of world peace might do well to consider what such an eventuality would mean, having regard to the critical position of this small country'.[20] American eyes were not then on Greece. But MacVeagh's well-written despatches helped to cause the Department of State to become so.

Sir Reginald Leeper, the Australian-born diplomatist with a strong political sense (as assistant to the director of wartime propaganda in London, Goebbels had presented him as his most dangerous opponent in London) who was British Ambassador in Athens, seemed to behave more like a colonial governor than an ordinary ambassador.[21] Believing that, for geographical and economic reasons, Greece could never be independent and, rejecting a permanent British occupation, he suggested that the country could join the British Commonwealth as a dominion.[22] His minister, Hector McNeil, Bevin's 'deputy', thought ordinary colonial status more appropriate. Bevin discounted both ideas. But he did think it was essential for Greece to remain 'with us politically'.[23] How could this be achieved? Did Britain have the money for it? The Chancellor of the Exchequer, Hugh Dalton, regarded Greece 'as a very poor investment for the British taxpayer'.* The consequences of this dilemma were not to be fully seen for a year. But the dilemma was there in 1946. Americans knew it, as well as the Greeks.

* A remark not made till April 18, 1947 but characteristic of Dalton in 1946.

A special problem affected the Republic of Turkey in these
post-war days. Turkey had been persuaded to declare war on
Germany in 1945, in order to gain a seat in the original United
Nations. Had Germany beaten Russia, however, she would
not have been unhappy. During the war, Turkey had seemed
'pro-Axis'. She had been Germany's main source of chromite.
German warships had been allowed by Turkey through the
Straits of Gallipoli into the Black Sea, and Allied warships had
been kept out, until the end of 1944. Russia looked on this
behaviour, understandably, as distinctly unfriendly. In 1943, the
Allies had made an effort to persuade the Turks to join them in
the war. Their failure had left all the Allies suspicious of one
another. Now Turkey represented the principal westerly gap in
the Soviet system of defence in depth along its borders. Until
Turkey was under Russian domination, and the Black Sea a
Soviet lake, the Russians would find themselves strategically
vulnerable in the South-West. But in the absence of any following

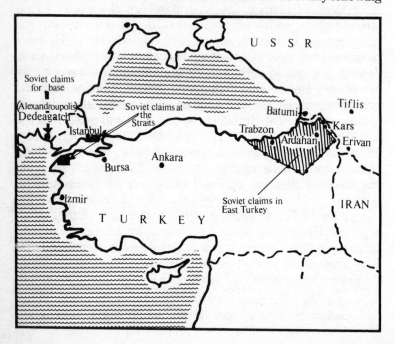

at all in Turkey – there was no Communist Party, to speak of – the Soviet Union would have to rely on potentially discontented elements, real or artificially created, such as Kurds or Armenians, the former being linked to the Persian Kurds (affected by Soviet moves there), the latter to be attracted by Soviet Armenia.[24]

Turkey was then a strong, if still parochial, state, created in 1923 on the ruins of the Ottoman Empire by the radical colonel, Mustapha Kemal, whose long-serving Prime Minister, Ismet Inonu (Ismet Pasha before the compulsory adoption of surnames as part of the programme of modernisation) had in 1946 been President for the eight years since Kemal's death. Inonu had steered the Turkish state cleverly past the shoals of the world war, maintained neutrality, and kept reasonable relations, and signed Treaties, with both Britain and Russia.[25] There was wisdom in this caution: the Ottoman Empire had fought twelve wars with Tsarist Russia over three centuries and generally had been the loser, of much territory. The new Turkey had not forgotten the past. Existing territorial disputes forbade it. But they had not sought officiously to revive it. All the same, it was scarcely a surprise when, on March 19, 1945, the Soviet Union had announced that they would denounce the Turco-Soviet Treaty of Friendship of 1925 (which would have had to have been renewed, since it was a ten-year Treaty, in November 1945, as it had been in 1935). Later, in June 1945, Molotov revived an old demand for a revision of the Treaty of Montreux (whereby control of the Dardanelles passed to the Turks, who were to be permitted to fortify them if they needed to)* to allow for a Soviet base at the Dardanelles; and also for certain

---

* The Montreux Convention of 1936 brought to an end the international control of the straits established in the Treaty of Lausanne (1925). By the Convention, effective control passed to Turkey; but (Article 19) belligerent warships, during a war in which Turkey was neutral, might pass the straits to fulfil obligations under the Covenant of the League of Nations or to help states which Turkey had to assist, under treaties concluded within the frame of the Covenant. If Turkey were herself at war, she could control the passage of warships as she liked (Article 20). Turkey could also exercise this control if she considered herself in imminent danger of war. In time of peace, all Black Sea nations could pass as they wished.

territorial concessions: namely, Kars and Ardahan in East Turkey, including 300,000 people in 6,500 square miles on the
borders of Georgia and Armenia. These two Soviet republics
each put in further claims: first, for 25,000 square miles of
north-east Turkey, with 1.25 million people; second, for Turkish
Armenia, claiming about the same size of area, with nearly
700,000 people.

Kars and Ardahan were classic places of rivalry between
Turks and Russians. The population was a mixture, as is the
entire Caucasus (and indeed the Balkans), but was primarily
Armenian, Kurdish, Greek or Kara-papak. Kars, a fortified town
of great age, had been captured by the Russians in 1828, 1856
and 1877, and had been transferred to Russia in 1878. The
Turks recaptured it in 1920, in their intervention against the
Soviet Republic of Armenia, and were permitted to hold it, along
with Ardahan, a similar but smaller city, by the Treaty of 1921.
The two large areas claimed by the Soviet republics had never
been Russian, but the one contained a medley of peoples,
including Kurds and Georgians, with national associates north
of the Russian border; and the other included still, despite the
Turkish massacres, a large number of Armenians.

These Soviet demands to expand territory, or to recover
their old losses, in the south, as well as in the west, were
accompanied by a menacing concentration of Russian and Bulgarian troops along the Bulgarian-Turkish frontier; by a campaign
against Turkey in the Russian press; by patriotic sermons from
the Soviet puppet Patriarch of the Armenian Church; and by
further mutterings by Molotov to the ambassador of Turkey in
Moscow to the effect that Turkey and Russia should make
a treaty of friendship. The American ambassador Laurence
Steinhardt, who had previously been in Moscow, believed that
Russia looked on Turkey in the same light as it did Poland and
the Balkans.[26] By the summer of 1945, the daily denunciations
by Russia of Turkey were so strong as to remind Steinhardt's
successor, Edwin Wilson, of Hitler's 'war of nerves' in the late
1930s.[27] The Turkish leaders thought that the Russians, 'like
Hitler', had become 'victory-drunk' and were seeking 'world
domination'.[28] A subsequent Russian demand followed for the

ancient Greek city of Trebizond and for a settlement, to their satisfaction, of the Kurdish problem. Russia had raised the revision of the Montreux Convention with Churchill in Moscow in October 1944. But most of these other demands were unexpected. Both Stalin and Beria were, of course, Georgians. Stalin, when Commissar of Nationalities in 1921, had himself negotiated the very Treaty with Turkey which he was now seeking to revise.[29] Beria, says Khrushchev, was, being a Georgian and knowledgeable about the Caucasus, able to influence Stalin's foreign policy. He used this advantage for 'all his worth'. At one of 'those interminable suppers' at Stalin's dacha, Beria started harping on how certain territories, now part of Turkey, had used to belong to Georgia and how the Soviet Union ought to demand their return. Khrushchev said (forgetting Kars and Ardahan) that it had been a long time since Georgia had had those lands; not since the mediaeval flourishing of the Bagratid dynasty before the Mongol invasion in the late XIVth century. But Beria 'kept bringing this subject up, teasing Stalin with it, goading him into doing something. He convinced Stalin that . . . Turkey had been weakened by the Second World War and would not be able to resist'.[30] Stalin anyway disliked the Turks.[31] He spoke of them, indeed, in his farewell talk with Sir Archie Clark Kerr, in January 1946, as 'cowards and intriguers'.[32]

The question of Turkey, therefore, was raised at Potsdam. Stalin said that the Russians needed a base at the Dardanelles. Churchill, generally ineffective at that conference, was tolerant of Russia's desire to have a major maritime presence. He recognised Russia was 'a giant with his nostrils pinched by the narrow exits from the Baltic and the Black Sea.'[33] But he could not agree to a Russian base near Constantinople even if he gave support to Stalin's wish to revise the Treaty of Montreux.[34] Stalin was then evasive. He could not understand why the Turks should be worried. They had 600,000 men under arms. The Russians had only 30,000 troops in Bulgaria, compared to 40,000 British troops in Greece. If the Turks desired friendship with Russia, as they seemed to, a rectification of the Eastern frontier to restore the line of 1914 would surely be desirable. Stalin followed up his requests in respect of the Dardanelles with an expression of interest in other Mediterranean properties: a trusteeship in one of Italy's colonies, say, a Mediterranean base, or a share in Tangier.[35]

The subject of the Straits, meantime, gave President Truman an opportunity at Potsdam to present his theory that wars might generally be prevented by ensuring free and unrestricted navigation of all enclosed, as well as international, waterways.[36] Churchill agreed. Stalin was in the end unenthusiastic, even rude, about that idea. It was one of the things which led to Truman's disillusionment with Stalin at Potsdam. Meantime, over a toast at a banquet, Stalin said to Churchill: 'If you find it impossible to give us a fortified position in the Marmora, could we not have a base at Dedéagach?' (That was Alexandroúpolis, on the Aegean coast of Greek Thrace.)[37] There was no further discussion between them on such dangerous details.

At the Conference of Foreign Ministers at London, Molotov returned to the Turkish question: why did Britain refuse to let Russia now have that access to the Straits which they had offered the Tsar (in the secret treaty of London in 1915)? Ernest Bevin's secretary, Pierson Dixon, decided that 'the main objective of Russia is access to a base in the Mediterranean'; it constituted 'a real Russian challenge'.[38]

These matters remained unresolved. In October 1945, Soviet demands for the plateau of Kars were repeated, while Soviet troops in both Bulgaria and Russia were said to have been increased. The Turks, knowing that their Treaty of non-aggression with Russia was due to come to an end in November, feared an attack. They asked for British help. Truman was apprised. Suddenly, the Russians withdrew their troop reinforcements. But, all the same, the Soviet Ambassador Vinogradov renewed his diplomatic demands for a revision of the Treaty of Montreux. Meantime, Soviet demands on, and activity within, Persia seemed to some specialists to be directed at Turkey. The State Department in November worked on a scheme for the revision of the Montreux Convention: a conciliatory scheme, whose interest lies in the fact that it was the United States not Britain who initiated it.[39]

Turkey's pronounced desire to maintain close relations with

Britain and the United States during these months acted as a motor for internal change towards representative government. In January 1946, the government admitted the desirability of a party of opposition and the Democratic Party, under Jelal Bayar, was therefore allowed to be formed. The Treaty of Montreux remained unchanged. Bevin, in February in the House of Commons, would fire a warning shot against Russia: 'it is said that we are drifting into war with Russia'. He did not want that. But 'I must really be frank and say that I do not want Turkey converted into a satellite state'.[40] A British intelligence report of March would describe how it was to be expected that Russia's plan would be to 'seek to support Turkey's neighbours, encourage her minorities and, in a continuing war of nerves, hope that the strain on the Turkish economy caused by the maintenance of large armed forces would eventually force her to agree to Russia's terms'.[41] Problems with Turkey would continue to overshadow the relations between Russia and the Mediterranean for the next forty years: with Turkey realising early that her liberty depended on her strength.

The most acute problem in international affairs in the winter of 1945–46 turned out to be neither Poland nor Germany, neither Manchuria nor Indo-China, but Persia.* Here, there were two problems: the first, that of Russian troops in the country; the second, that of autonomy 'in the most important Persian province', Azerbaijan, which borders on Russia. The two matters were permitted by Russia to merge one into another so that they became together a deeply disturbing affair.

The importance of these matters was enhanced by the fact that Persia produced more oil in 1945 than the rest of the Arab countries combined. (Persian oil amounted to 16.8 million tons,

* Persia was always so called by the West, following the ancient Greek usage. But 'Fars' or 'Persia' is really only one of the provinces of what the population calls Iran. In 1935 Reza Shah made Iran the official name of the country. Churchill directed the official use of 'Persia' in 1941. In 1949 the new Shah made both names equally correct. In this book, Persia and Iran are used as synonymous. 'Persia' was very frequent in the late 1940s.

Saudi-Arabian only 2.8 million.) The Anglo-Iranian Oil Company was one of the great multinational companies, with its own fleet, system of communication and even a regiment of highly-trained men. The refinery at Abadan was the largest in the world. The British colony at Abadan lived independently of the rest of the Persian economy, sustained by their own hospitals, guards, schools and clubs. The British Chiefs of Staff, who did not concern themselves much about Eastern Europe, regarded oil from the Middle East, and Persia in particular, as essential for both war and peace and were prepared to threaten resignation rather than abandon their position.[42] Ernest Bevin, a good nationalising Socialist of his epoch, disliked the idea that the government of which he was a member should own 51 per cent of the shares in the Anglo-Iranian Oil Company. But he was bound to support the management there if the Persian government should ever seek to nationalise it.[43]

Russia had in the past considered expansion in every direction, including southwards. The alleged will of Peter the Great had encouraged his successors to think carefully of Persia: 'Excite continual wars not only in Turkey but in Persia and, in the decadence of Persia, penetrate as far as the Persian Gulf . . .'[44] Peter had himself temporarily occupied the province of Gilan, along the South-West of the Caspian Sea. In the early XIXth century, Persia lost all her dependencies in the Caucasus to Russia: concessions of territory so large as to make the Treaty of Turkmanchai, which confirmed them in 1828, one of the decisive treaties of the world. Had it not occurred, Stalin and Gorki, Mikoyan and Beria, might all have been born Persian.

There was thereafter also steady pressure on Persia from the North-East. Tribes such as the Turkomans (dependent on Persian rulers for hundreds of years), and the cities of Samarkand, Bokhara, Tashkent and finally Merv – 'queen of cities' – were all captured by Russia in the mid-XIXth century. Britain made occasional, if ineffective, attempts to assist Persia against these inroads.

These attempts culminated in the Anglo-Russian entente of 1907 at the expense of Persia. By this unhappy instrument of

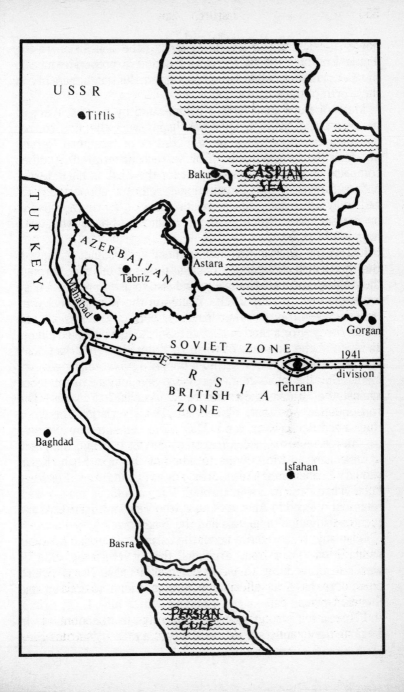

power politics (which led, however, to the conclusion of the Triple Entente) Russia recognised Britain's preponderance in the Persian Gulf, while Britain accepted Russian suzerainty in the North of the country.

Matters were soon further complicated by the discovery of oil on a large scale. Britain was happy with the Russian, or international, acceptance of her control of Southern Persia, in which the largest fields of oil were concentrated. Another complication was Russia's support for the Shah in his determination to resist the constitutional reforms supported half-heartedly by Britain, and more forcefully, if more improbably, by certain tribes, such as the nomadic Bakhtiári, who were friends of Britain.

During the Russian Revolution, these understandings lapsed. But the British continued to manage the great oilfields, through the Anglo-Iranian Oil Company, and also to use Persia as a base for operations to support the Whites in the Russian civil war. Russia looked, on the other hand, for both oil concessions and for territory. For a time in 1920 the Bolsheviks occupied almost as much of the province of Gilan as Peter the Great had done 200 years before. They set up a puppet revolutionary government. But the next year, partly to gain long-term influence against the British, they withdrew, cancelling all claims. The consequence was that, till the late 1930s, relations between Russia and Persia were good. They were cemented by effective commerce, as usual accompanied by Soviet bullying, mitigated by indecision in Moscow as to whether the new Shah, Reza, should be considered a reactionary, or a revolutionary. For Reza Pahlevi had risen to power through being an officer in a Cossack regiment offered to Ahmed Shah by the Tsar of Russia to assist in the subjugation of liberals and the Bakhtiári.

Germany, true to form, upset the balance of Persian relations with Russia. Their trade exceeded that of Russia by 1939. It was encouraged by an increasingly nationalist Persia which desired to have an alternative foreign friend to Britain and Russia. German espionage was active. After June 1941, Britain and Russia felt strong enough to stop this from continuing. In August, they jointly staged, as it were, a *coup d'état*, designed to force the Persians to expel the Germans. Insisting that they themselves had no long-term designs on Persian territory, they demanded an occupation of Persia for the duration of the war which would enable Russia to develop fisheries on the Caspian and Britain to use the oilfields with no hindrance, as well as to use the country as a route for their and American supplies to Russia. Germans were to be handed over to them or expelled. The Shah accepted under duress, delivered the peacock throne to his young son and abandoned the country in ignominy (he died in Johannesburg in 1944). He left behind a deep resentment against both Russia and Britain, the Communists and the West, which, especially when ordinary nationalism merged with Islamic fundamentalism, has never since been appeased.

Anglo-Russian control in Persia during the war was a real condominium; and, even outside the British and Russian 'zones', the occupying powers were all-powerful. Troops from both countries were posted in Tehran. The civil and military airports there were in 'Allied hands', as was passport control and immigration. When the three great powers chose Tehran for their conference in September 1943, the Persian Prime Minister heard of the plan by accident. The United States Persian Gulf Command carried 7.9 long tons of imports into Russia between 1941 and 1945. Most of this were Lend Lease goods, including 180,000 trucks and nearly 5,000 aircraft.[45]

The Russians managed their 'zone as if it were a colony.' They also assisted the revival of the Persian Communist Party (Tudeh) in 1942, an encouragement without ambiguity since this group of experienced revolutionaries for the moment eschewed all advocacy of revolutionary aims. The Tudeh spoke of liberty, constitutions and democracy, as well as of Russian friendship. Some of these new Communists were immigrants from the Russian Caucasus, some were young intellectuals, some were veterans of the old wild days of the early 1920s. They had a following in both the Southern British-dominated 'zone' and the Northern, Russian one. They supported Persian nationalism against the British as they did later against the Americans; and they backed by rhetoric the Kurdish, Armenian, Assyrian, and Turkish-speaking Azerbaijani minorities against the government in Tehran. They customarily denied that they had much contact with the Russians and had a habit of saying that they wished 'to introduce democratic principles in Iran, such as they are in the United States'; a formulation which irritated the English. They supported the Russians' claim for new concessions for oil in the regions bordering the Soviet Union (which the Persian parliament, the Majlis, in October 1944 bestirred themselves to refuse), and they attacked the pro-Western newspapers of the brilliant polemicist, Seyyid Zia.

In the Communist newspapers, it was obvious, in a hundred small ways, that Russia was contemplating after the war staying where they had been allowed to penetrate; the arrest of political refugees, the mysterious disappearance of prominent personages, the compulsory purchase of grain, the measures taken to encourage the departure of landholders and the ban on 'exports' of food to other parts of the country, all characterised Persian Azerbaijan in 1945. The British zone was no less imperial, though in its own way: paternal, not totalitarian.

The recovery of Persian self-esteem began with the 'concession crisis' of 1944. Sir Reader Bullard, the experienced British Ambassador, gave the Persian government a good deal of support. Bullard realistically saw the Russian demands as ones which, if conceded, would lead to their control of all Northern Persia.*[46] The recovery was continued by the introduction, at the end of the year, into the Persian parliament, of a law making it a punishable crime for any minister to enter negotiation over concessions to foreigners without parliamentary approval. The key role here was played by Dr Mohammed Mossadegh, an eloquent opponent of both British and Russian imperialism.

The young Shah began to travel throughout his country. The quarter of Persia which still lived in tribal nomadism gave him an appearance of backing. The Shi'ite clergy launched a general anti-foreign crusade which for the moment combined well with the Shah's demand for independence. The army, unexerted by the world war, recovered self-confidence. Thus 1945 found a

* See below, page 548.

Persian public opinion both alive and willing to demand that its government refuse to accept delay in the wartime undertaking by which both Russia and Britain agreed to withdraw their troops six months after the defeat of Germany and her associates. Russian troops in 1945 approached 75,000 (of which 30,000 were in Azerbaijan), compared with 5,000 British and 6,000 Americans.[47]

By now it seemed that it was Russia, not Britain, which was likely to outstay her welcome in Persia. During the war British propaganda had supported the idea of 'allied unity' uncritically: 'London conducted a policy of friendship towards Russia at almost any cost', recalled an American of Polish origin, George Lenczowski, at that time in the United States Embassy in Tehran.[48] For example, the British newspaper, the *Tehran Daily News*, was entrusted for a long time to a man with 'appeasing tendencies. The manner in which he edited the paper should have brought a citation from the Soviet embassy'.[49] In the summer of 1945 the British, however, were beginning to close down all their cultural missions, and cut their broadcasting, as well as the numbers of their soldiers in Persia. The Russians, to whom there was no sharp difference between war and peace, took no such steps.

On May 19, 1945, the Persian government formally asked both Russia and Britain to withdraw their troops within six months as they had agreed in 1941, now that the war against Germany was over. Britain began to withdraw. Some Russians were also withdrawn from Tehran, technically part of neither of the two occupied 'zones'. But Russia replaced these troops with police in uniforms. On the main issue, the Russians procrastinated, declaring that they did not have to withdraw until Japan was defeated. When that event in turn occurred, they produced from their archives the treaty which the Soviet government had signed with Persia in 1921. By that document, Russia was permitted to send troops to Persia if the country were to become a base for a third country's war against Russia. Russian diplomats began to suggest that that was a serious possibility. Further, was not their oilfield at Baku only a hundred miles from the Russian frontier? Did that proximity not offer every possibility to the skilful saboteur? After all, there were in Russia some who remembered how, at the Peace Conference at Paris in 1919, a Persian representative had wished to raise the question of the Russian right to the one-time Persian province in the Caucasus.

Before the Persians and their Western friends had decided how to face these impertinent demands, a new issue arose. This was that of Azerbaijan. The importance of the province was not simply that it was rich and produced a quarter of Persia's wheat, and supplied Tehran with about a third of its needs. It was populated by a quarter of the nation, including large minorities, established in strategically important places. In August 1945, the representatives of the Tudeh Party in that province staged a *coup d'état* in its capital, Tabriz, a healthy city, for many centuries the emporium of trade between Persia and the West (and supposed by Marco Polo to be the largest city in the world). Armed 'partisans' captured several government buildings and issued a manifesto, requesting home rule for the Azerbaijanis who they alleged were being deprived of their rights. The Persian Governor of the province, Bayat, an ex-Prime Minister, was powerless, since the Shah's troops in Tabriz were prevented from leaving their barracks by Soviet soldiers. At the same time, there were riots among army officers in the province of Khorasan, in the east of Persia. The Russians also inspired, or assisted, much new restlessness among the Kurds, whose zone of activity extended through the west of both the Soviet and British 'zones'. The Americans noticed with concern that the German army's expert on Azerbaijan, *Sturmbahnführer* Roman Gamotta, had been kidnapped in Vienna that summer: and was perhaps used thereafter by Russia.[50]

The crisis of August 1945 was managed successfully, since the Soviet Union called off their encouragement of the Azerbaijanis. It was a test apparently, no more. In Southern Kurdistan, British agents among the Kurds seem to have easily re-established control by old methods. The Shah's army restored order in Khorasan. All the same, the Russians for a time dismantled the customs and frontier ports between the Soviet Union and Azerbaijan and set up military posts on the southern borders of the province.[51]

In October 1945 a new test began. The British carried on with their withdrawal of troops. But the Russians, on the contrary, sent in a new division. The Tudeh Party in Azerbaijan was formally dismantled and the Communists who had been members of it took the name of the 'Democratic Party'. They revived their old agitation both for home rule and for an agreement that schools in 'the province' should be taught in Turkish, not Farsi, though it would have been a hard task to decide exactly what fraction of those who lived in Azerbaijan spoke Turkish at home. The new party sought explicitly to capture the support of all who had opposed Reza Shah's centralising and detribalising policies as well as of those who wanted a revolution or could be encouraged to make one. (The population in 1914 had been described as 'mostly Turkish-speaking Tartars'.) The next month, Soviet army officers began to distribute arms to the members of the Democratic Party in Tabriz. Several headquarters of *gendarmes* were seized, government officials kidnapped, landowners and police killed: a train of events familiar to those who knew what was happening in the Balkans.

The Soviet commander at Miandowab in western Azerbaijan summoned the local Kurdish chieftains and had them carried off to Baku. There, they were harangued by the president of the Soviet Republic of Soviet Azerbaijan and urged to abandon their own Kurdish independence movement and to join the 'Democrats'. They were sent back to Mahabad, with a printing press and two tons of paper.[52] The meetings of the Democratic Party, for a time, seemed little more than rowdy appeals for autonomy. When the Governor ordered the Persian army to ban them, however, the Russians again intervened to prevent the Shah's writ from being carried out. 1500 men sent as military reinforcements from Tehran were turned back at the city of Qazvin by Russian troops. Something close to a local rising now took place. Roads were closed. It seems that the Russians exercised their control through their commandants in each town. These were responsible to the Soviet consul who was, in turn, at the orders of the political commissar of Soviet Azerbaijan.[53] On November 23, the Central Committee of the Democratic Party announced that they were aiming at the 'complete autonomy' of Azerbaijan. In elections shortly held for an assembly in the province, there was a crude campaign of terror. Only 'Democrats' stood. The Communist paper *Khavar-i-No* went so far as to list the old officials to be killed after the full autonomy was achieved.

The new provincial assembly met at Tabriz on December 15. All 101 deputies were Democrats. They proclaimed 'the autonomous Republic of Azerbaijan'. A 'people's army', they said, would be formed for local activities, Turkish would be the language of the state, a new constitution would be written, the powers of the assembly would be transferred to a provincial presidium, and land would be handed out to those who worked on it. Banks would be nationalised. It was clear that Azerbaijan would soon be a police state. Immediately that invariable product of such enterprises, refugees, began to show themselves on the road to Tehran. The support of Moscow for Azerbaijan was made more obvious from the glowing terms in which the report of the formation of the new revolutionary government was made in *Pravda*.

The men who had taken the initiative in these radical events in Azerbaijan were all Communists. Several of them were experienced. Thus Salamollah Javid, 'Minister of the Interior', was a veteran who had had his blooding in the temporary capture of revolutionary power in Gilan in 1919–20. General Danishyan, who led the 'Azerbaijan Peoples' Army', spoke no Farsi, a little Turkish and could converse adequately only in Russian. Finally, the animator of the whole adventure and 'Prime Minister' was Ja'afar Pishevari, whose long career in the Communist movement now seemed about to be crowned with success. Pishevari, born in Azerbaijan in 1889, went to Baku in search of work when aged sixteen and stayed there until 1912, when he joined the Bolsheviks, for whom he travelled, both in Russia proper and in Central Asia. He returned to Persia in 1918 with the Bolshevik army under the name of Seijo Ja'afar Badka Bayl and as such exercised authority as 'Minister of the Interior' of the Soviet 'Republic of Gilan'. In 1920, he instigated the foundation of the Persian Communist Party at a meeting at Enzeli, a port in Gilan, on the Caspian Sea. He indeed represented that party at the early meetings of the Comintern and became a member of that body's executive. In September 1920, he was at Baku for the famous Congress of the Toilers of the East and afterwards carried out various missions either for the Comintern or for the Soviet government. In those days he called himself 'Sultan-Zade'. Allowing it to be assumed that he had been a victim of Stalin's purges in 1938, he secretly returned under a new name to Persia and was there to help to refound the Communist party as the Tudeh Party, in 1941. Now he seemed at last to have at least provincial power in his hands. It seemed likely that his friends in Moscow would insist on the integration of Azerbaijan in the Soviet Empire. Thus the recently formed 'Society of Friends of Soviet Azerbaijan' was plainly concerned to foster understanding with Soviet officials, not people, across the River Aras. Its leader and founder, Muhammed Beria (soon to be Azerbaijan's Minister of Labour) denied it in conversation with the new American Vice Consul at Tabriz, Robert Rossow, but added 'provided, of course, the Central Government meets our demands'. Rossow, who was only twenty-seven but had been in both the United States Army and the OSS, concluded, on January 9, 1946, that 'unless some sort of energetic action is soon taken Azerbaijan must be written off'.[54] (Rossow had been sent to replace Samuel Ebling, who had seemed too weak in face of the Russians and who himself had replaced a Russian specialist Bertel Kuniholm, who had been withdrawn in 1943 at the Soviet request.)

Furthermore, the radical behaviour of the Communists of Azerbaijan was being echoed by their colleagues in Northern Kurdistan. A new secret society of Kurdish nationalists had been penetrated by the Russians in 1944. On December 15, also, Communist Kurds met at Mahabad and proclaimed there the Kurdish Peoples' Republic. Qazi Mohammad, the chief of the Kurds of Mahabad, a theologian more than a Communist, became 'President' in January.[55] Five Kurdish chieftains were named 'Marshals' and accepted Soviet uniforms.[56] Mahabad soon established an 'alliance' with Azerbaijan.

These extraordinary actions did not occur without protests by the Americans and British, despite their pre-occupations elsewhere. Thus, on November 24, Britain and United States, on President Truman's suggestion, proposed to Moscow that they and the Russians should jointly withdraw their troops by January 1, 1946.[57] The Russians rejected the idea. They talked more and more of their rights under the until recently half-forgotten Treaty of 1921. The Chief of Staff of the Persian Army saw the British Ambassador and asked what would happen if the Russians stayed, 'We are not going to declare war on Russia for that,' was his somewhat discouraging reply. 'But you have guaranteed our independence?' 'That is up to London', answered Bullard.[58]

At the Conference of Foreign Ministers at Moscow in December, Ernest Bevin bluntly told Stalin that Russia's claim to be afraid of sabotage in Baku was absurd. Was Stalin thinking of absorbing Azerbaijan? Stalin answered that, of course, he was not, but he really had to safeguard Baku.[59] Byrnes, in turn, told Stalin that, unless the three outside powers withdrew their troops, Persia would place its complaint before the United Nations at its first meeting, and the United States would feel bound to support Persia. He hoped no action would be taken to cause such a difference between them on such an occasion. Stalin said 'We will do nothing to make you blush'.[60] ('This will not cause us to blush' was Bohlen's rendering of these words.)[61] Bevin suggested a three-power commission which would go to Persia. It would assist the Persians to set up provisional councils, under their constitution of 1921.[62] The Russians seemed quite interested.[63] The Shah said later that he had been in favour but the nationalists such as Dr Mossadegh were against, as Russia would be in the end. Nothing was decided. President Truman, meantime, began to take the case of Persia seriously. After all, he thought, the country had been an invaluable ally, without whose (admittedly reluctant) agreement America's military aid would not have reached Russia. He saw the new Persian ambassador, Hussein Ala, on November 29.[64] Ala laboured the parallel of German expansionism before 1939 effectively with Dean Acheson on December 20.[65]

In January, therefore, the Persians prepared to put their case to the United Nations. Most remarkably, they took this decision without consultation with Britain and the United States. Britain opposed the idea. They even used considerable efforts to prevent it: for it seemed inauspicious to have the first meeting of the new world assembly cluttered by the evidence of such dissension between the 'Big Three'. But all the same the discussion went ahead. Hussein Ala had said to Acheson: it was not just Persia whose sovereignty was at stake; it was the prestige of the new international body.[66] His colleague Sayid Hassan Tadizadeh, head of the Persian delegation to the United Nations in London, placed the item of Persia on the agenda of that body. The Russians, as expected, answered by complaining about the British still in Greece. Vyshinsky repeated the substance of the complaint, talked of the Treaty of 1921, denounced 'Fascist propaganda', and suggested some kind of understanding between the British and Russia over Persia and the Balkans. Bevin refused, and commented, 'I know when I displease the Soviet Government, because all the shop stewards who are Communists send me resolutions in exactly the same language' as that used by Vyshinsky.[67] An acrimonious debate continued till January 30 when the Security Council recommended direct discussions between Persia and Russia: a somewhat risky procedure, in the light of Stalin's bullying habits.

The Americans had kept the Persians informed about the course of events in Moscow. In these weeks, and over Persia, they quietly assumed the leadership of the West from which they have never retreated since. Thus it was to the United States' Ambassador in Tehran, Wallace Murray, a career diplomat, that the Persian Prime Minister was at his most candid. The Shah told Murray on New Year's Day 1946 that British interference in South Persia placed him in almost as difficult a position *vis-à-vis* opinion in his country as with Russia.[68] Murray, who had been previously in the Department of State as head of its Near Eastern division and had a Rooseveltian view of the British Empire, wondered whether the British 'were in fact prepared to make a tacit deal leaving the Soviets a free hand in the North while they consolidated their position in the South; an autonomous Azerbaijan under Russia; an autonomous

Khurdistan under Britain'. At that time, the British and American embassies in Tehran, as is often the case in moments of difficulty in the Middle East, were on poor terms: Wallace Murray, a longtime friend of Persia from a long distance, becoming incensed at Persia's apparent ingratitude to him; and the wise but somewhat pessimistic British Ambassador, Bullard, laughing at his colleague's swift changes of attitude.[69] But Murray's recent experience in the Department of State had enabled him to see the problem of Iran more vividly against the background of what was happening in the Balkans.[70]

At the end of January 1946, the situation seemed bleak for Persia. After some tortuous and apparently irresponsible intrigues in the *Majlis* (in which the Soviet Embassy was probably implicated), the Shah was forced to change his Prime Minister. The new incumbent, Ahmad Qavam Al-Saltana, elderly, enigmatic and heavy, was chosen because he had a reputation for success in negotiating with Russia. He owned tea-growing estates in the Soviet zone of the country. He was experienced, having been a minister first in 1910 and having first been Prime Minister in 1921–22. He gained his place since, after a tie vote in the assembly, the Speaker 'sodden with opium', according to a report of Sir Reader Bullard, cast a deciding vote for him. The Chief of Staff, a pro-British General, Hassan Arfa Ed Dowlah, married to an Englishwoman, was also exchanged for the one-time pro-German General Agherit. Qavam told Wallace Murray that he would 'tame' Azerbaijan by giving them a provincial council. At much the same time, Pishevari was telling Vice-Consul Rossow that 'his people would not give up national existence and would fight for it to the last man and with sticks and stones if necessary'. His 'government' would 'not retreat one step in the struggle for national existence'.[71] From the end of January, he began 'a new tactic' of 'inflammatory and extraordinary belligerent pronouncements', even announcing conscription and asking religious leaders to declare a holy war against Tehran. The motive seemed to be to give the Russians an excuse for staying in occupation 'to prevent bloodshed, disorder and the terrors of holy war'. Meantime, Vice-Consul Rossow went on, 'opposition is almost unanimous, and many of military age have gone into hiding' in order to avoid conscription. Although independence as such had not been proclaimed, the wearing of imperial insignia and display of the Shah's portrait was forbidden.[72]

Some of Pishevari's plans were evidently popular: for example, the redistribution of large estates, the establishment of pensions, provision for work on roads, and nationalisation of banks. But the economic consequences were as clearly catastrophic.

On February 19, 1946, Qavam, accompanied by the Shah's sister, Princess Ashraf, set off for Moscow. No one expected them to be able to negotiate their way out of the difficulties that faced Persia. The British Ambassador, Sir Reader Bullard, told his Foreign Secretary that the Persians were 'ideal Stalin-fodder', being 'untruthful backbiters, undisciplined, incapable of unity, without a plan'.[73] He had much evidence to support him. But as events turned out, and as will be seen, he was wrong. An explanation for this may lie in the fact that both he and his Consul in Tabriz, John Wall, thought that the average Iranian might be better off materially under Russian rule than under the Shah.[74] But, even if that were so, material well-being was not the only factor to be considered in Russia.

In the Near and Middle East* generally neither Russia nor the United States had developed a policy in what was perceived by both, with some degree of annoyance, as still a British sphere of influence. The United States believed that that would not last. The British Chiefs of Staff might have protested against a hasty abandonment of the Persian Gulf in late 1945 and had won their case against their government. But the idea might recur.[75] That would offer an opportunity to Russia. George Kennan wrote of Soviet designs in the region as already being constituted by 'the endless fluid pursuit of power' as betokened by 'Russian

* Until World War II Egypt and the Levant were properly called the Near East, while Persia and the Gulf were the Middle East. The blurring of these two concepts apparently derives from the fact that Britain established a 'Middle East' command in Cairo.

statesmanship, ingrained in its national tradition, as in the ideology of the Communists, who looked on all other advanced countries as Russia's ultimate enemies, and all backward nations as pawns in a struggle for power'.[76]

Another view, also of late 1945, in the Department of State, written by Loy Henderson, the gifted head of the Near Eastern division, was that Britain was endeavouring to use the Near Eastern area as a great dam which serves both to hold back the flow of Russia towards the south and 'to maintain an avenue of communications with India and other British possessions. Russia was determined to break down this dam' so that her 'power and influence can sweep unimpeded across Turkey and through the Dardanelles into the Mediterranean, and across Iran and through the Persian Gulf into the Indian Ocean'. Loy Henderson, who believed that the United States should play an active part in the future of the region, thought that some in Britain wanted to compromise 'in the hope that the Soviet Union may be satisfied by obtaining the control of certain territory now belonging to third powers'. But 'the Russians, once in possession of the new positions conceded to them . . . would undoubtedly begin preparations for further attacks upon such barriers . . . as might remain'.[77]

Both the British and the United States embassies in Tehran assumed that the Soviet design to secure an outlet on the Persian Gulf and to control Southern Persian oil were long-term Russian objectives.[78] Both had recently studied the record of Soviet discussions with Germany during the era of the Nazi-Soviet pact and had observed that even the Germans had been willing to see Russia seek that outlet (if more reluctant to allow Soviet ambitions in Turkey).[79] On this subject, the Department of State had a policy, if not a principle: Cordell Hull had written to Roosevelt in 1944 that 'it is to our interest that no great power be established in the Persian Gulf opposite the important American petroleum development in Saudi Arabia'.[80]

The British were worried about the possibilities of other Russian involvement in the Middle East at the end of the war. They were themselves dependent on conservative *pashas* and *effendis* while the Russians could easily make friends with the rising generation, in the swiftly growing towns of the region. British officials wondered whether they could move from empire to confederacy and asked themselves why precisely did Russia want a port in Libya. Was it to get Britain out of Egypt? Might the Russians try to bomb Britain out of Egypt with an atom bomb? (This was a question put in 1948.)[81] Or could the quest for uranium in the Congo really be the explanation? Might a 'Jewish Palestine', as seemed just possible as a result of Lord Balfour's declaration of 1917, turn out a Soviet satellite, and Stalin send in there so many 'indoctrinated Jews to turn it into a Communist state in a very short time?'[82]

Ernest Bevin had some dreams for a reconstructed Middle East under British leadership to take the place of India, after that sub-continent became independent, in the British crown. His colleague Hugh Dalton, Chancellor of the Exchequer, who was less enthusiastic, noted that the Foreign Secretary was attracted 'by the idea of building a road from Lagos to Kenya, with the new centre of a new post-Indian Empire in the Sudan'.[83] Could the Arab League be the basis for that? Nearly everyone, though not Attlee, the Prime Minister, agreed with Bevin's chief adviser, Sir Orme Sargent, that, if Britain were to abandon the Mediterranean, 'the Russians would take our place there'.[84] Busy with considerations as to what to do in Greece as well as in Egypt (the famous last Proconsul there, Lord Killearn, would leave Cairo on March 6 and the government was considering withdrawals of troops) not to speak of the future of Palestine (an Anglo-American Committee of Enquiry was at work), the British were as uneasy as they were over-stretched. But nearly everyone agreed with Frank Roberts, their Minister in Moscow, when he spoke (with echoes of Rákosi in his mind) of the Soviet Union looking at the Middle East 'as an artichoke whose leaves are to be eaten one by one'.[85]

# NINETEEN

# THE EAST: CHINA, JAPAN, KOREA AND INDO-CHINA

In the Far East, four countries gave grounds for disquiet to the Western allies and opportunites to the Russians. These were China, Japan, Korea and Indo-China. The third and fourth would bedevil Americans in the 1950s and 1960s. The second, Japan, had a turbulent effect on both the United States and the rest of the developed world in the 1970s and 1980s. The hour of trial for the first, China, and for Chinese-American relations, was the 1940s. The Soviet Union had before 1939 already established one satellite state in the East in the shape of Outer Mongolia, while the tiny 'state' of Tuva had 'applied for entry into the Soviet Union' in 1944. It had been accepted.[1]

The dropping of the two atom bombs on Japan led to the surrender of that country's troops throughout the Far East: in particular, of the 1.2 million Japanese troops and 1,750,000 civilians who still garrisoned almost all the most valuable places in China, from Manchuria and Peking in the North to Shanghai and Canton in the South. These men were the last representatives of the drive for Japanese power on the continent of Asia which had begun seventy-five years before and which had come close to establishing the so-called 'co-prosperity sphere' which might have given them world power. The atom bombs were followed by the entry of the Red Army into Manchuria. It had been agreed by Stalin in general terms at Moscow in November 1943, and in detail at Yalta, that, 'two or three months after' the defeat of Germany, Russian troops would 'share the burden' of the other Allies in the war in the East. Within a week, they had occupied most of the industrial province of Manchuria without a fight.

In return for this intervention, it had been agreed at Yalta (in a Secret Protocol, signed on February 11), that Russia would receive the Kurile Islands and Southern Sakhalin (lost by her to Japan in 1904); the commercial port of Dairen would be 'free' but 'safeguarded' for Soviet interests; and Port Arthur would be leased as a Soviet naval port (both being in the southern Liaotung peninsula); while various other Russian interests would be preserved for her in railways and ports, though on a more modest scale than previously insisted upon by Stalin: for example, the Manchurian railway would be governed by ten directors, five from China and five from Russia with a Chinese Nationalist president, who would have two votes, if necessary.[2] This arrangement had been suggested by Roosevelt to Stalin at Tehran: Stalin then said 'he had never thought of this idea and thought it a splendid one'.[3] The plan did form the rough basis of the post-war settlement, though the text of what was agreed about the East at Yalta was, characteristically, it is to be feared, not available to President Truman at Potsdam.[4] Possession of the Kuriles would give the Russians a series of offshore outposts across the sea of Okhotsk which would thereby become in effect a Soviet lake. South Sakhalin had oil and minerals. A hundred years before, Britain would have made similar demands. But, neither at Yalta nor at Potsdam, there was no suggestion that she aspired to more territory. The impending collapse of the British Empire was graphically indicated by her silence in respect of acquisitions in the East.[5] The restoration to Russia of the right, once possessed by the Tsar, to control the Chinese Eastern and South Manchurian railways, and the lease of Port Arthur as a base, seemed like survivals of imperialism to the Chinese. They were concessions which would probably make it impossible for a unified China to exercise full sovereignty in Manchuria and seemed, even to Roosevelt's admirers, such as Sumner Welles and Hopkins (as they did to Churchill), mistaken.[6]

American policy towards the East was more confused than that towards Europe. This was because of almost open disputes

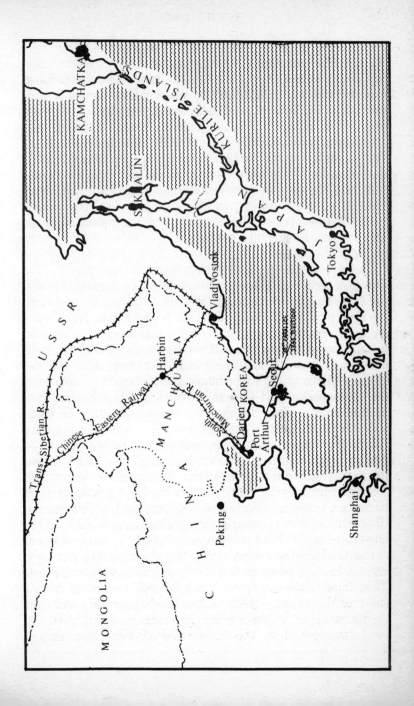

between the so-called 'Japan Crowd', composed of Under Secretary Grew and others in the Department of State who knew that country; and the 'China Crowd', headed by the Chinese experts, with whom Secretary Byrnes and Dean Acheson sympathised. The 'Japan Crowd' believed that Japanese militarism had been an unfortunate aberration in the history of the country. They were pre-eminent in policy-making till Roosevelt's death. The 'China Crowd' looked on Japanese aggression as deriving from fundamental tendencies in Japanese history. After Potsdam, and the retirement of Grew, they came into their own.[7] The consequences for the whole of the East were considerable since 'the China crowd' favoured, strongly, the pursuit of friendship with the Kuomintang in China.

The two enormous Chinese movements, the Kuomintang and the Communists, which sought in 1946 to benefit the one from the United States, the other from the Soviet Union, had several things in common. Both had fought the Japanese and had, on occasion, especially in 1937–38, collaborated against them. Both had large armies – the Communists claiming 475,000, the Peoples Militia of the Kuomintang 2.25 million.[8] Both Mao and the Communists, and Chiang Kai Shek and the Kuomintang, desired to rule a united China. No concessions could be made about that. The political entity first realised in the third century BC by the Napoleon of China, Shih Huang Ti, was not to be broken. Both claimed to respect the legacy of Dr Sun Yat Sen, the first president of modern China. Both talked of democracy, a verbal concession to a Western idea of whose appropriateness both were sceptical. ('Stalin had said both the Communists and Chiang . . . desired . . . to introduce democracy in China but in different ways'.)[9] Both sides believed really in force of arms, not persuasion. The United States indeed pinned their hopes for a stable East on the success of the Kuomintang as a government. Though both these powers had given their Chinese friends substantial assistance, the relations of both those allies with their clients were ambiguous. Both Communists and Kuomintang emphasised patriotism and the need for recovery after years of civil war and 'incidents'. The leaders of both came from the same social milieu. They had also tried to kill each other. On both sides, it is fair to say, there were elements of altruism and hope for the future of the country.

Yet the differences were great: first, the Kuomintang had been in power in much of China for twenty years or more; and the Chinese people knew many of these leaders to have shown themselves cynical, corrupt, cruel, lazy and incompetent. The 'Generalissimo' shut himself off from officials who gave unpalatable advice. 'Political tutelage', one of Dr Sun Yat Sen's ideas, had turned into an excuse for autocracy.

The Communists also had had their private enclave in the Western mountains for ten years, whence they had ruled a quarter of China in a way which promised patriotism, honesty and idealism to more than merely party members. The Communists looked, as Dean Acheson would put it later, to be a 'vast crusading movement which apparently has seemed to many Chinese to be wholly indigenous and national'.[10] That reputation was a trump card in the drama now to be played out.

For China, poor, backward, over-populous, divided and weary as it was, had a middle class, in the larger cities, which was anxious to articulate the higher ideals developed over the hundred years since the T'ai P'ing Rebellion had inaugurated an era of revolutionary change; and the Kuomintang had lost its old dynamism. In the battle against Japan, the population in the Communist areas had resisted, through what was in much of the country 'total guerrilla warfare aggressively waged by a totally mobilised population . . .', held together by what already amounted to 'an economic, political and social revolution'.[11]

The most acute matter in China in the winter of 1945–46 revolved around what seemed at first sight a different question: that was whether Japanese industries in the Chinese province of Manchuria should constitute war booty for Russia. Manchuria, it should be remembered, had been dominated by Japan since 1905. Since 1933, it had been a puppet state, 'Manchuoko', dependent on Japan. It had constituted the latter's industrial base for the invasion of China. It had scarcely been damaged in the war. It consistently produced agricultural surpluses, and was rich in raw materials as well as in developed industries. Manchuria had industry four times as large as that of China proper and a generating capacity three times as large. It housed seventy per cent of all the industry which Japan had in China.

The Soviet armies entered Manchuria on August 9, 1945. Japanese resistance was confined to the North. Southern Manchuria, which contained four-fifths of Manchurian industry, fell undamaged into Russian hands. The Soviet forces then began a systematic confiscation of food and other stockpiles and, in early September, set about the removal of machinery, just as they were doing or had done in Germany. They took the larger part of all functioning power-generating and transforming equipment, electric motors, experimental plants, hospitals and laboratories. They seized $3 billion worth of gold stocks and half a billion yuan from the banks. They acted with an extraordinary speed which showed that they might have wished to complete the business by December 3, the first date agreed for the withdrawal of their forces from China.[12] The Soviet Union then suggested joint development, with China, of what remained of Manchurian industry. The Chinese Communists kept quiet. The Nationalists opposed. The Russian definition of 'joint development' turned out to be to allow them 51 per cent of heavy industry, 49 per cent of light. The United States, not unreasonably, thought that these Japanese industries should have been available for reparations for the damage done to China, not go to Russia.[13]

There seemed to be other Russian threats. A British official remarked (to Ambassador Winant in London on February 10, 1946) that 'it was difficult to decide, on the basis of present information, whether the Russians intended to stay in Manchuria only until they had managed to get from that territory all that they wanted in the way of industrial equipment, or whether they intended to stay there permanently'.[14] The latter seemed improbable since the confiscation of food and stripping of industry, with no regard for the harmful effect on the Chinese population was leaving the province cold, idle and hungry. The Russians also permitted, and even encouraged, Chinese mobs to pillage in search of saleable objects or wood to burn in the cold Manchurian winter.

While the Nationalist Chinese complained about the Russians, the Communists criticised the policy whereby 50,000 American marines had recently landed in China: could it really be, as the United States insisted, that they were only there to assist in disarming and sending home the Japanese – from China proper, from Manchuria and from Formosa, the Chinese island which Japan had held as a dependency since 1895? (The Americans thought, even after Hiroshima and Nagasaki, that the Japanese might retain control of that island 'by their ability to tip the scales in the contest for power' if they were not sent quickly home.)[15] United States air transport also busied itself with ferrying Chiang's forces about China, while the marines controlled the important ports, to ensure that some forces of order were available. This work, of water-lift, relief and air-lift, was a thankless one of great magnitude, involving thousands of men, hundreds of ships and the consignment of vast quantities of food.

In 1945, the United States and the Russians had much the same views as each other about the chances of achieving unity in China. The United States had looked on China as a major ally, her favourite ally in many minds, as important as Britain, even as a great democratic ally of the future. Churchill told Roosevelt that he considered those views as utterly out of proportion. But Roosevelt, whose ancestors had been concerned with China, disagreed. FDR always attributed more importance to that country than many Americans. Even Stalin seemed to accept that peace in China depended on the Kuomintang, with whom he had had reasonable relations since 1927, as well as the Communists, to whom he had given sporadic help, throughout their struggle for survival in the 1930s. Perhaps, out of a coalition government between both, opportunities for Russia would arise, just as they had done in East Europe. China and Albania differed, it might seem in the 'nearby *dacha*' outside Moscow, only in size. Stalin had signed a treaty of friendship and alliance with Nationalist China as recently as August 14, 1945, as he had promised to do at Yalta.

Stalin was surely under no illusions as to the extent to which Russia could permanently control a Chinese Communist Party victorious in a civil war for the direction of the 500 million people in China. It would probably have been in the Russian interest to have China permanently divided, weak and with quarrelling military leaders.[16] 'Chip' Bohlen thought that Stalin 'did not want to see Mao successful', since the burden of aid to a Communist China would be great and since he foresaw the possibility of defection by Mao. That presumably explains much that was obscure at the time: for example, Russian assistance to the Chinese Nationalists in gaining control of the main Manchurian cities. Stalin had also, in conversation with Americans, called the Chinese comrades 'margarine Communists' in 1944,[17] and 'a bunch of fascists' in 1945.[18]

On January 23, 1946, Stalin had his last talk with Averell Harriman; he had, he insisted, 'poor contacts' with the Chinese Communists, ever since he had withdrawn his three representatives from Yenan.[19] Between April and August 1945, Stalin had agreed, perhaps even tried, to exclude the Chinese Communists from the post-war governments in China, even though, at the first Congress of the Chinese Communists for some years, in April of that year, Mao had supported the idea of a national coalition, in the style of East Europe.[20] At Potsdam, Stalin had declared Chiang's as the 'only possible government in China'.[21] Byrnes believed him.[22]

The Chinese Communists were then led by Mao Tse-Tung who, in 1946, was aged fifty-two. He was the son of a prosperous farmer in the province of Hunan. He had gone to a village school and, apparently against the wishes of his father, went on to a secondary school. He joined the Kuomintang when still very young, fought in the Republican army, studied, wrote poetry, and worked in the University Library at Peking. In 1921, he took part in the foundation of the Chinese Communist Party but, on Stalin's instructions, that Party continued to collaborate with the Kuomintang. Even after Chiang Kai Shek, with Soviet support, had surprised, and murdered, most of the Communists in Shanghai in 1926, the Communists sought an association with the Left of the Kuomintang. In late 1927, Mao, however, organised an armed peasant movement, in his own province of Hunan. Soon he established himself as the leader of a revolutionary group which was able to take over the direction of the

Chinese Communist movement; a coup which owed nothing to the support of Stalin. 'Moscow' did not like Mao's independence, nor his theoretical backing for the idea of revolts by peasants. For a time, Stalin openly supported Mao's rival, Li Li-San, an 'urbanist'. All the same, the Chinese Communists had to be accepted, since they existed. Li Li-San went in the end to Moscow, where he remained till 1945.

By the late 1930s, the Communists had organised the structure of their future state. They continued until after 1946 to stress the bourgeois and democratic nature of their revolution and to argue for a popular front of all – 'national bourgeoisie', peasants, workers and petty bourgeois – against Japan. But the idea of peasant guerrillas remained in the background of Mao's thought. Mao continued to believe that the Chinese revolution would spring out of the country, not from the town, and that the poor peasants would prove a natural revolutionary force. They would eventually 'encircle' the cities. Orthodox Communists, on the other hand – and there were many – continued to press the line which they believed was that of Moscow: that is, fomenting of strikes and revolts in the cities, as in Russia and Europe.

Mao's views seemed more those of a Nationalist, without many concessions to orthodox Marxism. Mao had never been out of China. He knew no foreign language. His dream of a peasant Utopia owed nothing to Europe.[23] The peasantry had not been allotted any permanent role by Marx. To identify the proletariat with it was scarcely a Marxist idea. Mao's two philosophical essays, 'On Practice', and 'On Contradiction', both written in 1937 in Yenan, were rough adaptations of Stalin and Lenin, without originality. Nevertheless, his will-power made him a formidable leader and opponent: 'one of the greatest, if not the very greatest manipulator of large masses of human beings in the XXth century,' wrote Leszek Kołakowski, though this quality would be seen only after he had gained power in all China.[24]

The policy of the United States to China was on the surface simple: on the basis of several generations of commerce and missionary activity, Americans desired to promote a democratic, reformist and united China. They believed that the Communists could be brought into this endeavour, not just to avoid civil war, nor just in order to unite the National and Communist armies under one commander to fight Japan, but because it was right. A few Americans (for example, General Wedemeyer), however, believed that China was not ready for a democratic form of government since, among other things, 95 per cent of her people were illiterate. They thought that some kind of continuing autocracy, preferably under Chiang, was the only hope.

The American Ambassador in 1945, General Patrick Hurley, Secretary for War under President Hoover, was a mercurial, vain, enthusiastic and reckless son of Oklahoma, of Irish blood, given to sudden Indian war whoops at unexpected moments. He had persuaded Mao Tse-Tung to meet Chiang Kai Shek in October and both of them to set up an interim council of forty people to run affairs till a new constitution could be devised. Chiang would have a veto, but a vote of three-fifths of the council would be able to override him. Nothing came of this idea since, in the field, the Communists were fighting to prevent the Nationalists from taking over the most important Japanese positions. Hurley soon resigned (on November 27), ranting that the State Department were sabotaging his work.[25] He had been Roosevelt's 'fact-finder' in Moscow and Tehran during the war. But he now affected to think that America was being 'sucked into a power bloc on the side of colonial imperialism' – a British or a Soviet one was unclear.

President Truman then decided to send the wartime Chief of Staff of the army, General Marshall, the American knight *sans peur et sans reproche*, whom he had determined that he wanted to succeed Byrnes as Secretary of State, to China to assist the 'unification of China by peaceful, democratic methods . . . as soon as possible'.[26] Byrnes did well over China at the Conference of Foreign Ministers at Moscow, though it was widely supposed that he had failed so far as that country was concerned: he secured a new Soviet agreement to withdraw their troops from Manchuria on February 1, 1946; and Stalin gave verbal support to the Nationalist government.

When Marshall arrived in China, the issues presented to him did not at first seem too difficult to resolve. The Kuomintang wanted a unification of Communist forces with the Nationalist army to precede the establishment of a coalition government; while the Communists were demanding that those things should be the other way round. The Kuomintang wanted the Communists to cease cutting their communications; the Communists wanted the Kuomintang to stop reinforcing their own forces in the North.[27] These seemed minor matters. Marshall believed that he would be able to impose unity on these presumably war-weary leaders. In January, a truce was indeed agreed. The Communists accepted that the government should move troops to Manchuria to re-establish Chinese sovereignty there. The government in turn requested the Russians to delay their own evacuation from Manchuria for a time, to preserve order. The economic situation also seemed to contain elements of hope. Production of food was close to pre-war levels, coal production had increased, the production of motor cars had increased too, pig iron capacity had gone up and, though in some sectors (cotton, shipping) there had been recent declines, those losses were more than compensated for by the recovery of Manchuria and of Formosa. Though inflation had caused retail prices to increase 2,000-fold between July 1937 and June 1945,[28] China's foreign exchange holdings, including gold reserves, were in 1945 the largest in their history.

General Marshall, therefore, wrote, in early February 1946, to Truman that 'affairs are progressing rather favourably'. The political consultative conference had worked out a 'fairly definite basis for a democratic coalition government', which would include a national assembly to meet in May. The 'nationalisation' of the armies seemed possible.[29] Marshall had also inspired a committee of three – himself; General Chou En-lai, who came from a mandarin family, for the Communists; and General Chang Chun, for the Kuomintang – and they too made some progress. Truman would tell Representative De Lacy on February 15, 1946, that 'if things continued going on favourably as they are going now, I believe we can have all our forces out of China before the year is out . . . with a unified China and a great friend in the Far East'.[30]

Yet, just as in Persia the issue of Azerbaijan blended with that of Soviet troops in the country as a whole, so in China the issue of Manchuria proved to be the one which turned a provincial problem into a national crisis. General Wedemeyer advised Chiang to consolidate his position in the South before he took on the North. Chiang feared a divided China and continued to send troops to Manchuria. The Russians, as has been indicated, had agreed at the Conference of Foreign Ministers in Moscow to withdraw troops from Manchuria by February 1. But they had not done so. With sporadic fighting in the controversial province, it looked as if real civil war would begin anew. Those with long memories (of whom there were many) recalled that the demand of the Communists for a place in the army had precipitated the break between the two groups in 1927.

The Chinese Communists then seemed to the United States a mystery. That that was so was partly the consequence of bad intelligence. But General Marshall found Mao in particular impenetrable: 'When he talked, I didn't get anything from it'.[31] Ambassador Hurley had implied in February 1945 that he agreed with Molotov that the Chinese Communists were 'not in fact Communists at all; that the Soviet government were giving no help to the Chinese Communists; and that Russia desired harmonious relations with the Chinese Nationalist government'.[32] Hurley, than whom nobody could have been more artless, appeared also to believe Mao's own remarks made, in April 1945, at the first Congress of the Chinese Communist Party for some years, that 'China cannot possibly have either a one-class dictatorship or a one-party government and therefore will not attempt it . . . there will exist a special form of state and political power . . . distinguished from the Russian system but perfectly . . . reasonable for us – namely, "the new democratic form" of state'.[33]

The juxtaposition of the adjective 'new' with the word 'democracy' is an enterprise always injurious to candour and freedom, and America should have had an ambassador experienced enough to know that. Hurley's predecessor had been better informed, though more gloomy: 'Pessimism of Ambassador Gauss' was the title of a whole chapter of the United States government's own history of her relations with China, published in 1949.

Numerous United States political officers were, however, far-sighted and knowledgeable: thus John Service had written, in April 1944, 'Chiang may be contributing to Russian dominance in Eastern Asia by internal and external policies which, if pursued in their present form, will render China too weak to serve as a possible counterweight to Russia.'[34] John Paton Davies had written: 'The Communists are in China to stay. And China's destiny is theirs'. Therefore, 'we must make a determined effort to capture politically the Chinese Communists rather than allow them to go by default wholly to the Russians'. But the United States was not prepared as yet to face this possibility. Marshall seemed to represent the last best hope. He knew China; he was patient; and he had a good heart. Later, the official treatment of both Davies and Service would prove that it is not only dictatorships which punish the bringers of bad news when they turn out to be correct.

Early 1946 was, however, a high point in United States post-war relations with China. Many Americans were confident that business and trade could easily be revived. Serious fighting had not yet begun between the two Chinese sides. The creation of Executive Headquarters, a tripartite agency, was an unprecedented achievement. Marshall had achieved a military cease-fire.

The reason why this achievement did not lead to peace was, partly, because the Nationalists had an intransigent self-confidence in their superior armaments; partly because an intelligent assessment was soon made by the Communists of Chiang's real weakness; and, partly no doubt, because of Russian determination to wage, wherever possible, 'a cold war of force and fraud against their former allies'.[35]

Japan was the one defeated country of the Second World War where, in 1945, the United States outmanoeuvred the Soviet Union. Immediately the President and his advisers knew that the atom bomb could be used, they realised that they did not need the Soviet Union to enter the war in the East in order to win it. Nor did they want it any more.[36] But by then it was too late to stop her. Russia had, in April, denounced her treaty with

Japan. As has been seen, her troops moved into Japanese-occupied Manchuria. Japan surrendered on August 14.

In these circumstances, Truman made up his mind that the American Supreme Commander in the Far East, General Douglas MacArthur, the most original of America's military men, an able and eloquent administrator as well as a veteran soldier, should be given full control after victory in Japan. Truman did not like MacArthur. Already, in July 1945, he was speaking of him as a 'primadonna' and comparing him adversely to the Lowells and Cabots who 'at least talked to themselves before they told God what to do'.[37] But, all the same, he kept him in his commmand, just as Roosevelt had, even though he had thought MacArthur 'one of the two most dangerous men in America'.[38] The truth was that, in 1945, MacArthur seemed irreplaceable. Truman wrote later that his experience at Potsdam over Germany, Bulgaria, Romania, Hungary and Poland 'was such that I decided to take no chances in a joint "set up" [in Japan] with the Russians'.[39]

After the dropping of the bombs, Truman and Attlee made an implicit alteration to Roosevelt's policy of unconditional surrender in respect of Japan. They let it be known that they would allow the Emperor Hirohito to remain head of the Japanese state; even if 'subject to the authority' of the American Supreme Commander. This concession to Japan, which might not have been made by Churchill, and would not have been by Stalin, could have been made earlier: Under Secretary of State Grew had suggested it on May 28.[40] Had it been so, the surrender might have been made before Potsdam; and before, and so without, the dropping of the atom bomb. The difficulty had been that, as many of the American policy-makers well knew, two-thirds of the United States public favoured the Emperor's execution or arrest.[41]

The Emperor, who took all the formal decisions leading to surrender, was worthy of the confidence shown in him. Had he had the mind of a Hitler, or even of his own Minister of War, Anami (who killed himself on August 15, 1945), matters might have been different. His actions, too, inspired the many responsible Japanese who had been in the shadows since the seizure of power by the 'fanatical military group' in 1931. They began soon to reappear in public.

Truman gave to General MacArthur effective authority from the moment of surrender. A United States declaration of September 6, 1945, stated, as if *ex cathedra*, that in Japan there would be no zones of occupation. Troops from other allies would formally be welcome: provided, however, that they served under MacArthur. That officer would be responsible for carrying out the agreed policy on the occupation, enshrined in SWNCC 150: disarmament, demilitarisation, punishment of war criminals, encouragement of democratic liberties and reparations.[42] It became immediately evident that the Japanese would be cooperative. Doubtless they considered themselves fortunate that the more violent suggestions for treating the Japanese after the war by some distinguished Americans looked like having been hyperbole (President Roosevelt had proposed enforced cross-breeding with South Sea islanders to eradicate the barbarism of Japanese: his son Elliott had thought of 'bombing until we have destroyed half the civilian population').[43]

The Russians took only a short time to complain. American troops began to land in Japan on August 28. As early as August 16, Stalin had requested a Soviet occupation of the northern part of the Japanese island of Hokkaido, in order to 'compensate the Russian people' for Japanese occupation of parts of Siberia between 1919 and 1922.[44] Presumably that was very much a 'first bid', the justification of which had been quite forgotten in the West. Then the Japanese surrender occurred on the battleship *USS Missouri* in Tokyo Bay on September 2. Molotov, calling on Secretary of State Byrnes in London a few weeks later, thought it dangerous 'merely to disarm the Japanese and send them home: they should be held as prisoners of war and made to work'.[45] The Russians for their part were beginning to send the half million or so Japanese whom they had captured in Manchuria to work in their vast archipelago of labour camps.

Molotov also wished to confirm at least the Russian occupation of Southern Sakhalin and the Kurile Islands. But Truman had told Stalin that the United States desired 'air base rights for land

and sea aircraft on one of the Kurile Islands, preferably in the central group, for military and commercial purposes'.[46] Stalin in reply reminded Truman of the agreement at Yalta on the subject. Byrnes, in language which, one of his biographers suggests, shows that he had not read the text of the relevant Secret Protocol, replied, in a conciliatory manner, that Truman knew that FDR had agreed to support this Soviet acquisition but it was to be 'in the peace settlement'.[47] Stalin then replied by sending troops to occupy both the Kuriles and Sakhalin. Asked at a press conference about this, Byrnes denied that the United States had made any commitment at Yalta about the Kuriles, but, all the same, the truth about the Protocol leaked. The American press divided in their attitudes, the *Chicago Tribune* denouncing Roosevelt as 'an even greater sucker than Churchill', the *New York Times* praising the agreement. This dispute led to attacks on Byrnes as well, because of his association with Yalta.[48] Subsequent discussion, and the ambiguity with which Byrnes answered, soon made this agreement one of the chief reasons for the growth of the 'black legend' of Yalta.

Molotov next proposed to Byrnes in London an Allied Control Council for Japan with strong powers. Russia would share all the responsibilities. The United States made no move. Molotov described the United States as trying to behave as the 'dictator of the world'.[49] He cited this intransigence when Byrnes complained of Soviet practices in East Europe. Stalin, who would have handled the surrender of Japan in a much more ruthless way, raised the question of Japan with Ambassador Harriman, at his private talk in Gagra on the Black Sea in October. He said that he had recalled his representative in Tokyo, General Kuzma Derevyanko, since he had been neither informed nor consulted by MacArthur (though the latter described Derevyanko as a man of 'considerable ability').[50] He was being treated as a 'piece of furniture'. Russia, he said, was being consulted as if it had been 'a satellite state', not an ally. The Japanese press was vilifying the Soviet Union. Changes in the Japanese government were being made without Stalin being consulted. Japanese banks had been closed without any information disclosed on the disposition of their assets. Yet Russia had maintained thirty to forty divisions on her Manchurian border throughout the war. She was surely entitled to better treatment.[51]

Harriman forebore to point out to Stalin that 'it was extremely difficult for any emissary', even from Washington, even President Truman himself, to 'get through to MacArthur'.[52] MacArthur had not been to the United States since 1937 and had twice refused to return home to receive the congratulations of the nation and to meet his new President for the first time;[53] and he had taken it upon himself to announce without reference to the Chiefs of Staff that Japan could only be occupied successfully by 200,000 troops.[54]

MacArthur, now SCAP (Supreme Commander for the Allied Powers), continued, indeed, to pursue a policy almost as independent of Washington as of Moscow. It is true that he followed a programme worked out in Washington before the Japanese surrender and that it had much in common with Roosevelt's New Deal. But MacArthur did not need further instructions. Now established in the Dai Ichi insurance company's building, opposite the Emperor's palace, he embarked on the creation of what was improbably called the 'Switzerland of the East'. He maintained the Japanese structure of government; kept the Emperor (relieved of most of his authority), and placed the country under a non-partisan government, led by an aged ex-diplomat, Baron Kijuro Shidehara. In a swift series of decrees, MacArthur restored civil liberties, freed political prisoners, dissolved the secret police, liberalised the educational curriculum, granted the franchise to all adults, encouraged the formation of trade unions, and abolished both the feudal land tenure and the compulsory adhesion to the Shinto religion. He imported food adequate to feed the half-destitute population. On January 1, 1946, the Emperor divested himself of the divinity which had been accredited to his ancestors since the Meiji Revolution of 1868.

MacArthur then stepped easily, as it were, into the place of the Shogun. He had garrisoned the West bank of the Rhine in 1918, he had known great American proconsuls, such as General Wood, and his father had been military governor of the Philippines. He had enemies, but he knew how to rule. He prepared for a general election to be held in April under a new constitution which he had commended to Japanese politicians in rough terms: while waiting for the Japanese confirmation, MacArthur's assistant, General Courtney Whitney, said that they would take a stroll in the garden to enjoy 'your atomic sunshine'.[55] A B29 roared overhead, completing the intimidation.

MacArthur also set on foot purges of 'active exponents' of aggressive nationalism from the civil service, universities and business, while an international military tribunal prepared for the trials of 'major war criminals'; separate British and Australian tribunals were to be set up in South-East Asia and the South Pacific respectively. He enfranchised women. He began the dismantlement of the *Zaibatsu* business monopolies. He embarked upon the demobilisation and disarmament of nearly seven million men, including two and a half million on the home islands. After all these things, and others, had been done, MacArthur did permit the formation of an inactive Council of Allies in Tokyo, and an equally ineffective Far East Commission in Washington (it would begin to function on February 26, 1946).[56] MacArthur only met the Council in Japan once in April 1946; and the Commission sent no 'Post Surrender Directives' to MacArthur till 1947. To allow the Russians to participate in these shadowy institutions was one of the 'achievements' of Byrnes at Moscow.[57] The British, who had wished to place the Emperor on the list of war criminals, were for a time almost as disturbed as the Russians,[58] but they could do nothing. Meantime, the United States Sixth Army left Japan on January 1, 1946, the Eighth Army, led by General Eichelberger, remaining as the sole garrison under MacArthur. No other Allied troops joined them.

In early 1946 the vexed question of the Kuriles came up again. On January 22, the Secretary of State being at the United Nations in London, the Acting Secretary, Dean Acheson, gave a press conference stating that, as he had understood the Yalta agreement, the United States had not agreed to give these islands to Russia. The Soviet news agency TASS quoted from the agreement itself to prove Acheson wrong. Byrnes, back in Washington on January 29, admitted by implication that, as the

*New York Times* put it, Roosevelt had made 'a secret gift of the Kuriles' to Russia.[59] In a later press conference, Truman dismissed the relevant Yalta agreement as merely 'a wartime understanding'. Even so, the text of the Protocol was published, on February 11, 1946: Truman successfully distanced himself; Byrnes found it harder to do so.

MacArthur had by then spent so much time in the East that he was convinced of its importance beyond comparison with any other part of the world. He believed that he had a unique knowledge of 'oriental psychology'. He did know Japan and the Philippines well. Early in 1945 he had told the then Under Secretary of the Navy, James Forrestal, that the Pacific would become a major economic sphere of development. He thought Washington 'guilty of treason and sabotage in not adequately supporting the Pacific, while hammering Germany . . . He never once referred to the "Americans" and the "Japanese" but always "the enemy and I"'.[60] He had absolute confidence in his mission in Japan, but soon fell a victim to his own legends, became increasingly theatrical, and in the end even irresponsible. Already in 1945 he had begun to be obsessed by phobias – that, for example, 'the Joint Chiefs of Staff, the Department of State, even the White House were under the domination of the Communists and the British Imperialists'.[61] To George Kennan, later, he cited Caesar's experience in the military occupation of Gaul as the only historical example of a productive military occupation besides his own. The Japanese, he believed, were 'thirsty for guidance and inspiration'. He thought that it was his mission to bring them both, as well as democracy and Christianity. Since they were now for the first time tasting freedom, they would never return to slavery. The Communists, he thought, had no influence in Japan apart from a minority of intellectuals.[62] Partly as a result, some members of MacArthur's loyal and often sycophantic staff began to look on Japan as a 'base for possible future military operations against Russia'.[63]

Japan is the only example in 1945 of policy being pressed to diplomatic victory because of the knowledge that superior industrial power gave the United States an advantage over the Soviet Union. Truman reluctantly gave MacArthur the opportunity. MacArthur, grandson of an immigrant from Scotland, and wholly Scottish in origin, seized the chance. The history of the Far East was thus transformed. This truth was masked at the time by the realisation that, for the first time in her history, Japan had tasted defeat, and that the surrender had occurred when the Japanese homeland still contained thousands of Kamikazis. Forty per cent of Japan's urban areas had been destroyed or seriously damaged, while industrial production in 1946 would be a third of the average between 1934 and 1936.[64] Japan had suffered from the worst ever 'conventional' air raid: that of March 9, 1945, when 83,000 people were killed in Tokyo and 40,000 injured. At Hiroshima 70,000–90,000 died immediately and many thousands died later from radiation. At Nagasaki, the figure approached 40,000 deaths.[65] Two million Japanese altogether had died since 1941, mostly at American hands. The country which had been the testing ground of America's most destructive weapon soon, however, became its favourite ally. History had rarely seen such a confounding of the expected.

The third Eastern country with an uncertain future at the end of the war was Korea, so placed between China, Japan and Russia that it is remarkable that it remained a separate entity at all. It is the Poland of the East. It had been from the XVIIth century a protectorate of China. Chinese weakness later gave Korea the illusion of independence. The United States prised Korea open to world trade in the 1870s. China and Japan went to war over her in 1894. After the Russo-Japanese War of 1904, Korea fell under control of the latter. She was absorbed by Japan in 1910. Her name was changed, to Chosen. A measure of prosperity ensued. Korean resentment continued. So did Korean emigration: 200,000 Koreans lived in Siberia in 1919, over 400,000 in Manchuria. From these centres, the remains of Korea's old 'Righteous Army' made occasional forays into Korea proper. Among these exile colonies, too, Korean socialism and Communism began in the 1920s. Korea itself remained Japanese.

During the Second World War, the Allies planned the dismantlement of all of Japan's Empire overseas. Roosevelt, Churchill and Chiang Kai Shek at Cairo proclaimed that, 'mindful of the enslavement of the people of Korea', they were determined that, 'in due course', Korea 'shall become free and independent'.[66] Roosevelt talked to Stalin about Korea at Yalta. He said that he had in mind for Korea a trusteeship composed of a Soviet, an American and a Chinese representative. Such an arrangement might last for thirty years. The Koreans could not be expected to govern themselves immediately after forty years of subjection to Japan. Stalin said that the shorter the period of trusteeship, the better he would be pleased. He mildly suggested that Britain ought to be included among the trustees.[67] The later 'Declaration at Potsdam' also called, by implication, for a Japanese withdrawal to its main islands. The 225,000 Japanese troops then in Korea would leave the country. At that time, the United States had no plan to send any troops there.

During August 1945, Korea was further discussed between the Russians and Americans. On the request of the United States administration (the SWNCC – State, War, Navy, Co-ordinating Committee), the Deputy Chief of Staff to General Stilwell, Dean Rusk (in civilian life Dean of the Faculty of Political Science at a small college in California), with Colonel Charles Bonesteel of the Department of State, worked out how, as an interim arrangement, Korea should be divided into two, between the United States and Russia, the temporary boundary being approximately the 38th Parallel; far enough to the north, Rusk insisted, to include the ancient capital, Seoul, in the southern, or American, zone.[68] The line drawn on a crude map, the only one available, lay approximately along the 38th Parallel – roughly the same point where Russia and Japan, under the Tsar and the Emperor, had proposed a division before 1904. Much to the United States' surprise, the Russians agreed. This conciliatory behaviour was no doubt due to Stalin's hope that such a division would strengthen his claim to similar arrangements in Japan. Secretary of State Byrnes had strongly supported the idea and over-rode the Army on the issue. MacArthur's General Order No. 1 on September 2 thus divided Korea into two.

On September 4, 1945, General John R. Hodge, one of the

successful American commanders in MacArthur's campaigns, landed at Inchon with the XXIV Army Corps and occupied South Korea up to the agreed line. Russian troops soon moved into the North, from Vladivostok and Manchuria. By the end of September, the country, formally a 'liberated territory' (like Austria), not an enemy one (like Japan), was divided. The North was the larger territory, 49,000 square miles to the South's 38,000. But the South's population was probably 16 million, the North's 9 million. The North had what heavy industry there was, plenty of hydro-electric power, and timber and minerals: the South had the rice fields and the light industry.

The Russians soon began to treat the 38th Parallel as a permanent line. They would allow no traffic across it except with express permission in each case. Their own reputation suffered as a result of the usual orgies of rape and destruction which characterised a Soviet 'liberation'.[69] Although they found radical nationalists in authority, they immediately proceeded to give support to the Communists, however few and inexperienced these were. Most of those in whom the Soviet supreme commander, General Ivan Chistiakov, had trust were in fact Russified Koreans who had, in most cases, been born in the Soviet Union as Korean immigrants. Soon, however, as sometimes occurred in the Balkans, these fell out with the Korean Communists who had spent the war in the country itself. The Russians – their political chief was General Romanenko, at the head of a '43-man' team – would have liked to have used at least for a time a good political neutral nationalist as a cover for their new order. But the obvious candidate, Cho Man-Sik, a learned man of character, refused. The Russians fell back on more amenable men.

General Hodge sought to open discussions with his Russian counterparts but failed. Hodge was not a patient man. But it is hard to believe that Job himself would have had any effect on events in the American zone of Korea.[70] He found the Koreans labouring under the belief that the Declaration of Cairo had prescribed immediate independence. (The Korean language, it seemed, had no phrase for 'in due course'.) Many organisations sprang up and offered to form governments. Indeed, there was one progressive group which, with Communist support, declared itself to be a government already: 'the People's Republic'. The concept of international trusteeship was discussed in the local press, but all Koreans consulted were bitterly opposed. Hodge suggested that both the United States and Russians should withdraw and leave Korea to its own devices.[71] The Communist party was then re-founded in Seoul, with a commitment to operate in both North and South Korea.

In November, 'the People's Republic', allowed itself, despite much protest, to dissolve into 'a movement', instead of a government, to avoid a clash with the Americans. Next month, Byrnes raised Korea with Molotov at Moscow. He proposed a trusteeship of four powers under the United Nations for the whole country. In five years, Korea would be independent. Though at first Molotov suggested a provisional government with the support of the two occupying authorities, in the end the conference decided in favour of both plans. Four-power trusteeship (China and Britain, as well as Russia and the United States) would last for 'up to five years'. But efforts would be made before that time was up to achieve a 'provisional democratic government' to be worked out by the occupying powers. The plan was to be submitted to China and Britain for approval, and then returned for a final confirmation by the occupiers. The compromise was a typical achievement of Byrnes. The Koreans – Left as well as Right – were persuaded by the Soviet High Command to make the most of it. Everything depended, however, on discussions between the occupiers on the spot. But these were held up over the question of Korean representation.

Hodge (who remained in Korea, formally as deputy to MacArthur who had the command of the whole of the Far East) found himself in a volatile political situation. He began to suspect that some of the Koreans with whom he had been working were Communists. Many were in fact radical nationalists, prepared at least to collaborate with the Communists. He permitted political meetings. These took the form of demonstrations against the idea of trusteeship and in favour of the immediate establishment of a Korean government. Trade unionists demanded the same. Hodge also found himself faced with bomb explosions, mysterious murders of people whom he trusted, and mob attacks against both Right and Left wing newspaper offices. The Korean Communist Party now claimed between 20,000 and 30,000 members but they had the use of several progressive 'fronts' which seemed much as they were in Eastern Europe. Exiles from the United States, such as Syngman Rhee (associated with the idea of independence for Korea since 1919) and Kim Koo, also plunged into political activity. They had not liked trusteeship any more than the Communists had done. The 'Democratic Council' formed by them in February articulated the views of what seemed increasingly a strong right-wing movement.

All the same, General Hodge was impressed by the efficiency of Soviet propaganda which he believed was having a critical effect on the 'poorly trained and poorly educated Orientals', for whom he was responsible.[72] He wanted American troops to leave as quickly as possible. But he did not want to leave confusion behind. By early 1946, Hodge was contemplating a special constabulary to control the explosive countryside. He was already using curfews to control the cities.

In the North, the Russians had obvious friends with whom to work. They were handing over control of municipalities to members of the growing Communist Party, now headed by Kim il-Sŏng. Kim had been a Party member since he was nineteen, in 1931, and was a 33-year-old guerrilla leader. He was launched into the North Korean leadership directly by General Roman-enko at a meeting in a Chinese restaurant in P'yŏngyang (the main town in the Russian zone) in early October 1945. Kim's dull speech, his youth, his Russian haircut, and his ill-fitting blue suit made a bad impression on the expectant Korean comrades. No matter! He was Romanenko's choice, the 'Korean Chapaev', and a man with no history of past deviations or 'factionalism'.[73]

By then, Korea looked as if it was on the brink of dividing itself by the 'twentieth century solution', as Ivone Kirkpatrick of the British Foreign Office bitterly called it, of partition.[74] By now, too, the Department of State had begun to hesitate about a withdrawal. The Office of Far Eastern Affairs, concerned mainly with China, looked on Korea as something to be bargained for with Russia, as part of the Soviet withdrawal from China.

Even after the failure of the talks, they insisted. Hodge and the Army wanted to leave. The State Department (and soon the President) thought otherwise.[75]

Korean Communism was well-established. Founded among exiles in Shanghai and New York, as well as Siberia and Manchuria, cells were planted in Korean cities by 1923. The party proper was founded in Seoul in 1925, also in a Chinese restaurant.[76] The young Koreans who took this step were nationalists, as much as socialists, who looked to Russia to help them against Japanese imperialism. The party experienced many tribulations and had to be re-founded several times. As in all small Communist parties, the struggles against 'factionalism' were bitter. In the 1920s and 1930s Korean Communists gave a great deal of trouble to the senior Communist in the Comintern charged to deal with it, the Finn, Otto Kuusinen. Nor was association with the Chinese and the Japanese Communist parties at all easy. Successful action by the police in Seoul prevented the activities of a Communist Party from 1928 till 1941. Among the hundreds of thousands of Korean exiles in Manchuria, a few remained in some kind of organisation, went to the 'University of the Toilers of the East' in Moscow, organised guerrilla groups in the areas of Manchuria occupied by the Japanese, and also organised terrorism in Shanghai (for example, the attempted murder of General Tanaka Giichi in Shanghai in 1933). It was out of this varied background that Kim il-Sŏng appeared: he figures as a 'Red Bandit', in Japanese police records, in 1937, for the first time.[77]

Like many Communist leaders in the East, as well as in the West, Kim was of a lower middle class origin, his family having been engaged in shopkeeping and schoolteaching, as well as farming, and also being interested in radical nationalist politics. Kim became a *guerrillero* in 1930 in Manchuria and fought in numerous petty skirmishes against the Japanese throughout the next fifteen years. In 1936, Kim was directing a band of about sixty men and women, backed by several hundred more, many of them Chinese, operating along the Yalu river. He remained concerned with such activities on a growing scale till about 1941.[78] Then he spent several years in Russia, apparently being trained.[79]

Kim did meet some difficulties in North Korea in the winter of 1945–46, particularly with the domestic Communists headed by the intellectual Pak Hŏn-Yŭng, but also with certain Communists with Chinese background. Both distrusted a 'Muscovite'. But, by early February 1946, Kim, with Russian help, had triumphed both against them and 'reactionaries', such as Cho Man-Sik who, without lifting a finger against the new regime, vanished, being last seen in freedom on January 5, 1946. He must have been murdered, as a dangerous free spirit. Kim's speech, on February 8, 1946, at an 'Enlarged Conference of the North Korean Democratic Parties, Social Organisations, the Five Provinces' Administrative Bureau and the People's Political Committees' in P'Yŏngyang seems to have been as unyieldingly doctrinaire as Stalin's the next day in Moscow; or, indeed, as his now disciplined audience was. By this time, the governing Provisional People's Committee in North Korea were all Communists except two.

A series of reforms were immediately put under way. These would soon ruin the old rural gentry, and transform industry and education. Russianised Koreans maintained discipline as advisers in most ministries: in these the Russian adviser was usually a KGB officer, such as Colonel Bodyagin, in the Ministry of Internal Affairs. North Korea thus vanished into the anonymity of subservience to Moscow, a plight darkened by Western neglect and ignorance of the country.


Finally, among the old kingdoms of the East which seemed in 1946 a possible source of trouble, there was Indo-China; though none could have foreseen how much trouble such a place, so remote to most Americans, would one day cause.

Indo-China was returned, at the end of the war in 1945, to France; or, rather, to the 14,000 or so French civil servants who ran it. French planters returned to their rubber plantations. Vietnamese notables went-back to their villages. The cities of Cochin-China became once more places of considerable sophistication.[80]

The shadow of ruin was nevertheless present. That was

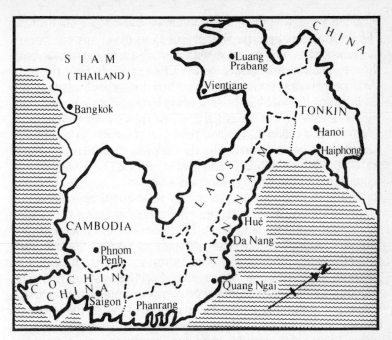

because, in the countryside, French imperial control was never fully restored. French troops could move about only in convoys. At night, officials, planters and merchants were being murdered. Vietnamese nationalist guerrillas, awoken by the war to opportunity, were already well established. These were led by Communists, and they by a certain Ho Chi Minh, 'he who makes things clear', a revolutionary who had proclaimed himself 'President of the Provisional Democratic Republic of Vietnam' the preceding summer; and who, as 'Nguyen Ai Quoc', had had a long reputation as a Communist leader.[81] Son of a middle-class mandarin, Ho Chi Minh had lived for some years in Paris working as a photographer's assistant. He had begun to denounce French rule in Indo-China before 1914 and published his first pamphlet, *Cahiers de Revendications du Peuple Annamite*, in 1918. He joined the French Communist Party at its foundation in 1920 and worked in China as an assistant to the legendary 'Borodin': whom Malraux made a hero and Stalin a victim. In 1945, Ho

planned a united Vietnam both Communist and free from France.
To achieve this end, he was prepared to make any temporary
concession: to make peace with France or to make war with
her; to use the Americans, or the Chinese; or to fight them.

How this opportunity in the East had come about was curious.
Indo-China in 1939 had been a jewel in the French crown; 'not
really a colony, but an empire', Governor-General Alexandre
Varenne had called it, echoing Josephine's conversation in Mar-
tinique with her fortune teller. His successor, General Catroux,
in 1940 offered Indo-China to Britain. Britain was pleased but
counselled him to avoid risking a conflict with Japan. So Catroux
accepted a Japanese ultimatum, in June 1940, and planned a
disarmed Indo-China. Catroux was then dismissed by Pétain.
He joined de Gaulle in London. His successor in Hanoi, General
Decoux, conceded Japanese demands to occupy the northern
Indo-Chinese airfields and other strategic points, in order to
support their Chinese operations. For the rest of the war,
Decoux maintained a shadowy *pétainiste* regime – authoritarianism at home married to appeasement abroad – while the Japanese
did as they wished in their '*stationnement*' (not precisely an
occupation). An equally shadowy resistance movement of
Frenchmen began. Behind that war of hesitations, the Vietminh
(Front of Independence) took shape, backed by the Communists,
whose headquarters were then in China, on the border with
Vietnam; which gave the British and Americans some indiscriminate help; and which had much in common with the National
Council of the Resistance in France.

Early in 1945, Japan demanded the transfer to themselves of
all Indo-China. The French in Hanoi hesitated. Japanese troops
moved to forestall an Allied invasion. The French sought to
oppose that. There was some modest local French resistance,
followed by a massacre of French prisoners in Japanese hands.
There were several acts of bravery among the French. But
Japan occupied Hanoi. For the Vietnamese, French rule was at
an end.

Japan, having in these improbable circumstances of March
1945 defeated France, turned to Bao Dai, a former puppet
Emperor of Annam. They offered him the control of all Indo-

China. He accepted. He declared Vietnam independent, under Japanese tutelage. His timing was imperfect, since Japan surrendered to the Allies in August.

The United States, meantime, had evolved a variety of plans for Indo-China. Roosevelt had not wished to restore the territory to France 'because', he believed, 'France had done nothing to improve the natives since she had the colony', a comment which had little relation to truth.[82] Roosevelt, however, accepted Chiang Kai Shek's belief that Indo-China was not 'ready for independence'. He offered Indo-China to China both by telegram and in person at Cairo in 1943.[83] Chiang Kai Shek refused the offer: a reticence for which his countrymen were doubtless subsequently grateful. So the idea of trusteeship was then mooted. Roosevelt told Stalin at Yalta that he had a policy in mind for that. But these plans were incomplete. France sought to send back her own directors. Alas, Cédile, the designated High Commissioner, was arrested by the Japanese; and Messner, his replacement, kidnapped by the Vietnamese, in Hanoi. In the moment of hesitation, Ho Chi Minh also declared the country independent; this time under no tutelage.

By prior arrangement, the only two powers which had hitherto done nothing over Vietnam, the Chinese and the British, were now requested, at Potsdam, by the three Great Powers to divide administration of Indo-China between them at the 16th Parallel. The rough, realistic but unsubtle General Leclerc, who had just before been sent out by de Gaulle to command the French land forces in Indo-China, heard the news of this diplomatic blunder at Karachi. Lord Louis Mountbatten, Allied Supreme Commander, sought to comfort him: he remarked, 'if Roosevelt had been alive, you would never enter Indo-China'. Leclerc continued to Saigon. Some United States troops followed him there too, under the auspices of the OSS. OSS Colonel Peter Dewey was, indeed, the first American fatal casualty in Vietnam then with the Vietminh, in September 1945.

De Gaulle was incensed. He despatched more French troops, to 'reestablish the greatness of France'. Fortunately, Britain brought herself to accept French jurisdiction south of the 16th Parallel on September 5. On October 5, Leclerc entered Saigon and sent his armoured troops through the city, to cheer the long-neglected French colonial families. On October 31, after tortuous negotiations rather than fighting, the French High Commissioner, Admiral Thierry d'Argenlieu, thoughtful and literate, was installed in his palace: *'En Indochine, la France réapparait, à present, dans sa dignité'*.[84] Between then and February, Leclerc, privately doubting, with the realism for which he was known, whether anywhere in the East could again become European as once it had been, reconquered the country, in the famous *'chevauchée cochinchinoise'*. Officers such as Colonels Massu and Lecomte made their names in a swift campaign, which lost 630 French dead or vanished, and 1,000 wounded. The King of Cambodia made an accord with France. So did his colleague in Laos. British troops tactfully withdrew from Indo-China in January 1946.

There remained Vietnam north of the 16th Parallel. There, Chinese troops had formally established themselves on September 15, 1945. A Chinese general took up his headquarters at Hanoi. The French Commissioner, with no forces, could do nothing. The 40,000 French citizens who lived in the province had no protection. The Commissioner, Monsieur Jean Sainteny, cultivated and acute, tried to negotiate with Ho Chi Minh. A conversation began. It did not get far. Leclerc wanted to reconquer the north. But he wisely did not drag France into war with China. The question remained poised. Assuming that Leclerc managed to secure a Chinese withdrawal, the next stage, it was hoped in Paris, would be the constitution of all Indo-China as a federation; of Vietnam as a free state within that federation; and referendums in the three provinces of Vietnam, Tonkin, Annam and Cochin-China, as to their form of association.[85]

The French position in Indo-China had in early 1946 been re-established. This was the consequence of a great effort of will on the part of France, particularly of de Gaulle and Leclerc. That act of will ruined Indo-China in the end. But it helped France to recover control over her own destiny, in the face of her recent defeats.

# BOOK FOUR

# A PROFESSOR'S DREAM

I do not think it will be as effective as is expected. It sounds like a professor's dream.

Admiral Leahy, *I was there*.

I shudder to think of what will happen to humanity including ourselves if this war ends in an inconclusive peace and another war breaks out when the babies of today have grown to fighting age.

Roosevelt in his annual State of the Union speech, January 7, 1943 (he had just heard of the first self-maintaining nuclear reaction at Staff Field, Chicago).

To slacken the tempo would mean falling behind. And those who fall behind get beaten . . . One feature of old Russia was the continual beatings she suffered because of her backwardness. She was beaten by the Mongol Khans. By the Turkish beys. By the Swedish feudal lords. By the Polish and the Lithuanian gentry. By the British and French capitalists. By the Japanese barons . . . because of her backwardness . . . That is why we must no longer lag behind.

Stalin, 'The Tasks of Business Executives' speech, February 4, 1931.

# TWENTY

# THE MANHATTAN PROJECT

The discovery of radioactivity in the late 1890s showed that one chemical element could decay into another by a series of changes which gives off new sources of energy. A small amount of matter, Albert Einstein observed in 1905, might, therefore, be transformed into much energy. In 1914, H. G. Wells, in a novel *The World Set Free*, forecast that this source of energy could be used for both 'atomic bombs' and reactors for peace.

Few took the implied prophecy seriously. Most scientists changed their views backwards and forwards. The great physicist, Rutherford, thought, in 1933, that the idea that weapons could be made in consequence of nuclear energy was 'the merest moonshine'. But in 1903 he had made the 'playful suggestion that, if a proper detonator could be found, this old world could vanish in smoke':[1] a good example of pessimistic youth giving way to optimistic old age.

The discovery that fission could artificially be achieved was made in Berlin by two German physicists, Otto Hahn and Fritz Strassmann, late in 1938. Their findings were published in the learned German journal, *Naturwissenschaften*, in early 1939. In August of that year, Einstein, then in the United States, wrote to President Roosevelt about the possible military consequences.[2] Soon British, American and Canadian scientists began to work on the 'atomic bomb' chiefly because they feared that the Germans were also doing so, though, in practice, neither the Germans nor the Japanese went far along the road. After the war, the distinguished German physicist, Werner Heisenberg, explained that 'the undertaking could not have been initiated against the psychological background of the men responsible for German war policy'.[3] Japanese efforts were similarly abandoned. The decision in the United States to work on a major programme designed to manufacture an atomic weapon was nevertheless made, in November 1941. 'The Manhattan Project', as the programme to build the bombs was secretly called, was then under way.

The leaders of the world knew, four years later, after the first atomic bomb had been dropped on Hiroshima, on August 6, 1945, that they were living in a new epoch. Here was a real turning point in the history of the world which for once was instantly perceived as such. The great scientists in the United States had known that that would probably be so from the beginning of the wartime activities, which, by 1945, had cost over $2 billion, and employed 600,000 men and women, in thirty-seven installations established throughout the United States and Canada.

Senior scientists already knew too that atomic energy would require 'extraordinary means of control'. Few had doubted, however, that the bomb, when completed, should be used. Prominent American scientific administrators, such as Dr Vannevar Bush and Dr James Conant, President of the Carnegie Institution and of Harvard University respectively, who had both been occupied with the Manhattan Project from the beginning, had concluded, in the summer of 1944, 'that they ought to discuss both domestic and international control'.[4] (Bush had previously been Dean of Engineering at the Massachusetts Institute of Technology. He had been impelled to press for action in 1940 out of a concern that a mixture of Hitler's successes and American isolationism might enable Nazism to win the day.)[5] Those who knew anything of nuclear energy – or rather the leaders of the scientific side of things – began to consult unofficially with one another. Thus the 'Jeffries' Committee (headed by Zay Jeffries, of General Electric) in late 1944, hoped for a world-wide organisation to prevent the atom bomb from becoming the 'destroyer of nations'; at the same time, it hoped that scientists in the United States would seek to keep the lead in research and industrial applications. A second committee (headed by Dr Richard Tolman) concluded that the United States should seek to maintain military superiority in atomic energy after the war. Doctors Bush and Conant, in touch with both the President and the scientists, began to talk among themselves of a post-war international agency of control. The Danish physicist, Niels Bohr, whose theoretical work had been fundamental to the original project, and who had escaped from Nazi-occupied Denmark in the bomb-bay of a fast Mosquito aircraft, personally urged Roosevelt to break the news about the atomic possibilities to Russia, in order to make it easier to achieve post-war international control and thus prevent what he already called 'an arms' race'. Bohr believed that the development of the atomic bomb necessitated a quite new international order. To secure that, it was surely essential to tell Stalin of the weapon well before it was used: at least in outline. He did not suggest any exchange of details, only an offer of cooperation.[6] Science, he believed, was approaching 'the realisation of a project which may bring either disaster or benefit on a scale unimaginable to the future of mankind'.[7]

As with many of Roosevelt's activities, the President's conduct towards both Bohr and atomic weapons in general is open to several interpretations. But it seems that, while Churchill met, misunderstood and mistrusted Bohr, and made no secret of it,[8] Roosevelt charmed and encouraged him but also sought to control him; one of those double games which he so much enjoyed.[9] Bohr may not have made himself clear to Churchill. He often did mumble. Roosevelt also thought that Bohr, innocently or not, would anyway pass on what he, Roosevelt, thought to the Russians, through his old scientific acquaintance Peter Kapitsa, then back in Russia.[10]

At all events, the President agreed with Churchill, at Roosevelt's house, Hyde Park in September 1943, that no one, the Russians least of all, should be told of the work on the bomb for the time being. Churchill was determined to maintain an Anglo-American monopoly of atomic power as a diplomatic counter to Soviet military strength. When the bomb became available, Roosevelt and Churchill were then thinking, 'it might perhaps, after mature consideration, be used against the Japanese, who should be warned that this bombardment will be repeated till they surrender' – an approximate anticipation of what did in the end occur.[11] Churchill himself was primarily concerned already about the chances of securing continuous British collaboration on atomic development with the United States – the beginning of a long but most unsatisfactory relation between the two Anglo-Saxon states.[12] Roosevelt, who confessed that the 'whole post-war atomic problem worried him to death',[13] told Bush a few days later that he wanted to keep the British Empire going – a preoccupation which he otherwise kept to himself – by encouraging it to use atomic energy as much as by giving it economic aid. But Bush thought that 'collaborating too closely with the British without considering the world situation might lead to most undesirable relations with the Russians'. He did not know that arrangements for collaboration with Britain had been, in theory, settled in 1943. Bush also worried lest an attempt to 'hoard' nuclear technology might lead to extraordinary efforts by the Russians to develop the bomb secretly and so to 'a catastrophic conflict' twenty years thence.[14] Yet the Russians were already receiving information about the Manhattan Project through espionage. Some of that activity was known at the time to the security departments in the American government, though perhaps not the scale.[15] Roosevelt received news of it also.[16]

On September 30, 1944, Bush and Conant wrote to the Secretary of War, Henry Stimson. They not only described the potential damage which might be caused by an atomic bomb, but discussed the chances of achieving a thermonuclear bomb, which might be many times more powerful. Such a bomb promised to place every city in the world 'at the mercy of the nation which struck first'. The Anglo-American advantage in the matter might be only temporary. Supplies of heavy hydrogen were, after all, almost unlimited. So, mere control of the raw materials would be impossible. The two scientists advocated disclosure of all but the manufacturing details of the bomb immediately that development was shown to be feasible. A demonstration might be made over enemy territory, or that of the United States. By making available all the information, as Bohr had argued, the United States might persuade the Russians to collaborate.

Stimson mulled over the matter. He was one of the wisest and most experienced of American statesmen, having first been Secretary of War under President Taft before 1914, and Secretary of State under Hoover in 1929–1933. 'The Colonel', had remained a Republican and had been brought in (along with Secretary Knox) by Roosevelt to broaden the administration in June 1941, to his Republican colleagues' fury. Stimson was a realistic conservative, doubtful about the possibilities of resisting Russia in East Europe, but determined to secure presidential support for rational policies. He was, however, by then old, shaky, and given to terrible headaches. His personality, all the same, was the most important one in the formulation of America's atomic policy during much of the critical year 1945.

Stimson talked about control of nuclear energy with Roosevelt, on December 29, 1944. By then, he had been much impressed by a note from General Deane of the American military mission in Moscow arguing that further concessions (over Poland, for example) to Stalin would gain them nothing. With alacrity Roosevelt agreed with him that it was not the time to share the atomic secret with Russia.[17] All the same, in deference to Bush and Conant, Stimson decided to set up a committee to advise him exclusively on the post-war implications. But, in these busy last weeks of the war, he could discuss the matter only once again with Roosevelt, on March 15. That talk bore no fruit. Nothing happened. Roosevelt died. By that time, United States intelligence had established that German atomic scientists had made little progress in respect of atomic research for weapons during the war.[18]

Byrnes mentioned the atom bomb to Truman on the day of Roosevelt's funeral. Stimson briefed the President in detail on April 25. He left a memorandum with Truman which went a long way towards satisfying Bush's desire for post-war planning. Stimson accepted that the United States could not enjoy an atomic monopoly for long. Russia might, for example, 'have the bomb' in a few years. A wilful nation, even a small one, might construct a bomb secretly. Those trying to create any kind of new world organisation had to remember that 'American leaders had a moral obligation' to consider the atomic question, a duty 'which they could not shirk, without incurring responsibility for any disaster that might follow'. So the committee already proposed ought to be set up. Stimson went on to argue that 'no system of control heretofore considered would be adequate to control this menace'. What was needed was 'such thorough-going rights of inspection and international control as we have never heretofore contemplated'.[19] Truman was told something of Soviet spying on the project[20] and also how the United States and Britain, according to General Groves, the energetic and competent, if secretive and autocratic, director of the Manhattan Project, controlled most of the world's known stores of uranium (and thorium), the essential ores needed for fission. On May 2, Truman approved the establishment of the much-discussed post-war policy committee: the 'Interim Committee'.[21]

Niels Bohr, back again in America, continued to urge speed. International control should be discussed 'while it could be done in a spirit of friendly advice'. If the United States were to delay, such advice might seem like a kind of 'coercion' which no great nation such as Russia could accept. Negotiation, Bohr believed, had to begin before any bomb was dropped. When and if that did happen, a vision of what control in peace would be should immediately be put to public opinion. Another scientist who knew what was happening, O. C. Brewster, argued that, unless controls were quickly established, the subsequent competition for atomic weapons would soon turn the whole world into 'a flaming inferno'.[22]

The long-awaited Interim Committee met several times, on May 14, May 18, May 31, June 1 and June 21. Four remarkable scientists (Arthur Compton, Robert Oppenheimer, Ernest Lawrence, and Enrico Fermi) acted as its advisory panel. The committee itself consisted of Karl Compton (President of the Massachusetts Institute of Technology), James Byrnes, Stimson, Conant, Bush, Ralph Bard (Under Secretary of the Navy), and Will Clayton, Assistant Secretary of State. On occasion,

Generals Marshall and Groves, together with some officials (Harvey Bundy and Page), also attended.

On the Committee itself, Dr Conant was the only scientist. Even so, it is difficult to believe that a more sensible team of scientists and public men could at that time have been assembled in any country. If the Committee was inadequate, so was human nature.

The early meetings of this body were concerned with how to announce the atomic bomb when it was dropped. The other meetings looked into the future. Compton thought that a competitor nation could make an atom bomb within six years. Marshall, believing at that time that Russia's extraordinary political unhelpfulness derived from anxiety over security, suggested that the Russians should be invited to the planned atomic test, at Alamogordo. Byrnes, already the President's representative and the most powerful political individual present, if still an *éminence grise*, not Secretary of State, thought that the best policy 'was to push production', 'stay ahead' and only then make every effort to improve political relations with Russia. (He himself had been told about the project of making the bomb by Roosevelt on a 'hot summer afternoon' in 1943, for no apparent reason, he said, other than that FDR desired 'to see my amazed reaction'.)[23]

The Interim Committee became a committee on all aspects of the bomb. It eventually agreed that United States policy should be based on a three-pronged plan: there should be freedom of research 'consistent with the needs of security'; 'a combination of democratic powers' for cooperation in atomic energy; and then, an understanding with Russia. The idea of a demonstrative first use of the bomb was discussed but dismissed. The bomb might turn out not to work. The Japanese might shoot down the bomber which was delivering it; or, they might bring Allied prisoners-of-war into the designated area. The Committee recommended, on Byrnes's proposal, that the bomb should be used in a way to cause the maximum psychological effect; for example, on a Japanese war plant, surrounded by workers' homes, and without warning. As for control afterwards: 'each country would promise to make public all work being done on atomic energy; an international control committee, with complete power to inspect,' should be set up. The Committee recommended that the Russians should be told, at the conference planned for Potsdam, that the United States had been working on the atom bomb and that they expected to use it against Japan. The President was to add that 'he hoped for future discussion to ensure that the weapon would become an aid to peace'.[24]

There were some dissenters. Ralph Bard, Under-Secretary of the Navy, an industrial financier from Chicago, believed that the war in the Far East was already won. Nor did he like dropping the bomb without warning Japan. He told Stimson so. Truman did not agree and Bard resigned on July 1.[25] Bard was replaced by Admiral Lewis Strauss, who also had unconventional views. He proposed the bomb be demonstrated to show the Japanese what would happen: in, for example, the forest of cryptomeria trees, near Tokyo.[26] General Marshall suggested that the weapon should be used first against a 'straight military area', such as a naval installation.[27] But the conventional view – in effect, Byrnes's view – triumphed.

Alongside the atomic project proper, the military commander of that project, General Groves, had been energetically seeking to build a United States monopoly of atomic raw materials. He had spent several million dollars – sometimes using his own bank account to avoid detection by spies – on purchasing all the available uranium and thorium from seven separate countries, shipping it as far as possible to the United States and securing agreements to buy all production thereafter indefinitely. Far and away the largest source of uranium ore in the western world was the Belgian Congo where the large mining consortium, Union Minière, controlled mining. Groves managed this diplomacy with both skill and secrecy: he let the sellers assume that the United States needed the ore for glass or as a colouring for ceramics.[28]

The culmination of the work on the bomb naturally cast a shadow over the coming end of the war in the Far East, affecting the issue of how much Soviet help would be needed in order to defeat Japan. The Secretary of War, Stimson, continued to advocate inaction on this till the bomb was tested and till it could be seen whether it would constitute 'a weapon in our hands or not': it seemed 'a terrible thing to gamble with such big stakes in diplomacy without having your master card in your hand'.[29] Truman made this concession to Stimson. The knowledge that the bomb would be tested by then must have been one factor which inspired Truman to delay going to Potsdam by another fortnight, from July 1 to July 15 – much to Churchill's annoyance.[30] On the boat on the way to Europe in July, Truman told his friends: 'if it goes off as I think it will I'll have a hammer on those boys':[31] presumably Russian boys. But he had also decided before leaving America that, as Stimson had recommended, 'if he thought Stalin on good enough terms with him, he would shoot off at him what we had arranged . . . that we were pretty nearly ready and we intended to use . . . the bomb . . . against the enemy, Japan; that if it was satisfactory, we proposed to them to talk it over with Stalin afterwards, with the purpose of having it make the world peaceful and safe'.[32]

When Truman got to Potsdam, Churchill was still against the idea of telling the Russians anything about the bomb. Stimson observed Soviet soldiers, read reports about the behaviour of the Red Army in Germany and himself wondered whether the United States ought to contemplate sharing any nuclear secrets with this unpredictable power until the latter had, say, carried into effect its liberal-sounding constitution of 1936.

The news then came of the successful test of the bomb on July 15, in a remote section of an air base at Alamogordo, in New Mexico. On July 24, Truman, 'much fortified' in Churchill's words to Stimson,[33] told Stalin 'casually' that the United States had 'a bomb of unusual destructive force'.* The bomb was not in any sense of the word an item on the agenda of the conference in Potsdam. Nor, against the recommendation of the Interim Committee, did Truman suggest any negotiations on international control to Stalin. The Declaration of Potsdam was then issued calling on Japan to surrender. It threatened retribution if she did not do so.

* See below, for Soviet reaction, pages 646-7.

Japan did not surrender. She neither quite accepted nor refused outright the opportunity offered. The peace party there, though active, as Americans knew from intercepted telegrams from Tokyo to Moscow, was not strong enough.

Like most of those concerned, Truman apparently had no hesitation about using the bomb: he regarded it 'as a military weapon and never had any doubt that it should be used' – confirming earlier decisions that use would go ahead when ready: not initiating a new idea.[34] Churchill had approved use on July 4, as was necessary under the Quebec agreement.[35] He was admitted even by the anti-British General Groves to be 'probably the best friend' that the atomic project in the war ever had, 'since he had seemed to be able to sense any lag in our work' and then stimulate the managers to renewed efforts.[36] No one questioned the assumption about use except, apparently, for General Eisenhower and Admiral Leahy. But the former spoke only to Stimson, the latter apparently doubted whether the bomb would work.[37] The Air Force Chief of Staff, General 'Hap' Arnold, also thought (as Ralph Bard had done) that Japan would probably surrender by October, even if the bomb did not exist: a judgement endorsed by subsequent enquiry.[38] The Far Eastern Department of the Foreign Office criticised the bombing in private memoranda, while the Vatican did so in *L'Osservatoro Romano*.[39]

The bombs were used on Hiroshima and Nagasaki on August 6 and 8 in the way that is now well known; and the Russians entered the war in the East on August 9: a week earlier than expected. The Japanese peace party captured power in Tokyo and, perhaps almost as much as a result of the Russian entry into Manchuria as of the dropping of the bomb, accepted the Declaration of Potsdam, on the understanding that the prerogatives of the Emperor were not affected. Thus as Robert Murphy put it, and Truman always maintained, 'unnumbered thousands of Americans and Japanese who would have surely been killed in a conventional assault on the islands lived to see the peace'.[40] To the world, the events seemed to prove that the atom bomb was a supreme weapon. To the makers of policy, above all Americans, the event presented a series of difficulties for which they were naturally ill-equipped. The great intellectual efforts of the internationalists during the war, the disputes between those who supported power politics based on alliances and force, such as Lippmann, and those who favoured international organisations seemed suddenly irrelevant: 'like the preparations some little girls might make for a lawn party as a thunderhead gathers'.[41]

Truman greeted the news of the bombings, after initial exultation, with a short statement which told the world of a 'new era in man's understanding of nature's forces'. Normally, he said, all data would have been made public. But, in the circumstances, that could not happen, pending examination of 'possible methods of protecting us and the rest of the world from the danger of sudden destruction'. He would develop plans which would make nuclear energy 'a forceful influence for world peace'. Stimson was more sombre than Truman had been, at a press conference on August 9. In his diary, he wrote 'the world is changed and it is time for sober thought'. Still shocked by what he had learned in Europe about Soviet conduct, he felt no exhilaration. The Manhattan Project itself was continued at full force: expenditure on it even rose, from $43 million a month in August, to $51 million in October. Work was also now under way on the potentially more powerful thermonuclear, or hydrogen, bomb. A candid report written by Professor Henry D. Smyth was published by the administration describing the scientific achievement behind the bomb in considerable detail.

Attlee in London sounded at first more optimistic. He wrote to Truman on August 9, 'the attack on Hiroshima has now demonstrated to the world that a new factor pregnant with immense possibilities for good or evil has come into existence'. The letter ended with the suggestion that Truman and Attlee should both declare their intentions to use 'this great power' as 'trustees for humanity' (like Stalin, he had not heard that the atom bomb was ready before he got to Potsdam). Attlee's public declaration (drafted beforehand by Churchill) the next day spoke of atomic energy as a possibly 'perennial fountain of prosperity'.

Attlee's views were important. Had it not been for Britain,

the Americans might not have seen the urgency for making the bomb, nor the practical possibility of one.[42] But despite that act of ignition, and Churchill's encouragement, Britain was now only a junior partner in the enterprise. So Truman replied, guardedly: 'until means have been found to control the bomb so as to protect ourselves and the rest of the world from . . . total destruction' neither Britain nor the United States should 'reveal the secret of its production'.[43] It was not till August 15, after all, that Japan surrendered. On the 14th the President told some British visitors, the Duke of Windsor and Sir 'Jock' Balfour, the minister at the Embassy, that, since the Japanese had still not accepted the Allied proposals for peace, 'he now had no alternative but to order an atomic bomb to be dropped on Tokyo'.[44] He did not have to give a new order. That was just as well if only because a third bomb may not yet have existed.[45]

The British government made no immediate claims about the power of the atom bomb. Attlee was wary; Bevin, cautious. Churchill, however, had been as invigorated as Truman, at least initially: 'now we could say "if you insist on doing this or that, well . . .". And then where would be the Russians?'[46] But, in the Commons on August 16, he soberly said that he believed there to be only three or four years before the work done in the United States could be overtaken by another power. In those years 'we must remould the relationships of all men, wherever they dwell, in all the nations'.[47]

In August 1945, also, the same month as the end of the war in the East, the American Joint Chiefs of Staff (JCS) prepared, meantime, their first paper on post-war military policy. They thought primarily of the Western hemisphere, but they conceded that the only serious potential enemy was the Soviet Union. Since these new weapons (and others) favoured surprises such as the United States had suffered four years before at Pearl Harbour, the Joint Chiefs thought that the United States would need above all the security of overseas bases for a long time, as well as both a system of intelligence and a national organisation for research and development.

These men were groping in the dark. They passed on the paper to the State Department who thought it too pessimistic and complained that it did not consider all the Allies. The JCS set about redrafting the paper. A Senate Committee on Atomic Energy, meantime, was formed, with elected members, headed by Senator Brian McMahon of Connecticut, a freshman legislator elected the previous year, anxious to make his name.[48]

In the weeks immediately following the ruin of Hiroshima, Secretary of State Byrnes apparently believed that the atom bomb would give his country a capacity for influencing events in Europe against Russia. Truman had also expressed that opinion to de Gaulle* and had even said the same before July: for example, he had suggested to Stimson in June that the bomb would be a critical thing in resolution of the crisis not only in Poland but also in Romania, Yugoslavia and Manchuria.[49] But Byrnes had held that view for six months. Thus he had assured Truman, as early as April, that the bomb 'might well put us in a position to dictate our own terms at the end of the war . . .'.[50] Byrnes also told the great Hungarian scientist, Leo Szilard, on May 28, that Russia might become more manageable in Europe 'if impressed by American military might': a point of view which 'flabbergasted' the Hungarian.[51] At Potsdam, Byrnes had too, unwisely, told Joseph Davies that he thought that 'the atomic bomb assured ultimate success in negotiations';[52] though, like Stimson, he had been so affected by Russia's behaviour that he formed the view that her promises on everything could be discounted.[53] Byrnes left for London in September in the same state of mind: with, as Stimson put it, the 'bomb in his pocket'.[54] He hoped that Truman would not say anything about international control till he had returned from London.[55] But, as has been seen earlier, the Russians made no concessions of any sort in London. On the contrary, they made demands. Byrnes explained the Russian interest in Italian colonies as a desire for a stepping stone towards the uranium in the Belgian Congo: a view which does not suggest that his knowledge of African geography, or a Mediterranean strategy, was a profound one.[56] He more acutely explained that, if even ordinary journalists could not enter Poland or Hungary, international inspectors

* See above, page 194.

could not be expected to reach Russian bomb factories: Science might not know frontiers, but Russia did.[57]

In all these attitudes, Byrnes was publicly operating a 'tough' policy in the knowledge that he was seen by the public as the man used by Roosevelt to put over the Yalta settlement to the Americans and to Congress. In private, with soft-hearted congressmen or Walter Lippmann or Joseph Davies, he was still claiming that his policy was one of co-operation with Russia. This was certainly an 'elaborate masquerade',[58] no doubt explicable as the inevitably confused reaction of a clever politician who found both Russia and the nuclear problem beyond his normal experience. Byrnes did not know at that time just how few atom bombs the United States had. Nor could he, or anyone, have had any real sense then of the consequences of a Hiroshima-scale attack on a nation of vast geographical dimensions.

The dropping of the bomb had meantime had an adverse effect on General Groves's attempt to establish a world monopoly of atomic raw materials. It was now out in the open as to why the United States had so much wanted those two previously unloved minerals, uranium and thorium. Sweden, who had been negotiating for more sales of her modest deposits, broke off discussions in September, out of consideration for her policy of neutrality: 'political considerations' made it impossible to give an option on uranium exclusively to two great powers.[59] Even so, at the end of the war the position seemed encouraging to the Americans. General Groves believed that his Combined Development Trust held 97 per cent of the world's high grade uranium ore. As to deposits of low grade ore, of those susceptible to swift development, most were either Swedish or in the British Empire.[60] True, there were countries with large deposits of this low grade material which could be used if there were no consideration of costs. Here the trust held only 35 per cent, with the rest in Latin America or Russia. But Russian sources of raw materials were then said to be inferior to those held by the United States.[61]

Not all the scientists in the United States agreed with Groves's estimate. Even a panel of atomic scientists, headed by Dr James Franck, which had earlier counselled the explosion of the bomb on an uninhabited island, for the purposes of demonstration thought that a monopoly of raw materials would be impossible (Franck was an eminent German Jewish scientist, Nobel prize-winner, who, in 1934, had left home to teach at the University of Chicago). The likelihood that the Russians would take a long time to discover how to process low grade ore, however, caused Groves to repeat his judgement that the Americans had a generation or so in hand before they would have to face a Russian bomb. Byrnes, having no personal access to scientists whom he trusted, believed Groves. But Groves was wrong in this estimate, as he was in his equally firm judgement that atomic energy would not be practicable for peaceful purposes for many years.[62]

Stimson did not believe Groves on the Russian issue. He for his part was in touch with Dr Vannevar Bush. In the light of what he believed to be Byrnes's policy, and taking advantage of Byrnes's absence in London, Stimson, now about to retire, wrote in early September to Truman, suggesting a forthright approach to the Soviet Union about nuclear weapons. Byrnes had managed to keep Stimson away from the President at Potsdam, along with Harriman.[63] Now was the time for an initiative. Further, perhaps under the influence of Bush, perhaps out of a salutary sense of dread following the bombing of Hiroshima and Nagasaki, Stimson had changed his own mind about atomic policy. Where he had previously been against talking to the Russians about atomic matters, he was now strongly in favour: to 'hang on to the bomb' and its secrets 'was by far the most dangerous course'.[64] Byrnes's approach would mean that the United States would be reverting, brutally, to 'power politics'.[65] Stimson thought that Russia would 'be more apt to respond *sincerely* to such a direct approach from America . . . if the policy were proposed as part of a general international scheme'. The United States might still offer to stop all work on the nuclear weapon (and impound what bombs they now had) provided the Russians and British did so too. Thereafter, the Russians, he hoped, would collaborate with their wartime allies on 'the development of atomic power for peaceful purposes'.[66]

Stimson's suggestion was the product of private discussion

with scientists and others who all thought that, if there were any other course, the Russians would embark upon 'an arms race'. Stimson recognised the likelihood of Soviet lack of enthusiasm or dishonesty. But the effort at diplomacy had to be made. The bomb, he now recognised, could not be used as a method to hasten changes towards liberty in Russia. The Russians had to be taken, in these unique circumstances, on their own terms: 'The chief lesson I have learned in a long life is that the only way you can make a man trustworthy is to trust him'.[67] That comment would have been fair in most circumstances. But it had no application to Russia. All the same, Stimson had backed away from the position which he had held in the spring; when, for example, he had thought Russia might have to be handled 'in a pretty rough and realistic way' by a United States which had, in the international poker game, a 'royal straight flush'.[68] On September 11, he specifically rejected Byrnes's idea that 'having this weapon rather ostentatiously on our hip' would yield results.[69] With any other politician in the United States it might be said that Stimson had changed his policies out of protest against a rival. But, with Stimson, that could not be so.

There were then, in America, two important discussions about nuclear weapons; they raised almost all the questions implicit in the matter which would trouble thinking people thereafter. The first discussion was in Chicago, on September 18, between about fifty scientists and other intelligent laymen (including, curiously, Charles Lindbergh, the pioneer of Atlantic flight, the prophet of 'America First', and a fanatical opponent of Roosevelt and intervention in the war). This was a meeting organised by the President of the university in that city, Robert Hutchins, the country's foremost exponent of liberal education, whose reaction to the dropping of the bomb had been that 'only through the monopoly of atomic power can one hope to abolish war'.[70] The second discussion, on September 21, was a Cabinet meeting, a leisurely and informal meeting so characteristic of the still easy-going world of American politics, called by Truman to discuss Stimson's paper.[71]

The scientists were the more thoughtful; and no less practical.

They had been distressed by what they considered to be superficial ideas in Washington. They believed that no one who had not worked on the Manhattan Project knew enough of the atomic 'predicament' to make any judgements about it, political or otherwise.[72] They had, in a petition by sixty-four signatories (headed by Franck), called on President Truman to share the secret of the bomb with other nations in order 'to avoid an armaments race'. Chicago was appropriate for their conference since it had been there that the first atomic chain reaction had been achieved nearly three years before by Enrico Fermi; and many of the University's scientists had worked on the Manhattan Project.

Appropriately, though, given the era, the first speaker was an economist from Chicago, Jacob Viner. He argued, rightly, that there were now only two 'giant' powers; the United States and Russia. With two such giants, any scheme for world government, which most people would not accept but which presumably could outlaw atomic weapons, was impossible. Atomic weapons might, however, have a 'peacemaking effect', because of their 'deterrent power'. Small powers might in future 'do damage'; not win wars. The fact that there was 'now no ambiguity as to the enemy that the United States would have to fear' – Russia obviously – had had a psychological effect on events. An agricultural economist, Theodore Schultz, agreed that the psychological consequences of the atomic bomb was to render the United States 'more insecure than ever before'. But Russia's behaviour would be more than just that of an insecure people because of their land mass and because they would soon have bombs too. A sociologist, Edward Shils, suggested mutual inspection. But a philosopher, Kurt Riezler, argued that any effective system of inspection 'would be so contrary to the traditions of the Russians and their philosophy . . . that they would consider such a proposal as an attack on their whole system of government'. He thought that the process of negotiating with the Russians would breed suspicion: 'Stalin won't say "no". He will propose a defective system of inspection, which we will reject.' That was politically dangerous: a wholly correct interpretation. Franck thought that any kind of inspection might meet political difficulties in the United States as well as in Russia. An inventor and chemist, Irving Langmuir, who had been to Russia earlier in the year,[73] next argued that 'the first step' had to be improved relations with Russia, by all and every means. The Americans should try and reach a point whereby, if Russia were to secure the bomb, neither she nor the United States would use it: 'at least for fifteen to twenty years, while we are developing world government'. If, during the next two years (when they would still be monopolists), the United States did not use nuclear weapons, they would be able to point to one important demonstration: 'we *did not* use our weapons when we had them and they did not'. The world was surely just enough to give the just a good reputation.

The next to speak was a mathematician, Oswald Veblen, who argued that Denmark (through Professor Bohr) and Britain had made a greater contribution to the preparation for the bomb than the United States. Franck, after discussing what a secret was in the process of manufacture, thought that, 'for another nation to make such weapons, two years is the minimum, if it is not revealed; six to eight years, as a maximum . . . these are only trade secrets'. Edward Earle, the Director of the Institute of Advanced Study at Princeton, a fine historian of France, reminded his colleagues that jellied gasoline in the terrible raid of March had been as destructive to Tokyo as if it had been an atom bomb. He thought a peace conference with Russia was needed: because 'we're on our way to talk ourselves into a war with Russia'.

There followed some discussion about the danger to science if there were to be security controls over discussion of ideas. Leo Szilard, who had worked with Einstein in Berlin, and who had drafted Einstein's letter to Roosevelt recommending that atom bombs be made, thought that, sooner or later, methods would be discovered of making combustible the earth, the sea and the air. Then, recalling that Oswald Veblen had said that in some circumstances a realistic approach might be the quixotic one, he wisely added that, if the Russians were to develop atomic weapons, there would be 'an armed peace and it will be a durable one. But we will not have permanent peace at a lesser cost than world government. That cannot come without the changed loyalty of people. If we can't have that, all we can have is a durable peace'. The chief purpose of a durable peace would be perhaps to 'create conditions, twenty to thirty years from now, which can bring about world government. That requires a shift of loyalties.' He added, with irresistible logic, 'If we are sure to get a Third World War' (and the chance of avoiding it, he thought, was only ten per cent) 'the later it comes, the worse' it would be. The victor of such a war would impose a world government, even if that victor was the United States, and had lost twenty-five million people dead. Dr Viner returned: world government was not 'in the picture at present'; but it was 'not inherently impossible'.[74]

The breadth of this discussion was worthy of the theme. Its inadequacy was also characteristic of humanity at any early stage of a new industrial development. The only result was the establishment of a society, subsequently influential, called 'The Atomic Scientists of Chicago', and a magazine.

The second critical meeting of that time was that of the American Cabinet on September 21, called to discuss Stimson's paper of the 12th. The occasion was Secretary Stimson's last official meeting. He was seventy-eight that day. He was presented with the Distinguished Service Medal by Truman, in the Rose Garden of the White House, just before the beginning of these discussions. He was to retire immediately afterwards. White-haired, infinitely experienced and willing to admit that he had often changed his mind, 'the Colonel', full of memories of Theodore Roosevelt that day, as of Hoover, of the 'era of good feelings' when Washington had scarcely been more than a village, had nothing to lose by candour. The only important addition, though, which he made to the memorandum which he had earlier sent to the President, was that he did not now think that the 'secrets concealed in atomic weapons were really such', since they could be easily apprehended by all serious scientists. He also told the Cabinet that, in future, thermonuclear bombs might be made which would be more destructive – so powerful as to ignite the atmosphere and put an end to the world.

In the discussion which followed, six men (Robert E.

Hannegan, Postmaster General; Robert Patterson, Stimson's successor-elect as Secretary of War; Lewis Schwellenbach, Secretary of Labour; General Fleming, Administrator of the Federal Works Agency; Abe Fortas, Under-Secretary of the Interior since 1942, sitting in for the Secretary of that office, Harold Ickes; and Paul McNutt, Chairman of the War Manpower Commission) agreed with Stimson. Dean Acheson, the Under Secretary of State, standing in, as he so often did, for Secretary Byrnes (then in London), accepted that an approach should be made to Russia, but added that under no circumstances should there be any one-sided exchange of information. He suggested that America and Russia should work out an exchange of information to proceed gradually, and on condition that weapons were renounced with an adequate opportunity for inspection. The rest of the Cabinet divided three ways: first, there were those who, like the Secretary of the Treasury, Fred Vinson; the Attorney General, Tom Clark; and the Secretary for Agriculture, Clinton Anderson, were opposed to any kind of approach to the Russians which might result in their receiving American secrets. Vinson questioned whether Russia could be seriously expected to make the bomb at all soon. Secretary Anderson thought that the Russians would never reciprocate any arrangement. He did not trust them at all. He told the meeting that the previous day he had been talking at Decatur, Illinois, and 'everyone' had been against telling the Russians 'anything'.

The second group was Forrestal, Secretary of the Navy; Julius Krug, Chairman of the War Production Board; John Snyder, directing OWMR (Office of War Mobilisation and Reconversion); and the septuagenarian acting President of the Senate, Kenneth MacKellar; who all wanted time to think about Stimson's ideas. Forrestal, who had a distrust of Russia (though uncertain what to do in consequence), was in fact close to Vinson, Clark and Anderson. On this occasion apparently he did not express himself harshly (Henry Wallace claimed, late that, 'as usual', he did). Since the bomb, and the knowledge which produced it, were 'the property of the American people', the Administration could not give it away till they knew that it was 'the sense of the people' that they should do so. In World War I, Japan had been an ally. But since then they had not kept their agreements. The moral was clear. Russia, like Japan, was an oriental nation; 'until we have a longer experience with them on the validity of their engagements', Forrestal thought, it was doubtful whether 'we should endeavour to buy their understanding and sympathy'. He believed the United States right to act as a sole trustee of the new energy for the time being.

A third point of view was represented by Henry Wallace, Secretary of Commerce. He now argued in favour of an open policy towards Russia. He agreed with Forrestal that the Russians were orientals. He doubted, too, whether the United States had adequate knowledge of their motives. But the atomic secret, he said, was bound to spread throughout the world. Atomic research had originated, after all, in Europe. Failure to give Russia 'our knowledge would make them embittered and sour'. He believed that there was a danger of a 'Maginot Line attitude', which would give 'us a false confidence'. Dr Vannevar Bush was also present. He seems on this occasion not to have spoken. But, perhaps more important, and equally appropriate, he had with him a memorandum which argued that, if the United States made no proposal for the exchange of scientific information which would lead to international collaboration in, and control of, atomic energy, there would be 'an atomic bomb race'. (That phrase, as will be seen, aptly or not, now became often used.) The question as to whether the United States could work with, and trust, the Russians would be determined by how they received such a proposal; even if they were unhelpful, the fact that it had been made would rebound to the American moral advantage.[75] At the end of the discussion, Truman asked the participants to send their suggestions in writing. Stimson, curiously enough, thought that most of the others had agreed with him. Acheson, on the other hand, thought the discussion unworthy of the subject. Apart from Stimson and Acheson, nobody present understood the technological issues or the diplomatic consequences of 'the bomb'. Wallace knew some science, and had known of the atomic project in 1942 but knew no atomic physics.[76]

Reading this account it is easy to be struck, as the Italian historian, Luigi Albertini, was, in writing of the causes of the First World War, and the makers of decisions then, by the apparent 'disproportion between their intellectual and moral endowments, and the gravity of the problems which faced them, between their acts and the results thereof'.[77] But the question of who was indeed up to the gravity of the problems is impossible to answer. After all, the Cabinet of September was, just as the Interim Committee had been, as broadly based as a jury. The United States were well represented geographically: there were present men from Washington State (Schwellenbach), Kentucky (Vinson), Missouri (Truman and Snyder), New Mexico (Anderson), Louisiana (Hannegan), Alabama (Mackellar) as well as the East Coast (only represented in its pure form by Acheson). There were arch-conservatives, such as Paul McNutt, one-time commander of the American Legion, a handsome, ambitious man who had been used by Roosevelt in numerous capacities. Patterson and Forrestal had both fought in the First World War and, if both had been unsympathetic to the New Deal, had served Roosevelt well throughout the second war. Henry Wallace and Julius Krug stood for the New Deal and the former might easily have been President in 1945 – had it not been for an intemperate attack on Jesse Jones, Secretary of Commerce, in 1943. Krug had been Roosevelt's nominee at the War Production Board. Hannegan, as chairman of the Democratic National Committee, a democratic party organiser from St Louis, who had once been Commissioner of Internal Revenue, had 'managed' the Democratic Convention in Chicago, which had led to Truman's nomination. Schwellenbach, like Truman, had been both a senator and a judge. Both Vinson and Anderson had been congressmen as well as judges. Clark might be, like Hannegan, a machine politician, and Snyder a Missouri friend of Truman's. But Abe Fortas and Dean Acheson could redress the balance. Stimson, the most radical person present, apart from Wallace, was the most experienced. Poetry and painting might not have been well represented; but they were no more so in Attlee's Cabinet in London. Truman and Acheson were well-read men. If one combines this group of men with the scientists at Chicago, it would be as good a collection of men as human nature could provide. The absence of any women, and black Americans, may seem strange to the modern reader but it is hard to believe that their presence would have altered the conclusion.

The next day, the news of the discussion in the Cabinet was out in open. The President's press secretary, or Forrestal, had told friends on the *New York Times*, whose headline was: 'PLEA TO GIVE SOVIET ATOM BOMB SECRET STIRS DEBATE IN CABINET: NO DECISION MADE ON WALLACE PLAN TO SHARE BOMB DATA AS PEACE INSURANCE'.

A little later, the Joint Chiefs of Staff sent Truman, at his request, a paper with their views on these matters. They opposed any release of secrets which would hasten the day when 'any new power' might develop an atomic bomb. Even though the principles of nuclear physics might be known, the manufacturing processes were not. In the absence of agreement with Russia on 'fundamental political problems', the release of such information would promote 'an atomic armament race'. The Joint Chiefs argued that, during the 'probably limited period' of American monopoly, the United States should use their technological advantage to bring about international control.[78] In a more considered document, finished on September 19 and sent later to the Secretaries of State, Navy and War, as well as the President, the Chiefs of Staff did not mention atomic weapons specifically. Yet they did say then that the 'power, range and prospective development of "modern" weapons' – a frequent euphemism – would favour a surprise attack against the United States if there were ever to be a power which would wish 'to dominate the world'. There was in consequence 'a marked reduction in the degree of invulnerability to . . . attack that has been provided in the past by our geographical position'. Fundamental changes were, therefore, needed in traditional policies. The Joint Chiefs again recommended an 'intelligence system which would assure this government information concerning military, political, economic and technological developments abroad and hence provide the necessary forewarning of hostile intent and capability'; and the 'maintenance of an adequate system of overseas bases'. The Chiefs of Staff added: 'when it becomes evident that forces of aggression are being arrayed against us by a potential enemy, we cannot afford, through any misguided and perilous idea of avoiding an aggressive attitude, to permit the first blow to be struck against us. Our government, under such conditions, should press the issue to a prompt political decision, while making all preparations to strike the first blow if necessary'.[79]

This paper was never adopted. Indeed, it does not seem to have been properly discussed,[80] but it clearly did represent the then views of clever staff officers as of the Joint Chiefs. All looked by then on the ambiguous power of the atom bomb as part of the protection of a peaceful United States unable, or at least unwilling, to maintain 'overwhelmingly strong forces in time of peace',[81] but anxious to defend itself by the best technological methods. This approach characterised United States policy for over twenty years.[82]

The only 'cabinet officer' to write to Truman after the meeting on September 24 was Henry Wallace. He repeated that he thought that there could be no secrets about the bomb, that both the United States and the world would gain from the free exchange of scientific information and that a failure to be generous on the subject would cause the rest of the world to hate the Anglo-Saxons. He hoped that there could be 'a full exchange' with Russia, including exchanges of scientists. The situation would become dangerous 'if we continue to follow our policy of . . . useless secrecy and, at the same time, building up a stockpile of atomic weapons'. Wallace had been to Chicago since the Cabinet meeting and talked to several of the scientists who had met in that city on September 18: Leo Szilard and James Franck, as well as Fermi.[83] He ended by giving support to Stimson.

The only other document of significance to reach Truman after the meeting of the Cabinet on September 21 was a memorandum of the 25th, from Acheson. His chief reflection was: 'the advantage of being ahead in such a race is nothing compared with not having the race'. Long-range cooperation with Russia would be impossible under a policy of Anglo-American exclusion of that country from atomic collaboration. If it was impossible there would be no peace but an 'armed truce'. So Russia, who would be bound to get the secret one day, ought to be directly approached in a conciliatory way. [84]

President Truman did not commit himself to any special view in the course of these discussions. But he could see that American development of atomic energy ought to be under a specific government agency; it was 'too important . . . to be made the subject of profit-seeking', he told Senators Connally, Vandenberg and Lucas. [85] He agreed that international control, as Stimson and Acheson requested, just might be achieved as a result of an approach to the Russians. [86] But he was moving away from any optimism about that.

When still making up his mind as to what precisely to do about these colossal problems, the President received a letter from Attlee in London. Attlee urgently wanted a discussion. He thought that the 'development of usable weapons by powers not friendly to our two nations had to be expected'. Anglo-American control of uranium and thorium might not last. The harnessing of atomic energy as a source of power, after all, could not be achieved without the simultaneous production of material capable of being used in a bomb. [87] If mankind were to continue to make the atomic bomb without changing the political relationships of states, sooner or later it would be used for mutual annihilation. The political problem in consequence was 'momentous'. Surely he and Truman should meet.

Attlee had taken a lot of trouble over this letter. He had shown it to Churchill in draft. Churchill also thought it essential to work matters out with the United States. Attlee would tell Bertrand Russell, on October 15, that he found the whole question of nuclear weapons 'one of the most difficult and perplexing problems with which statesmen have ever been faced'. [88] So Attlee was annoyed, even worried, that no reply came from Truman for three weeks. It exacerbated the bad blood between the ex-allies already worsened by the end of Lend Lease and the United States' slowness to concede a generous loan. But Truman had not decided what to do. He wanted to make up his own mind before he met Attlee again. There was a second inconclusive Cabinet meeting in Washington on the subject on September 25. Truman reported Byrnes's failure to make any headway in London with the Russians. As has been seen, in another context, he did not seem overly concerned.*

In the next few days Truman made up his mind that an open approach to Russia along the lines of Stimson's, Acheson's and Wallace's ideas would not be worthwhile. It is not at all clear exactly how this happened: a talk with General Groves? The apprehension that Russia might be going to challenge the United States in Turkey and in Persia? A series of chats with Admiral Leahy? Secretary Byrnes's report on the London conference was not the critical element. Though Byrnes had believed in the usefulness of the bomb as 'a lever' of policy, before the Conference of Foreign Ministers in London, he no longer did so after its failure. He was, indeed, about to embark on a hastily conceived, but nonetheless understandable, effort to go at least halfway to meet the Russians on atomic matters. But Truman took his decision, or rather took up his attitudes, independently.

Truman's change of line, vague but certain, towards one of cold realism, was probably affected by the news which reached him secretly (as it did Attlee) in September as a result of the defection of the Soviet intelligence official, Guzenko, in Canada, that the Allied atomic project (and many other things) had been penetrated during the war by Russian spies; of whom one, Dr Allan Nunn May, was under observation (though not as yet arrest) in London. (May had made three visits to the Chicago metallurgical laboratory in 1944, and had given the Russians a small quantity of enriched uranium ore.)[89] 'This Canadian business', as Lord Halifax called it, was shocking but it did not alter any judgements about the 'right course':[90] whatever that 'right course' might be. Truman had heard, as has been seen,† of Soviet espionage on the atom project earlier, even if the scale of the Canadian operation was larger than he could have anticipated. The Canadian Prime Minister, Mackenzie King, said that, at first, Truman did not seem surprised, nor inclined towards any action against the spies. He even advised King

* See above, page 195.
† See above, page 608.

against 'premature action'.[91] The British were less resigned: this news changed Bevin from being initially enthusiastic for sharing secrets with Russia to being sceptical; his belief was that Nunn May should be swiftly arrested and interrogated. 'I think we are being too tender', he said.[92] Truman, also seems at this time to have grasped the fact – surprisingly, in view of his reliance on Leahy and Groves in these weeks – that, as he mentioned to Stettinius, there was 'no precious secret' for the Soviet Union to steal.[93]

There was, however, a requirement to find some way of preserving for the national benefit 'the huge investment in brains and plant' assembled during the war, as well as to control the development of atomic power for peace and against war. That was the problem, however one put it.

On October 3, after many delays,[94] the President sent a message to Congress calling for the establishment of a national Atomic Energy Commission to deal with all relevant matters. He said also that he proposed to discuss these matters on an international level, first with Britain and Canada, then with others. There was no specific mention, as Stimson and Acheson had thought essential, of any approach to Russia. All the same, the message did, on Acheson's insistence, imply that international and national aspects of control should be intertwined. The next day, an already much discussed bill, giving the military a strong representation in any United States agency to manage atomic energy, was introduced to Congress by Congressman Andrew May and Senator Edwin Johnson: a draft had been prepared some time before, before indeed the bomb had been used, by two lawyers at the Department of War, Kenneth Royall (a future Secretary for War) and William Marbury. The draft bill had pleased the Secretaries for War and Navy, as it had General Groves; but it had worried Acheson and his colleagues in the Department of State. They set about stimulating Senator Brian McMahon of Connecticut to finish his own draft, giving civilian control, as soon as possible. These events meant that the debate about future nuclear policy was soon a public one. Walter Lippmann, probably the most widely-read columnist, had written on October 2: 'if the secret cannot be kept, it is unnecessary to argue whether it ought to be kept . . . it would be in the highest degree dangerous to suppose we were keeping the secret if in fact we were not'.[95] Such thoughts needed a response from the President, if not necessarily an answer. On October 5, Truman gave some indication of his thinking when he told the Director of the Budget that he wondered whether the United States might be demobilising too fast: 'there are some people in the world who do not seem to understand anything except the number of divisions you have', he said. The Director, Harold Smith, said, 'Mr President, you have an atomic bomb up your sleeve'. 'Yes', said Truman, 'but I am not sure that it can ever be used'.[96]

Less than a week later, President Truman made a short political tour; and, in the curious surroundings of Linda Lodge, Reelfort Lake, a fishing resort near Tiptonville, in Tennessee, he had an 'old-fashioned bull session' with reporters. In the course of it, on October 8, he said that, while scientific knowledge, and even engineering secrets, could be made available to Russia, the knowledge how to set up industrial plant for nuclear weapons would never be. Nor would the raw materials be made available. If other countries were to catch up with the United States, they would have 'to do it on their own hook, just as we did'. The atomic bomb would not be given up because it was the only means of countering Russian strength in Europe, while American troops were being cut rapidly, in response to public demands for demobilisation.

The press published this statement under the headline 'US WILL NOT SHARE ATOM BOMB SECRET, PRESIDENT ASSERTS'. On this occasion, it seems, headlines did not mislead: though he had not said what was attributed to him, Truman recognised privately to an old friend that that meant 'the armament race is on', but, he added, 'we would stay ahead'. Perhaps, Truman continued, world government might one day achieve peace and abolish nuclear weapons. At the moment, it was a dream only.[97]

After a few more weeks, during which the chief arguments in this field were those in public over the question of civilian or military control, Truman alluded again, briefly, to the atom bomb in his speech on Navy Day, October 27: his first major speech on foreign policy as President. He said that the United States would look on the possession of the bomb as 'a sacred trust', until the achievement of international control. *The Nation* commented sharply that the President had thus decided to conduct foreign policy simultaneously according to the principles of Theodore Roosevelt and Saint Francis.[98]

Some of these remarks were rash. Truman himself did not know how many atomic bombs the United States had at that time. Only General Groves did. Had he known, he would not have talked of anything like an armament race, since the nation's atomic capacity was soon going to run down as fast as its conventional one. So was the capacity to deliver the bombs. There were only about twenty-five bombers capable of delivering atom bombs that autumn. Production of both uranium and plutonium declined.[99] The individuals trained to assemble atom bombs were returning to civilian life like everyone else. The Joint Chiefs of Staff, responsible for integrating atomic capability into strategy, perhaps did not know of those facts.

Wrangling as to how to cope continued throughout the autumn of 1945, with Acheson and the State Department, and the senior scientists determined to transfer responsibility for atomic energy from the Department of War to civilian control – to 'men of demonstrated wisdom and judgement who would accept appointment not because of any emoluments that might attend their membership but . . . because of a profound recognition of the significance of atomic power to the future of civilisation'. The scientists, largely unconsulted on all subjects, and wanting to return to unregulated research, came to Washington to give evidence at Congressional hearings in October. They wrote letters of complaint. They levied what Secretary of War Patterson described as 'well-nigh hysterical criticism' of the bill before Congress. They lobbied. They formed associations. Senators 'pontificated'. Senator Connally thought that civilian control of atomic energy would be risky. The American debate about the future of nuclear energy continued that autumn to have a domestic character. Discussion of the international dimension was confined to rhetoric: Representative Merrow was characteristic when he argued that the idea of giving away the knowledge 'we have acquired by our genius and our industry' was 'beyond comprehension'. Senator Vandenberg also thought that to give Russia atomic secrets was 'unthinkable'.[100] The alternatives were scarcely discussed.

Attlee kept on pressing for a meeting with Truman about nuclear weapons. He was seriously concerned. He himself needed to decide British policy on the subject. Whitehall was perturbed. His thoughtful official, Sir Orme Sargent, believed that, 'with the arrival of the atomic bomb, civilisation was finished. It was merely a question of years – anything, say, from five years to twenty-five years'.[101] Alec Cadogan thought much the same.[102] There was less comment in the English press on the long-term significance of the bombs than in the United States. Doubtless this was because the British had not felt safe in their island since the invention of military air power. George Orwell had, however, suggested in *Tribune* that atom bombs were likely 'to put an end to large scale wars at the cost of prolonging indefinitely a peace that is no peace'.[103] The press contained little discussion as to whether Britain should have its own atomic bomb programme.[104] Perhaps such action was taken for granted. All the same, Attlee won approval in his Cabinet for the view that 'there was no prospect of controlling the use of this new weapon unless we succeeded in establishing an effective world organisation with both the will and the power effectively to preserve the peace'. In this long and important discussion in the British Cabinet on November 8, of the same character as that in Washington in September, some ministers thought that there should be an immediate offer to disclose information about the bomb to the Russians. They were over-ruled.[105]

Attlee kept his real decision-making on atomic policy to a tiny group of ministers ('Gen 75' was the name of the Cabinet Committee).[106] This was partly because of fear of indiscretion if matters were talked of in a larger group; partly because some of Attlee's colleagues were on the unreliable Left of his party. Attlee did not want to be told by Americans that the British could not keep atomic secrets.

It was as a result of a series of meetings in October at which Attlee and Anderson were the protagonists that, possibly in the light of Truman's procrastination over a meeting, the decisions were taken which led to independent British atomic energy and to a British atomic weapon. Harwell had been selected as the site for the first of these endeavours. Nothing was yet certain. But, just as the dropping of the bomb had been assumed as the right course when it was ready, so the understanding soon was that Britain would herself build one. Attlee did tell the House of Commons in October 1945 that a research and development committee would cover all aspects of atomic energy.[107] But he said nothing more to the public. He easily also secured the conservative opposition's support in ensuring that parliamentary questions about material for atomic research did not get put down.[108] He had a 'dislike of seeing almost anything about atomic energy in print';[109] perhaps because, as his biographer puts it, of 'his profound sense of unease on the subject'.[110] The Guzenko case probably did not tip the balance of Cabinet opinion in favour of the making of weapons. But it hardened Attlee's mind against trusting Russia.

The Anglo-American meeting was eventually held in mid-November. Sir John Anderson went with Attlee. (Rather unfortunately, Lord Keynes, chief adviser to the Treasury, was in Washington at the same time seeking a major loan to Britain in humiliating conditions.) The Prime Minister of Canada, Mackenzie King, also attended: he was disappointed that the meeting was not primarily concerned with atom spies. After some days of general discussion, a plan devised at the last minute by Dr Vannevar Bush was adopted. The three statesmen announced in public that, though they favoured the general dispersion of scientific knowledge, detailed information concerning the practical application of atomic energy should await 'reciprocal and enforceable safeguards'. They agreed jointly to propose a 'commission' of the United Nations to work out what these might be.[111] That commission, the statesmen thought, should investigate the best way of ensuring the elimination of all atomic weapons. For this, Bush favoured, for the time being, a three-part plan: first, a United Nations organisation; second, a committee of inspection which would have the right to look at any laboratory engaged in atomic research; thirdly, all nations would stockpile materials capable of atomic fission and release them for peaceful purposes only. The United States would still then be able to make atomic material but would promise not to assemble it for weapons.[112] This cautious document, with its emphasis on staged changes, formed the basis of policy for some time. There was no suggestion of further American collaboration with Britain except for sharing of raw materials.

Attlee agreed with this approach. He saw no point in simply outlawing the bomb. No rules, he knew, would apply when a nation was fighting for its existence. For the rest, a combined Anglo-American-Canadian committee of officials – the 'Central Policy Committee', established in 1944 – would continue to decide policy on these matters in Washington. The agreement between Roosevelt and Churchill at Quebec in 1943, that there would be full collaboration after the war between the United States and Britain in developing atomic energy for both war and peace was, however, not confirmed: it appears that no one knew of that agreement in Washington, that the American copy of it had been lost (because of the code-name for the project 'Tube Alloys', the papers had been filed in the archives at Hyde Park as concerning torpedoes) and that apparently it did not bind Truman.[113] The complementary agreement at Roosevelt's house, Hyde Park, in 1943, pledging the United States and Britain to consult before any bomb was used, was held to be obsolete now the war was over.

The Americans at this conference showed themselves far from being anglophiles. Byrnes, being Irish, had no vision of any special relation between the two countries. Dr Bush thought that Britain might seek to become the United States's rival. General Groves had, the previous year, opposed the Quebec agreement. The delegations seemed in the beginning even likely to quarrel. In the end, however, two 'memoranda of intention' were signed which provided respectively, in vague terms, for Anglo-American, and for Anglo-Canadian-American, cooperation. The only thing that the two parties agreed upon, however, was the fact of the bad organisation of the conference itself: the fault of Truman and Leahy, who perhaps thought that they were in the tradition of Roosevelt in refusing to work out a detailed agenda. It looks too as if Attlee was deceived by the appearance of good feelings to suppose that real concessions to him were being made.[114]

A swift Soviet accusation was that the United States and Britain had formed an anti-Russian bloc concerned to use 'atomic diplomacy' (apparently the first use of the phrase). It was an accusation on this occasion specially wide of the mark. Attlee returned to London, fairly content: to find, on his arrival, a memorandum from Professor P. M. S. Blackett, the charming and brilliant future Nobel Prize Winner, on the Left in politics, at that time in the Ministry of Defence, who argued that a decision to produce, or to acquire, atomic bombs would decrease, not increase, British security.*[115] Attlee would not, however, accept Blackett's recommendation that Britain could not, or should not, keep up with the United States and Russia on atomic matters. He regarded him as a layman with inadequate political judgement. All the same Blackett was right in principle. The British decision to manufacture atomic weapons, however understandable in the light of the Cabinet's perception of the country's power and of their belief that a neglectful America might leave Europe unprotected against Russia, was a first step towards the proliferation of the weapons.

One characteristic of the Anglo-American conference in Washington was that Secretary Byrnes had excluded the British from his thinking on these questions. Partly that was because his thinking was inchoate. But he had also determined that the best chance of making a successful approach to Russia would be if he avoided collaboration with other allies. That anyway was to his

---

* Blackett's reported assumption for possible numbers of bombs 1946–1955 was:

Cumulative stocks of Bombs assumed in January of each year

|      | 1946 | 1947 | 1948 | 1949 | 1950 | 1951 | 1952 | 1953 | 1954 | 1955 |
|------|------|------|------|------|------|------|------|------|------|------|
| US   | 40   | 120  | 200  | 280  | 300  | 440  | 520  | 600  | 680  | 760  |
| UK   | 0    | 0    | 0    | 40   | 80   | 120  | 160  | 200  | 240  | 280  |
| USSR | 0    | 0    | 0    | 0    | 0    | 0    | 40   | 80   | 120  | 160  |

liking. It seems a rational enough approach, if considered in the abstract. Although the British were later understandably angry, Byrnes made up his mind without collaboration with his own President or even his own staff. At all events, towards the end of November, as we have seen,* on Thanksgiving Day, according to his own account, he conceived his plan of making a direct approach to Russia over nuclear weapons. He then suggested, on November 23, that the Council of Foreign Ministers meet again in Moscow in December; and that there should be discussion with Russia of the idea for a United Nations commission to study control of the bomb.[116]

This led to, or coincided with, a series of 'policy plans': at least two by the new 'USSR division' in the Department of State; the other by the Joint Intelligence Committee.

The Department of State's main paper was interesting and well-written. 'Chip' Bohlen's hand can be detected in it. It began with a proper sense of humility. The problem of Russian capabilities and intentions was so complex, and the unknowns so numerous, that it was difficult to grasp the situation fully. Yet great risk was involved if all the United States's Russian problems were dealt with independently of each other. The paper assumed that the chief power centres of the world were now Russia and the United States; there was no nonsense about Britain, and no suggestion that the United States might withdraw into isolation, as she had in 1919. The paper assumed that, for several years ('perhaps five or even ten'), the Soviet Union would be unable to produce atom bombs in significant quantities and so be unable to prevent, by any measures of defence, the delivery of a significant proportion of atomic weapons to American (or British) bases. But all the same, soon after that, the Soviet Union would 'attain something like equality with the United States in the production of atom bombs, long-range bomb-carriers and facilities for active defence in atomic warfare'. Later still, in 'one or two decades', the Russians would probably be able to 'match the total production of the United States in essential lines'. Both sides would then have large offensive

* See above, page 207.

capabilities. If war should break out, and a ruinous stalemate be achieved, in which the Soviet state both survived and had been able to establish control over all Europe, the conflict would have to be accounted a Russian victory.

Perhaps, thereafter, a new phase in military affairs might be achieved in which one or both sides would have means of defence against each other's atom bombs. That would give the power which achieved it first an overwhelming superiority, since it could attack the other without itself being attacked.

War just might return to 'pre-atomic' conditions if both sides had bombs, but had no effective means of neutralising them; or, if both sides had the means of neutralising them in flight (or, indeed, if both sides had exhausted their capacity for bombing). In such a non-atomic war, Russia's capabilities might grow more rapidly than those of Britain, or the United States, because they would have maintained a high level of industrial expansion. In a conflict in Europe, the logistical advantage would lie with the Russians, especially after American and British demobilisation; nor would a Russian success in Europe be counterbalanced by the United States's control of East Asia.

The paper described the role of ideology in Russia. The principal factor of uncertainty was not that of her capability in war but the special one of an official Soviet ideology 'in process of change'. That ideology was basically the Marxist one of inevitable conflict. But that philosophy did not prescribe overt conflict at all times, and in all places. On the contrary, it contained obscure, often contradictory, ideas respecting the strategy, and timing, of compromise and collision in different conditions. Power politics of the old sort might still determine several actions. It was, however, unsafe to assume that the future attitudes of the Russians towards non-Soviet states, and towards the domestic forces and movements within them, would *not* be determined by Marxist ideology. At the least, ideological considerations would cause the Soviet leaders to construe some of the friendly acts of non-Soviet states as sinister in design. That would not only make them arm more heavily, but also cause them to continue to seek expansion in the name of security, more so than if no ideology were influencing them.

The paper also argued that, unless something could be done to improve material life in western Europe, a reaction in favour of Communism, which at least offered something new, might occur; but the authors of the paper thought that the Soviet leadership's interest in western Europe was less pronounced than it had been a few months earlier.

As to American policies, the Americans could choose between sharing immediately with the Soviet Union all knowledge of the nuclear weapons; or they could give them only information about practical industrial applications. The United States could take an initiative in specific diplomatic problems and, 'by asking substantially less than the current capabilities of the United States might require', could promote the establishment of 'stable, buffer regimes acceptable to both the United States and the USSR'. The United States could, alternatively, 'withhold all knowledge . . . that would contribute to the development of Soviet capabilities' and exert 'all the pressure, short of war, that American capabilities would permit, in attempting to build up, at home and abroad, a balance of power so strong that the USSR would be held in check for the foreseeable future'.

The report favoured the first, more moderate policy. The unconditional sharing of atomic energy with the Russians would be an irreversible action. Unquestionably, the Soviet government would welcome that. But what would they do if their capabilities were quickly, and substantially, increased? Their foreign policy might certainly be strengthened. Was it not possible that, in those circumstances, the United States could take advantage of some years of Soviet inferiority in weapons to accustom her to a system of stable relations? Would that system, even if achieved, be satisfactory once the Russians had gained an adequate capacity to make, and to deliver, nuclear weapons? The authors of this paper believed that it was best to make available a little technical knowledge to Russia and to keep on giving it, in proportion to Russian good behaviour; and to adopt a generally conciliatory policy. It was 'by no means certain' that Soviet intentions were 'set irrevocably in the pattern of expansion facilitated by revolution'. Even if they appeared to lean in that direction, a long period of a conciliatory policy might moderate the intentions of the Soviet Union 'before its capabilities were largely increased'. If that policy were to fail, a shift could always be made to a harder policy, before the Soviet Union achieved equality of capabilities with the United States. But the immediate application of such a hard policy would surely fix Soviet intentions in a policy of expansion. The authors thought too that an indecisive, or fluctuating, combination of a hard and a soft line of policy might have an inflammatory effect on Soviet intentions, without the corresponding effect of achieving balance of capabilities as a check.

The Department concluded that, in the course of a few years of independent development, 'the USSR will probably have offensive capabilities not greatly different from those of the United States'. The bomb had upset all previous estimates. The Department had 'formed the impression that this is an era of headlong change where still other new weapons may at any time affect the international balance'. A system of defence against the bomb might have the same effect.

The paper by the Department of State finally discussed the nature of a world in which both Russians and Americans would have the bomb. The United States might have an advantage in its new system of forward bases. Both sides would, however, have 'large offensive capabilities'. In such circumstances, any war would be enormously destructive for both sides. The outcome would be frankly uncertain. Perhaps neither side would be able to win. In a 'ruinous stalemate, one or both states' would collapse. In a more distant period, one or both sides would probably have an active defence adequate to 'neutralise' the enemy's bombs. Yet it was improbable that either the Americans or the Russians would remain 'in exclusive possession of such a defence for long enough to win a war'.[117]

Another paper in the Department suggested a direct bid for Soviet collaboration and it was apparently that which Byrnes planned to use as a brief for his visit to Moscow. The Secretary for the Navy, Forrestal, and the new Secretary for War, Patterson, criticised this approach. So did Senators Connally and Vandenberg, who thought that Byrnes was proposing to disclose scientific information. When they challenged Truman, after

Byrnes had left for Moscow, the President denied it. They remained perturbed.

The Joint Intelligence Committee, reporting to the Joint Chiefs of Staff, had a different interpretation of Soviet motives to that of the Department of State. They treated the Soviet Union much more as an old-fashioned imperial power. Its 'fundamental aims', in the next five years, were to 'round out and consolidate the recent territorial acquisitions on the periphery of the USSR'; to 'complete arrangements ensuring Soviet dominance over border areas in Eastern Europe, the Middle East and the Far East'; and to secure, at the least, equality with the West in influence in Germany, China and Japan. The Russians would seek air and naval bases beyond their frontiers to counterbalance the establishment of American bases near the Soviet Union; to expand Soviet influence in Western zones of influence; to divide, or win over, non-Communist Left-wing parties; to gain the support of organised labour; to increase Soviet standing among colonial peoples; and, to work for Soviet prestige inside the international agencies.

To realise these aims, the Committee did not believe that the Soviet Union was prepared deliberately now to risk a major conflict with either Britain or the United States. But such a thing might occur, particularly by miscalculation, deriving from an accident.[118]

These papers seem, like the discussions in September in Chicago and Washington, to have dictated policy on these matters for many years.

There were also by that time officers in the American services who had developed theories to suit the new atomic technology. General Carl Spaatz, the planner of the United States bombing offensive against Germany, for example, believed that the post-war air force should be built round methods of delivering the atom bomb; and that all defence should in turn revolve round the air force. General 'Hap' Arnold, about to retire, as the air force representative on the JCS, the post he had held throughout the war, believed that the post-war United States air force should be an aerial police force for the world. In November 1945, he told Secretary of War Patterson that the future security of the United States depended on making it evident to any aggressor that 'an attack on the United States would be immediately followed by an immensely devastating air-atomic attack on him. To do that, the United States should maintain its present air force', should establish a worldwide service of intelligence and remain in the forefront of research and development of all weapons.[119] Arnold's closest colleague, General Curtis Le May, commander of that 20th Air Force which had destroyed so much of Tokyo in March 1945, agreed with him. Le May himself suggested 'an army-navy agency' for co-ordinating the adaptation of atomic weapons to intercontinental ballistic missiles which he believed it would soon be possible to make.[120] That was on the basis of what the Americans had learned of German efforts on that subject.

Dr Arthur Hugh Compton, a scientist involved in policy-making on the Manhattan Project from early on gave, meantime, a powerful lecture to the National Academy of Sciences, on November 11. To it, he remarked: 'now for the first time . . . it becomes feasible for a central authority to enforce peace throughout the world. Before the Second World War, many parts of the earth were difficult for access by a world police. Today, this has changed. Fast aeroplanes, long-range rockets and atomic bombs have now solved the technical problem of bringing to bear on any area, at any time, whatever destructive force may be required . . . A central authority having critical monopoly of these major means of warfare can now be equipped to enforce international peace. The fact is that the United States now has in its possession a sufficient monopoly of the weapons needed for such policing that it might be able to act in this capacity of world policeman'.[121] The prospect might have seemed heady to anyone, even if Dr Compton excluded the idea from practical politics.

Against this background of conflicting advice and speculation, including some very radical suggestions, Secretary of State Byrnes made his controversial visit to Moscow, with the purpose of dealing there with 'the bomb'.

# TWENTY-ONE

# THE SOVIET WEAPON: FIRST STEPS IN NUCLEAR DIPLOMACY

The subject of these speculations, the Soviet Union, had long ago in 1930 begun to work seriously on nuclear physics, at the Physio-Technical Institute in Leningrad, under the direction of Professor Abram Ioffe.[1] One of Ioffe's pupils, Igor Kurchatov, was performing original research in the field by 1935. Soviet scientists had the use of a small cyclotron or 'atom smasher' by 1937, and were planning two more elaborate ones by the time that Russia entered the war in 1941. The design of these suggests that, both in theory and in application, the Russian nuclear physicists were, at that time, the equal of their counterparts in the West.[2] Reports reaching the West of a conference on atomic physics, in November 1939, at Kharkov, show that the Soviet Academicians and professors present also knew what had been demonstrated in nuclear physics outside the Soviet Union.[3]

The following year, two of Kurchatov's students proved for themselves the existence of spontaneous fission in uranium. A state fund to find uranium in Central Asia was set up. In early 1941, the study of how to separate the isotopes of uranium was continuing in Russia at about the same pace as in the United States. The Russians may, however, 'have been somewhat in the lead' in respect of the theoretical exploration of these methods.[4]

The war halted these Soviet activities. While the United States was able to turn vast resources, and a large number of scientists, into the Manhattan Project, the Russians turned over their institutes and academicians to more immediate concerns. Kurchatov, for example, was sent to the Black Sea to work on protection of ships from mines. There was an almost complete end of nuclear research in Russia: even indifference to the subject, as the publication of a speech by the Cambridge-educated scientist Peter Kapitsa in October 1941 suggested.[5]

In late 1943, this neglect came to an end: perhaps because of the Soviet discovery through espionage that the United States were taking seriously the possibilities of making an atomic bomb for use in the current war: the early channels of information included Klaus Fuchs, Allan Nunn May, and perhaps certain Communists in San Francisco.[6] But it remains uncertain how exactly the Soviet government became informed of Western activities: presumably Stalin decided against a full-scale attempt to make the weapons before the end of the war. Perhaps, considering the multitude of his other concerns, he was not informed in any detail of this product of his country's espionage: even perhaps not at all.[7] Had the Soviet Union been accurately informed, they might not have been impressed by the activities of the United States, before the test of the bomb at Alamogordo. It seems likely, nevertheless, that the news of the world's first chain reaction at Chicago on December 1942 became known in Moscow. In consequence of that, or of some other indication that nuclear weapons were possible, Kurchatov returned to nuclear physics in February 1943 and went to Moscow.[8] From then onwards, the hitherto remarkably open attitude in the Soviet Union towards nuclear physics changed.[9]

Espionage, it is known, continued: probably on an ever more intensive scale. Secretary Stimson told Roosevelt, in September 1943, that Soviet secret agents 'were already getting information about vital secrets and sending them to Russia'.[10] Perhaps Vice President Henry Wallace, one of the few Americans who knew anything of the project in the United States, was careless in talk. An article in *Time* in November 1944 'would', according to General Groves, 'have indicated that the way to produce an atom bomb was to take care that it was based on "implosion"'.[11] Conversations between Professor Bohr and an attaché of the Soviet embassy in London in 1944 (and correspondence between the former and Peter Kapitsa the same year) showed the extent of Soviet curiosity. William White, a United States businessman, visited the Electrosila plant in Leningrad in the summer of 1944. His guide, in the style of a true *faux-naïf*, said: 'Behind Urals, we have many big things. We have, like you call in America, "Manhattan Project" . . . you know of this?' White, who did not, replied, 'But . . . of course, I know Manhattan, I live there'.[12]

Concern about Russia dictated very early the attitudes of senior officials dealing with the Manhattan Project in the United States. General Groves, for example, freely admitted: 'There was never, from about two weeks from the time that I took charge of this project, any illusion on my part but that Russia was our enemy'. He did not go along with 'the attitude of the country as a whole that Russia was our gallant ally. I always had suspicions'.[13] Groves, all-powerful throughout the war in all that concerned atomic energy, went to considerable lengths to discover what the Russians were doing in the field: even sending over, under a pretext, half a ton of uranium salts and two pounds of low-grade uranium to Russia to observe their reaction.[14] There were also secret but apparently unsuccessful operations within Russia to try to discover the extent of deposits there of the sought after metals.[15] It is odd that, using the knowledge generally available about Soviet activities in these things before 1942, Groves did not conclude that the Russian scientists could soon build a bomb on their own.

In February 1945, Dr Klaus Fuchs, then in Los Alamos, told the Russians of the success being encountered there.[16] Other information continued to pass, probably through the later famous espionage network run by Julius Rosenberg. So the Soviet work was given a further impetus. Even so, the project remained theoretical. It occupied only twenty physicists and a staff of fifty.[17] In Germany, United States specialist officers were doing what they could to prevent as many German physicists as they could from falling into Russian hands.[18] The scientists concerned were, under 'Operation Paperclip', to be allowed asylum in the United States. The same policy was extended to France. All these arrangements were directed by the omnicompetent Groves.[19] Other groups concerned themselves with rocket scientists, who would devise the means of delivering the nuclear weapons of the 1960s and 1970s.

In May 1945, the Russian army found in Berlin some laboratories in which the Germans had been working on the breaking of the atom with what Stalin described as modest results. A number of German physicists such as Dr Nikolaus Riehl and Professor R. Döpel were, however, carried off from Berlin to Russia and soon began to work on nuclear physics in Moscow.[20] In June, Klaus Fuchs passed on a detailed description of the plutonium bomb which would be used at Nagasaki[21] and then in July, as has been seen, Truman 'casually' at Potsdam asked his interpreter: 'will you tell the Generalissimo that we have perfected a very powerful explosive, which we are going to use against the Japanese and we think it will end the war'.[22] Stalin as casually answered: he hoped that 'we would make good use of it against the Japanese'. Had Russian conduct at Potsdam been amiable, the President might perhaps have talked of future international control before the bomb was used.[23] The journalist Alexander Werth asked Molotov, in 1947, about this conversation; Molotov said, 'We were told of a "superbomb", the like of which had not been seen. But the word "atom" was not used'.[24]

According to Marshal Zhukov, Molotov said to Stalin, after they had returned to their quarters from the Cecilienhof in Potsdam, 'we'll have to talk it over with Kurchatov and hurry things up'.[25] Another Soviet commander, General Shtemenko, wrote, however, that 'neither Stalin nor Antonov, his Chief of Staff, realised that this was "an entirely new type of weapon"; and the General Staff then received no special instructions'.[26] Whether or no Stalin had been informed about nuclear questions before, he may have thought that the United States were developing the bomb as a threat, and that it would not be used. Perhaps Shtemenko merely meant that the Soviet General Staff knew nothing of the matter.

Khrushchev recalled that 'Stalin was frightened to the point of cowardice' after the actual explosion. The day after the bombing of Hiroshima, Svetlana Stalin went to her father's dacha. Everyone was so busy with the problem of the atom bomb that 'my father paid hardly any attention to me' even though she had just had a new baby.[27] Beria was put in overall direction of the Soviet version of the Manhattan Project. Stalin ordered 'all' Russian technology to be directed towards developing 'atomic weapons of our own'.[28] In mid-August Kurchatov and the People's Commissar for Munitions, Boris Vannikov were ordered by Stalin to 'provide us with the atomic weapons in the shortest possible time'. He also apparently said, 'If we don't manage to do all these things very quickly, the British and the Americans will crush us'.[29] Harriman saw Stalin on August 8. The latter thought that the atom bomb might give the Japanese a pretext for making an end of the war.[30] He showed 'great interest' in the bomb. But the Soviet press did not.[31] Neither Stalin nor Molotov showed any outward sign of concern. Thus on August 7 Molotov said: 'This is American propaganda. From a military point of view, it has no important meaning whatsoever'.[32] Even more interesting was the international Communist press. At first, Communist papers all over the world hailed the dropping of the bomb as an act of charity since it shortened the war and saved lives.[33] *Unita* in Rome went so far as to castigate the Vatican for their criticism: such criticism was 'a submission to a certain kind of abstract humanitarianism'.[34] But a few weeks later the same papers were saying the contrary.

George Kennan telegraphed Washington on September 30 that 'the Soviet government will undoubtedly endeavor with every means at its disposal to learn the secrets of atomic energy'.[35] Acheson reflected 'it seems most unlikely that, even if given complete control of method and means, Colonel Stimson could have persuaded Stalin to have foregone a Soviet nuclear armament system'.[36] Kennan added, in that same telegram, that 'the men in power in Russia, or those who have chances of gaining power within the foreseeable future, would not hesitate for a moment to apply this power against us if, by doing so, they thought that they might materially improve their power position in the world. To assume that the Soviet leaders would be restrained by scruples of gratitude or humanitarianism would be to fly in the face of overwhelming contrary evidence on a matter vital to the future of our country'. Kennan concluded that, because of the completeness of Soviet security, 'large scale, special efforts of intelligence, on various planes' were therefore essential. He offered to make detailed suggestions. Acheson agreed that would be desirable but, for the moment, nothing was done. There was as yet no such intelligence agency.

Now at that time, as has been seen, there was no agreement in the West as to when Russia might be able to finish her own bomb. Dr Conant had told the Interim Committee that Russia could catch up in three to five years. Most scientists agreed. General Groves – because he thought that he had captured most of the raw material, and that Russian scientists were backward – still thought that it might be a generation. Groves influenced Truman on the matter, and Byrnes also.[37]

In September 1945, Dr Fuchs – who remained in Los Alamos until June 1946 – told his Soviet 'control' how he had seen the great test at Alamogordo; and gave other information about the size of the bomb. Other agents, such as David Greengrass, gave confirmatory details. All this was presumably useful to Beria and to Kurchatov. Whether it enabled the Soviet scientists to 'catch up' more quickly with the West than they might otherwise have done can only be a matter for speculation. The explosion of the bomb itself must have been the greatest propaganda in favour of the realisation that it could be made: and that was the most important thing for a country which already had the capacity needed. At all events, also in September, Molotov permitted himself several curious indiscretions: thus he disconcertingly asked Byrnes at the London Conference if he had an atomic bomb in his side pocket. Byrnes replied that most southerners like him had artillery in their side pockets; but he had an atom bomb in his 'hip pocket'. Laughter followed uneasily. Then, later that same night, Molotov gave a toast at a party: 'Here's to the atom bomb: we've got it'.[38] Molotov also said that Russia would like a colony 'somewhere in Africa' and, 'if you won't give us one of the Italian colonies, we should be quite content to have the Belgian Congo'.[39] The implication was clear, if crude, and Byrnes made much of it.

During the course of October, the FBI sent a report to Truman obtained from Latin America. It told the White House that Russian experiments in atomic matters had begun in 1940, that there had even been an (accidental) atomic explosion there in 1943, that in Russia there were substantial deposits of both uranium and thorium, and that German scientists had recently been assisting the Russians.[40] Perhaps this information, along with the news of espionage, helped to make up Truman's mind about what to do.

On November 6 Molotov, to whom general responsibility for talk on all these things had plainly been allocated, addressed the Central Committee of the Communist Party of the Soviet Union in St Andrew's Hall – the one-time 'Throne Room of St Andrew' named by Peter the Great for the order of that Saint – in the Great Kremlin Palace, and warned the West against both setting up foreign bases and using the bomb as an instrument of power politics. Atomic energy could not remain a secret possession of one country: he said, 'we will have atomic energy and much else'. At which, there followed 'tumultuous and prolonged applause. Everyone rose'.[41] The Moscow press was accordingly negative about the Anglo-American-Canadian meetings in Washington. The conclusions were summarised in *Pravda* by the single comment that the Anglo-American view was that bomb production should remain a secret, with no qualifications at all.[42]

The American possession of the bomb naturally troubled the Russians. As in 1815, because of the industrial revolution, so in 1945, because of Anglo-Saxon technological superiority it seemed that a great Russian military victory could not be exploited to the full: in the case of 1815, the industrial revolution. Perhaps Stalin feared that his colleagues would think the West had outmanoeuvred him. If so, he needed to show himself specially resolute. Certainly it must have seemed in 1945 that someone had blundered when Kurchatov and other scientists were taken away from nuclear physics in 1941. The fear that he himself might be blamed was perhaps one reason why he gave the West (and his own colleagues) the impression in the coming months that he had every capacity to move on the Channel Ports. One informant (or disinformant) of Averell Harriman, a

Bulgarian working in Moscow, George Andreychine, sought to attribute the 'changes' in Soviet policy in later 1945 'primarily' to the atomic bomb.[43] Doubtless that at least was what the Soviet Union wanted Americans to think. Harriman may have for a time done so. Andreychine, born in Macedonia in 1894, was an old Comintern man. He had drifted into socialism through Macedonian revolutionary movements. He had helped to found the American Communist Party when he was working in Minnesota. He joined the Executive Committee of the Profintern (international trade union movement in 1921) as chief of its Anglo-Saxon section. Anarcho-syndicalist, Trotskyite and an 'informant' of Bullitt in Moscow, Andreychine would soon return to Sofia to work in the foreign ministry there and be purged in the late 1940s. Harriman meantime reported to Byrnes on November 27, that the bomb was recognised in Russia as 'an offset to the power of the Red Army'. It revived their sense of insecurity. Harriman thought that that partly explained Molotov's aggressiveness in London; 'the Russian people have been aroused to feel that they again face an antagonistic' world.[44] The same was expressed by Clark Kerr, the British ambassador: 'Plumb came the atom bomb', he telegraphed in December, 'when Russians had supposed themselves at last secure'.[45]

The atom bomb would ultimately cause the Soviet government to revise fundamentally one of Marxism-Leninism's most important doctrines: the view that war is merely a violent method of carrying through political designs. Of this change, there was in 1945 no sign. As late as September 1946, Stalin would say that atomic bombs 'are intended to frighten the weak-nerved but they cannot decide the outcome of war'.[46] A Soviet lawyer, E. A. Korovin, in a learned article in early 1946, derided British ideas as stated in a debate in the House of Commons in late November: Anthony Eden had said that only an abatement of sovereignty to take 'the sting out of nationalism' could make the world 'safe from atomic power'.[47] Korovin wondered whether, 'at the bottom of these political fantasies', there did not lie 'an extremely shrewd calculation, in the realm of political arithmetic and voting games, whereby the eager troubadours of a world parliament' dream of dictating 'their will to the rest of mankind'.


It will be recalled that, while the grandfather clock ticked in Byrnes's library on Thanksgiving Day 1945, the Secretary of State had conceived the idea of a direct approach about atomic energy to the Russians; and that he had earlier abandoned the rough line of unyielding diplomacy to exert concessions in East Europe, and elsewhere, because of Molotov's equal toughness in London. He had decided to ask Molotov for a meeting of foreign ministers in December and made the request (to try and please Molotov) without telling Ernest Bevin or the British ambassador; and he would go to Moscow definitely without the French. Preparations began and, in keeping with his plan, the British were told only at the last minute. Indeed, they heard first of the planned meeting from the Russians. Nor did the British learn anything of Byrnes's proposals on atomic questions till they got to Moscow.

Byrnes made a preliminary speech on November 16 in Washington in which he as it were emptied his 'hip pocket' of any suspicion of supporting 'atomic diplomacy' by saying that the peace-loving temper of Americans would assure the impeachment of any President who used atomic weapons in defiance of the Charter of the United Nations.

This meeting of Secretary of State Byrnes was carried out with none of the tact with which he was usually associated. His attentions were so fixed on Russia that he neglected those courtesies towards senators and officials in Washington at which he was customarily so adept. He appears to have taken into his confidence only his Rooseveltian counsellors, Benjamin Cohen and Leo Pasvolsky, and also Dr James Conant, the scientific member of the old Interim Commitee. Byrnes proposed to take Conant with him to Moscow in order to show that he meant business (and also to gain such information as he could about Russian atomic activities). It may be that the Secretary's tactlessness in refusing to talk to the leaders of the Senate, was due to the fact that he had not made up his mind what he would

do in Moscow till the last minute.[48] But this domestic mistake
damaged the mission. As noticed earlier, Senators Vandenberg
and Connally were irritated by Byrnes when they saw him before
he set off. They subsequently complained to Truman. The
Secretary could have mollified them. As he did not, they made
a special point of the fact that there was what they perceived as
a dangerous change in the plan to be put to the Russians from
that agreed with Attlee and Mackenzie King: instead of each
stage of atomic disarmament being dependent for initiation on
the completion of the last, that was no longer to be a prerequisite.[49]
The stages would follow automatically. In consequence, Truman
had to follow Byrnes to Moscow with a telegram saying that he
had assured Senators Vandenberg and Connally that 'there
was no intention to disclose any scientific information' without
safeguards.[50]

There was, in the end, however, no more detailed discussion
about atomic matters at Moscow than there had been at Paris.
Molotov wanted to talk about China and Greece, not atomic
energy. But one change was forthcoming. Until December 1945,
the Russians had denigrated the value of the atomic bomb. No
member of the Soviet delegation in London, for example, had
shown the slightest curiosity about atomic energy.[51] To begin
with in Moscow it was the same. No one in Moscow showed
any interest in Dr Conant's presence, even though he had been
actually present at the test at Alamogordo. Molotov in Moscow
pursued this line. He even joked that Dr Conant or Byrnes might
have in the pocket of their waistcoats a piece of fissile material.
At that, Stalin rose; nuclear fission, he said bleakly, spoiling the
party, was 'much too serious a matter to be the subject of jokes'
(especially, he might have added, jokes which had been used
before). He praised the American and British scientists for their
'great invention'.[52] Molotov's face did not change its expression.
But Soviet policy did. Thenceforward, the Russians seemed to
give the atomic bomb the consideration that it deserved.

The three foreign ministers at Moscow agreed in the end,
among other things, that they would all support a special commission of the United Nations to deal with atomic energy, and
that it should operate under the auspices of the Security Council,

whose other permanent members, France and China, would be asked to co-sponsor the idea.[53] The Russians agreed to this American plan almost without discussion. Byrnes had thus neither passed on scientific information, nor even promised to discuss it. His proposals now indeed scarcely seem adequate. Cohen later said that they had not been generous enough.[54] But no proposal could then have been generous enough for the Soviet Union to have accepted them. If Britain believed, as a 'great nation', that she had to enter the atomic field, it is scarcely surprising that Russia should feel the same.

Byrnes's policies in Moscow designed to slight Britain had been observed by Russia. Stalin commented to the Secretary of State that he knew that this was 'obviously only a cloak to hide the reality of the bloc' which was being built by the two Anglo-Saxon nations. He also told Byrnes that the French would be welcome at future meetings of the foreign ministers: a masterly remark discomforting the Secretary of State, who would personally not have much minded if France had been permanently excluded, particularly if blame could have been attributed to Russia.[55]

The internal debate in the United States also changed during December: for the worse, from the point of view of the military influence; for the better, so far as the scientists and the advocates of civilian control were concerned. Senator Brian McMahon had opened hearings on his bill for control of atomic energy by a civilian body in October. On November 28, he challenged the army at an 'Atomic Age Dinner' in New York, and called for the United States to adopt a civilian and an international approach to atomic questions just as Acheson had argued. On December 20, McMahon denounced the draft May-Johnson bill, now also before Congress, and formally introduced his own alternative. Controversy swirled around all the possibilities, fears and opportunities connected with this subject over Christmas and the New Year. Columnists, meantime, wrote of the danger of military control over atomic energy in the United States more than they did of the desirability of international control. They worried about the supposed ambitions of General Groves; and of the risks of state control to scientific research. Truman meanwhile told a meeting of his Cabinet in December that he personally did not know how many bombs the United States had and 'didn't want to know either'.[56] Only General Groves knew. The admission caused consternation. Patterson, the Secretary of War, even said that the United States had no bombs, only materials which could be assembled, in less than a day, to make them.[57] At that stage, Truman had taken no part in the debate over the respective merits of the bills introduced by McMahon or May-Johnson: but by refusing to let General Groves give McMahon access to atomic 'secrets' he had seemed to have opposed his bill.

The modesty of the achievements of the Moscow Conference had been a relief to the interested members of the United States Congress, who had feared that Byrnes would go 'too far'.[58] But Senators Connally and Vandenberg believed that Congress, that is, they themselves, should make foreign policy, not just the Department of State. They were unlikely to be easily appeased, since they had seen a great opportunity for themselves. Vandenberg greeted Byrnes's return from Moscow by assuring his wife that it had been simply 'one more American "give-away"' (over Romania and Bulgaria, not 'the bomb').[59] Had Byrnes taken the trouble to court Vandenberg on these things beforehand, he might have been more successful: Truman would not have opposed anything upon which Vandenberg and Byrnes agreed.[60]

In Washington the arguments continued. On January 2, General Groves, still in command of the Manhattan Project, produced his own paper on the future of atomic weapons. In this, he first, bravely, discussed military policy on the assumption that 'satisfactory world agreements with respect to atomic energy had been made to ensure that such weapons would never be used'. All rights of privacy would have been given up, all existing stocks of weapons destroyed. That in turn surely had to assume that the United Nations had established a measure of world government *or* that that world government, or the United States, or a group of great powers, would hold nuclear weapons for the purpose of enforcing peace. But what if there were a failure to achieve agreement? Each of the 'three major nations' would presumably possess atomic weapons within fifteen or twenty years; possibly, Groves now admitted, even five or ten. An atomic 'armament race' would follow. In those circumstances, Groves said that the United States must ('for all time') maintain absolute supremacy in atomic weapons, including number, size, and power, both for immediate offensive use and for defence against attack.

Groves's final reflections were stark. 'If we were truly realistic, instead of idealistic', he said sharply, '. . . we would not permit any foreign power with which we are not firmly allied, and in which we do not have absolute confidence, to make or possess atomic weapons. If such a country started to make atomic weapons, we would destroy its capacity to make them before it had progressed far enough to threaten us'.[61] He went on, 'either we must have a hard-boiled realistic enforceable, world-agreement ensuring the outlawing of atomic weapons or we and our dependable allies must have an exclusive supremacy . . . which means that no other nation can be permitted to have atomic weapons'. The United States could enforce one of those alternatives. Five years from then it would be too late.

The bleakness of Groves's suggestions was scarcely relieved by his argument that world government (in which he plainly did not believe) was the real answer to the innovatory terror of nuclear weapons. But his paper made no bones about the risks of a competition in atomic arms, and of the likely consequences as a whole, should the race turn into war. He added, 'if there are to be atomic weapons in the world, we must have the best, the biggest and the most'.[62] Groves's realism was too much for most of his colleagues. He had anyway offended Dean Acheson who, on January 16, complained that Groves was 'determining and almost running foreign policy'. Acheson made a determined effort to recapture direction of these atomic matters for the Department of State. He persuaded Byrnes, still shaken by the aftermath of Moscow, and his dispute with Truman, to name a special advisory panel on Atomic Energy. When that took shape, in January 1946, Acheson's, and the administration's, choice for its chairman was the brilliant, imaginative, sympathetic, and liberal David Lilienthal, who, as successful Director of the Tennessee Valley Authority, had been responsible for one of the prime achievements of the New Deal. Lilienthal was the son of Jewish immigrants from Moravia, of the same stock, therefore, as Mahler, Freud, Mach, Schönberg, Zweig and so many other men of genius, who had made good. He was a man with the imagination to make sense of all this. He was now to work, and report, to another committee, also appointed by Byrnes, comprising Groves, Conant and Bush as well as Acheson. The plan was to 'see, in the light of the facts that are known, what is possible, in the way of safeguards and control, before discussing what is desirable'.[63] Vandenberg and Connally were not concerned in this. That was just as well since Lilienthal, as Acheson knew, had heretical views on almost every subject: his 'hunch', for example, about atomic energy was that 'in the real sense there are no secrets . . . nothing that is not known or knowable'.[64] Acheson saw the committee as a way to ensure that diplomacy on nuclear questions could be brought back to the Department of State and so towards the possibility of reasonable negotiation.

Lilienthal's committee included three businessmen: Chester Barnard, President of the New Jersey Telephone Company; Charles Thomas, Vice President of the Montsanto Chemical Company, who had worked on the chemical side of the Manhattan Project at Los Alamos; and Harry Winne, Vice President of the General Electrical Company, who had worked on the electromagnetic side of the Manhattan Project. The last member of the panel was Dr Robert Oppenheimer, the Director of the atomic laboratory at Los Alamos, who by this time had gone back to the University of California: 'an extraordinary personage and a really great teacher' as Lilienthal thought. General Groves was unimpressed. He considered Oppenheimer to be nervous and, at the moment, almost hysterical about the prospects of nuclear war. Nor did he think that a committee on which he, Bush and Conant served needed any panel to report to it. Acheson told Lilienthal to get to work and not to worry about Byrnes: 'neither Byrnes nor Truman . . . understand anything about the bomb', he remarked, 'particularly not Byrnes'.[65] But Byrnes was naturally sympathetic to Acheson's plans to regain control of atomic policy for the Department of State. Groves agreed grudgingly to collaborate, being himself busy with the preparations for the next, and first post-war, atomic test at Bikini Atoll in the Pacific, planned for the early summer.[66]

The United States and the Russians met to discuss atomic energy at the first meeting in London of the United Nations. Byrnes, who had now made his private decision to resign at some as yet unknown point in the future, was in a weaker position than he had been in Moscow. He had Senators Vandenberg and Connally on the United States delegation alongside him, as well as the Republican lawyer, Foster Dulles. These men preceded their visit to London with the complaint that the proposal for atomic energy made by Byrnes in Moscow had inadequate safeguards. Using his old charm, so successful in the past, so recently neglected, Byrnes sought to persuade them that the veto in the Security Council would always be able to safeguard the American position in the proposed United Nations Commission. He also promised to introduce an amendment into his plan marking the stages of disarmament. These concessions met the objections of Senator Vandenberg; who now, as in the past, was more often angry at not being consulted about subjects than because he disliked the proposals themselves. The United Nations Commission was, therefore, set up.[67] Twelve members would be represented, including the five permanent members of the Security Council. It remained for the participants to decide their position on it. Presumably the American position would be decided by Acheson's committee and panel.

The panel had already got to work. Their imagination was fired by what they saw as 'the need to devise a danger signal – a red light flashing, so to say – when some power moved towards manufacture of a nuclear weapon', in Dr Conant's words.[68] During February 1946, they produced a preliminary report. This was based on a paper written by Oppenheimer.* The originality of this document was that the provision 'for constructive development in the field of atomic energy' – that is, peaceful uses – would turn out, he thought, to be essential for the operation of any system of safeguards. The prohibition of further work on

* See Appendix IX.

atomic energy as demanded by some people to avoid an 'atomic arms race' was 'so contrary to the human patterns of exploration' that such a scheme would command neither the interest nor the cooperation of people in general (at least in the West: Japan in the first half of the XVIIth century might have judged differently). Inspection, in which such faith was placed by so many, would be negative, dull work, and would inevitably be done by people inferior in wit to those who would seek to evade the controls. Development and control, therefore, should be done by a single international agency. That body should have a monopoly of the study, development and exploitation of uranium; possibly of thorium. A coordinated consideration on the problem on a world scale would be the best way of exploiting raw materials.[69] Peaceful activity would be allowed to states by the provision to them of 'de-natured' material: a process then believed to be irreversible.*

This paper appeared idealistic. In fact, it was realistic. Ineffective negotiations since 1946 have shown that no system of atomic disarmament is likely to be achieved without international ownership of material. Human nature, in particular Communist nature, was not ready for the leap forward into collaboration which this last would need. The paper of Dr Oppenheimer became the basis for the panel's report to the Committee. That would be delivered on March 7, 1946.

That document made some additional points: though men throughout the world had at first agreed that nuclear weapons should be outlawed, most had seen on reflection that mere agreements could not give security. The chief difficulty was that developments of atomic energy for peace and for war were interchangeable and interdependent. A nation might promise not to use nuclear energy for bombs. But there was only its good faith to assure other nations that there would be no diversion of material provided for peace, for bombs. So, it would seem, inspection would be essential. Such inspection, however, would have to be on a great scale, would cause such irritations, would constitute a permanent challenge to the good faith of peoples and

* It seems likely that that is not so.

would probably not prevent national managers from misdirecting 'dangerous quantities of uranium 235 or of plutonium'. The panel, therefore, following Oppenheimer, proposed the complete international ownership of all deposits of uranium and thorium. Uranium was essential for all foreseeable applications of nuclear energy. Even if one were to set about fusing light nuclei, and produce a thermonuclear reaction, the ignition would have to be promoted by uranium. Thorium also could be made into fissionable material only by the use of uranium. Even so, thorium should be controlled, as a double safeguard, in case, after all, uranium were illegally secreted. It would not be too difficult to identify, and control of it would assist inspection in special geological conditions where high concentrations of the two minerals occur. An agency of control which included development as well as inspection would be able to attract high-quality men, whereas a mere inspectorate might be able to recruit only the second-rate.

The panel sought to 'eliminate the right of individual nations or their citizens to engage in activities intrinsically dangerous'. These would be defined as providing the raw materials, producing U-235, plutonium, or U-233, in any quantity or of any quality, and incorporating these fissionable materials in a bomb. The possibility of 'denaturing' the minerals would introduce flexibility. Uranium which was below the concentration required for weapons was safe. So was plutonium with a high concentration of plutonium 240. Radioactive isotopes were equally safe. The international agency alone would have the authority to own, lease or develop uranium ore. The agency would carry out continuous surveys of all stockpiles, and sell the by-products. Inspection would be an essential part of these surveys. The agency would be staffed on an international basis; would compensate nations financially which had lost advantages; and would turn over all transmission and use of the energy into national or private hands.[70]

No more intelligent plan for the control of atomic weapons has yet been devised. Had atomic energy been achieved in 1900, a reasonable compromise between the great states might have been made. But the world of the two 'supreme powers' and five declining European empires was a less stable one that that of the Concert of Europe. The recommendation of the panel, however, would have meant not only a cessation of all Soviet efforts in the field; but the early abandonment of the United States' temporary nuclear monopoly in favour of cooperative international control. That might have been difficult to achieve too, judging from what happened when, in January 1946, Senator McMahon's bill for civilian control came to special hearings of Congress. The Secretary of the Navy, Forrestal, complained at the exclusion of his, and the War Department from the discussion. Senator Millikin, supporting those departments' favourite, the May-Johnson Bill, thought that United States atomic energy should remain in military hands till it had shown whether international control was possible. The White House was apparently concerned primarily with ensuring a governmental monopoly. Henry Wallace wished to be certain that any bill passed was consistent with international policy; he criticised the other plans as risking military dictatorship in the United States. In the end, Truman gave his backing to the McMahon bill, which soon began to hear hours of testimony on domestic legislation. The bill seemed to have been won. Secretary of Navy Forrestal and Secretary of War Patterson seemed resigned. But the issue was then influenced by a series of rumours that the Canadian Government had decided upon the arrest of no less than twenty-two people for disclosing secret information, allegedly about atomic energy, to the Soviet embassy.

These new consequences of the defection of Guzenko proved to many in the United States that the Soviet Union was quite untrustworthy. Most people began to think that all secrets should be kept, whatever happened. The result was to make even those who supported the McMahon bill sympathetic to the idea of a strong military representation on the proposed United States Atomic Energy Commission; and make some senators argue for a return to the May-Johnson bill. There was no sophisticated discussion about what an atomic secret might be. Mackenzie King in Canada, shocked by the leak of what were indeed his plans, allowed himself sardonic reflections as to what a *political* secret might be in the United States. Almost certainly, the leak in the United States administration came from General Groves: who knew exactly what he was doing.

Understandably, under new pressure, Senator McMahon became perturbed: the failure of the United States to transfer the management of atomic energy to a civilian body would tell the world, he said, that a 'race' in atomic armaments had begun. Tempers rose in Washington, not for the first time nor for the last time on this matter. So did worries. For those who read the learned press there was, for example, cause for alarm in the newly founded *Bulletin of Atomic Scientists* for February, where an article, 'The Distribution of Uranium in Nature', ended up with a direct contradiction of General Groves's optimism about the duration of the United States monopoly: 'any country can secure as much uranium as would be necessary for atomic warfare'.[71] The *New York Times* later carried a simpler version of the article: 'There are abundant sources of uranium for those . . . willing to pay a high price'.[72]

February 1946, as has been earlier noted, had also been the occasion for Stalin's implicit pledge about the future of nuclear research, contained in his speech of the 9th of that month.* Western observers seem scarcely to have noticed that at the time. But whatever decisions had been made by then, and whatever use the Russians had made of their capture of scientists in Germany and Austria, the first Russian chain reactor must, as became known from subsequent events, have been begun in the spring of 1946; it was completed a year later and was in full operation by August of that year.[73] In the spring of 1946, the Soviet Union went ahead with a programme of research for guided missiles.[74] Once again German scientists in captivity played a part. The use of talented foreigners had, of course, been a characteristic part of Russian governmental practice for two centuries: St Petersburg owed a great deal to an Italian; Tsarskoe Selo to a Scot; the Baku Oil wells to a Swede. All the same Russian endeavours in this field were well-advanced before 1939. The Soviet leaders began to contemplate the possibility of a kind of atomic diplomacy of their own: Stalin is said to have told the technical staffs, working on what

* See above, page 43.

would become the intercontinental ballistic missile, that its satis-factory development would give him a decisive advantage over Truman at a future conference: much as the possession of the atom bomb had, for a fleeting moment, seemed to Byrnes, and Truman, just another such.[75]

Despite Russian propaganda about an Allied, or Western, or 'Anglo-Saxon' bloc, Britain and the United States, in the Com-bined Policy Committee, had meanwhile not yet reached agree-ment about their own policy towards each other. They were much further apart than the tripartite declaration of November had promised. Britain had been discomforted in December by a refusal of the United States to help her build a plant for nuclear material. The sticking point was now held to be Article 102 of the Charter of the United Nations: the paragraph which required that every treaty and international agreement be registered with the United Nations and published. Mention of this was flung into the discussions between the two allies, on February 13, as a 'monkey wrench' by General Groves.[76] With some disingenous-ness, he argued that the British were apparently asking for a secret agreement between themselves and the United States which would constitute a military alliance with Britain and have to be registered. Groves also pointed out that relations between the British and the United States had been kept by Roosevelt from the American people and Congress.[77] That too could not be justified in time of peace. By the spring of 1946, the Commit-tee was in effect deadlocked. Attlee complained. Truman replied that the 'fully effective exchange of information' provided for in the statement between himself, Attlee and King did not mean any cooperation at all in building and operating atomic plants. Anglo-American cooperation thus 'withered away'.[78] Acheson, instinctively friendly to the British, was disturbed at the realis-ation that his government 'was not keeping its word'. 'Even so', he added, 'if a secret arrangement were carried out, it would blow the Administration out of the water'.[79]

The British Labour government therefore embarked definitely on their own atomic programme. Some British scientists remained in the United States (including the nominally British Dr Klaus Fuchs); and some would even be present at the next

United States atomic test in July 1946 at Bikini. But the most significant communication in these matters that spring was Truman's letter to Attlee which explained that the expression in the communiqué of November, 'full and effective collaboration', was 'very general'. The implication was that it could be interpreted to mean no collaboration at all.[80] Britain's name in the United States had by then been damaged by the arrest of Dr Nunn May.* The McMahon bill would soon be so altered in the congressional committee, to prevent the exchange of any information, as to make it a good excuse to bring the old wartime association on these matters between Britain and the United States to an explicit end.

By this time in London, Lord Portal, a wartime Chief of Air Staff, had been designated Controller of Atomic Energy to start in March 1946. In January 1946, Sir John Cockroft had been named Director of the proposed research establishment at Harwell. An engineer, Christopher Hinton, was to build the energy plants. Not only had Britain taken the first steps towards domestic production of nuclear energy, but her Chiefs of Staff had recommended, on January 1, 1946, that the best method of defence against atomic bombs was the deterrent effect of retaliation: 'We must be prepared for aggressors who have widely dispersed industries and populations. This means that in order to be effective as a deterrent, we must have a considerable number of bombs at our disposal . . . we are convinced that we should aim to have as soon as possible stock in the order of hundreds, not scores'.[81] So Britain's programme to create the possibility of manufacturing nuclear weapons went ahead. There was a 'general assumption' that there would be a British bomb, as early as February 1946.[82] (A final decision to go ahead only followed in January 1947, at a secret meeting between Attlee, Bevin, Herbert Morrison, A. V. Alexander, Lord Addison and John Wilmot; the Chancellor of the Exchequer, Dalton, was absent.)[83]

This 'general assumption' was a fateful one. But it never occurred to men such as Penney, Cockroft and Hinton, pioneers

* See below, page 717.

of British nuclear energy, to doubt that Britain ought to make nuclear weapons; any more than it did to Attlee, Bevin and Dalton. These men looked upon themselves as the leaders of a nation whose power could only be an influence for good. Cockroft also believed that 'the overwhelming danger and evil of our time' derived from the Soviet Union which had 'taken over the practices of the Nazis – concentration camps, slave labour, . . . in every street'.[84] Thus the world moved towards a fateful state of affairs in which not only the chief antagonist, but the chief ally, of the United States would have atomic bombs.

# BOOK FIVE


# WORLDS APART


We move above the moving tree
In light upon the figured leaf
And hear upon the sodden floor
Below, the boarhound and the boar
Pursue their pattern as before
But reconciled among the stars.

T. S. Eliot *Four Quartets, Burnt Norton, II*

# TWENTY-TWO

# THE ROAD TO FULTON: 'THE LONG TELEGRAM'

President Truman did not take Stalin's speech of February 9, 1946, very seriously. At a Women's Press Club dinner, he commented that the speech reminded him of the Senator who said, 'Hell, you know we all have to demagogue a little some-times'.[1] Secretary of State Byrnes, however, claimed to find the speech 'a shock', since the proposed new five year plan emphasised rearmament, not production of consumer goods.[2] The unfortunate man must, by that time, have been so confused as to have lost all capacity for independent judgement. Secretary of Commerce Henry Wallace believed that Stalin was offering 'a race – with America – in furnishing the needs of the common people without war or business crisis'.[3] He also thought 'it was obvious our military are getting ready for war with Russia . . . bases all the way down from Greenland, Iceland, North Canada and Alaska to Okinawa . . . Stalin knew what these bases meant . . . We are challenging him, and his speech was taking up the challenge'.[4] The Secretary for the Navy, James Forrestal, natur-ally did not agree. He chatted about the speech to Justice Douglas of the Supreme Court. He asked him what he thought of Stalin's speech: 'the declaration of World War III', said the Justice. Forrestal, his privately commissioned memorandum on Russia on his desk, agreed: 'This speech', he wrote, 'and the programme which it laid down, came close to convincing me that there was no way in which democracy and Communism could live together'.[5] Dean Acheson, already closer to Truman than

Byrnes was, but uneasy about his place between them, thought that the speech confirmed that 'Stalin was steering foreign policy on an ominous course'.[6] As for the officials in the Department of State, Elbridge Durbrow, the head of the East European division, remarked that Stalin had concentrated on denouncing capitalism but added, 'in view of the clear indication of the new Soviet line we should be most diligent to counteract Soviet propaganda and political moves directed primarily at dividing the British and ourselves'.[7] He thought that the speech was aimed at Russians and did not think it necessarily indicated that the Russian government would abandon 'its type of collaboration in the international field'.[8] His superior, 'Doc' Matthews, Director of the Department of State's Office of European Affairs, thought the speech 'the most important and authoritative guide to post-war Soviet policy . . . It should be given great weight in any plans which may be under consideration for extending credits or other forms of economic assistance to the Soviet Union'.[9]

The reaction of the former United States Ambassador to Russia, Averell Harriman, was calmer. Since his talks in Gagra with Stalin, and in Moscow with George Andreychine, Harriman, perhaps influenced by his dislike of the unpredictable Secretary of State, had been heading back towards the congenial shores of wartime memories of Soviet-American collaboration. He was also free now from Kennan's urgent influence, and was by then in the Far East. Asked by a reporter for his views about Stalin's speech, he warned that it was important to remember that public statements by high Soviet officials were 'primarily directed to their own people'. The Russians were tired, he added, and they had made great sacrifices in the war. Now they were 'being asked to begin another Five Year Plan'.[10] There were obviously more sacrifices ahead.

In Britain, the speech was viewed equally calmly. All the same, the head of the northern department within the Foreign Office, which dealt with Russia, Christopher Warner, who during the war had often given that country the benefit of the doubt, minuted that 'he did not find these speeches at all encouraging'. The new head of the Foreign Office, Sir Orme Sargent, agreed, but echoed Truman, at the Women's Press Club: 'certain allowances must be made for election speeches, even in Russia'.[11] In Moscow, the British Embassy thought the most notable feature of this speech was 'the omission of all reference to current international affairs or to the strengthening of Soviet military might'.[12]

The international press mostly concentrated on the promising side of the speech: thus *The Times* – or Ralph Parker – in its report, described 'Mr Stalin' as taking stock, and as drawing attention to the 'success of Soviet Communism'. In Paris, *Le Monde*, still preferring to speak of Stalin as '*Le Maréchal*', described the speech as 'a great electoral' one, ('*un grand discours électoral*') made 'in his electoral constituency in Moscow'. The end of rationing and a restoration of the standard of living ('*il a promis la suppression du rationnement et le relève-ment du niveau de vie*') would soon be forthcoming: 'The great speech which Joseph Stalin delivered to the Moscow electors will inspire all who desire to participate in a speedy advance to Socialism'.[13] *L'Humanité*, the Communist newspaper, was no more enthusiastic.

The American press, however, was generally as hostile as the administration was. *Time*, for example, called it 'the most warlike pronouncement by any top-rank statesman since V-J day':[14] Communists everywhere could be expected 'to take a tip from "Uncle Joe's" speech and sharpen their opposition to non-Communist governments'. Doubtless, however, Stalin had 'purely Russian reasons for pointing outward toward imagined enemies'. A surprisingly hostile interpretation of Stalin's speech was made in his column by Walter Lippmann. He had recently been insisting that the West and the Russians ought to be able to agree on fundamental questions. But now, since there was no ground for supposing that the Russians lacked either will, or desire, for 'military superiority', the West would have to undertake 'a mighty upsurge of national economy' to withstand it.[15] This comment created a sensation. *Business Week* thought that Lippmann 'had gone berserk and virtually declared war on Russia'. *Pravda* in reply named Lippmann 'a notorious representative of imperialist ideology' and described his call for an American economic transformation to face Russia as one which 'surpassed all records of hypocrisy and cynicism'.[16] Anne O'Hare McCormick, another widely-read columnist, said the same as Lippmann: 'if, against all our hopes, the world is to stay divided, its Western half must begin swiftly to look to its defences'.[17] But it was Lippmann's change of heart that seemed significant; even if it was improbable that he would maintain that line.

These diverse reactions indicated a Western world confused, divided and as yet in no fit state to make a wise assessment of Soviet intentions.

The conclusion of the 'election' in Russia can be briefly noted. Cheered, or cowed, by the speeches and agitation, over 100 million Soviet citizens voted: 99.7 per cent of the registered electors. The candidates of 'the Party and the non-Party bloc' received 99.18 per cent of those votes. A little over 800,000 votes were cast against the 'bloc' and a few thousand voting papers were spoiled. Even in Lithuania, then still in semi-civil war, over 90 per cent were held to have voted. The election results, the British minister in Moscow reported to London, drily, constituted an 'improvement on 1937', when candidates of 'the Party and non-Party bloc' received 98.6 per cent of the votes cast.[18]

The explanation of the harsh judgements made in the West of the speech by Stalin lay less in what it said explicitly than in the fact that it used a tone which Stalin had employed in the 1930s: a tone indicating a desire for isolation from, and distrust of, foreigners. There had been no word of gratitude for the help in the war: no word of polite mention of the Allies nor of the United Nations. No chestnuts out of the fire for them, as Malenkov had said. No, capitalism led to war; the Soviet system was best. There was no mention of the misunderstandings with the West which had made the end of the war so disappointing everywhere to the west of the River Bug; no mention of Poland; nor of Persia; neither of Yugoslavia nor Albania; nor explicitly of the atom bomb. No concessions to religion or the Russian soul were now needed. Away with the rotten liberalism of the war years! Away to camps or even the firing squad all Soviet citizens who had seen, as prisoners of war of the Germans, what the West was really like!

Part of the explanation for these harsh interpretations was, as has been shown, that rumours of Soviet espionage, on a colossal scale, within the United States, Canada and Britain were beginning to seize hold of the imaginations of many Western statesmen, worried lest they had in the past been too lax. Thus on February 6 Truman learned of the FBI's suspicions about his Assistant Secretary of the Treasury (and United States Executive Director 'elect' of the International Monetary Fund), Harry White;[19] he talked to Vinson and Byrnes about the matter but was understandably undecided what to do, bearing in mind that White had just been approved in this capacity by the Senate.[20] Then, on February 16, the story of the Canadian spy case was carried further with confirmation of the leak earlier noticed. Sixteen people were arrested on charges of seeking to steal information about the atomic bomb for Russia. Mackenzie King explained in a press conference that the arrests were made in consequence of the leaks a week earlier. Next day, a columnist, Frank McNaughton, alleged in his column that the Canadian spy ring had had United States atomic secrets as their real goal; and also that another spy ring was still active in the United States (General Groves was the author of this leak). On February 20 the scientist Dr Allan Nunn May, arrested in London, was persuaded by MI5 to confess that he had used his position on the National Research Council of Canada to gather information about nuclear energy for Russia; and confirmed that he had given a small sample of enriched uranium ore to the Russians. The public announcement of this further news was delayed but the other revelations created something almost like hysteria. Truman told Admiral Leahy that these stories (which, of course, he had himself known about in September), together with the 'insulting treatment' of American officials in Bulgaria and Yugoslavia, were convincing him of the need to take 'a strong attitude' towards Russia 'without delay'. He strongly disapproved of 'recent attitudes of appeasement' towards that country.[21] Truman's confidant, Joseph Davies, did nothing to help his reputation when, in an extraordinary article on February 19, he argued that Russia had 'every moral right' to seek atom bomb secrets through espionage if she were excluded from such information by her 'former fighting allies'.[22] After this outburst, he saw the President less often.

The Russians themselves now made an equally curious and never repeated admission about their past spying: they agreed that they had received 'insignificant secret data' through espionage but it had not yielded anything which was not in the Smyth Report published in August. The 'post-war behaviour' of Britain, and the United States had anyway made such conduct acceptable.[23]

On February 21 the Joint Chiefs of Staff, who now included General Eisenhower (who had succeeded Marshall), forwarded to Truman a report which commented on the paper written earlier in the year by the Department of State about the Soviet Union (SM:5062). This important and realistic document stated explicitly, for the first time, that 'from a military point of view, the consolidation and development of the power of Russia is the greatest threat to the United States in the foreseeable future'. The Joint Chiefs had previously only referred to Russia as a possible future menace; now they had fewer inhibitions. They thought that the expansion of Russia in the Far East might bring about direct conflict with the United States, while her expansion 'to the West and South' might involve clashes with Britain into which the United States might be drawn. Collaboration with Russia, the Joint Chiefs said, should stop short not only of compromise of principle but also of condoning any expansion in these areas. Support of threatened nations should be extended not only through the United Nations but (a clear anticipation of the Truman doctrine) also by direct economic support; though 'military support at present would be difficult if not impracticable'. Countries already penetrated by Soviet influence 'should be recognised' as a fact of life, in order that 'a position of antagonism may not be unfruitfully assumed'. The Joint Chiefs added, firmly, 'reliance cannot be placed upon the efficacy of the United Nations Organization to prevent war'; for power was lacking there for the arbitrary settlement of a major conflict of policy among major nations. So, 'one of the fundamentals of national power and prestige must be borne in mind, namely, the ability to back with force the policies and commitments undertaken by our government'. In two world wars 'a fortunate geographical position, and the fact of our allies holding the enemy at bay have given us the time in which to gather our strength for the offensive'. But, in future, 'neither geography nor allies will render a nation immune from sudden and paralysing attack, should an aggressor arise'. So United States foreign policy should give consideration to the government's capacity to 'support policy by arms if the occasion should demand', rather than to 'our long term potential which, owing to the length of time required for mobilisation . . . might not be sufficient to avert disaster in another war . . . The greatest single military factor in the security of the world', the paper concluded, 'is the absolute military security of the United States'.[24] No more interesting state paper has been written in the XXth century. It asserted the need for a permanent sense of global responsibility and for its backing by adequate force, and avoided any euphemisms about the need to be seen to operate under the auspices of the United Nations.

The Director of the FBI, Edgar Hoover, conferred with the Attorney General, Tom Clark, and Secretary of the Treasury, Fred Vinson, on both February 22 and 26 as to what action to take in respect of Harry White. Clark thought that the best thing would be to let White become the United States director at the International Monetary Fund and ensure that he was 'surrounded with persons who were specifically selected and were not security risks'.[25] Other investigations were embarked upon about the loyalty of Alger Hiss in the department of State.

That the democratic cause was in decline in Europe was meantime confirmed by recent events in Germany. By mid-February, the Socialist leader in Berlin, Grotewohl, had concluded that he could not hold out against the bullying, the threats and the powerful propaganda of the Communists and resist the unification of his Socialists in East Germany with the Communists. He made that evident at a public meeting on February 21. He was violently interrupted. All the same, he and those of his colleagues who supported the merger naturally carried the day. That was so even though, in Berlin, the Communists were practising what seemed to Western officials to be 'violently racial nationalism', which openly attacked the Western powers under the guise of an attack on capitalism. Jakob Kaiser, the beleaguered leader of the Christian Democrats, then still in East Berlin, described his enemies as having 'the same point of departure from which Hitler began after the last war, with the added temptation of having the great, powerful, ruthless Russians on their side'.[26]

This was more than just propaganda. Marshal Zhukov gave a party in February at his *Schloss* outside Berlin to about fifty Communists and Socialists, mostly trade unionists or party officials; the scenes were extraordinary, with 'Russian generals embracing their former enemies in a way which could no longer be called mere fraternisation'.[27] Following that, the Secretary of the Bavarian Communist Party, Fritz Sperling, made an offer to 'decent Nazis'; he told them that they could join the Communists if they wished to rebuild a democratic party.[28] The same occurred in Berlin, after an equally explicit appeal from Wilhelm Pieck.[29]

Continuing Communist support for the reunification of Germany also kept the officials and generals of the Western Allies in a state of perpetual unease. They were not well prepared for these waves of professionally organised propaganda, supported by vague menaces. Sir Orme Sargent even went so far as to ask, on February 21, 'if we cannot prevent the German government from becoming Communist-controlled, ought we to try and rescue at any rate the Ruhr from the wreckage, by removing it (a) from the economic control, (b) from the political control, of the German government?' The Socialist Schumacher might tell Sir William Strang, the British senior civilian in Germany, that 'democracy should become as natural as shaving';[30] but natural events did not yet always occur in Germany.

It was in these circumstances that another important document was written, in Moscow; this time, by a single man, not a committee. The man was George Kennan, United States Chargé d'Affaires in Moscow. Harriman, whom he had so influenced, was back in Washington. Harriman's successor, General Bedell Smith, sometime Chief of Staff to Eisenhower, had not yet arrived. Kennan who himself knew that he would soon return home, was asked for his comments on Stalin's speech of February by Byrnes.[31] He had also, he says in his memoirs, received a request from the Department of State for an explanation of the fact, bewildering to the Treasury, that the Russians were reluctant to join the two new world economic institutions, the World Bank and the International Monetary Fund,* despite the tenacious hopes in the United States Treasury and the friendly attitudes of officials of that institution.

Kennan's reply was 8,000 words long. He had by then developed a sense of scorn for the unpredictable behaviour of the administration which he served. He justified this 'long telegram' because the answer involved 'questions so intricate, so delicate, so strange to our form of thought and so important to the analysis of our international environment' that oversimplification would lead to unwisdom. The long document was circulated through the United States government at the end of February, on the initiative of James Forrestal, Secretary for the Navy. 'It was', wrote its author years later, 'one of those moments when official Washington, whose states of receptivity, or the opposite, are determined by subjective emotional currents as intricately imbedded as those of the most complicated of Sigmund Freud's erstwhile patients, was ready to receive a given message'. Forrestal made the telegram required reading for thousands of senior officers in the armed services. It was thus one of the most influential diplomatic despatches ever written and affected judgements long after the author had changed the views that it expressed. A bowdlerised version appeared in *Time* magazine in April.[32] A year later, a revised version appeared in the journal *Foreign Affairs* under the pseudonym 'Mr X'.[33] Almost the only prominent American to challenge its conclusions was, curiously enough, General Lucius Clay in Germany, who had been recently successful in negotiating certain low-level agreements with Russia in Germany.[34] The telegram expressed, in primitive form, the essence of the so-called

* Inaugural meetings of the Fund and of the Bank would be held at Savannah, Georgia, March 8 to 18.

policy of 'Containment' of the Soviet Union, though that word was not used in it.

Kennan began by pointing out that the leaders of the Soviet Union lived in the belief that it was encircled by inimical capitalists with whom they one day would have to fight. These men also thought that the capitalists were bound one day to fight with each other. Intervention against Russia would then be sought by clever capitalists as a way of escaping their internal conflicts. That action would be eventually disastrous for the interveners. But it would delay the achievement of Soviet Socialism. So it should be avoided. Conflicts between capitalist states, on the other hand, should be generally promoted, because they held out other possibilities for the advancement of the Soviet cause.

Kennan thought that this view of the world, combined with the insecurity natural to an agricultural people trying to live on an exposed plain in the neighbourhood of traditionally nomadic peoples, made for a specially dangerous challenge to Americans. The Soviet Government's fear of an economically and technologically advanced West, and the anxiety of Russian leaders as to what would happen if ordinary Russians learnt the truth about the world outside also affected the matter. A nation which had never known a friendly neighbour was promising ground for a doctrine such as Marxism, which viewed conflicts as insoluble by peaceful means. So, those rulers had, under Communism, 'learned to seek security only in a patient but deadly struggle for the total destruction of their rivals'. In this dogma of Marxism-Leninism, the Bolsheviks had found 'justification for their instinctive fear of the outside world, for the dictatorship without which they did not know how to rule, for the cruelties [which] they did not dare not to inflict, for the sacrifices [which] they felt bound to demand'. In the name of Marx, the Bolsheviks sacrificed every ethical value; 'no one should underrate the importance of dogma', Kennan wrote, 'because, without it, they would stand before the world as only the last of a long succession of cruel tyrants who have driven their people on to ever more military activities in order to guarantee external security for internally weak regimes'. Under the cloak of international Marxism, with 'its honeyed' promises, old Russian nationalism was more dangerous and more insidious than ever. The Russian leaders were ignorant of the outside world and too dependent intellectually to question their self-hypnotism. So they had no difficulty in making themselves believe what they found it comfortable to believe.

Kennan reminded his readers too of the different agencies which the Soviet government had at its disposal: the inner circle of Communist leaders abroad, 'in reality working closely together as an underground operating directorate of world Communism, a concealed Comintern tightly coordinated and directed by Moscow'; a wide variety of associations such as trade unions, youth leagues, religious societies, publishers, which could be penetrated by Communists; similar international organisations; the Orthodox Church; the Pan-Slav movement and other movements based on racial groupings within the Soviet Union; governments or governing groups willing to place their propaganda machines or their entire governments at the Soviets' disposal, such as the Bulgarians or Yugoslavs. This far flung apparatus, argued the Chargé d'Affaires, would be used to stimulate all forms of disunity in the countries of the West. Persons with grievances would be urged to seek redress not in mediation, but in defiant struggle. Efforts would be made to undermine strategic potential, to disrupt national self-confidence and to increase social and industrial unrest. Special efforts would be made to weaken the power and influence of the West over colonial, backward or dependent peoples: 'Here', said Kennan, 'we have a political force committed fanatically to the belief that, with the United States there can be no permanent *modus vivendi*, that it is necessary and desirable that the internal harmony of our society be disrupted, our traditional way of life destroyed, the international authority of our state broken, if Soviet power is to be secure'.

The Communists had complete control of one of the world's greatest nations, with vast resources at its disposal. Their force was one inaccessible to considerations of reality in its basic reactions. The problem of how to cope with this force was 'undoubtedly the greatest task our diplomacy has ever faced and probably the greatest which it will ever have to face'. It was a task which should be approached 'with the same thoroughness and care as the solution of a major strategic problem in war'.

Kennan then made suggestions as to how this should be done: the American public 'should be educated to the realities of the Russian situation'. The task should be done by the government. Then 'we' should 'formulate and put forward for other nations a much more positive and constructive picture of the world which we would like to see than we have put forward in the past'. He did not, however, recommend economic or military aid to countries which might seem under threat, as the Joint Chiefs of Staff had done on February 27. There were also some ambiguities in the telegram: Kennan did not mean to imply that there were no circumstances in which negotiations should be undertaken with Russia. But probably Forrestal read it as saying just that.[35] The success of the telegram was due to the fact that it gave an answer to those who, like Senator Vandenberg (in a speech in Congress, on February 27), were asking, 'What is Russia up to now? We ask it in Manchuria. We ask it in Italy. We ask it in Iran. We ask it in Tripolitania. We ask it in the Baltic and the Balkans. We ask it in Poland. We ask it in Canada. We . . . ask it sometimes . . . in our own United States . . . It is, of course, the supreme conundrum of our time'.[36] The telegram gave an ideological basis for United States policy which then was still floundering between the changes of mood of the Secretary of State, the hesitations of the President, and the conspiratorial fears of Admiral Leahy and General Groves. For four years, it would govern the attitudes of most American officials. One such, Louis Halle, recalled, 'There was a universal feeling that "this was it" . . . the appreciation of the situation that had long been needed'.[37] There is, however, no evidence that Truman read the long telegram.[38] Byrnes's comments were perfunctory.[39] Acheson remarked that, while Kennan's predictions could not have been improved upon, 'we responded to them slowly'.[40]

Kennan was not the only man to have put pen to paper in late February 1946. Stalin was giving some answers to a certain Captain Razin who had posed questions about Lenin's views on the subject of Clausewitz. This exotic topic provided the Vozhd with an opportunity both to show his knowledge and to rebuke certain errant Party members. Presumably the exchange was devised as a pretext. Nothing more was ever heard of this army officer, Captain Razin, if indeed he ever existed. (The name reminded any Russian with a sense of history of Stenka Razin who had led a peasants' revolt in the XVIIth century and who was the subject of a famous folk song.)* The question which he had raised was: Lenin had talked often of Clausewitz, whom he had plainly admired. He had been particularly fond of Clausewitz's reflection that the best victory for a commander was one in which the enemy surrendered without a fight.[41] But Captain Razin had believed that Communists surely had to consider all German militarist doctrine, including the writings of Clausewitz, to be false. Was it possible to make the two views consistent?

Stalin replied that Lenin had admired Clausewitz since he had stated that retreat, in unfavourable conditions, was as valid a form of fighting as an attack. But here Lenin was talking of Clausewitz as a politician, not as a soldier. So those who criticised Clausewitz – and, normally, one should do so for the very reasons that Captain Razin mentioned – could benefit as well. Clausewitz substantiated in his works the familiar Marxist thesis that there is a direct connection between war and politics, that politics gives birth to war, that war is the continuation of politics by violent means. (Clausewitz could scarcely have 'substantiated' anything written by Marx, since he began to write *On War* the year that Marx was born.) Stalin added: 'It is impossible to move science forward without subjecting the outdated positions and sayings of well-known authors to critical analysis. This applies not only to military writers but to the Marxist classics also. For example, Engels once said that, among the Russian leaders of 1812, only Barclay de Tolly was capable as an army leader. Obviously, Engels erred because, in reality, Kutusov was two heads above Barclay as an army leader!'

Since Stalin never wrote anything without due thought, it is likely that he wished at this stage of his dealings with his colleagues to remind them that Clausewitz's, and Lenin's, axiom

* To be later put to good use by Shostakovich.

about victories without conflict could easily apply to what had happened in Eastern Europe; to recall in time for Army Day (February 27) how knowledgeable he was about military matters: and so to make them accept unquestionably his establishment of a united defence commissariat and the abolition of the previously independent commissariats for army, air force and navy announced on February 28. (The fact that Stalin's letter to Razin was not published for a year does not mean that it was not seen by the comrade colleagues.)[42]

Several problems now brought the difficulties between the United States and Russia to something like a head. These were inaugurated on February 28 by two events in Washington: first the Secretary of the Navy, Forrestal, apparently with Lippmann's article about Stalin's speech of February 9 in mind, probably after a discussion with Lippmann himself,[43] and certainly thinking of Kennan's telegram, asked the President and Byrnes if they would support the despatch of a small naval task force to the East Mediterranean to give encouragement, by its mere presence, to the governments of Greece and Turkey apparently threatened by Communism. Both Byrnes and the President agreed. The battleship *USS Missouri*, the same 45,000-ton vessel on which the Japanese had surrendered to General MacArthur, was on its way to Turkey carrying, as a special consideration to the Turks, the ashes of Mehmet Ertegün, the deceased Turkish ambassador to Washington. The task force was to follow the *Missouri*.

In the event, it proved impossible to assemble the proposed flotilla: a commentary on how far the United States was from real preparedness. But the decision to send it was a new departure: a sign that the United States would be prepared to supplement the traditional role of Britain in the Mediterranean.[44] Naval forces were ever afterwards deployed in the Mediterranean by the United States as a 'presence', in Captain Mahan's phrasing.

The same day, Byrnes made a speech in New York to the Overseas Press Club. The Secretary had decided that the accusations of appeasement which he daily received had to be rebutted. However unfair it might seem, and however firmly he had decided that he would retire, the repeated criticisms made of him, not just by Senator Vandenberg, since his visit to Moscow, had wounded him. In this speech, Byrnes said that the United States would not, and could not, stand aloof 'if force, or the threat of force, is used contrary to the purposes and principles' of the United Nations Charter. No nation had the right to place troops on the soil of another state without its consent. No nation had the right to seize property of the late enemy before agreement on reparations had been reached. 'If we are to be a great power', Byrnes concluded (and how many traditions were finally abandoned by the use of that studiedly hypothetical clause?), 'if we are to be a great power, we must act as a great power, not only to ensure our own security, but in order to preserve the peace of the world'. Essentially, this speech marked the launching of Byrnes's policy of 'patience and firmness' which characterised the rest of his term of office, even though he did not then use the words.[45] Henceforth Soviet outrages would be publicised, not ignored.[46] The speech was not an accidental occasion. The text, for the first time in the chequered life of this unfortunate Secretary of State, had been shown to the President in draft; 'I've read it and I like it', Truman had noted on his copy.[47] (He told his staff that he himself had 'edited' Byrnes's speech and told Byrnes to 'stiffen up', and 'try for three months not to make any compromises'.)[48] It was certainly the speech which Leahy wanted to hear. The Alsop brothers thought that 'American foreign policy is at, or near, some sort of turning point' in consequence.[49] Another commentator considered the speech the most important since Woodrow Wilson's Fourteen Points.[50] Others were more sceptical: was it a speech or a policy?[51] An official in the Foreign Office in London, John Donnelly, thought that Byrnes's speech, along with Vandenberg's, was an example of 'the democratic force at work', since the pressure to make them had come from below. Events and public opinion had forced an uncertain administration into affording 'a measure of the leadership which the United States ought to be providing'.[52]

Some thought the speech a reply to that of Senator Vandenberg; and later Vandenberg claimed that 'almost everybody' conceded to him 'the major influence in changing the American attitude from "appeasement" to firm resistance'. [53] But Byrnes had been planning so to speak for some weeks. Vandenberg had discovered approximately what Byrnes was going to say and spoke himself first in the light of what he anticipated would happen. [54] The ironic comment that the speech was 'the second Vandenberg Concerto' was, therefore, inappropriate.

All such speeches reflect a statesman's consideration of a range of concerns which he might not think it necessary to specify. Byrnes, though partly responding to what he took to be the demands of American public opinion, in those days, had seen reports about most of the countries which Vandenberg had been asking about. He had to face the fact that Germany was settling for good into watertight compartments, [55] a particularly irritating state of affairs since it seemed to oblige the United States to pay indefinitely, in their zone at least, for food which could have been imported from the Russian zone. Byrnes would have heard of a new French refusal to countenance the establishment of central government, on the continuing grounds of a fear that one day the United States would lose interest in Europe, and 'some fine morning they will wake up and find themselves face to face with the Russians on the Rhine'. [56] Then, though the United States military authorities in Germany were congratulating themselves on having already 'repatriated' from Germany over 5.5 million 'displaced persons' – persons imported into the Third Reich to work like slaves in the Nazi war factories – there were still 60,000 or so Poles left behind: Poles whose old homes were east of the Curzon Line and who showed 'no desire to become Soviet citizens or resettle' in the new Poland. Nor, unsurprisingly, did Jewish Polish refugees want to return home to the proximity of scenes of German mass murder. [57] Baltic 'displaced' persons 'appeared to have moved to Germany willingly' to evade the Russians. Their repatriation was more complicated than that of others. They should not presumably be settled *en bloc* in a Western country where they might form a dangerously active anti-Soviet nucleus. [58]

Korea also constituted a great anxiety to the Secretary of State since, on February 12, the Russians had announced a new

Korean central government to take office in the North and be their model for the government of the whole country. This body was entirely composed of Communists; many having been brought back from long exile in Russia. The 'black-out over North Korea', General Hodge reported to Washington, was being greatly intensified. Travellers from the South were often arrested as 'American spies'.[59] On February 23, Hodge predicted that Russia would force the United States to accept their government as democratic representatives of North Korea while trying to secure enough Communist representation in the South to obtain control there too.[60] Truman told his staff playfully on February 25 that 'we were going to war with Russia. On two fronts: one, [is] Korea'.[61] In early March, Max Bishop, of the office of the United States political adviser on Japan, would tell Byrnes that Russian forces in Northern Korea were ready to move rapidly. Activity of troops was reported on North-South railroads and on roads leading to South Korea. The Russians had by then completed their familiar programme of transferring all moveable machinery and capital goods to Russia and were busy ensuring that, in Northern Korean schools, 'revolutionary doctrine' was being taught: that is anti-Americanism, the need to destroy the United States, and the greatness of the USSR.[62]

Nor was there reason to feel in any way comforted by news from East Europe. Mikołajczyk, the only hope for Polish freedom, had dined with the American Ambassador, Bliss Lane, on February 25 in Warsaw. He had explained that the Polish Cabinet had proposed that, at the forthcoming general elections, each of the four major parties would be allocated twenty per cent of the seats; and that the remaining seats would be divided between the minor parties. Mikołajczyk had rejected this scheme since he knew that his party in truth commanded much more than twenty per cent of the electorate and since the Socialists were now dependent allies of the Communists. He had asked for seventy-five per cent of the seats for himself and his ally, the PEL. He had told Bliss Lane that he thought that, once he came out publicly against these plans, the government would exclude him from the Cabinet.[63]

In Hungary, the situation was deteriorating fast: faster than the Department of State had anticipated. Rákosi's 'salami tactics' had been taken a stage further by his Party's demand that the 'reactionary elements' – the Communist word for overt anti-Communists – in the government be disavowed. Their particular target was Dezsö Sulyok, a Smallholder who was a most outspoken foe of Russia. If he did not leave his ministry, the Communists would withdraw from the coalition. The Prime Minister, Nagy, was exhausted and procrastinatory. He was no Karl Renner. It was also understandable that he might shrink from precipitating, so soon after the war, a real crisis. The American and British missions both favoured a policy of backing the Smallholders government, with no Communists, as was in effect the case in Austria next door. Nagy demurred.[64] Sulyok was duly dismissed. Just possibly it was a great chance lost.

There was similar cause for anxiety in respect of Trieste. The British commander there had told the Supreme Allied Commander in Italy that 'many responsible citizens . . . are fearful of outbreaks of disorder and even urged intervention by Yugoslav forces in the near future' to avoid a breakdown of order. There were rumours of a run on the banks. The demobilisation of United States troops in Italy was demoralising. The Italians in Trieste's population were becoming hysterical. The Supreme Commander drily commented early in March that 'he would certainly want all the troops he could get . . . if the Yugoslavs should attack'.[65]

Then, in Romania, the government seemed to have decided to do all possible (which was a good deal) to delay elections until they could be sure to win them through manipulation. Political violence was interrupting the large Peasant and Liberal Party meetings even more than before, while smaller ones were broken up completely. These old parties still had no access to the radio. As for Bulgaria, the news was more disturbing than ever: further detachments of Soviet troops had been reported moving into the country. Hospitals in Bucharest were instructed to send home their convalescents and to be fully equipped by the end of the month. A move into Turkey and Greece or to the Dardanelles was surely possible.[66]

Nor was the rest of the world free from anxiety about Soviet action. In faraway Argentina, Colonel Juan Perón had founded a government which was closer than any other in the world to a Fascist one, more so than the execrated Catholic monarchist General Franco in Spain. But an official in the British Foreign Office noted, on March 1, that, for some time past, there had been increasing evidence of 'an impending rapprochement between the Soviet and Argentine governments'. In the previous August, the Communist Party of Argentina had been given equal status with other political movements. A Soviet trade delegation to Buenos Aires was announced as shortly to arrive. The retiring United States Ambassador to Brazil, Adolf A. Berle, who had as an ex-under secretary of state much experience of the Americas, thought that the Russians were now planning to establish themselves in the 'most anti-American country in Latin America';[67] and there was always such a chance while Perón lived, since Communism makes the best ally for, as well as the most natural successor to, Fascism.

Despite these myriad problems which made Secretary Byrnes's past life with recalcitrant congressmen seem in retrospect relatively simple, it was, however, the concern caused by Russia's activities in Persia, above all in Azerbaijan, which most troubled the Secretary of State and which lay behind his warnings in New York on February 28. By that time, the autonomous Communist principality of Azerbaijan run by Pishevari had a neighbour in north Persia in Qazi Mohammed's state of Kurdistan, already making a bid for leadership of the Kurds both in Turkey and in Iraq as well as in Persia; the threat to Turkey, embattled herself in other ways, being taken seriously by all who knew that region.

On February 19, the new Prime Minister of Persia, Qavam, had flown to Moscow where he would stay till March 11. His prime aim was to make concessions in order to secure the withdrawal of Soviet troops on the deadline of March 2. As earlier noticed, Qavam had a reputation as a weak man, and one believed by many to be a friend of Russia. In order to soothe his unmanageable Northern neighbour, he had introduced Communists into the government. At the same time, Princess Ashraf, sister of the young Shah, also went to Russia and played, not for the last time, a part in international politics. She seems to have impressed Stalin. 'After a long wait, in a sinister room', she wrote later, referring to the antichamber of Stalin's office in the yellow Nikolai Palace, in the Kremlin, 'suddenly, a door opened and I caught sight of a man with a moustache . . . It was Stalin . . . what a relief! Stalin was soft, and fat, and, above all, he was small!' Later Stalin spoke very favourably of Ashraf: 'Look at that tiny little woman. She's a real patriot'.[68]

Qavam on the other hand seemed to make less impression. He saw Stalin once in his first week in Moscow, Molotov twice. Stalin was 'very rough' – very much, as several Americans recalled, with memories of the 1930s ever in their minds, as Hitler had treated the Austrian Chancellor Schuschnigg in 1938. Instead of making concessions, Stalin made demands: that Persia recognise the autonomy of the area then in the hands of insurgents – both Azerbaijan and Kurdistan; that Persia agree to the presence of Russian troops beyond March 2; and that they grant the oil concessions requested by the Russians in 1944.[69] In justification of these requests, Stalin spoke of the Persian-Soviet Treaty of 1921. Qavam was well able to reply to that citation, since he had himself been prime minister when that treaty had been signed, just before the *coup d'état* of Reza Khan. The clause giving the Russians the right to have troops in Persia if Soviet frontiers were threatened by a third power through the country was plainly inapplicable. As to Azerbaijan, Qavam said that the constitution of Persia proscribed autonomy. If Azerbaijan became autonomous, other provinces would seek to follow. The central government would lose control. The other Allies would protest. At this point Stalin burst in with the remark, 'We don't care what the United States and Britain think and we are not afraid of them'.[70]

Some haggling followed these demands. Thus, at one moment, Molotov said that Russia might abandon its demand for oil concessions if Persia were to agree to reconsider an old idea of a joint Persian-Russian stock company, with 51 per cent Russian shares, 49 per cent Persian. Moscow Radio unexpectedly announced that Qavam had been assured that Russian troops would leave east Persia but would remain in the west of the country, pending 'further examination of the situation': an Orwellian use of language as forbidding as it was unclear. At another point, Molotov intimated that the Soviet Union might withdrew all their troops if only the demand for oil concessions alone were granted. The Russians agreed that the Prime Minister of Azerbaijan might be called the Governor-General: that he need not have either a foreign ministry or a war ministry; that all foreign dealing with Azerbaijan would go through the central government in Tehran; and that thirty per cent of Azerbaijan's revenues would go to the central government too.

These were, of course, reasonable demands for any genuine autonomous movement. But the proximity of Russia, and the fact that the leaders of Azerbaijan included men who were primarily Russian agents, made the details irrelevant. Qavam recalled that there was a Persian law which forbade discussion of new oil concessions to a country whose troops were on the national territory. The Majlis had insisted on passing that in 1943. Similarly, he said, he had no authority from the Shah to discuss the matter of autonomy. He then asked the Russians how, seriously, they could justify the idea of troops remaining. Molotov replied that the Russian delegate at the Peace Conference in Paris in 1919, Moshavar-ol-Mamalek, had raised the question of the return to Persia of most of the Caucasus, including Georgia. So Russia could not feel secure against Persian plans of aggression. The very same Moshavar-ol-Mamalek had later become Foreign Minister. So, of course, Russian troops had to be left in the country.[71] Qavam replied that Moshavar-ol-Mamalek had also negotiated and signed the treaty of 1921. That had put relations between the two countries on a good footing. The conversations continued. Qavam was proving a more sturdy negotiator than anyone had supposed possible.

Byrnes had talked of Iran with Molotov and Vyshinsky in February at a dinner at the Hotel Meurice in Paris. Molotov had complained about United States support for the Iranians over this issue, in the United Nations. 'Keeping troops in Iran beyond the treaty deadline was too trivial a matter to disturb relations between the United States and the Soviet Union', he insisted. Molotov did not attempt to defend the illegality of the Soviet action. Byrnes explained that the United States had signed the Charter of the United Nations specifically in order to help small nations; he, as Secretary of State, could not think of turning his back on the Iranians in what they believed to be their hour of need.[72] But what would happen? It looked on the surface as if Britain for her part had decided to take a risk with the future of Iran. Thus Bevin sent a minute to Attlee on February 22 which made it evident that he wanted to be in a position to say publicly that all British forces had left that country by March 2, in accordance with the treaty of 1941. Bevin added, 'The matter is of such political importance that there must be no possibility of things going wrong. Our forces must all be out of Persia by the 2nd March, whatever happens, and whatever last minute difficulties may arise. I would, therefore, be grateful if you would impress this on the Chief of Staff. I want to be sure that all will go according to plan and that we do not have to make any excuses afterwards'.[73]

On March 2, with Qavam still in Moscow, the British War Office did announce that their troops had withdrawn across the border with Iraq – where, at that time, they had bases. The British had not, however, abandoned Persia completely to Russian mercies, since in the south-west the powerful Anglo-Iranian Oil Company continued to pump out its thousands of barrels a day; and, by their customary judicious support of their favoured tribes in that part of the country, they had some surrogate military support under cover. Britain accompanied these actions by drafting a note of protest to Russia over the Soviet violation of the Treaty of 1941. This document was shown to the Department of State.

On March 2 in the evening, the Persian Ambassador in Washington, Ala, himself went to the Department of State to say that his government too would 'appreciate it if we [the United States] would register [an] immediate protest to [the] Soviet government for its failure to withdraw [its] troops . . . in accordance with [its] treaty obligations'. But Byrnes had to hesitate. He did not know, as a matter of fact, whether Qavam had by then given in, in Moscow on the issue, nor whether Russian troops might now be remaining in Persia with the agreement, however reluctant, of Qavam and the Shah.[74] So he instructed Kennan to find out how the land lay.

Kennan went to see Qavam in the Persian Embassy in Moscow on March 4. Qavam told him that he was making a formal protest to Russia that very day. He was demanding a withdrawal of troops at once. This news was swiftly passed to Washington. The Persian ambassador in that capital, having been told by telegram from Tehran what his Prime Minister had done in Moscow, returned to the Department to tell Byrnes, 'It would appear, therefore, that there is no longer any obstacle to prevent Your Excellency from issuing the necessary instructions to Kennan to make the United States' protest'. The suggestion was given extra force by the news from Tehran that several thousand Russian Communists of the Tudeh party had prevented the Majlis from meeting on March 4. Such scenes continued.

Robert Rossow, the young new United States Vice-Consul in Tabriz, the capital of Azerbaijan, was meantime busy informing himself, and his government, of Russian activity in the region. On the night of March 3, he noticed that 450 Russian trucks, heavily laden with supplies, mainly ammunition, had left Tabriz on the road to Tehran. On March 4, twenty tanks left Tabriz with another hundred trucks, in the same direction. Two regiments of cavalry and batteries of artillery left probably for Kurdistan. Rossow was told that the Kurds were 'preparing to assert a claim to Turkish Kurdistan' and planned to begin military operations to that end shortly.[75] That day, the Kurdish government in Mahābād indeed proclaimed rights of sovereignty over the Kurdish regions of South-Eastern Turkey: a statement which caused consternation in Ankara: and was not entirely popular among the Turkish Kurds who, unlike those of Azerbaijan, were principally Sunni Muslims, not Shi'ite.[76] On the 6th, Rossow reported that Soviet troop reinforcements, including tanks, were continuing to arrive in Tabriz night and day by both road and rail. Furthermore, Marshal Ivan Bagramyan, a Soviet military commander with a 'spectacular combat record', was said to have reached Tabriz to take command of Soviet troops there, taking over from General Glinsky, who had little experience of war. Marshal Bagramyan was a specialist in tank warfare. He had been deputy commander on the Eastern Prussian front a year previously. He had even led the 11th Guards at Kursk. Rossow, who took a lot of trouble with his investigations,[77] concluded a telegram on March 6 with the terse comment, 'all observations and reports indicate inescapably that Soviets are preparing for major military operations'.[78]

Before the alarming message had reached Washington, the United States had taken the action for which the Persian ambassador there had been pressing. Truman and Byrnes discussed the whole question on March 4.[79] The Secretary had already decided to make a stand on Persia, after a meeting at which Loy Henderson had taken his usual firm view and Byrnes's own adviser, Benjamin Cohen, a moderate one.[80] Afterwards, Secretary Byrnes sent his note of protest to Russia. It was much the strongest communication made by the United States since the war: in many ways the strongest ever made up to then. The decision of the Soviet government to retain troops in Persia beyond the period stipulated by the Tripartite Treaty, Byrnes said, had created a situation with regard to which the United States could 'not remain indifferent'. That icy phrase of the old diplomacy was thus wheeled once more into use. The government of the United States, 'in the spirit of friendly association which developed between the United States and the Soviet Union in the successful effort against the common enemy, expresses the earnest hope that the government of the Soviet Union will do its part by withdrawing immediately all Soviet forces from the territory of Iran, to promote the international confidence, necessary for peaceful progress'. The United States requested 'that it be promptly advised of the decision of the government the Soviet Union which it hopes will be in accord with the views herein expressed'.[81] The American Cabinet did not meet to discuss this matter: just as well perhaps for peace in Washington if not in the world, since, at this time, the Secretary for Commerce, Wallace, was wondering whether the people in Russian Azerbaijan were 'living better than those in Persian Azerbaijan'.[82]

Byrnes despatched this document to Moscow; and appropriately it was George Kennan who carried it to Molotov on the morning of March 6. The fact that the message had been sent was announced publicly, but its contents were not. The British made a similar but less strong enquiry of the Soviet Union.[83] It was of great significance, however, that the United States took these major decisions without their being co-ordinated with Britain, despite the importance which Britain always had in the past in the country concerned: another major change in United States policy. Qavam had by then seen Stalin again. But nothing much had been said. The occasion had been at a banquet, with 'many toasts and speeches'. Stalin and Qavam merely agreed that fuller discussions would follow in Tehran between the new Soviet ambassador and the Persian government. These would not be a substitute for discussions in the United Nations if matters came to that, though the Russians would naturally have liked it.

There was one surprising element in the Soviet reaction to this crisis, and perhaps more notice should have been taken of it: the Soviet press had revealed little of any international difference having arisen in Persia.[84] Happily insulated from public opinion, Stalin was able to decide exactly what he wanted: to go forward; or to go back.

It was in these dramatic circumstances that Winston Churchill made one of his most famous speeches, at Fulton, Missouri.

# TWENTY-THREE

# FULTON AND CHURCHILL

Churchill's shadow lay over Britain then as heavily as Roosevelt's did over the United States. Young politicians had begun, unconsciously as well as deliberately, to model their style on his. His attitudes to the Soviet Union over the four and three-quarter years since that day in June when the Germans had attacked Russia had, however, been almost as unpredictable as Roosevelt's. His physician summed this up in a note in 1944, pointing out that his patient seemed 'torn between two lines of action . . . At one moment he will plead with the President for a common front against Communism and the next he will make a bid for Stalin's friendship. Sometimes the two policies alternate with bewildering rapidity'.[1] This great orator, who wrote as he spoke, in the classic mode, never indeed settled how to manage the shoemaker's son from Gori until it was too late to secure from him any concessions. The uncertainty did not derive from 'the burbling of the brandy in his sinuses' in the formulation of Henry Wallace;[2] it derived from a real clash of calculations.

Rational, far-sighted, well-read and witty, Churchill had, twenty-five years before, been the most vigorous proponent in Britain, after Lloyd George, of intervention in the Russian Civil War against 'that little set of Communist criminals'.[3] 'Of all tyrannies', he told the Aldwych Club in 1919, 'the Bolshevik tyranny is the worst, the most destructive, the most degrading'.[4] By May 1939, Churchill was, however, hoping for Soviet intervention to help to save Europe from the Nazis, against the ideas of Chamberlain.[5] As soon as he became Prime Minister in 1940, he made a bid for a Soviet rapprochement; Sir Stafford Cripps, his first Ambassador to Moscow, saw Stalin on July 1, 1940, and allowed him to think that Britain would not mind if Stalin were to obtain hegemony in the Balkans, if only they drew away from Germany. Perhaps Cripps exceeded his instructions. Anyway Stalin told the German ambassador with relish.[6] In 1941 Churchill, like most of Britain (with the exception of Evelyn Waugh's famous character Guy Crouchback in *Sword of Honour*), was much relieved by the German attack on Russia.* Britain at last had a powerful ally. Churchill's speech on June 22, 1941, on the radio, pictured a happier Russia than had existed for at least twenty-five years: 'I see the ten thousand villages of Russia where the means of existence is wrung so heavily from the soil, but where there are still primordial human joys'.[7] The Russian danger was, therefore, 'our danger'. He had, after all, decided that, as his private secretary recalled, 'if Hitler invaded Hell he would at least make one favourable reference to the Devil'.[8] A perceptive critic, Isaiah Berlin, however, considered that Churchill had in truth 'always looked on the Russians as a formless, quasi-Asiatic mass beyond the walls of European civilisation'.[9]

Churchill then set about creating an alliance between his country and the Soviet Union. The engineer of this improbable association, to begin with, was his friend and benefactor, Lord Beaverbrook, who, despite his love of empire, and his successful practice of capitalism, established a rapport with Stalin on the visit there: 'a proper villain' but 'a very jovial man', he afterwards seemed to him.[10]

It was Beaverbrook who argued that, unless Britain created a second front in 1941, Russia would either make a separate peace with Germany, or be defeated.[11] Churchill initiated several concessions of principle (including as has been seen, over the Baltic States) to make this alliance work effectively.

Churchill did not, however, suspend his critical faculties:

---

* 22 June – 'a day of apocalypse for all the world for numberless generations' (*Sword of Honour*, 530).

'I am getting tired of these repeated scoldings', he told his ambassador in Moscow in June 1942 (from Stalin about the second front) considering that 'they have never been activated by anything but cold-blooded self interest'.[12] In July 1943, he was thinking that a federation in Eastern Europe might still be created 'to restrain those Mongols'. He was disturbed by the tone of Stalin's complaints about the delay in the second front: 'Stalin is an unnatural man', he remarked in August 1943, 'there will be grave troubles'.[13] Even so, by that time, he had made the major concession, deriving from a consideration of the Baltic States, that the Atlantic Charter would not apply to the defeated countries of the Axis.[14]

In the latter part of 1943 there occurred the first of those 'woolly and bibulous',[15] ill-mannered and ill-prepared, international conferences between the 'Big Three', at Tehran. Churchill had there his celebrated discussion with Stalin about Poland's frontier, with Roosevelt refusing to become engaged. Churchill also 'volunteered the suggestion that so large a landmass [as the Soviet Union] deserved access to warm water ports'.[16] Although he had not raised the matter, Stalin agreed wholeheartedly and asked whether Britain would now relax the provisions of the Convention of Montreux. Churchill said that he hoped 'to see Russian fleets, both naval and merchant, on all seas of the world'.[17] After Roosevelt had said that the Kiel Canal should also be equally open to all ships, and the Chinese port of Dairen a free port under international guarantee, Churchill added that the important thing was that Russia's legitimate needs should be satisfied. Great powers should be satisfied and have no territorial or other ambitions. Hungry and ambitious nations were dangerous. He would like to see the leading nations of the world in the position of rich, happy men.[18]

These remarks have four explanations: first, Churchill was unhappy that he had not managed to organise – indeed, still opposed – a second front in Western Europe to take the pressure off Russia. Second, he feared that, if he did not make concessions, the Allies might, as Beaverbrook argued, throw Russia into the hands of the Germans with whom they might make a separate peace. Third, Churchill, like most other people, was partly charmed by Stalin when in his presence and so sometimes said things he did not mean. Fourthly, he allowed himself to believe, like Roosevelt and like most of his countrymen, that the peace might be made acceptable to Russia. He was not going to live in Yugoslavia after the war, he told Fitzroy Maclean in December 1943 in Cairo, and so what interested him, as to the comparative merits say of Mihailović or Tito, was 'which of them is doing most harm to the Germans'.[19] He did not, however, have a starry-eyed view: 'I hope you are not one of those men who think we are going to have a better world after the war. It is going to be pretty bad', he told a New Deal economist, Isador Lubin, in 1943.[20]

1944 was a year of ambiguity over Russia for Churchill. Thus, in January, he was talking to his secretary of the 'new confidence which has grown in our hearts about Stalin'.[21] But by March he was noticing that, in relation to Poland, 'it is perfectly clear that to argue with the Russians only infuriates them'; adding that 'although I have tried in every way to put myself in sympathy with these Communist leaders, I cannot feel the slightest trust or confidence in them. Force and facts are their only realities';[22] and he recognised that 'our, and especially my, very courteous and even effusive personal approaches may have had a bad effect'.[23]

In May 1944 he was found telling Anthony Eden, 'broadly speaking, the issue is: are we going to acquiesce in the communisation of the Balkans and perhaps of Italy? . . . If we resist the communist infusion and invasion, we should put it to them pretty plainly, at the best moment that military events permit'.[24] In July, though, officials in the Foreign Office were finding his telegrams to Stalin 'much too soft-soapy' and his approach to foreign policy in general, and in particular to Tito, too romantic.[25] By the autumn he was dismayed at the Soviet callous treatment of the rising by the Home Army in Warsaw.[26] All the same, he sought a new meeting with Stalin.

Roosevelt wanted to delay such a discussion till after his re-election in November and fourth inauguration in January. So Churchill went alone to Moscow in October and, inspired by General Smuts to think in large-scale terms, there made the 'percentages agreement' with Stalin, so often referred to in this volume. The Americans had been against such a concession on 'spheres of influence' throughout the war, and had opposed the proposal.[27] Churchill insisted, saying that it was not a suggestion for permanent spheres, but only temporary ones, needed for 'local military considerations'. Churchill began to talk of the idea to the Russians the previous summer, confining the idea to Romania and Greece. What Churchill really sought, and obtained, was a free hand in Greece, in exchange for leaving Russia the same in Romania, Bulgaria and Hungary. The United States attempted to ignore what had happened.[28] Hindsight makes the historian wonder whether the figures were fair to the West: could the British influence in Yugoslavia not have been raised to eighty per cent? And might that not have saved many lives had it been put into effect?

Churchill considered his meeting in Moscow a success. It showed, he told Stalin, 'that there are no matters which cannot be adjusted between us when we meet together in a frank and intimate discussion'.[29] He reported that Stalin and he talked 'with an ease, freedom and cordiality never attained before between our two countries'. Churchill seemed this time to have been charmed by Stalin;[30] or, as his biographer put it, 'he in his mind created a Stalin who had other pressures on him, not merely his own decisions'.[31]

At Yalta, Churchill stood up for the interests of small powers in making his famous, if ineffective, suggestion that eagles 'such as Russia' should permit small birds (Poland) to sing.[32] But Cadogan recalls Churchill 'plunging into a long harangue' about the proposed United Nations knowing nothing of what he was talking.[33] He showed an extraordinary confidence in Stalin. Thus he said, 'I know that, under the leaders of these powers represented here, we may feel safe. But . . . in ten years' time, we may disappear'.[34] This attitude is to be explained by the fear that even then Russia might hesitate, withdraw from the war, make a deal with Hitler, or otherwise give the Western Allies extra work and so extra loss of lives. (He had earlier said much the same to de Gaulle on November 11, 1944, only in reverse; namely that he trusted Stalin but, in ten years' time, when Stalin would be as old as he, Churchill, then things would be different: '*Je le crois sincère aujourd'hui.*\* *Peut-être dans dix ans, lorsque Stalin sera aussi vieux que je suis, les choses changeront-elles*'. This trust was expressed in respect of 'formal assurances' which Churchill told de Gaulle that he had received in respect of Polish independence).[35]

Like Tehran, Yalta had been a badly organised conference with no proper agenda and no real preparation. On his return to England, Churchill gave his ministerial colleagues an encouraging picture. So long as Stalin lasted, he repeated, Anglo-Russian friendship would be maintained. 'Poor Neville Chamberlain believed that he could trust Hitler. He was wrong. But I don't think I'm wrong about Stalin'.[36] In the House of Commons, in a debate on these 'Crimean Agreements', Churchill continued in this mellow mood; 'Marshal Stalin and the Soviet leaders wish to live in honourable friendship and equality with the Western democracies. I feel that their word is their bond. I know of no government which stands to its obligations, even in its own despite, more solidly than the Russian Soviet government'.[37] By then Churchill and most of the Cabinet in England were exhausted; Churchill in particular (according to the weary Permanent Under-Secretary at the Foreign Office, Cadogan) was 'spending hours of his own and other people's time simply drivelling, welcoming every red herring so as only to have the pleasure of more irrelevant, redundant talk'.[38] Still, even in February 1945, there might just have been a reconciliation between the Germans and the Russians. It was still likely that the Western Allies would want the Russians in the Far East war, which many believed might have lasted two more years. Churchill had, as has been seen, maintained an absolutely consistent view over holding onto the 'atom secrets' and not offering them to the Russians, to the disgust of Professor Bohr. Even so, his attitude to Stalin reads strangely. Great men nod.

In March 1945, the Polish situation went from bad to worse. Churchill cabled to Roosevelt, 'I advised critics of the Yalta

---

\* He had said the same to King Peter: he had 'always found Stalin a man of his word'.

settlement to trust Stalin'. If rebutted what could he do?[39] His letters to Stalin in April and May were fine arguments in admirable prose: 'do not I beg you, my friend Stalin,' one concluded, 'underrate the divergencies which are opening about matters which you may think are small to us but which are symbolic of the way the English-speaking democracies look at things'.

All through April, Churchill was begging the Americans to advance as far east as they could within the collapsing German Empire for the subsequent political and psychological benefits. By May 1945, he was already speaking of an 'iron curtain drawn along the line Lübeck-Trieste-Corfu', together with 'the further enormous area conquered by the American armies between Eisenach and the Elbe', which would fall to Russia after the United States had withdrawn from their 'tactical' zone to their zone of 'occupation'.* It was also in May that he inspired the stand of Field Marshal Alexander against Yugoslav inroads against Austria and Italy, with the reflection: 'If once we let it be thought that there is no point beyond which we cannot be pushed about, there will be no future for Europe, except by another war more terrible than the world has yet seen'.†[40] He repeated the phrase 'iron curtain', in June 1945, in a telegram to Truman, hoping that what became the Conference of Potsdam might be held earlier than the end of July.

The image of an 'iron curtain' had been used in the 1920s and recently by Goebbels, in an article in *Das Reich* in March: 'Should the German people lay down their arms according to Yalta, the Soviets would occupy the whole of Eastern and South East Europe plus the largest part of the Reich. In front of these territories, which, if one includes the Soviet Union, are gigantic, an iron curtain would come down at once behind which the mass slaughter of the people would take place.'[41]

Cadogan recalls a Cabinet meeting, in June, at which Churchill, looking pale, 'indulged in a long monologue in a depressed undertone – all about the menace of Russia sprawling all over

* On May 12 the first use of the phrase by an official appears to be that of D. Allen (FO371/47592 N6065) May 30, 1945.

† See above, page 432.

Europe'.[42] Joseph Davies also found Churchill gloomy and pessi-mistic, faced with an 'event in the history of Europe to which there has been no parallel and which has not been faced by the Allies in their long and hazardous struggle.'[43] The imposition of Gestapo-like methods in the liberated territories was 'more horrible' than Communism itself.[44]

At Potsdam, Churchill was still moody, ill-prepared and inef-fective, due to apprehensions over the election at home (which he lost). He suffered, according to one official, from 'the belief that he knew everything and need not read briefs'.[45] He had been seriously flummoxed by Truman's proposal for a Soviet-American meeting before the conference as such. He had wanted London, 'the greatest city in the world', to house the conference. He once again, nevertheless, showed a weakness for Stalin: 'I like that man', he said several times to his passionate, cultivated but temperamental Foreign Secretary, Anthony Eden, who, by then realistic about Soviet policies, passed their infrequent private discussions together trying to toughen his leader.[46] He then employed again the metaphor of 'an iron curtain'; 'fairy tales', said Stalin.[47] On July 18, as at Tehran, Churchill told Stalin that he looked forward to Russia becoming a great sea power. Eden did not dissent but told Churchill: 'I am deeply concerned at the pattern of Russian policy, which becomes clearer as they become more brazen every day'.[48]

By mid-August, having lost power, Churchill was again realistic; 'it is not impossible that tragedy on a prodigious scale is unfolding itself behind the iron curtain', he told the House of Commons, in their first debate on foreign policy since the formation of the new government.[49] In October, Churchill was telling Mackenzie King how the Russians were 'realist lizards', all belonging 'to the crocodile family'. They would be 'as pleasant with you as they could be, though prepared to destroy you'.[50] Yet in November his affection for Stalin apparently returned: 'How glad we all are to know and feel that Generalissimo Stalin is still strongly holding the helm . . . Personally I cannot feel anything but the most lively admiration for this truly great man, the father of his country, the ruler of its destinies . . .'[51]

By February 1946, nevertheless, and independent of anything

that Stalin himself had said, Churchill had made up his mind that Russia constituted the most serious problem for the West. Dining on holiday in Havana on February 6, for example, he explained to the American minister there that his great fear was that 'Russia will not only master the secret of atomic warfare but will not hesitate to use it for her own ends'. He thought that the only hope would be for 'some definite working agreement between the American and the British governments'. Any formal merger, or alliance, might be impracticable but some joint understanding was surely necessary.[52] Churchill's protégé, Harold Macmillan, had said in London in a debate on foreign affairs, on February 20, that the Anglo-Soviet alliance was in virtual abeyance.[53] Perhaps the Anglo-American one should be revived.

Stalin's view of Churchill was a good deal more consistently hostile: 'Churchill', Stalin told Djilas at the same time in March 1945 that Churchill was telling his Cabinet to trust 'Uncle Joe', 'Churchill is the kind of man who will pick your pocket of a kopeck if you don't watch him. Yes, pick your pocket of a kopeck. By God, pick your pocket of a kopeck'.[54] He told Mikołajczyk at Potsdam that Churchill did not 'trust us and in consequence, we could not fully trust him'.[55]

Churchill's speech in Fulton was made because of an indirect invitation by Truman himself. Margaret Truman, in her fine biography of her father, describes how 'not long after Dad returned from Potsdam, the President of Westminster College in Fulton, Missouri, paid a visit to General Vaughan', Truman's amiable military aide at the White House. Fulton is a tiny town. All the same, the President of Westminster College there wanted to offer Churchill an honorary degree. Vaughan took the President of the College to see the President of the United States. Truman read the former's letter of invitation and scribbled on the bottom: 'Dear Winnie, this is a fine old school out in my state. If you come and make a speech there, I'll take you out and introduce you.'[56] Churchill accepted, being determined, as the son of an American mother, to remind the world of the benefits of Anglo-Saxon civilisation and to do so now in the peace, as he had done in the war.

Churchill was beginning a long holiday from politics. He had

temporarily handed over the leadership of the Conservative
Party to Anthony Eden. He had in conversation implied that, if
Eden were to be a success in this, he would resign in his favour.[57]
He went to Florida. He revisited Cuba, scene of his first encoun-
ter with arms, when he rode with the Spanish army fighting the
Cuban rebels in 1895. He was available for speeches. So, on
March 4, Truman, having earlier that day given his approval to
Byrnes's protest to Russia over Iran, set out with Churchill, and
the usual presidential entourage from the White House, to
Missouri. On the train they drank and played poker. Truman
read the text of Churchill's speech, as Byrnes and Leahy (with
approval) had done before they set off (Byrnes, significantly,
before his own speech of February 28).[58] Churchill had talked
about the speech beforehand with the Canadian Ambassador in
Washington, Lester Pearson, and on the telephone, with his
wartime comrade, Mackenzie King.[59] Lord Halifax in the British
Embassy, Churchill's rival for the prime ministership in 1940,
read the text and asked his old colleague, unsuccessfully, to
tone down the language.[60] Joseph Davies had urged Truman to
look at the text in advance; but Truman had said it would not
be necessary, since it would only be 'the usual "hands across
the sea stuff"'.[61]

At Fulton, on March 5 – with yet another round of the
Guzenko case, the Canadian enquiry into it, in all American
papers – Truman introduced Churchill: 'I had never met Mr
Churchill personally until a conference we had with Mr Stalin. I
became very fond of both of them. They are men, and they are
leaders in a world that needs leadership . . . I understand that
Mr Churchill is going to talk about the sinews of peace'.[62]
Churchill, dressed in the red robes of an honorary doctor of
philosophy, then threw to the winds all the ambiguities about
Stalin and Russia which had characterised his utterances in the
six months following the war. 'Uncle Joe' was indeed now buried.
The elaborate presents which he (and his family) had exchanged
with Stalin (and Svetlana Stalin) were forgotten. So were the
compliments and embraces. Only eighteen months before,
Churchill had been in Moscow. He and Stalin had divided up
Eastern Europe on a half sheet of paper. Now, however, said

Churchill, a shadow had fallen over the scenes 'so lately lighted by the allied victory'.

The most famous passage in the speech referred to the 'iron curtain' which had descended across the continent of Europe 'from Stettin in the Baltic, to Trieste, in the Adriatic'. Despite its original manufacture in the Reich Ministry of Propaganda, it was a figure of speech which Churchill had begun to believe was his own. It had even been used by the Socialist leader Grotewohl in connection with what divided that country (on February 4 at a dinner in Berlin with the political adviser to the Commander in Chief).[63] It was now in common parlance among British officials. (The line 'From Stettin to Trieste' had as a concept a difficult history: Marx spoke of it as 'the national frontier' of imperial Russia, which he hated, in an article in the *New York Daily News* in 1853.)[64]

Churchill explained how all the capitals of Central and Eastern Europe had become 'subject, in one form or another, not only to Soviet influence, but to a very high and increasing measure of control from Moscow'. 'Police governments' were in control. Communist parties had been raised to power far beyond their deserts. The Poles were expelling Germans on a 'grievious and undreamt of' scale. The future even of Italy hung in the balance. Churchill did not believe that the Soviet leaders desired war. But they plainly did want its fruits: which as, has been seen, Clausewitz, Lenin, and Stalin had declared were their preferred victories. They also wanted the indefinite expansion of Soviet power and doctrines. Churchill sought to stir a sense of alarm in every 'cottage home' in Europe as well as in the United States. What was to be done? Churchill remarked, 'from what I have seen of our Russian friends and others during the war, I am convinced that there is nothing they admire so much as strength, and there is nothing for which they have less respect than military weakness'. But, in ruined Europe, the old idea of the balance of power no longer had application. Everything had to be looked at anew. He urged what sounded very like a new Anglo-American alliance, even if he called it 'a fraternal association under the United Nations', to stop Russia's persistent aggression. Time was short. The Dark Ages could return.

All the same, 'opportunity is here, now, clear and shining for both our countries'. He attacked any policy of conciliation with Russia over the atom bomb. It was 'wrong and imprudent to entrust the secret knowledge or experience of the atomic bomb to the United Nations' and 'criminal madness to cast it adrift in this still agitated and ununited world'.[65] Churchill had not gone quite so far as he had two and a half years before, when receiving an honorary degree at Harvard, and suggested that there might one day be 'common citizenship' between Britain and the United States. But he had gone a long way.[66]

Truman applauded, the audience cheered, and a new era in international relations began. The speech had been broadcast on the national radio. The Canadian Cabinet even listened to it while it was delivered.[67] The speech made, so Lord Halifax was constrained to admit, 'a very profound impact'. It was generally assumed that both the governments of Britain and of President Truman were privy to the text beforehand. The fact that Truman was seen applauding seemed to show that he agreed with it.[68] The *Herald Tribune* commented that Churchill had flung 'a block-buster into the disordered and tottering streets of the city of man'. Although 'the bulk of the press and Congress are clearly unwilling to endorse it as an adequate solution to present troubles, it has given the sharpest jolt to American thinking of any utterance since the war', Lord Halifax reported, on March 10.[69] Arthur Krock, the experienced columnist on the *New York Times* said that the general opinion in Washington was that Churchill should not have made his proposal for a new alliance in the United States (Henry Wallace thought that too); should not have made it in Truman's presence; that it was likely to have a contrary effect to that desired; that it should not have been made then; and that the speech would adversely affect the working of the United Nations.[70] Republicans, like Senator Taft, who approved Churchill's diagnosis, opposed the idea of an alliance. The young Richard Nixon 'at first wondered if he had not gone too far'.[71] The *Chicago Sun* rejected Churchill's 'poisonous doctrines' and hoped that Truman would also do so. The *Boston Globe*, in a characteristic judgement, thought Churchill was inviting the United States to become the heir of 'collapsing colonialism'. The *Washington Post* expostulated that Churchill's idea for an international police limited to Britain and America was a suggestion for an illegal appendage to the United Nations. Walter Lippmann was also critical, and later committed himself to the view that Churchill was saying that 'it was important to fight the Russians sometime during the next five years'.[72] Senators Brewster and Pepper believed that the United States ought to be 'orientating her policies towards the other great world power other than towards Britain'. Ex-Ambassador Joseph Kennedy wrote in *Life* in March 1946: 'Russia does not want a major war now nor in the near future'. He warned America against becoming involved in a world crusade for democracy which could lead to 'war-breeding'.[73] James Roosevelt, eldest son of the late President, said that 'it is up to us and to every peace-loving man and woman in the entire world to stand up now and repudiate the words, the schemes, and the political allies' of Churchill.[74] At a dinner the night after the speech, in Dean Acheson's house in Georgetown, Acheson, Bohlen, and the Australian minister to Washington, Richard Casey, all gave the impression, at least to their fellow guest Henry Wallace, that they believed that the 'United States and England should run the risk of immediate war with Russia by taking a very hard-boiled stand, and being willing to use force if Russia should go beyond a certain point'. Wallace demurred. He himself thought Churchill's speech 'very unfortunate'.[75] Senator Hugh Mitchell, of Washington State, asked him if the proposed American loan to Britain, then being discussed 'on the Hill', was intended to underpin this new Alliance which Churchill wanted. Mrs Eleanor Roosevelt was also critical: 'very much put out with Churchill'.[76]

President Truman himself, though applauding at the time and warmly congratulating Churchill afterwards, also plainly wanted to express some hesitations. He wrote on March 11, to his mother and sister. 'I'm glad you enjoyed Fulton', he said, 'so did I, and I think it did some good, although I am not ready to endorse Mr Churchill's speech'. Truman later invited Stalin to come to Missouri for 'exactly the same kind of reception, the same opportunity to speak your mind'.[77] In a press conference on March 8, he was asked: 'Mr President, your presence on the stage at Fulton has led to some speculation that you endorse the principles of Mr Churchill's speech'. Truman warily, and untruthfully, replied, 'I didn't know what would be Mr Churchill's speech. This is a country of free speech'.[78] He said the same to Henry Wallace, but added that he had been 'sucked in'.[79] That, of course, was what the President still thought that he had to say to the man who was now the last of the 'New Dealers' in the Cabinet (Harold Ickes had resigned in February). Truman was that day primarily perplexed no doubt over what to do about the fact that, unprecedently, on March 9, the new Secretary for War, Patterson, had endorsed the May-Johnson bill for atomic energy, not the McMahon draft which he, Truman, had backed. On March 12, however, in a talk to Adolf A. Berle, the outgoing ambassador in Brazil, the President said that 'he had decided on a policy towards Russia: to keep every agreement we make and to expect them to keep every agreement they make . . . He thought that the Russians were bluffing in the sense of not being willing to risk a new world war; but that they would carry on local aggression unless world opinion stopped them'.[80] Presumably, this was the real Truman, rather than the more hesitant person whom he still exposed in conversation with Henry Wallace and with Joseph Davies. At this time, it seems as if Secretary Byrnes was expressing the President's policy, while the President himself was waiting to see what would happen.

Truman thus said nothing about Russia in public for the moment. Neither he, nor Byrnes, had any desire for an alliance with Britain, whatever they might think about Russia. Even so, Willmott Lewis, the Washington correspondent of *The Times* of London wrote that 'the administration is ready to accept a "special relationship" between the United States and the British Commonwealth'. (It was the first time, apparently, that that comfortable phrase was used.)[81] While Truman did not publicly agree with Churchill, he did not disown him either, on any score.

The timing of Churchill's speech was undoubtedly apposite. American opinion had been perturbed by the spy scandals and their unresolved sequels, by the Soviet disregard of the wartime agreement in Persia, and by the alarming reports from Manchuria. There were few who did not see some *arrière-pensée* in the plan to despatch the *USS Missouri* to Turkey with the ambassador's body. News of British manoeuvres off Gibraltar increased the sensation that the world was back to moving about armed forces for strategic purposes. On March 6, the Department of War had felt constrained to issue a statement denying that demobilisation had been halted, that army reserves had been altered, and that leave had been cancelled.[82] Unfortunately, for Britain, however, men such as Leahy and Groves, who agreed with Churchill's general diagnosis, were as yet ill-disposed to the idea of any new alliance across the sea, and, as has been seen, were indeed busily cutting away the few links which remained of Anglo-American collaboration in essential atomic matters.

These Americans, of course, liked Churchill's speech in itself. William Bullitt, still most 'disturbed about the Russian situation', when lunching with Leahy and Forrestal, on March 10, hoped that Truman would 'create some small group to make an appraisal and evaluation of American policy *vis-à-vis* Russia, with particular emphasis on the balancing of our capabilities with our commitments'. Leahy thought that there was 'a difficulty in getting enough of the President's time to deal adequately with the problem':[83] a familiar complaint of the political adviser. Forrestal believed 'either we make the United Nations work, or we face a world in which we must maintain such overwhelming military power as to make it abundantly clear that future aggressors will eventually suffer the ruinous fate of Germany'.[84] Harriman also made a speech on March 13 which showed that, whatever his doubts about Stalin a month before, he now agreed with Churchill, his old friend: the important thing to do was to stop Russia 'before she expands any further', even at the risk of war.[85]

Churchill personally told Forrestal, in similar terms, that he was gloomy about the chance of reaching any accommodation unless it was made clear that Russia would be met by force if she continued her expansion. He was glad that the *USS Missouri* had been sent, though disappointed that it had gone alone: 'a gesture of power not fully implemented is almost less effective than no gesture at all'. Churchill assured Forrestal that the Russians had no understanding of such words as 'honesty', 'honour', 'truth' and 'trust'. They regarded those as negative virtues. They will, he said, 'try every door in the house, enter all the rooms which are not locked and, when they come to one that is barred, if they are unsuccessful in breaking through it, they will withdraw and invite you to dine genially the same evening'!*[86] The Canadian government, beset by their Royal Commission on Guzenko, meantime, were relieved at Churchill's speech. Though Mackenzie King thought that he should have made the speech himself, he telephoned Churchill to say that it had been the most courageous made by any man at any time.[87]

British opinion was critical. Even Churchill's deputy, Anthony Eden, thought that, 'when Labour was quarrelling with Russia, there was no need for the Opposition to get embroiled'.[88] The new head of the Foreign Office, Sargent, thought that the speech 'would be harmful in America but might possibly do some good in Russia'.[89] Grand old men of letters such as J. B. Priestley and George Bernard Shaw were also hostile. E. H. Carr began by asking (in an unsigned leader in *The Times*, on March 6) whether it was valid to regard Western democracy and Communism as irreconcilable opposites. They had much to learn from each other: 'Communism in the working of political institutions; Western democracy in the development of economic and social planning'. Such was Carr's general approach to politics at the time. On March 9, another writer in *The Times*, Rushbrook Williams, wrote a leader arguing self-protection to be the prime motive of Soviet behaviour in Germany, Persia and Manchuria. Churchill's call for an Anglo-American military understanding would be taken by Russia as confirmation of their fears; 'If Britain and America can discover directly from the Russians how timely and natural are the fears that underlie Russian policy, they may be able to show that these fears are susceptible of ready alleviation'.[90] This kind of voice, preaching unrealisable goals, often heard before, would be heard equally often again. The author, once an Indian civil servant, George Orwell's superior in the Indian service of

---

* He said exactly the same to United States businessmen on March 18.

the BBC in the war, believed, above all the historian of *The Times* noted, 'in the power of reasoned argument to influence men and events'.[91] But the age of reason had come to an end.

Far away in Nuremberg, the major Nazi war criminals on trial for their lives, sitting in the dock during a conference between their judges, were elated when they heard of Churchill's speech. Ex-*Reichmarschall* Goering slapped his thigh and predicted that their difficulties would soon be at an end. Rudolf Hess for a time ceased behaving as an amnesiac and reminded his colleagues how he had always predicted a great turning point which would return all the defendants to their lost ranks. Albrecht Speer reflected bitterly that Churchill was talking of the same Soviet Union whose representatives still confronted them on the judges' bench.[92]

The British Cabinet considered Churchill's speech on the morning of March 11. They had to do so because of the repeated suggestions that they had beforehand approved its terms. Attlee and Bevin both pledged themselves to say that they had not seen the text before delivery.[93] Most of the leading members of that government, however, agreed with the general tone of Churchill's argument. Bevin had been annoyed by its arrogance: Churchill 'thinks he is Prime Minister of the world', he told his private secretary.[94] On March 2, Attlee, the least imperial in thinking of his colleagues, had circulated a paper to his Defence Committee which suggested that a British Empire built in the era of seapower should reconsider its role in the Mediterranean. Bevin expostulated, 'if we withdrew, we would allow France, Italy, Yugoslavia, Greece, Turkey and Spain all under a totalitarian yoke'. There followed a discussion about policy on the assumption that 'it might soon be necessary to defend ourselves against Russia'.[95]

The same day, the Editor of *The Times*, Robin Barrington-Ward, went to see Ernest Bevin in the Foreign Office. The Editor was denounced by the Foreign Secretary. *The Times* did great harm, Bevin said. It was read abroad as if it were the national newspaper. Bevin was going to tell the House of Commons that it was not and that it was pro-Russian and not pro-British. Barrington-Ward was taken aback: 'too calm', he thought afterwards. He continued privately to believe, on no very good grounds – on his own judgement, as well as on E. H. Carr's advice – that 'the Russians do in fact intend cooperation with the West'.[96]

Trygve Lie, just preparing to move the United Nations Secretariat from London to New York, its permanent site, also visited Bevin to ask him to repudiate Churchill's speech. Trygve Lie said that he agreed with the sentiments of Churchill but thought that he had played into the hands of 'anti-Western elements' in Moscow by broadcasting them.[97]

Bevin did not wish to repudiate Churchill.[98] He was himself in a Churchillian mood at that time. On March 13, for example, whilst dealing with the question of Greece, he wrote, 'the Mediterranean is the passage through which we bring influence to bear on Southern Europe, the soft underbelly of France, Italy, Yugoslavia, Greece and Turkey. Without our physical presence in the Mediterranean, we should cut little ice with those states which would fall like Eastern Europe, under the totalitarian yoke . . . In the European scene . . . we are the last bastion of social democracy. It may be said that this represents our way of life against the red tooth and claw of American capitalism and Communist dictatorship of Soviet Russia'.[99] A recent recruit to the Labour Party, Harold Nicolson, brilliant writer, ex-diplomatist and adviser to a generation of young diplomatists, had written, a day or two before, in gloomy terms, that he could not decide between two views: the optimistic, that Russia was being troublesome in the Middle East merely to secure concessions in East Europe; the pessimistic, being that a war between the United States and Russia for world mastery was inevitable and that the 'Panslav and world revolution elements' had gained the upper hand in Moscow.[100]

It may be that the most positive immediate effect of Churchill's speech was to make it easier for the Administration to win approval of the $3.75 billion loan to Britain. The growing mood of anti-Communism, so swiftly assumed, after so much recent exultant pro-Russian sentiment, and now encouraged by anti-spy hysteria, helped Britain, through Churchill: a rare example of an opposition leader affecting policy. Congressmen were soon

persuaded that a bankrupt Britain would be an easy prey for
Communism, a connection of ideas which was not proved though,
in the next few years, it would be frequently assumed. This
view was easier to put forward following the British government's offer of independence to India on March 15. The United
States administration embarked on an effort of public relations
to educate the American public on the economic benefits of the
loan and on the wisdom generally of a multilateral economic
approach. But Representative Christian Herter was surely right
when he told Assistant Under-Secretary William Clayton that
he found 'the economic arguments in favour of the loan are on
the whole much less convincing (to Republican congressmen)
than the feeling that the loan may serve us in good stead in
holding up a hand to a nation whom we may need badly as a friend
because of impending Russian troubles'. Clayton answered: 'I
am sure you are right'.[101]

# TWENTY-FOUR

# DENOUEMENT IN PERSIA

The two occurrences of March 5 and 6, 1946, Byrnes's protest about Persia and Churchill's speech at Fulton, following Byrnes's speech the previous week, made the same point. 'After that nothing was the same again', wrote Alan Bullock, the biographer of Ernest Bevin.[1] For, after all, if a country formally tells another that it 'cannot be indifferent' to the other's actions, it has to be able to do something in consequence. In the course of March the United States prepared so to be. To carry that through in the administration in Washington it needed a philosophy, and a rhetoric. The philosophy was now provided, by Kennan's 'long telegram'; the rhetoric, by Churchill's speech at Fulton, as well as Byrnes's in New York. Truman, hankering after Roosevelt's 'Grand Design', still hoping that Stalin might turn out to be comparable to Boss Pendergast rather than Jenghiz Khan, and so would keep his word, might still be hesitant.[2] But, though he was silent, his policy had been made.

A new meeting on Persia was held by Secretary Byrnes in his office on March 8 in the evening. An experienced official, Edwin Wright, had prepared a large-scale map of Azerbaijan indicating the movement of Soviet troops.[3] On careful enquiry, it seemed that these movements were directed towards the Turkish border, the Iraqi border, and the southern oil fields, as much as Tehran. There were differences of opinion: 'Chip' Bohlen thought Persia the wrong place to challenge Russia, for geographical reasons. Benjamin Cohen again urged caution.

After all, what troops did the United States have available anywhere near? Perhaps only one combat division. Even so Byrnes remarked, after looking again at the recent telegrams from Rossow in Tabriz, that the Russians were adding military invasion to political subversion in Persia; 'now we'll give it to them with both barrels', he said.

Next morning, more telegrams came in from Rossow about Soviet troop movements. One stated, 'I cannot overstress the seriousness and magnitude of current Soviet troop movements here'.[4] The Azerbaijan 'government' also publicly announced the incorporation into their realm of the small strip of coastal plain which separates Azerbaijan proper from the Caspian.

There were more meetings, and more suggestions. One official thought that 'we ought to let the USSR know that we were aware of its moves but to leave a graceful way out'. Alger Hiss, who was present as adviser to Byrnes on the affairs of the United Nations, scribbled a draft statement and passed it to Loy Henderson. The consequence was that Byrnes sent another terse telegram: his government desired to know whether, instead of withdrawing troops, it was bringing in additional troops; in which case, why?[5] The British were told that, unless the United States received a satisfactory reply, they would take the matter immediately to the Security Council. The telegrams from Tabriz were shown to the British Embassy in Washington: but again Britain was not really consulted.[6] Perhaps that was because Britain did not take the rumours so seriously: 'a gross interference' in Persian affairs did not, it seemed to the British, 'necessarily amount to major Russian military operations'.[7] All the same, Ernest Bevin seemed 'in a great state' about this time saying that the Russians were advancing in full force on Tehran, and that 'this means war'. Attlee and the Chancellor thought Bevin too 'strung up'.[8]

Presumably, thanks to Donald Maclean (then acting Head of Chancery at the British Embassy in Washington) or other agents (or both), the Russians received information about these discussions in the Secretary's room in the Department of State. That Maclean was entirely informed of what was happening over Persia is suggested by the fact that it was he who signed on

March 9 a top secret letter on behalf of the ambassador Lord Halifax to Byrnes which ended: 'I am to add that so far as Mr Bevin is concerned he would strongly deprecate putting to Monsieur Molotov any proposal for a four power meeting until we have had some moderately satisfactory reply . . . regarding Persia'.[9]

On March 10, the Prime Minister of Persia, Qavam, at last returned home from Moscow to Tehran. He was, in one sense, in a strong position, since he had been seen to negotiate with Russia and apparently had given nothing away. In addition, the Majlis were to adjourn the next day, the 11th, and Qavam would be left as, in effect, the ruler of the country with no parliamentary criticism and with at least the nominal backing of the Shah. No new election could take place for a new Majlis (by the Majlis' own law of 1942) so long as foreign troops were in the country. That law had been introduced to avoid any packing of parliament. But the absence of a parliament would make the Prime Minister both a potential dictator and at the same time amenable to outside pressure. A majority of the Majlis could see that. So did the Communists, who continued to stage successful demonstrations to prevent the deputies from arriving for their adjournment, in order to try and prolong their term.[10]

On the afternoon of March 10, Wallace Murray, the United States Ambassador in Tehran, saw Qavam at the latter's private house. He gave him the essential assurance that, if the Russians were to maintain troops in Persia contrary to Persian wishes, the United States would support the Shah's government by placing the matter before the Security Council. For his part, Qavam gave an account of his dealings in Russia which partially satisfied the Ambassador; who, however, went to see the young Shah, and told him that he 'would like him to make sure Qavam understood the situation and the vital importance of placing the case of the Russian troops before the United Nations'. The Shah agreed. He himself was concerned lest the Russians stage a *putsch* in Tehran to take over the government, as they had done in Bucharest and Sofia. On March 13, Qavam promised Murray that, in 'two or three days', he would instruct his ambassador in the United States to place the issue of Persia on the agenda of the Security Council. He would tell the Soviet embassy that this was being done because the constitution forbade the presence of foreign troops unless approved by the Majlis.

Qavam then asked Murray what he, Murray, would do in his place if the Russians were to occupy Tehran on the ground that the lives of Russian citizens were in danger. The Russians, he believed, had thought of that excuse since several officials had already complained that they felt threatened. Murray replied that he thought that pretext obvious. Hitler had used it too often. The Prime Minister surely could not afford to allow any foreign government to assert that he was unable to maintain order with his army and gendarmerie available.

On March 14, the Soviet Chargé in Tehran called on Qavam to say that his government had heard that he planned to put the case of Persia to the Security Council. Moscow would look on this as 'an unfriendly and hostile act which would have unfortunate results'. Qavam took a strong line in reply, and said that the presence of foreign troops was unconstitutional. Murray insisted in telegrams to Byrnes that Persia's 'sole frail hope of salvation' lay in 'a quick appeal to the Security Council'. The recent 'direct and ominous threat' made that even more pressing.[11] The crisis was exacerbated by an attempt to bully Vice Consul Rossow in Tabriz by Russian soldiers, who stopped his car outside the city and held him up – in a manner very similar to the actions of Russians in East Europe. Rossow was personally attacked in the Soviet press for his 'wild' accusations.[12] The American press was sensational: *RED ARMY . . . BELIEVED TWENTY-FIVE MILES FROM TEHRAN* was a headline of the *New York Times* on March 13, 1946.

Qavam instructed his Ambassador in Washington, Hussein Ala, on March 18, to place the case of Persia on the agenda of the United Nations. The complaint was resolute. It referred not only to the Russian troops established in defiance of the tripartite treaty of 1942; but, 'furthermore, the USSR is continuing to interfere in the internal affairs of Iran through the medium of Soviet agents, officials and armed forces'.[13] Qavam hastened to send these instructions to the United States before he had seen the new Russian Ambassador, Sadchikov, who was to reach

Tehran that very day, in the evening. Obviously, he was influenced to take this action by a new communication from Secretary Byrnes to the effect that there was 'nothing to do . . . but immediately to file an appeal with the Security Council'. Byrnes also told Wallace Murray 'you should remind him [Qavam] that we have already given him assurances of our full support to such an appeal'.[14]

In the next day or two there was, as it were, a loaded pause in this crisis. Press commentators suggested that Truman seek to meet Stalin: 'never before, after a great war, have the leading men of the leading powers thought that they could make peace at a distance by occasional and breathless interviews, or through minor officials'.[15] Truman persuaded a half-reluctant Harriman to accept the post job of ambassador to London on the assumption 'it is important. We may be at war with the Soviet Union over Iran'.[16] George Kennan caused new alarm in the Department of State with a prediction, on March 17, that he thought it 'almost a foregone conclusion' that the Soviet Union would make some effort in the immediate future to bring to power in Iran a regime prepared to accede to immediate Soviet demands. But 'this would be done through subservient Iranian elements without direct responsibility on the Soviet side'. The Russians, however, would 'not blunder into a situation whose implications they had not thought through'.[17]

The answer to the crisis in Tehran lay in Moscow. There the mood seemed anything but promising. Churchill's speech had received substantial coverage in the press. Western diplomatists there were surprised at the freedom with which *Pravda* published so much on the subject, including several of Churchill's most effective phrases. Brooks Atkinson, temporarily the correspondent of the *New York Times* in Moscow, though the dramatic critic of that journal, explained that the remarks of Churchill had caused an 'outburst of fury'. The speech, he reported, had 'electrified and depressed everyone'. Moscow had received Churchill's speech 'hysterically', he said later, 'as if the atomic bombs might start there and then'.[17] On March 11 *Pravda* devoted a front-page editorial to Churchill's 'Anglo-American alliance' which, of course, would be directed against Russia; and the paper declared that any such association would mark the final breakdown of the wartime alliance, as of the United Nations. An editorial article couched in violent terms by Professor Evgeny Tarle followed in *Izvestiia* on the 12th. The observant, however, noticed that *Pravda* had carefully waited a week before making any comment and, when it did so, it specially drew attention to Truman's press conference of March 8 in which the President had to some extent dissociated himself from Churchill.

Among the Eastern European States, the reaction to Churchill's speech was also one of alarm. For example, in Bucharest it had been interpreted as a declaration of war on the Soviet Union. It was expected that war was now inevitable. That eventually might be welcomed by the parties of the opposition but even they were apprehensive. The Czechs seemed worried lest 'reaction' should be encouraged in their country;[18] while the Czech Ambassador in London, Count Max Lobkowicz, despite his aristocratic name, 'in general took the pro-Russian view' and so was 'against the speech'.[19]

Stalin gave a reply to Churchill in the form of an interview in *Pravda* (on March 14). This was a polemic of unparalleled virulence no doubt intended for Russian opinion. It was couched in the semi-liturgical style which, as has been seen, the Vozhd particularly liked. It seemed to Kennan in Moscow the most violent Soviet reaction to a foreign statement that he could remember. Stalin acknowledged, for the first time in some years, the 'laws' of historical development which were inevitably drawing the world towards revolution, and which Churchill was seeking to reverse. He compared Churchill to Hitler, named him a liar and a racist and recalled, for the benefit of his Soviet readers, how the 'little people' of England had rejected him in the last election.[20] Churchill wanted the Anglo-Saxons to dominate the world. That was an 'English race theory'. Well, Churchill only had to wait and see. Stalin thought that the speech was calculated to sow discord between the Allies. Churchill desired war. What Churchill had said about the police states of East Europe was 'not only slanderous but vulgarly tactless', since those countries had model democratic regimes; more so than Britain for, in Britain, only one party ruled, and the other parties were 'deprived of the right of participation in the government'; in East Europe there were many coalition governments; 'and that is called by Churchill "totalitarianism, tyranny and a police state"'.

No doubt Stalin, like Churchill himself, was speaking with the Persian problem partly in mind; preparing the Russians psychologically for any decision that he might make.[21] He would not have liked his countrymen to suppose that any showdown there with the West was the consequence of resistance to the 'expansionism' of which Churchill had been speaking. The Russian people, it is true, had still received no news officially of what was happening in Iran. But, in totalitarian regimes, rumour brings news fast. Many Russians had read of Churchill's speech, which had been well-publicised. Now they had to be assured that the 'broad masses' everywhere were against Churchill. Stalin said that 'serious attention cannot be paid to false statements of Mr Churchill's friends in Britain' about extending further the British alliance with Russia. On reporting this from Moscow, Frank Roberts stated in his telegram to Bevin that he feared that the allusion was intended to refer to him. Bevin noted on the document the words 'I do not think so'[22] and subsequently telegraphed Roberts to that effect.

So far as his own people were concerned, Stalin had done his work well. He had represented Churchill as an enemy of peace, but one who could not be regarded as constituting a serious threat of war; as a fomentor of discord but one without the backing of his own common people. Stalin had also discredited Bevin's proposal for an extension of the Anglo-Soviet treaty by attributing it to Churchill.[23]

Of course, it may be that pique had entered into Stalin's reaction. Only six weeks before, he had been telling the lighthearted departing British Ambassador, Sir Archie Clark Kerr, that he had been able to discuss difficult matters amicably with Churchill and with Eden; but the Labour government was different. If he went to London, for example, he doubted whether the Labour government would like to see him; he 'would have been sure of his reception under Churchill and Eden'.[24] Now such pleasantries would be impossible.

Years later Khrushchev, who saw Stalin regularly in those days, reported that 'it was largely because of Churchill's speech that Stalin exaggerated our enemies' strength and their intention to unleash war on us . . . he became obsessed with shoring up our defences . . . Churchill's speech marked a return to pre-war attitudes, so far as Stalin was concerned'.[25] So the Russians in consequence (Khrushchev argued) ceased to cooperate with their old allies of the Second World War; 'we dropped all pretence of friendship . . . Stalin was convinced that the West was deliberately creating tensions. He began to assume that another war was not only possible but inevitable'. The argument was dishonest. Churchill's speech came at the end of a process of growing bad relations, not at the beginning.

It was at this moment that the new Supreme Soviet, which had been 'elected' in February, assembled for the first time in Moscow. To this unreal gathering, Stalin formally submitted his resignation as head of his government and that of his fellow commissars. The same gathering immediately asked him to form a new administration. He agreed. But the commissars in the new adminstration were to be named 'Ministers', the 'Council of Peoples' Commissars' becoming, for the first time since 1917, a 'Council of Ministers', just as if it had been a Western cabinet. Nikolai Shvernik, the 'First Assistant Chairman of the Presidium of the Supreme Council of the Soviet Union' (Deputy President), gave the reason; the old nomenclature had been associated with the radical destruction of the old Tsarist administration. But it had given rise to confusions. The real reasons for this change is obscure. It did not result in any change of function; nor in the number of ministers, at least for the moment.[26]

A new Politburo of the Party was also now announced, Beria and Malenkov joining that body (of which they had previously been 'candidates') which now would number eleven for the first time.* New emphasis was also given to the Organisation Bureau,

---

* Stalin, Andreev, Beria, Kaganovich, Malenkov, Voroshilov, Kalinin, Khrushchev, Mikoyan, Molotov and Zhdanov. Shvernik, Bulganin, Kosygin and Voznesensky were candidate members (Shvernik and Voznesensky had also been so in 1941–6).

*Orgburo*, the body which supervised Party affairs and was supposed to meet weekly. There was a new emphasis on the role of the government at the expense of the Party. That represented the discomfiture, however, of the newly promoted Malenkov, as against that of Zhdanov within the inner discussions of the Soviet leaders. Once again, it would seem that Stalin had successfully covered all his possible successors by inter-relating checks. Thus the new *Orgburo* did not include any friends of Malenkov. It was full of 'Zhdanovites'; and six of those men were regional Party secretaries, such as Suslov (Karelia) and Zhdanov's ex-deputy and protégé, A. N. Kutznetzov (Leningrad):* Stalin had thus sought to balance the interests of his two most powerful deputies, and possible heirs, in his usual clever tactical arrangement.[27] Since the Politburo still did not meet regularly, much power lay with this *Orgburo*. At the same time the armed service commissariat – navy, air force and army, which had been merged the previous month – was transformed into a Ministry of Defence, with six deputy ministers; the united department which neither the United States nor her allies would achieve without much anguish.

Finally, Kalinin, the oldest and most venerable member of the Politburo, who for twenty years had held what was nominally the highest position in the Soviet state, Chairman of the Presidium of the Supreme Soviet, was dropped from that post, without a single speech of tribute to him. He was succeeded by Shvernik, an equally grey personality. No one seemed to notice the change. No Soviet leader had yet managed to retire in dignity. Kalinin might have wished to retire merely out of old age. Yet he was a symbolic figure of the regime all the same. He had been a prominent Bolshevik since 1912, when he had become an alternate member of the Central Committee of the Party. Kindhearted but weak, he had tried sometimes to defend colleagues arrested in the purges. Stalin had told him not to interfere and had his wife arrested. She was still in a camp in 1946. A head

---

* The Buro was: Stalin, Zhdanov, A. A. Kuznetsov, Popov, Malenkov (Secretariat members); and Aleksandrov, Andrianov, Bulganin, V. V. Kutznetzov, Mekhlis, Mikhailov, Patolichev, Radionov and Shatalin.

of state with a wife in prison was unusual even for Russia. But
Kalinin himself had been under near house arrest for years, on
the pretext of guarding him.[28]

Kennan incidentally thought that this session of the Supreme
Soviet was the most formalistic and most stereotyped of any
such meeting that Moscow had seen. There was no 'pretence
of spontaneous sentiment or action on [the] part of the deputies.
No proposal . . . failed to find unanimous support'.[29] Now that
these arrangements had been carried through, Stalin was ready
for other decisions.

In most of the world, things were going his way. For example,
the government of Yugoslavia on the 13th captured the missing
leader of their rivals, the Chetnik General Mihailović. They
announced on March 25 that they would proceed to try him –
an event which led to widespread protest in the United States.[30]
(Mihailović had been betrayed by one of his own 'devoted'
commanders, Nikola Kalabić, who, recruited by Rancović's
dreaded ONZA, had led him into a trap).[31] In France, the
Communist Party had a veto over the actions of Félix Gouin's
weak coalition: 'would a Communist government recognise
obligations contracted towards the United States,' the noble old
Socialist Léon Blum felt constrained to ask Thorez, when he set
off on a humiliating journey to Washington in early March ('*Cela
va de soi!*' was Thorez's answer).[32] In Berlin, the Communist
pressure towards fusion of Socialists and Communists was continuing remorselessly. Thus, on March 15, the Berlin Socialist
Grotewohl, for example, told the Secretary of the Social Democrats of Spandau of a plan to be introduced if and when the united
party were formed. A new Communist-Socialist Party would be
established. Of the 4,000 East German factories destined to
be dismantled under the reparations arrangements, 3,600 would
be put into use as part of a Russian five-year plan for the
production of war equipment.[33] The Americans and British were
doing what they could in Berlin to fight back. They planned to
give the anti-fusionist Socialists paper on which to print a million
leaflets. Social Democrats dismissed by the Communist-
controlled administration of Berlin would be provided with jobs
in the British sector. But the truth was that, by the end of March

1946, the chances of a free election in East Germany, whether held soon or later, were nil.

Between March 15 and 22 there were many rumours that the much-talked-of Soviet-inspired *putsch* in Persia would indeed be carried through. Ernest Bevin, earlier slow to feel alarm over this issue, told the British Cabinet on March 18 that he thought 'recent Soviet activity in Persia' was to be explained by their desire either for oil or for an outlet to warm water ports.[34] Bullard, convinced, at last, by delayed reports from Consul Wall, of the seriousness of the situation, telegraphed from Tehran that the Russians were intensifying their hold on Azerbaijan (March 20). But the publicity given to the movement of troops, and the dispositions of the American commander of the Persian gendarmerie in Tehran, Colonel Norman Schwarzkopf, seem to have had a dampening effect. All the same, March 23, a Saturday, was a most difficult day in Washington, since the Security Council was to meet on Tuesday the 26th. Truman (heavily engaged with the Vandenberg Amendment and the McMahon Bill) bade goodbye to General Walter Bedell Smith, then leaving for Moscow as Ambassador. He told him to tell Stalin that 'I had always held him to be a man to keep his word'. The troops left behind in Persia after March 2 upset that theory. Could not Stalin do something about it?[35]

Byrnes was then enjoying a popularity in Washington which he had not experienced during his conciliatory period: Admiral Leahy even denied rumours that he had wanted Byrnes dismissed and assured him personally that he was his friend.[36] Harriman would soon assert Byrnes to have become a stronger man.[37] Information that, at long last, President and Secretary of State – or at least White House and Department of State – were seeing eye to eye perhaps reached Moscow.

Stalin then made a decision over Persia: to climb down. He gave some indication that this was going to happen when, on March 23, he permitted the publication of another interview, replying to questions by the journalist, Eddie Gilmore, of United Press. He sought to play down the dangers of which he had himself spoken in his interview of March 13. There was, he said, no danger of war. Neither nations nor governments were aiming at new conflicts. The present fear of war was caused by the actions of 'certain political groups who were busy with propaganda'. Peoples and states should organise 'a broad counter-propaganda' in consequence.[38] The change in tone between the interview in reply to Churchill and this one could not have been greater.

Students of the Soviet Union had not fully absorbed that statement when the new Soviet Ambassador to Iran, Ivan Sadchikov, called on Qavam. Instead of more threats, he brought three notes. As in an old-fashioned fairy story, Qavam read them one after another. The first note announced that the Soviet government would evacuate all troops from Iranian territory within five or six weeks 'if nothing further happened'.[39] The second note proposed an Iranian-Soviet oil company to be formed to develop oil; 51 per cent to be Russian, 49 per cent Iranian. The third note suggested that Russia might 'intercede to adjust the Azerbaijan situation' on the basis that the 'Prime Minister of Azerbaijan' should be known as 'Governor-General', his cabinet ministers should be known as 'Directors' of Offices and the local Majlis should be known as the 'Provincial Council'.[40]

Qavam was astonished. Tehran was at that time in such a state of nerves that he had begun to fear a right-wing *coup d'état*, perhaps organised by Britain and carried through by the great friend of that country, Seyyid Zia. In consequence, he had placed Seyyid under preventive arrest. His reply to Russia was to request evacuation in four weeks, not five or six. He also asked that the new Russian decision be formally communicated to the Security Council. He would make a counter-proposal about the development of oil, would refuse Russian intercession over Azerbaijan and would negotiate direct with that 'government' once Russian troops were truly withdrawn. He did not modify Ala's instructions at the Security Council.[41]

In case anyone thought that the Russians were still bluffing, the Soviet press the next day stated that the evacuation of Soviet troops had 'begun' on March 2 and was, 'in some districts, complete'. The evacuation would continue and be complete, as the Ambassador had stated. A *Tass* despatch reported Qavam (untruthfully) as having reprimanded his ambassador in the

United Nations for placing the item of Persia on the agenda.

This Soviet withdrawal is mysterious. It surely did not happen because, as President Truman himself subsequently claimed, he sent Russia an ultimatum. Of that, as the historian of the Department of State drily says, there is no trace in the archives.[42] Probably Truman was confusing Byrnes's stiff note with such an action. Could it have been, to take an extreme suggestion, that it was because the United States despatched a small carrier force ('Operation Frostbite') into the Arctic?[43] It is improbable. Nor could it have been fear of 'Operation Deepfreeze', designed to carry another task force from Alaska to Norway, abandoned because there were not enough ships.[44] The answer must be that Stalin felt that he could afford such a withdrawal when, after all, no hint that there was anything like a crisis in Persia had appeared in the Russian press. His probe had drawn a strong United States reaction. That was what he wanted to know. Perhaps that was what he wanted. But perhaps too he wanted to explore just at what point the Americans would resist. He had to know that in order to deal with Communists in France or Italy who, tempted by 'left wing infantilism', might be desirous of carrying out a revolution there.[45] He may have abandoned Azerbaijan in the hope of being able to obtain Persia itself later.

Evidently Stalin hoped in these circumstances that the debate in the United Nations would not go ahead. But it did, being held at the new, temporary headquarters of the United Nations at Hunter College, in the Bronx. It was broadcast. Andrei Gromyko, the new Soviet Permanent Representative to the United Nations, said that an agreement between Persia and Russia had been reached about the withdrawal of the latter's troops. Once again came the promise of completion 'within five or six weeks unless unforeseen circumstances' occurred. Gromyko evidently expected that the item would be withdrawn. Secretary Byrnes insisted that it should remain on the agenda till the last Russian soldier had left Persia. That was Qavam's instruction too. Gromyko, thereupon, withdrew in dudgeon – and in some disarray, as the Secretary-General of the UN, Trygve Lie, pointed out in his memoirs.[46] It was not the last, but it was the first, time that a Soviet official would leave the table in the United Nations in anger.

There was criticism inside the United States of Byrnes's firmness. Lippmann, for example, ever provocative, ever mercurial, had recently again changed the thrust of his anxieties. He now thought that 'any confrontation between the great powers contained the theoretical danger of war'. He thus reversed his position from that of February. His wife challenged 'Chip' Bohlen, at a dinner in Washington during these weeks, with the words 'Well, Chip, all I can say is that, in your war, I will not be a nurse's aide'.[47] The aged businessman friend of all successful men, Bernard Baruch, sought to give comfort to Byrnes: 'You proved yourself a David in meeting the Goliath of disintegration'. He added: 'Let us not fear the Philistines, of whom Samson slew a thousand with the jawbone of an ass'.[48]

The Security Council, in Gromyko's absence, adopted a United States proposal calling on Russia and Persia to report to them in time for their next meeting on April 3; while, in Tehran, Qavam was beginning detailed negotiations with Pishevari about the future status of Azerbaijan and the oil concession, knowing that the Soviet troops really did seem to be being withdrawn;[49] and indeed the United States ambassador on March 30 was to report that a general Soviet evacuation was under way: save, for the time being, in Azerbaijan itself.[50]

Although much remained to be done, the case of Persia in March 1946 seemed to promise a victory to the West and so a reward for a 'firm line'. The moral was everywhere borne in mind. On April 3 Byrnes nevertheless agreed to defer further proceedings in the Security Council till May 6 when, six weeks after March 24, Persia and Russia would be asked whether they could report on the withdrawal of troops; and the Soviet ambassador agreed that, assuming the Red Army was withdrawn by the time specified, a joint Soviet-Iranian oil company would be established, with 51 per cent Soviet interest and 49 per cent Persian. A new Majlis, however, would have to ratify these arrangements, within seven months. As for Azerbaijan, that province would make arrangements with Persia about autonomy as soon as possible. Pishevari and Qavam would meet.

Victory for 'patience and firmness'! Kennan left Moscow at the end of his service there too soon to comment on his Secretary of State's success. But, though he disliked Byrnes, he applauded. In almost the last of his innumerable telegrams to Washington, on March 20,[51] he had made known his views about recent articles inspired by Churchill's speech (say, by Lippmann) which had suggested that there was something which the Western governments should do to persuade Stalin that 'we are not trying to form an anti-Soviet bloc'. Kennan exploded at hearing these comments. 'Belief that Soviet "suspicions" are of such a character, that they can be altered or assuaged by personal contacts, rational arguments or official assurances, reflect a serious misunderstanding about Soviet realities and constitutes . . . the most insidious and dangerous single error which Americans can make in their thinking about this country'. The official Soviet thesis that the outside world was hostile and menacing to the Soviet people was not a conclusion that Russian leaders had reluctantly arrived at, after an honest and objective appraisal of the facts made available to them, but an *a priori* tactical position, deliberately taken up and hotly advanced by them, for 'impelling selfish reasons of a domestic political nature'. A hostile international environment was 'the breath of life' for the internal system. The country still had a vested interest dedicated to the view that Russia was walking a dangerous path among implacable foes. The eclipse of Germany and Japan, the only two real dangers, left this vested interest no choice but to build up Britain and the United States so that it could fill the gap. Nothing short of complete disarmament, delivery of their air and naval forces to Russia and the resignation of powers of government to American Communists would dent the suspicion which the leaders in Moscow had of everyone. Even then, they would smell a trap. Suspicion in one way or another was an integral part of the Soviet system. It would not yield to any form of rational persuasion or assurance. Thus there could be no more dangerous tendency in American opinion than one which placed on their government the obligation to accomplish the impossible by gestures of good will and conciliation towards a political entity so constitutionally incapable of being conciliated. Of course, there was no tendency more agreeable to the purpose of Moscow. The Kremlin had no reason to discourage a delusion so useful to its purpose: 'we may therefore expect the Moscow propaganda apparatus to cultivate it assiduously'. Kennan returned the next week to Washington to receive the congratulations of his colleagues, and an appointment at the new National War College where, within six months, he would be speaking of his policy as being one to 'contain' the Soviet Union in the style for which he became well known (in September 1946, he told a gathering in the State Department that he sought policies 'to "contain" the Russians' for a long time to come).[52] The world which he would lecture about was one which he had undoubtedly helped, through his learning, eloquence and persistence, to form: no greater tribute could have been made to this powerful intellectual than that men of power took him seriously.

# TWENTY-FIVE

# 'PATIENCE AND FIRMNESS': OR, 'STRENGTH WITHOUT OSTENTATION'

Henry Wallace, Secretary for Commerce, was still, in mid-March 1946, fighting a rearguard action by means of public speeches, letters to the President and conversations with him, in favour of 'better understanding of Russia'. 'The common people of the world', he told an audience honouring Averell Harriman on March 19, 'would not tolerate any recrudescence of imperialism even under enlightened Anglo-Saxon auspices'. Truman said that he had agreed with this; and Wallace had sent him a long letter on March 15, arguing for a new approach to Russia, 'along economic and trade lines'. A great many people, Wallace told himself, 'seem to have reached the conclusion that I could do a lot of good by going to Russia'.[1]

The mood of official America nevertheless can be better gathered from a request of the Joint Chiefs of Staff to the Department of State on March 14. Following the discussion summed up in their paper in February,* they were considering 'courses of action which our armed forces may be called on to pursue in support of government policy'. Obviously, Russia was the main factor external to the United States in these considerations. The Joint Chiefs wanted the Department of State to provide them with a new estimate of the intentions of Russia,

* See above, page 672.

an outline of future United States policy with reference to it, and any requirement for its implementation by the armed forces.[2]

'Doc' Matthews gave a lengthy reply on April 1, the theme of which evidently derived from the long telegram of Kennan. It recommended that steps should be taken in the immediate future 'to reconstitute our military establishment', so that it can resist Soviet expansion by force of arms 'in areas of our own choosing', should such action prove necessary, and to protect, during the period of diplomacy, areas which would be strategically essential in any armed conflict with the Soviet Union; secondly, to create as soon as possible an informed public opinion concerning the issues involved. If the United States were to be successful, in checking physical Soviet expansion, Matthews concluded, and in bringing about a reorientation of Soviet political thinking, thus implicating them in the acceptance of the thesis that the two systems of economies and politics could peacefully co-exist, the United States could, after all, put into effect 'a positive and constructive programme of relations with the Soviet Union designed to produce maximum cooperation and harmony in international relations'.[3]

From then onwards, therefore, there came to be discussion within the Departments of War and the Navy, inside the Joint Chiefs of Staff secretariat and in the State War Navy Coordinating Committee (SWNCC), of specific areas of the world where war with the USSR might have to be fought. A new world of 'contingency plans' began. At the same time United States intelligence abroad – primarily a military or naval undertaking, despite Truman's establishment of the Central Intelligence Group in January – began to prepare themselves for new directions. The British and the Americans began to negotiate, in a more amicable manner than before, for the settlement of the unresolved question of bases in the Pacific and elsewhere. The first meeting was held in Washington on March 13. (It could not have passed unnoticed in the Soviet Union, since again Maclean was well placed: the third senior official in the British party.)[4] The British were chiefly worried lest the United States request for bases abroad might lead the Russians to make similar demands in other islands belonging to Denmark and Norway.[5]

There was still opposition to the new line in American policy other than from Henry Wallace. Churchill's speech had made that opposition more, not less, urgent, to those so preoccupied. A big 'anti-Churchill' demonstration was, for example, held in Madison Square Park in New York on March 18. Henry Wallace's speech on March 19 seemed to suggest to the columnist Joe Alsop, that 'he was diametrically opposed' to Truman and Byrnes in foreign policy. Alsop told Wallace that he was in 'an indefensible position' in the Cabinet.[6] Truman still tolerated Wallace. Indeed, when they met, he continued to agree with him. But he ignored his suggestions. He was close to a break; not just with an old friend, but with an old attitude of his own.

The President could avoid less easily the consequences of a substantial decline in support for the McMahon bill, despite his own support of it. McMahon and the scientist Harold Urey argued, as indeed Henry Wallace had done, that military representation on the Atomic Energy Commission would lead to military domination: an accusation which moved General Groves to send a letter to one of his senatorial allies, Bourke Hickenlooper, who read it aloud in the Senate the following day. This contained the accusation that Dr Nunn May, arrested two weeks earlier in London, had had access to American secrets.[7] The resultant uproar in the Congress led quickly to the Senate's acceptance of Senator Vandenberg's latest amendment to the bill. That gave the supporters of the old May-Johnson bill nearly everything that they wanted, since it established a 'military liaison board', which would review the civilians' decisions. The widespread fear of Soviet espionage must have played a part in this. The atomic scientists reluctantly agreed. Senator McMahon was bitter. He had expected Truman's support. It seemed as if the President, who had taken no steps to staunch the frenzy about spies during February, was bowing to public opinion.[8] Wallace was also disturbed.

There was some evidence, too, of growing Communist activity, in the United States itself, to try to sway liberal, or democratic, movements by internal manipulation; it was in the

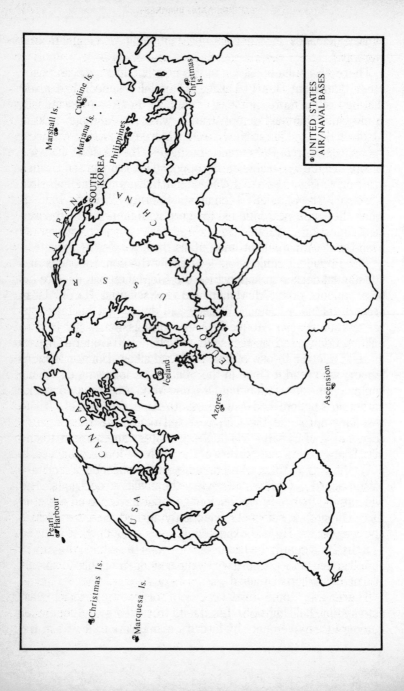

UNITED STATES
AIR/NAVAL BASES

spring of 1946, for example, that the Communists made a serious, if unsuccessful, effort to gain control of the American Veterans' Committee.[9]

In late March 1946, the British, independent of their transatlantic friends, also began to move towards a hard-headed view of Soviet behaviour.

The Foreign Office had been increasingly irritated by the anti-British and anti-imperial tone of Soviet propaganda ('in every channel open to the Soviet publicity machine').[10] A senior official on March 13 had been asking the ambassador in Paris what was the likelihood of large Communist gains at the elections.[11] The Guzenko case, debated in the Canadian parliament on March 21, continued to affect views in Britain. The case of Nunn May, waiting in prison for his trial – he would be sentenced on May 1 to ten years' confinement – affected the Foreign Office too. Thus the British official body known as JIC (Joint Intelligence Committee) Middle East telegraphed their appreciation that, while 'at present, Russian aims are primarily defensive', even that seemed to imply the inclusion of both Turkey and North Persia 'within their security belt'. In the long run, they thought Russia to be determined 'to challenge our predominant position in the Middle East'. That would include Persia, where the planners 'expected Russia to take every opportunity to encourage tribal disorder and labour unrest to increase the instability of the situation'.[12] Threats to the Middle East and Persia were far more disturbing, in the British view, than in East Europe.

On March 18 the designated new British Ambassador to Moscow, Sir Maurice Peterson, was briefed by his colleagues. Peterson was one of the few senior British diplomats who knew North America. He still nursed a grudge against the wartime government for suddenly, even unjustly, moving him from the embassy in Madrid in 1940.[13] He had a strong dislike of secret intelligence and had been inert during the unhappy dénouement of the Volkov affair the previous summer in Istanbul.[14] He was, however, a quick, even formidable, official. In the subsequent discussion, nearly all the ideas and questions which would be posed during the next forty years would be raised.[15]

This meeting showed, in general, what the government in London thought would happen next in Russia and what Britain should do about it: 'The extent to which we should be prepared to go on countering Soviet policy . . . would depend on how vital the Chiefs of Staff considered those areas for the security of the British Commonwealth'. It was thought probable 'but not certain that they would regard everything except the Middle East as less than of vital importance to us'. The officials considered the areas of 'Soviet expansion in the Middle East'. Were they primarily interested in oil? Were they hoping 'to establish a defensive glacis? Or, were they pursuing an offensive and expansionist policy?' How many times would these unanswerable questions be posed in the course of the next generation! Opinion was agreed that 'the Soviet General Staff had not yet been able to work out the desirability of a *glacis* in the light of modern weapons'.

How could Communism be countered? The trouble was that many of the Social Democrat leaders in Europe who headed the resistance to the Communists were old (Blum, Renner, Schumacher, for example) though, as events showed, old men sometimes have more moral courage than young and healthy ones. Weak governments in the Middle East also might encourage Communism. The officials then made the surprising judgement that 'we could not count on steady support from the United States in any policy designed to oppose Communism'. Nor could public opinion, even in Britain, be relied upon, since the Communists 'would have little difficulty in making people believe that, in the disputes which would inevitably arise as a result of following an explicit policy of anti-Communism, the British government, and not the Communists, were in the wrong'. This was an honest admission that the West had no effective agency of propaganda in peacetime.

British policy was then determined by a series of telegrams from its Chargé d'Affaires in Moscow, Frank Roberts – much as United States policy had been the previous month by Roberts's colleague, Kennan. Roberts was an experienced official who had served throughout the war, and before, at the heart of policy-making. He knew the 'London Poles' well and, before the war, had spent many tedious, frustrating and doubtless humiliating hours as British representative on the Non-Intervention Committee in the Spanish War. He was of the same frame of mind as Kennan, by whom he had been influenced.

Roberts's first telegrams considered Soviet policy in the Middle East and Far East. Then he made recommendations. Roberts could not believe that 'so dynamic a state' as Russia, convinced that 'she has a message for the world', was 'anywhere on the defensive, least of all in Asia'. But for the moment she was aiming at securing Soviet sympathisers in power in the states concerned and so gaining control at one remove.[16] Roberts did not think that, given the chance, Russia would stop short of absorbing the whole of Persia, 'with the goals of the warm water ports and the oil of the Persian Gulf just ahead'. Soviet attitudes to the Levant and Egypt, and a similar propaganda campaign just beginning in respect of Iraq, coupled with clumsy overtures in respect of the Dodecanese islands and of Tripolitania, suggested a design to extend Soviet influence throughout the Arab world, the Aegean and the Eastern Mediterranean. The Soviet appetite for oil would grow because of their proposed programme of industrialisation. They would look towards Iraq and Persia for those purposes. That was a 'clear pointer to future Soviet policy which we . . . neglect at our peril'.[17]

Another despatch from Roberts concluded by arguing that 'the Soviet regime was dynamic and still interested in expansion, though not *as yet* beyond the areas where Russian interests existed before 1917'; that Russian long-term ambitions were 'dangerous to British vital interests'; that security was the first consideration of Russia and that she would not endanger the realisation of long-term projects by pressing immediate issues to the point of serious conflict, except by miscalculation; that it was still possible, though difficult, to reconcile British and Soviet interests in any problem with which they were likely to be faced;

but that, except in the unlikely event of Germany or some other power becoming a menace to British and Russian survival, there was no longer any likelihood that Britain and Russia would ever be drawn together again as they had been in 1812, 1914 and 1941.[18]

Finally, in a third despatch, Roberts proposed a course of policy which echoed Kennan's recommendations to Washington Britain should eschew open hostility, cold aloofness and one-sided appeasement alike and, instead, 'embark on a close and coordinated study of every aspect of Soviet policy by a body specially set up whose knowledge would be at the disposal of all those responsible for formulating policy'. There should be a programme of 'education' of the public about the Soviet Union. Tactics in relation to the Soviet Union should include attempts to foster cultural and other contacts, 'propaganda in the Soviet Union', restoration of fair trade, 'friendship with the USA' and, above all, 'strength without ostentation'.[19]

These recommendations were supported by the young official then dealing with Russia at the Foreign Office (Thomas Brimelow) who knew that the arrangements for studying Soviet strategy were inadequate. This official had served in the British Consulate at Riga in 1939 (and in the consulate at Moscow later) and recalled, with unavailing remorse, how his Latvian friends (including the Foreign Minister) had, in 1940, vanished into the anonymity of Soviet camps.[20] There was, he now wrote, rarely 'any hard thinking on what the Russians were up to except when a paper (by the Joint Intelligence Committee) is on the stocks'. But, when such a paper was prepared, successive drafts of it were submitted to the northern department 'at hopelessly short notice': 'no fundamental works on Soviet policy are ready to hand in the northern department for reference when dealing with such papers. More important, there is no proper machinery for ensuring that decisions on topics which, at first sight, do not concern the Soviet Union are considered in advance from the standpoint of the opportunities which they afford to Communist-inspired anti-British propaganda'. Christopher Warner, head of the northern department, opposed Brimelow's and Frank

Roberts's suggestions. Nevertheless, on the recommendation of the Joint Intelligence Committee, a standing subcommitee of officials in the Foreign Office, the 'Russia Committee', was set up.[21] It met some of Roberts's and Brimelow's complaints. It had its first meeting on April 2.* After the First World War, there had been in Britain an interdepartmental Committee on Bolshevism, with a 'vigilance committee meeting fortnightly'.[22] This was a successor to it.

On April 2, this Committee of a dozen officials discussed the need for a 'coordinated defence against this longterm attack' and the adoption of a 'defensive-offensive [stance] in reply'. They urged that the Government co-ordinated its policy 'towards the Soviet Union in different parts of the world, since many of the elements of Soviet policy were much the same everywhere'. Mongolia was a Soviet satellite. Manchuria had been cleared of its factories and machinery. In Korea, the Russians were speaking less and less of four-power trusteeship and plainly hoped that the entire state would fall under their control. If the Americans were to withdraw in Japan, there was a danger that the Russians would come in to replace them. In China, the Communists would take all they could from Russia, even if, in the end, the Chinese Communists would 'bite the hand which fed them', since they had 'a nationalist tendency': an astute prediction. The Persian situation was still confused; whether or no Russia was still 'stirring up' the Kurds, the Kurdish question was dangerous since it affected both Turkey and Iraq. Communists were 'stirring up' labour troubles in the oil fields and seemed to be trying

* Its terms of reference were: to review weekly the developments of all aspects of Soviet policy and propaganda and Soviet activities throughout the world, more particularly with reference to the Soviet campaign against this country; to ensure a unified interpretation thereof throughout the political and economic departments of the Foreign Office; and to consider what action was required as a result of the Committee's review, with particular reference to the probable degree of support to be looked for from the United States and, to a lesser degree, from France and others; and to ensure that the necessary recommendations as to policy are made either by the departments of the office concerned or by the Committee to Sir Orme Sargent as may be appropriate. The Committee would maintain close contact with the JIC, with a view to coordinating intelligence and policy at every stage (April 12, 1946).

to control the food supply in all that country (as they were in Austria). As for Europe: in Albania, the Russians were developing a naval base in Valona while, in Bulgaria, they had intervened to prevent any agreement between government and opposition over the latter's representation in the government* In Scandinavia, the Russians were 'generally pursuing a policy of blandishments rather than threats', but were trying to penetrate the trade unions in Sweden (even if they had, however, begun to withdraw their occupying forces from the Danish island of Bornholm). In Austria, the Russians were being as difficult as possible, while the East Zone of Germany was being communised. Russia clearly wanted to turn Berlin into a communist stronghold. (Despite the evidence that Socialists opposed amalgamation with the Communists, German Communists and Socialists were expected to merge on April 22, Lenin's birthday).† General Montgomery's memorandum of March 25 pointed out that the 'Battle of the Winter' had been won in his zone, and nowhere had epidemics broken out. But the problem of food was as great as that of refugees.

Russia had taken no part in the work of the Food and Agriculture Organisation and had recently walked out of the Security Council (over Iran). They plainly did not want to reconstitute anything like the International Danube Commission. They were also being obstructive over all frontier questions and other provisions of the peace treaties. Finally, by means of their economic, financial, commercial and banking policies, they were tying the countries of East Europe to their own economic system

---

* Dr Georgiev had, on March 31, formed a new government, in which Communist control had been extended, with a new Communist Vice Prime Minister, in the shape of Traicho Kostov; a new Communist Minister of Finance, Ivan Stefanov; and a new Foreign Minister, who was so compromised by his old reputation as a Macedonian revolutionary advocate of German penetration into the Balkans as to have no independence left to him.

† On March 31 there was a 'plebiscite' of members of the Social Democrats in Berlin, but the Soviet commandant forebade participation in the Soviet sector. Of 32,547 SPD members who could vote, 2,937 were in favour of immediate unification; 14,763 for an alliance between two independent parties; and 5,559 against unification or alliance.

(particularly making use of Soviet-owned joint stock banks). All Western interests were being eliminated.*

As to Western responses, it would be difficult for Britain to pursue a similar policy of 'running stooge parties as we should be hampered by a barrage of parliamentary questions at home'.[23]

At that time, in fact, the Polish Peasants' Party would have very much liked such help. Both the United States and British ambassadors in Warsaw believed the life of that Party's leader, Mikojczyk, actually to be in danger. Summary courts were imprisoning persons of any prominence whatever who were not friends of the government, on allegations of having violated economic regulations – not necessarily a false charge in the intolerable circumstances of 1946 – but in truth because of affiliations with the Polish Peasants' Party.[24]

Curiously enough, this *tour d'horizon* omitted any mention of Greece, where elections had been held successfully on March 31. It was the first general election in the country which was subject to any kind of international scrutiny. It was a success. The Soviet Union had committed herself to recognition of the results in the spirit of the 'percentages agreement' of the previous year. The Western Allied missions in Athens thought that politically-inspired abstentions did not amount to ten per cent of the vote – though the Communists abstained. Tsaldaris, the Populist leader, won 251 seats out of 354 by a system of proportional representation. But there had been ominous warnings: the previous day, March 20, an armed band from Olympus had descended to attack Litochoro – in Greek Communist lore, subsequently, the 'first strike' in a new round of the Civil War.

---

* For example, a Hungarian-Soviet agreement on civil aviation was concluded on March 2, leaving to a jointly-owned civil air transport company responsibility for both domestic and international air traffic; giving landing rights without reciprocity to the Soviet Union. When the Hungarians asked that the United States should also be allowed to fly over Hungary, the Soviet minister, Pushkin, lost his temper, and said that the United States wanted such rights for military purposes, that the United States would not allow the Russians to operate in Italy or West Germany and that Russia would not allow any Western aircraft to fly within five hours' journey of Moscow.

The incident seemed at the time merely an onslaught by sixty bandits on a provincial city, in which eight innocent people were killed and many buildings (including the police station) burned down; and there were no further such incidents till July.[25] Bevin, in a subsequent paper, told his colleagues, 'I do not anticipate a direct Russian attack on Greece but I cannot put out of my mind the possibility of encirclement by Russia' in the rest of the Balkans in order 'to create trouble in Greece'. (Russian troops were, of course, still in Bulgaria in large numbers.) It would be unwise, Bevin thought, to commit Britain to withdrawing troops from there until the international situation was more clear.[26] Although Litochoro was not a turning point, the Greek Communist leader, Nikos Zachariades, had addressed a training camp for Greek guerrillas in Yugoslavia, at Bulkes, on March 25, telling the refugees there to be ready to return home.[27] Russian military assistance to the Greek Communists was observed on the Bulgarian/Greek border in February 1946 by a British Intelligence officer.[28]

The Russia Committee's *tour d'horizon* did not talk much of China, since it still seemed for the moment that, there, some of General Marshall's plans were coming to fruition. A basis had been achieved for the integration of the two armies, Communist and Nationalist (there would be fifty Kuomintang divisions, ten Communist, the rest would be demobilised and the united army would be established in certain approved numerical strengths in various parts of China). General Marshall had returned to Washington to try to find financial credits for an interim government in China. The Russians' withdrawal from Manchuria was also proceeding apace, still taking what they wanted on the way.[29] They would apparently have completed it by the end of April. No one anticipated that serious fighting would begin again in May.

In consequence of this discussion in London in early April, the Foreign Office prepared a paper entitled 'The Soviet Campaign Against This Country and Our Response to it'.[30] It argued that the new Russian posture was marked by a return to the pure doctrine of Marxism-Leninism, the concentration on building up the industrial and military strength of the Soviet Union, and the revival of the bogey of an external danger; 'we should be very unwise not to take the Russians at their word, just as we should have been wise to have taken *Mein Kampf* at its face value'. War-weary though Russia might be, she was practising 'vicious power politics' and would 'stick at nothing to obtain her objectives' – short of renewed war. The Soviet leaders were at pains to intensify their public suspicion of the outside world. They had embarked on a campaign not only against Britain but against all social democracy. 'It is submitted, therefore, that we must at once organise and coordinate our defences against all these and that we should not stop short of a defensive-offensive policy'.

This paper, signed by Christopher Warner, was circulated to several ministers. It was a note to which Attlee's great friend, Lord Addison, responded by suggesting 'an appropriate use of the Roman Catholic Church' in Western responses to Communism – an idea swiftly buried. Bevin sent a note to Attlee based on the paper of April 10.[31] During the war, Warner had seemed, on the evidence of earlier memoranda, ignorant of the nature of Soviet power. All the same, he appears, like many others, by now to have educated himself. He subsequently became a far more sagacious commentator of the Soviet scene.[32]

Thus the policy was decided, and the Russia Committee set about planning a 'counter-offensive designed to protect us' from Russian aggression. They checked first that the Cabinet did agree that Russia had become hostile; 'the importance of this becomes especially evident in dealing with publicity, since it is clear that any propaganda which may be done under our auspices must harmonise with the line taken by the Minister'. The conclusion was that 'we are authorised to take any defensive action that we think necessary although not yet to embark on an all-out anti-Communist offensive'.[33] That would be for the future.*

It is interesting, but not surprising, given the bad relations into which Britain had slipped with the United States on atomic matters, that there was little mention of the need or desirability of collaboration on these matters between the wartime friends

* See Appendix X.

across the Atlantic. The neglect to mention United States policy
in Persia was compounded by a reluctance to admit the certainty
of a United States role in the Middle East and elsewhere. The
British planners might have been living in the 1880s for all the
recognition that they gave to Washington. The same continued
to be true of Washington: Henry Wallace in a speech on April
12 would say that 'aside from our common language and common
literary tradition we have no more in common with Imperialistic
England than with Communistic Russia'. Such ranting might not
seem worthy of notice were it not for the fact that Truman,
still concerned to juggle with his New Deal friends, shown a
draft of this speech, told Wallace that he agreed with the
phrasing.[34]

The end of March, meantime, in the United States had seen,
equally without consultation with an ally, the completion of the
work of Lilienthal's panel of consultants about international
development and control of nuclear energy. The report was
finished as an outline on March 7. It was talked over by Acheson,
General Groves, Dr Vannevar Bush, John McCloy and Dr
Conant on that day and the next; and rewritten between the 7th
and the 16th, when it was discussed anew. Groves objected
(everyone on the panel knew that his objection was certain: the
uncertainty was what the objection would be) that nations using
undiscovered, or low-grade, ore could circumvent the authority.
Dr Bush had to remind his colleagues that the atom bomb was
a technological answer to Russian superiority in manpower.[35]
So the plan had to be made politically acceptable in the United
States. A progress by stages to the full achievement of the plan
was therefore desirable: particularly if Russia were to 'open up'
to the West as an initial sign of good faith. But, in the end, the
paper was agreed. Lilienthal accepted the staged plan. It was
left open how to ensure that one stage would succeed another.
Questions of punishment were left open also. As a result of a
virtual ultimatum by Lilienthal, the revised plan of the panel
was accepted by the Committee (even Groves) on March 17,
'miraculously', as all thought who were present. The paper was
then sent to Byrnes, to Truman, the Secretaries of War and the
Navy; and to the man whom Byrnes had just designated as the

United States representative on the proposed United Nations disarmament commission on March 21, Bernard Baruch, apparently on the suggestion of the President.[36] With all classified material removed, the report was released for publication, as the 'Acheson-Lilienthal Plan', on March 28. The excisions of classified material included reference to the possibility that there could well be, relatively easily, a bigger, or thermonuclear weapon.[37]

This plan was thoughtful and well-written. Had the Soviet Union wished to remove the threat of nuclear war, it would have been adopted. Following the recommendations in the first place of Oppenheimer, the paper again proposed that 'all dangerous activities – the mining, the ownership or leasing of nuclear material, the manufacture of bombs – would be carried on, not merely inspected, by a live functioning international authority'. The fact that development, as well as control, would be internationally managed meant that the authority would be sure to attract competent persons. This monopoly of dangerous activities in international hands would still leave a large field of safe activities open to individual nations, their industries and universities. The need for this international monopoly body was that the favoured position enjoyed by the United States would not last. The United States had, therefore, an obligation to promote international security while it was in a unique position.

The first trouble with the proposal was the position of Russia – and her allies. Acheson, who had shown Lilienthal a copy of Kennan's long telegram,[38] made clear what he thought when he discussed the first draft with the panel: that is, when McCloy thought that his colleagues might consider using international control to alter Russia's closed society. Perhaps, McCloy suggested, the United States could make disarmament a price for relinquishing its special position. Acheson replied there was no use chasing a will-o'-the-wisp. The 'Russian problem' could not be solved in one stroke. The Russian system as such could not be made a subject for negotiation. The United States was in for a long period of dealing with Leninism. It had to hope for Russia's gradual 'civilisation'.[39] Still, as Oppenheimer admitted later to Baruch, 'the plan was entirely incompatible with the present Russian system'. But the right course for the United States was 'to make an honourable proposal and find out whether the Russians had the will to cooperate'. [40]

The second trouble was Bernard Baruch. He might have been a friend of Roosevelt, as of Winston Churchill, and a strong supporter of both Woodrow Wilson and the League of Nations, but he was not the right man for this sensitive job. His once much-vaunted 'progressive' opinions were now limited to suspicions about the 'butter-mouthed Englishmen' advancing 'hypocritical arguments so that they could get in position to exploit subject peoples'. [41] He was vain and old as well as experienced, he liked popularity, and had helped many politicians, including Truman, with money; now he wanted to give the plan, which had been devised by Acheson and Lilienthal, his own style. When asked about the document after his appointment, by reporters outside the White House, Baruch turned off his hearing aid. Later, he insisted on writing into the document a provision whereby the use of the veto was prohibited when the Security Council was considering atomic energy. This damaged the scheme and made it easy for the Soviet Union to denounce it and gain a good deal of international sympathy. (Truman had considered asking for the abolition of the veto on other grounds in January:[42] so it is possible that Baruch thought that he was doing what the President wanted.) Baruch's nomination was 'the worst mistake I have ever made', Byrnes admitted to Acheson later. But he and Truman could not then go back on their designation. [43]

American opinion was, it was true, at first reassured by Baruch's appointment. 'Clear-eyed Bernie Baruch is on guard' so 'we can all sleep better at night', commented *The Chicago Tribune*. [44] They liked the anglophobe Baruch particularly because of his opposition to the big loan to Britain. But Lilienthal's reaction was characteristic of scientists: 'When I read the news of Baruch's nomination last night, I was quite sick . . . we need a man who is young, vigorous, not vain, and who the Russians feel isn't out simply to put them in a hole, not really caring about international cooperation'. [45] Oppenheimer later said that the day of Baruch's appointment was the day that he gave up hope.[46] It is almost certain that the Soviet Union would not have accepted any Western plan for atomic disarmament, for the reasons amply described, in 1946. But Baruch's appointment, and his corrections to the 'Acheson-Lilienthal Plan', gave them in the end a good excuse for not doing so.

The new American Ambassador, Walter Bedell Smith, arrived in Moscow at the end of March. Bedell Smith, a Catholic, had been a success as Eisenhower's Chief of Staff. He had a bad temper. But, like Baruch, he had begun life poor, and had sold newspapers on the streets of New York. The fact that 'Beetle' had worked with Eisenhower was assumed to make it easier for the Russians to deal with him, since many of them affected to admire Eisenhower. Smith began his mission by disliking his briefing by the Department of State, which, in the spirit of Kennan's telegram, had suggested 'that the Soviet Union, owing to its peculiar structure and the political philosophy which motivates it, is almost incapable of collaborating with other governments'. Smith was more optimistic.[47] Henry Wallace approved him.[48] His Minister, Elbridge Durbrow, ex-chief of the Soviet division in the Department, was, however, of Kennan's way of thinking. So, at that time, was the gifted Counsellor, John Paton Davies.

Smith called on Stalin on April 5, 1946. Once again the meeting was in the now famous office in the Yellow Nikolai Palace, so well-known to foreigners. Smith began with an exceptionally conciliatory statement. How much did the Americans appreciate the magnificent efforts of the Red Army against Hitler! How much did they sympathise with the sufferings of the Russians! The United States understood the desire of Russia for security and for a share in the world's raw materials. But Russian methods to gain those objectives were causing apprehension. Smith then talked about Persia, Turkey and the United Nations, while Stalin began to 'doodle' ominously with a red pencil (on this occasion, lopsided hearts in red with a question mark in the middle). It was wrong to suppose that, because the United States were peaceful, they were weak or unwilling to face their responsibilities. The United States would have to react against aggression on the part of any powerful nation, or group of nations, just as the Secretary had said.

Stalin replied at length. He justified Soviet behaviour in Persia, once again, by reason of the proximity of the Persian frontier to the Baku oil fields: 'Beria and others tell me that saboteurs – even a man with a box of matches – might cause us serious damage. We are not going to risk our oil supply'. The Soviet Union needed more oil from abroad but both Britain and the United States made obstacles when they sought concessions. The United States had given a false impression of the Soviet Union's actions at the United Nations. Russia had no intention of dominating her neighbours. It would indeed be difficult to do so. Churchill's speech at Fulton had been an unwarranted attack. But one should not be surprised: Churchill had tried to instigate war against Russia in 1919 and, 'latterly, he has been at it again'. Stalin believed the British and the United States were planning an alliance to thwart Russia.

Bedell Smith, after various explanations, said the question that the American people wanted to ask was 'how far is Russia going to go?' Stalin replied, 'We're not going much further'. He might have added: 'as far as you will let us go'.

Smith probed Stalin on Turkey. Stalin said that he had no intention of attacking Turkey. But Turkey was both weak and unfriendly to Russia. So Russia needed a base at the Dardanelles for her security. Just as well, Smith may have thought subsequently, that the United States battleship *Missouri* was due to arrive at Istanbul on April 6.[49]

Stalin's last words on this occasion to Smith were friendly; though there were differences in their political ideologies, the position of their two countries was not incompatible.[50] But he refused Truman's invitation to him to visit the United States; 'age has taken its toll. My doctors tell me I must not travel, and I am kept on a strict diet', he said.[51] Perhaps it was also just as well for the administration that that was the answer, since Truman did not consult his Secretary of State before taking this initiative.[52]

Three days later, on April 9, a significant clash came at the Allied Co-Ordinating Committee in Germany. General Clay, actually as angry with France as with Russia, gave notice that he objected to the further financing of reparations in the Soviet zone of Germany; and to continuing to strip the United States zone of its industrial capacity, unless he received the industrial and agricultural benefits from the amalgamation of all zones. 'We are struggling with a collapsed economy which cannot be revived piecemeal', he said. It was a statement which would soon lead him to order an end both to all delivery of reparations from the United States zone and to the dismantling of German industry there.[53] Truman might still be hoping that the 'patience and firmness' which his Secretary of State had shown could be carried out beneath the umbrella of the United Nations, as he said in a speech on Army Day (April 6); and as his experience at the Security Council over Persia suggested might be possible. But he knew from Acheson that a long struggle lay ahead; and, whatever soothing words he continued occasionally to express to Henry Wallace, he had begun to realise that a 'broad-ax' was, as he would tell a Cabinet meeting in May, 'the only language the Russians understood'.[54]

Two weeks later, the critical event of the first year of the clash between Russia and the West came with the merger of the Communists and Socialists in East Germany. Herr Pieck and Herr Grotewohl shook hands at a great meeting in the Admirals-Palast in Berlin. Not for the last time on such occasions, the orchestra played the overture to Beethoven's *Fidelio*. A certain Comrade Amborn from Leipzig presented the new joint leaders with a large wooden club of 'menacing appearance'. It had belonged to the heroic old Socialist, August Bebel. Bebel had cut it himself. He had even had it by his side at the Social Democratic conference at Erfurt in 1890. It was as good a symbol as any other for the age now beginning. So was the fact that the bearer of the club, executor of the comrade to whom Bebel had left it, was soon afterwards arrested for a doctrinal misdemeanour: the sin of 'Socialdemocratism'.[55]

*The future of the characters and subjects in this study will be treated in another volume, it is hoped, of this history. But, in the*

*meantime, the reader may like to know that the McMahon bill in the
end became law by incorporating in it the spirit of the May-Johnson
draft; that Bernard Baruch further damaged his chances of securing any agreement with the Soviet Union on weapons by incorporating, in his delegation, 'the old crowd' – Lilienthal's phrase for
associates of his in earlier ventures; that Secretary Byrnes presented a solid front with Senator Vandenberg, Foster Dulles and
Senator Connally at the Peace Conference of Paris and that that
unhappy Secretary of State formally submitted his resignation on
April 14, 1946, theoretically because his doctors had told him that
his heart was bad. But he was in fact well; and he remained
Secretary for another nine months, until General Marshall came
back from China to succeed him. Dean Acheson, who himself
would one day succeed Marshall, sought to resign in April 1946
because of the untidiness of his position as 'the ham in the sandwich'
between Truman and Byrnes. He later compared Byrnes's subsequent position to the lover of Aphrodite to whom the goddess had
given eternal life, but not eternal youth. The crisis in Persia
continued to boil, but came to an end with the arrival of governmental troops in Tabriz in December; when the Shah spoke of
Azerbaijan as the 'Stalingrad' of the Western democracies. The
European economies did well in 1946 but faltered in the bad winter
of 1946–47, making substantial economic aid necessary in 1947:
the Marshall Plan; and, President Truman showed himself willing to pick up the torch of protecting democracy in Greece and
Turkey, in March 1947, by his speech which proclaimed the
Truman Doctrine.*

# CONCLUSION TO
# THE ARMED TRUCE

By the spring of 1946, the attitudes and some of the institutions in the long conflict between the Soviet Union and the West, between the new ideological refinement of oriental despotism and the bruised but still resilient civilisation of the West, were falling into place. Even the origins of 'Titoism', the most successful Communist rebellion, could have been observed in the dispute between the Yugoslav government and Moscow's man in that country, Andrija Hebrang, over the relatively trivial matter of the leadership of a delegation to Moscow to discuss their five year plan in April 1946.[1]

A considerable burden faced the United States in 1946. Would they be capable of promulgating and working a long-term, consistent policy towards Russia? George Kennan, whose influence in events was so remarkable, thought it improbable. A high-minded American might, like J. P. Marquand's creation, George Apley, in 1917, become temporarily carried away by the need for intervention in world affairs.[2] But there was still a danger that, as Kennan thought, American actions in foreign affairs 'were no more than the convulsive reactions of politicians to an internal political life dominated by vocal minorities'.[3] The memory of isolationism was real. Every responsible American had read Washington's farewell address.* Dr Henry Kissinger years later would comment, 'No major nation has ever been so uncomfortable with the exercise of power as the United States'.[4] Americans tended to think of war as a brief if bitter interruption of peace, prosperity and liberty, not as something

* See page 171.

which might grumble on for generations; and they continued to think in terms of solutions.

It has been suggested that Stalin and the Soviet government which he directed might have conducted themselves, in 1945 or 1946, in a conciliatory way towards their erstwhile allies, Britain and the United States, had those allies been more friendly.

The evidence is against this interpretation. It is true that the United States government did not leap at the idea of offering a large loan to the Soviet Union; yet the Soviet Union did not persist in talking of it much (particularly after they had begun to loot so extensively as 'reparations') and neither Stalin nor Molotov was hesitant when speaking of things which they really coveted. The Soviet Union could have negotiated an arrangement for the purchase of non-military goods supplied under the Lend Lease agreements in 1944 but chose not to do so. They sought instead to avoid the terms by which they had obtained equipment under Lend Lease from 1941 and delay payment indefinitely. Their despatch of a Soviet delegation to Bretton Woods, and their later refusal to ratify the agreements on the World Bank and Monetary Fund, suggests that they took a deliberate decision to change policy. It is true that neither Roosevelt nor Churchill wanted in 1943 or 1944 to give Stalin the knowledge that their countries were working on an atomic weapon, as Professor Niels Bohr desired; yet once it was known that the weapon could be used, Roosevelt's successor, Truman, did inform Stalin. Nothing suggests that Stalin resented this lack of communication; it is almost the one thing for which he did not reproach the West: nor, it is fair to say, did he tell the West about his country's own activities in the atomic field during the war years or afterwards – though they had begun at much the same time as those in America; and it is obvious that, from his secret agents (whom he himself probably both despised and distrusted), he acquired some knowledge of what the United States and Britain were doing. Churchill and Roosevelt might, it is true, have launched a second front in Western Europe in 1943. But it could easily have failed. The United States could in theory have earlier recognised the dominance of the Soviet Union in Eastern Europe. But Americans, like many Englishmen, believed in Polish freedom, even if they might be doubtful about the precise whereabouts of Vilna, or Lvóv. The Russians, after all, had approved the Atlantic Charter as well as the other allies. Words mean much in democracies.

Perhaps it would have been more tactful if Allen Dulles had asked a Russian to join him in his discussions with General Wolff about German surrender in Italy in Switzerland in March 1945; perhaps Stalin heard of the contacts in Lisbon during the war between the German opposition and British intelligence: but the first of these were preliminary and the second led to nothing. Stalin did not pass onto the West news of his own fruitless contacts with the Germans in Stockholm: nor even did he pass on the news of Japanese peace offers made in Moscow by Japan's ambassador there in the summer of 1945. Britain kept Stalin informed about the peace negotiations with Himmler, and others in April and May 1945. Perhaps President Truman spoke roughly to Molotov when he saw him on April 24, 1945; but allowances must be made on behalf of a new President at the mercy of conflicting advice; sometimes, conflicting advice from the same person. Further, Molotov, in his long, terrible life, had met many who spoke more roughly than Truman did on that famous occasion. Molotov was not a child to be diverted from a chosen path by an unexpected rebuff.

It is true that Stalin and Molotov, having no understanding of idealism, and little knowledge of liberal idealists, could perhaps see the Western interest in the liberty of Poland only as a desire to gain an ally on the frontier of the Soviet Union and in an area which Stalin hoped to make part of a defensive *glacis* (with offensive possibilities). But Stalin knew, from his conversations in Tehran, that the Polish question constituted a political issue within the United States; and it was incompetence, at least, on his part if he did not know that the ideas enshrined in the Declaration on Liberated Europe, which he had himself signed at Yalta, were likely to seem of significance to the Americans and to many Englishmen; as Churchill reminded him, in vivid language in 1945, Britain had gone to war over liberty in Poland. The evident willingness of the United States to commit herself through membership of international organisations and the estab-

lishment of relatively permanent bases on a global scale may
have surprised and perhaps disturbed Stalin: it is improbable
that it was that which diverted him from a wartime emphasis on
traditional values, combined with international collaboration, to
a post-war one of ideology and intransigence.

The great nations of the West in 1945 or early 1946 indeed
took elaborate steps to remain on good terms with Russia.
There have been many reminders of that in this book. In
April 1945, the British Foreign Office, in a message to Stalin,
described themselves as having 'tried most earnestly to be
constructive and fair' over Poland;[5] the Poles believed that they
had exceeded their responsibilities in these efforts. Generals
Marshall and Eisenhower refused to contemplate political advantages when deciding on how to manage the last stages of the
fighting in Germany. The Germans tried, even in May 1945, to
use the hours before the final ceasefire to evacuate the largest
number of soldiers and civilians from the Russian front to within
the Western lines: Eisenhower refused to be party to that
understandable subterfuge. In July 1945, the Western Allies had
withdrawn from the regions of Germany which they had occupied
in their final advances; and President Truman had refused to
use the withdrawal of these troops as an instrument of pressure
on Russia, though Churchill urged him to (on June 11). The
United States and the British agreed to have the final meeting
of leaders of the war at Babelsberg, a suburb of Potsdam, which,
though technically Allied territory, and not in the Russian zone
of Germany, was managed by Russia, and could be reached by
train from Moscow by Stalin, without his having to run the risk
of passing at all through bourgeois territory. The Russians, in
turn, used the Western desire for the conference to ensure the
speed of the troop withdrawals.[6] After destructive arguments,
at the Conference of Foreign Ministers at London in September,
as to who should attend the subsequent Peace Conference,
Secretary Byrnes still thought it 'wise to give the Soviets the
benefit of every doubt' and so 'prepared a modification of our
proposals for a conference on the European peace treaties'.[7]
Secretary of State Byrnes's efforts to observe the cordialities
at Moscow in 1945, and at the United Nations in London in

1946, led him into difficulties with critics who thought him excessively pacific. Indeed, they ruined him. Efforts to please 'UJ' – Stalin – during the war were legion. The Polish emigré, General Anders, had even been disciplined when he told his troops in England that they would be sent to Siberia if they went back to Poland.[8]

It is not known what information the Soviet leaders received from their secret agents. But it must be supposed that they passed on documents giving an accurate impression of how business was handled in the government in London and in Washington. The directors of Soviet policy would, therefore, have realised that their wartime allies were, in the main, far from seeking occasions to quarrel with them. They might be confused. But they were not malign. Stalin would have known that Secretary Byrnes's flirtation with the idea of 'atomic diplomacy' in September 1945 was not a policy backed by the entire administration: nor even by the entire Department of State.

There is no sign that Stalin wanted, or expected, to remain on friendly terms with the Western Allies in peace as he had done in war; or indeed could have done, given his loyalties, career, and personality. He was a Communist; after his fashion, a sincere one. He believed in peaceful co-existence where suitable, war where appropriate, and hostility without outright war where it seemed profitable. He would keep agreements till the 'correlation of forces' dictated otherwise: 'the Soviet Union always honours its word', he once told Hopkins, adding *sotto voce*, 'except in case of extreme necessity'.[9] He did not seek a new war, but Lenin's recollection that Clausewitz believed that the greatest victory was one where the enemy surrendered without a fight had not, as had been seen, escaped him. Now that the great war against Germany was over, he could return to revive his Party, embellish the ideology where necessary, shut down relations with the rest of the world, except where that was inconvenient (rather as Japan had done in the XVIIth century) until reconstruction was complete. No information need be passed on outside Russia unless it could be useful. There was no need even to tell the West that Hitler's body had been identified; better, tell lies. (Just as the Polish officers had escaped to Manchuria, say that Hitler had escaped to Japan).[10] In a few years, another war might come and then there would be new opportunities (as he had candidly told Djilas, whom he obviously liked, in so far as he ever permitted himself such a personal indulgence as liking anyone).

For the moment, Stalin could put pressure on the West at many points; at all the points, indeed, mentioned by Senator Vandenberg, in the Senate, on February 27, 1946. Pressure could be of any sort. There was no need to press too far. Something would surely one day snap, somewhere. The myth of Soviet global strength would have a deterrent effect of sorts. The West would usually overestimate Soviet power. That would give Russia time to recuperate, to build new aircraft and to make atom bombs. The essential point though, which so few Western statesmen grasped (even when they were advised by men of Kennan's quality), was that Stalin, and Communism, needed an enemy; capitalism had to be 'menacing'; imperialism had to be 'on the march'; a 'Cold War' was in short not so much inevitable as essential.

Whether Stalin thought there was a serious possibility that the United States and her allies might seize the opportunity by their monopoly of nuclear weapons and strike against the Soviet world, as he might, no doubt indirectly through intimidation, have done had he been in their shoes, is obscure. But he probably did expect war with the West, sooner or later; so, he would overcome Russia's period of technological and economic weakness as fast as he could. Fortunately, captured German scientists could help him where his own experts might fail.

Stalin and Molotov were far from incompetent at dealing with friendly politicians from the capitalist West. On the contrary, they were clever at that, as the events of the war showed. In contrast with those who thought that the West had been too tough, it is likely that Stalin had decided that he was dealing with politicians ready to yield to pressure and often happy to settle for empty phrases.[11] He needed his capitalists to be bloody. Other behaviour was less easy to judge. Truman's hard line over Azerbaijan may thus have come as a relief.

The character of Stalin's Russia was not well understood in

the West in 1946. The complexity, distrust, and disposition to suspect, in every friendly move, a provocation, as well as the cruelty of the Soviet regime, were on a scale impossible to treat with by references to standards usual in Western debating chambers. Russia was not exactly comparable to Hitler's Germany. Yet, having exaggerated the chances of peacetime collaboration with the Soviet Union, while at war, during the years 1941 to 1945, many in the West, now in the time of 'armed truce', fell back on rash comparisons with the Nazi regime. Such comparisons were to be found among all political parties, and in all countries.[12] So many illusions had been entertained about Stalin's Russia in both the United States and Britain during the war that the discovery that the Stalin of 1946 was much as the Stalin of 1939, and nothing like the 'Uncle' of 1941–45, was certain to cause an outrage. Many in the West had 'compromised their perception of totalitarian reality'.[13] Thoughtless enthusiasm for the Grand Alliance now gave way to a sense of betrayal. Some Americans and Englishmen now felt guilty about the new 'betrayal of Poland'. This state of affairs was complicated by two new elements: first, the American possession of the atom bomb; and, second, the realisation by Americans, for the first time in earnest, that there could now be no turning back to isolation, and the 'era of good feelings', if they wanted the world in which they believed, and for which they had fought, to survive. In a search, conscious or not for the justification of permanent vigilance, many tended to exaggerate the risk of an immediate military attack on Western Europe and to underestimate the political threat. Thus they, like so many others, played into the hands of Stalin: who was, after all, in his way, a political genius.

There were some who thought that greater Western firmness towards the Soviet Union would have been more successful had it been embarked upon earlier. Admiral Standley, William Bullitt and George Kennan thought that. So, it seems, from what he said, did Maxim Litvinov. The European Division of the Department of State considered, in February 1942 that, 'at some time . . . the United States and Great Britain will be forced to state that they cannot agree, at least in advance, to all of its demands. It would seem that it is preferable to take a firm attitude now, rather than to retreat and to be compelled to take a firm attitude later when our position has been weakened by the abandonment of the general principles' of the Atlantic Charter.[14] At this distance of time, this line of argument is beguiling. Such a firm attitude might have included a refusal even to discuss the Baltic States or the Polish eastern frontier until a conference after the war in the style of Paris in 1919; a refusal to plan the future administration of liberated Germany and Austria as well as the Nazi satellite states; an instruction to all Western officials never to shake the hand of the prosecutor-turned-deputy foreign minister, Vyshinsky; and other such actions, or more moderate versions of them – for example Harriman's proposal to hold back the supply of petroleum to Russia until Stalin agreed to a tripartite commission to administer Romanian oil. Such policies were not pursued because they seemed likely to risk a Soviet *volte-face* with Germany, particularly when the Red Army had reached her frontiers of 1941. They might, therefore, have made for substantial Western losses in prolonged battles in 1945 and that might have risked the victorious end of the war generally. No major statesman in the West could have sustained a policy which incurred that risk. Such a policy would have made it impossible or, at all events, less easy, for the West to have secured Soviet participation in the Far Eastern war, a commitment which would have been important if the atom bombs had not been completed, and the war there had continued for two years, as many expected would be the case. A different policy would have been difficult to carry through against a public mood in both the United States and Britain profoundly grateful for the work of the Red Army in defeating Hitler's land armies. Had these policies been successful, they could not have avoided a 'Cold War', unless Stalin were overthrown by, for example, Marshal Zhukov. Even so, too, lines across Europe and the Far East would surely have been drawn, though they might have been drawn at different places. That would also have been the case had a Western Allied invasion been launched in, say 1943, in the Balkans, as was much discussed. Half Yugoslavia might have been saved for the West. The other half might, however, not have secured the relative independence obtained by Yugoslavia in 1948. Half Austria might thereby have been lost.

Some good might have come had a co-ordinated policy been worked out between the Western Allies towards Eastern Europe combining economic offers, propaganda, intense unremitting negotiation on every subject at issue, combined with threats. At that time, there would, however, have been very great public hostility to policies which would have delayed demobilisation. With a rapidly declining military establishment, the West was in no position to threaten Russia with 'conventional' forces. Even if the United States had wished to use 'atomic diplomacy' in the manner that some of Secretary of State Byrnes's most subtle critics have suggested that he wanted, there were few atom bombs ready for use. To drop an atom bomb on Russia or East Europe in 1945 or early 1946 was unthinkable and, therefore, not practical politics.

Nevertheless a co-ordinated policy adopted by the two main leading Western nations would have been both more wise and more just. One cannot refuse sympathy to Iuliu Maniu in Romania who, on several occasions, asked if he could be told whether the United States believed that his country was, or was not, subject to a policy embracing the idea of 'spheres of influence'. He was never told the truth. The policy of adopting a high moral tone in notional support of democracy without doing anything about it in practice was, as Sir Orme Sargent said, to get the worst of all worlds. It gave the impression to Stalin too that the West was led by the rhetoricians, not statesmen, and so encouraged him to embark on other ventures; and gave false hope to men who might otherwise have made a safer, if inglorious, acceptance of the realities of power. The reason why such Western plans were not even considered was the fault of the United States, both of whose presidents in the period concerned believed that they had a chance of achieving their ends by a conscious policy of distancing themselves from the British. President Truman later learned that intimate friendships with other Western nations were necessary even to the well-being of the United States. But in 1945 and 1946 he was still working in the shadow of trying to find out what were the real intentions of his great predecessor. Only when the influence of Admiral Leahy and Jimmy Byrnes, two men of Southern Irish origin, had been replaced by Dean Acheson whose ancestors coincidentally hailed from Ulster, was understanding between Britain and the United States made possible. Senators Connally and McMahon were also of Irish origin.

Atomic diplomacy in respect of Eastern Europe was, given the character of national politics in Britain and America, then out of the question. Atomic diplomacy in respect of Soviet possession of atomic weapons might not have been so. It was placed on the agenda by General Groves, as has been noticed. This would have needed the discovery of a pretext and the delivery of an ultimatum demanding, in the name of the United Nations, the termination of Soviet activities in this field. Such a policy would have required substantial preparation of the Western public, and a high level of courage, resolution and imagination. Public opinion would, however, have been hard to win to such a plan; and one cannot help thinking that something would have gone wrong. Human beings were ready in 1945 for neither world government nor a world empire.

The prime cause of the conflict opening up between the Russians and the Americans (and their allies) was the ideology of the Soviet leaders, and their consequent incapacity, rather than their reluctance, to make permanent arrangements with the leaders of capitalist states. This was stated by Maxim Litvinov in June 1946, in one of those strange, candid remarks of his: the 'root cause' of the trouble was 'the ideological conception prevailing here that conflict between communist and capitalist worlds is inevitable'.[15] When asked what would happen if the West were to concede to Russia all her aims in foreign policy, Litvinov replied: 'It would lead to the West being faced, in a more or less short time, with the next series of demands'.[16]

The second cause was the Soviet desire for a security against a third German invasion, which could be obtained only at the cost of insecurity, and lack of independence for their scarcely disposable neighbours. This security would prevent Poland or Romania being used as 'a corridor' for another German attack;

it ensured that the same countries could be used as a Russian corridor to the West.

It is necessary to face the question whether the policies of the United States, and to a lesser extent those of Britain, played any part: for example, the 'universalism' of US rhetoric; their atomic bombs and the use made of them; or, as Henry Wallace believed, the US policy for bases throughout the world. It seems unlikely that these policies did any more than to confirm Stalin and his associates in their suspicions. If the atomic bomb had not existed, Stalin would still have feared the success of the US wartime economy: which certainly seemed a fearsome obstacle to the success of the world Communism in 1945, whose revolutionary fatherland had after all suffered so much. There is also the question whether the changeability of the policies of the United States, or Britain, may not have played a part. That they changed, and that often, is obvious. Wilsonian idealism or 'Universalism' did make concessions to Stimson's realism. Both Truman's and Byrnes's moods changed backwards and forwards during 1945 and 1946, and neither saw eye to eye with the British, whose leaders they distrusted, or had been brought up to distrust, for reasons irrelevant to the issue of relations with the Soviet Union. When the American statesmen realised that the Russians would not accept, or could not accept, their vision of an open world, they moved towards supposing that the Russians were bent not so much on 'spheres of interest' as stepping stones to hegemony, as immediate world conquest. Stalin's probing could easily seem like the first steps of a revolutionary drive to the military conquest of the world; and it might have become that, had it not been resisted. But it was a political drive, not a military one, to be defeated by political means. Americans, and indeed Englishmen, could understand war; they could understand peace; but 'partial war', (as Lenin put it), including a wide variety of tactics including 'deception, concealed penetration and subversion, psychological warfare' and the 'adroit exploitation of every conceivable form of division in capitalist society'[17] was, to begin with, a concept too complicated for most of that era's public servants.

Under all these manoeuvres lay another truth: world power

was now narrowly concentrated in two nations. Before 1914, there were seven world powers: Russia and the empires centred upon France, Britain, and Germany; perhaps Italy; there were Austria-Hungary and the Ottoman Empire, sick men of Europe though they seemed; and China and Persia, sick men of Asia though they were. The United States then stood in the wings, hovering tentatively if powerfully, as if the central figure in a great novel by Henry James (liking, with Isabel Archer, 'complications – of the right sort'). So, less close, did Japan. Now most of these old edifices had been shattered. No more did power revolve between Vienna and Versailles, neither in time nor in space. This was not the work of international Communism. All the same, the process of concentration left the relatively inexperienced United States and the *rusé* Soviet Union the only possible contenders.[18] Britain, after all, was weaker than she seemed, and was about to embark upon a generation-long withdrawal from her empire, and upon economic stagnation. France, even if stronger than she appeared to be in 1946, could never again be more than a European power, if sometimes an international irritant. So the great Frenchman Alexis de Tocqueville's hackneyed but apposite, prediction in 1834 seemed about to be realised: 'There are at present two great nations in the world which, starting from different points, seem to be moving towards the same end – the Russians and the Americans . . . the principal means of action of the one is freedom; of the other, servitude. Their starting points are different and their courses are diverse. Yet each of them seems marked by a secret design of Providence to hold one day in their hand the destinies of half the world'.[19]

About sixty years after de Tocqueville wrote these words, the Russian reformer Peter Struve made a comparison between Russia and the United States; both were multinational states; both had expanded territorially in the previous century; both were ideologically disposed to ignore nationalism; but, even then, there was the difference that, whilst the United States, with her 38 million new immigrants from 1820 to 1930, had become the preferred home of millions of men and women born Russian, the chief export of the Russian Empire was refugees.

From 1917, another difference was added, the imposition on Russia of an all-explaining ideology, which itself welcomed, or demanded, a manichean view of the world.*

The phrase 'cold war' appears to have been invented in 1893 by the German Marxist, Edward Bernstein, when he said, 'this continual arming, compelling the others to keep up with Germany, is itself a kind of warfare. I do not know whether the expression has been used previously, but one could say it is "a cold war". There is no shooting, but there is bleeding'.[20] The phrase is often said to have been first used in its modern context in 1946 by Herbert Bayard Swope, Bernard Baruch's assistant during the First World War on the War Production Board and in 1946 on his ill-fated atomic panel; and to have then been taken up by Walter Lippmann in his book of that name.[21] That is not so. The credit for the current usage lies with George Orwell when describing, in an article in *Tribune*, dated October 19, 1945, the difficulties of coping with 'a state which was at once unconquerable and in a permanent state of "cold war" with its neighbours'.[22] That was the nature of the challenge mounted by the Soviet leadership. High-minded, experienced and cultivated men and women in Western administrations did not find it easy to face the consequences. They do not do so now.

---

* cf. Professor Saggs' comment in *The Glory that was Babylon*: 'the simultaneous expansion of Larsa in the south and Babylon in the north led in the end to conflict between these two powers but it would be an over-simplification to regard a struggle between these two city states as the key . . .'

# APPENDICES

# APPENDIX I

# STALIN'S FAMILY

# Appendix I  Stalin's Family

ZAZA DJUGASHVILI
active in anti-Russian rising.
Georgia c. 1810

VANO
tended vineyards at Didi-Lilo, near Tiflis

SEMYON SVANIDZE
railway worker at
Didi-Lilo, Tiflis.
Organised strike at
Alexandropol 1905

VISSARION DJUGASHVILI  =
settled Tiflis.
Shoemender in
leather factory,
Gori. d.1890 in brawl

MARIA KORONA  =
Jewish, soloist
at Tiflis theatre
d.in prison c. 1942

ALEXANDER 1886–1942
in Soviet financial
posts. Brought up by
Jakob. Executed
Orel 1942

EKATERINA SVANDIZE  =
'KETO' married 1902
d.1908

JOSIF DJUGASHVIL
'Soso'
'Kobo'
STALIN
only survivor of four
children
1879–1953

MARIKO
secretary to
A. Yenukidze

JOHNREED SVANIDZE
'Johnik', Ivan, Vano
b.1929
in psychiatric prison Kazan 1941–46
in copper mines 1946–51
returned Moscow 1956
Africa Institute 1960

?  =

JAKOB b.1908
d.Sachsenhausen
concentration camp 1944

=  YULIA
Jewish
In prison 1941–4

daughter
d.in infancy

YULIA

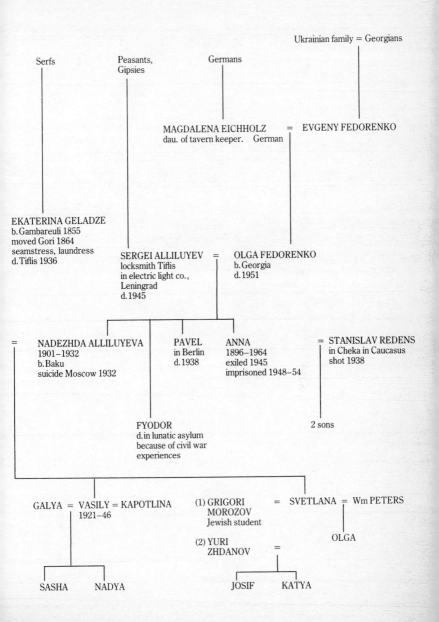

# APPENDIX II

# MACLEAN AND HISS

*Memorandum of Telephone Conversation, by the Director of the Office of Special Political Affairs (Hiss)\**

[Washington,] October 21, 1946.

Participants:

Mr D. D. Maclean, First Secretary of the British Embassy

Mr Alger Hiss

Mr Acheson informed me Friday evening that the Secretary had agreed with the recommendation made to him by the Department in Secdel 1075 of October 8 that we should not oppose the addition of the above item to the General Assembly agenda but instead should move for a clarification of it to ensure the inclusion of Austria as a non-enemy state and also for its expansion to cover troops in ex-enemy states. Mr Acheson agreed that the British Embassy should be notified promptly of our views and that the Delegation in New York should be instructed not to notify the Secretary General of our intentions until after giving the British advance notice. Mr Acheson suggested that we might simply notify the British that we intended to send our

* The file copy of the present document is accompanied by the following handwritten chit, addressed by Mr Byrnes to Mr Hiss, which is date-stamped Office of Special Political Affairs October 21, 1946: 'Bevin asks we do not talk to Lie about Soviet Resolution as to armed forces until he communicates with me. I have told Ambassador would delay action but urged that he advise me promptly.'

notification to the Secretary General on Tuesday or Wednesday and were giving the British advance information because of their interest in the matter.

Accordingly I informed Mr Maclean of the British Embassy last Saturday of our intentions and pointed out that we were giving consideration to making public our own troop dispositions in the course of the Assembly discussion, probably at an early date in the particular committee to which the matter would be referred.

Mr Maclean thanked me for this information and said he would immediately communicate it to London. He added that he thought our plans would be viewed with concern in London although he recognized the differences between the limited jurisdiction of the Security Council and the general authority of the General Assembly to discuss all subjects.

This morning Mr Maclean called to say that the Embassy had received a preliminary reply on this subject which stated that the Foreign Office is giving urgent consideration to the problem which they regard as a joint problem since the Russians' initiative in their opinion is aimed at the United States and Britain. Mr Bevin had expressed the hope that we would not make our communication to the Secretariat until we had heard further from him. Mr Maclean assured us that their further views would be forthcoming shortly. He added that the Ambassador was being instructed to take the matter up directly with the Secretary.

Mr Maclean said that in view of what I had said on Saturday, namely that we do not contemplate communicating our views to the Secretary General until Tuesday or Wednesday that he assumed we would be able to wait a short time further until Mr Bevin's further views had been received. I assured Mr Maclean this was the situation.

# APPENDIX III

# THE 'SPHERES OF INFLUENCE' AGREEMENT, OCTOBER 1944

# THE 'SPHERES OF INFLUENCE'

| Date: | Original Proposal 9 Oct. | | | | | Subsequent Proposals 10 Oct. |
|---|---|---|---|---|---|---|
| Proposer: *Country* | Churchill USSR:GB % | Molotov USSR:GB % | Molotov USSR:GB % | Molotov USSR:GB % | Eden USSR:GB % | Molotov USSR:GB % |
| Greece: | 10:90 | | | | | |
| Romania | 90:10 | | | | | |
| Hungary: | 50:50 | 75:25 | 75:25 | | 75:25 | |
| Bulgaria: | 75:25 | 90:10 | 75:25 | 90:10 | | 75:25 |
| Yugoslavia: | 50:50 | | 75:25 | 50:50 | | 60:40 |

[As designed by B. Kuniholm, *The Beginning of the Cold War in the Middle East*]

# AGREEMENT, OCTOBER 1944

| Eden USSR:GB % | USSR:GB % | Molotov (or) | USSR:GB % | *Last Proposal 11 Oct.* Molotov USSR:GB % | *Implicit Final Agreement* USSR:GB % | *Changes from Original Proposal* |
|---|---|---|---|---|---|---|
|  |  |  |  |  | 10:90 |  |
|  |  |  |  |  | 90:10 |  |
| 75:25 |  |  |  | 80:20 | 80:20 | +30% for USSR −30% for GB |
| 80:20 | 90:10 |  | 75:25 | 80:20 | 80:20 | + 5% for USSR − 5% for GB |
| 50:50 | 50:50 |  | 60:40 | 50:50 | 50:50 |  |

# APPENDIX IV

# THE ATLANTIC CHARTER, AUGUST 1941

*Declaration of Principles known as the Atlantic Charter, made public on 14 August 1941*

*Joint Declaration of the President of the United States of America and the Prime Minister, Mr Churchill, representing His Majesty's Government in the United Kingdom, being met together, deem it right to make known* certain common principles in the national policies of their respective countries for a better future for the world.

*First*, their countries seek no aggrandizement, territorial or other;

*Second*, they desire to see no territorial changes that do not accord with the freely expressed wishes of the peoples concerned;

*Third*, they respect the right of all peoples to choose the form of government under which they will live; and they wish to see sovereign rights and self-government restored to those who have been forcibly deprived of them;

*Fourth*, they will endeavour, with due respect for their existing obligations, to further the enjoyment by all States, great or small, victor or vanquished, of access, on equal terms, to the trade and to the raw materials of the world which are needed for their economic prosperity;

*Fifth*, they desire to bring about the fullest collaboration between all nations in the economic field with the object of securing, for all, improved labour standards, economic advancement and social security;

*Sixth*, after the final destruction of the Nazi tyranny, they hope to see established a peace which will afford to all nations the means of dwelling in safety within their own boundaries, and which will afford assurance that all the men in all the lands may live out their lives in freedom from fear and want;

*Seventh*, such a peace should enable all men to traverse the high seas and oceans without hindrance;

*Eighth*, they believe that all of the nations of the world, for realistic as well as spiritual reasons, must come to the abandonment of the use of force. Since no future peace can be maintained if land, sea or air armaments continue to be employed by nations which threaten, or may threaten, aggression outside of their frontiers, they believe, pending the establishment of a wider and permanent system of general security, that the disarmament of such nations is essential. They will likewise aid and encourage all other practicable measures which will lighten for peace-loving peoples the crushing burden of armaments.

# APPENDIX V

# THE DECLARATION ON LIBERATED EUROPE

*Report of the Crimea Conference 11 February, 1945*

For the past eight days Winston S. Churchill, Prime Minister of Great Britain, Franklin D. Roosevelt, President of the United States of America, and Marshal J. V. Stalin, Chairman of the Council of People's Commissars of the Union of Soviet Socialist Republics, have met with the Foreign Secretaries, Chiefs of Staff and other advisers in the Crimea . . .

## V. Declaration on Liberated Europe

We have drawn up and subscribed to a Declaration on Liberated Europe. This Declaration provides for concerting the policies of the Three Powers and for joint action by them in meeting the political and economic problems of liberated Europe in accordance with democratic principles. The text of the Declaration is as follows:

The Premier of the Union of Soviet Socialist Republics, the Prime Minister of the United Kingdom, and the President of the United States of America have consulted with each other in the common interests of the peoples of their countries and those of liberated Europe. They jointly declare their mutual agreement to concert during the temporary period of instability in liberated Europe the policies of their three Governments in assisting the peoples liberated from the domination of Nazi Germany and the peoples of the former Axis satellite States of Europe to solve by democratic means their pressing political and economic problems.

The establishment of order in Europe and the rebuilding of national economic life must be achieved by processes which will enable the liberated peoples to destroy the last vestiges of Nazism and Fascism and to create democratic institutions of their own choice. This is a principle of the Atlantic Charter – the right of all peoples to choose the form of government under which they will live – the restoration of sovereign rights and self-government to those peoples who have been forcibly deprived of them by the aggressor nations.

To foster the conditions in which the liberated peoples may exercise those rights, the three Governments will jointly assist the people in any European liberated State or former Axis satellite State in Europe where in their judgement conditions require: (a) to establish conditions of internal peace; (b) to carry out emergency measures for the relief of distressed peoples; (c) to form interim governmental authorities broadly representative of all democratic elements in the population and pledged to the earliest possible establishment through free elections of Governments responsive to the will of the people; and (d) to facilitate where necessary the holding of such elections.

The three Governments will consult the other United Nations and provisional authorities or other Governments in Europe when matters of direct interest to them are under consideration.

When, in the opinion of the three Governments, conditions in any European liberated State or any former Axis satellite State in Europe make such action necessary, they will immediately consult together on the measures necessary to discharge the joint responsibilities set forth in this Declaration.

By this Declaration we reaffirm our faith in the principles of the Atlantic Charter, our pledge in the Declaration by the United Nations, and our determination to build in cooperation with other peace-loving nations a world order under law, dedicated to peace, security, freedom and the general well-being of all mankind.

In issuing this Declaration, the Three Powers express the hope that the Provisional Government of the French Republic may be associated with them in the procedure suggested.

# APPENDIX VI

# SOVIET ENTRY INTO THE WAR IN THE EAST

*Yalta Agreement on the Kuriles and entry of the Soviet Union in the war against Japan, 11 February 1945 (released 11 February 1946)*

The leaders of the three Great Powers – the Soviet Union, the United States of America and Great Britain – have agreed that in two or three months after Germany has surrendered and the war in Europe has terminated the Soviet Union shall enter into the war against Japan on the side of the Allies on condition that:

1. The *status quo* in Outer Mongolia (The Mongolian People's Republic) shall be preserved;

2. The former rights of Russia violated by the treacherous attack of Japan in 1904 shall be restored, viz:

(a) the southern part of Sakhalin as well as all the islands adjacent to it shall be returned to the Soviet Union,

(b) the commercial port of Dairen shall be internationalized, the pre-eminent interests of the Soviet Union in this port being safeguarded and the lease of Port Arthur as a naval base of the USSR restored,

(c) the Chinese-Eastern Railroad and the South-Manchurian Railroad which provides an outlet to Dairen shall be jointly operated by the establishment of a joint Soviet-Chinese Company, it being understood that the pre-eminent interests of the Soviet Union shall be safeguarded and that China shall retain full sovereignty in Manchuria;

3. The Kurile islands shall be handed over to the Soviet Union.

It is understood that the agreement concerning Outer Mongolia and the ports and railroads referred to above will require concurrence of Generalissimo Chiang Kai Shek. The President will take measures in order to obtain this concurrence on advice from Marshal Stalin.

The Heads of the three Great Powers have agreed that these claims of the Soviet Union shall be unquestionably fulfilled after Japan has been defeated.

For its part, the Soviet Union expresses its readiness to conclude with the National Government of China a pact of friendship and alliance between the USSR and China in order to render assistance to China with its armed forces for the purpose of liberating China from the Japanese yoke.

*February 11, 1945*

J. Stalin
Franklin D. Roosevelt
Winston S. Churchill

# APPENDIX VII

# THE ANGLO-RUSSIAN TREATY, MAY 26, 1942*

*Treaty of Alliance in the War against Hitlerite Germany and her associates in Europe and of Collaboration and Mutual Assistance thereafter concluded between the Union of Soviet Socialist Republics and the United Kingdom of Great Britain and Northern Ireland*

His Majesty The King of Great Britain and the Presidium of the Supreme Council of the Union of Soviet Socialist Republics;

Desiring to confirm the stipulations of the Agreement between His Majesty's Government in the United Kingdom and the Government of the Union of Soviet Socialist Republics for joint action in the war against Germany, signed at Moscow on the 12th July 1941, and to replace them by a formal treaty;

Desiring to contribute after the war to the maintenance of peace and to the prevention of further aggression by Germany or the States associated with her in acts of aggression in Europe;

Desiring, moreover, to give expression to their intention to collaborate closely with one another as well as with the other United Nations at the peace settlement and during the ensuing period of reconstruction on the basis of the principles enunciated in the declaration made on the 14th August 1941, by the Presi-

* The treaty was ratified at Moscow on July 4, 1942 and published as Cmd. 6376 (Treaty Series). This Command paper includes not only the English and Russian texts but reproductions, at the end of the Russian text, of the signatures of Mr Eden and M. Molotov.

dent of the United States of America and the Prime Minister of Great Britain to which the Government of the Union of Soviet Socialist Republics has adhered;

Desiring, finally, to provide for mutual assistance in the event of an attack upon either High Contracting Party by Germany or any of the States associated with her in acts of aggression in Europe,

Have decided to conclude a treaty for that purpose and have appointed as their Plenipotentiaries: –

[Here follows a mention of Mr Eden and M. Molotov].

Who, having communicated their Full Powers, found in good and due form, have agreed as follows:

## PART I

### *Article 1*

In virtue of the alliance established between the United Kingdom and the Union of Soviet Socialist Republics the High Contracting Parties mutually undertake to afford one another military and other assistance and support of all kinds in the war against Germany and all those States which are associated with her in acts of aggression in Europe.

### *Article II*

The High Contracting Parties undertake not to enter into any negotiations with the Hitlerite Government or any other Government in Germany that does not clearly renounce all aggressive intentions, and not to negotiate or conclude except by mutual consent any armistice or peace treaty with Germany or any other State associated with her in acts of aggression in Europe.

## PART 2

### *Article III*

(1) The High Contracting Parties declare their desire to unite with other like-minded States in adopting proposals for common action to preserve peace and resist aggression in the post-war period.

(2) Pending the adoption of such proposals, they will after the

termination of hostilities take all the measures in their power to render impossible a repetition of aggression and violation of the peace by Germany or any of the States associated with her in acts of aggression in Europe.

### Article IV

Should one of the High Contracting Parties during the post-war period become involved in hostilities with Germany or any of the States mentioned in Article III (2) in consequence of an attack by that State against that Party, the other High Contracting Party will at once give to the Contracting Party so involved in hostilities all the military and other support and assistance in his power.

This Article shall remain in force until the High Contracting Parties, by mutual agreement, shall recognise that it is superseded by the adoption of the proposals contemplated in Article III (1). In default of the adoption of such proposals, it shall remain in force for a period of twenty years, and thereafter until terminated by either High Contracting Party, as provided in Article VIII.

### Article V

The High Contracting Parties, having regard to the interests of the security of each of them, agree to work together in close and friendly collaboration after the re-establishment of peace for the organisation of security and economic prosperity in Europe. They will take into account the interests of the United Nations in these objects, and they will act in accordance with the two principles of not seeking territorial aggrandisement for themselves and of non-interference in the internal affairs of other States.

### Article VI

The High Contracting Parties agree to render one another all possible economic assistance after the war.

### Article VII

Each High Contracting Party undertakes not to conclude any alliance and not to take part in any coalition directed against the other High Contracting Party.

## *Article VIII*

The present Treaty is subject to ratification in the shortest possible time and the instruments of ratification shall be exchanged in Moscow as soon as possible.

It comes into force immediately on the exchange of the instruments of ratification and shall thereupon replace the Agreement between the Government of the Union of Soviet Socialist Republics and His Majesty's Government in the United Kingdom, signed at Moscow on the 12th July, 1941.

Part I of the present Treaty shall remain in force until the re-establishment of peace between the High Contracting Parties and Germany and the Powers associated with her in acts of aggression in Europe.

Part II of the present Treaty shall remain in force for a period of twenty years. Thereafter, unless twelve months' notice has been given by either Party to terminate the Treaty at the end of the said period of twenty years, it shall continue in force until twelve months after either High Contracting Party shall have given notice to the other in writing of his intention to terminate it.

In witness whereof the above-named Plenipotentiaries have signed the present Treaty and have affixed thereto their seals.

Done in duplicate in London on the 26th day of May, 1942, in the English and Russian languages, both texts being equally authentic.

(L.S.) Anthony Eden

(L.S.) V. Molotov

# APPENDIX VIII

# SIS IN AUSTRIA, 1945

FO 371/46609   *Austria 1945*

C2226/141/G3   *W. H. B. Mack to [Oliver] Harvey, 3 May, 1945*
*Allied Commission for Austria* (British
Element)

My dear Oliver, I hope that you will be patient in regard to
political reporting in the early stages after our arrival in Vienna.
2. 'C''s representative for the Mediterranean, whom I have seen
here, tells me that from experience in other liberated countries
at least a month has elapsed before his people found it possible
to gather any useful information. In agreement with me he is
not proposing to send any of his people into Vienna for a month
or so after the arrival of the Mission. He naturally does not want
to repeat the unfortunate experience of the team which he sent
into Sofia. He tells me that he has a good man to send in when
the time comes.
3. I arranged with 'C' several months ago that we should have
one of his people camouflaged in one of the civil Divisions and
we shall also have one of his men in the Public Security Branch.
4. Much will of course depend on the contacts with Austrians
which I can make after my arrival. I fear that I shall find none
of my former friends and acquaintances of any value in Vienna.
I expect, however, that quite a few odd Austrians will come
round, but since on principle I take no Austrian at his (or her)

face-value, it is bound to take some little time to get one's impressions sorted out and to see below the surface of things. I am sure that you realise all this and that you will not expect too much for a bit.

# APPENDIX IX

# DR OPPENHEIMER'S PROPOSAL

[Submitted as a draft to the scientific panel of the Acheson
Committee, 1946]

*Memorandum by Dr J. Robert Oppenheimer*
[Washington, February 2, 1946.]

In these notes I shall write down some of the non-technical
things that have seemed to me relevant to the establishment of
effective international control of atomic energy, and make, in
rather broad terms, proposals on the basis of which a sound
solution can in my opinion be sought. I shall write these notes
against the background of our discussions in the past days, and
with the thought in mind that the technical basis of many of the
judgments will be provided in a separate report.

1. It is probable that the main desire of our Government is
the achievement of safety and protection against the threat of
atomic warfare. Even if it were possible to achieve this without
considering such positive features as the extension of knowledge
and its application to constructive purposes, it might be argued
that such a course should not be followed. It is my belief that
quite apart from its desirability, the provision for constructive
development of the field of atomic energy will turn out to be
essential for the operation of any system of safeguards. You
have seen in the last days evidence of the enthusiasm, inventiveness, and intelligence that has gone into the development of the
field in this country, and that has manifested itself even in such

relatively peripheral matters as the exploration of raw material resources. I believe that just these elements must be brought to bear on the problem of control if there is to be any chance for a real solution. In particular, it has become clear to us that not only politically, but scientifically and technically as well, the field of atomic energy has witnessed very rapid change and very rapid progress. I believe that this will be the case in the future, too, and that no organisation and no proposal can be effective which does not have a flexibility adequate to these changes. I further believe that any proposed organization must itself reflect the changing character of the problem and the constructive purposes which are a complement to control. It is clear that quite apart from any organizational details, the objectives here outlined will require a genuine cooperation and not a mere acquiescence on the part of the participating powers and agencies. As I understand it, the primary function of the United Nations Atomic Energy Commission must be to lay the basis for such cooperative approach to the problem.

2. The position of the three powers, the United States, the United Kingdom, and Canada, that have in the past collaborated in the development of atomic energy, is a rather special one, and that of the United States perhaps the most special of all. There are two parts to this: our technical advantage puts us in a position to exercise disproportionate influence in shaping the proposals made, and our greater scientific and technical mastery of the problem should give us greater insight into the implications of a proposed solution and the character of the steps necessary to achieve it.

It has from the first, seemed important to balance our technical superiority insofar as possible by allowing the proposals to be formulated as a result of multilateral discussion, rather than through acceptance of a plan elaborated unilaterally by us. It would seem to be inevitable that differences of opinion similar to those which appeared in the Panel, but far more profound, would be expressed in approaching the organizational problems of control. Here again it would seem to me neither desirable, nor in any long term practical, to avoid a discussion of these issues in an attempt at their constructive reconciliation. Just this possibility is in fact my ground for believing that the negotiations we are now discussing may provide a prototype for more difficult future problems.

I have a somewhat different view of the situation arising from our sole possession of the technical and scientific insight necessary to sound judgments. This problem is in part technical, since many of the facts at our disposal, but not now generally known, are indeed relevant to questions of feasibility, adequacy, and safety. It is also in part a psychological problem in that insight depends not only on having facts available, but on having a sense of assurance that the relevant facts have not been withheld. I believe that it is premature to discuss the precise extent to which basic scientific information should be made available to the Atomic Energy Commission. It is clear, on the one hand, that such information neither must, nor with propriety should, include detailed engineering specifications for plants and for weapons; on the other hand, our experience would indicate that the Smyth Report as it stands is probably far from sufficient. We shall be in a better position to judge this at our next meeting.

3. In order to evaluate the proposals that I should like to make, it may be well to consider extreme examples, which have been suggested from time to time, of proposals that I regard as unworkable. Almost everyone has, at one stage or another in his acquaintance with this problem, considered prohibiting further work on atomic energy, and devising a system of inspection adequate to insure that this prohibition is carried out. It is not only that this proposal would make impossible the application of existing knowledge to constructive ends; it would be so contrary to the human pattern of exploration and exploitation that no agreement entered into by heads of state could command the interest or the cooperation of the people of the world.

An apparently less radical solution would be the separation of the functions of development and of control according to which the only responsibility of an international authority would be the inspection of work carried out under a purely national or private initiative, and the possible prohibition of some of this work. The negative approach to the problem of control would leave the inspecting agency with inadequate insight, both into the technical state of the subject, and into its motivation and the organic characteristics of its growth. It would provide inspectors who are less informed and less enlightened than those whose evasions they were trying to prevent; it would provide inspectors with a motive pathetically inadequate to the immense and dreary task which such inspection would involve, and who would no doubt be in a poor position to apply to their work the technical ingenuity and inventiveness which alone can make it an undertaking of finite dimensions and some prospect of success. One sees these difficulties most clearly if the problem is considered as it may appear in the almost immediate future. On the one hand, I believe that no one would be willing to wait for the institution of a system of controls until such time as many nations had a flourishing atomic energy industry, and no doubt a flourishing atomic armaments program; on the other hand, it is probably true that at the present time there is pitifully little to inspect in any countries but the United States, the United Kingdom, and Canada. It is unclear what primary deposits would be exploited in the future, what plans would be made for the production of fissionable materials, and what laboratories and scientists will in the end be chosen to carry out this work. It is just this circumstance which would make the task of inspection so unenlightened and so vast as to be prohibitive. It is also clear that this approach to the problem would sacrifice almost wholly whatever advantages there are in the fact that atomic energy developments are nowhere else in the world an established and flourishing activity, representing a vested interest and a living organization.

4. Against this background of the difficulties of control as an isolated and negative function, I have thought it essential at least to consider combining the functions of development and of control in a single agency. It is fairly certain that there are now, and will increasingly be, activities having to do with atomic energy which are not vital to control and which, for human, or organization, or political, reasons should not be included among the functions of the controlling authority; but there are certainly several such functions which, as matters now appear, should be so included among them: the development of raw materials, the

exploration of atomic weapons, and the applications, in its more dangerous forms, of atomic energy to power and technology.

   *a*. I thus propose that the international authority have a monopoly on the study, development, and exploitation of uranium: That this could be an interesting activity some of our discussions of last week clearly showed, and apart from considerations of security a coordinated attack on a worldwide scale is the more appropriate way of exploiting the raw materials. An agency which was well informed about the location of deposits and the most highly developed means of working them, and their relation to each other, would be in a strong position to detect and discourage illegal enterprises of a more private nature. It would also be in a position to provide the basic accounting and material control for an ingredient which is at present, and probably will remain for a long time to come, uniquely necessary. Technical arguments suggest that the same machinery should be applied to the exploitation of thorium.

   *b*. A second activity of the international authority, which is doubtless far less urgent, but for which provision must ultimately be made, is research and study of atomic explosives. You will remember from our discussion that this is a field in which we are by no means confident of the facts; it is, of course, possible that such atomic explosives may be useful to the peacetime economy of the world, but quite apart from this it is only by their exploration that any agency can have a reasonable chance of ensuring that developments beyond its control are not of great danger to the world.

   *c*. It would be an essential function of the international authority to develop atomic energy for industrial purposes and as a source of power, and to carry out the technical advances necessary to make these developments practical, and to extend their range. In conducting this program, it is clear that economic, technological, and even sociological considerations will be as important as purely scientific ones, and it is further clear that the solution of the resulting conflicts will involve compromise and good will which only an agency with authority and adequate technical competence can bring to the problem.

   *d*. As we pointed out, there are a number of potential applications of atomic energy which can be made relatively safe, either by denaturing procedures, or because plants are involved which destroy, rather than create, atomic explosives; or because the scale of the operation is small enough to be immaterial for atomic weapons. There may be strong arguments (and there probably are) for conducting these developments under a license system, with nations or with more private organizations, but the line between safe and dangerous activities should not remain fixed where we would draw it today, so that I should be reluctant to make a final *a priori* definition at this time.

*e.* It would seem to me desirable and, in fact, essential, that the international authority cooperate with scientists, engineers, industrialists, and others who are not members of their organization but who have an interest in, or a contribution to make toward, the work of the authority. This openness would contribute in an important way to making the authority subject to enlightened criticism and to making its findings available for more private exploitation wherever this could be done effectively and safely.

5. There are a number of questions which probably should be discussed in connection with the above proposals, although I do not feel qualified to discuss them. In particular, the organizational structure of the international authority, whether it be a commission or a corporation (or take another form), will have to be settled in the light of conflicting views as to the best methods of providing initiative, responsibility, and integrity. The machinery set up for providing a reasonable, forward-looking allocation of atomic power and atomic products, the machinery required for financing undertakings, many of which in the earlier times may not be economically profitable, and the contributions that might be expected in the form of labor, technical competence, and raw materials, all would need a fairly prompt discussion. Other questions on which there will be differences of opinion are the appropriate scale of development and the priorities that should attach to various phases of the work. In all of these matters one will have to draw both on the technical ingenuity of those familiar with the field of atomic energy, and on all useful precedents of effective organization.

6. There are a few questions which it seems to me not very profitable to discuss at present. One has to do with the complex of problems that would arise should there be abrogation of agreements by a nation or a group of nations, or activities in serious violation of these agreements. Such discussions will inevitably bring one to the problem of sanctions, which seems to me essentially separable from the questions we have been asked to consider. Related to these questions is the provision of an adequate physical security for installations operated by the international authority but susceptible to diversion for military use, and the question of whether any useful purpose can be achieved by stockpiling atomic weapons to facilitate the application of sanctions. It is inevitable that all these questions will be asked; in my opinion their discussion cannot contribute in a constructive way to the solution of our primary problem.

*Foreign Relations of the United States,* 1946,
Volume I, pp. 960–964.

# APPENDIX X

# THE SOVIET POLICY OF BRITAIN, MAY 1946

FO 371/56784

N6733/140/38G *FO Minute: Russian policy of Cabinet*
Sir O. Sargent.

At the meeting on May 14th [1946] of the Committee on Policy towards Russia, it was suggested that it would be well to clear up a point of doubt regarding the Russian policy of the Cabinet.

Mr Hall-Patch said he had received the impression in a recent Cabinet meeting that there was not complete agreement in the Cabinet on this subject. Some Ministers, he said, took the line that it would be wrong to consider Russia to be 'hostile' to this country, that we should not treat the Soviet Union as an 'enemy' and so on.

Mr Warner's memorandum on 'The Soviet Campaign against this country', which has been approved by the PM for circulation to those taking part in discussions with the Dominion PMs, is of course based on the premise that Russia *is* at present 'hostile' to us in almost every possible way and has in fact launched an offensive against this country.

Action is, as you know, being taken, under the general supervision of the Russian Committee to put into effect a counter-offensive designed to protect us from Russian aggressive tactics. It is, in the Committee's view, essential that this policy should have the full backing of the Cabinet. The importance of this becomes especially evident in dealing with publicity, since it is clear that any propaganda which may be done under our auspices must harmonise with the line taken by Ministers, and would let us in for some very damaging criticism from this country if it did not.

It is possible that the PM and S/S may find it undesirable to discuss too openly with certain of their colleagues this aspect of our official policy, but it is so fundamental to the work of the Office that the Committee feels it should cover itself before embarking on any further activities, especially propaganda. The Committee has therefore directed that the matter should be submitted to you, and that you should be asked to consider whether it would not be advisable to speak to the S/S about it.

[This memorandum was signed by Oliver Harvey. From the distribution list held by the Cabinet Office, it appears that Mr Warner's memo was circulated to the following Mins: PM, S/S, LD Pres, Fst Ld, S/Ss Dominions, India, Colonies, War, Air and Scotland.]

# APPENDIX XI

# ROOSEVELT AND POST-WAR EUROPE

THE WHITE HOUSE
WASHINGTON
February 21, 1944

MEMORANDUM FOR THE ACTING
SECRETARY OF STATE

I disagree with the British proposal of the demarcation of boundaries which would go into effect in Germany after their surrender or after fighting has stopped.

1. I do not want the United States to have the post-war burden of reconstituting France, Italy and the Balkans. This is not our natural task at a distance of 3,500 miles or more. It is definitely a British task in which the British are far more vitally interested that we are.

2. From the point of view of the United States, our principal object is not to take part in the internal problems in southern Europe but is rather to take part in eliminating Germany at a possible and even probable cost of a third World War.

3. Various points have been raised about the difficulties of transferring our troops, etc., from a French front to a northern German front – what is called a 'leap-frog.' These objections are specious because no matter where British and American troops are on the day of Germany's surrender, it is physically easy for them to go anywhere north, east or south.

4. I have had to consider also the ease of maintaining American

troops in some part of Germany. All things considered, and remembering that all supplies have to come 3,500 miles or more by sea, the United States should use the ports of northern Germany, Hamburg and Bremen, and the ports of the Netherlands for this long range operation.

5. Therefore, I think the American policy should be to occupy northwestern Germany, the British occupying the area from the Rhine south, and also being responsible for the policing of France and Italy, if this should become necessary.

6. In regard to the long range security of Britain against Germany, this is not a part of the first occupation. The British will have plenty of time to work that out, including Helgoland, air fields, etc. The Americans by that time will be only too glad to retire all their military forces from Europe.

7. If anything further is needed to justify this disagreement with the British lines of demarcation, I can only add that political considerations in the United States makes my decision conclusive.

You might speak to me about this if the above is not wholly clear.

FDR

# NOTES

# REFERENCES

The full name of the author, title and place of publication (or deposit, if unpublished) of all sources are mentioned on the first citation. Thereafter, a reference to the chapter and footnote where those full details are given follow in square brackets after the name of the author: thus 'Eden [7:30]' means that the full title, place and date of publication are given in Chapter 7, footnote 30.

Abbreviations are employed thus:
DNB:      Dictionary of National Biography
DPSR:     Documents on Polish-Soviet relations 1939–45
          Edited by the Sikorski Institute, 2 vols (London 1968)
FRUS:     Foreign Relations of the United States (followed by year
          covered by the volume concerned)
HSTL:     Harry S. Truman Library, Independence, Missouri
L of C:   Library of Congress, Washington DC
NA:       National Archives of the United States
PRO:      Papers in the Public Record Office, Kew

*Notes to the epigraphs*
For Acheson: *Foreign Relations of the United States* 1945, Vol. (II, 49–50; for Litvinov, the same publication, 1946, Vol. VI, 763.

# BOOK ONE
# DESPOTISM AND IDEOLOGY
*Mr Laurence Kelly and Dr George Urban read some of these chapters
in typescript and made many useful suggestions.*

## CHAPTER 1 STALIN'S 'ELECTION'

1. Leonard Schapiro, *The Communist Party of the Soviet Union*, 2nd ed. (London 1970), 68–69. Axelrod was, paradoxically, worsted in a series of controversies with Lenin in the early years of the century. 'Soviet' in Russia means 'advice' or 'council'.

2. Robert Conquest, *Inside Stalin's Secret Police* (London 1985), 50

3. Another instance was the occasion when, in late December 1945, the presidium of the Supreme Soviet told the Polish provisional government that they would recognise it as soon as it was formally launched: 'This instance makes me powerless to fulfil your wish,' he told Roosevelt, when the latter said that neither the US government nor the US people would accept the Lublin committee as representative (FRUS, 1944, III, 1444). See also FRUS, 1945, I, 165; and Derek J. R. Scott, *Russian Political Institutions* (London 1965), 90–121

4. Printed as Appendix VII

5. FRUS, 1946, VI, 673 (January 3, 1946)

6. *Ibid.* These reports were Kennan's political summaries from Moscow.

7. Andrei Vyshinsky, *The Law of the Soviet State* (New York 1948), 722: 'never in a single country did the people manifest such activity in elections as did the Soviet people,' says Vyshinksy.

8. For the role of the theatre, see Fitzroy Maclean, *Eastern Approaches* (London 1949), 81; for Stalin and music, see Galina Vishnevskaya, *A Russian Story* (London 1985).

9. Svetlana Alliluyeva, *Twenty Letters to a Friend* (London 1967), 37

10. Svetlana Alliluyeva, *Only One Year* (London 1969), 339

11. *The Second World War Diary of Hugh Dalton*, ed. Ben Plimlott (London 1986), 842

12. Milovan Djilas, *Wartime* (London 1983), 386

13. William O. McCagg, *Stalin Embattled* (Detroit 1978), 205

14. Alliluyeva [1:9], 199

15. Averell Harriman in George Urban, *Stalinism* (London 1982), 59

16. Elliot R. Goodman, *The Soviet Design for a World State* (New York 1960), 46

17. B. R. Mitchell, *European Historical Statistics 1750–1970* (London 1975)

18. *Soviet Monitor*, February 10, 1946. I have corrected the translation.

19. Alexander Werth, *Russia at War 1941–1945* (London 1964), 11

20. Alexander Solzhenitsyn, *The Gulag Archipelago*, 3 vols. (London 1974–78), vol. I, 70. For Solzhenitsyn in February 1946, see Michael Scammell, *Solzhenitsyn, a Biography* (London 1985), 208

21. Suetonius, *Lives of the Twelve Caesars*, tr. by Robert Graves (London 1974), 196

22. W. Averell Harriman and Elie Abel, *Special Envoy to Churchill and Stalin, 1941–1946* (New York 1975), 521

23. Eric A. Johnston, *Readers' Digest*, vol. 45, No. 271, November 1944, 1–10; FRUS, 1944, IV, 973–74

24. This is none other than an early version of the 'Brezhnev doctrine'.

25. *Soviet Monitor*, February 10, 1946

26. Naum Korzhavin, qu. Roy Medvedev, *All Stalin's Men* (London 1983), 157

27. *Soviet Monitor*, February 10, 1946

## CHAPTER 2 NATIONAL SOVIETISM

1. Harriman [1:22], 540. This conversation was reported to Harriman by T. V. Soong in Shanghai on January 31, 1946.

2. Milovan Djilas, *Conversations with Stalin* (London 1962), 90, 91

3. See John Lowenhardt, *The Soviet Politburo* (New York 1982)

4. The phrase is that of Boris Nikolaevsky, *Power and the Soviet Elite* (London 1965), 132

5. Nikita Khrushchev, *Khrushchev Remembers*, vol. I (London 1974), 320. Early doubts that this work might be an invention have been allayed.

6. In his 'long telegram' of February 22, 1946 (see page 675)

7. Quoted Merle Fainsod, *How Russia is Ruled* (Harvard 1953), 235

8. Robert Conquest, *Power and Policy in the USSR* (London 1961)

9. Schapiro [1:1], 527

10. Figures in this paragraph are in Fainsod [2:7], 60, 249; for 1905, Adam Ulam, *Lenin and the Bolsheviks* (London 1966), 202

11. Isaiah Berlin, *Personal Impressions* (London 1980), 182

12. Fainsod [2:7], 234

13. Nikita Khrushchev's 'open' speech at the XXth Party Congress, February 1956

14. Fainsod [2:7], 250

15. Nikolaevsky [2:4], 105–119

16. Nikita Khrushchev, Secret Speech to the XXth Party Congress, published as 'The Dethronement of Stalin', by the *Manchester Guardian* (Manchester 1956), 10

17. John Erickson, *The Road to Berlin* (London 1983), 401

18. The best study of the party revival is in McCagg [1:13], *passim*

19. Schapiro [1:1], 75

20. Julius Braunthal, *History of the International*, II, 1914–1943 (London 1967), 541

21. Fainsod [2:7], 42

22. Neil McInnes, *Eurocommunism* (Beverly Hills 1976), 30–39

23. Leszek Kołakowski, *Varieties of Marxism*, 3 vols. (Oxford 1978), vol. 1, 153

24. *Ibid.*, vol. III, 90; Milovan Djilas, in Urban [1:15], 200

25. Alliluyeva [1:10], 177

26. Khrushchev, *Khrushchev Remembers*, vol. II (London 1974), 598

27. These points are developed in Conquest [2:8], 21

28. Solzhenitsyn [1:20], vol. 1, 174

29. Hedrick Smith, *The Russians* (New York 1983), 298

30. For the influence of Hegel, see Isaiah Berlin, *Karl Marx* (London 1939), especially Chapters III and IV

31. For example, in his *Critique of the Gotha Programme*, qu. Schapiro [1:1], 44–45, 208

32. Frederick Engels, *The Origin of the Family, Private Property and the State* (Chicago 1902), 212

33. Frederick Engels, *Herr Dühring's Revolution in Science* (London 1935), 315

34. Frederick Engels and Karl Marx, *The Russian Menace to Europe*, ed. by Paul Blackstock and Bert Hoselitz (London 1953), 28

35. Engels [2:33], 331

36. Karl Marx and Frederick Engels, *The German Ideology* (London 1938), 22

37. Karl Marx, *The Communist Manifesto* (London 1930), 50

38. Qu. Goodman [1:16], 9. For Khrushchev's view of a communist world, see Cyril Black in Thomas Hammond, *Anatomy of Communist Takeovers* (New Haven 1975), xii

39. This was conceded by Marx in a letter to the editor of *Notes on*

*the Fatherland* in 1877, published in Russia in 1886. It was something which he did not mention in *Capital* itself.

40. Fainsod [2:7], 32
41. In collaboration with Engels in 1882, in a new Russian translation of *The Communist Manifesto*, qu. Bertram Wolfe, *Three who made a Revolution* (Briarcliff 1984), 111
42. Preface to second edition of *Communist Manifesto*, qu. Goodman [1:16], 3
43. This summary is based on Kołakowski *Varieties of Marxism*, vols. I and II [2:23]
44. Elie Halévy, *The Era of Tyrannies* (London 1967), 206. Tkachev's fundamental idea was the seizure of power by a 'revolutionary minority'.
45. Otto Kuusinen in *Kommunisti*, Nos. 7–8, July/August 1925, qu. John H. Hodgson, *Communism in Finland* (Princeton 1967), 207
46. J. L. H. Keep, *The Rise of Social Democracy in Russia* (Oxford 1963), 6
47. Schapiro [1:1], 78
48. Schapiro [1:1], 619
49. Report on foreign policy, at All Russia Central Executive Committee of Moscow Soviet, May 14, 1918, V. I. Lenin, *Collected Works*, published in 35 vols. in English (Moscow 1960 onwards), vol. 27, 378
50. The 'Disarmament Slogan', written October 1916, in *ibid.*, vol. 23 (London 1964), 95
51. Speech at the First All-Russia Congress of Workers in Education, July 31, 1919. Published in *ibid.*, vol. 29, 535
52. *Ibid.*, vol. 31, 291, 294; Speech to Komsomol Congress, October 2, 1920.
53. See instances quoted in Kołakowski [2:23], II, 510
54. Lenin, 'Where to begin', in *Iskra* No. 4, May 1901, in *Collected Works* [2:50], vol. 5 (London 1961), 19. It is fair to add that he thought the use of terror inappropriate *then*.
55. Boris Souvarine, *Stalin, a Critical Biography* (London 1937), 251. It is worthwhile looking at his preface to his new edition, published Paris 1985, to see the difficulties which he met earlier in having this volume published.
56. Robert Tucker in Urban [1:15], 165
57. N. Krupskaya and others, *Souvenirs sur Lénine* (Paris 1956). See George Orwell's comment in *Collected Essays, Journalism and Letters* (London 1968), IV, 23
58. Souvarine [2:55], 355

59. Speech opening the eleventh Congress of the RCP(B), March 27, 1922, in *Collected Works* [2:49], vol. 33, 288

60. Milovan Djilas, *Memoir of a Revolutionary* (New York 1973), 276. Gorbachev in 1985 during his visit to France denied that 'Stalinism' had ever existed.

61. Souvarine (2:55), 308

62. Djilas, in Urban [1:15], 212. The first to speak of 'Leninism' were the enemies of Bolshevism in 1903 who counterposed Lenin's ideas against those of Marx. Zinoviev discussed those expressions in 1924 in his lectures on 'Leninism': see Fernando Claudín, *La crisis del movimento comunista* (Paris 1970) 95–96.

63. Annie Kriegel, *The French Communists* (Chicago 1972), 350; Nicolas Berdyaev, *Origins of Russian Communism* (Ann Arbor 1948), 41

64. Qu. in Schapiro [1:1], 385, from the memoir of 'N. Valentinov', to whom Piatakov made the remark.

65. Isaiah Berlin, *Personal Impressions* (London 1980), 170

66. Edward Crankshaw, *Khrushchev* (London 1966)

67. Lenin, actually quoting from Pasadovsky (an 'Iskra-ist of the minority'), in 'One step forward, two steps back', published in book form Geneva May, 1904, in *Collected Works* [2:49], vol. 7 (London 1961), 227.

68. Kołakowski [2:23], III, 97

69. Lenin, report of the Central Committee, to the Eighth Congress of the RCP(B), March 18, 1919, in *Collected Works* [2:49], vol. 29 (London 1965), 153

70. Lenin, July 4, 1920: 'Theses on Comintern fundamental tasks' in *Collected Works* [2:49], vol. 31, 186–87

71. Alexander Herzen, qu. Souvarine [2:55], 675

72. Maxim Gorki, *Life of a Useless Man*, tr. by Moura Budberg (London 1975), 51

73. Richard Pipes, *Russia under the Old Regime* (London 1974), 313–14

74. Vasili Klyuchevsky, *Peter the Great*, tr. Liliana Archibald (London 1958)

75. Pipes [2:73], 94

76. Ulam in Urban [1:15], *Stalinism*, 150

77. A. Leroy Beaulieu, cited Souvarine [2:55], 108

78. Edward Crankshaw, introduction to *Khrushchev* [2:26], 8

79. See Solzhenitsyn's *Letter to the Soviet Leaders* (London 1974), 147: 'Cast off this cracked ideology, relinquish it to your rivals'.

80. As it is put by Robert Tucker in Urban [1:15], 160

81. Kołakowski, in *ibid.*, 262
82. Robert Tucker in *ibid.*, 170–71
83. Count Raczyński in Michael Charlton, *The Eagle and the Small Birds* (London 1984), 18
84. Kołakowski [2:23], III, 241

CHAPTER 3 THE VOZHD

1. Bertrand Russell, *Freedom and Organisation* (London 1934), 431
2. Djilas [2:2], 171
3. Harriman [1:22], 536
4. Solzhenitsyn [1:20], II, 279
5. Djilas [2:2], 171
6. Adam Ulam, *Stalin and his era* (London 1974)
7. Robert Tucker in Urban [1:15], 172
8. Sir Alexander Cadogan, *Diaries of, 1938–1945* (edited by David Dilkes), 709
9. Robert Sherwood, *Roosevelt and Hopkins: an intimate history* (New York 1948), 2 vols, vol. I, 345
10. *Ibid.*, 392
11. Roy Medvedev, *Let History Judge* (London 1972), 547
12. Charles Bohlen, *Witness to History 1929–1961* (London 1973)
13. Winston S. Churchill, T*riumph and Tragedy* (London 1954), 206
14. Winston S. Churchill, *The Hinge of Fate* (London 1951), 440
15. Sir Llewellyn Woodward, *British Foreign Policy in the Second World War* (London 1970–76), III, 231
16. Sherwood [3:9], 346
17. Eduard Táborský in Charlton [2:83], 70
18. Sherwood [3:9], 390
19. Ulam [3:6], 560
20. Alliluyeva [1:10], 369
21. Ulam [3:6], 430
22. Sir William Hayter, *The Kremlin and the Embassy* (London, 1966), 29
23. James Byrnes, *Speaking Frankly* (New York 1947), 45. Anthony Eden also felt for Stalin 'a sympathy which I have never been entirely able to analyse' (Robert Rhodes James, *Anthony Eden*, London 1986, 144) while General Marshall thought him 'direct and reliable' (Joseph Davies Diaries, May 23, 1945).
24. Dalton [1:11], 349
25. This was Gladwyn Jebb. *Ibid.*, 843

26. Anton Antonov-Ovseenko, *The Time of Stalin* (New York 1980), 245

27. Djilas [2:2], 58

28. Djilas in Charlton [2:83], 92

29. John Morton Blum, *The Price of Vision, the Diary of Henry A. Wallace* (Boston 1973), 548

30. *Ibid.*, 172

31. Sherwood [3:9], 391; Walter Bedell Smith, *Moscow Mission* (London 1950), 38, believed the wolves to be 'lop-sided hearts'.

32. Solomon Volkov, *Testimony: The memoirs of Shostakovitch* (London 1979), 104

33. The only worthwhile picture is in Alliluyeva [1:9], 213 though there is also a chapter in Achmed Amba, *I was Stalin's bodyguard* (London 1952).

34. Nadezhda Mandelstam, *Hope Against Hope* (London 1971), 13

35. Antonov-Ovseenko [3:26], 230; Khrushchev [2:5], I, 323. There are rumours that Stalin was the illegitimate son of the explorer Nikolai Przhevalsky. See Alex de Jonge, *Stalin* (London 1986), 23.

36. Souvarine [2:55], 9

37. Baedeker's *Russia* (London 1914), 468

38. Souvarine [2:55], 168. Most great Russian writers went to Georgia; many young Russian officers went there to prove their virility.

39. Alliluyeva [1:10], 312

40. Hugh Seton-Watson, *The Russian Empire* (Oxford 1967), 363. Berdyaev made a slightly different point: 'among the seminarists of the second half of the 'fifties, and the beginning of the 'sixties, a violent protest against the decadent Orthodoxy of the nineteenth century was coming to a head' (Berdyaev, 48).

41. Souvarine [2:55], 191. There are other variations of the tale: cf. Boris Bajanov (Bazhanov) in Urban, *Stalinism* [1:15], 15–16. Those present when he spoke were, apparently, Dzerzhinsky and Kamenev.

42. For this skilful survivor, see his *Bajanov révèle Stalin* (Paris, 1979) and Gordon Brook-Shepherd, *The Storm Petrels* (London 1977), 19–84

43. Souvarine [2:55], 113; also Sverdlov, in Ulam [3:19], 129

44. N. N. Sukhanov, *The Russian Revolution 1917*. Abridged and edited by Joel Carmichael (London 1955), 230

45. Souvarine [2:55], 35

46. Engels in *Russian Menace* [2:34], 76

47. Harriman, in Urban [1:15], 55
48. Most of these descriptions derive from one or other of Svetlana Alliluyeva's books.
49. Popovíc in Vladimir Dedijer, *Tito speaks* (London 1953), 282
50. Djilas [3:2], 63
51. Khrushchev [2:5], I, 322
52. Khrushchev [2:5], 322. When with the Western leaders, Stalin often had his glass filled with water from a special decanter, on the pretence that it was vodka, as did his marshals on occasion. (See Charles Thayer, *Hands across the Caviar* (London 1953), 114
53. Teresa Toranska, 'They' (in *Granta*, 17, Autumn 1985), 48
54. Dedijer [3:49], 283
55. *Ibid.*, 281
56. Sherwood [3:9], I, 345
57. Djilas [2:2], 52
58. Robert Tucker, *Stalin as Revolutionary* (New York 1973), 132
59. The Alliluyev Memoirs (ed. by David Tutaev) (London 1968), 224
60. Cadogan [3:8], 706
61. Alliluyeva [1:10], *Only One Year*, 361
62. *Ibid.*, 350
63. Djilas [2:2], 85
64. For a discussion of numbers who died during the 'agricultural revolution' see Raphael Abramovich, *The Soviet Revolution 1917–1939* (London 1962), 345
65. Qu. Isaac Deutscher, *Stalin* (London 1961), 330 (March 2, 1930)
66. Stefan Staszewski in Toranska [3:53], 66
67. Hodgson [2:45], 47
68. Djilas [2:2], 85. He said the same to Roosevelt at Teheran: Sherwood [3:9], 777
69. Alliluyeva [1:10], 357
70. Khrushchev [2:16], in *Secret Speech*, 20
71. The theory of the 'weakest link' gave rise to a polemic between Stalin and Bukharin. See Goodman [1:16], 59
72. Medvedev, *Let history judge*, 501
73. Speech of November 6, 1941, qu. Deutscher [3:65], 468
74. Bohlen [3:12], 343
75. *Izvestiia*, July 3, 1941, qu. Alfred Rieber, *Stalin and the French Communist Party* (New York 1962), 6
76. FRUS, 1945, V, 826–29
77. Sherwood [3:9], 880

78. A remark when playing billiards with his brother-in-law, Alyosha Svanidze, quoted by Antonov-Ovseenko [3:26], 223

79. Vishnevskaya [1:7], 172

80. E. H. Carr, *The Bolshevik Revolution* (Oxford 1954 onwards), vol. III, 56

81. For a military assessment (by Alanbrooke) see Arthur Bryant, *Triumph in the West* (London 1954), 90–92

82. But see, for example, 'Un Caligula au Kremlin', in *Est et Ouest*, No. 98, November 1953 and No. 102, January 1954, by Nicolas Volski ('Valentinov') and Boris Souvarine.

## Chapter 4 HOMO STALIENS

1. Roy Medvedev, *All Stalin's Men* (Oxford 1983), 132

2. *Ibid.*, 348

3. Vishnevskaya [1:7], 117

4. Qu. in Nadezhda Mandelstam, *Hope Against Hope* (London 1971), 13: Beria was, however, of a usual size, apparently.

5. Arthur M. Schlesinger Jr., *A Thousand Days* (London 1965), 776

6. For instances of Molotov's personal brutality, see Medvedev [4:1], 345–46

7. Blum [3:29], 210

8. Sherwood [3:9], 563

9. Djilas [3:2], 66–67

10. Harrison Salisbury, *A journey for our times* (New York 1983), Werth [1:19] 753

11. Qu. Werth [1:19], 62–63

12. Sir Nicholas Henderson, *The Private Office* (London 1984), 46

13. Harold Macmillan, *War Diaries The Mediterranean 1942–45* (London 1985), 308; Maclean [1:8], 85: 'and play golf at Sunningdale every weekend'.

14. Ulam [3:6], 89

15. Antonov-Ovseenko [3:26], 239

16. Bohlen [3:12], 48

17. Solzhenitsyn [1:20], I, 34–35

18. Bohlen [3:12], 48. For a communist's reflection on these trials see Ernst Fischer, *An Opposing Man* (London 1974), 304–21.

19. George Kennan, *Memoirs 1924–1950* (London 1968), 39

20. *Report of Court Proceedings in the Case of the Anti-Soviet 'Bloc of Rightists and Trotskyites'* (Moscow 1938), 333, qu. Robert Conquest, *The Great Terror* (London 1968)

21. Bohlen [3:12], 181
22. Robert Murphy, *Diplomat among Warriors* (London 1964), 265
23. Bohlen [3:12], 48
24. Impressions of Mrs Babesi, the Russian born wife of the Romanian counsellor in Moscow, March 8, 1945, in FO 371/56782 N4160/140/38 (PRO)
25. PRO: PREM 4/24/5, 951. Churchill took Vyshinsky's word for it that Croce was unreadable! (Warren Kimball, *Churchill and Roosevelt: the complete correspondence*, three vols. (Princeton 1984), II, 56
26. Private information; Volkov [3:32], xxiv
27. See Conquest [1:2], 98 and Salisbury [4:10] 218–19, referring to samizdat memoirs by Litvinov's former secretary, Yevgeny Gnedin
28. Sherwood [3:9], 391
29. FRUS, 1943, III, 522–24
30. FDR asked Litvinov this time if he was prepared to abandon the League of Nations in favour of these ideas. 'Anything for the common cause', was his reply (Robert Divine, *Second Chance*, New York 1971), 86: this is the best study of the growth of US internationalism during the Second World War.
31. PRO: FO 371/47855; Maclean [1:8], 28
32. Harriman [1:22], 518; and FRUS, 1945, V, 921
33. Edgar Snow, *Journey to the Beginning* (London 1959), 357
34. See Frank Roberts's report of this private talk in FO 371/56833 B8027/605/38 (PRO)
35. See Vojtech Mastny 'The Cassandra in the Foreign Commissariat', *Foreign Affairs*, January 1976; 366–76, and, for 1947, Werth [1:19], 938. Ivy Litvinov told Mastny that these conversations were inconceivable.
36. Khrushchev, II [2:26], 262
37. Arkady Shevchenko, in Charlton [2:83], 139
38. See Salisbury [4:10], 232–37, where he is described as having 'dark hair and a broad face'; and Walter Bedell Smith [3:31], 31, where he is credited with 'blue eyes, blond hair and a pale face'.
39. Snow [4:33], 314
40. Djilas [2:2], 86
41. Nikolaevsky [2:4], 109; Medvedev [3:11], 348
42. Khrushchev [2:5], I, 114
43. *Ibid.*, 118
44. *Moscow News*, 22 February 1941, qu. Conquest [2:8], 89

45. Robert Slusser (ed.), *Soviet economic policy in post-war Germany* (New York 1953), 41–42
46. Djilas [2:2], 86
47. Khrushchev [2:5], I, 396
48. Bohlen [3:12], 370
49. Alliluyeva [1:10], 341
50. Khrushchev [2:5], I, 335–36
51. Alliluyeva [1:9], 16
52. Djilas [2:2], 100
53. Nikolaevsky [2:4], 113
54. Conquest [1:2], 107
55. Thaddaeus Wittlin, *Commissar, the Life and Death of Lavrenty Pavlovich Beria* (London 1973), 133–34
56. Khrushchev [2:5], I, 143
57. *Ibid.*, 337
58. FRUS, 1946, VI, 817. Perhaps this was because of its scientific responsibilities.
59. Alliluyeva [1:10], 354
60. Khrushchev, [2:5] I, 121
61. Khrushchev, [2:26] II, 91
62. The most extreme example of this is perhaps in 1941 when Beria took Stalin's side in misinterpreting German troop movements toward the East (*Memoirs of General Grigorenko*, qu. de Jonge [3:35]), 39
63. Conquest, *Inside*, 89
64. Nikolai Krasnov, *The Hidden Russia, my ten years as a slave laborer* (New York 1960), 72. This book deserves to be better known.
65. 'A. I. Romanov', *The Nights are Longest There* (London 1972), 238
66. Leopold Trepper, *The Great Game* (London 1977), 36
67. *Ibid.*, 367
68. PRO: F0371/47709 N2016
69. In a paper 'SOE-NKVD co-operation' there is the comment: 'A general rising, as distinct from resistance, can only be set in motion on the instructions of the Soviet Government and it will be for them to decide whether, and if so, when it will be required' (FO 371/47709 N2016/265/G55) (PRO)
70. See letter from Henry Sporborg to Christopher Warner in PRO: FO 371/47710 N4771.
71. Interview with Foreign Workers Delegation, qu. Fainsod [2:7], 423

72. Fainsod [2:7], 423–24
73. For an imaginative attempt at a life, see Thaddaeus Wittlin, *Commissar* [4:55]
74. *Ibid.*, 98; Alliluyeva [1:9], 148
75. Krushchev [2:5], I, 119–21, 330
76. Wittlin [4:55], 89
77. Medvedev [3:11], 243
78. L. Trotsky, *My Life* (New York 1930), 341
79. PRO: FO 371/4985 2M 5387
80. Corrigan to Washington, NA: 711061/4–1646. Since the Russians looked on foreign embassies in Moscow as centres of espionage, they saw no reason why they should not use their own service for that purpose. During the war the Soviet embassy in Washington went to great lengths to lobby individuals who might help them in their various designs. See Hazard in R. Dennett and J. Johnson, editors, *Negotiating with the Russians* (Boston 1951), 41
81. Ernst B. Haas and Allen S. Whiting, *Dynamics of International Relations* (New York 1956), 326. These telegrams were intercepted by the Japanese Government's consul in Harbin, 'we concluded an Agreement with Germany because a war is required in Europe', the telegram concludes.
82. Qu. Goodman [1:16], 169
83. Carr [3:80], III, 451
84. 'Lavotchka': Walter Krivitsky, *I was Stalin's Agent*, (New York 1940), 92. Claudín points out that Stalin mentioned the Comintern in speeches only twice after 1933, once ironically (in 1939), once when he ended it (1943). Fernando Claudín, 90
85. Wolfgang Leonhard, *Child of the Revolution* (New translation 1979) (London 1979), 218. The text of the declaration and favourable statements by e.g. Willkie and Eric Johnston are in the *New York Times*, May 23, 1943
86. Tom Connally and Alfred Steinberg, *My name is Tom Connally* (New York 1954)
87. May 23, 1943. See Claudín [2:62], 403, for a summary of the press.
88. For the view that the dissolution was genuine, on the grounds that the Comintern had finished its task, see Claudín, 18. Ernst Fischer said that it took years to understand that the real significance meant that 'the old concept of world revolution had in fact been superseded by a new concept – that of Russia as a world empire (Fischer [4:18], 401)
89. Leonhard [4:85], 253
90. Antonin Liehm, in George Urban, *The Communist Reformation*

(London 1979), 77. Earl Browder gave the transcript of discussions in the American Communist Party in January 1944 to Dimitrov in Moscow: see Joseph R. Starobin, *American Communism in Crisis 1943–1957* (Cambridge, Mass. 1972), 74

91. Other comments about the continuity of the system can be seen in Alfred Burmeister, *Dissolution and Aftermath of the Comintern* (New York 1955) and Enrique Castro Delgado, *Mi fe se perdió en Moscú* (Barcelona 1964), 258. The argument of Burmeister, who worked in the Comintern in 1937, was then sent with other Polish communists to the camps, and returned in 1945 to join the Polish embassy in Moscow, was that the institution was essentially destroyed in the late 1930s and was formally dissolved to enable the establishment of 'a more complex network designed to serve the same purpose'. See also Guzenko's evidence at the Canadian enquiry, where he testified that the abolition was 'the greatest farce', *Report of the Royal Commission (Canada) to investigate the facts relating to and the circumstances surrounding the communications, by public officials and other persons in positions of trust of secret and confidential information to agents of a foreign power June 27, 1946* (Ottawa 1946).

92. Djilas, *Memoir* [2:60], *passim*

93. Braunthal [2:20], 537–42. Lenin's views about the British Communists were revealing. They never understood why he wanted them to join the Labour Party and trade unions because they wanted open revolution.

94. Starobin [4:90], 31. See also for a good general picture Allen Weinstein, *Perjury: the Hiss Chambers Case* (London 1978), especially Chapter VI

95. Vladimir Lenin, *'Left-wing' Communism, an infantile disorder* (New York 1978), 38

96. William Deakin and G. R. Storry, *The Case of Richard Sorge* (London 1966), 41

97. See *The Rote Kappelle*: the CIA's history of Soviet intelligence and espionage networks in Western Europe 1936–1945 (Washington 1974); Nissan Oren, *Bulgarian Communism, the Road to Power 1934–1944* (New York 1971), 183–84

98. Djilas [2:60]

99. Igor Gouzenko (usually Guzenko), *This was my choice* (London 1948), 74

100. For the general history of Soviet penetration, see David Dallin, *Soviet Espionage* (New Haven 1955)

101. PRO: FO 371/60657 2M 382/382/22 Minute dated March 21,

1946. Burgess was private secretary to the Minister of State, Hector McNeil, for whom he prepared 'briefs on important subjects such as Stalinism' (Sulzberger [8:81], 571)

102. Weinstein makes this case convincingly.

103. For Maclean and the Persian crisis of March 1946, see pages 714–15, below. For Maclean as the 'almost too-perfect pattern of the trained diplomatist', see Sir John Balfour, *Not too correct an aureole* (Salisbury 1983), 43

104. Stettinius noted in his diary, *The diaries of Edward Stettinius*, edited by Thomas Campbell and George Herring (New York 1975), 416, that the Soviet ambassador to the US, Andrei Gromyko, told him that 'he would be very happy to see Alger Hiss appointed temporary secretary general (to UN) as he had a very high regard for him'.

105. Private information

106. M. Toscano, *Designs in Diplomacy* (Baltimore 1970), qu. David Dilkes, ed. *Retreat from Power* (London 1981), 151

107. James Callaghan in the House of Commons, November 21, 1979, on the occasion of the discussions about the case of Professor Anthony Blunt (Hansard, vol. 974, col. 504)

108. J. W. Pickersgill (and D. F. Forster), *The Mackenzie King Record*, 4 vols. (Toronto 1960–1970), vol. III, 13; Report of the Royal Commission lists the names and backgrounds (57–58)

109. David Rees, *Harry Dexter White* (London 1974), 22; Weinstein [4:94], 237–40; Morgenthau, Diaries, III, 89; Robert J. Lamphere, *The FBI–KGB War* (New York 1986), 283–85. For a defence of White, see I. F. Stone, *The Truman Era* (London 1953), 48–50

110. Sir Roy Harrod, *The Life of John Maynard Keynes* (London 1951), 537–41

111. Blum [3:29], 27

112. W. D. General Staff: 'The influence of Brigadier General Faymonville', in private papers of General 'Pa' Watson, University of Virginia, qu. Anthony Cave Brown and Charles B. Macdonald, *On a field of Red* (New York 1981), 336–37

113. Blum [3:29], 314

114. *Ibid.*, 315–16

115. Salisbury [4:10], 150; Sherwood [3:9], 397

116. See Robert Manne, 'The fortunes of Wilfred Burchetti', *Quadrant*, August 1985. I benefited from a discussion about the matters raised here with Mr Iverach Macdonald.

117. Raymond Radosh and Joyce Milton, *The Rosenberg File* (New

York 1983). In the same position, there was Fred Rose (born Rosenberg, in Russian Poland) the Communist party's organiser in Ottawa and a member of parliament; Sam Carr (born Kogan in the Ukraine), the Communist party organiser in Canada; and Jacob Golos (born Rasin in Ukraine), who ran a spy-ring in New York. See too Harry Rositske, *KGB, Eyes of Russia* (London 1982) and Roger Anders, 'The Rosenberg case revisited', *American Historical Review*, vol. 83, 2 (April 1978)

118. Maxim Gorki [2:72], 103. Most of the early Bolsheviks grew up in this atmosphere of conspiracy and were always conscious of the likelihood of penetration, by the Tsarist police.

119. Trepper [4:66], 103; Deakin and Storry [4:96], 351

120. Ulam [3:6], 611; Woodward [3:15], V, 376; Allen Dulles, *The Secret Surrender* (London 1967), 109, and 146–47, makes the point that the Russians received the report anyway *via* the Joint Chiefs of Staff. Stalin suggested that the Soviet Union should be represented by three generals who would have been difficult to secrete in wartime Switzerland. Stalin's anger may have been caused by the fact that any German surrender in Italy would have prevented Tito's forces from driving across Northern Italy to join up with French communists from coming to fruition. This is discussed in Silvio Bertoldi, *Gli Tedeschi in Italia*, Milano 1964, 186–87, and may have bearing on the Carinthia-Klagenfurt crisis.

121. Arnold Kramish, *Atomic Energy in the Soviet Union* (Stanford 1959), 66

122. See page 677. This is surely the most important of all points in dealing with the Soviet Union to remember.

123. Erickson [2:17], 152–54

124. Trepper [4:66], 130–31

125. See Christopher Andrew, *Secret Service* (London 1985), 427; Bohlen [3:12], 82

126. David Smiley, *Albanian assignment* (London 1984), 134

127. Trepper [4:66], 130–31; Alexander Foote, *Handbook for Spies* (London 1964), 155

128. Robert Cecil in Christopher Andrew and David Dilkes (ed.), *The missing dimension* (London 1984)

129. Private information from a retired member of that service.

130. Bohlen [3:12], 270

131. *Loc. cit.*

132. See George Lenczowski, *Russia and the West in Iran 1918–45* (Ithaca 1949). One weakness of Soviet espionage was its mistrustfulness: Alexander Foote described how, when the agent 'Rado'

had, in 1942, documents which would have been of value to the British as well as to the Russians, the material was so bulky that it was impossible to pass it to the latter by radio. 'Rado' suggested it be given to the British for shipment to Moscow. He received instructions to burn it all. If he could not pass it to Moscow direct, it had to be destroyed. Foote described his superiors as men among whom 'treachery, double-crossing, and betrayal were second nature' (Foote [4:127], 123, 150). There was also confusion: Guzenko says that there were nine separate intelligence networks in Canada operating directly to Moscow (*op. cit.* 242)

## CHAPTER 5  RUSSIA IN 1946

1. R. Pipes, *Communism and Russian History* (New York 1967), 14
2. Morton Schwartz, *The Foreign Policy of the USSR, domestic factors* (Encino, California 1975), 21–22
3. Qu. Goodman [1:16], 90
4. Boris Pasternak, *Dr Zhivago* (Fontana edition, London 1968), 555–56
5. Leonhard [4:85], 121
6. See Nicolas Timasheff, *Religion in Soviet Russia* (London 1943), 136
7. Bedell Smith [3:31], 37
8. Alexander Dallin, *German rule in Russia* (Wisconsin 2nd ed. 1981)
9. Qu. *ibid.*, 153. See also Johnnie von Herwarth, *Against Two Evils* (London 1981), 230, and Herwarth's remark to Charles Thayer: 'I don't know if we could ever really have conquered Russia but if Hitler had not been so stupid at least we might have destroyed Stalin' (Thayer [3:52], 171)
11. Dallin [5:8], 511. See page 248, for General Gehlen's comment on this 'error of the most grievous kind'.
12. Goodman [1:16], 108
13. Werth [1:19], 1003
14. This is a subject discussed in Vojtech Mastny, *Russia's Road to the Cold War* (New York 1979), an excellent work from which I have learned much.
15. James C. Hagerty, *The diary of:* (edited by Robert Ferrell) (Indiana University Press 1983), 191–92
16. Khrushchev, *Secret Speech* [2:16], 22
17. Antonov-Ovseenko [3:26], 292
18. Djilas [2:2], 132

19. PRO: FO 371/47917 N1 4101/558338
20. Malcolm Mackintosh, *Juggernaut: a history of the Soviet Armed Forces* (London 1967), 271
21. Kennan despatch, September 8, 1952, qu. 331–35, in his memoirs, vol. II (Boston 1972)
22. Harry Schwartz, *An Introduction to the Soviet Economy*, (Columbus, Ohio 1968), 21 (All figures rounded).
23. Qu. Alex Nove, *An Economic History of the USSR* (London 1969), 387
24. Fainsod [2:7], 101–3
25. Basil Liddell Hart, *History of the Second World War* (London 1970), 158
26. Roger Munting, *The Economic Development of the USSR* (London 1982), 117
27. FRUS, 1945, V, 844
28. Bruce Kuniholm, *Origins of the Cold War in the Near East* (Princeton 1980), 206 fn 181
29. Dallin [5:8], 426–27
30. Estimated figures in Dallin [5:8], 452. The most moving account of one of these slave labourers is in Zoë Polanska-Palmer's *Yalta Victim* (Edinburgh 1986)
31. Solzhenitsyn [1:20], I, 218
32. Sherwood [3:9], 562. This treatment of Russians exposed to the West had an echo of the realisation in the 1820s that the conspirators of 1825 came from members of secret officers' societies which sprang up at the end of the Napoleonic Wars.
33. See David Dallin and Borish Nikolaevsky, *Forced Labour in Soviet Russia* (New Haven 1947), 86
34. Frederick Engels in 'Democratic Slavism' in Marx and Engels *Russian Menace* [2:34], 70
35. Medvedev [3:11], 239
36. Secret speech [2:16], 23
37. For an account of Lithuanians as displaced persons, see J. A. Swettenham, *The Tragedy of the Baltic States* (London 1952), esp. 155–57
38. Erickson [2:17], 11
39. Recollection of the late Tibor Szamuely
40. A summary can be seen in *Ukraine, a Concise Encyclopaedia* (Toronto 1963) 2 vols., vol. I, 900–2
41. Harry Rositske, *The CIA's Secret Operations* (Readers' Digest Press 1977), 160–68
42. Figures in Fainsod [2:7], 541

43. Merle Fainsod, *Smolensk under Soviet rule* (London 1958), 248
44. *Ibid.*, 241
45. PRO: Frank Roberts' despatch, October 22, 1945
46. Khrushchev [2:5], I, 251
47. Dallin [5:8], 326–27
48. Fainsod [2:7], 535–36
49. Arnold Kramish [4:121]
50. Malcolm Mackintosh and Harry Willetts, 'Disarmament and Soviet Military Politics', in Louis Henkin, ed., *Arms Control* (Englewood Cliffs 1961), 144
51. John Prados, *The Soviet Estimate* (New York 1982), 38
52. There was then an element of barbarism in the Russian character which, if it should not be overstressed, should not be forgotten. Two illustrations will suffice: first, in Belgrade, in 1945 a Russian soldier was shot by an American military policeman for looting a shop. An American officer apologised. A Russian officer replied: 'Never mind, there are lots of us'. Second, in Bucharest in the late 1940s, the senior American general wished to assist a famine stricken region and asked the Russian command to help. General Susaikov laughed: 'Of course, I won't join you. We have famines in parts of Russia almost every year. The weak die, the strong survive. That is nature's way'. *Absit omen.* Petrovich in Thomas Hammond, *Witnesses to the Origins of the Cold War* (Seattle 1982), 41; General Schuyler, in *ibid.*, 154.

## Chapter 6 RUSSIA'S INTERNATIONAL POLICY

1. *Letters of Frederick the Great*, ed. Boutaric, II, 335, qu. Albert Sorel, *Europe and the French Revolution*, tr. by Alfred Cobban and J. W. Hunt (London 1969), 498. The Gepids were an ancient East German tribe who set up a kingdom in Dacia.
2. Frederick the Great, *Mémoires*, qu. *loc. cit.*
3. Qu. Harold Nicolson, *Congress of Vienna* (London 1946), 81 and 296
4. Heinrich Heine, *Works of Prose*, ed. by Hermann Kesten (New York 1943), 161
5. Qu. Norman Stone, *Europe Transformed* (London 1983), 197
6. Hugh Seton-Watson, in George Urban [4:90], 133
7. Sir Frank Roberts's comment in PRO: FO 371/56763 NA 4156/97/38
8. Qu. G. H. Bolsover, in Richard Pares and A. J. P. Taylor, *Essays for Namier* (London 1956), 322

9. Louis Eisenmann, *Le compromis austro-hongrois de 1867* (Paris 1904)

10. Robert A. Goldwin, ed., *Readings in Russian Foreign Policy* (New York 1959), 74

11. Paul Kennedy, *Strategy and Diplomacy* (London 1983), 46, 50

12. Qu. Mastny [5:14], 10

13. See Robert E. MacMaster, *Danilevsky: a Russian Totalitarian Philosopher* (Cambridge, Mass. 1967)

14. *Izvestiia*, December 25, 1918, qu. Goodman [1:16], 294. Berdyaev [2:63] wrote: 'Marxism, itself so un-Russian in origin, and character, assumed a Russian style, an oriental style approaching Slavophilism' (*Origin of Russian Communism*, 141)

15. Kennan [4:19], 522

16. Lenin, speech of July 26, 1918, in *Collected Works* [2:49], vol. 27, 551 (speech to a meeting in Khamovniki district)

17. Speech of Iuri Steklov, July 10, 1918, qu. Goodman [1:16], 30

18. The Soviet Union expanded in the East in the 1920s to make a satellite of the small territory of Tannu Tuva and Outer Mongolia, as well as to re-absorb Georgia. As Thomas Hammond says (*Anatomy* [2:38], 107) the West should not have forgotten Outer Mongolia, the only communist expansion between the wars

19. R. J. Sontag and J. S. Beddie (eds.), *Nazi-Soviet Relations 1939–1941: Documents from the Archives of the German Foreign Office* (Washington 1948), 222. This volume is the best chronicle of the two terrible years 1939–41 when Hitler and Stalin in collaboration dominate the Eurasian landmass.

20. *The Times*, October 2, 1939

21. Woodward [3:15], II, 592

22. *Ibid.*

23. Message to Churchill, June 12, 1944, in Kimball [4:25], 11, 183

24. Churchill, *Triumph and Tragedy* [3:13], 227

25. PREM 3.434/4 (PRO). For discussion, see *American Historical Review*, April 1978, Albert Resis, 'The Churchill-Stalin Percentages Agreement on the Balkans'. Churchill went to some lengths in *Triumph and Tragedy* (197) to insist that the plan was only meant to cover wartime arrangements. Despite the fact that William Deakin, who worked on Churchill's memoirs, has argued that the agreement was only 'a trial balloon', it really seems to have been more like a 'comprehensive informal understanding'

in which Britain gained (1) a temporary extension of the three-month Anglo-Soviet agreement, giving Britain a lead in Greece, and the Soviet Union the lead in Romania; and, (2) an understanding that Stalin would not back Bulgaria's territorial ambitions, at Greece's expense (and at Yugoslavia's). The other countries were not so nicely affected. Soviet historians later denied Stalin could have accepted such old-fashioned proposals

26. Speech on the 27th anniversary of the Bolshevik Revolution, November 6, 1944 (Moscow 1944), 20

27. *Bolshevik*, October 1944, article by Solodovnikov, qu. Werth [1:19], 942

28. *Zvezda*, September 27, 1944, qu. *ibid.*, 944

29. Erickson [2:17], II, 402–3

30. Fainsod [2:7], 114

31. Sherwood [3:9], 837

32. This is Lynn Ethridge Davis's interpretation (*The Cold War begins*, Princeton 1974)

33. FRUS 1945, *Yalta*, 93–101, 603. Stalin remarked at Potsdam: 'A freely elected government in any of these countries would be anti-Soviet and that we cannot allow': a remark made in the hearing of Philip Mosely; see his *Face to Face with Russia* (New York 1948), 23. For a precisely contrary remark, to Mikołajczyk, see Chapter 12, 133

33[A] Actually, as Thomas Hammond says (*Witnesses* [5:52], 296) that was not quite so. See also Herbert Feis, *From Trust to Terror* (London 1970), 22, for Stalin's motives.

34. Comment to the author by Sir Frank Roberts

35. This 'mystifying' article is in *Cahiers du Communisme*, April, 1945, and is discussed on page 244, below. For a disintoxicating view, see William Taubman, *Stalin's American Policy* (New York 1982), 98. *The Daily Worker* published on May 24, 1945. See commentary by Starobin [4:90], 86 and 272.

36. The author was Chuvikov, qu. Rieber [3:75], 192

37. Leonhard [4:85]

38. E. Iaroslavskii, in July 1945, qu. Rieber [3:75], 202

39. In *Bolshevik*, No. 16, 31, 35, qu. Rieber [3:75], 202–5

40. Published in *Bolshevik* and discussed by Frederick Barghorn, 'The Soviet Union between War and Cold War', in a special number, 'The Soviet Union since World War Two' of the *Annals of the American Academy of Political and Social Science*, vol. 263, May 1949, 4

41. Rieber's argument, 235 [3:75]

42. *Partiinoe Stroitel'stvo*, No. 5, qu. McCagg [1:13], 111–14. This was a monthly journal for provincial party officials.
43. *Pravda*, September 16, 1945, qu. Rieber [3:75]
44. Woodward [3:15], V, 405
45. McCagg [1:13], 205
46. See Stalin's article of January 21, 1905, qu. Goodman [1:16], 93
47. FRUS, 1945, V, 889–91
48. McCagg [1:13], 192–93
49. FRUS, 1945, V, 914
50. McCagg [1:13], 162–63
51. Alliluyeva [1:9], 194. Interpretation of Lord Hankey, then in the British Embassy, Warsaw.
52. NA: 711.61/12–1245, December 12, 1945
53. I. Lemin in *Mirovoe Khoziaistvo i Mirovaia Politika*, Nos. 1 and 2, January–February, 1946, qu. Rieber [3:75], 258
54. Report to the Fifteenth Congress of the CPSU(B), December 3, 1927, in J. V. Stalin, *Collected Works*, vol. 10 (Moscow 1954), 295
55. *Pravda*, March 5, 1936, 2, qu. Goodman [1:16], 176
56. 'Lenin's well known principle regarding the co-existence of the Soviet state and capitalist countries', Molotov describes it (*Pravda*, September 1, 1939, p. 1. Qu. Goodman [1:16], 176)
57. Thomas B. Trout, *Soviet Foreign Policy-Making and the Cold War* (PhD dissertation, Indiana University), qu. McCagg [1:13], 91 and 150
58. Alan Bullock, *Ernest Bevin, Foreign Secretary, 1945–51* (London 1983), 210
59. Byrnes [3:23], 228
60. McCagg [1:13], 232
61. PRO: FO 181/1922 197/1/46
62. John Lewis Gaddis, *The United States and the Origins of the Cold War* (New York 1972), 354–55, an outstanding work, for an astute summary
63. Robert A. Pollard, *Economic Security and the Origins of the Cold War* (New York 1985), 40. A lucid book
64. Goodman [1:16], 128
65. Volkov [3:32], 111
66. Talk with Emil Ludwig, December 13, 1931, in *Collected Works*, 13 (Moscow 1955), 116–17
67. *Stalin-Wells Talk*, with commentary by Bernard Shaw, Maynard Keynes, Dora Russell, and Ernst Toller (London 1934), 11

## BOOK TWO
## THE WEST

CHAPTER 7 THE COMING OF ENTANGLING ALLIANCES

1. Sir John Colville, *The Fringes of Power* (London 1985), 346–47. Hopkins did not, apparently, record the occasion.
2. Henry Steele Commager, *Documents of American History* (Englewood Cliffs 1973), 2 vols, I, 174
3. *Ibid.*, 188
4. Qu. Foster Rhea Dulles *America's Rise to World Power 1898–1954* (New York 1954), 7
5. *Loc. cit.*
6. Calvin Colton (ed.), *The Works of Henry Clay* (New York 1904), III, 224. This was Clay's last testament.
7. James D. Richardson, *A Compilation of the Messages and Papers of the Presidents 1789–1902* (Washington 1904) 10, vols, V, 180
8. Qu. Carl Degler, *Out of our past* (New York 1959), 124
9. J. W. Pratt, 'Origin of Manifest Destiny', *American Historical Review*, XXXII, July 1927. The first usage was in *The Democratic Review*, July–August 1945.
10. Merle Curti, 'Young America', *American Historical Review* XXXII, October 1926
11. Ralph Henry Gabriel, *The Course of American Democratic Thought* (New York 1956), 372
12. *Ibid.*, 108
13. Qu. Foster Rhea Dulles [7:4], 19
14. Ned Rosier in Henry James, *Portrait of a Lady* (Bodley Head ed., London 1968), 295
15. Qu. Margaret Leech, *In the days of McKinley* (New York 1959), 345
16. Works of Theodore Roosevelt, ed. H. Hagedorn New York 1926), 20 vols, XIV, 182–99, June 2, 1897
17. Commager [7:2], II, 33–34
18. R. S. Baker and W. E. Dodd, *The Public Papers of Woodrow Wilson* (New York 1925–27), 6 vols, V, 16, 138, 67
19. *Ibid.*, VI, 18–19
20. *Ibid.*, V, 552
21. Walter Lafeber, *America, Russia and the Cold War 1945–1950* 4th edition (New York 1980), 4
22. Inaugural Address, March 4, 1925, in *The Inaugural Addresses of the Presidents* (New York 1961)

23. Annual Message to Congress, January 4, 1939, in Samuel Rosenman, *The Public Papers and Addresses of Franklin D. Roosevelt* (New York 1941), 1

24. Arthur H. Vandenberg Jr., *The Private Papers of Senator Vandenberg* (London 1953), 10

25. Qu. in Sherwood [3:9], 383. Behind FDR there was a whole school of internationalists whose inter-war activities are brilliantly summarised in Divine, Chapters One and Two [4:30].

26. But, 'With due respect for existing obligations'. See Appendix IV

27. Cadogan [3:8], 398. See Divine [4:30], 43–44, for Welles' role.

28. Geoffrey Perrott, *Days of Sadness, Days of Triumph* (Madison, Wisconsin 1985), 168

29. House of Commons, September 9, 1941. Hansard, vol. 374, col. 69

30. Martin Herz, *Beginnings of the Cold War* (Bloomington, Ind. 1966), VII. In December 1941, the British foreign secretary, Anthony Eden, spoke of the Atlantic Charter to Stalin as a reason for avoiding discussion of the Russian western frontier (which the Russians wished to establish approximately as that of June 1941). Stalin remarked, 'I thought the Atlantic Charter was directed against those people who were trying to establish world dominion. It now looks as if the Charter was directed against the USSR'. (Anthony Eden, *The Eden Memoirs: the Reckoning* (London 1965), 296.) See also Woodward [3:15], II, 204, 206

31. Sherwood [3:9], 363. See also FRUS 1942 I, 1–9; and Woodward [3:15], II, 219

32. Sherwood [3:9], 363

33. Churchill to Roosevelt, March 7, 1942, in Churchill, *Hinge of Fate* [3:14], 293. Roosevelt resisted that interpretation. (FRUS, 1942, III, 512–14)

34. Woodward [3:15], II, 237

35. For the origins of the Atlantic Charter, see also Sherwood [3:9], 360–64; Sumner Welles, *Where are we heading?* (London 1947), 1–50; and for interpretation of the consequences see Lynn E. Davis, *The Cold War begins* [6:32]. A good summary of the 'universalist' vs. 'spheres of interest' argument is in Arthur Schlesinger, 'Origins of the Cold War', *Foreign Affairs*, vol. 46, No. 1, 22–53

36. Stalin thought unconditional surrender 'bad tactics' and believed

'we should together work out terms and let them be made known generally to the people of Germany' (Eden's telegram Nov. 30, 1943, qu. Kimball [4:25], II, 646.)

37. Cordell Hull, *Memoirs*, 2 vols. (New York 1948), II, 1314–15
38. Sumner Welles on armistice day, 1941, qu. Divine [4:30], 46
39. The argument as to the nature of this new commitment, whether it should be 'universalist' (or Wilsonian), or 'practical', giving importance to 'spheres of influence' (and other definitely non-Wilsonian concessions to *realpolitik*) was the main one within the American administration. Most Americans, Republicans as well as Democrats, were 'universalists': Russia, Britain, Argentina and France were all expected to carry out the same principles. The main exceptions to this view were: Henry Stimson, the realistic republican Secretary of War; and George Kennan, the outstanding diplomatist, minister in Moscow. (Later, there were those who, like the Secretary for Commerce, Henry Wallace, were prepared to concede Russia a 'sphere of influence' in the interests of maintaining good relations.)

## Chapter 8 THE NEW AMERICANS

1. Margaret Truman, *Harry S. Truman* (New York 1973), 16
2. Richard Lawrence Miller, *Truman, the Rise to Power* (New York 1985)
3. H. G. Nicholas (ed.), *Washington despatches 1941–45* (London 1981), 392
4. M. Truman [8:1], 58
5. *Ibid.*, 141
6. William Hillman, *Mr President* (New York 1952), 154
7. Harry S. Truman, *Year of Decisions* (New York 1955), 119
8. *The Federalist*, edited with introduction by Jacob E. Cooke (Middleton 1961)
9. Harry S. Truman, *Years of Trial and Hope* (London 1955), 305
10. Harriman, in Emmet Hughes, *Living Presidency*, qu. Robert J. Donovan, *Conflict and Crisis* (New York 1977), 347
11. Alfred Steinberg, *The Man from Missouri* (New York 1962), 246
12. Ernest May, *'Lessons' of the Past* (New York 1973), 75
13. David Lilienthal, *Journals*: II, *The Atomic Energy Years, 1945–50* (New York 1964)
14. Bohlen [3:12], 301
15. Adolf A. Berle, *Negotiating the Rapids 1928–71* (New York

1973), 573. Berle was the only survivor in the Government of Roosevelt's original 'Brains Trust'.

16. Dean Acheson, *Present at the Creation* (London 1970)
17. Truman [8:9], 5
18. Blum [3:29], 391–92
19. Pollard [6:63], 23
20. Robert Ferrell (ed.), *Off the Record* (Diaries of Harry S. Truman) (New York 1980), 98
21. *Ibid.*, 144; Joseph Davies Diary, May 13, 1945
22. Sherwood [3:9], 870
23. William E. Leuchtenberg, *In the shadow of Roosevelt: From Truman to Ronald Reagan* (Ithaca 1984), 18–19
24. Nicholas [8:3], 410
25. Minute of Cabinet, Sept. 7, 1945, qu. Donovan [8:10]
26. Truman [8:9], 104
27. *New York Times*, June 24, 1941, page 7
28. Robert Dallek, *Franklin Roosevelt and American foreign policy* (Oxford 1979), 278
29. Truman, [8:7] I
30. Leuchtenberg [8:23], 6
31. M. Truman [8:1], 236
32. Bohlen [3:12], 212
33. Truman, [8:7]
34. Joseph Davies, Library of Congress, Journal, April 30, 1945
35. D. F. Fleming, *The Cold War and its origins* (London 1961), 265. The first controversy over the causes of the Cold War was waged over this interview. See Arthur Schlesinger, 'Origins of the Cold War', *Foreign Affairs*, October 1967. Harriman's account is on p. 453 of Harriman and Abel [1:22].
36. Harriman [1:22], 444. See comment in M. Truman [8:1], 232. The conversation at lunch is important because many of FDR's 'written communications' on international matters after Yalta were written by the Department of State, and (or) Admiral Leahy, and perhaps only received perfunctory consideration by the President. See Kimball [4:25], III, 560 and 549 for discussion. The most authoritative historian of FDR's foreign policy, Robert Dallek, believes that Roosevelt would probably have moved more quickly than Truman to confront the Russians.
37. Kimball [4:25], III, 617
38. FRUS, *The Conference at Cairo and Tehran*, 1943, 253–55, Roosevelt, talking about the future of Germany, said: 'we should go as far as Berlin. The Soviets could then take the territory to

the South East herself. The US should have Berlin. There would definitely be a race for Berlin. We may have to put the US division into Berlin as soon as possible'.

39. Lynn E. Davis [6:32], 224
40. *Ibid.*
41. Joseph Davies, journal, April 30, 1945 (L of C)
42. Lynn E. Davis [6:32], 276–77. Schuyler's account is in his essay in Thomas Hammond's *Witnesses* [5:52], 138–39.
43. Henry Stimson Diary, May 11, 1945 (Yale University Library)
44. Woodward [3:15], III, 371
45. Davies, diary, May 13 (L of C). Davies had supper en famille with Truman on May 13. He told Truman that he feared that Russia had decided that Britain and the US would not work with the new president. 'What should be done?' asked Truman. Davies then proposed himself as an intermediary and privately proposed a top level meeting using the Russian embassy cipher; Hillman [8:6], 98
46. Blum [3:29], 448
47. Woodward [3:15], III, 375
48. Ferrell, *Off the Record* [8:20], 44
49. 'Ganging up' on the Russians was something that Roosevelt had also wanted to avoid in 1943. See below Chapter 10, footnote 42
50. Blum [3:29], 450
51. Davis [6:32], 278
52. Admiral William Leahy, *I was there* (London 1950), 363
53. FRUS, Conference of Berlin (1945) 12–13; W. Churchill, *Triumph and Tragedy* [3:13], 457
54. Jacob to Charlton in Michael Charlton [2:83], 43
55. Truman [8:7], I, 338
56. Sherwood [3:9], 877
57. Churchill, *Triumph and Tragedy* [3:13], 577. For Davies's account see his diaries May 26, 27 and 29.
58. Henry Wallace, Diary, 4, 5 and 6 June 1945 in Blum, *Price of Vision* [3:29]
59. Joseph Davies, Diary note of May 29, 1945 (L of C); Blum, *Price of Vision* [3:29], 454
60. Henry Stimson, Diary, May 16, 1945 (Yale University Library)
61. For example, Gar Alperowitz whose imaginative *Atomic Diplomacy* (new ed., 1985) stimulated so much controversy. The original idea was in Professor P. M. S. Blackett's *Military and*

*Political Consequences of Atomic Energy* (London 1948). This side of Truman's policy is discussed in Chapter 20

62. See Robert Maddox, *The New Left and the Origins of the Cold War* (New York 1973), especially 63–78; and Lynn E. Davis [6:32], 176n, 225, 230n.

63. The expression 'World War III', for a possible conflict between Russia and the US, was used at least as early as 1943: see instances in Divine [4:30], 127 (Senator Joseph Bull, July 15, 1943) and 154 (Henry Wallace) November, 1943.

64. Hillman [8:6], 105

65. M. Truman [8:1], 360

66. Qu. Deborah Welch Larson, *Origins of Containment* (Princeton 1985), 185. An excellent work.

67. Public Papers of the Presidents: Harry S. Truman, April 12–December 31, 1945 (Washington 1961), 123 (press conference June 13, 1945)

68. Bohlen [3:12], 216

69. Diary, July 17, 1945, in Ferrell, *Off the Record* [8:20], 53

70. Donovan [8:10], 76

71. Qu. Larson [8:66], 197

72. Byrnes [3:23], 69

73. Truman [8:9], 342; Murphy [4:22], 342, and Maynard Barnes in FRUS, 1945, Potsdam, I, 383

74. Truman [8:9], 412

75. Donovan [8:10], 76

76. Churchill, *Triumph and Tragedy* [3:13], 550

77. Truman [8:7], 300

78. *Ibid.*, 342

79. M. Truman [8:1], 360

80. Khrushchev [2:5], I, 242

81. Eben Ayers Diary (HSTL) August 7, 1945. Cyrus Sulzberger of *The New York Times* reminds us that this was Truman's one and only experience of negotiating with Russia (see C. L. Sulzberger, *A long row of candles*, New York 1969, 333). Truman told his staff at the White House that 'he did not want to live in Europe and was glad to be back' (Eben Ayers Diary, August 7).

82. Snow [4:33], 358

83. Larson [9:172], 202

84. Blum [3:29], 621

85. FRUS, 1945, IV, 710

86. See Davis [6:32], 374; this is the theme of Geir Lundestad's *The American non-policy towards Eastern Europe* (Oslo 1978)

87. Qu. Robert Messer, *The End of an alliance* (Chapel Hill 1982), 126. An outstanding study.

88. Stettinius [4:104], 438

89. *Ibid.*, 439

90. *Blum* [3:29], 490

91. *Ibid.*, 503.

92. *Public Papers of Harry S. Truman*, 1945 [8:67], 431

93. Forrestal Diary, December 4, 1945, in Walter Millis, *The Forrestal Diaries* (New York 1951)

94. Wallace Diary, November 28, 1945, in Blum [3:29]

95. Eben Ayers Diary, December 17, 1945. This followed an exchange which went thus: 'There's only one thing the Russians understand.' 'Divisions? . . .' The President nodded: 'we can't send any divisions over to prevent them moving from Bulgaria'.

97. Kuniholm [5:28], 281

98. Messer [8:87], 165

99. Truman [8:7], 492–93

100. Messer [8:87], 160. See Byrnes's article in *Colliers' Magazine*, April 26, 1952. According to Herbert Feis (*From Trust to Terror* [6:33], 55), Byrnes believed that this famous 'letter' was 'fabricated for the record' later by Truman.

101. Larson [8:66], 243

102. Truman [8:7], I, 120

103. *Washington Post*, January 5, 1946

104. This is the wording of Deborah Larson [8:66], with which I agree.

105. Blum [3:29], 492

106. This also is Professor Larson's judgement with which I agree.

107. Nicholas [8:3], 69

108. Cadogan [3:8], 675; Joseph Davies Diary, August 1, 1945

109. FRUS, *The Conferences at Malta and Yalta*, 1945, 107–8

110. Pickersgill and Forster [4:108], 133; Leahy [8:52], 515. Ayers's diary shows that Truman laughed at Leahy's doubts as to whether the bomb would go off. It does not give evidence of Leahy's qualms about use, even if it could work.

111. Leahy Diary, November 28 (L of C). He believed that there were at least 2000 Soviet agents in Los Angeles 'making some progress towards attracting the natives towards the Soviet philosophy'.

112. The best description of the curious events of December 31, 1945– January 5, 1946, is that in Donovan [8:10], 159–60.

113. Leahy Diary, January 1, 1946 (L of C)

114. *Ibid.*, February 21, 1946 (L of C)
115. See Larson [8:66], 57; and Ernest May, *'Lessons of the past'* [8:12], 19–51. This last book is a stimulating study of how to avoid such usages.
116. Messer [8:87], 119
117. Leahy [8:52], 500
118. *Ibid.*, 515
119. Blum [3:29], 462
120. *Ibid.*, 464. Roosevelt also told Stettinius that he did not make Byrnes Secretary of State because he had 'no understanding of geography' (Stettinius [4:104], 184)
121. M. Truman [8:1], 202
122. See Messer [8:87], 37; and Lloyd Gardner's essay on Byrnes, in *Architects of Illusion* (Chicago 1970), 84–112.
123. Qu. Patricia Dawson Ward, *The Threat of Peace* (Kent, Ohio 1979), 22
124. Nicholas [8:3], 92; Graham Stuart, *The Department of State: a history of its organization, procedure and personnel* (New York 1949), 425.
125. David S. McLennan, *Dean Acheson, The State Department Years* (New York 1976), 59
126. Blum [3:29], 565
127. Truman journal, published in Ferrell, *Off the Record* [8:20], 49
128. Vandenberg [7:24], 225
129. Kennan [4:19]
130. Messer [8:87], 236
131. George Herken, *The Winning Weapon: the atomic bomb in the Cold War 1945–1950* (New York 1980), 52. An excellent introduction
132. Byrnes, *Speaking frankly* [3:23], 116
133. Herken [8:131], 53
134. *Ibid.*, 55
135. Forrestal diary [8:93], November 6, 1945. Actually Byrnes's moment of truth may have come on September 30 in Claridge's Hotel, London, when he said to John Foster Dulles: 'well, pardner, I think we pushed these babies about as far as they will go and I think we better start thinking about a compromise' (Dulles papers, qu. Daniel Yergin, *Shattered peace* (London 1978), 129)
136. Pasvolsky had been in the Brookings Institution before entering government service with Roosevelt. Hull made him personal assistant in 1936.

137. See George Curry, *James F. Byrnes*, vol. XIV of Robert Ferrell and Samuel Flagg Bemis, eds., *The American Secretaries of State and their diplomacy* (New York 1965), 189–90, 362–64

138. Truman [8:7], 492–93

139. Byrnes [3:23], 109; *All in one Lifetime* (New York 1958), 326. Murphy, 367

140. Messer [8:87], 135

141. Kennan, diary for December 19, 1945, in his *Memoirs* [4:19], 287–88

142. Murphy [4:22], 369

143. Bohlen [3:12], 248

144. *Washington Post*, January 4, 1946; see Blum [3:29], for background

145. Messer [8:87], 167

CHAPTER 9 THE NEW AMERICANS II

I am grateful to Arthur Schlesinger Jr. for reading portions of this and the following two chapters in draft and making several helpful suggestions.

1. *Forrestal diaries* [8:93], 62; May [8:12], 176–77

2. Sherwood [3:9], 754

3. Joseph Grew, *Turbulent Era*, 2 vols. (Cambridge, Mass. 1953), vol. 1, 1455

4. NA: 740.00119 Control (Austria) /5–545

5. Grew, II, 1445

6. *Ibid.*, 1449

7. Dean Acheson, *Morning and Noon* (London 1967), 1–24

8. Acheson [8:16], 212

9. Berle [8:15], 586. For a quite different view see Eugene Rostow *Peace in the Balance* (New York 1972), 131. Rostow describes how he and Acheson, after negotiating lend-lease with the Russians discussed telling them 'Some home truths while we still have some military power'. They decided – in the spring of 1944 that they couldn't turn on allies at the end of a war and tell them to open up 'or else'.

10. McLennan [8:125], 79

11. Acheson [8:16], 380

12. *Ibid.*, 197

13. McLennan [8:125], 144

14. See Coral Bell, (*Negotiation from Strength*, London 1963, 18, 45) for a good assessment of Acheson.

15. Blum [3:29], 409
16. James MacGregor Burns, *Roosevelt, the Soldier of Freedom* (New York 1970), 398
17. Davis [6:32], 191. Matthews had been chargé at Vichy before Leahy.
18. May [8:12], 25
19. (PRO) FO 371/44574 AN 2438/35/45
20. Hickerson file, State Department Papers, qu. Yergin [8:135], 498
21. Arthur Bliss Lane, *I saw Poland betrayed* (Indianapolis 1948), 20
22. See Charlton [2:83], 45–46 for Hiss's views. Hiss at Yalta spoke as if he did not know that the Comintern had been formally abolished (Stettinius [4:104], 229). At San Francisco he opposed OSS intelligence operations against the foreign delegates (including the Russians) (*ibid.*, 303).
23. Kennan [4:19], 61
24. May [8:12], 28–29
25. Susan Mary Alsop, *To Marietta from Paris 1945–1960* (London 1976)
26. Bohlen [3:12], 531
27. *Ibid.*, 186
28. *Ibid.*, 202
28[A] Steinhardt's summary of Soviet attitudes in June 1941 (FRUS 1941, I, 765) was masterly and shows that it was unwillingness to consider carefully existing reports, not their absence, which characterised later policy. See Bernard Bellush, *He walked alone: a biography of John Gilbert Winant* (The Hague), 1968, 176
29. His polemic *I saw Poland betrayed* (London 1949) is the only memoir by an American ambassador of that time, apart from Harriman's book with Elie Abel. See also FRUS, 1946, V, 642, and VI, 53. Barnes had served in several trouble spots before Bulgaria including Paris (1940) and Smyrna in the Graeco-Turkish war.
30. May [8:12], 26–27
31. NA: 711–61/10–2645, for Gagra; FRUS, 1945, VI, 782–85
32. Harriman [1:22], 531
33. Khrushchev [2:26], 414
34. Bohlen [3:12], 142
35. Kennan [4:19], 234
36. Bohlen [3:12], 142
37. Salisbury [4:10], 242
38. Urban [1:15], 61

39. *Ibid.*, 34
40. For an interesting analysis of Harriman, see Larson [8:66], 66–125
41. FRUS, *Cairo and Tehran*, 152. In 1941, Harriman with Lord Beaverbrook had dispensed with their own interpreters in conversation with Stalin, as with their ambassadors, in order to try and gain trust: an action which must have evoked Stalin's 'puzzlement . . . and contempt' (Taubman [6:35], 43)
42. Harriman [1:22], 296
43. September 10, 1944. See comment in Urban [1:15], 61
44. FRUS, 1945, IV, 993
45. NA: R59 711.61.4.645, April 6, 1945
46. Sherwood [3:9], 391
47. Harriman [1:15], 444
48. *Forrestal* [8:93], 47
49. *Ibid.*, 78
50. FRUS, 1945, V, 930–33; Harriman [1:22], 521
51. *Komsomolskaya Pravda*, December 27, 1945, qu. FRUS, 1946, VI, 676–78
52. *Trud*, January 15, 1946, qu. *ibid.*
53. Harriman [1:22], 531
54. John R. Deane, *The Strange Alliance: the story of American efforts at wartime collaboration with Russia* (London 1947), 84 (this was in a letter to General Marshall, dated December 2, 1944)
55. *Ibid.*, 85
56. Daniel Yergin [8:135] makes play with the fact that Kennan, Bohlen *et al.* were educated in Riga (*The Shattered Peace*). But some came out of Riga with different views, e.g. E. H. Carr.
57. In a report from Moscow in 1936, 'The War Problem of the Soviet Union', Kennan predicted that Stalin would enter into pacts with non-communist nations (e.g. Nazi Germany) to try and make sure that the next war would be fought between those nations and not between the capitalist and communist worlds.
58. Bohlen [3:12], 161
59. *Ibid.*, 161
60. *Ibid.*, 175
61. Despatch, September 1, 1952, Kennan, *Memoirs*, vol. II [5:21], 331. One of Kennan's contemporaries, then in the British Embassy in Moscow, spoke of him as 'the most distinguished luminary ever of the diplomatic profession.'
62. Berle [8:15], 523
63. *Ibid.*, 542

64. Truman [8:9], II, 305
65. M. Truman [8:1], 353
66. Joseph Davies, *Mission to Moscow* (London 1942), 230
67. Lockhart, Sir Robert Bruce: *Diaries of* (Edited by Kenneth Young) (London 1980), 443. One of Davies's 'anxieties' in 1945 was the fear of an emergence of a 'Soviet Napoleon' (for example, Zhukov) who might overthrow and destroy 'the present altruistic ideological purposes of peace and brotherhood which the present government avows and in my opinion sustains' (FRUS *Potsdam*, I, 219).
68. Kennan [4:19], 32
69. Sherwood [3:9], 729
70. Dallek [8:28], 279; also see Yergin [8:135], 33–34; Sherwin [9:15], 178
71. Davies diary, April 30, 1945 (L of C). See John Downey and Susanne La Follette's review of *Mission to Moscow* (*New York Times* May 9, 1943), a reply defending Davies (*ibid.*, May 16, 1943) and their rebuttal (May 24, 1943)
72. He told Truman in 1945 that since 1941 he had 'acted as a kind of liaison between the President, the Soviet Embassy and the Secretary of State' and that he believed Russia wanted peace. It was known in Washington that Davies 'maintained close contact with the Soviet embassy there' (Stettinius [4:104], 157): by his own account, on FDR's instructions (Diary in the L of C, April 30, 1945).
73. See Davies diary for May 13, 1945 (L of C), and commentary by Sherwin [9:15], 178 ff.
74. *New York Times*, February 16, 1946
75. Founded in December 1944 on Stimson's intelligent initiative; Sherwood [3:9], 756
76. Robert Ferrell, *George C. Marshall* (New York 1966), 3
77. Truman [8:7], I, 130–31; Kimball [4:25], III, 602–3; Woodward [3:15], III, 572 fn. Stalin knew that the question of 'who is going to take Berlin, we or the Allies?' (as he put it to Zhukov and Konev on April 1, 1945, thus excluding himself from the terminology, 'the Allies') was far from 'unimportant' (S. Bialer, *Stalin and his generals*, 2nd ed., Epping 1984, 516–17).
78. Forrest Pogue, *The Supreme Command* (Washington 1954), 468. This was about a move into Prague.
79. E. Razin, *Bolshevik*, No. 1, January, p. 47, qu. Rieber [3:75], 35. As Feis says, 'No one suggested that military strategy be adjusted to serve the political purposes and settlements in mind'

*Churchill, Roosevelt, Stalin* (Princeton 1957), 125. For the
suggestion that Marshall knew what he was doing, and was
motivated by a desire to prevent Britain from reasserting herself
after the war, see Kimball [4:25], II, 480.

80. Nicholas [8:3], 301
81. Personal memories
82. Nicholas [8:3], 100
83. Lilienthal [8:13], 375
84. Qu. Gaddis [6:62], 103
85. NA: 711.61/11–1745
86. A remark to Hopkins, qu. Stephen Ambrose, *Eisenhower*, vol.
    1 (1890–1952) (New York 1984), 402
87. *Ibid.*, 400
88. *Ibid.*, 394. 'Monty' thought that 'Ike' should not be in command
    since he had never seen action before his nomination as supreme
    commander (comment of Brian Montgomery)
89. Nigel Hamilton (*Monty, The Field Marshal, 1944–1976*, London
    1986, 444) describes the shock of receiving Eisenhower's order
    on March 28 not to drive on to Berlin. Hamilton attributes the
    ambitions of Bradley as the reason for Eisenhower's sudden
    change (*ibid.*, 460). See also Stephen Ambrose's *Eisenhower and
    Berlin, 1945, The Decision to Halt at the Elbe* (New York 1967).
90. Ambrose [9:86], 400–3
91. Harriman [1:15], 502
92. Qu. Blanche W. Cook, *The Declassified Eisenhower* (Garden City
    1981), 51
93. NA: RG.59 740.00119
94. Michael S. Sherry, *Preparing for the Next War* (New Haven
    1977), 208
95. Lucius D. Clay, *Decision in Germany* (London 1950), 50
96. General Mark Clark, *From the Danube to the Yalu* (London,
    1954), 14
97. February 5, 1945, qu. Herken [8:133], 206
98. Nicholas [8:3], 62. Hull 'echoed and re-echoed' the views of the
    Soviet ambassador Gromyko in October 1943 that there was
    'no serious divergence of interest between the Soviet Union and
    the United States'. He wanted to 'talk Mr Stalin out of his
    shell'. (Quoted in Taubman [6:35], 59). See Divine [4:30],
    42–43.
99. Nicholas [8:3], 465. See Stettinius's *Diaries* [4:104], xvii.
    Stettinius had wanted to become a clergyman but lacked the
    degree required and so joined General Motors. Always philan-

thropic, Stettinius's life revolved round a beautiful estate, 'Horse-shoe', in the Blue Ridge mountains.

100. Dalton, *War Diaries* [1:11], 805. His senior officials nicknamed him derisively 'junior'.

101. Richard L. Walker, James F. Byrnes and George Curry, *E. R. Stettinius Jr.*, vol. 14 of the *American Secretaries of State and Their Diplomacy* (New York 1965), 60

102. Cadogan [3:8], 708. Stettinius, however considered Cadogan 'calm, intelligent, and . . . quick on the trigger'. (Stettinius, *Diaries* [4:104], 50).

103. Forrestal [8:93], 35

104. Bohlen [3:12], 165

105. Charles Yost, *History and Memory* (New York 1980), 115

106. George Ball, *The Past has Another Pattern* (New York 1982), 17. Stettinius did, however, tell Latin American diplomatists at San Francisco that 'the next war will be between Russia and the US' and thought that Soviet 'penetrations' would be made through South America. (Stettinius [4:104], 354).

107. Stettinius, *Diaries*, November 27, 1944 [4:104]. Stettinius was certainly naive about Russia but, in this matter, merely repeated what he heard Roosevelt say.

108. For these individuals, and their difficulties with Congress in 1944, see Divine [4:30], 254–55. See too Gardner, *Architects of Illusion* [8:122], 113–38

109. Sherwood [3:9], 753

110. Ferrell, *Off the Record* [8:20], 174; Daniels qu. Leuchtenberg [8:23], 14

111. Dwight Macdonald in *Henry Wallace*, qu. Irving Howe and Lewis Loser, *The American Communist Party* (Boston 1957), 472

112. Henry Wallace, *Soviet Asia Mission* (Cornwall 1946), 82

113. See Cave Brown and Macdonald [4:112], 618, qu. from FBI material

114. Blum [3:29], 625

115. Sherwin [9:15], 37

116. Blum [3:29], 4

116[A] The 'Common Man' speech was May 8, 1942. It was a reply to Henry Luce's speech calling for an 'American century'. For a sympathetic picture of Wallace, see Divine [4:30], 64–66.

117. David Rees, *Harry Dexter White* (London 1974), 373

118. Vernon Walters, *Silent Missions* (New York 1978), 110

119. Jonathan Daniels, *The man from Independence* (London 1951), 223

120. Forrestal [8:93], 8. See Gardner [8: 122], 270–78
121. *The Eisenhower Diaries*, edited by Robert Ferrell (New York 1981), 160
122. Donovan [8:10], 41
123. Forrestal [8:93], 52
124. *Ibid.*, 73
125. Frederic Eberhardt papers, Princeton
126. Gaddis, *Origins* [6:62], 60–1
127. Qu. *ibid.*, 49
128. Nicholas [8:3], 245. For a good picture see Divine [4:30], 196–97
129. Acheson [8:10], 223
130. Vandenberg [7:24], xix
131. Diary, March 24, 1943, in *ibid.*, 41
132. Qu. Gaddis, 146
133. *Ibid.*, 136
134. Vandenberg [7:24], 134. For a critical consideration of this speech's importance see Gardner, 49–50. It could be argued that Vandenberg's greatest service to the nation (and the world) was his support of, and work on, the Republican party's 'Mackinac declaration' of September pledging support for a future international organisation (Divine [4:30], 131–32).
135. Vandenberg [7:24], 182
138. *Ibid.*, 225
139. *Ibid.*, 244
140. This point is developed in Messer's book.
141. Speech in the Senate, November 27, 1945, Congressional Record, vol. 91, Part 8, 11013–36
142. Speech, December 4, 1945, in *ibid.*, part 9, 11371–81
143. Speech, November 28, 1945, *ibid.*, part 8, 11085–87
144. Dulles papers, qu. Yergin [8:135], 436, 124
145. John Foster Dulles, *War or Peace* (New York 1950), 29–30
146. Council on Foreign Relations' papers, qu. Yergin [8:135], 140
147. *Ibid.*, 173. Lippmann's *US War Aims* (1944) argued that with Russia as it was then constituted there could only be 'a modus vivendi, only compromises, bargains, specific settlements' no general understandings.
148. See Balfour to Halifax, May 21, 1945, in FO 371/44356 AN 1641/4/1945 (PRO)
149. Lippmann to Byrnes, in Ronald Steel, *Walter Lippmann and the American century* (New York 1980), 421
150. Nicholas [8:3], 562
151. Steel [9:149], 426

152. *Ibid.*, 426
153. Forrestal [8:93], 127
154. Nicholas [8:3], 157
155. Harriman [1:22], 457. They were Raymond Gram Swing and Walter Lippmann. Swing apologised within the year. Lippmann agreed with Harriman within six months.
156. *Life*, March 29, 1943. Written by Walter Graebner, with a special article by Joe Davies and a picture of Stalin on the cover, this influential issue spoke of Lenin as 'perhaps the greatest man of modern times' but one who was also 'a normal, well-balanced man [who] did what he set out to do – rescuing 140 million people from a brutal and incompetent tyranny'.
157. Gaddis [6:62], 42–43. For Chambers at *Time*, see Weinstein [4:102], 344–45
158. December 13, 1944; in NA: 700.0011 Peace/12–1344 qu. *ibid.*, 54
159. 'The World from Rome: the Eternal City fears a struggle between Christianity and Communism', *Life*, September 4, 1944
160. Blum [3:29], 286
161. Hopkins, however, apparently thought himself of his first visit to Moscow in July 1941 (Sherwood [3:9], 318). Roosevelt's words were actually to Wayne Coy of the Office of Emergency Management (Elliot Roosevelt, *FDR: his letters 1928–1945*, 3 vols. New York 1950, II, 1195–96)
162. Blum [3:29], 393
163. Lord Moran, *Winston Churchill, the struggle for survival* (London 1966), 132
164. Sherwood [3:9], 859
165. The most useful book on this period of the history of the Communist party in America is that of Joseph Starobin, *American Communism in Crisis 1943–1957* [4:90]
166. FRUS, 1942, III, 570–71. For the first generation of American communists, see Theodore Draper, *The Roots of American Communism* (New York 1957)
167. Qu. Gaddis [6:62], 57: 'Capitalism and Socialism have begun to find the way to peaceful coexistence and collaboration in the same world' (qu. Starobin, 55).
168. Blum [3:29], 305
169. *Cahiers du communisme*, April 1945. The essence of the article is that Browder thought that at Tehran, 'capitalism and socialism had begun to find means of peaceful co-existence'. That view was 'erroneous', and would have allowed the greater part of

Europe west of the Soviet Union to be 'reconstructed on a bourgeois democratic basis', not 'a fascist or Soviet basis'. See comments in Starobin [4:90], 79

170. Starobin [4:90], 113
171. This was based on a report by the US Embassy in Moscow shown to the British Embassy in June 1946; see FO 371/56833 N 7699/605/38G (PRO)
172. See Branko Lazitch, *Biographical Dictionary of the Comintern* (Stanford 1973), 4; an outstanding work (new edition 1987)
173. Sherwood [3:9], 226
174. James Bamford, *The Puzzle Palace* (New York 1973), 306–8. In February 1946 Sosthenes Benn of ITT offered Admiral Leahy his company for use for intelligence purposes (Leahy Diary February 7, 1946)
175. Dallek [8:28], 226
176. Allen Dulles, *The Secret Surrender* (London 1967), 8–11
177. Not least among OSS achievements was its handling of wartime agents in Germany, e.g. 'George Wood' in the German Foreign Office.
178. Truman, [8:9], I, 56
179. Thomas Troy, *Donovan and the CIA: A history of the establishment of the CIA* (Langley 1981), 153
180. *Ibid.*, 311
181. Acheson [8:10], 162
182. *Russia: 13,999 OSSDF*, qu. Anthony Cave Brown, *The Last Hero* (New York 1982), 417
183. See John Lewis Gaddis, *Strategies of Containment* (Oxford 1982), 19 fn.
184. Records of the War Dept., civil affairs Division, Record Group 165, File CAD 388 (9–17–43) (1) qu. Davis [6:32], 83
185. Cave Brown [9:182], 410–25
186. Sherwood [3:9], 744
187. Thus OSS obtained some Soviet ciphers from the Finnish Government. But Stettinius forced Donovan to give them back to Russia (Lamphere [4:109], 84; Cave Brown [9:182], 622
188. *Ibid.*, 641; Thayer [3:52], 105
189. *Ibid.*, 679
190. *Ibid.*, 735, 752
191. See Erickson [2:17], 343; Reinhard Gehlen, *The Service* (Tr.) (New York 1972); and Thomas Powers, *The Man who kept the Secrets: Richard Helms and the CIA* (New York 1979), 24.

Gehlen was a US prisoner, mostly in the US, between May 1945 and July 1946

192. Alexander Dallin [5:8], 545
193. Weinstein [4:94], 62, 341; Blum [3:29], 332
194. See, for example, the evidence which appeared during the case of Dr Oppenheimer in 1953 printed in, for example, Robert Williamson and Philip L. Cantelson, *The American Atom 1939–1984* (Philadelphia 1984)
195. Harry Rositke, *The CIA's Secret Operations* (Readers' Digest Press 1977), 20
196. Kennan despatch in FRUS, see also Groves, in FRUS, 1946, vol. I, 1203
197. Truman [8:9], 58
198. Powers [9: 191], 27; Donovan [8:10], 307
199. Forrestal [8:93], 36
200. Troy [9:179], 336
201. *Ibid.*, 361
202. Rees [4:109], 380
203. *Ibid.*, 380
204. *Ibid.*, 385
205. *Historical Statistics of the US: Colonial Times to 1957* (Washington 1960), 56–57
206. FRUS, 1943, *The Conferences at Cairo and Tehran*, 594
207. McMahon to Macleish, April 4, 1945, qu. Davis [6:32], 224
208. Nicholas [8:3], 267


## Chapter 10 THE LEGACY OF ROOSEVELT

1. Byrnes, qu. Messer [8:87], 17
2. Eden [7:30], 513
3. Hugh G. Gallagher, *FDR's Splendid Deception* (New York 1985) *passim*. FDR's influenza in 1944 and the discovery subsequently of his heart weakness, are discussed in Burns, *Soldier of Freedom*, 948–50 and Kimball, III, 138–39
4. Dallek [8:28], 102
5. Blum [3:29], 284
6. Bohlen [3:12], 210
7. Kennan [4:19], 123. Attlee thought the same: see Woodward [3:15], V, 45–46
8. Harriman in Urban [1:15], 31. Sumner Welles believed that Roosevelt thought that 'if one took the figure of 100 as representing the difference between American democracy and Soviet

communism in 1917, with the United States at 100 and the Soviet Union at 0, American democracy might eventually reach the figure 60 and the Soviet system might reach . . . 40.' (Qu. Taubman [6:25], 38)

9. There are indeed moments when it did seem as if Roosevelt believed in the possibility of some kind of global 'New Deal'.
10. Sherwood [3:29], 386
11. Kimball [4:25], II, 168 (FDR to Churchill, November 19, 1942)
12. Harriman [1:22], 172
13. Qu. Dallek [8:28], 81
14. Bohlen [3:12], 210
15. Urban [1:15], 36
16. Harriman [1:22], 191. FDR told Joseph Davies that he wanted a private meeting with Stalin in 1943 but then denied it: 'I did not suggest to "UJ" that we meet alone' (Kimball [4:25], II, 283)
17. This was essentially in criticism of President Johnson's use of US troops without authority.
18. Dallek [8:28], 289–90
19. *Ibid.*, 298
20. R. G. Hewlett and Oscar Anderson, *A History of the United States Atomic Energy Commission*: I, *The New World* (New York 1962), 323; see also Herbert Feis, *From Trust to Terror* [6:33], 32–33
21. Murphy [4:22], 546
22. *Ibid.*, 545. FDR did not tell his ambassador to Poland, Lane, what had been said at Tehran about that country (Lane [12:40], 43).
23. See Walker *et al.* [9:101], *Stettinius*, 14
24. Dallek [8:28], 532. But there were officials who deeply resented that, towards the end of the war, FDR gave the impression that 'recently anybody could get to the President to sign anything . . . often the President didn't know the contents of any document he signed' (Qu. Thorne [10:60], 508).
25. Roosevelt–Churchill, March 18, 1942, in Kimball [4:25], I
26. Murphy [4:22], 287
27. Blum [3:29], 348
28. See Burns [9:16], 350; Divine [4:30], 138; Blum [3:29], 383. Bullitt is treated by Lloyd Gardner in *Architects of Illusion* [23:101], 3–25. Whatever may be said of Bullitt's passions, he did know Russia, and had talked to Lenin, Bukharin, Radek *et al.* as well as Stalin and, of course, often Litvinov. Paradoxically,

Welles's resignation was considered by part of the press as a sign that the administration was embarking on an anti-Russian policy. For Standley, see George Herring, *Aid to Russia 1941–1946* (New York 1973), 80–109 and William Standley and Arthur A. Ageton, *Admiral Ambassador to Russia* (Chicago 1955). Standley's candid remark was at a press conference on March 8, 1943.

29. *Public Papers of the Presidents* [7:23] 1943 volume, 138
30. *Ibid.*, 1943 volume, 550
31. Bullitt (*Life*, XXV, August 30, 1948) described FDR as telling him . . . 'I just have a hunch that Stalin is not that kind of man. Harry says he's not . . . and I think that if I give him everything I possibly can and ask nothing from him in return, *noblesse oblige*, he won't try to annex anything and will work with me for a world of democracy and peace'. This comment was published five years after it was supposed to have been made. In 1941 he told Bullitt that commitments from Stalin would not be worth having; he would surely break promises when necessary. But by 1942 he was telling Morgenthau 'the whole Question whether we win or lose the war depends on the Russians' (Morgenthau Diaries, III, 85).
32. Sherwood [3:9], 871. After Yalta, Stettinius told the President of Brazil that FDR 'was confident that the Soviet Union had decided to take its place in the United Nations family'.
33. J. L. Gaddis, *Strategies of Containment* [9:183], 13. 'He distrusted everybody' said Walter Lippmann much later, 'what he thought he could do was outwit Stalin, which is quite a different thing'. (Lippmann memoir, oral history project, qu. Divine [4:30], 157).
34. Blum [3:29], 91
35. He told Lane the same when the latter was setting off to be ambassador to Poland (Lane [12:40], 42); *Public Papers of FDR, 1944–1945* [7:23], 570–86
36. Murphy [4:22], 261. On the last morning of the conference, FDR, finding Stalin 'stiff, solemn, not smiling', made jokes at Churchill's expense, got the Soviet leader to 'break into a deep hearty guffaw' and, 'from that time on, . . . we talked like men and brothers' – but *not* about Poland (Frances Perkins, *The Roosevelt I knew* (New York 1947), 84
37. Harriman [1:22], 263
38. Bohlen [3:12], 146
39. Gaddis [6:62], 139

40. Joseph Alsop, *FDR* (London 1984), 248; Stanislaw Mikołajczyk, *The Pattern of Soviet Domination* (London 1948), 66
41. Roosevelt to Churchill, April 11, 1945. Kimball [4:25], III, 630. This was one of the few messages drafted personally by FDR between Yalta and his death. As the editor of these messages to Churchill says, it was a good example of his 'creative procrastination'.
42. Roosevelt to Churchill, November 11, 1943, Kimball [4:25], II, 597
43. Harriman [1:22], 74
44. FRUS, 1941, I, 378. FDR made jokes about this qualification: See Stettinius diaries [4: 104], 234
45. Roosevelt privately began to talk of a new international body based on 'the Big Four' in 1942 (FRUS, 1942, III, 568–81). He first spoke in public of the need for a peace built on 'firmer foundations than good intentions alone' in his annual message to Congress in January 1943 (Divine [4:30], 84). Secretary of State Cordell Hull gave priority in Moscow in October 1943 to securing a confirmation of the Soviet promise of May 1942 to collaborate in the United Nations – not 'piddling little things', such as Poland. (Harriman [1:22], 236; Hull [7:37], II, 1170). Roosevelt pretended to Stalin that he wanted to keep those ideas from Churchill for the time being (see discussion in Divine [4:30], 159)
46. Sherwood [3:9], 780–84
47. The debates in the House of Representatives and the Senate of September and October 1943 are well analysed in Divine [4:30], 141–53. For Roosevelt's speech, see *Public Papers of FDR* [7:23] XII, 553–62. These metaphors were much on his mind. Compare his casual allusions before the Canadian parliament in August 1943 to the United Nations as a 'sheriff's posse to break up the gang in order that gangsterism may be eliminated' (*ibid.*, 1943 volume, 368).
48. Speech to Foreign Policy Association, October 21, 1944, qu. Sherwood [3:9], 817
49. *Ibid.*, 822. See also Forrest Davis, 'Roosevelt's World Blueprint' in *Saturday Evening Post*, April 10, 1943 and May 13 and May 20, 1944; and commentary by Gaddis, [6:62] 153 and Divine [4:30], 115–16. Davis had in December 1942 talked to FDR and the President had approved the article in draft.
50. Dallek [8:28], 3
51. Sherwood [3:9], I, 225
52. Dallek [8:28], 11

53. Woodward [3:15], V, 3–8, summarises. The first draft was prepared by Gladwyn Jebb. Churchill's ideas for post-war reconstruction were put in public for the first time on March 21, 1943, in a radio address, in which he called in general terms for an international body and for the early creation of a 'Council of Asia' and a 'Council of Europe'. He put more detailed plans to a conference at the British Embassy in Washington on May 22, 1943 (Kimball [4:25], II, 222)

54. The creation of the UN is outside the scope of this volume. See Woodward [3:15], V, 50–62, and 70–180.

55. Gaddis [6:62], 134. Roosevelt's views on the making of the United Nations can be studied in many works, but see especially Stettinius's diary [4:104], e.g. 108–14.

56. For Soviet support for the US site, see *ibid.*, especially p. 447

57. Stettinius's diary [4:104], 341–73

58. Last message to Stalin, April 12, 1945, in Kimball [4:25], III, 630

59. Statement at Yalta, February 5 in *Foreign Relations & the United States*. See Appendix XI

60. W. L. Louis, *Imperialism at Bay* (Oxford 1977); Christopher Thorne, *Allies of a Kind* (London 1978)

61. Hull [7:39], II, 1635

62. Samuel Rosenman, *Working with Roosevelt* (London 1952), 367–69

63. Keith Sainsbury, *The Turning Point* (Oxford 1985), 322–23

64. Truman [8:7], 66–67

65. FRUS, 1946, I, 1135

66. FRUS, 1946, I, 715

67. Churchill to FDR, June 11, 1944 in Kimball [4:25], III, 180

68. Henry Kissinger, *The White House Years* (New York 1979), 551

69. FRUS, 1946, VI, 721

70. Truman [8:7], 270; FRUS, Berlin II, 52–54. This Council was intended specifically by the Department of State 'to reduce the possibilities of unilateral action by either the Russians or the British, and would serve as a useful *interim* means through which the United States could work for the liquidation of spheres of influence' (FRUS, *Berlin*, 263).

71. Woodward [3:15], V, 402–3

72. Public Papers of FDR [10:29]

73. *New York Times*, July 23–24, 1944; Pollard [6:63], 15

74. Pollard [6:63], 17, 32

75. FRUS, 1943, III, 586–88

76. FRUS, 1944, IV, 1032–35, 1041–42. Harriman told Mikoyan the interest was 'far too low . . . The US Government itself paid more for its longterm borrowings'.

77. See Eugene Rostow's account, in *Peace in the Balance* [9:9], 117

78. *Fortune*, XXXI, January 1945, 'What Business with Russia?' In the same issue is, 'The Russians can manage'.

79. Gaddis [6:62], 189

80. FRUS, 1945, V, 942–44, 945–47

81. FRUS, *The Conferences at Malta and Yalta*, 608–11, for discussion of agenda

82. See Chapter 13

83. Gaddis [6:62], 194, fn 39

84. FRUS, 1945, V, 998

85. Sherwood [3:9], 882–83

86. Harriman [1:15], 467

87. Congresssional Record, July 20, 1945, vol. 91, part 6, 7827–41. Senator Wiley wanted the 'peace capital' in the United States in order to show that 'we intend to snap out of the inferiority complex which has dogged our relations with Europe'.

88. That is, items already procured contracted for or committed but not delivered. Pollard [6:63], 29–30. Little was used in combat.

89. FRUS, 1945, V, 881–84; and Colmer, in Appendix to the Congressional Record, August 2, 1946, A 4895–98

90. Kennan [4:19], *Memoirs*, I, 277

91. Appendix to the Congressional Record, November 26, 1945, A 5103–8

92. FRUS, 1945, V, 1031–44

93. Pollard [6:63], 52. One curious occurrence in these months was the remarks of Stalin to Leo Krzycki, President of the American Slav Congress, and Vice-President of the Amalgamated Clothing Workers of America, on January 3, 1946. Having asked about the role of Slavs in United States politics, he said that 'Russia could use thousands of engineers and mechanics from America' (Qu. Taubman [6:35], 136)

94. Pollard [6:63], 30

95. See William Appleton Williams, *The Tragedy of American Diplomacy* (Cleveland, Ohio 1953) Chapters VI–VII, for an alternative view.

96. See Davis [6:32], 194 for an interesting interpretation of FDR's policies

97. FRUS, 1945, *Yalta*, 848

98. FRUS, 1945, *Yalta*, 862

99. US Department of State, *Postwar Foreign Policy Preparation, 1939–1945*, Publication 3580 (Washington 1949), 372–73, 394–95. Roosevelt had been unhappy with the European Advisory Commission as he did not want anything to interfere with the United Nations and, above all, did not want the United States to have the post-war burden of reconstituting France, Italy and the Balkans: 'This is not our natural task at a distance of 3500 miles or more'. See Appendix XI

100. FRUS, 1945, Yalta, 503, 566, 863–64

101. Public Papers [10:29], 1944–45, 570–86

102. Davis [6:32], 295

103. Radio report of President Truman to the Nation, August 9, 1945 in *Public Papers of the Presidents* [8:67], 203–24

104. FRUS, 1945, II, 292

105. The relation between the 'percentages' agreement and the Declaration is discussed in Lundestad [12:12], 92

106. Policy Manual, December 1, 1945, qu. Davis [6:32], 326

107. As published in book form, with comments (New York, 1941). Despite the title, Luce was far from optimistic. He began: 'We Americans are unhappy. We are not happy about America. We are not happy about ourselves in relation to America . . . Roosevelt failed to make American democracy work;' So 'our only chance . . . to make it work is in terms of a vital international economy and in terms of an international moral order'.

108. Blum [3:29]

109. See Divine [4:30], *passim*

110. Gabriel and Joyce Kolko, *The Limits of Power. The World and United States Foreign Policy 1945–1954* (New York 1972), 2; and W. A. Williams [10:95], 150–51; who here argued that the policy of the 'open door' was at least as important as 'atomic diplomacy'. Most Americans in 1946 probably agreed with their President when he stated that both peace and prosperity could be best assured by world trade's restoration 'and it must be returned to private enterprise' (*Public Papers of Harry S. Truman* [8:67], 1946, 168). But that does not mean that a group of 'American leaders' had sat down in Washington to work out a policy.

111. Nicholas [8:3], 252

112. Sherwood [3:9], 878

113. Dallek [8:28], 109

114. *Ibid.*, 122

115. Wendell Willkie, *One World* (London 1943). As William Taubman

[6:35] says, Willkie's visit to Russia in 1942 was a textbook exercise in how *not* to treat the Kremlin. As well as accepting that Soviet persecution of religion was a thing of the past, Willkie made a scarcely disguised attack on Britain, saying that the only two countries which could be counted on to win the war were the Soviet Union and the United States. It was left to Vyshinsky to say that victory depended on the efforts of *three* allies. See FRUS 1943, III, 638–47 and commentary in Taubman, 56. For *One World*, see Divine [4:30], 103–05.

116. William Miller, *A New History of the United States* (London 1958)
117. *Historical Statistics* [9:205], 735
118. Murphy [4:22], 349
119. Robert Ferrell, *Harry S. Truman and the Modern American Presidency* (Boston 1983), 70
120. FRUS, 1946, I, 1111
121. Byrnes in FRUS, 1946, I, 1128–33
122. Forrestal, *Diaries* [8:93]

## Chapter 11 ANGLO-SAXON RELATIONS

1. For *malentendus* between Britain and the US, generally, and not just the East, see Christopher Thorne, *Allies of a Kind* [10:60] and Robert M. Hathaway, *Ambiguous Partnership* (New York 1981), Chapters 8 to 12.
2. Harriman [1:22], 570
3. Kennan, Diary, December 9, 1946, qu. in his *Memoirs* [4:19], *I*. It is fair to recall that, in February 1946, the new US intelligence authority discussed a plan to exchange intelligence with the British, and the Chiefs of staff of the US discussed with British colleagues the idea of collaboration 'during the peace that is rapidly approaching'.
4. Randall, Stockholm to Washington, January 16, 1946; NA: 711–61/1–1646
5. For Churchill, see Chapter 23
6. Kennan [4:19], *Memoirs*, I, 288
7. Nikolai Tolstoy, *Victims of Yalta* (London 1977), 82
8. This is discussed on pages 314–15
9. Volkov [3:32], xxiv
10. Davis [6:32], 207
11. Roberts to Bevin, September 28, 1945, in FO 371/47856 (PRO); and Koukin to Warner, May 19, 1945, in FO 371/4785 (PRO)
12. Bullock [6:58], 213

13. Matthews to Stettinius, June 6, 1945, 711.41/1–645 (NA)
14. Stettinius to Roosevelt, 711. 41/1/245 (NA)
15. OSS memorandum of April 1945, qu. Thorne [10:60], 599
16. PRO: PREM 8/120 1945, dated August 31, 1945, in COS (45) 200
17. See Woodward [3:15], I, 355–99: Churchill [3:13], Chapter 20; Balfour [4:103], 72–80; and Colville [7:1], 360 for details. The role in 1941 of William Stephenson is discussed in Andrew [4:125], 465.
18. See FRUS, 1945, VI, 206. FDR also spoke of the idea in conversation with de Gaulle in July 1944. According to de Gaulle, FDR 'thus intended to lure the Soviets into a group that would contain their ambitions': Charles de Gaulle, *Mémoires*, II, *l'Unité* (Paris 1956, 269). See Kimball [4:25], III, 237–38. He had spoken similarly to Molotov as early as 1942 (Sherwood, 572) as to Eden, of the need for 'strong points' for the four policemen (see Herbert Feis, *Churchill, Roosevelt, Stalin* (Princeton 1957), 121) in 1943.
19. Blum [3:29], 550
20. *Loc. cit.* See also Thorne's summary of US bases' policies (and visions) in *Allies* [10:60], 390–91, 490–92 and 663–65
21. See Keynes's telegram of September 27, 1945. Some of the islands concerned had been matters of dispute between Britain and New Zealand, on the one hand, and the US, on the other, throughout the interwar period. See, for example, the case of Canton island, needed by Pan American for an airport. The Americans took it despite British claims. 'Mr President, you can't do this', said the British Ambassador. 'But Ronny, we've done it', said FDR (Stettinius [4:104], 39)
22. In CAB 21/1916, extract from CM (46) January 11, 1946 (PRO)
23. Stimson diary, qu. Thorne [10:60], 665. Truman was asked about these bases in January 1946. The conversation went thus: Truman: 'Those that we do not need will be placed under UNO trusteeship'. 'And those that we need?' Truman: 'we will keep'. 'Forever?' Truman: 'That depends. As long as we need them'. (*Public Papers of Harry S. Truman* [8:67], 1946, 20–21)
24. Dallek [8:28], 139
25. Margaret Gowing, *Independence and Deterrence 1945–51*, vol. I: *Policy Making* (London 1974), 8
26. Pickersgill and Forster [4:108], III, 19. Gouzenko first went to the offices of *The Ottawa Journal*, where he was told 'nobody wants to say anything but nice things about Stalin' (Gouzenko [4:99], 312)

27. Pickersgill and Forster [4:108], 42
28. *Ibid.*, 51
29. *Ibid.*, 143
30. Gowing [11:23], I, 131–40
31. Sir A. Clark Kerr to Bevin, August 24, 1945 (PRO)
32. Kenneth Harris, *Attlee* (London 1982), 126
33. Letter to Fenner Brockway, September 1945, qu. *ibid.*, 295
34. Pickersgill and Forster [4:108], III, 71
35. Harris [11:32], 147
36. October 29, ATE/45/20 (PRO)
37. Sir William Hayter, *The Kremlin and the Embassy* (London 1966), 39
38. Pickersgill and Forster [4:108], III, 48
39. Gladwyn, Lord, *The Memoirs of*: (London 1972), 121
40. House of Commons, March 1, 1945, Hansard vol. 408, col. 1617
41. Manifesto in *British General Elections 1900–45*, 130–31
42. Trevor Burridge, *Clement Attlee* (London 1985), 221
43. Hansard, House of Commons, February 21, 1946, vol. 419, col. 1348–66
44. *The Times*, May 24, 1945
45. Hayter [11:37], 30; Hathaway [11:1], 178
46. Harold Nicolson, *Diaries*, January 31, 1945
47. Bullock [6:58], 92
48. Sir Nicholas Henderson, *The Private Office* (London 1984), 22
49. To Hector McNeil, qu. Bullock [6:58], 480
50. Cadogan [3:8], 785
51. Byrnes [3:23], 79
52. FO 371/56781 N 3694/140/38 (PRO)
53. Bullock [6:58], 221
54. See Harriman [1:22], 570
55. Duff Cooper diary, in Duff Cooper, *Old Men Forget* (London 1953), 363
56. Bullock [6:58], 235
57. FO 371/56780 N 1471 1/140/38 (PRO)
58. Bullock [6:58], 193. For FO origin of this, see FO 371/477857 N 15085/18/38 (PRO)
59. I owe this insight to Lord Annan.
60. Colville [7:1], 522
61. Gladwyn [11:39], 176
62. Bohlen [3:12], 123
63. Hugh Dalton, *Hugh Dalton, High Tide and After: Memoirs 1945–1960* (London 1962), 129

64. Eben Ayers diary, August 7, 1945. (HSTL) Truman compared Bevin to John L. Lewis.

65. Bullock [6:58], 231

66. W. L. Louis, *The British Empire in the Middle East 1945–51* (Oxford 1984), *passim*: When Molotov demanded an African trusteeship, Bevin told the House of Commons that 'a great power was cutting across the throat of the British Empire'.

67. Henderson [11:48], 28

68. Ben Plimlott, *Hugh Dalton* (London 1985).

69. Burridge [11:42], 189

70. Pickersgill and Forster [4:108], 49

71. Lockhart [9:67], 506

72. Private information

73. Truman [8:7], I, 412

74. Dalton, *War Diaries* [1:11], 626

75. Harold Nicolson to the author, c. 1955. See also Peter G. Boyle, 'The British Foreign Office View of Soviet-American relations 1945–46', *Diplomatic History*, Summer 1979, an article which takes a different view.

76. PRO: FO 371/123/5/34. An exception to this contrived innocence was Owen O'Malley, minister to the Polish government in exile. His despatch on the Katyn murders, arguing that it would be 'inconsistent with British interests that Russia should enjoy a sphere of influence stretching from Danzig to the Adriatic' was not widely circulated (it is published in Kimball [4:25], II, 389–402). For another letter of his, about Churchill's 'faulty' perspective, see de Jonge [3:35], 437–38.

77. Malcolm Mackintosh, *Strategy and Tactics of Soviet Foreign Policy* (London 1962), 311

78. Woodward [3:15], I, xlvi

79. PRO: FO 954/24A SU/36/6, February 19, 1936. Fitzroy Maclean [1:8], was 'assured that the Moscow Embassy was a dead end'. He was the first British diplomatist 'who had ever asked to go to such a notoriously unpleasant post'.

79A De Jonge [3:35], 252–53

80. Henderson [11:48], 22

81. *Ibid.*, 48

82. His minister 'Jock' Balfour, describes him as usually inclined 'to give the Soviets the benefit of the doubt' (*Not too Correct an Aureole* [4: 103])

83. See W. H. Auden and C. Isherwood, *Journey to a War* (London 1939), 156. A personal letter to Tadeusz Romer, foreign minister

of the Polish government in exile, then in Moscow, calling on the Poles to make numerous concessions to the Russian point of view, including 'some kind of withdrawal from the suggestion that the killing at Katyn was done by the Russians' (in J. K. Zawodny, *Nothing but Honour* (Stanford 1979, 218–19), makes sad reading. One member of Kerr's staff assured me that he 'could not believe that the Russians could have killed the Polish officers at Katyn', first, because he 'did not believe human nature could be so evil'; second, because he 'could not bring himself to think ill of an ally'. Kerr, like many others, made a number of erroneous predictions about Chinese communism and reported that it was an 'agrarian reform' movement (see Thorne [10:60], 68).

84. See his letter to Churchill, June 3, 1945; and Snow [4:33], 358, for his view of Truman.
85. Salisbury [4:10], 245
86. Churchill to Kerr, June 15, 1945 PRO
87. FO 181/1022.20.46 PRO
88. Dalton [1:11], 552
89. For this valet, see Frank Giles, *Sunday Times*, January 6, 1980. It seems barely believable that Most was never used by the Soviet Government; but it may be so.
90. Woodward [3:15], III, 561–63
91. *Ibid.*, 563
92. Dalton [1:11], 35
93. Cadogan [3:8], 132–33
94. FRUS, 1941, I, 355; Cadogan [3:8], 398. Cadogan was the strongest opponent in the Office of what he called 'crystal-gazing'.
95. Lord Vansittart, *The Mist Procession* (London 1958), 399
96. *Ibid.*, 399
97. Article on Sargent by Lord Gladwyn in *Dictionary of National Biography 1961–1970* (Oxford 1981), 924
98. Dalton [1:11], 630
99. Lockhart [9:67], 81
100. *Ibid.*, 134
101. FO 371/43636 R10483/68/67 (PRO)
102. Lockhart [9:67], 334
103. Minute of May 2, qu. Woodward [3:15], III, 587
104. Winant to Byrnes, August 23, 1945, qu. Davis [6:32], 314
105. Colville [7:1], 87; Woodward [3:15], I, 100–7
106. Churchill is treated in Chapter 23. I have reserved a full treatment of Anthony Eden for a later volume. In the meantime, for

speculation about his Polish and Soviet position see *Anthony Eden* (London 1981), de Jonge [3:35], 413–16, David Carlton [11:106], 183–96.

107. Woodward [3:15], III, 110 fn; Lockhart [9:67], 317. Warner was interested in Scandinavia. He was close to Sargent without having his intelligence, a bachelor reader of detective stories inclined to believe that Stalin was merely *primus inter pares*.

108. The attitude of Christopher Hill when serving in this department of the Foreign Office can perhaps be suggested by the last chapter, pages 236–37, of his *Lenin and the Russian Revolution* (in the Home University Library, published London 1947), where he concludes that the 'Russian Revolution has demonstrated that the common people of the earth . . . can take over power and run the state infinitely more effectively than their betters'.

109. This was a paper N 1908/36/38 of April 1944, qu. Woodward [3:15], III, 100; private information also. An interesting commentary on the difference between senior and junior officials comes from the briefing given during the war to Sir Giffard Martell *en route* to Moscow: from seniors, he received the advice that 'the best approach was to be very forthcoming and friendly . . . and give in to them, whenever one reasonably could do so'. But officials of medium seniority told him to be 'very forthright and outspoken'. (Sir Giffard Martell, *The Russian Outlook* (London 1947), 46. Policy in the Northern department was perhaps still decided by the old, charitable view of Sir Edward Grey that 'gullibility is better than suspicion'.

110. Woodward [3:15], III, 124

111. *Ibid.*, 344; Carlton, *Eden* [11:106], 254

112. Woodward [3:15], III, 124

113. *Ibid.*, II, 34

114. *Ibid.*, 42

115. Woodward [3:15], II, 227. See also Eden [7:30], 285–303; and the diaries of both his private secretary Oliver Harvey and Alexander Cadogan.

116. *Ibid.*, 241. For suggestions that Eden was influenced to take up a basically pro-Soviet position by his private secretary, Oliver Harvey, see Carlton [11:106], 184–92.

117. Woodward [3:15], II, 245. Churchill took full responsibility: 'under the pressure of events, I did not feel that this moral position could be physically maintained. In a deadly struggle, it is not right to assume more burdens than those who are fighting for a great cause can bear. My opinions about the Baltic states

were, are, unaltered, but I . . . could not carry them farther forward at this time'. (*Hinge of Fate* [3:14], 293)

118. Sir John Wheeler Bennet and Anthony Nicholls, *The Semblance of Peace* (London 1972)

119. Woodward [3:15], III, 110

120. This prophecy is summarised in *ibid.* [3:15], 123–31. Eden circulated it to the cabinet.

121. PRO: FO 371/43305 N 3246/36/38

122. PRO: FO 371/43306 N 5792/6/38. Woodward deals with (V, 205n)

123. Private information.

124. PRO: FO 371/43335: DHP (43) (0) Final (May 1, 1944)

125. PRO: FO 371/43384 N 3781/1120/38 June 6, 1944. This paper was prepared by Gladwyn Jebb (the chairman) C. C. C. Allen, F. C. Curtis, and P. Warburton. It was dated June 6, 1944.

126. JIC (44) 467 (0) (PRO)

127. Dalton [1:11], 609

128. Victor Serge, *Memoirs of a Revolutionary* (English edition, London 1984), xx

129. Pierson Dixon, September 24, 1945, in FO 3/1/47861 (PRO)

130. Memorandum at Potsdam, July 29, 1945 – (U 6311/2600/70 No. 459 of Potsdam Papers, 990). Elsewhere, Jebb remarked 'the stronger we are in general, the more likely the Soviet Government is to work with us' (qu. Thorne [10:60], 662)

131. Cadogan [3:8], 749

132. PRO: FO 371/49071 2336/14/17

133. Harold Nicolson, *Diaries and Letters 1945–62* (London 1968), entry for June 4, 1946

134. PRO: PREM 4/21/5: General Smuts to PM and Eden March 20, 1944. Churchill minuted 'Certainly a paper should be prepared.' April 3, 1944. Smuts's later paper on the subject can be seen in Kimball [4:25] III, 334–36

135. Private communication

136. PRO: FO 371/43579 R724

137. H. R. Trevor-Roper, *The Philby Affair* (London 1968); Robert Cecil in Dilkes and Andrew [4:128]. Philby was apparently instructed by his Soviet controller to gain this job at all costs. See his account of his intrigues to fulfil this order in his *My Silent War* (London 1968) and commentary in e.g. Lamphere [4:109], 228f.

138. This was 'F' section, concerned with 'both' political extremes

139. Leslie R. Groves, *Now it Can be Told* (New York 1962), 143.

This 'same reason' was one of many why a Soviet agent in MI5 was suspected. For discussion, see Chapman Pincher, *Too Secret Too Long* (London 1984) and the statement made in the House of Commons by the Prime Minister on the subject (March 1981, Hansard, House of Commons, vol. 1 (new series), col. 1079).

140. CAB 21/2554 DO (47) 25, COS, qu. Andrew [4:125], 40

141. PRO: FO 954/24 SOE/44/17 April 6, 1944

142. Trevor-Roper [11:137], 28–29

143. *The Times* obituary (May 31, 1968); and *DNB, 1961–1970*, 749–50

144. Trevor-Roper [11:137], 70–11

145. From a letter by the official concerned.

146. Blum [3:29], 492

147. G3982/72/G COS MED (PRO)

148. See Sporborg's letter to Warner in PRO: FO 371/47710 N4771/265/55G of April 27, 1945; and minute by Roger Allen, FO 371/46604 C6129/72/93. For suggestions that SOE 'outgunned SIS' in Greece, see Nigel Clive, *A Greek Experience* (London 1985), 29

149. PRO: FO 371/47710 N 4771/265/55 G

150. Andrew [4:125] 259 ff

151. House of Commons debate, Hansard 1927, vol. 206, cols. 2195–310

152. CAB 129/1 cp (45) 112, qu. in W. K. Hancock and M. M. Gowing, *British War Economy* (London 1952), 546–49. For Attlee's reaction to this 'bodyblow', as he put it, see his *As it Happened* (London, no date), 174–75

153. Urban [1:15], 235–36

154. Hugh Thomas, *John Strachey* (London 1973). The pamphlet was 'Why you should be a Socialist', first published 1938.

155. George Orwell [2:57], III

156. *Ibid.*, 176, 186. See Paul Addison, *The Road to 1945* (London 1975), 137; and, Bernard Crick, *George Orwell, A Life* (London 1981), 336

157. Gladwyn [11:39], 117–18

158. Addison [11:156], 134–42

159. Orwell [2:57], IV, 62

160. William Temple, *Christianity and Social Order* (London 1942), 34; J. B. Priestley, *Letter to a Returning Serviceman* (London 1945), 24; for Taylor, see *Listener*, November 22, 1945; G. D. H. Cole, *The Intelligent Man's Guide to Post-war Britain* (London

1948), 802. I owe all these references to Thomas Howarth, *Prospect and Reality: Great Britain 1945–55* (London 1984)

161. *The Times*, July 27, 1945 comments on Laski's expression in August of 'profoundly brotherly affection for the Soviet Union' see House of Commons, Hansard, vol. 413, col. 89, August 16, 1945

162. *Star*, August 6, 1945

163. PRO: FO 371/475905 N7540/6/55, June 29, 1945

164. Iverach McDonald, *The History of* The Times: *Struggles in War and Peace 1936–1966* (London 1984), 88; Julian Amery, *Approach March* (London 1973), 189–90

165. Salisbury [4:10], 249. Werth's book *Russia at War* [1:19] has many insights.

166. For example, 'The British and the Balkans', *New Statesman*, November 24, 1945

167. *The Times*, October 4, 1945 (for the leader quoted). I benefited from a discussion with Mr Iverach Macdonald for this picture of Barrington-Ward's character and his relations with 'Ted' Carr.

168. Summary of the conversation between Eden and Molotov October 16, 1944 in PRO: PREM 3.434/4, 35. Eden did not then seem to have any idea of the numbers concerned. The arrangements were confirmed to cover 'all Soviet citizens freed by forces operating under United States command,' on February 11, 1945 in a document signed at Yalta by Stalin, FDR and Churchill.

169. These decisions are treated in Carlton's *Eden*, [11:106] 240–42

170. Deane [9:54] was naturally primarily concerned with the freedom of the 15,000 American prisoners freed by the Russians (Deane, 40)

171. Tolstoy [11:7], 161

171A That something untoward occurred is suggested by the subsequent testimony of a Soviet NKVD officer who came to the West (looked on as a serious man in intelligence circles): 'The British lured them, about two thousand men in all, into a trap by inviting them supposedly to take part in a conference with Field Marshal Alexander. I found out these details later from our NKVD agents, who had been with Krasnov [the Cossack commander] for a long time. They had played the parts of anti-Soviet Cossack officers who had gone over to the Germans and were handed over to us along with the others. There were the same kind of agents in the Vlasov movement'. (A. I. 'Romanov', *The Nights are Longest There* (London 1971), 154). Notes for a draft Foreign Office 'White Paper' on the subject of conditions in immediate post-war Austria (FO

1020/792 ACA195/138 November 23, 1945), never published, says: '35. 55,000 Cossacks were repatriated at the end of May'. The rest of the draft paper discusses the confused conditions in Austria at that time, with the British commander finding himself responsible for '236,000 troops of more than 30 nationalities'. What happened may be best conveyed by a note in a chronicle of events prepared for the same unpublished paper: 'May 29, agreements reached: Germans to SHAEF; Cossacks to Russians; Croats to Jugs'. All the same, it is obvious from e.g. Stalin's conversation with Emil Ludwig in 1931 that Krasnov preoccupied him; and he wanted him back.

172. FRUS, 1945, V, 1097
173. *Ibid.*, 1946, V, 141–42
174. FO 1020/95 (PRO)
175. Tolstoy [11:7], 15
176. *Ibid.*, 394
177. Djilas, in Urban [1:15], 236
178. Comment of Lord Aldington (Brigadier Low)
179. The notes for the Foreign Office's (unpublished) draft 'White Paper' on conditions in Austria at the end of the war (FO 1020/792 ACA195/138) implies to my reading that, in the 'complete chaos' which then reigned, the Yugoslavs were returned (by General Keightley) to their homeland as a condition for Tito's withdrawal: thus: '5. At the same time, numbers of Croats [i.e. also Slovenes, Chetniks, etc.] were also invading the country from the south as Tito's armies drove them northwards. As a result of governmental decision, Tito eventually withdrew and the majority of the Croats were handed back to Yugoslavia'. SOE Yugoslavia then worked closely with Tito's forces.
180. Paul Kennedy, *Strategy and Diplomacy* (London 1984), 105
181. See 'Comment' (i.e. Cyril Connolly), in *Horizon*, vol. XII, No. 69 (September 1945)
182. The 'Dynamos' played: Chelsea (draw); Cardiff (Russians win); Arsenal (Russians win); Glasgow (draw). (*The Times*, November 21 and 30, 1945)

# BOOK THREE
## DISPUTED LANDS

CHAPTER 12 FAR AWAY COUNTRIES: EASTERN EUROPE, POLAND AND CZECHOSLOVAKIA

I am grateful to Dr Antony Polonsky for kindly reading the Polish section of this chapter, thereby saving me from many errors.

1. Private letter, September 2, 1945: Countess Nathalie Bencken-dorff to her mother. 'We are not afraid of the atomic bomb!' was also a slogan in the abortive election campaign in August 1945 in Sofia (FRUS, 1945, IV, 308)
2. Grew [9:5], II, 1465
3. e.g. Maisky to Frank Roberts, in Roberts to Christopher Warner, 30 June 1945 (PRO)
4. See Bevin's speech, February 22, 1946, House of Commons, Hansard, vol. 419, col. 1349
5. M. N. Roy, 'Joseph Stalin, Mephisto of Modern History', *The Radical Humanist* (Bombay) XIV, No. 49 (December 10, 1950), qu. Goodman [1:16], 298
6. FO 371/56832, March 18, 1946, Foreign Office briefing to Sir Maurice Peterson, ambassador-elect to Moscow
7. Bela Szasz in Charlton [2:83], 55
8. Gomułka's speech, October 20, 1956 to Polish Central Committee, qu. Paul Zinner, *National Communism* (New York 1956), 228
9. Jozsef, Cardinal Mindszenty, *Memoirs* (London 1975), 22
10. E. A. Radice in Martin McCauley, *Communist power in Europe 1944–49* (London 1977), 20; Antony Polonsky, *The Little Dictators* (London 1975)
11. This made the resumption of trade with the west more difficult too. See Margaret Dewar, *Soviet Trade with Eastern Europe 1945–1949* (London 1951), 2–3
12. Before 1940, Eastern Europe had only 5.5 per cent of US investment, sent 3.5 per cent of US imports, and received only 2 per cent of US exports. See Geir Lundestad, *The American Non-Policy towards Eastern Europe 1943–1947* (Oslo 1978), 71
13. Nissan Oren, *Bulgarian Communism* (New York 1971)
14. Djilas [2:60], 265
15. Artur London, *L'Aveu* (Paris 1968), 15; Trepper [4:66], *The Great Game* (London 1977), 147; Oren [12:13], 179. Young

revolutionaries in the Comintern schools were sent direct to Spain in 1936; and back to their own countries in 1944–45

16. Foote's *A Handbook for Spies* [4:127] includes a chapter entitled 'It all began in Spain'. Morris Cohen ('Peter Kroeger') was similarly recruited in Spain. So was at least one of the 'Canadians' revealed by Guzenko: Henning Sorensen, liaison officer in Spain between Dr Bethune's hospital group and the Spanish Republican Army.

17. Djilas, *Memoir* [2:60], 190

18. Murphy [4:22], 366

19. The helplessness of the *peoples* of the Balkans in the maelstrom of these world wars was not a factor which weighed much elsewhere.

20. Murphy [4:22], 367

21. Hegedus, conversation with Zoltan Zeille, qu. George Urban, *Encounter*, September–October 1985, 16

22. Fainsod [2:7], 87

23. Urban, *Stalinism* [1:15]

24. This was Kennan's reconstruction of what Stalin might have thought in his Despatch, September 3, 1952 (*Memoirs* [5:21], II)

25. Stephen Clissold, *Whirlwind* (London 1949), 240

26. Zbigniew Brzezinski, *The Soviet bloc: unity & conflict* (Cambridge, Mass. 1967), 6–7

27. For a summary of the old 'bourgeois' parties of East Europe, see Chapter II of Hugh Seton-Watson's *The East European Revolution* (2nd edition, London 1952)

28. I am indebted to Professor W. H. McNeil for this observation.

29. For the Outer Mongolian 'model', the role of Ivan Maisky there, and the proof that its experience was on the syllabus at Comintern schools, see Hammond, *Anatomy* [2:38], 110

30. For the forming of this army in Russia, see General Anders' memoir, *An Army in Exile* (London 1948), Chapters V to IX.

31. Seton-Watson, *The East European Revolution* [12:27], 115–19

32. For 'Revkom', see Lerner in Hammond, *Anatomy* [2:38], 101–3

33. See Teresa Toranska, *They* [3:53], 46

34. Djilas, *Memoir* [2:60], 115

35. Nicholas Bethell, *Gomułka* (London 1969), 2–5

36. Norman Davies, *God's Playground* (Oxford 1981), II, 558, where Gomułka is quoted as saying 'the masses do not regard us as Polish communists at all, but just as the most despicable agents of the NKVD'. He was often candid: he told Mikołajczyk in June

1945, 'Once we have attained power we shall never give it up' (Bethell [12:35], 102)

37. Lane, 105; FO 371/47707 NI 4864/211/55, October 24, 1945

38. Recollection of Lord Hankey. Radkiewicz told Lane that the Russians had 'lent him 200 NKVD instructors'.

39. Toranska [3:53], 52

40. For an account in which a Polish typist, employed in the British Consulate, was involved, see letter from Cavendish Bentinck to C. F. A. Warner, October 24, 1945, in FO 371/47707 NI 4864/211/55. For Lane's problems of the same sort, see *I saw Freedom Betrayed* [12:40], 126–27

41. See Mikołajczyk's *The Pattern of Soviet Domination* [10:40], 166–67, and in numerous secret reports to the British and US governments.

42. Milovan Djilas, *Rise and Fall* (New York 1985), 115; Lane [12:40], 99

43. Leonhard [4:85], 178

44. Qu. Andrej Korbonski, *Politics of Socialist Agriculture in Poland 1945–1960* (New York 1965), 109 fn. 41

45. Qu. Brzezinski [12:26]

46. Pollard [6:63], 42; Lane [12:40], 145. One of the difficulties about UNRRA in Poland was that it was directed by a Russian, V. Menshikov, who agreed with the Polish Government that it should be they who should administer the assistance concerned. Thus, though ninety per cent of the Poles were Catholics, Catholic schools received little help. Lane discusses this (pages 136–37).

47. See Patrick Howarth, *Intelligence Chief Extraordinary* (London 1986)

48. Recollection of Lord Hankey

49. Archbishop Adam Sapieha of Cracow's estimate to Ambassador Lane, FRUS, 1945, V, 389

50. Korbonski [12:44], 114

51. PRO: FO 371/41917 NI 4894/5541/38G (Cavendish-Bentinck to Bevin). Relations between communists and the Home Army had been exacerbated by the dropping into Poland of Russian-trained party members by parachute behind the German lines to carry out sabotage. This was not co-ordinated with the Home Army's command and led to German reprisals on civilians.

52. Polonsky [12:10], 28

53. Korbonski [12:44], 119

54. M. K. Dziewanowski, *The Communist Party of Poland* (Cam-

bridge, Mass. 1959), 196. See also S. Korbonski, *W Imieniu Kremla* (Paris 1956), qu. Brzezinski [12:26], 8 fn.

55. See Jozef Mackiewicz, *The Katyn Wood Murders* (London 1951), 49

56. PRO: FO 371/47709 NI 2446/256/G55

57. Report on interrogation of P. O. Hubert Brooks in PRO: FO 371/47709 78667

58. Werth describes a visit there in *Russia at War*, 889–99; Davies, in McCauley [12:10], 42

59. Major Pickles to D. Allen, January 24, 1945, in PRO: FO 371/47709 NI 002/265/G55

60. Sikorski was the one man who might have persuaded his country-men to have accepted the Curzon line (with compensation in the West), in return for a genuinely independent Poland. His removal was so convenient to the Soviet Union that it is understandable that many should conclude that he was murdered by Stalin. Characteristically, Stalin began to accuse the British of killing Sikorski by the end of 1943.

61. Comment by Count Raczyński, June 1986

62. DPSR, I, 274: Mikołajczyk, 25. Stalin offered Sikorski 'a very little agreement' which would hardly change Poland. Sikorski refused: his government could not accept it.

63. Woodward [3:15], II, 202

64. *Ibid.*, 232 and 657–62. The line appears in fact to have been drawn in 1919 by H. J. Paton, an Oxford philosopher.

65. FRUS, 1942, III, 509

66. DPSR, II, 11

67. Foreign office minute by Sir William Malkin, March 9, 1942, in FO 371/47704 (PRO)

68. FRUS 1943, III, 361–62, March 23, 1943. In February 1943, the communist playwright Korneytchuk spoke (*Radianska Ukraina*, February 19, 1943, qu. Mikołajczyk, 29) of Russia's claims in East Poland.

69. Sherwood [3:9], 707

70. Conquest in Charlton [2:83], 29

71. Woodward [3:15], II, 625–30; Mikołajczyk [10:40], 24; see, for this 'Manchurian candidacy', DPSR, I, 233. It is now difficult to understand how anyone could have doubted Soviet guilt. Yet even B. H. Sumner, the Russian specialist in the Foreign Office's Research Department, gave the Russians the benefit of the doubt. Churchill, who knew the truth, observed to Count Raczyński, 'the Russians are very cruel'. See Kimball [4:25], II, 389–99.

For the Soviet insertion of this into the Nuremberg indictment see Sidney Alderman in Dennett and Johnson [4:80], 96–97

72. PRO: FO 371/31091 C 12329/464/55 (December 19, 1942)

73. FRUS, 1943, III, 401

74. The subject was dismissed by *Izvestiia* in November 1943. For a discussion, see Goodman [1:16], 389–92

75. Sherwood [3:9], 776

76. Winston Churchill, *Closing the Ring* (vol. 5 of *The Second World War*) (London 1952), 319

77. *Ibid.*, 320

78. FRUS, 1943, Tehran, 594 (Bohlen recalled that this was the first time that anyone knew that FDR might run for a fourth term)

79. Dallek [8:28], 437

80. Bohlen [3:12], 152

81. For a discussion of the Curzon line, see Woodward [3:15], II, 657–62. In 1920, the Red Army drove across the 'line' when Curzon proclaimed it the ethnic frontier, subsequently to be driven back (see Lerner, in Hammond [2:38], *Anatomy*, 101).

82. Woodward [3:15], II, 651

83. Kennan [4:19], 215

84. Adam Ulam, *Expansion and Co-existence* (New York 1968), 355–57

85. Davis [6:32], 96

86. Churchill's figure at Potsdam (Woodward [3:15], V, 421)

87. Gaddis [6:62], 141. This territory (including Lvov) provided 63 per cent of Poland's oil in 1939, 90 per cent of its natural gas, and 42 per cent of its water power.

88. See Churchill's speech in the House of Commons, February 22, 1944 (Hansard, House of Commons, vol. 397, cols. 679–701) where he said that the Curzon line 'attempted to deal with the position and that he could not feel that the Russian demand for a reassurance about her Western frontiers goes beyond the limits of what is reasonable and just'.

89. Woodward [3:15], III, 191. It was on this occasion that Roosevelt assured Mikołajczyk that Stalin was no imperialist and 'doesn't intend to take freedom from Poland': 'I will see to it that Poland will not be hurt in this war and will emerge strongly independent', he added. See Taubman's commentary in *Stalin's American Policy* [6:35], 72.

90. Dziewanowski [12:54], 161; Korbonski [12:44], 51–55

91. Korbonski [12:44], 64

92. Jan Ciechanowski, *Defeat in Victory* (London 1947), 308

93. FRUS, 1944, III, 1414

94. R. F. Staar, *Poland 1944–1962* (Baton Rouge 1962), 167

95. Major Pickles's report in PRO: FO 371/47709 N3354/265/G55

96. Kennan [4:19], I, 211; FRUS, 1944, III, 1375 and 1386–89

97. Telegram of August 22, qu. Dallek [8:28], 464. He asked Mikołajczyk: 'Can you give me your word of honour that there is fighting going on in Warsaw? The Lublin Poles tell me there is no fighting at all' (Mikołajczyk [10:40], 85).

98. See John Ehrman, *History of the Second World War: Grand Strategy*, V (London 1956); J. K. Zawodny [11:83], Woodward [3:15], III, 203, 221

99. Woodward [3:15], III, 217, fn. 1. Since the Polish government in London had no diplomatic contacts with Moscow, Bohr could only have communicated, as he did, through the British. Hugh Seton-Watson thought (*The East European Revolution* [12:27], 116) that the reason for Soviet unwillingness to let the aircraft land may have been that they did not wish American airmen to see their primitive airfields.

100. Kennan [4:19], 211. He said the same in 1972 to Zawodny, *Nothing but Honour* [11:83], 223

101. Roosevelt to Churchill, August 26 (Kimball [4:25], III, 296); he said the same to the President of the Polish American Congress, Chas. Rozmarek, on October 28, 1944 (Lane [12:40], 39). The British historian of allied Grand Strategy concluded that relations between Britain and Russia now suffered a shock from which they never fully recovered (Ehrman [12:98], 376). Churchill wanted to suggest cutting off Western aid to Russia but the Foreign Office and Roosevelt persuaded him to think better of it (Woodward [3:15], III, 215 fn.).

102. e.g. report by Major Pickles in PRO: FO 371/47709 1007, January 26, 1945

103. Woodward [3:15], III, 224–31; Mikołajczyk [10:40], 104–7; DPSR, II, 405–30. This was the occasion when Churchill bullied Mikołajczyk mercilessly: 'You're a callous people who want to abandon your people at home. You are indifferent to their suffering'. He even told Mikołajczyk that he should be in a lunatic asylum.

104. Churchill, *Triumph and Tragedy* [3:13], 327; Woodward [3:15], III, 257

105. FRUS, 1945, *Yalta*, 776–79; 854; 973.

106. Cadogan [3:8], 707. Feis [6:33], 26, now thinks that 'it would have been better to have risked a break with Stalin at Yalta'.

107. Rosenman papers, qu. Davis [6:32], 190. Leahy was not optimis-

tic: 'Mr President, this is so elastic that the Russians can stretch it all the way from Yalta to Washington without technically breaking it.' 'I know, Bill, I know', said Roosevelt, 'but it's the best I can do for Poland at this time.'

108. Clark Kerr to Eden, March 23, 1945 (PRO)
109. Eden to Churchill, March 24, 1945 (PRO)
110. See Davis [6:32], 205–12; Woodward [3:15], III, 490–512
111. The letters are in Woodward [3:15], III, 515–23
112. PRO: FO 371/47589 N4976/6/55 (FO to Moscow, May 9, 1945)
113. NA: 711.61/6–1145, Hopkins report by Leahy to Byrnes. See also Sherwood [3:9], 878–902; FRUS, 1945, *Potsdam*, I, 21–62
114. Sherwood [3:9], 889; FRUS, *Potsdam*, 1945, 39
115. Woodward [3:15], III, 506
116. *Ibid.*, III, 531
117. *The Times*, June 22, 1945. Considering that the trial, in Moscow, was of Poles, for being anti-Soviet, in Poland, *The Times*'s attitude is incomprehensible.
118. This insolent treatment of brave men who had fought the Germans continuously since 1939, and who were known to be friendly to the Western Allies, should have awoken the latter to the realities of power in East Europe. See Woodward [3:15], III, 555, 556–58. For details of the trial, see DPSR II, 601–5 and Z. F. Ztypulowski, *Invitation to Moscow* (London 1951), 300–33. Lane discusses (pp. 74–5). Some of those concerned were ultimately released. But the fate of Okulicki, who refused to plead guilty, remains obscure. Presumably he died in prison. The proceedings were published in Moscow as '*The Trial of the Polish Conspirators*'.
119. Bethell [12:35], 104. Churchill told Mikołajczyk: 'I think you should use this last opportunity to get not only your foot but your leg in the door' (Mikołajczyk [10:40], 132).
120. *The Times*, June 25, 1945
121. Davis [6:32], 244
122. Clark Kerr to London, March 30, 1945 (PRO). Danzig and southern East Prussia had been similarly absorbed.
123. Woodward [3:15], III, 251–52; Churchill, *Triumph and Tragedy* [3:13], 581: 'Neither I nor Mr Eden would ever have agreed to the Western Neisse being the frontier line'. But would he really have had a 'showdown' on this issue?
124. Bierut said a million and a half in July (Woodward [3:15], V, 427)
125. Korbonski [12:44], 87
126. Qu. Bethell [12:35], 113

127. Churchill, *Triumph and Tragedy* [3:13], 575; Woodward [3:15], V, 425

128. Bethell [12:35], 120

129. As Marshal Tukhachevsky said in 1920: 'Across the corpse of White Poland lies the road to world conflagration' (Qu. Lerner, in Hammond, *Anatomy* [2:38], 99)

130. Seton-Watson, *Imperial Russia* [3:40], 288

131. Leahy to Byrnes, reporting on Hopkins's visit to Stalin in June 1945, NA 711.61/6–1145. In October 1944, Stalin had told Mikołajczyk: 'in 1914 we were much further to the West. Poland is fortunate that I am not asking for more'.

132. Marx and Engels, *The Russian Menace to Europe* [2:34]

133. DPSR, II, 432: 'Poland must have a democratic rule', said Stalin. 'Private ownership and a free economic life should be maintained'.

134. FRUS, 1946, VI, 404–5

135. Korbonski [12:44], 48–9

136. *Ibid.*, 35–37

137. Kołakowski in Charlton [2:38], 88

138. Mikołajczyk's comment to Clark Kerr in July 1945, qu. Woodward [3:15], V, 414

139. See Werth [1:19], 1018

140. 'Don't worry, I'll never forget Poland', Churchill had assured Mikołajczyk in 1944 [10:40], 118

141. Věra Olivová, *The Doomed Democracy* (London 1972), 189

142. Engels, 'Democratic Panslavism' in *The Russian Menace* [2:34], 77

143. J. Navratil and J. Domansky, qu. Vladimir Kusin in Martin McCauley [12:10]

144. Cave Brown, *Last Hero* [9:182], 655

145. McCagg [1:13], 61

146. Ducháček to Charlton, Charlton [2:83], 56

147. See Claire Sterling, *The Masaryk Case* (Boston 1982), for details.

148. See report by P. Nichols, June 18 in PRO: FO 371/47088 N7487/207/12

149. See Miss Gallacher's report in PRO: FO 371/47099 N1903/259/G/12

150. Foreign Office report on PRO: 'SOE–NKVD co-operation' in FO 371/47709 N2016/265/G55

151. Artur London, *L'Aveu* [12:15], 170

152. Frantisek Moravec, *Master of Spies* (London 1975), 240. Svoboda admitted (official record of the Central Committee of the Czech communist party (qu. Pavel Tigrid, in Hammond, *Anatomy*

[2:38], 420) in 1959) that he was in April 1945 a 'faithful and well-disciplined' communist who was not allowed formally to be a member because it was more convenient that he did not show himself as such.

153. Kennan, *Memoirs* [4: 19], I, 250; Lockhart [9:67], 411.

154. Moravec [12:152], 241

155. Pietro Nenni, *Tempo di Guerra Fredda, Diari, 1943–1956* (Milano 1981), 176. Masaryk's advocacy of the Lublin Polish Government in May 1945 at the San Francisco government indicated his support for Soviet policies even then.

157. Navratil and Domansky, qu. Kusin, in McCauley [12:10], 87–84

158. Pollard [6:63], 47. As will be remembered, Steinhardt had been ambassador to Moscow before Harriman, and had formed sober, cold views of the Soviet intentions in June 1941 (see fn. 28A of Chapter 9)

159. FRUS, 1946, VI, 179

160. Charlton [2:83], 84

161. Kusin in McCauley [12:10], 78

162. FRUS, 1945, IV, 446; and FRUS, 1945, IV, 449

163. Truman [8:7], I, 134; for Eisenhower's attitude, see Murphy [4:22], 313; FRUS, 1945, IV, 446, for Churchill's request; see Eden's letter to Winant of April 16, 1945, saying 'It would be most desirable politically for Prague to be liberated by the US Army' (FO 371/47121 N3797/650/12). There are also minutes on this arising from Churchill's conversation with Eisenhower on April 24, 1945, which, to my mind, do not suggest that there was a question of a 'Denmark–Prague trade-off', as is implied in David Eisenhower, *Eisenhower at war* (New York 1986), 771

164. Forrest Pogue, *The Supreme Command* (Washington 1954), 469. Antonov's ground was 'to avoid a possible confusion of forces'.

165. FO 371/47086 N5445/207/12

166. This was Smrkovsky's own story in 1968. But Eisenhower again restrained Patton: see David Eisenhower [12:163], 795–96.

167. Mastny [5:14], 278–79; Michael Charlton in *Encounter*, July 1983; Murphy [4:22], 313

168. PRO: FO 371/47086 N5571/307/12

169. Lockhart [9:67], 600

170. Report of Col. Harold Perkins of May 14, source same as cited in fn. 168

171. Charlton [2:83], 58. Duchaček had talked to a catholic jeweller who had just become a communist for opportunistic reasons.

172. See Frank Roberts's comment, March 1945, in Woodward [3:15], III, 564
173. Moravec [12:152], 249
174. Mastny [5:14], 135. Herbert Ripka's *East and West* (London 1944) was an argument for collaboration with Russia.
175. *New York Times*, May 29, 1943
176. See Eduard Táborský, 'A Polish–Czechoslovak Confederation: a story of the first Soviet veto', *Journal of Central European Affairs*, vol. IX, no. 4, Jan. 1950
177. Mastny [5:14], 227–28; Beneš on return to London was 'very hopeful about the Russian situation. The Russians are quite agreeable to Beneš having his old pre-Munich frontier back, with a slight military adjustment along the northern crests of the mountains and a little territory to the eastward linking them with Russia' (Churchill to Roosevelt, Kimball [4:25], II, 651)
178. The text of the treaty is to be seen in Holborn, *War aims of the United Nations*, 2 vols. (Boston 1943–48), vol. II, 761–63
179. Qu. Charlton [2:83], 73
180. Walter Laqueur, *The Terrible Secret* (London 1980), 163
181. Alfred de Zayas, *Nemesis at Potsdam* (London, 2nd edition 1979)
182. See Freda Utley, *The High Cost of Vengeance* (Chicago 1949), 206
183. This figure is from Statistisches Bundesamt, *Vertreibungsverluste*, 1958, 325, qu. Zayas 129.
184. Mackintosh in Hammond, *Anatomy* [2:38], 233–34; Seton-Watson, *The East European Revolution* [12:27], 146–47
185. Report of British officer in Czechoslovakia, dated June 2, 1945, in FO 371/47087 N6451/207/12 (PRO)
186. Cadogan [3:8], 100
187. Utley [12:182], 46
188. Kusin in McCauley [12:10], 77
189. Qu. William V. Wallace, *Czechoslovakia* (London 1977), 189
190. Stephen Kertesz, *Between Russia and the West* (Notre Dame 1984)
191. Táborský in Charlton [2:83], 73
192. For a detailed study see F. Němec and V. Moudry, *The Soviet Seizure of Subcarpathian Ruthenia* (Toronto 1955)
193. Miss Charles's report of June 8 in FO 371/47087 N6648/207/12 (PRO)
194. These mines were handed over, by officials of the communist-controlled Ministry of the Interior, to the Soviet govern-

ment without approval, or, apparently, consultation, of the cabinet.

195. Steinhardt to Byrnes, November 19, 1945, qu. Herken [8:133], 328

196. London [12:15], 440

197. Countess Nathalie Benckendorff to her mother, January 10, 1986.

## CHAPTER 13 NATIONS OF THE DANUBE: HUNGARY, ROMANIA, AND BULGARIA

I am grateful to Ian Roberts for his advice on the Hungarian section of this chapter and to Malcolm Mackintosh for his on the Bulgarian section. The latter kindly showed me his unpublished paper on Soviet policy on the Balkans in 1944: a British view which contains a clear account of the *coup* in Sofia of September 1944. Another unpublished paper which I found valuable was that by Ivor Porter on SOE and Romania.

1. Miklós Molnar, *A Short History of the Hungarian Communist Party* (Boulder 1978), 57

2. FRUS, 1945, IV, 904. For a Hungarian view, there is Ferenc Nagy, *The Struggle Behind the Iron Curtain* (New York 1948), chapters 37–38. This election was looked upon, in the American debate about the causes of the cold war, as an indication of Soviet capacity for moderation. See, for example, Barton J. Bernstein, ed. *Politics and Policies of the Truman Administration* (Chicago 1970), 38. See also Louis Mark in Hammond, *Witnesses* [5:32], 206–7; Harriman on his visit to Budapest at the time of the municipal elections, *op. cit.* 510.

3. McCagg [1:13], 286

4. FRUS, 1946, VI, 275

5. Szasz in Charlton [2:83], 67. Nagy had earned Rákosi's disapproval because his broadcasts from Moscow in the war had been nationalistic in tone.

6. FRUS, 1944, III, 907–55

7. FRUS, 1945, *Yalta*, 43, 238–39

8. Stephen Kertesz, *Between Russia and the West* (Notre Dame 1984), 38

9. The Armistice of 1944 had specified that 'Transylvania (or the greater part thereof) be returned to Romania'. The Americans thought that the pre-war boundaries should be redrawn to give to Hungary the territory in north Transylvania where there was

an Hungarian majority. Britain supported Russia in their backing for Romania, and the United States abandoned their modest stand (FRUS, 1946, VI, 272–73)

10. Szasz, in Charlton [2:83], 67

11. During the 'siege', the Germans and Hungarian fascists plundered and robbed the West, and the Russians the East, while artillery pounded in both directions.

12. Members of the last pre-1944 Hungarian government took refuge in the US zone of Germany, but most were handed over to the new régime and shot in 1945–46.

13. Mindszenty [12:9], 266–67

14. Hungary's usefulness to Germany had included the provision of good communications across her territory, of food and manufactures in a country free from Allied bombing till 1944.

15. Molnar [13:1], 43, 48

16. Paul Ignotus (in Hammond, *Anatomy* [2:38], 393) suggests that Rákosi put this interpretation around himself: 'if only that dogmatic Gerö didn't force our path', he was wont to say, he would be much more open to non-Communists.

17. General Key's report, FRUS, 1945, IV, 854

18. Speech, March 1952, at Party High School; Schöpflin in McCauley [12:10], 98, 109

19. *Ibid.*, 67. See Ignotus, in Hammond [2:38]. For Rajk's negotiations in the war with the Horthy government, see Imre Kovacs, *D'Une occupation à l'autre* (Paris 1949) (Tr. from German)

20. 'On the Character of our People's Democracy' by Jozsef Revai, in *Foreign Affairs*, vol. 28, 1949, 143–52

21. Mindszenty [12:9], 85

22. E. Reale, qu. Schöpflin in McCauley [12:10], 105

23. H. F. A. Schoenfeld, 'Soviet Imperialism in Hungary', *Foreign Affairs*, vol. 26 (1947–48), 554–66

24. Molnar [13:1], 27

25. David Lilienthal's impression; in Diaries [8:13], 61

26. FRUS, 1945, IV, 848–50

27. Khrushchev [2:5], I, 326. Rákosi was released from his prison in Hungary in 1940 in exchange for the Hungarian flags sent to Moscow after the surrender of the Hungarian army to the Russians at Világos in 1849.

28. Kertesz [13:8], 19

29. Molnar [13:1], 39

30. *Ibid.*, 42

31. *Ibid.*, 133

32. Orwell [2:57], IV, 83
33. Kertesz [13:8], 22
34. Harriman [1:22], 511
35. A Soviet colonel supervising the dismantling of a Hungarian factory was reminded of a small American interest in the concern. 'Where do you see any American troops?' was his reply (Mark in Hammond [5:52], *Witnesses*, 208)
36. Copock to Wilcox, NA: 711–61/11–1645
37. FRUS, 1946, VI, 258
38. Mindszenty [12:9], 47–50
39. There are acute pictures of both Dej and Ana Pauker in Enver Hoxha, *The Artful Albanian* (London 1986), 117: the former seemed 'tall . . . with black eyes, black brows and hair, well-dressed and cheerful, who gave the impression of a *perifani*, as we say in Girokastra about those people who are vigorous and energetic and speak with a sort of pride in themselves . . . Ana Pauker was . . . of a quieter nature . . . energetic too . . . big, heavy-featured . . . who looked as if she had suffered more in prison than Dej, her hair was grey and cut short . . . *à la garçonne.*' For a further discussion, see Ghita Ionescu, *Communism in Rumania 1944–1962* (London 1964) and Stephen Fischer-Galati, *The New Rumania* (Cambridge, Mass. 1967).
40. Le Rougetel to Bevin (PRO), November 28, 1945
41. Memorandum by Cloyce Haston, April 11, 1944, in FRUS, 1944, IV, 172. For General Schuyler's recollections of his vague instructions, see his essay in Hammond, *Witnesses* [5:52], 125 ('Well, Schuyler, you will be on your own, so don't get into trouble')
42. September 15, 1944; FRUS, 1944, IV, 235
43. FRUS, 1945, *Yalta*, 238 and 43
44. FO 371/43336; N8065/183/38 (PRO)
45. FRUS, V, 544–45
46. Schuyler to Washington, 711–61/2245 (NA)
47. FRUS, 1946, V, 630
48. Reuben Markham, *Rumania under the Soviet Yoke* (New York 1949), 435–38
49. See Elizabeth Barker, *British Policy in South East Europe in the Second World War* (London 1976), 230–32
50. Lynn E. Davis [6:32], 258–60
51. FRUS, 1945, V, 484–98. Churchill twice chided his Foreign Office and British diplomats in Bucharest for criticising Russia there (Carlton, *Eden* [11:106], 254, 255).

52. FO 371/48547 R4092/28/37 (PRO)
53. Markham [13:48], 456–58
54. *Ibid.*, 211. The King contemplated abdication but believed that he could still be helpful if he remained.
55. See Ivor Porter's memorandum, kindly lent to me by Malcolm Mackintosh.
56. FRUS, 1945, V, 553
57. *Ibid.*, 1944, 1V, 279–80
58. Kimball [4:25], III, 548
59. Franklin A. Lindsay, 'Unconventional War', *Foreign Affairs*, vol. 40 (1961), 268
60. FRUS, 1945, V, 556
61. FRUS, 1945, V, 575–86
62. FRUS, 1945, V, 603–4. He went with his mother Queen Helen who assured herself that they could both have asylum in the US legation if necessary. See Schuyler in Hammond, *Witnesses* [5:52], 146.
63. FRUS, 1946, V, 577
64. Markham [13:48], 258; *The Times*, November 9, 1945. Schuyler describes (p. 148).
65. FRUS, 1946, V, 630
66. Sulzberger [8:81], 92
67. Robert King, *A history of the Romanian Communist party* (Stanford 1980), 150. Schuyler, visiting Byrnes in Washington, had the impression that Byrnes 'was relieved that, with the Romanian problem no longer pressing, he could devote his efforts to other tasks'.
68. FRUS, 1946, V, 630
69. Markham [13:48], 272–321
70. Amery [11:164], 196
71. King [13:67], 64
72. FRUS, 1945, V, 556
73. Le Rougetel to Foreign Office, November 28, 1945 (PRO)
74. 'Geography made it possible to ensure a rescue of Jews from Romania during the war on a small but persistent scale' Martin Gilbert, *Auschwitz and the Allies* (London 1981), 294
75. Just as the leader of the fascists, Codreanu, had been.
76. Oren [4:97], 41
77. Report of British Military Mission, No. 3, 1944, in FO 371/43621 R17851/14916 (PRO)
78. C. M. Woodhouse, *Apple of Discord* (London 1948), 129
79. The role of the minister of war, General Marinov, suggests that

the Russians plotted to achieve this to ensure their own control of the armistice arrangements. See Cyril Black, 'The View from Bulgaria' in Hammond, *Witnesses* [5:52], 65, and Kimball [4:25], II, 714–15, for Bulgarian peace-feelers in February 1944.

80. 12,000 was the British SOE's estimate, see FO 371/43579 R4396/38/7. See discussion of other figures in Oren, 217. Many operated in Bulgarian-occupied Macedonia, not Bulgaria proper.

81. FO 371/43582 R20081/38/G7 (PRO)

82. Oren [4:97], 76–77

83. *Ibid.*, 184

84. *Ibid.*, 15

85. *Ibid.*, 132

86. Joseph Rothschild, *The Communist Party of Bulgaria 1883–1936* (New York 1959), 118. His adjutant was one morning found with his skull crushed: 'a gentle reminder to his minister . . . not to meddle' (Black in Hammond, *Witnesses* [5:52], 73).

87. Lord Moyne to Macmillan in FO 371/43579 R12759/38/G7. One was betrayed, the other withdrawn.

88. See Oren [4:97], 163, and B. Sweet Escott, *Baker Street Irregular* (London 1965), 205 ff. for OSS in Bulgaria, 1943–44

89. FRUS, 1944, III, 457–81. Woodward [3:15], III, 566; Black in Hammond, *Witnesses* [5:52] 67–68, gives another analysis.

90. FRUS, 1945, *Yalta*, 238–39

91. *Ibid.*, 1945, *Potsdam*, II, 555–56

92. Qu. Davis [6:32], 268

93. Oren [4:97], 165

94. Black in Hammond, *Witnesses* [5:52], 76–77

95. Schapiro [1:1], 218

96. Woodward [3:15], III, 556. The trials for 'war crimes' in December 1944 resulted in the sentencing to death of twenty-two ex-ministers and three Regents (including prince Kiril and Bogdan Filov), eight close advisers of ex-King Boris, and sixty-eight ex-members of the national assembly. These hundred executions were carried out in February 1945, with a British lieutenant present, with whom I have spoken. Light sentences were given to Muraviev and his government. These gross injustices, to which scant attention was paid in the West, then or since, were clearly intended to strike fear into the hearts of all. The Bulgarian Government announced that 2138 had been executed by March 1945, 1940 sentences of twenty years given, and 1689 of ten to fifteen years

97. FRUS, 1945, IV, 322–23

98. Oren [4:97], 259
99. FRUS, 1945, IV, 389
100. *Ibid.*, 1945, IV, 278–82
101. See the account of Malcolm Mackintosh of the British delegation to the control commission, in Hammond, *Anatomy* [2:38], 239–40. This shows that Barnes's account to Washington published in Foreign Relations, and emphasised by Lynne Davies, may be misleading. Stalin's telephone call came through at 2 in the morning. General Biruysov fainted. It would seem likely that Stalin, perturbed by the lack of overt opposition to him in Bulgaria, decided to back a real election campaign, in order to draw the opposition out.
102. FRUS, 1945, IV, 373
103. *Ibid.*, 399
104. *Ibid.*, 365
105. *Ibid.*, 410
106. Ethridge and Cyril Black, 'Negotiating on the Balkans 1945–1947', in R. Dennet and J. Johnson (eds), *Negotiating with the Russians* (Boston 1951), 185. Black accompanied Ethridge (see Black's essay in Hammond, *Witnesses* [5:52], esp. 83–84)
107. FO 371/47917 N10228/558/38 (PRO)
108. FRUS, 1946, VI, 68–71
109. Barnes to Secretary of State, February 18, FRUS, 1946, VI, 77
110. Both Petkov's father and brother had been assassinated for political reasons.
111. See also Charles A. Moser, *Dimitrov of Bulgaria: a political biography of Dr Georgi M. Dimitrov* (Ottowa, Illinois 1979) esp. 187–203; Amery [11:164], 150
112. Oren [4:97], 36–37
113. Rothschild [13:86], 302
114. FRUS, 1945, V, 543; Davis [6:32], 281
115. Davis [6:32], 282

## CHAPTER 14 HEIRS OF THE TURKISH EMPIRE

1. Djilas, in Urban [1:15], 202, gives a lower figure than usual, as in e.g. Dedijer [3:49], 244.
2. FRUS, 1945, V, 1281–82
3. *Ibid.*, Yalta, 900, 974
4. *Ibid.*, V, 1284; Seton-Watson, *The East European Revolution* [12:27], 222–23, has a good account of this election.

5. FRUS, 1945, V, 1292–93. See Petrovich's account in Hammond, *Witnesses* [5:52], 52–53. He was able to visit Croatia and other places, thanks to Tito himself.

6. This was Jozef Korbel, subsequently author of many studies of Communist activities in East Europe.

7. FRUS, 1946, VI, 879–81

8. *Ibid.*, 1945, V, 1302

9. 'These killings were sheer frenzy', Djilas wrote (*Wartime* [1:12], 447). Tito virtually admitted that when, at a meeting of the Central Committee in late 1945, he said 'enough of these sentences and all this killing' (*Ibid.* 449).

10. For Jovanović before 1941, see Djilas [2:60], 16–17; Amery [11: 164], 152–53

11. Djilas [2:60], 14. The character of the war is expressed in the fact that one town, Berane, is said to have changed hands forty-one times (Vane Ivanović, *LX Memoirs of a Yugoslav* (London 1977), 228)

12. Kestesz [13:8], 112. Djilas's characterisation is in *Wartime* [1:12], 140.

13. M. D. R. Foot, *SOE the Special Operations Executive* (London 1984), 239–40

14. Woodward [3:15], III, 287–319, summarises evidence: see Jozo Tomasevich, *The Chetniks* (Stanford 1975), 297–361; Michael Howard, *History of the Second World War: Grand Strategy*, vol. 4 (London 1972), 483–84; Ivanović [14:11], 249

15. Woodward [3:15], III, 290–91

16. *Ibid.*, 296–97. Deakin appears to have been the decisive influence with Churchill, in January 1943, on the question of Mihailović's disloyalty and Tito's fighting qualities.

17. *Ibid.*, 325

18. *Ibid.*, III, 325; Kimball [4:25], II, 549–51; and Maurice Matloff and Edwin Snell (eds), *Strategic planning for coalition warfare* (Washington 1953), 427. Churchill always wanted an American commitment to a major military move in the Balkans, more for 'general war reasons' than to thwart the Soviet expansion there. In June 1944, he returned to this theme, hoping to achieve his aims by advancing from Italy *via* the Ljubljana gap. See Kimball, III, 198–99. Roosevelt refused to listen to the idea. He wanted an attack in southern France. He added: 'for purely political reasons over here, I would never survive even a slight setback in OVERLORD . . . if it were because large forces had been

diverted to the Balkans.' Churchill was furious when ten divisions were transferred from Alexander's Command in Italy to FDR's pet offensive in the south of France. His own Chiefs of Staff, however, supported FDR, Eisenhower and Marshall (Kimball [4:25], III, 223–29, and 232).

19. See Chapter 18
20. Paul Shoup, *Communism and the National Question* (New York 1968), 104–05
21. Nikolai Tolstoy, *The Minister and the Massacres* (London 1986) has a moving account, in Chapter 7; FRUS, 1945, VI, 1256–57; Djilas in Urban, *Stalinism* [1:15], 235 and *Wartime* [1:12], 447
22. Werner Markert, *Osteurope Handbuch Jugoslawien* (Cologne 1954), qu. Shoup
23. Woodward [3:15], III, 366–73, 381
24. See Mark Clark, *Calculated Risk* (New York 1950), 443; also Allen Dulles [9:176], 236
25. This crisis is discussed on its British significance alone on page 325; Mark Clark drove past Yugoslav defences on May 22 (*ibid.*, 446)
26. See Bogdan Novak, *Trieste 1941–54* (Chicago 1970), 162
27. Blum [3:29], 463. But Patterson had an able counsellor, Harold Schantz, who knew Russia, and his military adviser Charles Thayer educated him a little in the brutalities of Balkan politics (*Hands across the Caviar* [3:52], 147)
28. Shoup [14:20], 102
29. Dedijer [3:49], 234
30. Djilas, *Memoir* [2:60], 6
31. Shoup [14:20], 13
32. Rebecca West, *Black Lamb and Grey Falcon* (London 1982), 479
33. Erickson [2:17], II, 379
34. Murphy [4:22], 273. Maclean, who had known Russia in the 1930s, quickly decided Tito was 'a principal, not a subordinate, with an odd lack of servility' (*Eastern Approaches* [1:8], 308, 317). Weil's colleague, Colonel Charles Thayer evidently shared his opinions about Tito (see *Hands across the Caviar* [3:52], 142). But General Donovan sent an OSS mission in August to Mihailović. It was eventually withdrawn on the British request (Kimball [4:25], III, 308–09)
35. Woodward [3:15], III, 336. Tito guilefully said that he would 'confine himself to the military sphere after the war'. Šubašić

was a 'gentle indecisive and not very bright diabetic' (Ivanović [14:11], 259). Some communists were candid about their plans. See Popović's remarks to Ivanović in 1944 (*op. cit.*, 222). Maclean was impressed by the fact that Tito made fun of the Soviet general Korneyev sent to advise him. See Michael Petrovich's account of Soviet official iciness to Yugoslav enthusiasm (Hammond, *Witnesses* [5:52], 38) and Thayer [3:52], 60, for a favourable account of Korneyev.

36. Djilas [12:42], 82–89; Djilas [2:2], 118; Dedijer, [3:49], 268–69
37. Djilas [12:42], 92
38. FRUS, 1946, VI, 867
39. *Ibid.*, 868
40. Davis [6:32], 349
41. For Tito in general, see Maclean [1:8], 308–16; and his subsequent *Disputed Barricades* (London 1957). For a wholly sceptical account, see Nora Beloff, *Tito's Flawed Legacy* (London 1985).
42. Djilas [12:42], 48
43. Dedijer [3:49], 268
44. Djilas, *Rise and Fall* [12:42], 105–06
45. Maclean [1:8], 326; Thayer [3:52], 142, speaks of 'Arso' as 'sour, sullen', the opposite of the affable Tito.
46. Kardelj published memoirs which do not mention that, in 1945, he was wont to believe that it was 'our greatest ambition to become the seventeenth republic of the Soviet Union' (Petrovich in Hammond, *Anatomy* [2:38], 93)
47. Mosha Pijade, *About the Legend that the Yugoslav Uprising Owed its Existence to Soviet Assistance* (London 1950)
48. Djilas [12:42], 39–41
49. Dedijer [3:49], 251
50. Sherwood [3:9], 708
51. Sir Fitzroy Maclean says that Tito was furious at hearing of Stalin's assertion of a fifty per cent interest in the country. Djilas says the opposite (*Wartime* [1:12], 422)
52. See his *The Artful Albanian* (London 1986). Hoxha's family belonged to the Bektashi, the most liberal form of Islam. See also Stephen Peters, *Ingredients of the Communist take-over in Albania*, in Hammond, *Anatomy* [2:38], 275, who argues that it is questionable whether there would have been a communist government in Albania had it not been for aid to Hoxha by the Western allies.
53. Dedijer [3:49], 280

54. FRUS, 1945, IV, 35–36. Britain before 1939 had substantial oil interests in Albania while British officers ran the gendarmerie of King Zog till 1938.

55. Jan Sejna, *We will bury you* (London 1982), 65

56. FRUS, 1946, VI, 5

57. On December 2, 1945, the 'National Liberation Front' won 50 per cent of the vote.

58. So he told the Spanish magazine *Interviu*, in 1976

59. FRUS, 1946, VI, 1–2: 'there are a number of technicians but with no known jobs that can be discovered'.

60. Shehu was in 1981 accused by Hoxha of having been a British agent. For discussions of Shehu's alleged contacts with Britain in the war, see Hoxha, 330.

61. Rositzke [5:41], 172; Nicholas Bethell, *The Great Betrayal* (London 1984), *passim*

62. Peter Kemp, *No Colours or Crest* (London 1958), 239. Equally, as in Yugoslavia, the British and Americans found it easy to believe that Hoxha was 'neither a communist nor a fellow traveller' (Hoxha [14:52], 357)

63. Dallek [5:8], 318

64. Report of Colonel Neil McLean, January 1944, qu. Hoxha [14:52], 351

65. Denis Mack Smith, *Mussolini's Roman Empire* (London 1976) 154–58

66. A clear analysis of the Albanian resistance is to be found in Seton-Watson's *The East European Revolution* [12:27], 139–46. A fine study of the Ghegs and the clan-like society of the north is to be found in Julian Amery's *Sons of the Eagle* (London 1948). See also Anthony Quayle's novel, *Eight Hours from England* (London 1948).

67. *Extra Note on Albania*
The situation was complicated by the fact that, when Italy collapsed in 1943, the Germans knew that they could not afford to leave the Adriatic coast unguarded. They sought to control Albania by conciliation, a stratagem which they rarely tried elsewhere. Thus they set up a Regency Council of men who seemed to be nationalists, and who gained the backing of many chiefs and old conservatives, organised in a national front (Balli Kombetar). The last year of the war was marked by fullscale fighting between, on the one hand, the Communists and their liberal supporters, and the forces of the Regency, the Balli, and other conservatives, among whom Abbas Kupi, leader of the

Ghegs was the outstanding man. Allied missions tried to secure the latter a place in the Hoxha's coalition but the Communists had no time for such independent men. He escaped to Italy in November 1944, and lived to fight another day.

CHAPTER 15 BALTIC HARBOURS: FINLAND, THE BALTIC STATES, EAST PRUSSIA

1. Max Jakobson, *The Diplomacy of the Winter War* (Cambridge, Mass. 1961), 258
2. *Ibid.*, 258
3. Hodgson [2:45], 212
4. Jakobson [15:1], 34
5. Seton-Watson [3:40], 669
6. Bohlen [3:12], 150
7. Dallek [8:28], 209
8. Perrott [7:28], 18–19
9. Woodward [3:15], I, 102
10. *Ibid.*, 109
11. Harriman [1:22], 314
12. Hull papers, qu. Davis [6:32], 81
13. *Mannerheim, Memoirs of Marshal*, tr. by Count Eric Lewenhaupt (London 1953), 489
14. Stalin received approval of this extension of Soviet influence as a result of the secret protocols to the Nazi–Soviet pact, in August and September 1939. See Jane Degras (ed.), *Soviet Documents on Foreign Policy*, vol. III, 1933–1941 (London 1953), 360, 378
15. A useful summary is in Munters in Hammond, *Anatomy* [2:38], 220–28
16. Alfred Maurice de Zayas, article on 'Forced Resettlement' in vol. I, 'Settlement of Disputes', *Encyclopedia of Public International Law* (Amsterdam 1981), 235. For the record of an English family in Riga, see Lucy Addison, *Letters from Latvia* (London 1986). For Latvia and the Soviet Union see the articles of that name by Mintauls Cakste in *Journal of Central European Affairs*, vol. 9, Nos. 1 and 2, April and July 1949
17. David Kirby, 'The Baltic States', in McCauley [12:10], 22–38
18. Woodward [3:15], II, 226; Cadogan [3:8], 438–39
19. Woodward [3:15], I, 475; Bronis Kaslas, *La Lithuanie et la seconde guerre mondiale* (Paris 1981), 201
20. *Ibid.*, 480–84
21. FRUS, 1942, III, 538–39

22. *Ibid.*, 505
23. Woodward [3:15], II, 250–54
24. Policy Summaries 'Soviet Union: Territorial Problems – Western Frontier of the Soviet Union', July 15, 1942 (H-22), qu. Davis [6:32], 73
25. Sherwood [3:9], 706
26. *Ibid.*, 713
27. James MacGregor Burns [9:16], 365
28. FRUS, *Tehran*, 594–95: 'He went on to say that the big issue in the US, insofar as public opinion was concerned, would be the questions of the referendum and the right of self determination'. The discussion at Tehran had been preceded by a confusion between 'Baltic Sea' and 'Baltic States' made by Stalin's interpreter. When FDR spoke of free access to the first, Stalin said categorically that these countries had 'voted' to join the USSR in 1940.
29. See Ādolfs Šilde, Resistance Movements in Latvia (1972), and R. J. Misiunas and R. Taagepera, *The Baltic States, Years of Dependence 1940–48* (Berkeley, 1983), and Medvedev, Suslov, in *All Stalin's men* [4:1]
30. FRUS, 1945, V, 887. Lithuanians in Britain, as in the US, were still thinking in 1944 that they might get the same kind of post-war treatment as Austria (see Conversation in Stettinius's diary [4: 104], January 24, 1944).
31. Eden's assistant private secretary, Valentine Lawford (Nicholas Lawford) wrote an admirable volume of memoirs, *Born for Diplomacy* (London 1963)
32. FO 371/47995 (PRO)
33. Caccia in discussion, March 18, 1946, in briefing Sir Maurice Peterson (PRO)
34. Woodward [3:15], II, 222
35. Sherwood [3:9], 708
36. Woodward [3:15], II, 651
37. Zayas [12:181], 61
38. Kennan [4:19], 266
39. Zayas [12:181], 20. See discussion in Michael Scammell, *Solzhenitsyn* [1:20], 139–41
40. FRUS, Berlin, II, 211
41. As quoted in FRUS, *Potsdam*, 1945, I, 6
42. *Ibid.*, 509–12
43. *Ibid.*, 521
44. Orwell [2:57], IV, 8

45. 'No levanteis mañana la bandera del perdón' in *Residencia en la tierra* (in the poem *Canto al ejército rojo a su llegada a las puertas de Prusia*). *Residence on Earth*, tr. by D. D. Walsh (London 1976)
46. Stettinius [4:104], 86
47. Lucy Addison [15:16], 7

CHAPTER 16 THE HEART OF EUROPE: GERMANY AND AUSTRIA
I am grateful to Lord Annan for kindly giving me his comments on a draft of the first half of this chapter.

1. Walter Millis, in John Gimbel, *The American Occupation of Germany* (Stanford 1968), 6
2. This figure is in Douglas Botting, *From the Ruins of the Reich* (New York 1985), 70
3. PRO: FO 371/49193 Z6693/3599/17
4. For description, see Konrad Adenauer, *Memoirs 1945–53* (London 1966), 24–25
5. This comes from FO: Compare Clarissa Churchill 'Berlin Letter', *Horizon*, March 1946, where the city is described as 'a different climatic zone, a mountain top where no living thing can survive'.
6. Truman [8:7], 105
7. Qu. Botting [16:2], 125
8. Pollard [6:63], 90
9. FRUS, 1946, V, 520–21
10. John Gimbel, *The Origin of the Marshall Plan* (Stanford 1976), 32
11. FRUS, 1943, III, 26
12. Gladwyn [11:39], 126
13. Burridge [11:42], 175
14. FRUS, 1945, *Yalta*, 899–900 and 936–37; Stephen Ambrose, *Eisenhower and Berlin* (New York 1967), 41–42
15. Truman [8:7], 63
16. This body had been suggested in Washington in March 1943 following Eden's visit there: as a 'UN Commission Europe' (Woodward [3:15], V, 37)
17. Kennan [4:19], 166. Such arrangements would have at least given legal arguments for demanding a Russian withdrawal to the east of Germany if their armies had reached France. (See Lord Gladwyn, *Halfway to 1984*, London 1966, 10.) The same thought was, apparently, in the mind of Hopkins (FRUS, 843, III, 36).
18. Murphy [4:22], 284. Roosevelt's ideas for dividing Germany into

zones were sketched on a map reproduced in Matloff and Snell [14:17], 341. They would have taken the Western zones up to Berlin. He did not press them, and Marshall and Chiefs of Staff opposed them. See Feis, *From Trust to Terror* [6:33], 31–33.

19. Truman [8:7], 63
20. John Blum, *From the Morgenthau Diaries* (New York 1967), III, 342. For White on these things, see Rees [4:9], 239, 260
21. Michael Schaller, *The American occupation of Japan* (New York 1985), 4
22. Blum, *Morgenthau Diaries* [16:20], III, 354. Churchill himself contributed the word 'pastoral'.
23. Blum [3:29], 202
24. For discussion, see Sherwood [3:9], 708–09, 789 and 893; Hull [7:37], II, 1265–66; FRUS, 1943, I, 541–43. A full analysis of the plans can be seen in Woodward [3:15], V, 198–214. The division which did emerge after 1945 never seems to have been contemplated, but see *ibid.*, 325–31, for the Tripartite Committee on Dismemberment
25. Murphy [4:22], 310–11
26. The character of Eisenhower has been discussed on pages 229–30
27. *Memoirs of Field Marshal Viscount Montgomery* (London 1958), 381
28. FRUS, *Potsdam*, I, 6–7
29. *Ibid.*, 1945, III, 313. It is obvious from a memorandum printed in Stettinius's diary [4:104], that it was James Dunn who made the firmest stand as to the benefits of not withdrawing (p. 327).
30. Cave Brown, *Last Hero* [9:182], 530
31. Werth [1:19], 984; and Murphy [4:22], 317–25
32. FRUS, 1945, III, 135
33. Murphy [4:22], 322
34. *Ibid.*, 323
35. *Ibid.*, 377
36. *Ibid.*, 336
37. Gadis [6:62], 96–97
38. Woodward [3:15], V, 280
39. Gimbel [16:1], 56
40. FRUS, *Potsdam*, II, 275, 1485–86; Pollard [6:63], 88–89; Bohlen [3:12], 233
41. See Vladimir Rudolph's memoir in Robert Slusser, *Soviet Economic Policy in Post-War Germany* (New York 1953), 10

42. Vladimir Alexandrov, in *ibid.*, 14–17
43. Zayas [12:181], ii
44. FRUS, 1945, *Potsdam*, vol. II, 1494, 1511; Woodward [3:15], V, 210–13
45. See pages 382–83
46. Golo Mann, *The History of Germany since 1789* (London 1972), 493
47. Woodward [3:15], V, 213
48. See minute by Gladwyn Jebb, January 11, 1943, in FO 371/21091 C12169/464/55 (PRO)
49. Alfred de Zayas, 'Population, Expulsion and Transfer', in *Encyclopedia of Public International Law*, vol. 5 (Amsterdam 1985), 442
50. Zayas, *Nemesis* [12:181], 123
51. *The Times*, October 19, 1945
52. Debate in House of Lords, December 5, 1945 (Hansard, vol. 138, col. 376)
53. Kennan, *Memoirs* [4:19], 178
54. Qu. Zayas, *Nemesis* [12:181], 133
55. FO 371/46868 (PRO)
56. Dallek [8:28], 472–73
57. The best general account is still Robert Jungk, *Brighter than a Thousand Suns* (London 1958)
58. Adenauer [16:4], 37
59. Kennan, *Memoirs* [4:19], 417
60. Murphy [4:22], 281
61. FRUS, *Potsdam*, II, 1503
62. Botting [16:2], 262
63. See Utley [12:182], 190–91, for affidavit of Hans Schmidt in Oberwesel, September–October 1945
64. Mann [16:46], 496
65. Kennan, *Memoirs* [4:19], 260–61
66. Murphy [4:22], 360
67. Murphy [4:22], 307–09
68. Blum, *Morgenthau* [16:20], III, 460
69. Jean Edward Smith, *The Papers of General Lucius D. Clay* (Bloomington 1974), 18–20
70. *Observer*, February 22, 1948, qu. Pollard [6:63], 90
71. Harold Zink, *The US in Germany* (Princeton 1957), 95, Zink was 'chief historian' to the US High Commissioner later.
72. Statement of December 12, 1945: See Gimbel [16:1], 32
73. *Ibid.*, 35–40

74. Yergin [8:135], 304
75. Montgomery [16:27], 400–02
76. *Ibid.*, 411
77. Labour Party, Conference Report for May 1945 (London 1945), 113
78. Pollard [6:63], 100
79. Adenauer [16:4], 25–26
80. *Ibid.*, 33
81. Recollection of Lord Annan
82. Adenauer [16:4], 42–47; Mann [16:46], 506–09
83. CAB 128/5 22 conclusions, March 8, 1946
84. Murphy [4:22], 360
85. Gimbel, *American Occupation* [16:1], 40 ff.
86. *Ibid.*, 45. There is a good summary of the French position in Feis [6:33], 56–59
87. Adenauer [16:4], 37
88. Leonhard [4:85], 303
89. *Ibid.*, 315–16
90. Ivor Pink to Bevin, December 27, 1945, in PRO: FO 371/55360 C72/2/18
91. PRO: FO 371/46910 C10128/2069/18
92. FRUS, 1946, V, 712
93. Jean Edward Smith [16:69], 38
94. FRUS, 1946, V, 701–02
95. Pink, as in footnote 90
96. *Ibid.*
97. FRUS, 1946, V, 711
98. Sir William Strang, despatch of January 15, 1945, PRO: FO 371/824/2/18
99. FRUS, 1946, V, 702–03
100. Speech of February 2, PRO: FO 371/55360 C1766/2/18
101. The German Communist Party in 1932 had 200,000 members and 6 million voters – higher by far than the votes of any communist party in any other election, except for the 9 million votes for the Bolsheviks in Russia in 1918.
102. For Ulbricht in Spain, see Ruth Fischer, *Stalin and German Communism* (London 1948), 500 fn. 2, and Branko Lazitch, *Biographical dictionary of the Comintern* [9:172], entry for Ulbricht.
103. Gustav Regler, *Owl of Minerva* (London 1959), 175
104. To Popović, in Dedijer [3:49], 283
105. Victor Serge, *Memoirs of a Revolutionary* (New York 1984), 162

106. Zaisser had been a teacher, drafted into the World War, which he left in 1918 as an officer, became a member of the KPD in 1920 and went to Russia first in 1924 as a member of the German delegation to the Profintern. He became an apprentice agent of the GRU in 1924 (Lazitch [9:172], 451)

107. Staimer had been interned during the war at Saint Gall in Switzerland.

108. Bohlen [3:12], 275

109. Trepper [4:66], 211; Heinz Höhne, *Codeword: Direktor* (London 1971), 249

110. Slusser [16:41], 53

110[A] NA: 704.00119 Control (Austria) 1–1145

111. NA: 740.00119 Control (Austria) /1–845

112. See William B. Bader, *Austria between East and West 1945–1955* (Stanford 1966), 11–25; Thayer, *Hands across the Caviar* [3:152]; and Renner's own account *Denkschrift ueber die Geschichte der Unabhaengigkeitserklaerung Oesterreichs* (Zurich 1946), 9–19. See also NA: 740.00119 Control: Austria, 5–515. Martin Herz, in Hammond, *Witnesses* [5:52], 166–67, suggests that it was chance, not long planning, that led the Russians to impose Renner on the Government.

113. Alexander Vodopiveć, *Wer Regiert in Oesterreich* (Vienna 1960), 73. Stalin would have known that Renner was almost a generic term in Lenin's vocabulary: 'the Renners and similar lackeys of the bourgeoisie' (Works 31, 268)

114. *War Diaries of Oliver Harvey* (London 1978), 380

115. See NA: 740.00119 Control Austria/10–2445

116. Adolf Schaerf, *Österreichs Erneurung 1945–1955* (Vienna 1955), 21–23

117. Radomir Luza, *The Resistance in Austria* (Minneapolis 1984), 274

118. *Ibid.*, 285 and note on the Wiederstand-Bewegung by Lieut. Kennedy in FO 371/46603 71263 (PRO)

119. Charles de Jaeger, *The Linz File* (London 1981)

120. Luza [16:117], 55

121. *Ibid.*, 151

122. Oskar Helmer, *50 Jahre erlebte Geschichte* (Vienna 1957), 203–95

123. PRO: FO 371/146610 C4126/141/G

124. Teltscher report in PRO: FO 371/46610 C3323/141/3

125. Letter from Countess Nathalie Benckendorff, December 10, 1945, to London.

126. PRO: FO 371/46665 C4635/4635/3

882

127. PRO: FO 181/1022 204/66/46
128. Orwell [2:57], IV, 1
129. Praeger, in Urban [1:15], *Stalinism*, 100
130. Martin Herz, *Understanding Austria* (Salzburg 1984), 26
131. PRO: COS 320/15, May 26, 1945
132. PRO: JCS 577/15
133. PRO: Letter Winant to FDR and Stettinius, December 8, 1944 in 740.00119 EW/12–844
134. FRUS, 1945, III, 586. For a discussion of negotiating the zonal borders in Austria see Philip E. Mosely, in Dennett and Johnson [4:80], 284
135. NA: 740.00119 Control (Austria)/4–1345 CS/LR
136. See Harriman to Stettinius, June 6, 1945 in RG 59 740.00119 (NA)
137. Truman [8:7], 223
138. FRUS, 1945, III, 571. One such was the Vienna–Salzburg train, the Mozart Express, which, it had been agreed, was American. Some Soviet officers and men insisted on boarding the train at the demarcation line, against General Clark's orders when they refused to leave an American policeman killed an officer and wounded another. The sergeant concerned was later cleared (Clark, *From the Danube to the Yalu*)
139. Comment of Dr Fritz Molden, then secretary to Dr Karl Gruber.
140. Ernst Trost, *Figl von Österreich* (Vienna 1985), 101–02
141. FRUS, 1945, III, 656
142. PRO: FO 371/466/11
143. Herz [16:130], 39
144. Comment by Dr Fritz Molden. Renner's decision, against communist opposition, to declare the old constitution revived, unless the minority indicated 'by their resignation that the proposals remained unacceptable' was, as Martin Herz says, a fine assertion of will-power. See Adolf Schaerf, *Zwischen Demokratie und Volksdemokratie* (Vienna 1950), 18
145. Bader [16:112], 47
146. FRUS, 1945, III, 687. For an outstanding essay on the characters of Austria in 1945, see Alan Pryce-Jones 'Letter from Vienna' (*Horizon*, vol. XIII, No. 75, March 1946)
147. Evidence of Michael Cullis
148. Harriman reported in 1945 that Soviet output of crude oil had fallen from 31·3 million metric tons to 21·5 million between 1940 and 1945 (FRUS, 1945, Potsdam, 943)
149. FO 371/55160 C 1252 124/3

150. FO 371/5518 C 190/189/2
151. FRUS, 1946, V, 310
152. FO 371/5518 C1890/189/3
153. Luza [16:117] 376–77
154. Renner, *Drei Monate*, qu. Luza, 315
155. Bader [16:112], 79
156. Schaerf [16:116] 147


CHAPTER 17  GARDENS OF THE WEST: FRANCE,
ITALY AND SPAIN

1. PRO: FO 371/49078 Z12231/14/17
2. See letter from Scarlett to Rumbold in FO 371/49076 Z10222/
   14/17 (PRO)
3. Alfred Rieber [3:75], 219
4. FO 371/49074 Z12922/14/17 Cooper to Bevin, November 22,
   1945 (PRO)
5. Georgette Elgey, *Histoire de la IVème République*, vol. 1, *La
   République des Illusions* (Paris 1965)
6. *Ibid.*, 116
7. Annie Kriegel, *The French Communists*, tr. by Elaine Halperin
   (Chicago 1974), 119–20; Auguste Lecoeur, *Le Partisan* (Paris
   1963), 93–95
8. *Ibid.*, 130
9. For the Communist party in this extraordinary year after the
   return of 'Maurice', see Philippe Robrieux, *Histoire intérieure du
   Parti Communiste, 1945–1972* (Paris 1981), 78–175
10. Rieber [3:75], 94
11. *Ibid.*, 151
12. Robert Aron, *Histoire de la Libération de la France* (Paris 1959),
    632
13. G. A. Tokaev, *Comrade X . . .* (London 1956), 280–81; See
    *Cahiers du Communisme*, 10, 1952, qu. *in extenso*, in Claudín,
    757–58
14. Jacques Dumaine, *Quai d'Orsay* (London 1958), 60
15. Theodore Zeldin, *France 1848–1945* (Oxford 1977), 1129–42
16. Rieber [3:75], 166
17. Jacques Fauvet, *Histoire du Parti Communiste Français* (Paris
    1964), 337. To read Thorez's speeches in 1945, wrote Claudín,
    is to gain the impression that 'the central task for workers was
    to get under way an economy which they already controlled'
    (Claudín [2:62], 332)

18. Rieber [3:75], 154
19. PRO: FO 371/49078 Z12746
20. Cooper [11:55], 366
21. PRO: FO 371/40978 Z12746/14/17
22. Fauvet, 369
23. Doubtless Stalin, who did not greatly admire Thorez (Dedijer [3:49], 283), used these shadowy figures as sources of information. See Lazitch [9:172], 441, and Jean Montaldo, *Les finances du PCF* (Paris 1977).
24. Cooper, 338–39
25. Rieber [3:75], 8, 15, 19
26. FRUS, 1945, IV, 661–65
27. *Ibid.*, 665
28. See Frank Roberts's despatch of May 12, 1945 in FO 371/49193 76693 (PRO)
29. Sherwood [3:9], 849
30. Pollard [6:63], 75. This 'distancing' from the United States was not, it should be recognised, shared by de Gaulle's great literary adviser and friend André Malraux: see his interview in *Horizon*, October 1945 (vol. XII, No. 70), where he talks of the coming of 'Atlantic culture'.
31. FO 371/49074 26025/14/17 (PRO)
32. Orwell to Philip Rahv, *Letters* [2:57], IV, April 9, 1946
33. Orwell to Koestler, in *ibid.*, January 10, 1946
34. Elgey [17:5], 17
35. Malraux to Cooper, November 10, 1945: FO 371/49071 317/14/g/7 (PRO)
36. Reported by Yves Farges to the Embassy, in FO 371/59956 Z690/21/17 (PRO). For an authoritative account, see Jean Lacouture, *De Gaulle*, 2; *Le politique* (Paris 1985), Chapter 10
37. FRUS, 1946, V, 402
38. FO 371/59956 Z621 (PRO)
39. FO 371/56887 (PRO)
40. *Ibid.*, Z1407/21/17 (PRO). Perhaps de Gaulle's holiday in the south of France where he read Saint-Simon, Retz and Von Bulow assisted him in these decisions: particularly Retz.
41. Elgey [17:5], 104–5
42. FRUS, 1945, IV, 666
43. Murphy [4:22], 290–94
44. FRUS, 1945, IV, 666–67
45. Gimbel [16:10], 34
46. See conversation with Truman, August 1945, in FRUS, 1945,

IV, 710; and with Stalin, in Charles de Gaulle, *Mémoires*, III, *Le Salut* (Paris 1959), 365

47. Elgey [17:5], 85
48. Jean Lacouture, *André Malraux, Une Vie dans le Siècle* (Paris 1973), 330
49. Elgey [17:5], 88
50. A variety of figures have been given, between 105,000, estimated by the minister responsible Adrien Tixier, and the 10,000 of Robert Aron in *Histoire de la Libération de la France* (Paris 1959), 651–53. The second figure, for Nazi executions, is in Kriegel, 124. The Bureau of Research on War Crimes at Nuremberg gave a total of 26,000. De Gaulle spoke of 60,000 executed (*Le Salut* [17:46], 107) as well as 150,000 died in deportation.
51. See Rieber [3:75], 144; Kriegel, 124; and Paul Viret, *Les 75,000 fusillés communistes*.
52. De Gaulle [17:46], 107–08
53. Elgey [17:5], 17
54. Harriman [1:22], 268
55. De Gaulle [17:46], Documents II, 603–06
56. FRUS, *Cairo & Tehran*, 485, 509
57. This case is summarised in Thierry Wolton, *Le KGB en France* (Paris 1986), 49. The Yugoslav was 'Louis', or Ljubmir Ilitch, 'veteran' of the Spanish War. Teulery was tried in 1950 and sentenced to five years in prison.
58. Rieber [3:75], 290–91
59. See below, page 594
60. See, for example, FRUS, 1946, VII, 52
61. Gowing, I, 157
62. De Gaulle, III [17:46], 289
63. Pollard (6:63], 77
64. PRO: FO 371/49772 ZM3557/3/22. Luigi Longo claimed in 1947 that there had been 300,000 partisans in northern Italy who for ten days of April 1945, had 'controlled northern Italy' (qu. Claudín [2:62], 361). This was a period looked back upon as a time of 'real' liberty by romantics.
65. FO 371/49825 ZM5357/19/22 (PRO)
66. Federico Chabod, *A History of Italian Fascism* (London 1961), 122
67. FO 371/49825 ZM5357 (PRO)
68. Churchill, June 15, 1945, in Minute to Sir Alexander Cadogan in FO 371/49771 ZM3244/3/22 (PRO). Churchill was extremely prejudiced, for no good reason, about both of these men.

69. FRUS, 1946, V, 875
70. Truman [8:7], 325
71. *Ibid.*, 302
72. Byrnes [3:23], 96
73. Unlike the two hundred Italian communists who died in Russia during the purges and whose fate is discussed in Guelfo Zaccaria's *A Mosca senza ritorno* (Milan 1983)
74. Dalton, *War Diary* [1:11], 811
75. Dedijer [3:49], 282
76. *Rinascita*, I, No. 3, 1944. For Togliatti (who returned to Italy on March 27, 1944) see *Opere* (Rome 1979), vol. IV. This volume is the first occasion that a leading international communist has published his despatches as a revolutionary (in Spain in Togliatti's case). His biographers Marcella and Maurizio Ferrara (*Palmiro Togliatti, essai biographique* (Paris 1954), 340, describe how astounded the local leaders were by this unexpected '*svolta*'.
77. Murphy [4:22], 265
78. Paolo Spriano, *Storia del partito comunista italiano vol. V* (Turin 1975), Chapter XII. Probably the Russians realised that an early communist capture of power in Italy would have risked their position in East Europe. A Soviet diplomat told General Mason-Macfarlane in Rome that, if his country had wished to do anything abnormal in Italy, they would 'not have been so stupid as to exchange representatives. They had . . . more effective ways of doing that sort of thing.'
79. Harold Macmillan, *War Diary*, 312–17
80. Nenni, *Diary 1945–56* [12:55], 162
81. FRUS, *Potsdam*, II, 43–44
82. OSS, XL, 35131, January 16, 1946, qu. Cave Brown, *Last Hero*
83. FRUS, 1946, V, 1043
84. *Ibid.*, 1032
85. *Ibid.*, 1034
86. FO 23091/1636/41/2 (PRO) March 2, 1946
87. Qu. in FO 371/60375 (PRO)
88. David Pike, *Jours de Gloire, Jours de Honte* (Paris 1984), 131–32
89. Santiago Carrillo, *Demain L'Espagne* (Paris 1974), 99–100
90. In January 1946, the Communist Party in Paris announced their willingness to support a bourgeois government.
91. See, for example, Martín Artajo's talk with Sir V. Mallet, FO 25292/45/41, June 9, 1946 (PRO)

92. FO 371/60379 289283/45/41; Kindelán's memoirs touch extensively on the subject (Alfredo Kindelán, *La verdad de mis relaciones con Franco*, Barcelona 1981).
93. See Cipriano Mera, *Memorias: Guerra, exilio y cárcel de un anarcosindicalista* (Paris 1976), 278–80.

CHAPTER 18 THE 'NORTHERN TIER': GREECE,
TURKEY AND IRAN

I am grateful to Mrs Robert Rossow for letting me see a copy of an unpublished manuscript written by her late husband about his time in Tabriz and Tehran and to Archie Roosevelt Jr. for his help.

1. Qu. C. M. Woodhouse, *Struggle for Greece* (London 1970), 143
2. FRUS, 1946, VII, 108–10
3. Bruce Kuniholm, *The Origins of the Cold War in the Near East* (Princeton 1980), 84; Woodward [3:15], III, 399
4. Woodhouse, *Apple of Discord* [13:78], 60. W. H. McNeil, then assistant US military attaché in Athens, writes 'most of the soldiers of ELAS were peasant boys, patriotic Greeks, eager to escape from poverty'. (McNeil in Hammond, *Witnesses* [2:38], 102). The military leaders of ELAS were the somewhat ambiguous ex-regular General Serafis and the more dramatic communist Velouchiotis (Ares). Woodhouse discusses the nice question of Zervas's alleged collaboration with the Germans, 75–81.
5. Woodward [3:15], III, 390–92; Clive, 41
6. Woodhouse [13:78], 57–58. Controversy surrounds all these decisions. The real communist opportunity was in October 1944. George Kousoulas believes (see Hammond, *Anatomy* [2:38], 298–99) it was deference to Russian wishes to give Britain her 'sphere of influence' that lost it.
7. The position of the clever Russian Colonel Popov and his self-control is clearly analysed in McNeil [2:38], 107–08
8. Churchill, *Triumph and Tragedy* [3:13], 288. Colonel Popov continued inactive in the centre of Athens.
9. FRUS, 1945, *Yalta*, 782. Stalin said that he had 'no intention of criticising British activities . . . in Greece but merely would like to know what was going on'.
10. Woodward [3:15], 38. A British intelligence officer of the time described to me how he saw crates of Soviet arms being shipped south from Bulgaria in February 1946 for the use of Greek communists.

11. R. Harris Smith, *OSS* (Berkeley 1972), 127; Cave Brown [4:112], 429
12. FRUS, 1945, VIII, 263
13. Woodhouse, *Struggle* [18:1], 157
14. Truman [8:9], 99
15. Acheson [8:16], 200
16. Kuniholm [5:28], 99
17. FRUS, 1946, VII, 91–92
18. MacVeagh to Byrnes August 1, 1946, qu. Lawrence Wittner, *American Intervention in Greece* (New York 1982), 34
19. See *op. cit.*, 333, for summary
20. FRUS, 1946, VII, 99
21. Clive [11:148], 166. Leeper's career had included the exchange of Sir Robert Bruce Lockhart for Litvinov in 1920 and being taught Russian by the latter.
22. Letter to Sir O. Sargent, February 27, 1946, in FO 371/58678 R3496, qu. Louis [11:66], 83–84
23. March 1946, qu. Louis [11:66], 88
24. FRUS, 1945, V, 901–02
25. Kuniholm [5:28], 20–72
26. FRUS, 1945, VIII, 122
27. Bullock [6:58], 157
28. Forrestal [8:93], 97
29. Kuniholm [5:28], 12
30. Khruschev [2:26], II, 348
31. Louis Fischer, *The Life of Lenin* (London 1964), 342
32. FO 181/1022.202.346
33. Churchill, *Triumph and Tragedy* [3:13], 261
34. FRUS, 1945, *Berlin*, II, 304
35. *Ibid.*, II, 303–04
36. See above, page 193
37. Churchill, *Triumph and Tragedy* [3:13], 669
38. Bullock [6:58], 134–35
39. FRUS, 1945, VIII, 1237–69
40. Qu. Bullock [6:58], 233
41. PRO: FO 371/56831 N4544/605/380
42. DO (46) 22, July 19, 1946, qu. Louis [11:66], 35
43. FO 371/52735 qu. *ibid.*, 56
44. Sir Percy Sykes, *History of Persia* (London 1930), II, 244
45. Pollard [6:63], 109
46. For this crisis, see Louis [11:66], 63
47. FRUS, 1945, VIII, 481–82

48. Lenczowski [4:132], 259
49. *Ibid.*, 261
50. Herz, *Understanding Austria* [16:130], 401
51. Report by Edwin Wright of OSS, qu. Kuniholm [5:28], 152
52. *Ibid.*, 274–75
53. *Ibid.*, 153
54. FRUS, 1946, VII, 299
55. See Archie Roosevelt Jr., 'The Kurdish Republic of Mahabad', *Middle East Journal*, July 1947
56. Lenczowski [4:132], 291
57. Truman, II [8:9], 93
58. Hassan Arfa, *Under Five Shahs* (London 1964), 349
59. Bullock [6:58], 207; see also FO 371/52661 E70/G for Bevin's report to the cabinet on this discussion.
60. Byrnes [3:23], 120
61. Bohlen [3:12], 251. There is doubt about this conversation. See FRUS, II, 1945, 750–51 and commentary in Gardner [8:122], 213–14
62. Bullock [6:58], 210
63. Byrnes [3:23], 120
64. Kuniholm [5:28], 283
65. FRUS, 1945, VIII, 508
66. *Ibid.*, 435. Ala told Loy Henderson that Iran was keen to gain a seat on the Security Council (November 19, 1945). See also Gary R. Hess, 'The Iranian Crisis of 1945–46 and the Cold War', *Political Science Quarterly*, March 1974.
67. Bullock [6:58], 221
68. FRUS, 1946, VII, 291
69. Louis [11:66], 67
70. FRUS, 1945, VIII, 417–19
71. *Ibid.*, 328–30
72. *Ibid.*, 333–34
73. Bullard to Bevin, March 15, 1946, in FO 371/522670/E2813, qu. Louis [11:66], 59–60
74. *Ibid.*, 62
75. Kuniholm [5:28], 188
76. Paper by Harriman, drafted by J. P. Davies and Kennan, October 23, 1945
77. FRUS, 1946, VII, 1–3. For Loy Henderson's role, see Kuniholm [5:28], 237–41
78. FO 371/36838 C 3756/605/38
79. Kuniholm [5:28], 293–94. See Protocol 1 of the Soviet-Nazi Pact

and discussion in Byrnes, *Speaking Frankly*, 284–90, and Edward M. Mark, 'Allied Relations in Iran' 1941–47, *Wisconsin Magazine of History*, Fall 1975

80. Cited in John R. O'Neal, *Foreign Policy-Making in Times of Crisis* (Ohio State University 1982), 81
81. Louis [11:66], 34
82. PRO: FO 800/509, October 15, 1947, qu. *ibid.*, 43
83. Dalton, *Diary*, March 22, 1946 (Library of the London School of Economics)
84. Minute, March 12, 1946, in PRO: FO 371/57173
85. Roberts, March 20, 1946, PRO: FO 371/56831 N3756/605/38

## Chapter 19 THE EAST: CHINA, JAPAN, KOREA AND INDO-CHINA

1. The best introduction is in the essays of Thomas Hammond and Robert Rupen in Hammond, *Anatomy* [2:38], 145
2. *United States Relations with China with Special Reference to the period 1944–1949* (Washington 1949), 589
3. FDR's report to the US Cabinet, December 17, 1943, qu. Blum [3:29], *Price of Vision*, 280
4. Messer [8:87], 100
5. One of Roosevelt's mistakes was that he did not realise this. He said that he believed that 'the British would take land anywhere in the world even if it were only a rock or sand bar' (Stettinius [4:104], 40).
6. Sherwood [3:9], 855; Welles, *Where are we heading?* [7:35]. See Thorne [10:60], for a lucid analysis (*Allies*, 525–28).
7. Pollard [6:63], 174–75
8. *United States Relations with China* [19:2], Annexe 41
9. Conversation with Harriman, January 23, 1944. Many Americans, from the 1930s onwards, would have agreed with this reported judgement of Stalin about the Chinese communists: see instances quoted in e.g. Thorne, *Allies* [10:60], 42, and 183. Clark Kerr also, as earlier mentioned, spoke of Chinese communism as 'mild radicalism'. Other references are in Thorne, 437–89, and 559. Even the experienced merchant, John Keswick, thought it 'unlikely that the Communists would interfere with private ownership of property'.
10. In the 'Letter of Transmittal', *US Relations with China* [19:2], xvi
11. John Stewart Service, in *ibid.*, 566

12. See Ed Pauley's report to President Truman, November 1946, in Annexe C to *ibid.*
13. FRUS, 1946, X, 1100
14. *Ibid.*, 1109
15. Truman, II [8:9], 60
16. Dallek [8:28], 328–29
17. Bohlen [3:12], 530
18. In a talk with Harriman, August 1944; see *US Relations with China* [19:2], 72
19. To Byrnes, in Blum [3:29], 506
20. Harriman [1:22], 531
21. McCagg [1:13], 198
22. Byrnes [3:23], 228
23. Acheson [8:16], 202
24. Kołakowski [2:23], III, 496–97
25. *US Relations with China* [19:2], Annexe 50, 582–84; Forrestal [8:93], 113. See Thorne [10:60], *Allies*, 373
26. Letter of Truman to Marshall, December 15, 1945, qu. Truman, II [8:9], 671–78
27. Acheson [8:16], 145
28. Pollard [6:63], 171
29. *Ibid.*, 146
30. Donovan [8:10], 246
31. Qu. Ferrell, *Marshall* [9:76], 30
32. *US Relations with China* [19:2], 86, 93
33. Qu. McCagg [1:13], 195
34. Annexe 47 of *US Relations with China* [19:2]
35. These are John Fairbanks's words in his admirable *The US and China* (Cambridge 1958), 267
36. John Ehrman, *Grand Strategy* [12:98], V, 292
37. Ferrell, *Off the Record* [8:20], 47
38. Schaller [16:21], 20
39. Truman [8:7], 342
40. Grew, II [91:5], 1421–38; FRUS, 1945, 6, 545–47
41. Schaller [16:21], 16
42. Pollard [6:63], 175; see Acheson [8:16], 426–27
43. Schaller [16:21], 3–4. For an engaging summary of FDR's views on sterilisation ('people pass through a narrow passage and . . . brrrrr of an electrical apparatus'), see Thorne, *Allies* [10:60], 159 and 167–68
44. FRUS, 1945, 6, 667–68
45. Byrnes [9:16], 214

46. Truman to Stalin, August 18, 1945 in FRUS, 1945, 6, 670
47. This was on August 27, 1945
48. Messer [8:87], 120–24
49. Harriman [1:22], 509
50. Douglas MacArthur, *Reminiscences* (New York 1964), 263
51. Harriman [1:22], 782–85; FRUS, 1945, 6, 787–95
52. *Ibid.*, 866
53. Truman [8:9], 459
54. Schaller [16:21], 66–67
55. Courtney Whitney, *MacArthur: his Rendezvous with History* (New York 1956), 251
56. Schaller [16:21], 63
57. FRUS, 1945, VII, 835–50
58. MacArthur [19:50], 291
59. Messer [8:87], 167
60. Forrestal [8:93], 18
61. Sherwood [3:9], 867
62. Kennan [4:19], 384
63. Schaller [16:21], 68
64. Pollard [6:63], 175
65. Figures in *The Effects of the Atomic Bombs on Hiroshima and Nagasaki*, published by the Home Office and the Air Ministry (London 1946). Compare 30,000 killed from bombing in London between 1939 and 1945, 60,000 in all Britain.
66. Annexe 33 in *US Relations with China* [19:2]
67. The exchange showed Stalin at his most feline: thus, Roosevelt said that he 'personally did not feel it was necessary to invite the British to participate . . .' Stalin said 'they would most certainly be offended. In fact the Prime Minister might kill us . . . the British should be invited'. FRUS, *Malta and Yalta*, 1945, 770
68. *Ibid.*, 1945, VI, 1039
69. Robert A. Scalapino and Chung-Sik Lee, *Communism in Korea* (Berkeley 1972), 315. The best introduction to a complicated subject.
70. Truman [8:9], 317
71. *Ibid.*, 318
72. FRUS, 1946, VIII, 629
73. Scalapino [19:69], 323–24
74. He made the remark (about Cyprus) in the hearing of the author.
75. May [8:12], 55–56
76. Scalapino [19:69], 58

76. Scalapino [19:69], 202
77. *Ibid.*, 202–32
78. *Ibid.*, 326
79. *Ibid.*, 383
80. Ellen Hammer, *The Struggle for Indo-China 1930–1955* (Stanford 1968), 120–21
81. For Ho's early life as Comintern revolutionary, see Duncanson in Hammond, *Anatomy* [2:38], 492
82. FRUS, 1945, *Yalta*, 770. Equally wide of the mark, as it turned out, was his comment that the people there were 'not warlike'. Stalin earlier remarked that he thought Indochina an important area.
83. Blum [3:29], 308
84. De Gaulle, III [17:46], 231
85. See discussion in FRUS, 1946, VIII, 32

# BOOK FOUR
# A PROFESSOR'S DREAM

## CHAPTER 20 THE MANHATTAN PROJECT

1. Sir Marcus Oliphant, *Rutherford: recollections of the old days at Cambridge* (London 1972), 135
2. Williams, Robert C. and Philip L. Cantelson, *The American Atom*, 1939–44 (Philadelphia 1984), 12–13
3. *Nature*, August 16, 1947; S. A. Goudsmit, *Alsos* (New York 1947), 106; Robert Jungk, *Brighter than a Thousand Suns*; and David Irving, *The German Atomic Bomb* (New York 1968), 11–18
4. A. G. Hewlett and Oscar E. Anderson [10:20], I, 322
5. Sherwood [3:9], 155
6. A. P. French and P. J. Kennedy, *Niels Bohr: A Centenary Volume* (Cambridge, Mass. 1985)
7. Sir Henry Dale to Churchill, on the basis of Bohr's briefing in Ruth Moore, *Niels Bohr* (London 1967), 339
8. *Ibid.*, 343–44
9. *Ibid.*, 349
10. *Ibid.*, 350
11. Hewlett and Anderson [10:20], 327
12. Dallek [8:28], 416–17
13. Moore [20:7], 332

14. *Ibid.*, 328
15. Leslie R. Groves, *Now it can be told* (New York 1962), 141
16. Sherwin [9:15], Chapter IV
17. Henry Stimson Diary, December 31, 1945 (Yale University Library).
18. Goudsmit, *Alsos* [20:3]; Groves [20:15], 230–49
19. Henry L. Stimson and McGeorge Bundy, *On Active Service in Peace and War* (New York 1947), 636
20. Groves to congressional sub-committee 1948, qu. Herken [8:133], 14
21. Hewlett and Anderson [10:20], 343
22. *Ibid.*, 345
23. Byrnes [3:23], 257
24. Hewlett and Anderson [10:20], 365
25. R. A. Bard sent a dissenting memorandum printed in Lewis Strauss, *Men and Decisions* (Garden City 1962), 192. See also 'War was really won before we used A-bomb', *US News and World Report*, August 15, 1960.
26. Strauss, 193
27. *Ibid.*, 270
28. Margaret Gowing [11:25], 393–445
29. Henry Stimson Diary, May 15, 1945 (Yale University Library)
30. The Stimson diaries say that Truman told him that he had postponed the Potsdam meeting for two weeks 'until the 15th July on purpose to give us more time' (Stimson Diary, Yale, June 6, 1945). See also Woodward [3:15], V, 523
31. Daniels [9:119], 266
32. Henry Stimson Diary, July 3, 1945 (Yale University Library)
33. *Ibid.*, July 23, 1945. Churchill added: 'Now I know what happened to Truman yesterday. I couldn't understand it. When he got to the meeting after having read this report he was a changed man. He told the Russians just where they got on and off and generally bossed the whole meeting'.
34. Truman [8:7], 419; M. Truman [8:1], 273; Ferrell, *Truman* [10:119], 55
35. Churchill, *Triumph and Tragedy* [3:13], 639; Woodward [3:15], V, 524; Ehrman, *Grand Strategy* [12:98], VI, 275–313
36. Groves [20:15], 408. For the Welsh contribution to the atom bomb, see Arnold Kramish, *The Nuclear Motive: International Security Studies Program* (Washington 1982)
37. Eisenhower's doubts are seen in Ambrose, I, 36; David Eisenhower [12:163], 691 discusses. Truman told his staff on August

8 that Leahy 'said up to the last, that it wouldn't go off'. (Ayers diary, HSTL, August 8, 1945).

38. Omar Bradley, *A General's Life* (London 1983), 444; Leahy [8:52], 505

39. Thorne, *Allies* [10:60], 533–34. There was some controversy in the English press: see for example Niels Bohr's warning of a challenge 'perhaps more serious than ever before' (*The Times*, August 11, 1945 and John Watson's letter the same day to the same journal.

40. Murphy [4:22], 589

41. This was E. B. White, a writer in the *New Yorker*, an ardent advocate of world government, qu. Divine [4:30], 314–15

42. Gowing [11:25], I, 2

43. Ernest Bevin papers, FO 800/438

44. PRO: FO 800/461 FE/4/23. Balfour also has an account in *Not too Correct an Aureole* [4:103], 108.

45. Henry Stimson, 'The decision to use the Atomic Bomb', *Harper's Magazine*, February 1947

46. Arthur Bryant, *Triumph in the West* [3:81], 477

47. Hansard, House of Commons, vol. 413, col. 80

48. NA: Joint Planners Staff to JCS, August 30, 1945. McMahon had made a fine speech in the debate on the United Nations in the Charter: how rare it was for a man 'to be given a second chance in his lifetime to correct a great mistake. It is even more seldom that the chance comes to a nation . . .' (qu. Divine [4:30], 311)

49. Henry Stimson Diary, June 6, 1945 (Yale University Library). On the way back from Potsdam, Truman told the officers on board *USS Augusta* 'because the US now had developed an entirely new weapon . . . we did not need the Russians – or any other nation' (Fletcher Knebel and Charles Bailey, *No high ground* (New York 1960), 2–3)

50. Truman [8:7], 87

51. Gertrude Szilard, *Leo Szilard, his version of the facts* (Cambridge, Mass. 1978), 186

52. Joseph Davies diary, July 28, 1945 (L of C)

53. Hewlett and Anderson, I [10:20], 418

54. In conversation with J. J. McCloy and Stimson; in Stimson diary, September 4 (Yale)

55. FRUS, 1945, II, 55–56

56. In conversation with Patterson and Forrestal.

57. Hewlett and Anderson, I [10:20], 456

58. Messer [8:87], 253
59. FRUS, 1945, II, 45–47
60. Gowing [11:25], I, 355–57
61. FRUS, 1945, II, 84–89; see also Hewlett and Anderson [10:20]
62. Blum, *The Price of Vision* [3:29], 480. Byrnes told Stettinius in London that though the Russians might have the secret of the bomb in four years or so 'they couldn't produce the thing before about eight years' (Stettinius [4:104], 428).
63. Harriman [1:22], 133
64. Stimson Diary, September 17 (Yale)
65. Stimson Diary, September 5 (Yale). It is obvious from these and other entries that Stimson was greatly influenced by Under-Secretary J. J. McCloy in these views.
66. Truman [8:7], 462–63. See Acheson [8:16], 124
67. FRUS, 1945, II, 42
68. Stimson Diary, May 14, 1945 (Yale)
69. FRUS, 1945, II, 40–44
70. Hewlett and Anderson [10:20], I, 416
71. Blum, *Price of Vision* [3:29], 481
72. Hewlett and Anderson [10:20], I, 423
73. Kramish [4:121]
74. For this conference, see notes on it in Appendix A, to Lilienthal Diaries, vol. II [8:13], 637–45; and Sziland [10:51], 223 where the meeting is described as 'one of the best . . . he attended'.
75. Acheson [8:16], 124–25
76. This is a point made by Deborah Larson. For this meeting, there are accounts by Truman [8:7], I, 463–64; Wallace in Blum [3:29], 482–85; Acheson [8:16], 124; Stimson in his diary at Yale; and Forrestal [8:93], 94–96
77. As quoted James Joll, *The Origins of the First World War* (London 1984), 6. Feis describes Truman's own account of this meeting as 'inane' (*From Trust to Terror*, 97): Truman said 'The discussions had been lively and it was the kind of interchange of opinion that I liked to see at Cabinet meetings . . .' ([8:7], 527)
78. *Ibid.*, 863–64
79. SWNCC 282, dated March 27, 1946, but actually approved September 19, 1945, published in FRUS 1946, I, 1163.
80. *Ibid.*, 1160, fn. 69
81. *Ibid.*, 1162
82. FRUS, 1945, II, 48–50
83. Blum [3:29], 485–87
84. FRUS, 1945, II, 48–50

85. Truman [8:7], 467
86. Letter of Lord Halifax to Anderson, September 20, 1945
87. Margaret Gowing [11:25], I, 78–81 for text
88. Bertrand Russell, *Autobiography*, vol. III (London 1969), 45
89. Hewlett and Anderson [10:20], I, 501
90. Halifax to Sir J. Anderson, in Gowing [11:25], 85
91. Pickersgill, and Forster [4:108], III, 40–41
92. Bullock [6:58], 187
93. Qu. Gaddis [6:62], 253
94. Hewlett and Anderson [10:20], I, 425–27
95. *Washington Post*, Oct. 2, 1945
96. Harold Smith diary (HSTL) October 5, 1945
97. See Truman, *Public Papers*, 1945 [8:67], 381–88 and discussion in Herken [8:133], 39; Gardner [8:122], 185–86
98. *Nation*, November 3, 1945, qu. Gaddis [6:62], 269
99. David Rosenberg's estimate for January 1946 was twenty-seven, in 'American Atomic Strategy and the Hydrogen Bomb Decision', *Journal of American History*, May 1979. The number of bombs available remains classified but there were probably twelve according to General Carl Spaatz – a figure which remained till April 1948.
100. Vandenberg [7:24], 223; Connally [4:86], 306
101. Lockhart [9:67], 495
102. Private recollection
103. Orwell, October 19, 1945 (Orwell [2:57], IV, 10)
104. Gowing [11:25], I, 53
105. CAB 128/4. CM(45) 52 Conclusions – Minute 4, November 8, 1945. See also Burridge [11:42], 241–42; and Gowing [11:25], 71–73. Dalton noted in his diary: 'we have had several meetings of an Inner Cabinet on this and the outcome is that the only possible course, if the world is to be saved from further and greater disasters, is to put all our force behind a real United Nations Organisation with power and determination to smash any aggressor by every means . . . It is quite idle, most of us feel, to make rules to secure that war, if it comes, shall be constructed without the use of this new weapon'. (Diary dated December 7, 1945, but obviously November 7, 1945).
106. See Gowing [11:25], I, 21
107. House of Commons, Hansard, vol. 415, cols. 38–39 (October 29, 1945). See also debate of November 7 in *ibid.*, cols. 1290–1390.
108. Burridge [11:42], 235

109. Gowing [11:25], I, 279
110. Burridge [11:42], 236
111. Truman [8:7], I, 482
112. FRUS, 1945, II, 71–73
113. Groves [20:15], 402
114. Gowing [11:25], I, 209
115. Burridge [11:42], 247
116. Byrnes, *Speaking Frankly* [3:23], 109
117. *The Challenges and Intentions of the Soviet Union as affected by American Policy*, typescript given to Bohlen, December 10, 1945, FW 711. 61/12–1045 (NA)
118. This paper was entitled *Aims and Sequence of Soviet Military Moves*, JIC 314, in CCS 092 USSR 3–276 (section 5) (NA)
119. Qu. Herken [8:133], 212, 375
120. Report of November 26, 1945, File 1945/2/322 AF RG 341 (NA); qu. *ibid.*, 23
121. Published in *Nature*, 157, issue for February 9, 1946, 146–50: 'world government has become inevitable,' he said, 'the choice before us is whether this government will be agreed upon; or whether we shall elect to fight a catastrophic third world war to determine who shall be masters'.

## Chapter 21 THE SOVIET WEAPON: FIRST STEPS IN NUCLEAR DIPLOMACY

1. A. F. Ioffe, *Moscow News*, June 16, 1945, qu. Kramish [4:121], 7
2. Kramish [4:121], 21
3. *Ibid.*, 23
4. *Ibid.*, 30
5. *Ibid.*, 57
6. Groves, 143; summary of the case against Nunn May in Report of the Canadian Commission (iv, 91)
7. Kramish [4:121], 70–71
8. Erikson [2:17], II, 79–80
9. A. I. Olryish, I. D. Morokhov and S. K. Ivanov, *A-bomba* (Moscow 1980), 376–77, qu. Robin Edmonds, 'Yalta and Potsdam', *International Affairs*, vol. 62, No. 2, 215
10. See Stimson, Diary, September 9, 1943 (Yale University)
11. *Time*, November 27, 1944; Groves qu. Kramish [4:121], 62
12. W. L. White's book, *Report on the Russians* (London 1944), had compared Russia adversely to life in the Kansas State

Penitentiary and received the most violent response (see Stettinius [4:104], 178). But all the same the book reports Russian intentions as likely to be friendly.

14. *House Un-American Activities Committee*, 81st Congress, 2nd Session, Washington 1950, 935–50; qu. Herken [8:133], 107

15. Lilienthal to Herken, in *ibid.*, 358. It is hard to believe that the Soviet absorption in 1944 of the previously 'independent' satellite state of Tuna in October 1944 was quite unrelated to the uranium deposits there, even though these were *said* only to have been discovered definitely in 1944 (Hammond in *Anatomy* [2:38], 147)

16. Radosh [4:117], 18

17. Sherwin [9:15], 113

18. Groves [20:15], 242

19. *Ibid.*, 244

20. Stalin to Harriman, in Truman [8:7], I, 357. See also David Holloway *Entering the Nuclear Arms Race: the Soviet Decision to build the Atomic Bomb* (Washington, The Wilson Center, 1979) 33–34. Several German scientists (for example, Manfred von Ardenne and Peter Adolf Thiessen, apparently made the decision to join the Russians willingly. (See Holloway *op. cit.*) These included the 1925 Nobel Prize-winner, Gustav Hertz.

21. Radosh [4:117], 442–43

22. Donovan [8:10], 93

23. Hewlett and Anderson [10:20], I, 7

24. Werth [1:19], 1034

25. Marshal Zhukov, *Reminiscences and Reflections* (London 1985), vol. 2, 449

26. Qu. Ulam [3:6], 425

27. Alliluyeva [1:9], 199. The biographer of the Soviet master scientist Kurchatov, Igor Golovin, writes (I. V. Kurchatov; tr. William Dougherty (Bloomington, Indiana) 1968) that work was undertaken at a feverish rate after the Alamogordo explosion

28. Khrushchev [2:26], II, 92

29. Holloway [21:20], 110, quoting from an unpublished biography of Vannikov. Abakumov to 'Romanov' [4:65], 238. A more *vraisemblable* source suggested that Stalin told Kurchatov that 'the balance has been destroyed. Provide the bomb. It will remove a great danger . . .' (qu. Edmonds [21:9], 215)

30. Truman [8:7], I, 357

31. Werth [1:19], 1037

32. Molotov to Mikołajczyk, in Kramish [4:121], 87

33. *Daily Worker*, August 10, qu. *ibid.*, 88

34. *Loc. cit.*

35. FRUS, 1945, V, 885

36. Acheson [8:16], 126

36[A] See evidence summarised in Nunn May in Report of Canadian Commission [4:91], 450

37. Scientists were also divided: e.g. Dr Irving Langmuir, of General Electric, told the Senate Special Committee on Atomic Energy on November 3, 1945, that the knowledge that he had that all the prominent scientists in Russia were *not* working on atomic energy showed 'they are not carrying out a Manhattan Project' (Hearings, November 30, part I, 118)

38. Dalton diary, October 17, 1945, recalling events of two weeks before (LSE)

39. Dalton diary, October 5, 1945 (LSE)

40. Hoover to General Vaughan, October 11, 1946, 'FBI-Atomic Bomb' folder, Box 167, PSF, 4 STL, cited Herken [8:133], 128

41. *New York Times*, November 7, 1945

42. Harriman to Byrnes, November 17, 1945 FRUS, 000

43. Harriman [1:22], 519

44. Harriman [1:22], 521

45. Gowing [11:25], I, 68

46. *Pravda*, September 25, 1945, qu. Bohlen [3:12], 249

47. House of Commons, November 22, 1945, Hansard vol. 416, col. 613: 'I have been unable to see . . . any final solution which will make the world safe for atomic power save that we all abate our ideas of sovereignty'.

48. Gaddis [6:62], 278, note 60

49. Acheson's report to Byrnes of his disagreeable conversation between Truman and the Senate Atomic Energy Commission on December 14. FRUS, 1945, II, 609

50. Truman [8:7], 488

51. Byrnes [3:23], 267

52. Bohlen [3:12], 249; Byrnes [3:23], 268, for a slightly different description

53. Byrnes [3:23], 268

54. Herken [8:133], 33, fn. 6

55. Byrnes [3:23], 116–17

56. Blum, *Price of Vision* [3:29], 530

57. *Ibid.*, 527

58. Vandenberg [7:24], 229

59. *Ibid.*, 231

60. Herken [8:133], 93–94
61. FRUS, 1946, I, 1198–99
62. *Ibid.*, 1203
63. Lilienthal [8:13], 10–11
64. *Ibid.*, 16 (diary, January 24)
65. *Ibid.*, 11
66. *Loc. cit.*
67. Groves [20:15], 411
68. Hewlett and Anderson [10:20]
69. FRUS, 1946, I, 749–54, February 2, 1946
70. Summary in Hewlett and Anderson [10:20], I, 533–57
71. *Bulletin of the Atomic Scientists*, February 1946
72. *New York Times*, February 24, 1946
73. Kramish [4:121], 97–102
74. In 1947, Stalin is supposed to have said: '[an intercontinental] rocket would change the fate [*sic*] of the war. It could be an effective straightjacket for that noisy shopkeeper, Harry Truman. We must go ahead with it, comrades!' (Michael Stoiko, *Soviet Rocketry: Past, Present and Future*, New York 1972). The Soviet occupation of Peenemunde was a great help. V2s were again being made there before the end of 1945. In 1946, Helmut Goettrup and the entire staff of 6000 plus 20,000 dependants were shipped to Russia.
75. See Asher Lee, *The Soviet Air force* (London 1961), 195 'bludgeon Truman at a conference' were supposed to be Stalin's words. The fact that the Soviet government had criticised the United States of 'atomic diplomacy' might have been an indication that they were themselves contemplating it.
76. Herken [8:133], 145
77. Acheson [8:16], 151
78. Hewlett and Anderson [10:20], 480
79. Acheson [8:16], 164
80. FRUS, 1946, I, 1236–37
81. Gowing [11:25], 170–71
82. *Ibid.*, 173–77. Compare France which also drifted towards the possession of an atomic bomb without the project ever receiving official sanction at cabinet level (Laurence Scheinman, *Atomic Energy Policy in France under the Fourth Republic*, Oxford
83. *Ibid.*, 182–83
84. *Ibid.*, 184
85. Adam Ulam wrote: 'The early monopoly of the new weapon debilitated rather than helped American foreign policy . . . It

encouraged . . . a Maginot Line psychology . . . led to a feeling
of national guilt . . . America hugged the evanescent atom monopoly to its bosom equally unable to exploit it or to exchange it
for something useful.' (*The Rivals*, New York 1971, 103–5.)

## BOOK FIVE
## WORLDS APART

### CHAPTER 22 THE ROAD TO FULTON: 'THE LONG TELEGRAM'

1. Joseph Davies Diary, February 9, 1946 (L of C). This comment
   followed some anecdotes about Potsdam. Davies, as was sometimes his strange practice, gave two versions of this diary entry.
2. Byrnes [3:23], 256
3. Blum [3:29], 563 fn.
4. *Ibid.*, 547: conversation of February 12
5. Forrestal [8:93], 135
6. Acheson [8:16], 150
7. FRUS, 1946, VI, 695 fn.
8. Comment on Stalin's election speech in Matthews-Hickerson files
   'Russia', RG59 qu. Larson [8:66], 253. Anyone who consulted the
   American Communist Party's theoretical texts would have seen
   that its leader, W. Z. Foster, agreed with Stalin: the basic
   premises of Lenin's view of 'imperialism' were as accurate in
   1945 as they were in 1915. See *Political Affairs*, February 1946,
   and commentary by Starobin [4:90], 122.
9. 761.00/2–1146, qu. Larson. A year later, a new Foreign Service
   Officer thought the speech 'seemed to convey marching orders
   to all who followed Moscow's dictate' (Armitage in Hammond,
   *Witnesses* [5:52], 214)
10. Harriman [1:22], 546. His public position seems to have been at
    odds with his private, darker thoughts, as expressed to Leahy
    on February 21. (See Leahy diary for that day, L of C)
11. FO 371/56725, N1876/24/38
12. Roberts to Foreign Office, February 10, 1946 in PRO: FO 371/
    56725
13. *Le Monde*, February 12, 1946
14. *Time*, February 18, 1946
15. 'Today and Tomorrow', February 12, 1946, qu. Steel [9:149],
    427

16. Soviet Home Service, February 2, 1946, qu. *ibid.*, Lippmann's book, *US War Aims* (London 1944), had anticipated this line.
17. PRO: FO 371/51606 AN 423/1/45
18. PRO: FO 371/56728 N. Roberts to London, February 14, 1946
19. Pickersgill and Forster [4:108], III, 147. See *New York Times*, February 16, 17, 18 and 24, for Drew Pearson's leaks in 'Washington Merry Go Round'
20. Truman statement, November 16, 1953, qu. Rees [4:109], 439. Nunn May's confession is on pp. 455–56 of the Canadian Royal Commission Report.
21. Leahy diary, Feb. 20, 1946 (L of C)
22. *Time*, March 4, 1946
23. *New York Times*, February 21, 1946 qu. David Dallin [4:100], 296–98
24. SWN–4096 in FRUS, 1946, I, 1165–66, dated February 21 but forwarded by State-War-Navy Coordinating Committee on March 29, 1946
25. Edgar Hoover testimony in 83rd Congress, Senate Committee on Judiciary, Sub-Committee on Internal Security, 'Interlocking Subversion in Government Departments', 1142–46
26. PRO: FO 371/55362 C2517/2/18
27. *Ibid.*, 371/55360 C1782/2/18
28. *Ibid.*, 371/55361 C1995/2/18
29. *Ibid.*, C2159/2/18
30. PRO: FO 371/55361 C236/2/18, February 21
31. NA: 868.001/2–1246 in RG 59
32. Kennan [4:19], 294. The relation between Kennan and Forrestal is discussed in Gardner [8:122], 278–79. See *Time*, April 1, 1946
33. See also NA: 711.61/2–2746 for K. W. Hamilton's minute to Clayton on the telegram; Harriman [1:22], 547–48; and Acheson [8:16], 151. For the significance of the later revisions, and Forrestal's role in them, see Gardner [8:122], 282–83.
34. Murphy to Matthews, 861.00/346
35. See Gardner [8:122], *loc. cit.*
36. Donovan [8:10], 185
37. Louis Halle, *The Cold War as History* (New York 1967), 105
38. Larson [8:66], 352
39. NA: 861.00/2–2246
40. Acheson [8:16], 209
41. For example, in an article of 1915 on 'The collapse of the Second International', qu. Kołakowski [2:23], II, 496

42. Qu. McCagg [1:13], 234. Note: 'Reply to Razin' was published in February 1947, but dated February 23, 1946

43. Steel [9:149], 427

44. Donovan [8:10], 190

45. *New York Times*, March 1, 1946: see discussion in Larson [8:66], 259–62

46. Gaddis, *Strategy* [9:183], 21

47. Donovan [8:10], 185

48. Eben Ayers Diary, February 28, 1946 (HSTL)

49. *Washington Post*, March 1, 1946

50. *Ibid.*, March 2, 1946 (Barnett Nover's article). It is significant that at the end of February 1946 the German Intelligence General Gehlen's offer to organise counter-espionage against Russia on German soil with American support was accepted (Gehlen [9:191], 10–17, 110)

51. *New York Times*, March 3, 1946 (James Reston's article)

52. FO 371/51606, AN587, qu. Larson [8:66], 262

53. Qu. Gaddis [6:62], 305–6

54. Stettinius diary, February 28, 1946, in Stettinius [4:104], 280

55. Byrnes [3:23], 170–71

56. FRUS, 1946, V, 506

57. *Ibid.*, 144–45

58. *Ibid.*, 150

59. *Ibid.*, VIII, 641

60. *Loc. cit.*

61. Eben Ayers Diary, February 25, 1946 (HSTL): 'The President pulled a number of telegrams or cablegrams out of the holder on his desk when we were in at the staff meeting this morning, with a comment that we were going to war with Russia or words to that effect . . . on two fronts, one Korea.'

62. FRUS, 1946, VIII, 647

63. *Ibid.*, VI, 406–07

64. *Ibid.*, 271–72; Paul Zinner, *Revolution in Hungary* (New York 1962), 29–49

65. FRUS, 1946, VI, 878

66. *Ibid.*, VII, 818–19

67. PRO: FO 371/51832 AS1507/842–2 Crombie Minute

68. See Gerald de Villiers, *The Imperial Shah* (London 1976), 126–27. Princess Ashraf was the first member of any royal family to enter the Kremlin since 1917.

69. Kennan to State Department, March 2, 1946, in FRUS, 1946, VII, 337–39

70. *Ibid.*, 352
71. *Ibid.*, 338
72. Bohlen [3:12], 212
73. PRO: E 1959/18/34 COS (46) 58
74. FRUS, 1946, VII, 336
75. *Ibid.*, 340
76. Kuniholm [5:28], 315
77. *Ibid.*, 318–19
78. *Ibid.*, 343
79. Truman [8:9], II, 94
80. Loy Henderson interview with Yergin, in *Shattered Peace*, 186
81. FRUS, 1946, VII, 340–2
82. Blum [3:29], 554
83. PRO: FO 371/52666 E1990/5/34
84. FRUS, 1946, VI, 712

CHAPTER 23 FULTON AND CHURCHILL

1. Lord Moran, *The Struggle for Survival* (London 1966), 206 (Diary note, October 30, 1944)
2. Blum [3:29], 223
3. Martin Gilbert, *Winston S. Churchill*, vol. IV (London 1975), 915
4. *Ibid.*, 278
5. *Ibid.*, vol. V (London 1976), 1054
6. Mastny [5:14], 30
7. Martin Gilbert, vol. V (London 1983), 1120
8. Colville diary, June 21, 1941 [7:1], 404
9. Isaiah Berlin, *Personal Impressions* (London 1980), 8
10. A. J. P. Taylor, *Beaverbrook* (London 1972), 666. Beaverbrook described the Baltic State as 'Russia's Ireland' (FO memorandum; qu. de Jonge [3:35], 416).
11. Lockhart [9:67], 217
12. Woodward [3:15], II, 556
13. Dalton [1:11], 621; Dallek [8:28], 415
14. Churchill, *Hinge of Fate* [3:14], 293
15. Cadogan [3:8], 580
16. Harriman [1:22], 279
17. FRUS, *Tehran*, 1943, 567
18. *Ibid.*, 567–68
19. Maclean, *Eastern Approaches* [1:8], 405: 'Few people', Churchill rather condescendingly said, 'are going to be more cheerful or

more downcast because of the future constitution of Yugoslavia'.
20. Blum [3:29], 174
21. PRO: PREM 3/399/6
22. PRO: FO 371/43304 N2128/36/28
23. Woodward [3:15], III, 110
24. PRO: FO 371/43636 RY380/68/67
25. Dalton [1:11], 764
26. See the Chapter entitled 'the Martyrdom of Warsaw', in *Triumph and Tragedy* [3:13], 113. Either out of guile or a desire to please Stalin, the record of Anglo-Russian discussions in October [see fn. 25 to Chapter VI] shows that Churchill presented himself as exasperated with the London Poles.
27. Kimball [4:25], III, 343
28. Bohlen [3:12], 164. Bohlen said (wrongly) that no-one in the Dept. of State knew of it. But the way it reached Washington was confused. The first whiff the Americans had of the matter was in June 1944 when Churchill told FDR that 'we . . . suggested to the Soviet Ambassador here that we should agree, as a practical matter, that the Soviet Government would take the lead in Romanian matters, while we would take the lead in Greek affairs, each government giving the other help in the respective countries'. (Kimball [4:25], III, 153: Churchill to FDR, May 31, 1944.) See Resis's article in *The American Historical Review*, summarised in fn. 25 to Chapter 6.
29. Churchill, *Triumph and Tragedy* [3:13], 211
30. Private discussion with Sir John Colville
31. Martin Gilbert, in Charlton [2:83], 31
32. Charlton makes this expression the title for his book [2:83], but Churchill's interest in the small countries of East Europe does not bear examination.
33. Cadogan [3:8], 705
34. Stettinius [4:104], 243
35. De Gaulle, III, *Le Salut* [17:46], 355. Churchill's and Stalin's remarks were thus almost identical in language. One must assume that Stalin knew what Churchill had said and adapted himself accordingly.
36. Dalton [1:11], 836
37. Hansard, House of Commons, February 27, 1945, vol. 408, cols., 1283–84. After this, Tokaev wrote, restless anti-Stalinist Russians 'felt that Stalin's home-grown apologists and boosters might as well retire . . .' (Tokaev [17:13], 277).
38. Cadogan [3:8], 720. For a subtle argument about Churchill's

concern with domestic politics over Poland, see Kimball [4:25], III, 546–47.

39. *Ibid.*, 588
40. Woodward [3:15], III, 536. It seems though that it was only in February 1945 at Malta that Churchill for the first time suggested to the US that Allied forces should be positioned so as to limit later Soviet expansion (FRUS, *Yalta*, 543).
41. See 'Das Jahr 2000', in *Das Reich*, February 25, 1945, qu. Ernest Kohn Bramsted, *Goebbels and National Socialist Propaganda 1925–1945* (London 1965), 336. Vladimir Rozanov in 1918 wrote 'with a great clanking scraping and squeaking, an iron curtain is descending across the history of Russia. The performance is over . . .'
42. Cadogan [3:8], 752. An unsent telegram of protest of May 30 (Woodward [3:15], III, 583) explains his position.
43. Truman [8:7], 180; Letter of May 9 to Eden and Attlee, qu. Woodward [3:15], III, 574–75
44. Leahy [8:52], 441–45
45. Hayter [3:22], 29
46. Cadogan [3:8], 764
47. Truman [8:7], 314
48. PRO: Eden papers, FO/800954/26, SU/45/136, PM/45/27, Eden to PM, July 17, 1945
49. Hansard, House of Commons, August 16, 1945, vol. 413, col. 83–84.
50. Pickersgill and Forster [4:108], III, 86
51. House of Commons, November 7, 1945, Hansard, vol. 415, col. 1291
52. Letter dated February 7, NA: 711.41/2–45 from US Minister in Havana, Cuba
53. Hansard, House of Commons, February 20, 1946, vol. 419, col. 1158–59
54. Djilas [3:2], 70
55. FRUS, 1945, *Potsdam* II, 1531. It is likely that Stalin knew from espionage of Churchill's suggestion to Truman that the Western armies remain where they were at the end of the war and not withdraw to the pre-arranged Zones (Adam Ulam, *A History of Soviet Russia* (New York 1976), 181).
56. M. Truman [8:1], 311
57. Lockhart [9:67], 510
58. Messer [8:87], 190; Leahy diary, March 3, 1946
59. Pickersgill and Forster [4:108], III, 182

60. DNB entry on Lord Halifax
61. Joseph Davies Diary, February 11, 1946 (L of C)
62. *The Times*, March 6, 1945
63. PRO: FO 370/55360 C1674/2/18
64. *New York Daily News*, April 12, 1953, qu. Charlton [2:83], 181
65. *The Times*, March 6, 1946: Governor Dewey had, during the war, said that he favoured a permanent alliance with Britain. That was at the Republican Postwar Advisory Council in September 1943 (Divine [4:30], 130)
66. Sherwood [3:9], 746
67. Pickersgill and Forster [4:108], III, 180–85. King was too busy with the Guzenko case to come to see Churchill in person.
68. Burt Andrews in *The New York Herald Tribune*, qu. M. Truman [8:1], 312
69. AN 656/1/45 in PRO: FO 371/51696
70. *The New York Times*, March 13, 1946
71. Richard Nixon, *Memoirs* (New York 1978), 45
72. Blum [3:29], 573
73. Qu. Arthur M. Schlesinger Jr., *Robert Kennedy and his Times* (Boston 1978), 89
74. *New York Times*, March 17, 1946
75. Blum [3:29], 556–57
76. Blum [3:29], 561
77. M. Truman [8:1], 312; he said to Mackenzie King 'that was a fine speech a great speech' (Pickersgill and Forster [4:108], III, 186)
78. Presidential papers [8:67], 1946 volume (Washington 1962), 145
79. Blum [3:29], 558–59
80. A. A. Berle [8:15], 573
81. *The Times*, March 6, 1946. For Willmott Lewis, see Iverach Macdonald, *The History of The Times*, V (London 1984), 151–53
82. Halifax at place cited
83. Forrestal [8:93], 144
84. Speech on March 23, 1946
85. Blum [3:29], 560
86. *Ibid.*, 153
87. Pickersgill and Forster [4:108], III, 184
88. Carlton [11:106], 266
89. Lockhart [9:67], 530
90. *The Times*, March 9, 1946
91. Macdonald [23:81], 139

92. Albrecht Speer, *Spandau: The Secret Diaries* (London 1976), 62
93. PRO: CAB 23(46) March 11
94. Nicholas Henderson [4:12], 27
95. Bullock [6:58], 242–44
96. Barrington-Ward, Diary October 25, 1945, qu. Macdonald [23:81], 141–42
97. Gladwyn [11:39], 185. That was March 15.
98. PRO: FO 371/56781/ N3847/140/38 (Conversation Bevin–Lie, March 15, 1945)
99. PRO CO(46)40, March 13, 1947, CAB 131/2
100. Harold Nicolson, *Diaries and Letters 1945–1962* (London 1968), entry for March 4, 1946
101. Richard N. Gardner, *Sterling-Dollar Diplomacy* (New York 1969), 250

## Chapter 24 DENOUEMENT IN PERSIA

1. Bullock [6:58], 238
2. Larson [8:66], 323, for the continued influence of the 'Pendergast persona'
3. Kuniholm [5:28], 320
4. FRUS, 1946, VII, 344
5. Telegram to Kennan [4:19], *ibid.*, 348. The text was released and published in the American press on March 7. It would seem probable that this discussion was the last attended by Alger Hiss while in possession of a blameless reputation. An FBI statement reporting Whittaker Chambers's accusations about him reached Byrnes about now; Byrnes questioned him, sent him to be cross-examined by Hoover and kept 'certain matters of importance' from him thereafter. (Byrnes, *All in One Lifetime* [8:139], 324
6. PRO: E2060/5 34, March 6, 1946
7. PRO: E2149/5/34
8. Dalton diary March 22, 1946 (London School of Economics). See also Kuniholm [5:28], 324, where it is shown how the British Vice Consul in Tabriz, John Wall, attributed his shortage of information to shortage of money!
9. D. D. Maclean p.p. Lord Halifax to Byrnes in FRUS, 1946, VII, 355–56
10. Lenczowski [4:132], 291
11. FRUS, 1946, VII, 357
12. *Ibid.*, 358–59

13. *Ibid.*, 365
14. *Ibid.*, 360
15. Walter Lippmann, in *Washington Post*, March 14, 1946
16. Harriman memorandum in Feis, *From Trust to Terror* [6:33], 83
17. FRUS, 1946, VII, 362–64; *New York Times*, March 17 and July 8, 1946; the latter article written on his return to America.
18. Roberts to Warner in PRO: FO 181/1022, March 26
19. Lockhart [9:67], 530
20. McCagg [1:13], 236; and FRUS, 1946, VI, 716
21. FRUS, 1946, VI, 717
22. PRO: FO 371/56781 and 3442/140/38
23. *Loc. cit.*
24. PRO: FO 181/1022 202/346
25. Khrushchev [2:5], I, 386–87
26. Fainsod [2:7], 392
27. Nikolaevesky [2:4], 256; McCagg [1:13], 93, 232
28. Medvedev, *All Stalin's Men* [4:1], 349
29. FRUS, 1946, VI, 720
30. David Martin, *Ally Betrayed* (New York 1946)
31. Djilas, *Rise* [12:42], 35. Tomasevich [14:14], 457–59. Kolabić, an ex-regular officer, had collaborated with both the Serbian government of Nedić and the Germans.
32. Elgey [17:5], 137
33. Reported to Stell *via* Germer in PRO: C3147/2/18 March 19
34. PRO: E2501/2/34
35. Truman papers in HSTL, qu. Donovan [8:10], I, 194
36. Diary, March 13, 18, 1946 (L of C)
37. On April 22 to Sulzberger in Sulzberger [8:81], 290
38. Qu. McCagg [1:13], 236
39. FRUS, 1946, VII, 379
40. *Ibid.*, 380
41. *Ibid.*, 381
42. FRUS, 1946, VII, 348. Truman's remarks can be found in a press conference on April 24, 1952 and an article in *The New York Times*, August 25, 1957. They are discussed by Rouhollah Romazini in Hammond, *Anatomy* [2:38], 465–66. Truman claimed to have 'laid down an ultimatum' in conversation with Herbert Feis, Feis [6:33]. Loy Henderson told Feis that so far as he knew, Truman never sent an admonitory note to Stalin (*op. cit.*, 94). Professor Herbert Druks (*Harry S. Truman and the Russians*, New York 1966, 125) says that Truman told him in 1962 that he had told Stalin that, unless the Russians withdrew,

he would send back US troops to Persia and dispatch a fleet to the Persian Gulf.

43. Herken [8:133], 374
44. *Ibid.*, 374
45. Italy always gave trouble to Moscow: 'keep calm. Avoid premature revolutionary upheavals' was Lenin's advice to Serrati in 1920 (Angelica Balabanoff, *Impressions of Lenin*, Ann Arbor 1964, 85)
46. Trygyve Lie, *Seven Years with the United Nations* (London 1954), 78. Stettinius was not unnaturally furious to be brushed aside here by Byrnes and contemplated resignation: it occurred in June.
47. Bohlen [3:12], 252
48. Baruch MSS., qu. Gaddis [6:62], 314
49. See FRUS, 1946, VII, 394–95, 393–99
50. *Ibid.*, 399
51. My paraphrase comes from *ibid.*, VI, 721–23
52. Kennan [4:19], 304

CHAPTER 25 'PATIENCE AND FIRMNESS': OR, 'STRENGTH WITHOUT OSTENTATION'

1. Blum [3:29], 562–63
2. Memorandum for the SWN Coordinating Committee 711. 61/3–1446, entitled *'US Security Interests in the East Mediterranean'*. This paper is printed in FRUS, 1946, I, 1167–71
3. *Loc. cit.*
4. *Ibid.*, V, 13
5. PRO: CAB 1217 in CM (46), 27
6. Blum [3:29], 567
7. *The New York Times*, March 20
8. Hewlett and Anderson [10:20], I, 510
9. Cord Meyer, *Facing Reality* (New York 1980), 51
10. Roberts to Warner, March 8, 1946 in PRO: FO 371/56781/140/38
11. PRO: FO 371/59959 Z24107/21/17
12. N4544/605/38 G, in FO 371/5683 (PRO)
13. See his *Both sides of the curtain* (London 1950), 254; DNB entry
14. Robert Cecil, in Dilkes and Andrew [4:128]
15. FO 371/56832 N5572/605/38G (PRO)
16. FO 371/56831 N3756/605/38 (PRO)
17. N3812/605/38 of March 21, 1946 (PRO)

18. Despatch in FO 371/5673/68855 N4156/97/38, March 28, 1946 (PRO)
19. Despatch in FO 371/5673/68855 N4157/97/38 (PRO)
20. Personal communication
21. See FO 371/6763 N4157/97/38; FO 371/56885 N5170/51691 360; and FO 371/56885 N5169/-/G (PRO). The minutes that I have studied do not make it precisely clear how the Russian Committee was formed against Warner's advice.
22. Andrew [4:125], 280
23. FO 371/56885 N5169/-/G, Minutes of the First Meeting of the Russia Committee held on April 2, 1946 in Mr Oliver Harvey's Room. Those present at this first meeting of the Russia Committee were Oliver Harvey, Sir Nigel Ronald, Edward Hall-Patch, Ivone Kirkpatrick, Christopher Warner, and John Sterndale-Bennett.
24. Conversation between Mikołajczyk and Ambassador Lane, after a dinner for Herbert Hoover, in the US Embassy, Warsaw, March 30 (FRUS, 1946, VI, 418). See Lane [12:40], 141–42
25. Woodhouse [18:1], 170
26. CP (46), 213, qu. Bullock [6:58], 244
27. Kuniholm [5:28], 402
28. Private communication from the intelligence officer concerned
29. Acheson [8:16], 206, 146–47
30. FO 371/56832 N6344/605/38
31. Qu. Bullock [6:58], 234
32. That this paper was written by Warner was confirmed by his successor as head of department, Lord Hankey.
33. FO 371/56784 N6733/140/38G; and, FO 371/56784 7199/140/38G (PRO)
34. Blum [3:29], 570
35. Dr Vannevar Bush, *Pieces of the Action* (London 1972), 298
36. Hewlett and Anderson [10:20], I, 540–59
37. *Ibid.*, 540
38. Lilienthal [8:13], 26
39. Hewlett and Anderson [10:20], I, 548
40. *Ibid.*, 562
41. Blum [3:29], 279. Baruch was a bitter opponent of a loan to Britain (see Gardner 123–25) and one cannot help wondering whether he did not get his appointment to the Atomic Energy Commission to stop him lobbying against that.
42. See papers summarised in Larson [8:66], 252. The use of the veto had been the most contentious issue between the Western

Allies and the Russians at the Dumbarton Oaks' conference in 1944. See Divine [4:30], 225–26.

43. Bernard Baruch, *The Public Years* (New York 1961), 361–64, 366. Lilienthal [8:13], 125; Leahy diary, January 12, 1948.
44. Qu. Herken [8:133], 159
45. Lilienthal, Diaries [8:13], March 18, 1946
46. Oppenheimer was, however, asked by Baruch to work with him.
47. Bedell Smith [3:31], 30–31
48. Blum [3:29], 561
49. Kuniholm [5:28], 335
50. Bedell Smith [3:31], 40–43
51. M. Truman [8:1], 313
52. Larson [8:66], 269
53. FRUS, 1946, V, 550–55; Clay [9:45], 120–25
54. Blum [3:29], 572
55. Leonhard [4:85], 353–54

## CONCLUSION TO THE ARMED TRUCE

1. Djilas, *Rise and Fall* [12:42], 101
2. J. P. Marquand, *The Late George Apley* (London 1937)
3. Kennan, *Memoirs* [4:19], I, 185
4. Henry Kissinger, *The Years of Upheaval* (London 1982), 38
5. FO 371/47588 N4384/6/55G (PRO)
6. Murphy [4:22], 329
7. This was the theme of Truman's letter to Stalin, delivered by Byrnes [8:139], 332
8. Churchill at Potsdam, qu. Woodward [3:15], V, 417
9. Bohlen [3:12], 219
10. See page 91 above.
11. André Fontaine, *Histoire de la Guerre froide* (Paris 1966), I, 256
12. See Ernest May, *'Lessons' of the Past* (New York 1973), for a study of these comparisons.
13. Marshall Shulman, *Beyond the Cold War* (New Haven 1966), 4. Another historian of Russia wrote (Seton-Watson, *Eastern European Revolution*, 166), that Western policy towards East Europe in the 1941–1945 war was 'neither very clever nor very noble but, with military facts and public opinion as they were, it is hard to see how to see how it could have been much different'.
14. Bullitt [10:31]; FRUS, 1942, III, 510. The West's reluctance to take a stand over the trial of Okulicki and the Poles in the Home Army was a sad concession, whatever the reasons.

15. European Division to Hall, August 10, 1943, in 840.50/2521 qu. Davis [6:32], 80. The 'real surprise' wrote Arthur Schlesinger Jr., 'would have been if there had been no Cold War' *(New York Review*, October 25, 1979).

16. Litvinov in conversation with Richard Hottelet of CBS News, June 1946, published by him in the *Washington Post*, January 21–25, 1952, but mentioned in FRUS, 1946, VI, 763–65

17. This is quoted in Kennan's despatch, September 8, 1952. I have benefited from Kennan's reconsideration of 1944–46 in his 'The view from Russia', in T. T. Hammond (ed.), *Witnesses* [5:52], especially pp. 32–33.

18. Orwell says the same in '*You and the Atom Bomb*', in Orwell [2:57], IV, 8.

19. This is my translation from *De la Démocratie en Amérique*, I (Paris 1986), pp. 597–98. One can with benefit compare Brooks Adams, *American Economic Supremacy* (new ed., New York 1947) in which the author suggests a final struggle between the US and Russia and, as pointed out by Theodor Draper (*Present History*, New York 1982, 378) by others beginning with Baron Friedrich von Grimm in a letter to Catherine the Great in 1790 and not excluding Napoleon, who believed Europe had only a choice between being '*américanisée*' and '*cosaque*'.

20. Eduard Bernstein, *Die internationale Bedeutung des Wahlkampfs in Deutschland*, 1893, qu. James Joll, *The Origins of the First World War* [20:77], 67

21. Ferrell [8:20], 60

22. Orwell [2:57], IV, 9. Victor Serge spoke of 'permanent war' between the West and the Soviet Union in October 1944 (Serge [11:28], xx).

# INDEX